Attitudes

Ohio State

Published titles

Attitudes: Insights from the New Implicit Measures (2009), Petty, Fazio & Brinol

Attitude Strength: Antecedents and Consequences (1995), Petty & Krosnick

Attitude Structure and Function (1989), Pratkanis, Breckler & Greenwald

Cognitive Responses in Persuasion (1981), Petty, Ostrom & Brock

Psychological Foundations of Attitudes (1968), Greenwald, Brock & Ostrom

Attitudes

Insights from the New Implicit Measures

Edited by

Richard E. Petty ◆ *Russell H. Fazio* ◆ *Pablo Briñol*

Psychology Press
Taylor & Francis Group

New York   Hove

Psychology Press
Taylor & Francis Group
270 Madison Avenue
New York, NY 10016

Psychology Press
Taylor & Francis Group
27 Church Road
Hove, East Sussex BN3 2FA

© 2009 by Taylor & Francis Group, LLC

Printed in the United States of America on acid-free paper
10 9 8 7 6 5 4 3 2

International Standard Book Number-13: 978-0-8058-5845-7 (0)

Library of Congress Cataloging-in-Publication Data

Attitudes : insights from the new implicit measures / edited by Richard E. Petty,
Russell H. Fazio, Pablo Brinol.
  p. cm.
Includes bibliographical references.
ISBN 978-0-8058-5845-7
 1. Attitude (Psychology) I. Petty, Richard E. II. Fazio, Russell H. III. Brinol, Pablo.

BF327.A894 2008
152.4028'7--dc22
                                                                2008006827

Visit the Taylor & Francis Web site at
http://www.taylorandfrancis.com

and the Psychology Press Web site at
http://www.psypress.com

Dedication

To:
Annette, Dianna, and Lynn
Michael, Daniel, Lisa, and Barbara
Dolores and Julio

Contents

Section VI   Implicit Measurement: Conceptual Issues

Section VII   Additional Measures

Preface

This volume is the fifth in a series of books edited at Ohio State University that deal with attitudes. Each volume appeared at a time when a new approach—conceptual or methodological—had captured the attention of the field. The first volume (Greenwald, Brock, & Ostrom, 1968), which appeared 40 years ago, celebrated conceptual alternatives to the dominant cognitive consistency approaches of the 1960s. The next two volumes, dealing with cognitive responses to persuasion (Petty, Ostrom, & Brock, 1981) and cognitive structure and function (Pratkanis, Breckler, & Greenwald, 1989), appeared in the 1980s and demonstrated the impact of the cognitive revolution on the field of attitudes. The fourth volume (Petty & Krosnick, 1995) appeared in the 1990s and focused on aspects of attitudes that determined whether they were consequential (i.e., attitude strength). In each case, the volume aimed to represent not just a hot topic in the field, but a topic that had become a dominant one among attitudes researchers.

The current book, like its predecessors, tackles a subject that has captured the imagination of many researchers in the field. Specifically, although the field has always recognized that people's attitudes could be assessed in different ways—from direct self-reports to disguised observations of behavior—in the past decade several new approaches to attitude measurement have been identified. One new type of measure focused on the automatic evaluative associations that came to mind when people were exposed to the attitude object. These automatic evaluative reactions, though sometimes consistent with the self-reports that people provided, were at times inconsistent. Yet, both kinds of measures proved predictive of people's behavior in different situations. What did these new measures mean? Why did they predict behaviors that explicit self-reports could not? Were all discrepancies due to the fact that these measures bypassed social desirability concerns or did these measures tap into a new kind of attitude, or an attitude that was unconscious? This book deals with these issues.

In addition to completely new implicit measures that focused on automatic activation of attitudes, other measures were developed in the past decade that aimed to perfect an approach that was introduced much earlier. For example, although researchers in the field have long used physiological measures of one sort or another (e.g., skin conductance), new, more sophisticated approaches were developed that relied on brain imaging techniques to examine evaluative processes. This book also addresses this new wave of implicit measures and the contribution they have made to understanding attitudes and attitude change.

Many of the authors who contributed to this volume attended a 2004 conference on implicit attitudes sponsored by the European Association of Experimental Social Psychology (EAESP), Cardiff University, the Universidad Autónoma de Madrid, and The Ohio State University. The meeting was held in an ideal conference venue, La Cristalera, on the outskirts of Madrid. The editors of this book, along with Gregory Maio and Geoffrey Haddock, invited individuals who had made significant contributions to the topic to take part in this book, and also included a diversity of perspectives and approaches. Following the conference, when we finalized our long-standing plan to prepare this volume, we also solicited chapters from some scholars who had not attended the meeting but who were also major contributors to the literature. Because of the many researchers working in this area, and the ever-growing list of notable investigators, we could not include everyone in the volume who has made important contributions to the topic.

Nevertheless, we have attempted to represent some of the best work being done in the area. Particular chapters focus largely on individual research programs. We have not attempted to impose any uniformity in definitions or conceptual approaches. However, we have asked all authors to be clear in their intended meanings. Despite the fact that there is no monolithic point of view with respect to implicit attitudes or measures, we hope that the book will prove informative in capturing the exciting developments that have taken place over the past decade and point the way for future exploration. We anticipate that the volume will be of interest both to graduate students initiating work on attitudes as well as to established scholars in the field. In addition, because of the many potential directions for application of the work on implicit attitudes and measures to health issues, consumer behavior, and the legal system, the book may be of interest to scholars in these and other applied disciplines as well.

Richard E. Petty
Russell H. Fazio
Pablo Briñol

References

Greenwald, A. G., Brock, T. C., & Ostrom, T. M. (Eds.). (1968). *Psychological foundations of attitudes.* New York: Academic Press.

Petty, R. E., & Krosnick, J. A. (Eds.). (1981). *Attitude strength: Antecedents and consequences.* Hillsdale, NJ: Erlbaum.

Petty, R. E., Ostrom, T. M., & Brock, T. C. (Eds.). (1981). *Cognitive responses in persuasion.* Hillsdale, NJ: Erlbaum.

Pratkanis, A. R., Breckler, S. J., & Greenwald A. G. (Eds.). (1989). *Attitude structure and function.* Hillsdale, NJ: Erlbaum.

Acknowledgments

As usual, there are many people to thank for their contributions to this volume. First, we are grateful to the sponsors of the European Association of Experimental Social Psychology (EAESP) Conference on Implicit Attitudes, which brought many of the book's contributors together in June 2004. We are especially appreciative for the role that Gregory Maio and Geoffrey Haddock played in securing funding from EAESP. We are also indebted to our chapter authors, who prepared outstanding first drafts and were very cooperative in clarifying their use of various key terms. In addition, we are most appreciative of our colleagues and students at The Ohio State University and Universidad Autónoma de Madrid, who provided an amazingly supportive and stimulating atmosphere in which to work. This book was also facilitated by the dedicated editors at Erlbaum Associates and Psychology Press. The enthusiasm shown first by Debra Riegert and then by Paul Dukes made working with them a pleasure.

Contributors

Luuk W. Albers
Social Psychology Program
University of Amsterdam
Amsterdam, the Netherlands

David Amodio
New York University
New York, New York

Galen V. Bodenhausen
Northwestern University
Evanston, Illinois

Karin C.A. Bongers
Social Psychology Program
University of Amsterdam
Amsterdam, the Netherlands

Pablo Briñol
Department of Psychology
Universidad Autónoma de
    Madrid
Madrid, Spain

William A. Cunningham
Department of Psychology
The Ohio State University
Columbus, Ohio

Jan De Houwer
Department of Psychology
Ghent University
Ghent, Belgium

Patricia G. Devine
University of
    Wisconsin–Madison
Madison, Wisconsin

Ap Dijksterhuis
Social Psychology Program
University of Amsterdam
Amsterdam, the Netherlands

John F. Dovidio
Department of Psychology
Yale University
New Haven, Connecticut

Russell H. Fazio
Department of Psychology
The Ohio State University
Columbus, Ohio

Samuel L. Gaertner
Department of Psychology
University of Delaware
Newark, Delaware

Bertram Gawronski
Department of Psychology
University of Western Ontario
London, Ontario

Anthony G. Greenwald
University of Washington
Seattle, Washington

Geoffrey Haddock
School of Psychology
Cardiff University
Cardiff, Wales

Miles Hewstone
School of Psychology
Oxford University
Oxford, England

Christian H. Jordan
Department of Psychology
Wilfrid Laurier University
Waterloo, Ontario

Kerry Kawakami
Department of Psychology
York University
Toronto, Ontario

Amanda Kesek
The University of Minnesota
Minneapolis, Minnesota

Christine Logel
Department of Psychology
University of Waterloo
Waterloo, Ontario

Gregory R. Maio
School of Psychology
Cardiff University
Cardiff, Wales

Michael J. McCaslin
Department of Psychology
The Ohio State University
Columbus, Ohio

Brian A. Nosek
University of Virginia
Charlottesville, Virginia

Michael A. Olson
University of Tennessee
Knoxville, Tennessee

Dominic J. Packer
The Ohio State University
Columbus, Ohio

B. Keith Payne
Department of Psychology
University of North Carolina
Chapel Hill, North Carolina

Richard E. Petty
Department of Psychology
The Ohio State University
Columbus, Ohio

Kerry J. Rees
University of Gloucestershire
Cheltenham, England

Denise Sekaquaptewa
Department of Psychology
University of Michigan
Ann Arbor, Michigan

Jeffrey W. Sherman
Department of Psychology
University of California, Davis
Davis, California

Natalie Smoak
Department of Psychology
Illinois Wesleyan University
Bloomington, Illinois

Steven J. Spencer
Department of Psychology
University of Waterloo
Waterloo, Ontario

Fritz Strack
Lehrstuhl fuer Psychologie II
University of Würzburg
Würzburg, Germany

Susan E. Watt
University of New England
Armidale, Australia

Mervyn L. Whitfield
Department of Psychology
Wilfrid Laurier University
Waterloo, Ontario

Jay J. Van Bavel
The Ohio State University
Columbus, Ohio

Patrick T. Vargas
Department of Advertising
University of Illinois at
    Urbana-Champaign
Urbana-Champaign, Illinois

William von Hippel
School of Psychology
University of Queensland
Brisbane, Australia

Susan E. Watt
School of Psychology
University of New England
Armidale, Australia

Mark P. Zanna
Department of Psychology
University of Waterloo
Waterloo, Ontario

Section I

Overview

1

The New Implicit Measures
An Overview

Richard E. Petty
Russell H. Fazio
Pablo Briñol

Numerous contemporary attitude theorists have made a distinction between implicit and explicit measures of attitudes, and sometimes a related distinction between implicit and explicit attitudes as well. Research on this topic is exploding at a phenomenal rate (see Fazio & Olson, 2003; Wittenbrink & Schwarz, 2007). Thus, it is interesting to note that although the implicit-explicit distinction has become very popular recently, it actually has been around in one form or another for a long time. For example, in their classic treatise on persuasion, Hovland, Janis, and Kelley (1953) defined *attitudes* as "implicit responses" that were "sometimes unconscious" and were "oriented toward approaching or avoiding a given object" (p. 7). Attitudes were contrasted with *opinions*, which were "verbal answers that one covertly expresses to (oneself)" (p. 8). These private opinions were further distinguished from public opinions, which could be susceptible to social desirability motives.

Contemporary Meanings of Implicit

In current literature, the term *implicit* is sometimes applied to the attitude itself (as was the case with the usage of Hovland and colleagues) and is sometimes applied to the attitude measure (Fazio & Olson, 2003; Petty, Wheeler, & Tormala, 2003). When applied to the measure, the most common meaning of the term implicit is that people are unaware of what the measure is assessing, in contrast to an explicit measure, in which people are fully aware that a self-report of their attitude is being requested. In this sense, there is full overlap with what prior texts on attitudes have called *indirect* or *unobtrusive* measures of attitudes (e.g., Petty & Cacioppo, 1981; Webb, Campbell, Schwartz, & Sechrest, 1966). Direct attitude measures are those that simply ask respondents to report their attitudes. Because these measures are transparent and make it obvious that attitudes are being assessed, they can be considered *explicit* measures. Included in this category are attitude measurement devices such as the semantic differential (Osgood, Suci, & Tannenbaum, 1957), the Likert scale (Likert, 1932), the Thurstone scale (Thurstone, 1928), and the ubiquitous one-item rating scale.

Indirect attitude measures, on the other hand, are those that do not directly ask the individual to report his or her attitude. Such measures were to be used when it was either impractical or undesirable to ask people what their opinions were (e.g., assessing interpersonal attraction with seating distance so as not to disturb the interaction), or there was some possibility that people might not be willing to tell you what their attitudes were (e.g., because of social desirability concerns or fear of retribution). When using indirect measurement approaches, the individual's attitude is inferred from his or her judgments, bodily responses, or overt behaviors. Because these measures do not make it obvious that attitudes are being assessed, they can be considered implicit measures.

A person completing an implicit measure is presumably unaware that the measure is assessing attitudes. Included in this category are a wide variety of methods such as the Thematic Apperception Test (TAT; Proshansky, 1943) and the information error test (Hammond, 1948); physical behaviors such as nonverbal gestures, eye contact, or seating distance (e.g., Dovidio, Kawakami, Johnson, Johnson, & Howard, 1997); picking up "lost letters" (Milgram, Mann, & Harter, 1965); and physiological measures such as skin conductance (Rankin & Campbell, 1955), pupillary dilation versus constriction (Hess & Polt, 1960), and facial muscle activity assessed with electromyography (EMG; Cacioppo & Petty, 1979). By the criterion of lack of awareness of what the attitude measure assesses, the new implicit measures are seen primarily as an attempt to improve upon the earlier and now classic indirect approaches.

In addition to accepting the idea that an implicit measure should be one that does not obviously assess attitudes, some researchers further emphasize that some implicit measures tap into an automatic evaluative reaction—one that comes to mind spontaneously upon the mere presentation of the attitude object (e.g., Fazio, Sanbonmatsu, Powell & Kardes, 1986; see De Houwer, 2006), rather than a more deliberative assessment that comes to mind upon some reflection. Although in Hovland's day, all that could be measured were explicit or deliberative evaluations (what Hovland called "opinions"), today it is possible to assess automatic evaluative reactions. It is difficult to know exactly what was the first shot fired in establishing the current wave of research on automatic measures of attitudes, but it likely had to do with the growing acceptance of the idea that attitudes could be characterized as object-evaluation associations in memory that could vary in their accessibility (see Fazio, 1995). Furthermore, the voluminous research on associative priming in cognitive psychology (e.g., *doctor-nurse*; Meyer & Schvaneveldt, 1971) inspired efforts in social psychology to examine the automatic associations people had to social objects rather than just physical ones.

One of the earliest examples of this approach was provided by Gaertner and McLaughlin (1983), who attempted to assess automatic racial stereotypes. In their research the goal was to see if presenting participants with either the words *white* or *black* would facilitate lexical decisions about positive and negative stereotype words. One finding was that people were faster to identify positive words (e.g., *smart*) as words when primed with white rather than black, suggesting the presence of automatic stereotypes at least with respect to differential possession of positive traits.

Although various priming tasks continue to be used to assess specific beliefs that automatically come to mind (e.g., Wittenbrink, Judd, & Park, 1997), this volume is concerned with an even more popular topic: assessing the general evaluations that automatically come to mind when people are exposed to an attitude object. Two implicit measurement approaches have attained widespread use. The first, called the *evaluative priming measure* (Fazio, Jackson, Dunton, & Williams, 1995), examines the extent to which attitude objects selectively facilitate categorization of common words as positive or negative. The basic idea is that priming people with stimuli that they evaluate positively (e.g., *puppies*) should make it easier to categorize other positive stimuli as good, but make it more difficult to categorize negative stimuli as bad. For negative targets (e.g., *cancer*), the opposite should be the case.

In the second popular measure, the Implicit Association Test, or IAT (Greenwald, McGhee, & Schwartz, 1998), researchers compare how quickly people can categorize attitude objects of interest (e.g., male versus female names) when the target categories are paired with the good versus the bad response on a computer keyboard. For example, if one computer key represents both *female* and *good*, and the other key represents both *male* and *bad*, will a person categorize the female name

Linda faster or slower than when one computer key represents female and bad and the other key represents male and good? The assumption of the IAT is that if people evaluate females more positively than males, they should be faster to categorize the name Linda in the first situation than the second. Although conceptual analyses regarding exactly what the evaluative priming measure and the IAT assess and why they work can be complex, both measures assume that attitude objects can be linked to evaluative associations in memory that vary in strength.

It is important to note that the automatic versus deliberative distinction is not the same as the indirect versus direct one. This is because both direct and indirect attitude assessments can vary in the extent to which they permit deliberative responding (Vargas, von Hippel, & Petty, 2001; Vargas, 2004). For example, experimenters could require individuals to report their attitudes on a direct one-item rating scale with plenty of time for thinking, or extremely quickly with no time for deliberation. The one-item rating scale is a direct measure in that it explicitly asks people for their attitudes, but the circumstances under which it is completed could facilitate getting at a quick gut reaction or a more deliberative assessment (Wilson, Lindsey, & Schooler, 2000). Similarly, some indirect attitude measures permit relatively slow and deliberate responding (e.g., the Thematic Apperception Test or information error test), whereas others require very fast responses (e.g., the IAT or evaluative priming measure). Thus, when some theorists speak of implicit measures, they are referring to measures that both are indirect and tap into automatic evaluative reactions, whereas explicit measures are characterized by requiring a self-report and encouraging at least some deliberation. The natural confounding of these two categorizations could explain why implicit (indirect/automatic) measures tend to predict spontaneous behavior better than deliberative behavior, whereas explicit (direct/deliberative) measures tend to do the reverse (e.g., Dovidio et al., 1997). That is, prediction of behavior from attitudes is best the closer the correspondence in measurement each construct is.

The third and most controversial meaning that is sometimes applied to implicit measures is that they are assumed to assess an attitude of which people are unaware. Recall that Hovland, Janis, and Kelley noted that attitudes were sometimes unconscious (1953), and it is this possible aspect of attitudes that has intrigued some contemporary theorists as well (e.g., see Kihlstrom, 2004). That is, just as cognitive psychologists have shown that people can show traces of memory for some past event without any conscious recollection of that event (implicit memory; see Schacter 1987; Roediger 1990), so too might people show evidence of attitudes without having any conscious access to the attitude itself. However, just because some implicit memory or attitude measure detects an effect of memory or attitudes, it does not mean that an explicit measure would not detect the same memory or attitude.

In the domain of memory, if an implicit measure detects an effect of the memory but people report no recollection of the memory, it seems reasonable to conclude that people have no conscious awareness of the memory. However, if an explicit measure of attitudes shows no evidence of the attitude but an implicit measure does, the conclusion that people are not aware of the attitude is less clear. That is, although it is possible that people would not want to report certain memories that they actually have due to social desirability concerns, this seems all the more likely with respect to certain attitudes. The fact that correlations between explicit and implicit measures of attitudes are reduced for just those attitude issues for which social desirability is a concern (see Chapter 3, this volume) suggests that social desirability attenuates the correlation between explicit and implicit measures. On the other hand, some might argue that it is in just these sensitive areas where people would be most likely to repress or deny their true attitudes, leading to the discrepancy.

In general, the three views of implicit attitude measures (indirect, automatic, unconscious) vary in the extent to which implicit and explicit measures should be correlated with each other. If implicit measures assessed attitudes of which people were completely unaware, by definition implicit measures should not correlate with explicit measures at all. The fact that correlations are often not zero suggests that it is unwise to rely on an implicit measure to necessarily tap an unconscious attitude. On the other hand, if the correlation between an implicit and explicit measure in some domain or in a given experiment actually is zero, does this mean that the implicit measure is assessing an unconscious attitude? This inference is also not certain because there are many ways in which a zero correlation can come about. The most obvious is poor reliability or validity of either or both measures.

However, what if the correlation between an explicit and an implicit measure is zero, but each measure is predictive of some type of outcome, thereby demonstrating some reliability and validity? This effectively rules out the garbage measure possibility. Nevertheless, this too is not sufficient to argue that the implicit measure is tapping an unconscious evaluation. People could be completely aware of the evaluation that comes to mind, but deny its validity or applicability to the self. Furthermore, people could be aware of the evaluation that comes to mind, accept it as their own, but have different motives regarding reporting it, leading some to report more favorable attitudes than they actually have and some to report less favorable attitudes, producing a zero correlation with the implicit measure. Thus, to infer that an implicit measure is tapping an unconscious attitude requires not only a zero correlation, but other evidence that people have no access to the opinion. Demonstrating this could involve using various other attitude measurement techniques designed to control for social desirability (e.g., the bogus pipeline; Jones & Sigall, 1971).

Although with respect to the awareness criterion, most attention has been paid to the idea that implicit measures might tap attitudes of which people are unaware, various theorists have emphasized other aspects of awareness. For example, Wilson and colleagues (2000) emphasized that implicit attitudes were automatic evaluations for which people were unaware of the origins of the evaluation even if they were aware of the attitude itself. Because individuals rarely, if ever, have complete access to all of the influences on their judgments (see Wilson & Hodges, 1992; Nisbett & Wilson, 1977), this criterion may not represent a viable means of making a distinction between implicit and explicit attitudes.

Still other researchers have highlighted the idea that implicit attitudes were automatic evaluations for which people were unaware of the consequences or impact of the evaluation on other judgments and behavior (e.g., Greenwald and Banaji, 1995; Greenwald et al., 1998). Again, because individuals are unlikely to be aware of all of the consequences of their attitudes, this criterion would seem to render nearly every attitude implicit. Furthermore, by this criterion, whether the attitude was considered implicit could vary from context to context (e.g., the person could be aware that a negative attitude was influential in one situation but not another). Consequently, this feature does not appear to be an optimal criterion for distinguishing implicit from explicit attitudes.

In sum, automaticity in addition to a dimension on which some theorists have argued that implicit attitudes differ from explicit attitudes is in awareness. That is, implicit attitudes are viewed as automatic evaluations for which people are unaware of what the attitude is, or where it comes from, or what effects it has. Only the first criterion appears to provide a unique role for implicit versus explicit attitudes, but this one is the most difficult to instantiate. Finally, it is important to note that these three types of awareness are not mutually exclusive. Any attitude can be characterized by all, none, or some subset of these criteria (Fazio & Olson, 2003; Petty et al., 2003). If people are not aware of what their attitudes are, they certainly cannot be aware of where the attitudes come from or what effect they have. However, if people are completely aware of their attitudes, they might not be aware of their origins or consequences.*

The Chapters in This Book

This book highlights the past decade of research in social psychology on implicit measures of attitudes. If explicit and implicit measures of attitudes always showed the same effects, then implicit measures would not be of much use. The fact that there has been a groundswell of interest in implicit measures of attitudes suggests that they do not invariably show the same results. But, as the chapters in this book indicate, there is no consensus on how to understand these discrepancies. How one interprets discrepancies between implicit and explicit measures depends in part on one's assumptions about the nature of attitudes.

The two chapters in this book that immediately follow this introduction discuss two different ways to think about implicit versus explicit measures and any discrepancies that arise between them. As noted earlier, one common approach to attitude representation asserts that attitudes are best conceptualized as object-evaluation links in memory (e.g., Fazio, 1995; Fazio, Chen, McDonel, & Sherman, 1982; Fiske & Pavelchak, 1986). This idea helped set the stage for the new implicit measures that aim to assess automatic attitudes and is perhaps best represented by the Motivation and Ability as Determinants (MODE) model (Fazio, 1990). In brief, the MODE model holds that automatic measures of attitudes (e.g., evaluative priming; Fazio et al., 1995) tend to assess the stored evaluation that is associated with the attitude object, whereas more deliberative measures (e.g., semantic differential; Osgood, Suci, & Tannenbaum, 1957) tap the retrieved evaluative association along with the outcome of any downstream cognitive processes. Thus, if people express different attitudes on a deliberative measure compared with an automatic measure, it is presumably because they have engaged in some thought that modifies the initial automatic evaluative reaction that comes to mind. This thought can reflect additional mental contents that are activated by the context, or it can stem from impression management or correc-

---

* One can ask similar questions regarding automaticity as one can for awareness. For example, in addition to asking whether the attitude or measure is an automatic or deliberative one, one can ask if the process of attitude formation is automatic or deliberative, or whether the attitude exerts its influence on behavior by an automatic or deliberative process.

tion motives. In Chapter 2, Olson and Fazio review work on the MODE model and explain how it can account for numerous outcomes on both implicit and explicit measures, along with their discrepancies.

A second approach to attitudes that has captured the attention of social psychologists more recently argues that people can hold separate explicit (conscious, deliberative) and implicit (unconscious, automatic) attitudes (e.g., Greenwald & Banaji, 1995; Wilson et al., 2000), which can take on different values. Although there are several versions of the dual attitudes approach, one or more of the following assumptions about attitudes are usually made (see Petty, Briñol, & DeMarree, 2007). First, the dual attitudes (implicit and explicit) are thought to have separate mental representations that are stored in separate brain regions (e.g., see DeCoster, Banner, Smith, & Semin, 2006; Wilson et al., 2000). A second common assumption is that the two attitudes stem from distinct mental processes. Implicit attitudes are said to result from relatively automatic associative processes, whereas explicit attitudes stem from more deliberative propositional processes (e.g., Rydell, McConnell, Mackie, & Strain, 2006). Third, implicit and explicit attitudes are postulated to be relatively independent and to operate in different situations (see Dovidio et al., 1997). When considering all of these assumptions together, the dual attitudes framework suggests that attitudes assessed with automatic and deliberative measures are quite different. The issue of whether implicit and explicit measures tap into a single- or a dual-attitudes structure is addressed by Greenwald and Nosek in Chapter 3. After reviewing some relevant evidence, they explain why they believe that the single-versus-dual-representation debate cannot be resolved with behavioral data alone. Nevertheless, they argue that the available evidence, though not requiring dual representations, is consistent with the idea that implicit and explicit attitudes are best conceptualized as distinct constructs.

Following these chapters, the book moves to a series of chapters dealing with a variety of classic issues in the attitudes literature. Each chapter discusses a particular domain in which implicit measures have enriched our understanding beyond what explicit measures have revealed. We have grouped these chapters thematically into those dealing with (a) ambivalence and consistency, (b) prejudice, (c) self-esteem, (d) attitude change, (e) methodological issues, and (f) alternatives to the reaction time measures.

The two chapters in the next section deal with issues involving cognitive consistency and ambivalence. What can implicit measures tell us about these classic phenomena? In Chapter 4, Gawronski, Strack, and Bodenhausen explain how implicit measures can contribute to our understanding of cognitive consistency paradigms such as those involving cognitive balance (Heider, 1958) and dissonance (Festinger, 1957). Gawronski and colleagues explain how both simple associative processes as well as more cognitively complex propositional processes play an important role.

In their approach to consistency, Gawronski and colleagues rely on their Associative Propositional Evaluation (APE) model of attitudes (Gawronski & Bodenhausen, 2007). This framework holds that people can respond positively or negatively to some attitude object based solely on the affect that is activated by that object, or based on the propositions that come to mind with respect to the object. The affect associated with an object can be detected directly by measures of automatic attitudes. Or, the affect can be detected by deliberative measures after it is translated into propositional form (e.g., "I like this.") and then checked for validity by an on-line process that examines whether the evaluative proposition is consistent with other salient propositions. In this framework, there are no stored evaluations (attitudes) per se, only stored affects and beliefs (propositions) that serve as input to the evaluations tapped by implicit and explicit measures.

Because the APE does not assume that there are stored evaluations, this perspective takes a very different approach to attitudes than the single- (MODE) or dual-attitudes models already described. That is, the APE focuses not on attitude structure but on the processes leading to evaluation.* In this constructivist perspective, attitudes are expressed, as needed, based on currently salient feelings and beliefs (see also Schwarz & Bohner, 2001; Wilson & Hodges, 1992). According to this approach, different contexts make different emotions or knowledge accessible, resulting in changes in people's evaluations. Any consistency in implicit or explicit attitude measures across contexts, according to this perspective, comes from the same set of building blocks being retrieved each time and being reflected in the current evaluation.

In Chapter 5, Petty and Briñol discuss the concept of implicit ambivalence and use yet another approach to attitudes to guide understanding of this phenomenon. This approach is referred to as the Meta-Cognitive Model (MCM; Petty & Briñol, 2006; Petty et al., 2007). The MCM shares some features with each of the approaches just described,

---

* If one assumes that the "affect" that forms the basis of the evaluation under automatic conditions is a stored evaluation, then the APE is similar to the MODE model described earlier.

but also has some differences. In brief, the MCM holds that attitude objects can be linked in memory to both positive and negative evaluations that can vary in the degree to which they are endorsed. Thus, in common with the MODE model, people are assumed to have stored evaluative representations. In common with dual-attitudes approaches, an attitude object can be linked to both positive and negative evaluative associations. In contrast with the dual-attitudes approach, however, the MCM assumes that any object can be linked to and thus jointly activate both evaluations rather than each evaluation being compartmentalized or isolated. In common with the APE, the MCM assumes that people assess the validity of their evaluations, but in contrast to the APE, the MCM holds that people can store validity information rather than necessarily constructing a new validity assessment on each occasion. If positive and negative evaluations are associated with an attitude object, but one valence is invalidated, automatic and deliberative attitude measures would yield different attitudes. The focus of Chapter 5 is on how these implicit-explicit discrepancies can lead to a state of implicit ambivalence. The chapter addresses how this differs from the more commonly studied explicit ambivalence in both origins and consequences.

Chapters 6 and 7 deal with prejudice. This is the domain in which the new implicit measures were first applied and is the research area in which more work has accumulated than any other. In Chapter 6, Dovidio, Kawakami, Smoak, and Gaertner provide an overview of a long-standing program of research on racial prejudice using implicit measures. The studies they review point to the utility of using implicit measures in this domain, allowing prediction of various outcomes that would not be expected from explicit measures alone. Chapter 7 by Amodio and Devine further explores the domain of prejudice. Amodio and Devine argue that to understand prejudice, it is necessary to distinguish between stereotyping and more general evaluative forms of racial biases. They argue that these core components of racial prejudice stem from affective processes versus semantic associations, and that these two forms of racial bias interact with behavior in different ways.

Besides prejudice, the topic where implicit and explicit measures have been most popular is in the domain of self-esteem. The next two chapters tackle this subject. In Chapter 8, Dijksterhuis, Albers, and Bongers examine the meaning of implicit and explicit measures of self-esteem. In accord with the MODE model, they argue that implicit measures tap one's core self-esteem, whereas explicit measures are more influenced by self-deception and impression management. In Chapter 9, Jordan, Logel, Spencer, Zanna, and Whitfield take a somewhat different approach, arguing that implicit and explicit self-esteem represent distinct self-evaluations that operate within separate, though interacting, psychological systems. Their chapter focuses on the behavioral consequences of having discrepant implicit and explicit self-esteem, with special attention paid to individuals who have high explicit but low implicit self-esteem.

The next two chapters address the topic of attitude change. Although hundreds of studies examine attitude change and persuasion with explicit measures, it is only recently that persuasion work has begun to examine the impact of attitude change techniques on implicit measures and to examine the mechanisms by which these measures are impacted. In Chapter 10, Briñol, Petty, and McCaslin consider attitude change processes that range from those using simple automatic associations (e.g., evaluative conditioning) to those involving more deliberative forms of reasoning (e.g., elaborating the arguments in a persuasive message), and how these processes influence both automatic and deliberative assessments of attitudes. In reviewing the research on this issue, the conditions under which the different processes of change affect both kinds of measures versus just one are articulated. In Chapter 11, Maio, Haddock, Watt, and Hewstone first provide an overview of the use of implicit measures in applied persuasion contexts such as consumer attitudes and health disorders. Then, they describe a case study demonstrating the utility of using implicit measures to assess the effectiveness of an antiracism media campaign.

The next chapters address various conceptual and methodological issues that have arisen in understanding exactly what the new wave of implicit measures—especially those aiming to tap automatic evaluations—actually measure. In Chapter 12, De Houwer describes two levels at which different implicit measures can be compared. One is at the functional level. De Houwer considers what functional properties are assumed by researchers using different implicit measures (e.g., "Is the measure controllable?") and what are the conditions under which the various measures operate as intended. Second, measures are compared at the procedural level. For example, De Houwer argues that depending on the specific procedure used, an implicit measure might better assess attitudes at the category level (e.g., *insect*) or at the exemplar level (e.g., *cockroach*). In Chapter 13, Sherman also addresses some important methodological issues. In particular, he explains that although many researchers have assumed that implicit measures uniquely tap into automatic processes, such measures are not process-pure; that is, these measures can also be influenced by more deliberative processes. In his chapter, Sherman articulates the Quadruple Process (Quad) Model (Conrey, Sherman, Gawronski, Hugenberg, & Groom, 2005) as a means of estimating the extent of various automatic and controlled influences on implicit measures.

All of the chapters in the volume to this point have focused primarily on implicit measures that aim to assess automatic evaluative reactions with procedures relying on reaction times (e.g., how quickly can people categorize *beauty* as a positive word after being primed with *Chinese*). Although these measures have proven amazingly popular and useful, they are not the only new measurement techniques developed in the last decade. Our final set of chapters tackles alternative approaches to the implicit measurement of attitudes. In Chapter 14, von Hippel, Sekaqua-ptewa, and Vargas examine the ways in which a person's use of language can provide implicit assessments. For example, the spontaneous use of *we* versus *I* can be employed to assess the extent to which a person feels part of a group. In their chapter, von Hippel and colleagues provide a fresh perspective on some classic indirect approaches such as projec-tive tests and also review more contemporary indirect techniques that rely on linguistic markers of attitudes. In Chapter 15, Payne presents his Affect Misattribution Procedure (AMP). In brief, with this technique, inferences about people's attitudes are made based on how they judge ambiguous objects after being exposed to the attitude object of real interest. The key idea is that a person's reaction to the target object (e.g., a picture of a presidential candidate) can be misattributed to the subse-quently presented ambiguous object (e.g., a Chinese ideograph; see Mur-phy & Zajonc, 1993). In Chapter 16, Cunningham, Packer, Kesek, and Van Bavel provide an overview of the various physiological measures of attitudes that have been used over the years from skin conductance to state-of-the-art brain imaging approaches. Cunningham and colleagues view evaluations of attitude objects as continually being updated, with implicit evaluations involving relatively few iterations of the evaluative system and a reduced set of cognitive operations, whereas explicit evalu-ations involve many iterations and more cognitive operations.

Conclusion

As should be evident by now, the goal of this book is not to provide a "how to" handbook on using implicit measures. There are many good sources available for this. Rather, the chapters in this book outline sev-eral conceptual approaches for understanding what implicit measures assess and how they are useful in understanding classic as well as very new phenomena in the attitudes literature.

It is important to note that the chapter authors do not necessarily agree on the most appropriate and productive definition of implicit attitudes and measures and how they should be conceptualized. To avoid confusion, however, we have asked each author to be as clear as possible in making his or her underlying assumptions and definitions transparent. Thus, as a reader, we hope that by the time you have finished this volume, you will find that one approach is more appealing than another, or you will formulate and adopt your own unique perspective on the new implicit measures and their utility.

References

Cacioppo, J. T., & Petty, R. E. (1979). Attitudes and cognitive response: An electro-physiological approach. *Journal of Personality and Social Psychology, 37,* 2181–2199.

Conrey, F. R., Sherman, J. W., Gawronski, B., Hugenberg, K., & Groom, C. (2005). Separating multiple processes in implicit social cognition: The Quad Model of implicit task performance. *Journal of Personality and Social Psychology, 89,* 469–487.

DeCoster, J., Banner, M. J., Smith, E. R., & Semin, G. R. (2006). On the inexplicability of the implicit: Differences in the information provided by implicit and explicit tests. *Social Cognition, 24,* 5–21.

De Houwer, J. (2006). What are implicit measures and why are we using them? In R. W. Wiers & A. W. Stacy (Eds.), *The handbook of implicit cognition and addiction* (pp. 11–28). Thousand Oaks, CA: Sage Publishers.

Dovidio, J., Kawakami, K., Johnson, C., Johnson, B., & Howard, A. (1997). On the nature of prejudice: Automatic and controlled processes. *Journal of Experimental Social Psychology, 33,* 510–540.

Fazio, R. H. (1990). Multiple processes by which attitudes guide behavior: The MODE model as an integrative framework. In M. Zanna (Ed.), *Advances in experimental social psychology* (Vol. 23, pp. 75–109). San Diego: Academic Press.

Fazio, R. H. (1995). Attitudes as object-evaluation associations: Determinants, consequences, and correlates of attitude accessibility. In R. E. Petty & J. A. Krosnick (Eds.), *Attitude strength: Antecedents and consequences* (pp. 247–283). Hillsdale, NJ: Erlbaum.

Fazio, R. H., Chen, J., McDonel, E. C., & Sherman, S. J. (1982). Attitude accessibility, attitude-behavior consistency, and the strength of the object-evaluation association. *Journal of Experimental Social Psychology, 18,* 339–357.

Fazio, R. H., Jackson, J. R., Dunton, B. C., & Williams, C. J. (1995). Variability in automatic activation as an unobtrusive measure of racial attitudes: A bona fide pipeline? *Journal of Personality and Social Psychology, 69,* 1013–1027.

Fazio, R. H., & Olson, M. A. (2003). Implicit measures in social cognition research: Their meaning and use. *Annual Review of Psychology, 54,* 297–327.

Fazio, R. H., Sanbonmatsu, D. M., Powell, M. C., & Kardes, F. R. (1986). On the automatic activation of attitudes. *Journal of Personality and Social Psychology, 50,* 229–238.

Festinger, L. (1957). *A theory of cognitive dissonance.* Stanford, CA: Stanford University Press.

Fiske, S. T., & Pavelchak, M. A. (1986). Category-based versus piecemeal-based affective responses: Developments in schema driven affect. In R. M. Sorrentino & E. T. Higgins (Eds.), *Handbook of motivation and cognition: Foundations of social behavior* (pp. 167–203). New York: Guilford Press.

Gaertner, S. L., & McLaughlin, J. P. (1983). Racial stereotypes: Associations and ascriptions of positive and negative characteristics. *Social Psychology Quarterly, 46,* 23–30.

Gawronski, B., & Bodenhausen, G. V. (2007). Unraveling the processes underlying evaluation: Attitudes from the perspective of the APE model. *Social Cognition, 25,* 687–717.

Greenwald, A. G., & Banaji, M. (1995). Implicit social cognition: Attitudes, self-esteem, and stereotypes. *Psychological Review, 102,* 4–27.

Greenwald, A. G., McGhee, D. E., & Schwartz, J. L. K. (1998). Measuring individual differences in implicit cognition: The Implicit Association Test. *Journal of Personality and Social Psychology, 74,* 1464–1480.

Greenwald, A. G., & Nosek, B. (in press). *Attitudinal dissociation: What does it mean?* In R. E. Petty, R. H. Fazio, & P. Briñol (Eds.), *Attitudes: Insights from the new implicit measures.* Hillsdale, NJ: Erlbaum.

Hammond, K. R. (1948). Subject and object sampling: A note. *Psychological Bulletin, 45,* 530–533.

Heider, F. (1958). *The psychology of interpersonal relations.* New York: Wiley.

Hess, E. H., & Polt, J. M. (1960). Pupil size as related to interest value of visual stimuli. *Science, 132,* 349–350.

Hovland, C. I., Janis, I. L., & Kelley, H. H. (1953). *Communication and persuasion: Psychological studies of opinion change.* New Haven, CT: Yale University Press.

Jones, E. E., & Sigall, H. (1971) The bogus pipeline: A new paradigm for measuring affect and attitude. *Psychological Bulletin, 76,* 349–364.

Khilstrom, J. F. (2004). Implicit methods in social psychology. In C. Sansone, C. C. Morf, & A. T. Panter (Eds.), *The Sage handbook of methods in social psychology* (pp. 195–212). Thousand Oaks, CA: Sage Publications.

Likert, R. (1932). A technique for the measurement of attitudes. *Archives of Psychology, 140*, 1–55.

Meyer, D. E., & Schvaneveldt, R. W. (1971). Facilitation in recognizing pairs of words: Evidence of dependence between retrieval operations. *Journal of Experimental Psychology, 90*, 227–234.

Milgram, S., Mann, L., & Harter, S. (1965). The lost-letter technique: A tool of social research. *Public Opinion Quarterly, 29*(3), 437.

Murphy, S. T., & Zajonc, R. B. (1993). Affect, cognition, and awareness: Affective priming with optimal and suboptimal stimulus exposures. *Journal of Personality and Social Psychology, 64*, 723–739.

Nisbett, R. E., & Wilson, T. D. (1977). Telling more than we can know: Verbal reports on mental processes. *Psychological Review, 84*, 231–259.

Osgood, C. E., Suci, G. J., & Tanenbaum, P. H. (1957). *The measurement of meaning.* Urbana: University of Illinois Press.

Petty, R. E., & Briñol, P. (2006). A meta-cognitive approach to "implicit" and "explicit" evaluations: Comment on Gawronski and Bodenhausen (2006). *Psychological Bulletin, 132*, 740–744.

Petty, R. E., Briñol, P., & DeMarree, K. G. (2007). The Meta-Cognitive Model (MCM) of attitudes: Implications for attitude measurement, change, and strength. *Social Cognition, 25*, 657–686.

Petty, R. E., & Cacioppo, J. T. (1981). *Attitudes and persuasion: Classics and contemporary approaches.* Dubuque, IA: Win. C. Brown.

Petty, R. E., Wheeler, S. C., & Tormala, Z. L. (2003). Persuasion and attitude change. In T. Millon & M. J. Lerner (Eds.), *Handbook of psychology, Vol. 5. Personality and social psychology* (pp. 353–382). Hoboken, NJ: John Wiley and Sons.

Proshansky, H. M. (1943). A projective method for the study of attitudes. *Journal of Abnormal and Social Psychology, 38*, 393–395.

Rankin, R. E., & Campbell, D. T. (1955). Psychophysiological evaluation of stigma towards schizophrenia. *Schizophrenia Research, 76*, 317–327.

Roediger, H. L. (1990). Implicit memory: Retention without remembering. *American Psychologist, 45*, 1043–1056.

Rydell, R. J., McConnell, A. R., Mackie, D. M., & Strain, L. M. (2006). Of two minds: Forming and changing valence-inconsistent implicit and explicit attitudes. *Psychological Science, 17*, 954–958.

Schacter, D. L. (1987). Implicit memory: History and current status. *Journal of Experimental Psychology: Learning, Memory, and Cognition, 13*, 501–518.

Schwarz, N., & Bohner, G. (2001). The construction of attitudes. In A. Tesser & N. Schwarz (Eds.), *Blackwell Handbook of Social Psychology: Intrapersonal Processes* (pp. 436–457). Oxford, UK: Blackwell.

Thurstone, L. L. (1928). Attitudes can be measured. *American Journal of Sociology, 33*, 529–554.

Vargas, P. T. (2004). On the relationship between implicit attitudes and behavior: Some lessons from the past and directions for the future. In G. Haddock & G. R. Maio (Eds.), *Contemporary perspectives on the psychology of attitudes* (pp. 275–297). New York: Psychology Press.

Vargas, P. T., von Hippel, W., & Petty, R. E. (2001). It's not just what you think, it's also how you think: Implicit attitude measures tapping biased information processing. In S. E. Heckler & S. Shapiro (Eds.), *Proceedings of the Society for Consumer Psychology Winter Conference* (pp. 82–88). Tempe, AZ: Society for Consumer Psychology.

Webb, E. J., Campbell, D. T., Schwartz, R. D., & Sechrest, L. (1966). Unobtrusive measures: Nonreactive research in the social sciences. *The Annals of the American Academy of Political and Social Science, 368,* 229–230.

Wilson, T. D., & Hodges, S. D. (1992). Attitudes as temporary constructions. In L. L. Martin & A. Tesser (Eds.), *The construction of social judgments* (pp. 37–65). Hillsdale, NJ: Lawrence Erlbaum Associates.

Wilson, T. D., Lindsey, S., & Schooler, T. Y. (2000). A model of dual attitudes. *Psychological Review, 107,* 101–126.

Wittenbrink, B., Judd, C. M., & Park, B. (1997). Evidence for racial prejudice at the implicit level and its relationship with questionnaire measures. *Journal of Personality and Social Psychology, 72,* 262–274.

Wittenbrink, B., & Schwarz, N. (Eds.). (2007). *Implicit measures of attitudes.* New York: Guilford Press.

2

Implicit and Explicit Measures of Attitudes
The Perspective of the MODE Model

Michael A. Olson
Russell H. Fazio

Introduction

Strong or weak, extreme or mild, certain or uncertain, attitudes are as richly diverse as the judgments and behavior they often influence. Years of systematic study of these attitudinal qualities have tackled the age-old questions of when and how attitudes relate to behavior. What sorts of attitudes relate reliably to judgments and behavior? Under what conditions is attitude–behavior correspondence most likely to occur? By what processes do attitudes exert their influence? The MODE model (Motivation and Opportunity as Determinants of the attitude-behavior relation) was developed to address these historical and fundamental questions (Fazio, 1990; Fazio & Towles-Schwen, 1999). We will describe the tenets of the model in this chapter, and in so doing illuminate the multiple paths from attitude to behavior delineated by the MODE model.

However, in addition to these historical issues, the present volume also tackles a more contemporary set of questions. Premised on the potentially important distinction between implicit and explicit attitudinal processes, the various authors represented in these pages ponder questions like: Can one harbor both conscious and unconscious attitudes toward the same object? Might such attitudes relate differently to judgments and behavior? What sorts of consequences result from discrepancies between the two attitudes? Also, one would be remiss to overlook the energizing role that recent advances in implicit measurement have played in this research. How might we make sense of discrepancies between implicit and explicit measure of attitudes, and how might the different measures map onto the processes operating within the mind?

We argue that, despite its predating the surge in research on implicit measures, the MODE model provides a cogent and compelling account of many of the attitudinal phenomena that recently have been the focus of attention. These include conceptual issues currently couched in conscious and unconscious terms, as well as inferences premised on dissociations between implicit and explicit measures. The chapter is organized in three major sections. We first will provide a brief review of the MODE model. Then, we will summarize a lengthy series of investigations we have conducted in which implicit measures have been used to test the MODE model, largely in the domain of racial prejudice. In the third and final section, we will broaden the discussion from the initial focus on prejudice to more general issues that have arisen regarding implicit measures. In particular, we will consider the implications of both the MODE model and the associated empirical findings for the interpretation of observed dissociations between implicit and explicit measures of attitude. In so doing, we hope to illuminate how contemporary research findings are consistent with the model.

The MODE Model

Before describing the MODE model, some definitional clarity is in order, particularly with respect to the term *attitude*. It has seen varied definitions over the years (Eagly & Chaiken, 1993), but all of them describe some way in which positivity or negativity is linked to some attitude object. The MODE model identifies this link explicitly by defining attitude as an association in memory between an object and one's evaluation of it (see Fazio, 2007, for an extensive recent discussion of this definition). The strength of this object-evaluation association, as we will see, has some important implications for attitude-behavior processes.

Every attitude can be located somewhere along a strength dimension. Relative to weak attitudes, strong attitudes are stable, are resistant to persuasive appeals, and more reliably predict behavior (Petty & Krosnick, 1995). The MODE model's definition of attitude captures this critical dimension via the object-evaluation association. The weak end of the continuum is marked by the nonattitude, where there is simply no object-evaluation association (such as one's evaluation of the window pane on the left side of one's office window). When asked about one's attitude toward such objects, a respondent must construct an attitudinal response on the spot, even if that were to mean nothing more than shrugging one's shoulders and claiming perfect neutrality toward the object. As we move along this strength dimension, one finds attitudes with more accessible object-evaluation associations. Such attitudes can be sufficiently accessible that the mere perception of the attitude object automatically and inescapably evokes an evaluative response (such as when the sight of a cigarette immediately prompts cravings in a smoker; Fazio, Sanbonmatsu, Powell, & Kardes, 1986). An abundance of empirical evidence attests to the pervasiveness of this automatic activation effect, as well as its downstream consequences for attitude-behavior processes (see Fazio, 2001 for a review). Indeed, it is with basic cognitive phenomena of attention, perception, and categorization that a relatively spontaneous attitude-behavior process begins.

Spontaneous Attitude-Behavior Processes

The MODE model distinguishes two basic classes of attitude-to-behavior processes. The difference centers on the extent to which pursuing a particular course of action involves a spontaneous reaction to one's perception of the immediate situation versus deliberation regarding the behavioral alternatives. Details regarding the model and relevant empirical findings are available in earlier chapters (Fazio, 1990; Fazio & Towles-Schwen, 1999). Briefly, however, the model postulates that attitudes can guide behavior in a spontaneous manner, without the individual actively considering the relevant attitude and without the individual's necessary awareness of its influence. Instead, the attitude may be activated from memory automatically upon the individual's encountering the attitude object. The automatically activated attitude will influence how the person construes the object in the immediate situation: either directly, as when the activated evaluation forms the immediate appraisal (e.g., an immediate "Yuk" reaction), or indirectly, as when the activated attitude biases perceptions of the qualities exhibited by the object. Ultimately, this construal will affect the person's behavioral response.

Thus, the model postulates that for attitudes strong enough to be automatically activated upon perception of the object, attitude-relevant behavior can flow spontaneously from the attitude, unimpeded by more controlled processes. Clearly, the reasoning is premised on the notion of constructive social cognition first championed by the "New Look" movement (Bruner, 1957) and followed by several decades' worth of fascinating research illuminating the effects of temporarily and chronically accessible constructs on perception, judgments, and behavior (see Higgins, 1996, for a review). Over the years, our research program has documented many fundamental consequences of accessible attitudes that contribute to this spontaneous attitude-behavior relation. Consistent with this theme, we have demonstrated that accessible attitudes can orient attention (Roskos-Ewoldsen & Fazio, 1992), influence categorization of the attitude object (Smith, Fazio, & Cejka, 1996; Fazio & Dunton, 1997), and bias visual perceptions of the object (Fazio, Ledbetter, & Towles-Schwen, 2000). In addition, they have the potential to influence the processing of information related to the attitude object. That is, the more accessible the attitude, the more likely it is that new information about the object will be disambiguated in an attitudinally congruent manner (e.g., Fazio & Williams, 1986; Houston & Fazio, 1989; Schuette & Fazio, 1995).

This sometimes unwitting tendency to attend to attitude-congruent aspects of an object and to twist its ambiguous qualities into alignment with our attitudes is central to the MODE model's postulate regarding a spontaneous attitude-to-behavior process. By shaping construals of the object in the immediate situation, automatically activated attitudes can influence behavior without any necessary reflection on our parts and without any necessary awareness of the biasing influence of our attitudes. It is important to reiterate, however, that attitude accessibility exerts a critical moderating role. Any such spontaneous process is predicated upon automatic activation of the attitude upon encountering the attitude object. In fact, considerable evidence has accumulated indicating that the extent of biased information processing about an object varies as a function of attitude accessibility (see Fazio, 1995, for a review). For example, in a study of the 1984 presidential election, Fazio and Williams (1986) found that respondents' attitudes toward the candidates predicted impressions of their debate performance, but this relationship grew stronger as attitude accessibility increased.

Deliberate Attitude-Behavior Processes

As apparent as the automatic ways in which attitudes can steer behavior may be, it is also clear that much of our behavior is more thoughtfully determined. That is, instead of a "top-down," attitude-driven process, oftentimes a "bottom-up" process of scrutiny and deliberation precedes a behavioral response. In this latter case, behavior toward a given object is influenced less by the evaluation it may automatically evoke and more by a deliberative comparison of the behavioral alternatives. Under some circumstances, individuals analyze the costs and benefits of a particular behavior and, in so doing, deliberately reflect upon the attitudes relevant to the behavioral decision so as to arrive at a behavior plan, which they may then choose to enact (see Ajzen, 1991; Ajzen & Fishbein, 1980, 2005).

In contrast to the more spontaneous process we described earlier, what is central to the deliberative mode is the exertion of effort. Indeed, it is clear that humans can be as reflective as they are impulsive and that sometimes they are a little of both (Strack & Deutsch, 2004). The critical questions, and those most central to the MODE model, are under what conditions one or the other orientation predominates, and how these processes interact on the path from attitudes to behavior.

The Role of Motivation and Opportunity

Given the effortful reflection required by the deliberative alternative, some motivating force is necessary to induce individuals to engage in the reasoning. The MODE model posits that a variety of motivational factors might push an individual toward a more deliberative scrutiny of behavioral options. Perhaps the most fundamental of these motives is the desire to be accurate: that is, to reach valid conclusions. The MODE model is certainly not alone in arguing for the importance of accuracy motivation. A good example is Kruglanski's (1989) theory of lay epistemics, which identifies "fear of invalidity" as a motive that drives individuals to seek out and consider relevant knowledge. Contemporary models of persuasion such as the Heuristic-Systematic Model (HSM; Chen & Chaiken, 1999) and Elaboration Likelihood Model (ELM; Petty & Wegener, 1999) also assume an accuracy motive. However, other motives—such as the need to belong (Baumeister & Leary, 1995) and to feel positively toward the self (Sedikides & Strube, 1997)—may be similarly capable of pushing the perceiver in a more deliberative direction. But the goals entailed in these motives aren't to arrive at a more accurate conclusion in general, but to reach a more specific and desired conclusion. A motive to belong, for example, might lead one to arrive at a behavioral decision to ingratiate others or to highlight their similarities. As we shall see later, a motivation to avoid prejudice against a given group may lend itself to more positive behavioral responses to its members. The critical similarity among these various motives, however, is that they all imply the exertion of effort for the purpose of reaching (or avoiding reaching) a given conclusion, whether to be right, liked, accepted, or something else.

Of course, motives do not make behaviors. In order for any motivation to overcome the influence of one's attitude, an opportunity for this motive to exert its influence must also be available. And again, the model views "opportunity" broadly; it manifests in a variety of ways. Opportunity can simply amount to a matter of time; careful consideration of information simply cannot be done quickly (e.g., Jamieson & Zanna, 1989). But opportunity also comes in psychological forms. Because our cognitive resources are limited, fatigue, distraction, and other factors can interfere with one's ability to process information. For example, Baumeister and colleagues' work on self-regulation suggests that "ego-depletion" might compromise one's processing resources, thus limiting the potential impact one's motivated intentions can have on judgments and behaviors (Baumeister, Bratlavasky, Muraven, & Tice, 1998).

According to the MODE model, these two moderating factors—motivation and opportunity—determine the extent to which the attitude-to-behavior process is primarily spontaneous versus deliberative in nature. Moreover, as implied by the preceding analysis and illustrated by subsequent research, a shift toward a more deliberate mode of processing requires both motivation and opportunity. For example, Sanbonmatsu and Fazio (1990) found that when participants were deciding between two alternatives, they engaged in the effort of retrieving specific attribute information from memory (beliefs about the alternatives) only under conditions in which motivation to reach a valid decision was heightened and no time pressure was applied. When their fear of invalidity was relatively low or when their decision-making was done under time pressure, participants showed evidence of relying on their global attitudes instead of specific attribute knowledge (see Fabrigar, Petty, Smith, & Crites, 2006, for related evidence).

In addition to delineating two distinct classes of attitude-behavior processes, the MODE model explicitly postulates the possibility of processes that are neither purely spontaneous nor purely deliberative, but instead are what we refer to as *mixed* processes, ones that involve a combination of automatic and controlled components. Any controlled component within a mixed sequence requires, once again, that the individual both be motivated to engage in the necessary cognitive effort

The MODE Model

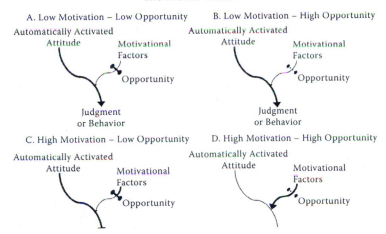

FIGURE 2.1 Depictions of the MODE model as a function of high versus low motivation and opportunity.

and have the opportunity to do so. Figure 2.1 provides a graphical summary of the MODE model, illustrating the potential interplay between automatic and controlled processes. The model views an automatically activated attitude as a "starting point" for judgment and behavior. However, the "downstream" consequences of the automatically activated attitude—that is, its influence on overt judgments—can be moderated by motivation and opportunity. In the figure, the thickness of a "stream" is intended to convey the extent of influence. As depicted in the top two panels, when little or no motivation to deliberate is evoked in a given situation, overt judgments and behavior are hypothesized to reflect the direct influence of the automatically activated attitude. These downstream consequences of attitude activation would occur via the mechanisms discussed earlier as comprising a spontaneous attitude-to-behavior process. Any motivational factors that might be evoked can exert an influence on the overtly expressed judgment, assuming that the situation and behavior in question provide sufficient opportunity for controlled, deliberative processing. Essentially, the opportunity factor can be viewed as a gating mechanism that determines the extent to which motivational factors can influence the overt judgment. When the gate is open, as in panel D of the figure, motivational goals can have a strong influence on their overt judgments, potentially attenuating the influence of the automatically activated attitude. However, such motivated efforts will be thwarted when the opportunity to deliberate is minimal, as in panel C.

One of the first experiments to examine such mixed processes was conducted by Schuette and Fazio (1995), who tested the hypothesis that attitudinally biased information processing should be jointly affected by attitude accessibility and motivation to deliberate. Schuette and Fazio employed the paradigm developed by Lord, Ross, and Lepper (1979), in which participants' judgments of the quality of presumed scientific studies concerning the deterrent efficacy of capital punishment are potentially biased by their own attitudes toward the death penalty. On the basis of the MODE model, Schuette and Fazio reasoned that any such biasing effects should depend on the accessibility of those attitudes and the presence of motivation. In some conditions, the accessibility of participants' attitudes toward the death penalty was enhanced by having them repeatedly express their attitudes in an early phase of the experiment. Such repeated expression is known to increase the likelihood of automatic attitude activation when the attitude object is later encountered (Fazio et al., 1986). Replicating earlier findings (Houston & Fazio, 1989), participants in the repeated-expression condition displayed greater attitudinally biased processing than did those in a condition in which attitudes had been earlier expressed only a single time. That is, the correlation between attitudes and judgments of the research quality was stronger for individuals with more accessible attitudes. However, the MODE model predicts that such attitudinal bias should be minimized in the presence of motivation and opportunity. In this study, participants in all conditions were provided ample opportunity to digest the information, but some participants were particularly motivated to process the information carefully. These individuals were told that their responses would be made public and compared to the judgments rendered by a panel of experts. No such fear of invalidity was invoked for participants in the low-motivation conditions, and it was within these conditions that those with more accessible attitudes exhibited biased processing. They judged the quality of the research in accordance with their attitudes, agreeing with research supporting their views and criticizing research that contradicted them. (Note that this finding accords with panel B of Figure 2.1.) The more motivated participants, on the other hand, were able to overcome the biasing effects of their attitudes and presumably judge the research more objectively, even when their attitudes were highly accessible. (This latter finding matches the predictions depicted in panel D.)

This interplay between the biasing effects of automatically activated attitudes and "corrective" measures prompted by a relevant motivational factor lies at the heart of the MODE model. Automatically activated attitudes can have a potent effect on overt judgments and behavior, but their influence can be attenuated when some relevant motivational goal arises. In the Schuette and Fazio (1995) research, both motivation and the attitude's capacity for automatic activation were manipulated experimentally. In subsequent work, we adopted an individual difference approach to testing the MODE model. Automatically activated attitudes were assessed via an implicit measure. In addition, individuals who experienced varying levels of motivation to counter the influence of their automatically activated attitudes were identified. Such an approach required that there was variability across individuals with respect to both their automatically activated attitudes and relevant motivations. The domain of racial prejudice—a richly active area of social psychological research—proved very well suited to these research aims. We now have accumulated a series of empirical findings confirming the predicted moderating role of motivation on the relation between automatically activated racial attitudes and various race-related judgments. Essentially, the estimates of racial attitude provided by an implicit measure are predictive for individuals low in motivation to control prejudiced reactions, but the relation is attenuated, and often reversed (a pattern indicative of motivated overcorrection), as motivation increases.

MODE Model Applications to Racial Prejudice

Most social psychological treatments of prejudice entail both automatic and controlled components. Devine (1989), for example, argued that the automatic component of prejudice is acquired through passive socialization processes, and that nonprejudiced individuals are marked by a controlled, value-driven system to avoid allowing automatic prejudices from influencing their behavior. Most "modern" theories of racism hint at the dual interplay of automatic and controlled processes, but the theory of aversive racism posits explicitly that aversive racists tend to be prejudiced at more automatic (and perhaps less conscious) levels, but still think of themselves as egalitarian (Dovidio & Gaertner, 1998). We argue that the MODE model provides a broad, overarching means of conceptualizing and explaining the various roles that automatic and controlled processes play in such discriminatory behavior. Because many individuals wish to avoid prejudiced responses (or at least their appearance), motivational forces should interact with automatically activated racial attitudes in predicting race-related behavior—at least when opportunity allows. Because we view attitudes as the starting point of race-related behavior, we first discuss how we have conceptualized and assessed racial attitudes, particularly their automatic properties.

Automatically Activated Racial Attitudes

The priming measure. The research involves not only the application of the MODE model to the domain of racial attitudes, but also our technique for assessing automatic attitude activation. The studies concern the direct assessment of the evaluations that are automatically activated in response to Blacks. They employ a priming procedure that was first developed in the mid-1980s (Fazio et al., 1986) and has since been used widely to study automatic attitude activation (see Fazio, 2001, for a review). Briefly, the participants' task on each trial is to indicate the connotation of an adjective as quickly as possible: Does it mean "good" or "bad"? We are concerned with the latency with which this judgment is made and, more specifically, the extent to which responding is facilitated by the prior presentation of a prime. The pattern of facilitation that is exhibited on positive versus negative adjectives provides an indication of the individual's attitude toward the primed object. Relatively more facilitation on positive adjectives is indicative of a more positive attitude and relatively more facilitation on negative adjectives is indicative of a negative attitude. Furthermore, these estimates are obtained without the individual's awareness that his or her attitude is even being assessed; the participant is not asked to consider his or her attitude toward the prime during the task. Yet, it is possible to infer from the facilitation data the degree to which positive or negative evaluations are activated when the object is presented.

We have applied this methodology to the assessment of racial attitudes. We will provide only a brief sketch of the procedure here; details are available in Fazio, Jackson, Dunton, and Williams (1995). Participants are told that the experiment concerns word meaning as an automatic skill and that a variety of tasks will be performed. The procedure consists of four phases, the last being the actual priming task. The purpose of the first task is to obtain baseline latency data. On each trial, the participant is presented with an adjective (e.g., *attractive, likable, disgusting, offensive*) and asked to indicate as quickly as possible whether it means "good" or "bad." The next two phases are intended to prepare participants for the priming task, which involves the presentation of faces as primes and adjectives as targets. The second phase is presented to the participants as involving the ability to learn faces. They simply attend to a series of head-shots of individuals presented on the computer screen. The third phase is a recognition test. Participants are presented with a face and asked to indicate whether the face was one that they had or had not seen in the previous task. Next, the actual priming task occurs. Participants are told that the previous tasks will now be combined, in the interest of determining the degree to which judging word meaning is an automatic skill. The experimenter indicates that if it truly is, individuals should be able to perform just as well as in the very first phase of the experiment, even if they have to do something else at the same time. In this case, the task to be performed simultaneously is learning faces. Thus, this phase of the experiment is said to involve both the learning of faces and the judgment of adjectives. On the target trials, images of White and Black students serve as the primes, again followed by positive and negative adjectives. We record the latency to respond to the adjectives as a function of prime race.

This procedure yields a multitude of observations for each participant. We routinely have reduced the data from any given respondent to a single index that serves as the estimate of the individual's attitude toward Blacks. To do so, average facilitation scores are computed for each person on positive and negative adjectives for each face that was presented. This preliminary step yields mean facilitation scores for each of the multiple White and Black faces. Thus, it is possible to examine the interaction of race of photo × valence of adjective for each participant. The effect size of this interaction is computed and serves as our estimate of the individual's attitude. Given the computational procedure, more negative scores reflect a pattern of facilitation indicating greater negativity toward Blacks: relatively more facilitation on negative adjectives when they were preceded by a Black face than a White face and relatively less facilitation on positive adjectives when they were preceded by a Black face. The opposite pattern yields a positive score.

Predictive validity of the priming measure. In adopting this paradigm to the study of racial attitudes, we were questioning the assumption that evaluative responses to Blacks reflected the cultural stereotype and, hence, were universally negative (Devine, 1989). Instead, we advocated that meaningful individual differences in White individuals' automatic evaluative responses might be observed. Indeed, across many studies to date, wide variability has been found across hundreds of participants, with many individuals exhibiting various degrees of automatically activated negativity toward Blacks, but others exhibiting more positive automatic responses.

This variability we observe is meaningful. Given the MODE model's emphasis on the "early" influences of automatically activated attitudes, these attitudes should operate subtly, guiding attention, defining situations, and often guiding behavior in a relatively spontaneous fashion. Consistent with this reasoning, attitude indices derived from the priming measure have proven predictive of a race-related behavior across a number of studies. For example, in one such study, participants were "debriefed" by a Black experimenter after completing the priming measure. After a several-minute interaction with a given participant, the experimenter rated the extent to which the participant seemed interested and friendly, paying particular attention to nonverbal behavior such as smiling, eye contact, and distance. These experimenter ratings showed clear correspondence with the attitude index—participants characterized by negativity toward Blacks produced a less friendly and interested impression in the eyes of the Black experimenter (Fazio et al., 1995).

Additional evidence of construals being shaped by automatically activated racial attitudes was found in a study in which White participants were charged with rating the quality of essays purportedly written by a Black undergraduate (Jackson, 1997). After completing the priming measure, participants returned for a second session, where they were told that they would be serving as judges for an essay contest. After reviewing biographical information about the author that revealed his race, participants rated how interesting, well-written, and persuasive the essay was, as well as how deserving it was to win the contest. A composite index of participants' ratings was again correlated with their attitude estimates: negative automatically activated racial attitudes appeared to guide participants' impressions of the work created by a Black student.

We recently reported similar findings in the context of a study about committee selection procedures (Olson & Fazio, 2007a). As in Jackson's research, participants had completed the priming measure prior to returning to the lab for a "second study." Upon returning, they were told that they would be simulating the work of committee members, who must review a large number of applications in a limited amount of time. Applications of four individuals who were applying to work in the Peace Corps were provided for them to review. The first two applicants consisted of highly qualified and poorly qualified White females. The critical applicants were the final two: moderately qualified Black and White males. After reviewing the extensive application materials (including school transcripts, work history, personal statement, and an interview summary purportedly provided by a Peace Corps official), they rated each applicant on a number of dimensions including their credentials, likeability, and suitability for Peace Corps work. These ratings were averaged and a relative preference score for the Black versus the White critical applicants was computed for each participant. As expected, the attitude index predicted their ratings: negativity toward Blacks according to the priming measure corresponded to a preference for the White relative to the Black applicant.

Comparable findings can be found in research employing variations of the priming measure. For example, Dovidio, Kawakami, Johnson, Johnson, and Howard (1997) reported correspondence between the nonverbal behaviors exhibited by White participants when interacting with a Black experimenter and a priming measure using composite sketches of Blacks and Whites as primes. Individuals characterized by negative attitude indices showed reduced eye contact, among other things, when interacting with a Black relative to a White (see also Dovidio, Kawakami, & Gaertner, 2002).

In addition to attesting to the predictive validity of the priming measure, these studies also validate the role of attitude accessibility in the attitude-behavior process. Instead of manipulating or measuring attitude accessibility and then examining how it moderated the relation between self-reported attitudes and behavior, as in early MODE model research, the more recent work essentially incorporated accessibility into the very measure of attitude itself. That is, the priming measure assessed the evaluation automatically activated by the presentation of African-American faces, and the resulting attitude estimates proved predictive of race-related judgments and behavior. Thus, these findings provide support for the MODE model's postulate that behavior can be a direct reflection of the attitude automatically activated from memory upon exposure to the target.

But this, of course, is only part of the story. Despite the correspondence we have observed between automatically activated attitudes and race-related judgments and behavior, oftentimes we see no evidence for that simple relationship. The MODE model predicts that additional processes, afforded by motivation and opportunity, can be evoked to steer behavior somewhere other than where the automatically activated attitude would imply. We turn to these motivational factors next.

Motivation to Control Prejudiced Reactions

According to the MODE model, deliberative processes enter into the attitude-behavior relation given the presence of some relevant motivation. Earlier we described some of the motives (e.g., accuracy) that operate in a variety of attitude domains. Although they probably operate in the prejudice domain as well, additional motivational forces are uniquely at work when it comes to prejudice and make it all the more useful as an arena for testing the MODE model. Specifically, many White individuals wish not to appear prejudiced, either to themselves or to others. Others are more motivated to avoid conflict or dispute with respect to race. We have employed our Motivation to Control Prejudiced Reactions (MCPR) scale as a means of assessing these motives. The MCPR consists of two orthogonal factors (Dunton & Fazio, 1997). The first, concern with acting prejudiced, reflects a personal commitment to avoid reactions that others and oneself might consider prejudiced, and contains items such as, "I feel guilty when I have a negative thought or feeling about a Black person." The second factor, restraint to avoid dispute, involves a willingness to inhibit the expression of one's own thoughts and feelings in the interest of avoiding dispute with or about Blacks, and contains items like, "If I were participating in a class discussion and a Black student expressed an opinion with which I disagreed, I would be hesitant to express my viewpoint." Importantly, neither factor correlates with the priming estimates of automatically activated racial attitudes.

Before turning to research examining the moderating influence of these motivational factors, we'll review some of what we have learned about the two factors. First of all, they have very different correlates. A correlation of .50 was observed between scores on the concern factor and the endorsement of egalitarian values, as assessed by Katz and Hass's (1988) Humanitarianism-Egalitarianism Scale (see Fazio & Hilden, 2001, footnote 1). Restraint factor scores, on the other hand, were independent of egalitarianism, $r = -.01$. Additional correlates were identified in a study in which some 150 college students completed the MCPR during a mass survey, the priming procedure in an initial lab session, and a survey regarding their race-related childhood experiences in yet another session (Towles-Schwen & Fazio, 2001). A number of intriguing relations emerged. For example, the attitude estimates correlated significantly with the positivity of relatively recent interactions with Blacks, those during the high school years. What may have been most interesting about the study, however, was that the two factors of the MCPR related in very different ways to the past experience variables. Higher scores on the concern factor were associated with reports of more positive interactions with Blacks at all school levels and reports of little parental prejudice. Scores on the restraint factor correlated with these same variables, but in the reverse direction. Greater restraint was associated with relatively infrequent interactions, which (when they occurred) were less positive, and with relatively high parental prejudice. Thus, higher restraint seems to be associated with a lack of contact with, and possible avoidance of, African Americans.

Further evidence that high-restraint individuals adopt an avoidance strategy comes from a study in which White individuals provided private evaluations of Black and White job applicants prior to making videotaped public statements evaluating their credentials (Olson & Fazio, 2007b). Not surprisingly, according to naïve judges who rated the transcripts of the White participants' spoken words, participants' public statements corresponded with their private evaluations of the job applicants. However, this relation was moderated by scores on the restraint factor. When discussing a Black candidate (relative to a similarly qualified White target), high-restraint individuals showed less correspondence between their privately reported beliefs about those individuals and the words they chose to utter publicly about them. It appears, then, that high-restraint individuals obfuscate their private views when speaking publicly about Blacks, perhaps in an attempt to avoid controversy or dispute. The concern factor showed no such pattern.

We also have examined how the two motivational factors, as well as automatically activated racial attitudes, relate to individuals' emotional reactions following their exhibiting a seemingly prejudiced response (Fazio & Hilden, 2001). In a study about "emotional reactions to television commercials," participants were exposed to a series of Clio Award-winning ads, including the target public service ad. This ad induces viewers to assume wrongly that the African American who is pictured and the criminal who is described in the scrolling text next to the image are one and the same individual. Instead, viewers eventually learn that the photo is actually of the police officer who apprehended the criminal. Emotional reactions to the ad varied as a function of automatically activated racial attitudes and the two MCPR factors. More positive attitudes were associated with feelings of guilt. Individuals characterized by higher scores on the concern with acting prejudiced factor reported both greater guilt and greater agitation. Those with higher scores on the restraint to avoid dispute factor experienced agitation but not guilt. Thus, the unique experience of guilt (unaccompanied by any other feelings of agitation) was associated with positive racial attitudes, ones that were so well-internalized that they were capable of automatic activation. Guilt and agitation were more pronounced among those for whom the ad provoked violation of a valued "ought" standard (Higgins, 1987) regarding egalitarianism (higher concern), whereas agitation alone was accentuated among those for whom the ad was reminiscent of the very race-related dispute they seek to avoid (higher restraint).

Mixed Processes in the Racial Prejudice Domain

We turn now to the evidence for mixed processes in racial prejudice. In the research we review in this section, participants typically completed both the priming measure of racial prejudice and the MCPR prior to performing some race-related judgment or behavior. Our analytic approach has been to regress these judgments or behaviors onto the attitude estimate provided by the priming measure, scores from the MCPR factors, and importantly, their interaction terms. Mixed processes are revealed in interaction effects, whereby the direct effect of the attitude estimate is reduced (or even reversed) as motivation increases. Throughout these studies we have found consistent evidence for the MODE model's predictions regarding these mixed processes. However, these interaction effects can take varied forms, which, as we shall see, reveals interesting insights about the correctional goals involved in motivation to control prejudiced reactions.

Moderating effects of the concern factor. Some of the first evidence of these mixed processes in the racial prejudice arena was found with respect to participants' responses on what has been indisputably the most popular self-report measure of racial prejudice: the Modern Racism Scale (MRS, McConahay, 1986). This seven-item measure prompts respondents to indicate their agreement with statements like "Over the past few years, Blacks have gotten more economically than they deserve," and "Blacks should not push themselves where they are not wanted."

It is important to note that indicating responses to such statements is itself race-related verbal behavior. From the MODE model's perspective, such verbal expressions occur further "downstream" in the attitude-behavior process, after any automatic activation of racial attitudes, and after any motivation to control prejudiced reactions has been evoked. Thus, responses to these statements—and any explicit measure of prejudice—have the potential to be influenced by both automatic and more motivated forces. Indeed, evidence suggests that the MRS, contrary to how it was originally portrayed, is a reactive measure; White participants report less prejudice on it in the presence of a Black experimenter (Fazio et al., 1995; see Olson, in press, for a more extensive review). The MODE model predicts that in the absence of motivation, automatically activated racial attitudes should directly influence responses on the MRS.

However, motivated individuals should wish to avoid the influence of any automatic racial prejudice and respond differently to the items.

This is just what we found (Dunton & Fazio, 1997). Individuals who were relatively unconcerned about acting prejudiced responded to the MRS items in a manner that was consistent with the attitude index provided by the priming measure. Those with negative automatically activated racial attitudes reported more prejudicial beliefs on the MRS, and those with relatively positive racial attitudes reported less prejudice. However, as concern with acting prejudiced increased, correspondence between the two measures decreased, so much so, in fact, that participants characterized by more negative attitudes and higher scores on the concern factor seemed to have gone out of their way to avoid the appearance of prejudice. They responded even more positively to the MRS items than did participants who displayed positivity in response to photos of African Americans during the priming procedure. (Although we will be discussing Figure 2.2 extensively in a subsequent section, readers who wish to see a graphical depiction of the form of the obtained interaction will find it represented in panel B of the figure.)

A similar moderating effect of the concern factor was observed in a study concerning people's expressed willingness to enter situations

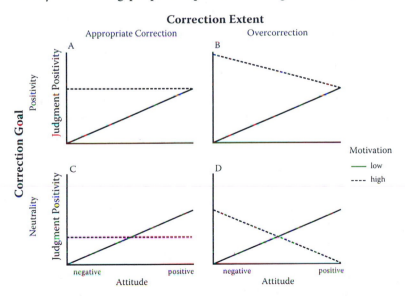

FIGURE 2.2 Hypothetical forms of attitude × motivation interactions predicting race-related judgments and behaviors. Reprinted from Olson & Fazio (2004).

involving a Black interaction partner (Towles-Schwen & Fazio, 2003). As Snyder and Gangestad (1982) emphasized, the social situations we choose to enter, or avoid entering, can be a reflection of the social worlds we wish to create. Towles-Schwen and Fazio speculated that the choice to enter or avoid certain social situations involving Blacks might be determined by the mixed processes posited by the MODE model. Participants were invited to imagine themselves about to enter a variety of social situations (e.g., granting a maintenance worker access to one's home, sharing a small dorm room, sitting down at a crowded table where someone is already seated). They were asked to rate how comfortable they would be to enter these situations. After responding to these situations in the absence of any specification of the interaction partner, participants rated their comfort with the situations again, this time imagining each of a variety of hypothetical interaction partners, one of whom happened to be Black. Interestingly, a marked difference was observed when participants imagined a Black partner relative to their ratings when the partner was left unspecified. In general, participants claimed that they would find the social interaction more comfortable when a Black partner was involved. However, the extent to which they did so varied as a function of automatically activated attitudes and concern with acting prejudiced. Consistent with the MODE model, more positive attitude estimates corresponded to greater anticipated comfort interacting with a Black partner, but only among participants with relatively low scores on the concern factor. Participants who were more concerned about acting prejudiced tended to show a reverse pattern. Those claiming the most comfort were those marked by negative automatically activated attitudes and high concern (again, see panel B of Figure 2.2). It appears that these individuals were overcompensating for their prejudice when indicating their willingness to pursue an interaction with a Black partner.

Moderating effects of the restraint factor. Moderating effects of motivation on the relation between automatically activated racial attitudes and a race-related judgment have been observed in additional studies. In the two we wish to highlight now, the driving motivational force proved to be restraint to avoid dispute. Dunton and Fazio (1997) asked participants to list the feelings that came to mind when they thought of the "typical Black male undergraduate." They then rated their own thoughts in terms of their positivity and negativity, which were averaged to form an overall index of their self-reported evaluations. In later sessions, participants completed the priming measure of racial attitudes and the MCPR. The regression analysis revealed a significant interaction between attitudes and the restraint to avoid dispute factor of the motivation scale. Correspondence between estimates of automatically activated racial attitudes and participants' ratings of their feelings toward the typical Black male undergraduate increased as restraint decreased. Those with low restraint scores appeared to be guided simply by their attitudes. More motivated participants, on the other hand, showed a reverse pattern, indicative of correction for their automatically activated attitudes. (The form that the interaction assumed is represented in panel D of Figure 2.2, which will be discussed shortly.)

We observed a conceptually parallel finding in a study that we conducted concerning "first impressions" (Olson & Fazio, 2004). We asked participants to offer their first impressions of a series of individuals depicted in photographs that were presented on their computer screens. These were images of various people—men, women, Blacks, Whites, and people of other races—in various occupational settings. Included therein were several Black-White pairs, matched in terms of the status and independence of their occupational roles (e.g., a Black male potter and a White male bricklayer; a Black male minister and a White male professor). Participants recorded their impressions of each target individually on a variety of scales (e.g., likeability, competence) as they appeared on the screen. The analyses focused on the difference in the ratings of the Black target persons relative to the matched White targets. In general, participants reported viewing the Black targets as more positive than the White targets. However, we also observed an interaction indicating that this preference for Blacks was more characteristic of some kinds of individuals than others. Among individuals with low scores on the restraint to avoid dispute factor, racial attitudes corresponded with the trait inferences. Those with more positive attitudes judged the Black targets more positively than the White targets. This relation was attenuated and, once again, even reversed, as restraint to avoid dispute increased (see panel D of Figure 2.2). Thus, a correction process appeared to be at work among the more motivated participants.

Correctional goals implied by the motivational factors. We now have seen repeated instances of motivation to control prejudiced reactions moderating the relation between automatically activated racial attitudes and some race-related judgment or behavior. In some cases, concern for acting prejudiced seemed to do the work, and in other cases it was restraint to avoid dispute. For example, it was the concern factor that interacted with attitude estimates in predicting MRS scores (Dunton & Fazio, 1997) and reported comfort in entering social situations with a Black individual (Towles-Schwen & Fazio, 2003). Restraint, on the other hand, played a moderating role in predicting evaluations of a Black male undergraduate (Dunton & Fazio) and first impressions of Black individuals (Olson & Fazio, 2004).

We have hesitated to make predictions about the sorts of social judgments and behaviors that might be more likely to evoke one or the other motivational factor. Looking back across several studies, however, some patterns have emerged that we believe provide some insight as to the sorts of situations that lend themselves to the influence of the two motivational factors, as well as the sorts of corrective goals each motivation implies. Our speculations hinge on whether the Black social target in question is construed at the category or the individual level. Take, for example, the items included in the MRS. They prompt respondents to consider Blacks as a group, at the category level. In Towles-Schwen and Fazio's (2003) work, the social target with whom participants were imagining interacting was described simply as Black, and described only at the category level. In research involving restraint factor interactions, on the other hand, the Black social targets were depicted more as individuals (albeit as members of a category). So while the concern factor's focus appears to be Blacks as a group, restraint works at the individual level.

The relevance of this individual-versus-group distinction becomes apparent when considering the underlying bases of each of the motivational factors. Recall the concern factor's relatively strong correlation with egalitarianism. If one's impetus to avoid prejudice is based on the institutional factors implicated in egalitarian beliefs (such as a belief in Blacks' historical plight and continued educational and economic disadvantages), then one is more likely to see prejudice at the group level and aim one's own responses to it commensurately. Restraint, on the other hand, is premised on the desire to avoid dispute, conflict, and confrontation. With few exceptions, an individual comes into conflict not with categories of people, but with individuals. If it is the fear of being accused of prejudice, or of being offensive in some way, that characterizes people high in restraint motivation, then such motivation is more likely to be evoked in the interpersonal situations, where conflict actually occurs. So while speculative, we believe that concern motivation is more aligned with the possibility of prejudice toward the group, whereas restraint motivation stems from desire to avoid dispute at the individual level.

Another difference that seems to emerge between the concern and the restraint factors is the pattern of interactions we have observed involving attitude estimates and the motivational factor. As we noted parenthetically earlier, the interactions involving concern and those involving restraint have assumed somewhat different forms. Although admittedly speculative, consideration of these differential patterns provides some further insights regarding the specific correctional goals involved with each motive. The analysis we have offered (Olson & Fazio, 2004) rests heavily on Wegener and Petty's (1995) flexible correction model, which suggests that upon suspicion that they are falling prey to an undesired judgmental bias, individuals may attempt to correct for the bias. They may adjust their judgments on the basis of naïve theories that they hold regarding the direction and magnitude of the unwanted influence.

Hypothetically, the attitude by motivation interaction implying motivated correction can assume one of several potential forms. These are illustrated in Figure 2.2. Common to all the panels of the figure, correspondence between automatically activated racial attitudes and judgments is evident at low levels of motivation, in accordance with the MODE model. The slopes and intercepts of the high-motivation regression lines, on the other hand, vary. The top two panels (A and B) depict correction for negativity only. In panel A, the line is flat, suggesting appropriate correction for negativity. Panel B also implies correction for the purpose of avoiding negative judgments, but in this case, judgments of Blacks among prejudiced individuals are particularly positive—more positive than even low-prejudiced participants. That is, overcorrection is apparent. Findings involving interactions between attitude estimates and the concern factor have shared a remarkably similar form, that of panel B. Here, participants appear to have corrected for automatically activated negativity toward Blacks, but not for positivity.

Panels C and D, on the other hand, depict correction for both negativity and positivity. For example, in panel C respondents with negative attitudes toward Blacks have adjusted their responses in a positive direction, and those with positive attitudes have adjusted their responses in a negative direction, in both cases coming to more closely resemble respondents with neutral attitudes. Panel D also depicts correction for both positive and negative prejudices, but respondents here, as in panel B, appear to have "overshot" their goal, such that the relationship between attitudes and judgments for high-motivation respondents is actually negative. Findings involving interactions between attitude estimates and the restraint factor have also shared a similar form, that of panel D. Here, participants appear to have corrected for both negativity and positivity toward Blacks. It appears, then, that two general correctional goals underlie motivation to control prejudiced reactions, positivity and neutrality, and these motives align, respectively, with concern and restraint.

Why are the two motives associated with different correctional goals? Given its strong ties to egalitarianism beliefs, as described earlier, we suspect that the historical mistreatment of Blacks is a salient belief among individuals characterized with concern motivation. Their goal is to treat such disadvantaged individuals more favorably. Hence, those motivated by egalitarian values may correct for any negativity that they experience. On the other hand, individuals with more positive attitudes believe they have nothing to correct for; their automatically activated positivity toward Blacks is concordant with their goals.

Restraint motivation, on the other hand, has a more bidirectional quality to it. Recall that the primary motive in the case of restraint is to avoid dispute, not redress historic inequalities. Here our suspicion is that individuals characterized by such motivation may fear accusations of "reverse discrimination" in addition to the more straightforward accusation of prejudice. Indeed, both our research and others' suggest that Whites are often willing to "bend over backwards" to avoid the appearance of prejudice (Biernat & Vescio, 1993; Gaertner & Dovidio, 1977; Jussim, Coleman, & Lerch, 1987; Olson & Fazio, 2004). It's likely, then, that overtly positive treatment of Blacks might sometimes be met with suspicion that such treatment is because of race. Thus, race-related disputes can stem from the appearance of either mistreatment or special treatment of Blacks. High-restraint individuals appear to respond to such dispute-provoking situations by either appearing more positive toward Blacks (if their underlying, automatically activated racial sentiments are negative) or appearing more negative toward Blacks (if their underlying racial sentiments are positive).

Interestingly, a commonality that has emerged across the unidirectional corrective nature of concern and bidirectional corrective nature of restraint is that of overcorrection, as displayed in panels B and D of Figure 2.1. In terms of Wegener and Petty's (1995) flexible correction model, it appears that motivated perceivers believe their automatically activated attitudes to be a potent source of judgmental bias.

Setting the specifics of the correctional process aside for the moment, the studies summarized above have provided support for the MODE model's postulate regarding mixed processes. Verbally expressed judgments—whether they be responses to an explicit measure of racial attitude, first impression ratings, or behavioral intentions regarding a willingness to initiate interaction—all occur farther "downstream" than the automatic activation of any relevant attitude. They can be influenced by automatically activated racial attitudes. But such explicit judgments also may be influenced by motivational factors that can override the effect of the automatically activated attitude.

The Role of Opportunity

In the research summarized above, we have focused on the interactive roles of automatically activated racial attitudes and motivation to control prejudiced reactions. The outcome variables concerned verbally expressed judgments, and these judgments were offered under conditions in which the opportunity parameter of the MODE model was high. That is, it is not at all difficult to monitor and control one's responses to the simple judgmental scales that participants completed. Thus, in all these cases, ample opportunity (e.g., time and cognitive resources) was available for motivated processes to influence race-related judgments.

In the complexity of real-world interracial contact, however, opportunity may be limited. Some of these limits stem from the confines of our cognitive endowments. For example, in contrast to verbal judgments, the nonverbal behavior one emits is less likely to be monitored and, to some extent, is less susceptible to conscious control (DePaulo & Friedman, 1998). Thus, even if one is motivated to control prejudiced reactions, automatically activated negativity might "leak" into the nonverbal channels in interracial settings because there is less opportunity for behavioral control. This is just what Dovidio and colleagues (1997) found in research that employed a priming measure of racial prejudice quite similar to our own. Participants in this research also completed explicit questionnaire measures on racial attitudes prior to interacting with Black and White confederates. Although the explicit measure predicted self-reported liking of the confederates, the priming measure predicted nonverbal expressions like blinking and eye contact (see also Dovidio et al., 2002). Thus, in accordance with the MODE model, motivation is unable to overcome one's automatically activated attitudes when opportunity is not available.

The multiple demands of social life also mean that opportunity is likely to wax and wane. Those with whom we have long-term relationships are likely to see us when we are tired or preoccupied, that is, when our "true colors" are likely to emerge. It is unlikely that Whites in long-term relationships with Blacks are always able to suppress any underlying automatic negativity toward Blacks in these low-opportunity moments. Thus, automatic prejudice is likely to emerge periodically in real interracial relationships that extend over time, and influence the quality—and longevity—of those relationships, even when the White individual is motivated to control prejudiced reactions. That is, when opportunity is low, as it sometimes is in real relationships, motivation to control prejudice will be impotent to overcome automatic prejudice.

The desire to examine automatically activated attitudes and motivation in the context of real-life relationships prompted Towles-Schwen and Fazio (2006) to conduct a pair of logistically complex field investigations that proved very informative. The studies took advantage of the fact that Indiana University randomly pairs any freshmen who have requested a double dormitory room and not specified a roommate by name. Hence, with the cooperation of the Housing Office, it was possible to identify dyads consisting of an African American and a White freshman who had been randomly paired to share a room. The White member of such dyads was recruited to participate, for monetary payment, in a study presumably concerned with satisfaction with college life. A comparison sample of Whites who had been randomly paired with another White also was recruited. The initial study confirmed the presumption that these interracial relationships are problematic. At the end of the fall semester, Whites paired with an African American reported less satisfaction with their roommates, as well as a lower frequency of engaging in various joint activities. However, the most striking evidence of the difficulties faced by the interracial dyads came from a very simple objective variable: the sheer likelihood of the relationship remaining intact. By the end of the semester, a number of these relationships had simply dissolved; one or the other person had moved out. In fact, 28% of the interracial dyads had split up, a dissolution rate that was significantly higher than the 9% observed for the same-race dyads.

Study 2 focused on whether knowledge of the White partner's automatically activated racial attitudes, as assessed early in the semester, could predict the success of the interracial roommate relationships. Again, the students were recruited for a study presumably concerned with satisfaction with college life. In an initial session, they completed a number of computer tasks and questionnaires, many of which were intended to obscure the interest in racial attitudes and in their roommate relationships. The priming measure of racial attitudes was embedded within a series of speeded computer tasks that presumably assessed cognitive skills potentially related to doing well in college. Participants also completed opinion surveys regarding a wide array of social and political issues, and the MCPR was embedded within those items.

Housing Office records revealed that nearly 30% of the interracial roommate relationships had dissolved by the end of the first semester;

57% of the dyads failed to remain intact for the entire academic year. The number of days the roommates were together, which ranged from 24 to 252 days, provided a very useful continuous measure of the success of the relationship. The measure of automatically activated attitudes correlated significantly with this duration index; the more positive the attitudes, the greater the longevity of the relationship. Importantly, neither factor of the MCPR bore any relation to the duration of the relationship, nor did either of these motivational factors moderate the relation between attitude and status of the relationship. As suggested earlier, this lack of effect for motivation likely stems from the opportunity factor. No matter how well intentioned one might be, no matter how much one may wish to monitor one's behavior carefully, no matter how much one might try to control seemingly prejudiced reactions, it is just not possible to do so in the sort of intimate, continuous interaction context that characterizes sharing a dorm room.

Although all of this research attests to the importance of the impact of the opportunity factor, in our research on racial prejudice we have not pursued experimental manipulations of opportunity to provide a more rigorous test of its moderating role. However, as we shall see later, other researchers have pursued just this in research on "ego-depletion" and related constructs.

Failures to Evoke Relevant Motivations

The MODE model describes opportunity as a factor moderating the influence of automatically activated attitudes on judgments and behavior, and it can vary by person, situation, or judgment/behavior type. We have argued that in cases where verbal judgments are made with unlimited time and no source of distraction, opportunity is quite high and hence should not limit the influence of motivational forces aimed at curbing the influence of automatically activated attitudes. However, in the laboratory's own research, we have seen two cases where motivation failed to influence judgments even under such "ideal" conditions. In Jackson's (1997) research, where participants rated the quality of an essay purportedly written by a Black student, attitudes proved influential but motivation to control prejudice did not. Olson and Fazio (2007a) reported a similar pattern of findings regarding White participants' ratings of a Black relative to a White applicant to a volunteer position. Estimates of automatically activated racial attitudes derived from our standard priming procedure predicted the evaluations, but this relation was not moderated by either factor of the MCPR.

Why, with such a controllable judgment and no time pressure, did motivation essentially "fail" to act? We suspect that in order for motivation to control prejudice to influence one's race-related judgments, those judgments must be construed as race related. In Jackson's research, participants had the essay before them and their task was to evaluate it. In Olson and Fazio's research (2007a), a wealth of information about the targets was provided, including transcripts, a personal statement, and an interviewer's report. In both cases, it is likely that participants simply failed to consider the possibility that their judgments might be at all influenced by the race of the target person, and hence, no motivation was evoked. According to most models of social judgment, one of the first steps in correcting bias is noticing it (e.g., Wegener & Petty, 1995; Wilson & Brekke, 1994). The richness of the information that is available as a basis for one's judgment may render a potential source of bias relatively subtle and, hence, difficult to discover. Thus, the informational context can prevent motivation from being evoked.

Perspectives of the MODE Model on Contemporary Research

Early tests of the MODE model were conducted with the historic issue of attitude-behavior processes in mind, before implicit measures of attitudes and debates about their relation to explicit measures, conscious versus unconscious attitudes, and related issues examined in this volume came to the fore. As we have seen, the model has fared well in more recent tests employing an implicit measure of attitudes; the research has yielded supportive findings across a variety of judgmental and behavioral contexts. Given this success, it is our belief that the MODE model provides a valuable perspective concerning issues that have arisen regarding the meaning and interpretation of implicit measures. Below, we address some of these contemporary issues and consider how they are informed by the MODE model and our research findings.

Explicit Measures and Their Relation to Implicit Measures

A few years ago we reviewed what we referred to as the "burgeoning" research on implicit and explicit measures of attitudes (Fazio & Olson, 2003). As exemplified by this volume, this research has expanded to include a number of related research questions involving issues of both measurement and the underlying cognitive processes presumably tapped by different measures. Myriad claims have been made about what these implicit measures actually measure (for extended reviews, see Fazio & Olson; Olson, 2003). As the popularity of implicit measurement tools has driven this research forward at a staggering pace, it is no irony that one of the age-old tools of attitude research—the questionnaire—has been thrust into the spotlight. As supposed measures of attitudes, it was natural for researchers to wonder whether implicit measures would reflect the same attitude reported on an explicit measure (for reviews, see Blair, 2001; Dovidio, Kawakami, & Beach, 2001). Thus, one question to come from implicit measurement research was this: What is the relation between implicit and explicit measures? Are they getting at the same thing?

The MODE model has a ready answer. Recall our earlier point that responses to a questionnaire necessarily involve overt expressions of one's attitudes. These responses are verbal behaviors. As such, they fall directly under the intended purview of the MODE model. Like any other behavior, verbal expressions can be affected by both one's automatically activated attitude toward the object and, opportunity willing, motivational factors. In the absence of motivation and opportunity, the evaluation automatically activated by the object should guide verbal responses. Thus, it is under conditions of low motivation or low opportunity (or both) that one should find correspondence between implicit and explicit measures, and this is precisely what a substantial body of research has shown.

The most obvious place to look for the MODE model's predictions of implicit-explicit correspondence is in research domains where motivational forces are likely to be completely absent. In early work (e.g., Fazio et al., 1986), the priming measure was employed to assess the automatic activation of attitudes toward objects for which there were few barriers to honest attitude reporting (e.g., puppies and cockroaches). This work indicated that just as explicit measures revealed a preference for puppies and a distaste for cockroaches, so did the (implicit) priming measure. There is little demand, either personally or socially, to adjust verbal reports of one's liking for such objects away from one's true attitudes. In contrast, research that has directly compared such attitude objects to more socially sensitive issues (e.g., abortion, Blacks, contraceptives, homosexuality, pornography) has observed far less correspondence between the implicit and explicit measures in the latter case (Dovidio & Fazio, 1992). Hence, we find that individuals' responses on explicit measures flow directly from the attitude the object automatically evokes onto the questionnaire page when there is little motivation to report otherwise, but automatically activated attitudes are less likely to be openly expressed when the issues are more sensitive in nature. The same conclusion has been reached in research employing the IAT as an implicit measure of attitudes. For example, correspondence with explicit measures has been observed with respect to food and beverage preferences among other socially tame domains (Maison, Greenwald, & Bruin, 2001). More recent research, as well as meta-analyses, support the view that motivational factors presumably derived from social sensibilities moderate the relationship between the IAT and explicit measures (Hoffman, Gawronski, Gschwendner, Le, & Schmitt, 2005; Nosek, 2005).

Even in cases where one may be motivated to respond a certain way on an explicit measure, a lack of opportunity to do so will inhibit the influence of motivational processes, leaving only one's automatically activated attitudes to influence responses on an explicit measure. For example, Koole, Dijksterhuis, and van Knippenberg (2001) demonstrated that implicit and explicit measures of self-esteem correspond better when responses on the explicit measure are made very quickly or while distracted (see also Ranganath, Smith, & Nosek, 2008). Again, and as the MODE model predicts, correspondence between implicit and explicit measures appears when motivational factors have minimal impact on responses to the explicit measure.

According to the MODE model, such correspondence should be minimal or altogether absent to the extent that motivation and opportunity factors are both present. Again, this is what the research indicates. For example, in the motivationally volatile domain of racial prejudice in particular, where much of this research has been conducted, little correspondence has been observed between implicit and explicit measures (e.g., Fazio et al., 1995; Greenwald, McGhee, & Schwartz, 1998; Dovidio et al., 2002), and where it has been observed, correlations tend to be weak (e.g., McConnell & Liebold, 2001; Lepore & Brown, 1997; Wittenbrink, Judd, & Park, 1997). Of course, people vary in their motivation to control prejudice, and the MODE model would expect that dissociations between the two measure types would be observed only among individuals with relatively strong motivation to control prejudiced reactions. As we described earlier, this is precisely what Fazio and colleagues reported in 1995 with respect to an implicit priming measure of racial attitudes and the explicit Modern Racism Scale, well before debates about the relationship between implicit and explicit measures reached its current prominence.

Such moderating effects of the MCPR—with low-motivation respondents showing correspondence between implicit and explicit measures—have now been demonstrated across a variety of implicit and explicit measures (e.g., Banse, Seise, & Zerbes, 2001; Gawronski, Geschke, & Banse, 2003; Payne, 2001; Payne, Cheng, Govorun, & Stewart, 2005). For example, Payne et al. found the relation between estimates of racial attitudes assessed through their affect misattribution procedure and self-reported evaluations of Blacks to be moderated by MCPR scores. Similarly, Payne (2001) found that the relation between scores on the Modern Racism Scale and the extent to which performance in a weapons identification task was affected by Black versus White primes to vary as a function of MCPR scores. Correspondence was observed among those with lower motivation scores, but those higher in motivation to control prejudiced reactions displayed an inverse relation, indicative of motivated overcorrection.

Further evidence of the mixed processes predicted by the MODE model has accumulated from multiple laboratories and has demonstrated the joint influence of implicitly measured attitudes and motivation across a variety of measures and domains. For example, Florack, Scarabis, and Bless (2001) examined the relation between German students' attitudes toward Turkish immigrants, as assessed via an IAT, and their judgments of a Turkish juvenile delinquent whose criminal behavior was described in a lengthy newspaper article. The relation was moderated by scores on the need for cognition scale (Cacioppo, Petty, Feinstein, & Jarvis, 1996). The implicit measure proved predictive of assessments of the Turkish offender among those lower in need for cognition, but not among those more motivated to process information extensively. Dasgupta and Rivera (2006) assessed the impact of automatically activated prejudice toward gays and lesbians (also via an IAT) toward a gay interviewer. Consistent with the MODE model, this relation was influenced by two more motivationally oriented moderating variables, the extent to which participants endorsed egalitarian beliefs regarding gender and gender identity, and the extent to which they reported a commitment to monitoring and controlling their potentially prejudicial behavior. It was among individuals who lacked such motivation that a relation was observed.

Intriguingly, recent research by Scinta and Gable (2007) has yielded conceptually parallel findings in a very different domain: that of romantic relationships. Estimates of participants' automatically activated attitudes toward their romantic partners (obtained via an IAT in one study and an evaluative priming procedure involving the subliminal presentation

of images of the partner in a second study) were employed as predictors
of reported satisfaction with the relationship. As expected, those with
more positive attitudes reported greater satisfaction. However, this was
true only among participants who were not entrapped in the relationship.
Among participants who had invested heavily in the relationship and
foresaw poor alternatives to their current partner, the relation between
automatically activated attitudes toward the partner and relationship satisfaction was reversed. Using Scinta and Gable's terminology, such individuals faced formidable "barriers to exit" the relationship and, hence,
were motivated to view the relationship favorably. Those characterized
by relatively negative automatically activated attitudes and such motivational pressure actually reported the greatest satisfaction with the relationship. Indeed, across a variety of self-reports concerning satisfaction
with the relationship, the moderating effects of barriers to exit yielded
regression lines of the form depicted in panel B of Figure 2.2. Once again,
then, we see evidence of differential correspondence between implicit
measures (automatically activated attitudes toward the partner, in this
case) and explicit measures (reports of relationship satisfaction) as function of motivational forces (barriers to exit the relationship).

This is not to say that the MODE model's two moderating factors,
motivation and opportunity, can account for the universe of observed
dissociations between implicit and explicit measures. Dissociations can
occur for any number of reasons. For example, reiterating Azjen and
Fishbein's (1977) argument regarding the importance of measuring
attitudes and behavior at equivalent levels of specificity, Hofmann and
colleagues (2005) pointed out that dissociations will occur if implicit
and explicit measures do not correspond conceptually—one would not
expect correspondence between two measures if they are measuring
attitudes toward two different objects. Similarly, one would expect correspondence to be relatively weaker if the two measures fail to encourage the same categorization of the attitude object. Most people, objects,
and issues are multiply categorizable, and contextual factors can pro-
mote one categorization over another. For example, if one measure were
to encourage categorization of stimulus persons by race, but the other
not, dissociations are more likely to be observed (see Fazio & Dunton,
1997; Olson & Fazio, 2003, for discussions of categorization by race).

Implications for Awareness of the Attitude

Observed dissociations between implicit and explicit measures have
prompted many claims about the sorts of attitudes assessed by implicit

measures. One of the more provocative strikes us as also one of the least tenable: that individuals lack introspective access to their automatically activated attitudes. As we first argued a few years ago (Fazio & Olson, 2003), dissociations can easily be explained without invoking unawareness, and the use of an implicit measure does not, in and of itself, guarantee that individuals are unaware of their attitudes. Implicit measures simply provide estimates of individuals' attitudes without our having to ask them directly for such information. The measures themselves are silent with respect to the question of whether individuals are or are not aware of the evaluations they show evidence of associating with the attitude object (see Gawronski, Hofmann, & Wilbur, 2006, for a similar analysis and review). Indeed, the position of the MODE model stands contrary to the tenet that implicit measures reflect unconscious attitudes. Instead, the model maintains that people tend to generally be aware of their attitudes and that it is motivational forces, not some consciousness-impervious shield, that prevents their verbal expression. The evidence, as we describe next, supports the MODE model's perspective.

Perhaps the most direct way of testing the hypothesis that countervailing motivation, and not a lack of awareness, prevents the expression of automatically activated attitudes is to remove the source of motivation. Under such conditions, the explicit measure should then reflect the implicit measure. In other words, if one is aware of a given attitude, then an effective exhortation to report it honestly should reveal it. This is precisely what Nier (2005) demonstrated. Participants in his study completed both an IAT designed to assess racial prejudice and the Modern Racism Scale. Some participants completed the MRS under bogus pipeline conditions, where they were led to believe that the experimenter could identify any dishonesties in reporting, thus effectively rendering motivation impotent to conceal respondents' underlying sentiments. When participants completed the MRS under standard circumstances, no implicit-explicit correspondence was observed. However, when participants had been induced to be honest, IAT and MRS measures of racial prejudice showed clear correspondence ($r =$ .51). Such a pattern would not have been apparent had participants been unaware of their implicit racial biases.

Additional evidence that people are aware of their implicitly measured attitudes comes from research demonstrating motivated correction for those attitudes, which, of course, is precisely what the research we reviewed earlier shows. For example, motivated participants in Olson and Fazio's (2004) study on first impressions of Blacks and Whites actively corrected for their implicitly assessed prejudice according to their initial level of prejudice; motivated individuals with a greater degree of prejudice showed greater correction. Such corrective measures could not be taken had participants been unaware of the existence of their biases. Indeed, theories of bias correction in social judgments explicitly highlight the essential role that awareness of one's biases plays in corrective processes (e.g., Wegener & Petty, 1995; Wilson & Brekke, 1994). It is upon the suspicion that their judgments are being unduly influenced by some biasing force that individuals engage in correction. That such corrective processes have been observed repeatedly in the MODE model research suggests that people are aware of their implicitly measured attitudes. Importantly, we do not argue that people are always correct in estimating their biases, and it is interesting that the consistent pattern of overcorrection that we and others have observed time and again suggests that some Whites might actually overestimate the magnitude of influence exerted by their automatically activated attitudes toward Blacks.

We also do not claim that attitudes cannot form unconsciously—indeed, we have provided replicable evidence that attitudes can form and change unconsciously (Olson & Fazio, 2001, 2002, 2006). Evaluative conditioning can lead to the development of automatically activated attitudes that reflect pairings to which individuals have been exposed, even if they are unable to report any awareness of those pairings. In one such experiment (Olson & Fazio, 2002), participants underwent our evaluative conditioning procedure, and immediately thereafter their attitudes toward the conditioned stimuli (CS) were assessed via a subliminal priming measure. As a result, they never had any reason to consider their attitudes toward the CS and were not even aware of the presence of the CS during the performance of the implicit measure. Nevertheless, they showed evidence of greater positivity having been activated in response to the positive CS than the negative CS. Thus, the entire process, from attitude formation to attitude activation, can occur outside of conscious awareness. Yet, as demonstrated by the finding that explicit measures of attitude toward the CS also are sensitive to the evaluative conditioning (Olson & Fazio, 2001), once attention is called to feelings about the objects, such attitudes can be reported.

Unconscious processes unquestionably play a role in judgment and behavior. In any given instance, people may be unaware that their attitudes have been activated from memory. Moreover, they may be unaware that their attitudes are exerting some influence on their construals of the object in the immediate situation, or unaware of the magnitude of that influence. And there certainly is no reason to believe that individuals are necessarily cognizant of the origins of their attitudes, that is, why they came to like or dislike some object. Yet, none of these possibilities necessitates the inference that individuals lack awareness of their attitudes per se.

Implicit Measures of Self-Esteem: A Case in Point

The MODE model has analogous implications for implicitly measured self-esteem, another domain in which lofty claims have been made about implicit measures' ability to penetrate the unconscious. Similar to claims of "unconscious prejudice," researchers have argued that the self-esteem tapped by implicit measures is unconscious and independent of one's conscious self-views, an argument bolstered by the low correlations observed between implicit and explicit measures of self-esteem (e.g., Bosson, Swann, & Pennebaker, 2000; Kernis, 2003; Koole and Pelham, 2003). Do we all have two independent attitudes toward the self, one conscious and one unconscious?

Again, the MODE model's perspective on the separation between implicit and explicit measures of self-esteem has little to do with unconsciousness versus consciousness or the existence of two independent self-attitudes. Instead, we argue that one's automatic self-views are accessible to conscious awareness and that motivated processes often interfere with forthright reporting on explicit measures. That is, explicit measures of self-esteem reflect not only automatically activated self-evaluations but also downstream forces. Our view is similar to that put forth by Dijksterhuis, Albers, and Bongers (see Chapter 8, this volume), who described implicit measures as more likely to reach "core" self-esteem, with responses on explicit measures more likely to be colored by a variety of motives.

One particularly strong motive is to view oneself in a positive light. Western culture in particular aims to champion and empower the individual, resulting in the social expectation that one view the self positively. Indeed, the mean response to traditional explicit measures of self-esteem is typically near the ceiling of the scale. On the other hand, modesty is another valued trait, and it is likely that some individuals strategically underpresent themselves in service of this motive, particularly in non-Western cultures (Kitayama & Uchida, 2003). The former motive might cause one to appear more positive toward the self than one's automatic reactions toward the self might imply. The latter, on the other hand, would encourage explicit reports that are more negative than those assessed implicitly.

Across two studies, we demonstrated that motivational forces such as these, and not separate conscious and unconscious self-attitudes, underlie dissociations between implicit and explicit measures of self-esteem (Olson, Fazio, & Hermann, 2007). First, we asked respondents to rate themselves on a variety of trait variables relating to over- (e.g., proud, boastful) and underpresenting (e.g., modest, meek) styles after completing implicit (IAT) and explicit (Rosenberg, feeling thermometer) measures of self-esteem. As expected, those who reported more positive self-views on the explicit measure than their implicitly measured self-esteem would imply admitted to being more proud and boastful, and less modest and meek (see Lambird & Mann, 2006, for a similar analysis). In a second study, we directly manipulated the operation of participants' self-presentational motives. Some participants completed implicit and explicit measures under the usual conditions, without any special instructions. Others were implored to be honest when completing the explicit measure. More specifically, they were told that when answering self-related questions, some people tend to overpresent themselves by being proud or boastful and others tend to underpresent themselves by being modest or humble. They were urged to do neither. In the control condition, little correspondence was found between the two measure types, replicating much past research. However, when urged to be honest, participants' implicit and explicit responses showed greater convergence. It would be difficult to explain this pattern of relations if one were to assume the existence of two independent self-attitudes, one of which was hidden from introspective access.

This is not to say that dissociations between implicit and explicit measures of self-esteem are not interesting or important. Quite the contrary, the presence of a discrepancy can serve as a very informative marker. Pursuing such an approach, Jordan and colleagues (e.g., Jordan, Spencer, Zanna, Hoshino-Browne, & Correll, 2003; see Chapter 9, this volume) have provided a fascinating window into individuals characterized by relatively high scores on an explicit measure of self-esteem, but relatively low scores on an implicit measure. These individuals exhibit what can be termed a narcissistic, fragile, or defensive form of high self-esteem (see also Kernis, Abend, Goldman, Shrira, Paradise, & Hampton, 2005). Their defensiveness can lead to outgroup derogation, pronounced dissonance reduction effects, and more (see also Jordan, Spencer, & Zanna, 2005). We would argue that the high self-esteem such individuals report on the explicit measure of self-esteem is a product of this very same defensive style. Thus, it is not the discrepancy per se that motivates their defensive reactions. Instead, the discrepancy is itself symptomatic of the defensive style with which they respond to their less-than-desired automatically activated self-views and to self-related threats more generally. Our point is that, as verbal behaviors, responses to explicit measures of self-esteem are necessarily an exercise in self-presentation. Hence, they may not offer an accurate portrait of automatically activated self-evaluations, but instead may be behavioral manifestations of additional phenomena, such as narcissism. From the perspective of the MODE model, it is the schism between the attitude that is activated automatically and more motivated processes that produce the behavior under study, not some schism between the conscious and the unconscious.

Single versus Dual Attitudes

As should be abundantly obvious by now, the MODE model stands in contrast to the stance of models that postulate the existence of dual representations of attitude in memory (e.g., Wilson, Lindsey, & Schooler, 2000). Our perspective does not view responses to an explicit measure as indicative of a representation in memory that is distinct from the automatically activated attitude. Instead, such responses are viewed as verbal behaviors that, under appropriate circumstances, can be influenced by considerations other than, or in addition to, the automatically activated attitude. We continue to believe, just as we argued earlier (Fazio & Olson, 2003), that "implicit" and "explicit" are best viewed as properties of the measure, not properties of the construct that is being measured. Such terms as "implicit attitude" and "explicit attitude," and "implicit self-esteem" and "explicit self-esteem," invite misinterpretation, because they imply the existence of dual representations. Within the context of the MODE model, such references are inappropriate; the model views automatically activated attitudes as the representations captured by an implicit measure and as the starting point for verbal responses to an explicit measure.

Implications for Predicting Behavior

A consensus appears to be emerging from recent research on implicit and explicit attitudinal processes. Most succinctly, it is the view that implicit attitudes predict automatic behavior, and explicit attitudes predict controlled behavior. Findings by Dovidio and colleagues (1997, 2002), McConnell and Liebold (2001), Neumann, Hülsenbeck, and Seibt (2004), and others seem to support such a view. Here and elsewhere, implicit measures were found to correlate with nonverbal behavior like looking and smiling, whereas explicit measures related more strongly to controllable behaviors.

However, a look through the literature indicates that a mere "mapping" of implicit measures to uncontrollable behavior and explicit measures to controllable behavior is a simplistic characterization of the research findings. Clearly, implicit measures have been shown to predict more than the merely less-controllable classes of behavior. As we reviewed earlier, the priming measure of racial prejudice we employ has related to explicit judgments of the quality of a Black student's writing, reported first impressions of Black and White social targets, evaluations of job candidates, and the longevity of interracial roommate relationships. Other implicit measures employed in other labs have similarly shown that even behaviors fully susceptible to conscious control can be guided by the automatic processes assessed by implicit measures (e.g., Vanman, Saltz, Nathan, & Warren, 2004). Thus, the view that implicit measures (and the constructs they measure) are limited to the prediction of less-controllable behavior grossly underestimates their predictive power.

From the MODE model's perspective, the attitude that is automatically evoked upon encountering an object can, if unimpeded by motivation, determine behavior of all sorts, from approach/avoidance behavior to smiles and frowns to verbal declarations of admiration or disgust. For example, recall the research we reviewed earlier indicating that the influence of automatically activated attitudes begins early in the attention and perceptual process, coloring construals of the object and the situation at hand. These early influences can have a cascading effect on later judgments and behaviors, whether they be controlled or automatic in nature.

Such downstream consequences of automatic processes are particularly well illustrated by a class of research demonstrating stronger relations between automatically activated attitudes (as measured by some implicit measure) and some judgment or behavior when the individual's resources have been depleted in some way. For example, Hofmann, Rauch, and Gawronski (2007) assessed participants' automatic attitudes toward candy (using an IAT) as well as their personal "dietary restraint standards," that is, the extent to which they were motivated to monitor and control their diet. All participants were exposed to a dramatic movie scene, but those in the resource-depletion condition were instructed to suppress the expression of emotion while viewing the clip. Later, in a product testing phase of the experiment, participants were provided with an opportunity to consume candy. Just as the MODE model would predict, resource-depleted participants' candy consumption was primarily predicted by their automatic candy attitudes, whereas those with fuller resources ate according to their dietary standards. Similar findings supportive of the MODE model are now beginning to appear in the substance use and abuse literature (see Wiers & Stacy, 2006, for an overview). For example, Hofmann, Gschwendner, Friese, and Schmitt (2007) reported that automatically activated attitudes toward alcohol predict consumption behavior particularly when cognitive resources are diminished from an ego-demanding task. Govorun and Payne (2006) demonstrated that a resource-depleting Stroop color-naming task diminished the controlled component of a process-dissociation procedure in a weapons identification task, leaving a greater role for automatic processes to guide judgments. Essentially, these depletion manipulations represent manipulation of the opportunity factor. So, when the opportunity for downstream motivational forces to be influential is minimized, stronger relations between automatically activated attitudes and behavior emerge.

Conclusion

It was nearly two decades ago that the MODE model was first formalized (Fazio, 1990). We believe the theory continues not only to be relevant, but also to provide a general theoretical framework for addressing some of the more contemporary questions addressed in this volume. The model considers the evaluation automatically evoked upon encountering an object as the starting point of the perceptual, cognitive, and motivational processes that guide object-related behavior. It considers responses to explicit measures of attitudes a form of verbal behavior, comparable to other social judgments. As such, they are susceptible to the same sorts of influences of motivated processes that, opportunity permitting, can steer one's behavior away from that implied by the attitude.

The MODE model provides input on many of the issues discussed in this volume, including the relation between implicit and explicit measures, the nature of the constructs tapped by each, the role of the unconscious in attitudes, and the sorts of important social behaviors guided by the various attitudinal processes. Our view is that many of these debates are not new; they have parallels in earlier literature regarding the attitude-behavior relation and, hence, can be informed by earlier theory and research. The advent of implicit measures has added important tools by which these questions can be pursued with greater precision and rigor. However, it takes theory to ground the rapidly accumulating research findings to basic principles, which is what we believe the MODE model provides.

References

Ajzen, I., & Fishbein, M. (1977). Attitude-behavior relations: A theoretical analysis and review of empirical research. *Psychological Bulletin, 84,* 888–918.

Ajzen, I., & Fishbein, M. (1980). *Understanding attitudes and predicting social behavior.* Englewood Cliffs, NJ: Prentice Hall.

Ajzen, I., & Fishbein, M. (2005). The influence of attitudes on behavior. In D. Albarracín, B. T. Johnson, & M. P. Zanna (Eds.), *The handbook of attitudes* (pp. 173–222). Mahwah, NJ: Erlbaum.

Ajzen, I., & Sexton, J. (1999). Depth of processing, belief congruence, and attitude-behavior correspondence. In S. Chaiken & Y. Trope (Ed.), *Dual-process theories in social psychology* (pp. 117–138). New York: Guilford Press.

Banse, R., Seise, J., & Zerbes, N. (2001). Implicit attitudes towards homosexuality: Reliability, validity, and controllability of the IAT. *Zeitschrift fur Experimentelle Psychologie, 48,* 145–160.

Baumeister, R. F., Bratlavasky, M., Muraven, M., & Tice, D. M. (1998). Ego depletion: Is the active self a limited resource? *Journal of Personality & Social Psychology, 74,* 1252–1265.

Baumeister, R. F., & Leary, M. R. (1995). The need to belong: Desire for interpersonal attachments as a fundamental human motivation. *Psychological Bulletin, 117,* 497–529.

Biernat, M., & Vescio, T. K. (1993). Categorization and stereotyping: Effects of group context on memory and social judgment. *Journal of Experimental Social Psychology, 29,* 166–202.

Blair, I. V. (2001). Implicit stereotypes and prejudice. In G. B. Moskowitz (Ed.), *Cognitive social psychology: The Princeton Symposium on the legacy and future of social cognition* (pp. 359–374). Mahwah, NJ: Erlbaum.

Bosson, J. K., Swann, W. B., Jr., & Pennebaker, J. (2000). Stalking the perfect measure of implicit self-esteem: The blind men and the elephant revisited? *Journal of Personality & Social Psychology, 79,* 631–643.

Bruner, J. S. (1957). On perceptual readiness. *Psychological Review, 64,* 123–152.

Cacioppo, J. T., Petty, R. E., Feinstein, J. A., & Jarvis, B. W. (1996). Dispositional differences in cognitive motivation: The life and times of individuals varying in the need for cognition. *Psychological Bulletin, 119,* 197–253.

Carretta, T. R., & Moreland, R. L. (1982). Nixon and Watergate: A field demonstration of belief perseverance. *Personality & Social Psychology Bulletin, 8,* 446–453.

Chen, S., & Chaiken, S. (1999). The heuristic-systematic model in its broader context. In S. Chaiken & Y. Trope (Eds.), *Dual-process theories in social psychology* (pp. 73–96). New York: Guilford Press.

Dasgupta, N., & Rivera, L. M. (2006). From automatic antigay prejudice to behavior: The moderating role of conscious beliefs about gender and behavioral control. *Journal of Personality & Social Psychology, 91,* 268–280.

DePaulo, B. M., & Friedman, H. S. (1998). Nonverbal communication. In D. Gilbert, S. T. Fiske, & G. Lindzey (Eds.), *Handbook of social psychology* (4th ed., Vol. 2, pp. 3–40). New York: Random House.

Devine, P. G. (1989). Stereotypes and prejudice: Their automatic and controlled components. *Journal of Personality & Social Psychology, 56,* 5–18.

Dovidio, J. F., & Fazio, R. H. (1992). New technologies for the direct and indirect assessment of attitudes. In J. M. Tanur (Ed.), *Questions about questions: Inquiries into the cognitive bases of surveys* (pp. 204–237). New York: Russell Sage Foundation.

Dovidio, J. F., & Gaertner, S. L. (1998). On the nature of contemporary prejudice: The causes, consequences, and challenges of aversive racism. In J. Eberhardt & S. T. Fiske (Eds.), *Confronting racism: The problem and the response* (pp. 3–32). Newbury Park, CA: Sage.

Dovidio, J. F., Kawakami, K., & Beach, K. R. (2001). Implicit and explicit attitudes: Examination of the relationship between measures of intergroup bias. In R. Brown & S. L. Gaertner (Eds.), *Blackwell handbook of social psychology: Vol. 4. Intergroup processes* (pp. 175–197). Malden, MA: Blackwell.

Dovidio, J. F., Kawakami, K., & Gaertner, S. L. (2002). Implicit and explicit prejudice and interracial interactions. *Journal of Personality & Social Psychology, 82,* 62–68.

Dovidio, J. F., Kawakami, K., Johnson, C., Johnson, B., & Howard, A. (1997). On the nature of prejudice: Automatic and controlled processes. *Journal of Experimental Social Psychology, 33,* 510–540.

Dunton, B. C., & Fazio, R. H. (1997). An individual difference measure of motivation to control prejudiced reactions. *Personality & Social Psychology Bulletin, 23,* 316–326.

Eagly, A. H., & Chaiken, S. (1993). *The psychology of attitudes.* Fort Worth, TX: Harcourt Brace Jovanovich.

Fabrigar, L., Petty, R. E., Smith, S. M., & Crites, S. L. (2006). Understanding knowledge effects on attitude-behavior consistency: The role of relevance, complexity, and amount of knowledge. *Journal of Personality and Social Psychology, 90,* 556–577.

Fazio, R. H. (1990). Multiple processes by which attitudes guide behavior: The MODE model as an integrative framework. In M. P. Zanna (Ed.), *Advances in experimental social psychology* (Vol. 23, pp. 75–109). San Diego: Academic Press.

Fazio, R. H. (1995). Attitudes as object-evaluation associations: Determinants, consequences, and correlates of attitude accessibility. In R. E. Petty & J. A. Krosnick (Eds.), *Attitude strength: Antecedents and consequences* (pp. 247–282). Hillsdale, NJ: Erlbaum.

Fazio, R. H. (2001). On the automatic activation of associated evaluations: An overview. *Cognition and Emotion, 15,* 115–141.

Fazio, R. H. (2007). Attitudes as object-evaluation associations of varying strength. *Social Cognition, 25,* 664–703.

Fazio, R. H., & Dunton, B. C. (1997). Categorization by race: The impact of automatic and controlled components of racial prejudice. *Journal of Experimental Social Psychology, 33,* 451–470.

Fazio R. H., & Hilden, L. (2001). Emotional reactions to a seemingly prejudiced response. *Personality & Social Psychology Bulletin, 27,* 538–549.

Fazio, R. H., & Williams, C. J. (1986). Attitude accessibility as a moderator of the attitude-perception and attitude-behavior relations: An investigation of the 1984 presidential election. *Journal of Personality and Social Psychology, 51,* 505–514.

Fazio, R. H., Jackson, J. R., Dunton, B. C., & Williams, C. J. (1995). Variability in automatic activation as an unobtrusive measure of racial attitudes: A bona fide pipeline? *Journal of Personality & Social Psychology, 69,* 1013–1027.

Fazio, R. H., Ledbetter, J. E., & Towles-Schwen, T. (2000). On the costs of accessible attitudes: Detecting that the attitude object has changed. *Journal of Personality and Social Psychology, 78,* 197–210.

Fazio, R. H., & Olson, M. A. (2003). Implicit measures in social cognition research: Their meaning and use. *Annual Review of Psychology, 54,* 297–327.

Fazio, R. H., Sanbonmatsu, D. M., Powell, M. C., & Kardes, F. R. (1986). On the automatic activation of attitudes. *Journal of Personality & Social Psychology, 50,* 229–238.

Fazio, R. H., & Towles-Schwen, T. (1999). The MODE model of attitude-behavior processes. In S. Chaiken & Y. Trope (Eds.), *Dual-process theories in social psychology* (pp. 97–116). New York: Guilford Press.

Florack, A., Scarabis, M., & Bless, H. (2001). When do associations matter? The use of implicit associations toward ethnic groups in person judgments. *Journal of Experimental Social Psychology, 37,* 518–524.

Gaertner, S. L., & Dovidio, J. F. (1977). The subtlety of white racism, arousal and helping behavior. *Journal of Personality & Social Psychology, 35,* 691–707.

Gawronski, B., Geschke, D., & Banse, R. (2003). Implicit bias in impression formation: Associations influence the construal of individuating information. *European Journal of Social Psychology, 33,* 573–589.

Gawronski, B., Hofmann, W., & Wilbur, C. J. (2006). Are "implicit" attitudes unconscious? *Consciousness and Cognition, 15,* 485–499.

Govorun, O., & Payne, B. K. (2006). Ego depletion and prejudice: Separating automatic and controlled components. *Social Cognition, 24,* 111–136.

Greenwald, A. G., McGhee, D., & Schwartz, J. L. K. (1998). Measuring individual differences in implicit cognition: The Implicit Association Task. *Journal of Personality & Social Psychology, 74,* 1469–1480.

Hastorf, A. H., & Cantril, H. (1954). They saw a game: A case study. *Journal of Abnormal and Social Psychology, 49,* 129–134.

Higgins, E. T. (1987). Self-discrepancy: A theory relating self and affect. *Psychological Review, 94,* 319–340.

Higgins, E. T. (1996). Knowledge activation: Accessibility, applicability, and salience. In E. T. Higgins & A. W. Kruglanski (Eds.), *Social psychology: Handbook of basic principles.* New York: Guilford Press.

Hofmann, W., Gawronski, B., Gschwendner, T., Le, H., & Schmitt, M. (2005). A meta-analysis on the correlation between the Implicit Association Test and explicit self-report measures. *Personality & Social Psychology Bulletin, 31,* 1369–1385.

Hofmann, W., Gschwendner, T., Friese, M., & Schmitt, M. (2007, January). *Impulsive and reflective paths to behavior: Available control resources moderate the predictive validity of implicit and explicit attitudes.* Paper presented at the annual meeting of the Society of Personality and Social Psychology, Memphis, TN.

Hofmann, W., Rauch, W., & Gawronski, B. (2007). And deplete us not into temptation: Automatic attitudes, dietary restraint, and self-regulatory resources as determinants of eating behavior. *Journal of Experimental Social Psychology, 43,* 497–504.

Houston, D. A., & Fazio, R. H. (1989). Biased processing as a function of attitude accessibility: Making objective judgments subjectively. *Social Cognition, 7,* 51–66.

Jackson, J. R. (1997). *Automatically activated racial attitudes.* Unpublished doctoral dissertation, Indiana University.

Jamieson, D. W., & Zanna, M. P. (1989). Need for structure in attitude formation and expression. In A. R. Pratkanis, S. J. Breckler, & A. G. Greenwald (Eds.), *Attitude structure and function* (pp. 383–406). Hillsdale, NJ: Erlbaum.

Jordan, C. H., Spencer, S. J., & Zanna, M. P. (2005). Types of high self-esteem and prejudice: How implicit self-esteem relates to racial discrimination among high explicit self-esteem individuals. *Personality & Social Psychology Bulletin, 31,* 693–702.

Jordan, C. H., Spencer, S. J., Zanna, M. P., Hoshino-Browne, E., & Correll, J. (2003). Secure and defensive self-esteem. *Journal of Personality & Social Psychology, 85,* 969–978.

Jussim, L., Coleman, L. M., & Lerch, L. (1987). The nature of stereotypes: A comparison and integration of three theories. *Journal of Personality & Social Psychology, 52,* 536–546.

Katz, I., & Hass, R. G. (1988). Racial ambivalence and American value conflict: Correlational and priming studies of dual cognitive structures. *Journal of Personality & Social Psychology, 55,* 893–905.

Kernis, M. H. (2003). Toward a conceptualization of optimal self-esteem. *Psychological Inquiry, 14,* 1–26.

Kernis, M. H., Abend, T. A., Goldman, B. M., Shrira, I., Paradise, A. N., & Hampton, C. (2005). Self-serving responses arising from discrepancies between explicit and implicit self-esteem. *Self and Identity, 4,* 311–330.

Kitayama, S., & Uchida, Y. (2003). Explicit self-criticism and implicit self-regard: Evaluating self and friend in two cultures. *Journal of Experimental Social Psychology, 39,* 476–482.

Koole, S. L., Dijksterhuis, A., & van Knippenberg, A. (2001). What's in a name: Implicit self-esteem and the automatic self. *Journal of Personality & Social Psychology, 80,* 669–685.

Koole, S. L., & Pelham, B. W. (2003). On the nature of implicit self-esteem: The case of the name-letter effect. In S. Spencer, S. Fein, & M. P. Zanna (Eds.), *Motivated social perception: The Ontario Symposium* (pp. 93–116). Hillsdale, NJ: Lawrence Erlbaum.

Kruglanski, A. W. (1989). *Lay epistemics and human knowledge: Cognitive and motivational bases.* New York: Plenum Press.

Lambird, K. H., & Mann, T. (2006). When do ego threats lead to self-regulation failure? Negative consequences of defensive high self-esteem. *Personality & Social Psychology Bulletin, 32,* 1177–1187.

Lepore L., & Brown, R. (1997). Category and stereotype activation: Is prejudice inevitable? *Journal of Personality & Social Psychology, 72,* 275–87.

Lord, C. G., Ross, L., & Lepper, M. R. (1979). Biased assimilation and attitude polarization: The effects of prior theories on subsequently considered evidence. *Journal of Personality & Social Psychology, 37,* 2098–2109.

Maison, D., Greenwald, A.G., & Bruin, R. (2001). The Implicit Association Test as a measure of consumer attitudes. *Polish Psychological Bulletin, 2,* 61–79.

McConahay, J. B. (1986). Modern racism, ambivalence, and the modern racism scale. In J. F. Dovidio & S. L. Gaertner (Eds.), *Prejudice, discrimination, and racism* (pp. 91–125). Orlando, FL: Academic Press.

McConnell, A. R., & Liebold, J. M. (2001). Relations between the Implicit Association Test, explicit racial attitudes, and discriminatory behavior. *Journal of Experimental Social Psychology, 37,* 435–442.

Neumann, R., Hülsenbeck, K., & Seibt, B. (2004). Attitudes towards people with AIDS and avoidance behavior: Automatic and reflective bases of behavior. *Journal of Experimental Social Psychology, 40,* 543–550.

Nier, J. A. (2005). How dissociated are implicit and explicit racial attitudes? A bogus pipeline approach. *Group Processes & Intergroup Relations, 8,* 39–52.

Nosek, B. A. (2005). Moderators of the relationship between implicit and explicit evaluation. *Journal of Experimental Psychology: General, 134,* 565–584.

Olson, M. A. (in press). Measures of prejudice. In T. Nelson (Ed.), *Handbook of Prejudice.* Hillsdale, NJ: Erlbaum.

Olson, M. A., & Fazio, R. H. (2001). Implicit attitude formation through classical conditioning. *Psychological Science, 12,* 413–417.

Olson, M. A., & Fazio, R. H. (2002). Implicit acquisition and manifestation of classically conditioned attitudes. *Social Cognition, 20,* 89–103.

Olson, M. A., & Fazio, R. H. (2003). Relations between implicit measures of prejudice: What are we measuring? *Psychological Science, 14,* 636–639.

Olson, M. A., & Fazio, R. H. (2004). Trait inferences as a function of automatically activated racial attitudes and motivation to control prejudiced reactions. *Basic and Applied Social Psychology, 26,* 1–12.

Olson, M. A., & Fazio, R. H. (2006). Reducing automatically activated racial prejudice through implicit evaluative conditioning. *Personality & Social Psychology Bulletin, 32,* 421–433.

Olson, M. A., & Fazio, R. H. (2007a). Discordant evaluations of Blacks affect nonverbal behavior. *Personality & Social Psychology Bulletin,* 33, 1214–1224.

Olson, M. A., & Fazio, R. H. (2007b). Unpublished raw data. University of Tennessee.

Olson, M. A., Fazio, R. H., & Hermann, A. D. (2007). Reporting tendencies underlie discrepancies between implicit and explicit measures of self-esteem. *Psychological Science, 18,* 287–291.

Payne, B. K. (2001). Prejudice and perception: The role of automatic and controlled processes in misperceiving a weapon. *Journal of Personality Social Psychology, 81,* 181–192.

Payne, B. K., Cheng, C. M., Govorun, O., & Stewart, B. (2005). An inkblot for attitudes: Affect misattribution as implicit measurement. *Journal of Personality & Social Psychology, 89,* 277–293.

Petty, R. E., & Krosnick, J. A. (Eds.). (1995). *Attitude strength: Antecedents and consequences.* Hillsdale, NJ: Erlbaum.

Petty, R. E., & Wegener, D. T. (1999). The elaboration likelihood model: Current status and controversies. In S. Chaiken & Y. Trope (Eds.), *Dual-process theories in social psychology* (pp. 41–72). New York: Guilford Press.

Ranganath, K. A., Smith, C. T., & Nosek, B. A. (2008). Distinguishing automatic and controlled components of attitudes from direct and indirect measurement methods. *Journal of Experimental Social Psychology, 44,* 386–396.

Roskos-Ewoldsen, D. R., & Fazio, R. H. (1992). On the orienting value of attitudes: Attitude accessibility as a determinant of an object's attraction of visual attention. *Journal of Personality & Social Psychology, 63,* 198–211.

Sanbonmatsu, D. M., & Fazio, R. H. (1990). The role of attitudes in memory-based decision making. *Journal of Personality & Social Psychology, 59,* 614–622.

Schuette, R. A., & Fazio, R. H. (1995). Attitude accessibility and motivation as determinants of biased processing: A test of the MODE model. *Personality & Social Psychology Bulletin, 21,* 704–710.

Scinta, A., & Gable, L. (2007). Automatic and self-reported attitudes in romantic relationships. *Personality and Social Psychology Bulletin, 33,* 1008–1022.

Sedikides, C., & Strube, M. J. (1997). Self-evaluation: To thine own self be good, to thine own self be sure, to thine own self be true, and to thine own self be better. *Advances in Experimental Social Psychology, 29,* 209–269.

Smith, E. R., Fazio, R. H., & Cejka, M. A. (1996). Accessible attitudes influence categorization of multiply categorizable objects. *Journal of Personality & Social Psychology, 71,* 888–898.

Snyder, M., & Gangestad, S. (1982). Choosing social situations: Two investigations of self-monitoring processes. *Journal of Personality & Social Psychology, 43,* 123–135.

Strack, F., & Deutsch, R. (2004). Reflective and impulsive determinants of social behavior. *Personality and Social Psychology Review, 8,* 220–247.

Towles-Schwen, T., & Fazio, R. H. (2001). On the origins of racial attitudes: Correlates of childhood experiences. *Personality & Social Psychology Bulletin, 27,* 162–175.

Towles-Schwen, T., & Fazio, R. H. (2003). Choosing social situations: The relation between automatically activated racial attitudes and anticipated comfort interacting with African Americans. *Personality & Social Psychology Bulletin, 29,* 170–182.

Towles-Schwen, T., & Fazio, R. H. (2006). Automatically activated racial attitudes as predictors of the success of interracial roommate relationships. *Journal of Experimental Social Psychology, 42,* 698–705.

Vanman, E. J., Saltz, J. L., Nathan, L. R., & Warren, J. A. (2004). Racial discrimination by low-prejudiced Whites: Facial movements as implicit measures of attitudes related to behavior. *Psychological Science, 15,* 711–714.

Wegener, D. T., & Petty, R. E. (1995). Flexible correction processes in social judgment: The role of naive theories in corrections for perceived bias. *Journal of Personality & Social Psychology, 68,* 36–51.

Wiers, R. W & Stacy, A. W. (Eds.). (2006). *Handbook of implicit cognition and addiction.* Thousand Oaks, CA: Sage Publishers.

Wilson, T. D., & Brekke, N. (1994). Mental contamination and mental correction: Unwanted influences on judgments and evaluations. *Psychological Bulletin, 116,* 117–142.

Wilson, T. D., Lindsey, S., & Schooler, T. Y. (2000). A model of dual attitudes. *Psychological Review, 107,* 101–126.

Wittenbrink, B., Judd, C. M., & Park, B. (1997). Evidence for racial prejudice at the implicit level and its relationship with questionnaire measures. *Journal of Personality & Social Psychology, 72,* 262–274.

3

Attitudinal Dissociation
What Does It Mean?

Anthony G. Greenwald
Brian A. Nosek

Introduction

A by-product of increasing recent attention to implicit measures of attitudes is the controversial hypothesis of dissociated attitude representations (i.e., dual attitudes). This reference to *dissociation* implies the existence of distinct structural representations underlying distinguishable classes of attitude manifestations. In psychology, appeals to dissociation range from the mundane to the exotic. At the mundane end, the dissociation label may be attached to the simple absence or weakness of correlation between presumably related measures. At the exotic end, dissociation may be understood as a split in consciousness, such as mutually unaware person systems occupying the same brain. While recognizing this breadth of uses, we focus in this chapter on the specific usage in which dissociation refers to structurally separate and presumably independently functioning mental representations within the same brain. We shall keep this focus in sight by frequently referring to *structural dissociation.*

Empirical Data Patterns and Dissociation

Consider a research finding that might be observed in a person whose cerebral hemispheres have been surgically separated to control epileptic seizures. This hypothetical subject is asked to view words and then attempt immediately to recognize each word by pointing to it in a list containing additional distracter words. If the to-be-identified word is briefly flashed to the left of a visual fixation point (and is therefore transmitted by optic nerves to the right cerebral hemisphere), performance will be excellent if the left hand (under control of the right hemisphere) does the pointing but will be at chance if the right hand does the pointing. The reverse pattern (excellent with right hand, but at chance with left hand) will result for words flashed to the right half of the visual field. This result illustrates *double dissociation*, a pattern of directionally opposite effects of an independent variable under two levels of a second independent variable. Double-dissociation data patterns are often taken to justify a conclusion that structurally separate mental systems are involved in the performances. In this case, the separate systems would be ones operating independently within the left and right cerebral hemispheres.*

More ordinary (i.e., single) dissociation data patterns also take the form of a statistical interaction effect, but one lacking the juxtaposed opposite-direction effects that identify double dissociation. Two measures show an *empirical dissociation* pattern when they respond differently to procedural variations or when they have different observed relationships to other measured variables. At the level of data (rather than theory), dissociation corresponds approximately to the notion of *discriminant validity*. Discriminant validity refers to the distinctness of *empirical constructs* (Cronbach & Meehl, 1955), whereas structural dissociation refers to distinctness of hypothesized *mental representations*. In the split-brain illustration of double dissociation, one can describe the left-hand and right-hand response measures not only as having discriminant validity as measures, but also as corresponding to structurally distinct (dissociated) right and left hemisphere operations.

---

* A conclusion of structurally distinct systems does not require that the distinction be identified as one between conscious and unconscious systems. The left hemisphere of the split-brain subject may not know what the right hemisphere is doing, but this does not mean either that one hemisphere has an unconscious representation of the other's conscious knowledge or that one hemisphere is operating consciously and the other unconsciously. Implicit and explicit attitude measures may likewise show double dissociations (e.g., Perugini, 2005), which, likewise, do not oblige a conclusion that one attitudinal system is conscious and the other is not.

AGE ATTITUDE

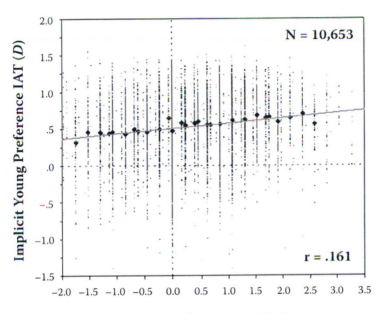

FIGURE 3.1 Regression of an IAT measure of implicit age attitude on a parallel self-report measure. This analysis is based on data from Greenwald, Nosek, and Banaji (2003). The regression reveals both a weak positive correlation between the IAT and self-report measures and a wide separation between their means on standardized scales for which the zero points of both indicate evaluative indifference between young and old. The self-report measure shows much weaker attitudinal preference for young relative to old. See text for further discussion.

Evidence for Implicit–Explicit Dissociation

Figure 3.1 shows the regression of an IAT measure of implicit age attitude onto a parallel explicit (self-report) measure. For both measures a score of 0 is interpreted as indicating attitudinal indifference between the concepts *young* and *old*. For the IAT measure, the 0 score indicates that the respondent is equally fast at classifying young-appearing faces together with pleasant-meaning words and old-appearing faces together with pleasant-meaning words. The data set is one for which methods and samples were described by Greenwald, Nosek, and Banaji (2003), and the IAT measure is Greenwald et al.'s D measure. The self-report measure was based on three items (Greenwald et al., p. 216). The first of the three items used a 5-point Likert format in which the middle alternative (scored 0) was "I like young people and old people equally"; the other two items used 11-point thermometer rating scales for the concepts young and old, combined subtractively into a difference score. The explicit measure in Figure 3.1 averaged the Likert and difference scores, with each measure divided by its standard deviation (SD; i.e., preserving the 0-point locations) before averaging.

Although a positive relationship between the two measures (a positive regression slope) is visible in Figure 3.1, it is a decidedly weak positive relationship, corresponding to a correlation of $r = .16$. A correlation this weak is sometimes taken to indicate implicit-explicit dissociation. A second possible indicator of dissociation in Figure 3.1 is that the regression function deviates substantially from passing through the origin. Alternately described, there was a substantial difference in means for the two measures. In standard deviation units on scales for which 0 indicates evaluative indifference between young and old and positive scores indicate preference for young, the mean of the explicit measure was 0.39, whereas the mean of the implicit measure was 1.35. This is nearly a full standard deviation difference, with the implicit measure showing substantially greater relative positivity for young than the explicit measure, $t(10,254) = 75.5$ (a value of t that leaves p too small to be computed by standard statistical software).

Figure 3.2 shows still a third possible indicator of dissociation, in the form of the finding that a demographic variable, chronological age, has a well-defined relation with the explicit age attitude measure ($r = -.194$, $N = 10,266$, $p = 10^{-87}$), but no relation with the implicit age attitude measure ($r = -.012$, $N = 10,266$, $p = .23$). The data in Figure 3.2 can also be described as showing an interaction effect of age and the implicit-explicit attitude variation, $t(10,188) = 14.11$, $p = 10^{-44}$.

A weakness of the evidence for dissociation in Figure 3.2 is the lack of any sure indication that the explicit measure's relation to age has something to do with attitudes. Perhaps older subjects, who may be more conservative than young subjects, are reluctant to use responses at the end points of self-report measures. An age difference in response style could therefore explain Figure 3.2's data pattern without concluding that there is less explicit favorableness toward the young with increasing age. The explanation just offered is perhaps implausible because (a) the explicit measures are not extreme even for younger subjects and (b) subjects of greater age may have a good reason (approaching old age) for having genuinely increased explicit favorableness toward the

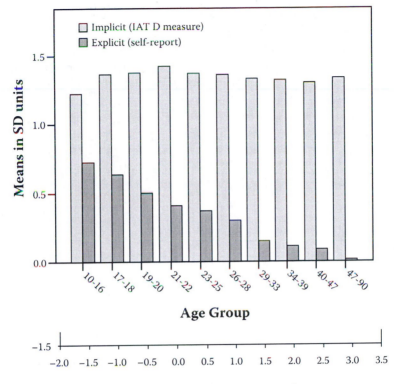

Combined Explicit Young Preference

FIGURE 3.2 IAT and self-report age attitude measures of Figure 3.1, plotted to reveal that the IAT measure is unrelated to variations in age of respondents, whereas the self-report attitude measure shows a regular reduction in relative preference for young as respondent age increases. Such distinctive patterns of correlation with other variables suggest dissociation of mental representations underlying the implicit and explicit attitude measures.

concept *old*. For these reasons, even the small correlation between the two measures shown in Figure 3.1 suggests that the two measures have something in common.

The evidence for attitudinal dissociation would be stronger if Figure 3.2 showed not just a lack of relation between age and implicit attitude, but a relationship opposite in direction to that found for age and explicit attitude (i.e., a double dissociation). An opposite-direction relation could not readily be dismissed by supposing that it could be due to the implicit measure being a poor measure. Even with such a (hypothetical) double-dissociation pattern, however, it might be assumed that the opposite-direction relationship with the implicit measure was due to some nonattitudinal process associated with age that affects the IAT measure.*

In summary, Figures 3.1 and 3.2 provide an implicit-explicit data pattern that includes three components: (a) low intercorrelation, (b) separation of means, and (c) different relationships to a third variable. How compelling is this collection of patterns as evidence for two structurally distinct attitude representations? The collection of three patterns is certainly more compelling than is the low correlation by itself, but nevertheless, it is less than fully compelling. As we shall now show, one also needs some assurance that the data for both measures are relevant to attitudes.

Discriminant and Convergent Validity

The foregoing hopefully establishes that considerations of construct validity are essential in interpreting empirical data patterns. To justify interpretation of empirically distinct implicit and explicit attitude constructs, data must meet an unusual combination of two validity-related criteria. They must show both (a) *discriminant validity*, such as by having different patterns of relationship to other variables, thereby establishing that the two measures are not measures of identically the same construct, and (b) *convergent validity*, which establishes that the two measures also warrant interpretation as reflecting the same type of construct. This is an interesting paradox of dissociation; one must demonstrate that two measures assess the same *type* of construct while, simultaneously, demonstrating that they must represent different *forms* of that construct.

For the split-brain case that we are treating as a prototype of structural dissociation, most observers will readily agree that both the discriminant and convergent empirical validity criteria are met. The data directly provide evidence for discriminant validity: The right-hand and left-hand recognition measures have opposite patterns of relation to the independent variable of left versus right visual hemifield stimulus presentation. Also, the convergent validity criterion is satisfied intuitively, because the two measures are identical except for the right-left switch;

---

* The original scoring procedure for the IAT might well have contained such an undesired effect of age, due to the characteristic slower responding of elderly subjects. Slower responding on RT measures tends to produce artifactually large differences in RTs between experimental conditions. However, introduction of the D measure sharply reduced that obviously nonattitudinal influence on IAT measures (cf. Greenwald et al., 2003).

there is no plausible alternative to viewing them both as measures of recognition memory.

What about the situation for implicit and explicit attitude measures? How can the discriminant and convergent validity criteria be met simultaneously? Demonstrating discriminant validity—which requires showing different patterns of relationship to other variables—is straight-forward. Figure 3.2's data illustrate this. Discriminant validity justifies the use of the distinct construct terminology, in this case implicit and explicit, though it does not establish difference in the process(es) or representation(s) that generate the data. More difficult is meeting the convergent validity criterion; that is, what justifies a conclusion that the constructs legitimately share use of the term attitude? The weak positive correlation between implicit and explicit measures (shown in Figure 3.1) helps, but does not suffice both because of its weakness and because the correlation could be due to some shared nonattitudinal influence. Each measure must also correlate with other variables in a way that makes plausible that the measures are both attitude measures. However, these correlations cannot be with the *same* other variable for each measure—if they were, then the discriminant validity require-ment for dissociation would be undermined.

Not all data sets that include implicit and explicit measures show the dissociation-suggestive patterns of Figures 3.1 and 3.2. Figure 3.3 shows a regression of implicit on explicit attitude from a data set obtained with procedures very similar to those that obtained in Figure 3.1's data, dif-fering only in the attitude object. Unlike Figure 3.1, Figure 3.3 reveals a high implicit-explicit correlation ($r = .73$). Also unlike Figure 3.1, the difference between means of the implicit and explicit measures is very small: 0.04 SD units, quite unlike the 0.96 SD units for the data in Figure 3.1. The same data set of Figure 3.3 can be seen in Figure 3.4 to show patterns in which the implicit and explicit measures have virtually identical relations to another variable, education level. Quite clearly, the data in Figures 3.3 and 3.4 do not show even one of the three dissocia-tion-suggestive patterns evident in Figures 3.1 and 3.2.

Three Interpretations

Interpretations that we here label *single-representation, dual-represen-tation,* and *person versus culture* have received the greatest attention in discussions of published data that, like the prior examples, show either relationship or lack of relationship between implicit and explicit atti-tude measures.

ELECTION 2004

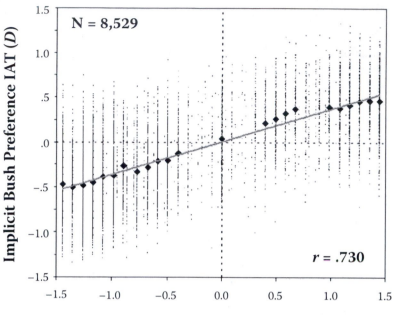

Combined Explicit Bush Preference

FIGURE 3.3 Regression of an IAT measure of implicit attitudinal preference for George W. Bush, relative to John F. Kerry, on a parallel self-report measure. Data from Greenwald, Nosek, and Sriram (2006). This regression illustrates both a strong positive correlation between IAT and self-report measures, and no separation between their means on standardized scales for which the zero points of both indicate evaluative indifference between the two presidential candidates. These observations suggest lack of implicit–explicit dissociation. See text for further discussion.

Single-representation interpretations treat all appearances of attitudinal dissociation as illusory. All attitude manifestations—implicit and explicit—are attributed to a single form of mental attitude representation. Appearances of dissociation such as weak correlation and differing relationships with other variables are interpreted in terms of processes that are assumed to be different in the implicit and explicit measurement situations. In the most fully developed analysis of the single-representation type, Fazio (1990; Fazio & Olson, 2003; Olson & Fazio, in press) interprets explicit measures as subject to motivational and ability or opportunity influences that differ from the influences on implicit measures.

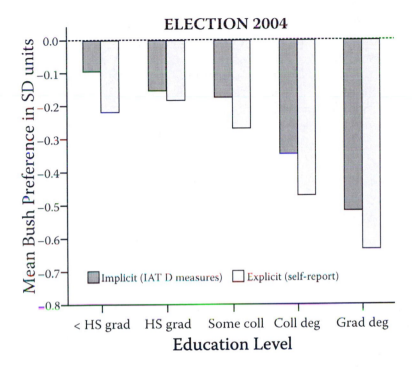

FIGURE 3.4 IAT and self-report political preference measures of Figure 3.3, plotted to reveal that both measures have the same relation to variations in education level of respondents. Such similar patterns of correlation with other variables suggest singleness (lack of dissociation) of mental representations underlying the implicit and explicit attitude measures.

> [F]rom the perspective of the MODE model, [overt, explicit expressions of attitude] are, for want of any better expression, farther "downstream" than automatically activated attitudes [i.e., implicit measures]. Responding to an explicit measure is itself a verbal behavior that can be affected by motivation and opportunity, as well as whatever is automatically activated. (Fazio & Olson, 2003, p. 305)

The second interpretation of empirical dissociation patterns identifies implicit and explicit measures of attitude with structurally distinct mental representations of attitudes. Several such two-attitude views have been offered (see Chaiken & Trope, 1999; Wilson, Lindsey, & Schooler, 2000). These views often characterize the representations underlying implicit measures as operating automatically and perhaps unconsciously, while treating representations underlying explicit measures as operating consciously and with deliberate thought (see also Strack & Deutsch, 2004).

The third interpretation conceives implicit and explicit measures as due to distinct categories of influences that are represented by the labels *culture* and *person*. Implicit measures (and perhaps the IAT more than other implicit measures) are assumed to represent the influence of culture, whereas explicit measures capture influences operating within the person. This person-versus-culture interpretation has sometimes been stated so as to suggest that influences from culture are in the category of semantic knowledge (like one's knowledge of names of countries and meanings of words) rather than in the category of attitudes (cf. Karpinski & Hilton, 2001; Olson & Fazio, 2004). However, the person and culture labels can fit equally well with their being conceived as two varieties of attitudinal knowledge, making it a variant of the dual-representation position.

Evaluating the Three Interpretations

To what extent can behavioral evidence for dissociation resolve questions of how many attitude representations exist? Perhaps the most discomforting conclusion of this chapter is that there is actually no possibility for using behavioral evidence to choose decisively among the single-representation, dual-representation, and person-versus-culture interpretations of dissociation data patterns.*

Although demonstrations of simultaneous convergent and discriminant validity contribute toward a conclusion in favor of structural dissociation, they do not oblige such a conclusion. It is possible to explain the empirically distinct constructs in terms of a single type of structure. Nosek and Smyth (2007) illustrated the possibility of having distinguishable empirical constructs based on a single structure with the physics of H_2O. Snow, ice, water, and steam are empirically distinct phenomena that share a single structural form: H_2O. The differences among the four phases of H_2O are explained, not as differences in molecular structure, but as the result of *processes*—triggered

---

* Dunn and Kirsner (1988) are more sanguine about demonstrating structural dissociation with behavioral measures. They describe a "reversed association" data pattern that can justify concluding that different "processes" are involved in two performances. Their analysis does not consider the distinction between processes and structural representations. In our view (which is not developed formally here in parallel fashion to that of Dunn & Kirsner), this added layer of distinctions removes the possibility of using behavioral data to choose between single- and dual-representation structural views.

by environmental variations of temperature and pressure—operating on a single molecular structure. Even without distinct structural representation, it is quite useful to treat the four phases as distinct constructs for many applications.

The H_2O example illustrates that empirically distinct constructs can derive from a single representation. The reverse is also true. Behavioral evidence suggesting consistency between measures could obscure the existence of distinct underlying representations. The data in Figures 3.3 and 3.4 might be taken to reveal the operation of one and the same attitudinal representation underlying both the implicit (IAT) and explicit (self-report) measures. Nevertheless, nothing about those data patterns demands the conclusion that a single representation underlies both types of measure. The measures could reflect representations that, despite being structurally dissociated, have been shaped by the same experiences. For example, imagine that the explicit measure in Figures 3.3 and 3.4 was not self-rated attitude, but a sibling's estimate of the participant's IAT-assessed attitude. A strong correlation would indicate that persons may have accurate knowledge of their siblings' attitudes as measured by the IAT. Despite the strong correlation, there is most certainly a structural dissociation in the underlying data: They reside in different brains (see Nosek, 2005).

Returning to our original example of structural dissociation with split-brain patients, why is it that we can be confident in interpreting a structural dissociation in that case, but not in the case of attitudes? There is an important feature that distinguishes brains and attitudes: Brains are physical entities, attitudes are not. Attitudes, like other psychological constructs, are hypothetical and unobservable. This means that resolution of "how many structural representations" is not possible for latent constructs because they do not (at least, not yet) correspond to known physical structures.

In summary, impressive as the double-dissociation data pattern is, there is nothing in that empirical pattern that, by itself, requires an interpretation in terms of structurally distinct underlying representations. The only meaningful inferences from behavioral data are discriminant and convergent validation of empirical constructs. The empirical constructs *implicit attitudes* and *explicit attitudes* can reasonably be interpreted as deriving from either a single-representation or a dual-representation structure. No behavioral evidence can demand a conclusion that one view is right and the other is not.

Convergent and Discriminant Validity Evidence
Supports Two Attitude Constructs

As already described, even an empirically clear double-dissociation finding does not demand theoretical interpretation as the product of structurally distinct representations. And the lack of dissociation might, in isolation, decrease the plausibility of distinct structural representations, but it does not require such a conclusion (i.e., highly correlated sibling responses does not mean that they share a brain). A nonstructural theoretical interpretation for double-dissociation empirical data requires only some plausible explanation of distinct influences operating on each type of measure, such as an explanation in terms of differences in processes engaged by the measurement procedures. In the case of implicit and explicit attitude measures, there are generally numerous differences in measurement procedure. Also, as was previously explained, even quite clear nondissociation data patterns (as in Figures 3.3 and 3.4) are open to interpretation as being produced by structurally distinct representations.

Although these issues have been regularly discussed in philosophy of science, they are still frequently misapplied. For example, on distinguishing implicit and explicit attitude measures, Fazio and Olson (2003, pp. 302–303) conflate constructs with representations, stating that:

> A second troublesome aspect of the implicit–explicit distinction is that it implies pre-existing dual attitudes (or whatever the construct of interest might be) in memory. That is, if the terms refer to the constructs themselves, then both an implicit and an explicit attitude presumably exist in memory (see Wilson et al., 2000).

Fazio and Olson (2003) continue: "For these reasons, it is more appropriate to view the *measure* as implicit or explicit, *not* the attitude (or whatever other construct)" (p. 303; italics in original; see also Chapter 2, this volume).

Following the discussion above, the construct terms implicit attitude and explicit attitude do not, as Fazio and Olson (2003) worry, commit attitudes to originating from dual representations. Their preference to limit the implicit–explicit (or indirect–direct) terminology to measures appeals to a distinction that is methodological, not theoretical. Psychological theories explain relations among constructs, not measures.*

---

* For example, one does not discuss solid and liquid measures of H_2O. More useful are the constructs ice and water, and explaining their relationship involves a theory in which processes such as heat application or removal lead to transformation of one to the other.

Procedural differences between measures can be understood without conducting empirical research and have no direct implications for psychological theory or construct validation (De Houwer, in press). In other words, the description of measures as implicit–explicit (or indirect-direct) holds no matter what behavioral evidence is gathered.

With the ambiguity of behavioral data, is any purpose served by debating whether behavioral data patterns such as Figures 3.1 and 3.2 are usefully interpreted as evidence for structurally dissociated underlying attitudinal representations? Even though the behavioral evidence does not afford a conclusion that one of the three theoretical interpretations is the correct one, nevertheless it is reasonable to use behavioral evidence to compare the three interpretations in terms of construct validity.

As a broad methodological topic, validity deals with justification for descriptions of research findings. Construct validity refers to the justifications for statements about research conclusions offered in the language of theoretical constructs. Without being able to declare in any decisive way that any of the structural interpretations of dissociation data patterns can be dismissed as incorrect, it is still possible to talk about empirically distinguishing constructs. So, instead of resolving single versus dual representations, convergent and discriminant validity can help distinguish the value of single versus dual attitude constructs.

In appraising construct validity of the implicit–explicit relation, the most important construct validity evidence is provided by studies that have reported correlations of IAT and self-report measures with attitude-relevant behaviors. Greenwald, Poehlman, Uhlmann, and Banaji (in press) collected and meta-analyzed these studies, yielding four conclusions that bear on evaluating the three interpretations of dissociation, at the level of constructs, not representations:

1. IAT measures showed consistent positive correlations with behavioral indicators of attitude at moderate levels (average effect size between $r = .25$ and $r = .30$). These relationships were not significantly influenced by any of several potential moderators that were examined.

2. Correlations of explicit measures with behavioral measures of attitude (average effect size between $r = .30$ and $r = .35$) were on average slightly and significantly higher than those of IAT measures, but several significant moderating effects were found. Especially, correlations of explicit attitude measures with behavior significantly weakened in socially sensitive outcome domains.

3. IAT measures significantly outperformed self-report measures in predicting behavior in the heavily researched domain of intergroup

      discrimination—a domain that is widely understood to be socially sensitive.

4. When self-report and IAT measures were highly correlated with each other—a circumstance occurring especially in domains of political and consumer attitudes—both types of measures were more strongly correlated with behavior than when implicit–explicit correlations were low.

These meta-analytic conclusions conform to the unusual combination of convergent and discriminant validity described previously. The convergent validity evidence that justifies interpreting both IAT and self-report as measures of attitude is that both types of measure display reliable positive correlations with measures of attitude-relevant behavior. The consistent finding of positive correlations between IAT and self-report measures that has been found in other meta-analyses (Hofmann, Gawronski, Gschwendner, Le, & Schmitt, 2005; Hofmann, Gschwendner, Nosek, & Schmitt, 2005; Nosek, 2005) further supports convergent validity.

Part of the discriminant validity evidence that justifies interpreting the measures as assessments of distinct constructs (implicit and explicit) is finding that correlations between IAT and self-report measures are only modestly positive on average. This type of finding (illustrated in Figure 3.1) is not by itself convincing evidence of discriminant validity of implicit and explicit measures, because it has the possibly uninteresting explanation that one or both of the measures are psychometrically weak. More important for discriminant validity, therefore, were Greenwald et al.'s (in press) meta-analytic findings that IAT and self-report attitude measures differed in their relations with other variables. Correlations involving explicit attitude measures, but not IAT measures, were moderated by judged social desirability pressures of the measurement situation. A useful summary of the overall meta-analytic evidence is one that has previously been offered by several researchers—IAT measures appear especially useful in predicting attitude-relevant behavior that plausibly occurs without planning and deliberation, whereas self-report best predicts the complementary category of attitude-relevant behaviors that are deliberate or planned (Asendorpf, Banse, & Mücke, 2002; Perugini, 2005).

The summary statement just given fits well with a dual-construct conception in which IAT and self-report measures reflect different types of attitudes. However—to restate a point made a few times previously in this chapter—the behavioral meta-analytic findings cannot be taken as disproving one or another of the different representation interpretations. The interpretation of multiple representations is an arbitrary decision about the psychological taxonomy on which psychological processes operate. Psychological taxonomies are organizational schemes, not theories (Willingham & Goedert, 2001). Constructs are hypothetical and tentative at the same time that they are useful and powerful. Whether implicit and explicit attitudes are conceived as dual representation or a single representation might be based on explanatory power and parsimony of the resulting theory, rather than more directly on empirical findings. If one theory must postulate dozens of interacting processes in order to maintain a sensible single-representation account of existing data, and another theory can account for the same data more directly by use of a dual-representation conception, then the latter theory might justifiably be preferred to the former. In both cases, however, the empirical data would support an interpretation of dual constructs.*

Greenwald et al.'s (in press) meta-analysis also sheds light on interpretation of the person-versus-culture distinction of the difference between IAT and self-report measures. The meta-analytic finding that IAT attitude measures effectively predicted attitude-relevant behavior is difficult to reconcile with the interpretation that the IAT provides a measure of cultural knowledge that is distinct from the person's own evaluations (i.e., attitudes). Nevertheless, an advocate of the person-versus-culture interpretation might explain the IAT's ability to predict attitude-relevant behavior by suggesting that nonattitudinal cultural knowledge can influence behavior outside of awareness. This stipulation would bring the person-versus-culture interpretation into agreement with the meta-analytic findings. Although this variant of the person-versus-culture interpretation cannot be faulted on logical grounds, it does render that interpretation empirically indistinguishable from one in which the culturally produced knowledge is regarded as affective or attitudinal in nature. Said another way, with the stipulation that nonattitudinal cultural knowledge can influence attitude-relevant behavior, the term cultural knowledge serves only to describe the presumed origins of the knowledge, not its implications for behavior (Nosek & Hansen, 2008). This theoretical flexibility is just

---

* Importantly, the meta-analytic evidence does not resolve what is responsible for the discriminant validity such as whether awareness, controllability, or some other factor(s) differentiate the constructs.

one more symptom of the difficulty of using behavioral data to choose between theoretical interpretations.

Conclusion

Two issues make the question of "How many attitude representations are there?" unresolvable. First, psychological constructs are hypothetical, resisting definitive decisions about number or form. Theories can explain the same behavioral data as multiple processes operating on a single representation, one process operating on multiple representations, or any admixture of representations and processes. Selection among theories is based on explanatory power and parsimony, not clarification of how many representations actually exist. Second, even if psychological constructs were treated as physical entities, behavioral dissociation data is not sufficient to determine whether one, two, or more representations are operating. Dissociation increases the potential utility of conceiving of multiple representations, and association decreases the potential utility. But, as described, convergent validity can mask underlying multiple representations (e.g., self-ratings and sibling judgments), and discriminant validity can mask underlying singular representations.

Although we are confident that the single-representation versus dual-representation debate will not be resolved decisively by behavioral data, fortunately no such uncertainty attends the question of whether two theoretical constructs are needed to map the implicit–explicit attitude domain. It appears unequivocally established that two constructs are needed. The relevant data are those that establish discriminant validity of the implicit–explicit distinction for attitudes described above. Even staunch adherents of the single-representation view must concede that the implicit–explicit distinction has been established at the level of empirical constructs. Among such advocates, Fazio and Olson (for example) account theoretically for the contrast between implicit and explicit attitudes by appealing to distinct processes—ones involving motivation and ability or situational opportunity—that can be applied to a single type of structural attitude representation (Fazio & Olson, 2003). Others prefer to treat the two constructs not as process variations applied to a single type of mental structure, but as structurally distinct attitude representations. Among those taking the latter structural dissociation view, there are two camps: one that describes the two types of representations as being attitudinal in nature and another that describes the distinction in terms of the contrast between an attitudinal representation and a cultural or semantic-knowledge representation.

References

Asendorpf, J. B., Banse, R., & Mucke, D. (2002). Double dissociation between implicit and explicit personality self-concept: The case of shy behavior. *Journal of Personality and Social Psychology, 83,* 380–393.

Chaiken, S., & Trope, Y. (Eds.) (1999). *Dual-process theories in social psychology.* New York: Guilford Press.

Cronbach, L. J., & Meehl, P. E. (1955). Construct validity in psychological tests. *Psychological Bulletin, 52,* 281–302.

De Houwer, J. (2005). What are implicit measures and indirect measures of attitudes? *A Comment on Spence Social Psychological Review, 7,* 18–20.

Dunn, J. C., & Kirsner, K. (1988). Discovering functionally independent mental processes: The principle of reversed association. *Psychological Review, 95,* 91–101.

Fazio, R. H. (1990). Multiple processes by which attitudes guide behavior: The MODE model as an integrative framework. *Advances in Experimental Social Psychology, 23,* 75–109.

Fazio, R. H. & Olson, M. A. (2003). Implicit measures in social cognition research: Their meaning and use. *Annual Review of Psychology, 54,* 297–327.

Greenwald, A. G., Nosek, B. A., & Banaji, M. R. (2003). Understanding and using the Implicit Association Test: I. An improved scoring algorithm. *Journal of Personality and Social Psychology, 85,* 197–216.

Greenwald, A. G., Nosek, B. A., & Sriram, N. (2006). Consequential validity of the Implicit Association Test: Comment on the article by Blanton and Jaccard. *American Psychologist, 61*(1), 56–61.

Greenwald, A. G., Poehlman, T. A., Uhlmann, E., & Banaji, M. R. (in press). Understanding and using the Implicit Association Test: III. Meta-analysis of predictive validity. *Journal or Personality and Social Psychology.*

Hofmann, W., Gawronski, B., Gschwendner, T., Le, H., & Schmitt, M. (2005). A meta-analysis on the correlation between the Implicit Association Test and explicit self-report measures. *Personality and Social Psychology Bulletin, 31,* 1369–1385.

Hofmann, W., Gschwendner, T., Nosek, B. A., & Schmitt, M. (2005). What moderates implicit–explicit consistency? *European Review of Social Psychology, 16*(10), 335–390.

Karpinski, A., & Hilton, J. L. (2001). Attitudes and the Implicit Association Test. *Journal of Personality and Social Psychology, 81,* 774–788.

Nosek, B. A. (2005). Moderators of the relationship between implicit and explicit evaluation. *Journal of Experimental Psychology: General, 134,* 565–584.

Nosek, B. A., & Smyth, F. L. (2007). A multitrait-multimethod validation of the Implicit Association Test: Implicit and explicit attitudes are related but distinct constructs. *Experimental Psychology, 54,* 14–29.

Nosek, B. A., & Hansen, J. J. (2008). The associations in our heads belong to us: Searching for attitudes and knowledge in implicit evaluation. *Cognition and Emotion, 22,* 553–594.

Olson, M. A., & Fazio, R. H. (2004). Reducing the influence of extrapersonal associations on the Implicit Association Test: Personalizing the IAT. *Journal of Personality and Social Psychology, 86,* 653–667.

Olson, M. A., & Fazio, R. H. (in press). Implicit and explicit measures of attitudes: The perspective of the MODE model. In R. E. Petty, R. H. Fazio, & P. Briñol (Eds.), *Attitudes: Insights from the new implicit measures.* Hillsdale, NJ: Erlbaum.

Perugini, M. (2005). Predictive models of implicit and explicit attitudes. *British Journal of Social Psychology, 44,* 29–45.

Strack, F., & Deutsch, R. (2004). Reflective and impulsive determinants of social behavior. *Personality and Social Psychology Review, 8*(3), 220–247.

Willingham, D. B., & Goedert, K. (2001). The role of taxonomies in the study of human memory. *Cognitive, Affective, and Behavioral Neuroscience, 1*(3), 250–265.

Wilson, T. D., Lindsey, S., & Schooler, T. Y. (2000). A model of dual attitudes. *Psychological Review, 107,* 101–126.

Section II

Ambivalence/Consistency

4

Attitudes and Cognitive Consistency[*]
The Role of Associative and Propositional Processes

Bertram Gawronski
Fritz Strack
Galen V. Bodenhausen

Introduction

Since the early 1950s, cognitive consistency has been a topic of continuing interest in social psychology. Notwithstanding some fundamental differences between different theories of cognitive consistency (Abelson, Aronson, McGuire, Newcomb, Rosenberg, & Tannenbaum, 1968), most of them share the assumption that cognitive inconsistency causes aversive feelings that, in turn, are assumed to have a powerful influence on judgments, decisions, and behavior. Research on cognitive dissonance (Festinger, 1957), for example, has repeatedly shown that people change their attitudes or their behavior in order to reduce the uncomfortable feeling caused by inconsistent cognitions (for an overview, see Harmon-Jones & Mills, 1999).

Until recently, research investigating the impact of cognitive consistency on attitudes primarily employed explicit attitude measures. In these studies, participants were simply asked to report their attitude toward a given object. With the recent development of implicit attitude

---

[*] Preparation of this chapter was supported by grants from Canada Research Chairs Program (CRC), the Social Sciences and Humanities Research Council of Canada (SSHRC), the Academic Development Fund of the University of Western Ontario (ADF), and the TransCoop Program of the Alexander von Humboldt Foundation.

measures (Fazio & Olson, 2003), however, researchers have become increasingly interested in the dynamics of cognitive consistency at the automatic level. This application of implicit attitude measures to investigate consistency phenomena was expected to improve our understanding of both implicit measures (e.g., Greenwald, Banaji, Rudman, Farnham, Nosek, & Mellott, 2002) and cognitive consistency in general (e.g., Gawronski & Strack, 2004).

The main goal of the present chapter is to provide an integrative review of research on cognitive consistency employing implicit attitude measures. This review is guided by a theoretical framework proposing that implicit and explicit attitude measures tap two distinct evaluative tendencies that have their roots in qualitatively different, though interrelated, processes: associative and propositional processes (Gawronski & Bodenhausen, 2006; Strack & Deutsch, 2004). Specifically, we argue that a distinction between associative and propositional processes offers a deeper understanding of several phenomena commonly explained in terms of consistency theories, thereby providing a new perspective on how cognitive consistency influences basic attitudinal processes. In addition, we argue that an application of consistency principles to research comparing explicit and implicit attitude measures can provide deeper insights into the distinct nature of their underlying processes. For this purpose, we first outline our theoretical framework in terms of associative and propositional processes, and how cognitive consistency is related to the two kinds of mental processes. Drawing on these assumptions, we then employ the proposed distinction as an integrative framework to review research that used implicit attitude measures to study cognitive consistency.

Associative and Propositional Processes

The theoretical framework employed in our review is based on the Reflective-Impulsive Model (RIM; Strack & Deutsch, 2004) and its recent derivative, the Associative-Propositional Evaluation (APE) Model (Gawronski & Bodenhausen, 2006). A central notion in these models is the distinction between two qualitatively different kinds of mental processes (see also Kahneman, 2003; Lieberman, Gaunt, Gilbert, & Trope, 2002; Sloman, 1996; Smith & DeCoster, 2000). Specifically, we argue that implicitly and explicitly assessed attitudes should be understood in terms of their underlying processes. Whereas implicit attitude measures—such as affective priming tasks (Fazio, Jackson, Dunton, & Williams, 1995) or the Implicit Association Test (Greenwald, McGhee, & Schwartz, 1998)—are assumed to tap evaluations that have their roots in associative processes, explicit attitude measures are assumed to tap evaluations that have their roots in propositional processes. This conceptualization resembles Eagly and Chaiken's (1993) definition of attitude as a psychological tendency to evaluate a given entity with some degree of favor or disfavor. However, the present model goes beyond this definition by arguing that such evaluative tendencies can be rooted in two different kinds of mental processes.

Nature of Associative and Propositional Processes

The first source of evaluative tendencies is represented by associative processes, which build the basis for evaluations reflected in implicit attitude measures. Such associative evaluations are best characterized as the automatic affective reactions resulting from the particular associations that are activated automatically upon encountering a relevant stimulus (Fazio, 1995). As such, associative evaluations require neither a high amount of cognitive capacity nor the intention to evaluate a specific object. The most important feature of associative evaluations, however, is that they are independent of the assignment of truth values (Strack & Deutsch, 2004). That is, associative evaluations can get activated irrespective of whether a person considers these evaluations as accurate or inaccurate. For example, the activation level of negative associations regarding African Americans may be high even though an individual may regard these associations as being incorrect or undesirable (Devine, 1989).

The second source of evaluative tendencies resides in propositional processes, which build the basis for evaluations reflected in explicit attitude measures. Evaluations resulting from propositional processes can be characterized as evaluative judgments that have their roots in syllogistic inferences from any kind of propositional information that is considered relevant for a given judgment. In the Reflective-Impulsive Model (Strack & Deutsch, 2004), such transformations are assumed to occur in a reflective system that is superordinate to an associative store. Specifically, the reflective system is assumed to transform inputs from the associative store into propositional format (e.g., a negative affective reaction toward X is translated into the proposition "I dislike X."). The resulting propositions are then subjected to syllogistic inferences to assess their validity (Gawronski & Bodenhausen, 2006). Thus, the most important feature that distinguishes propositional from associative processes is their dependency on truth values. Whereas the activation of associations can occur regardless of whether a person considers these associations to be true or false, propositional reasoning is generally concerned with the validation of evaluations and beliefs. Moreover, whether or not a given proposition will be explicitly endorsed depends on its subjective validity, as determined by processes of propositional reasoning.

Interplay Between Associative and Propositional Processes

An important aspect of the distinction between associative and propositional processes is their mutual interplay. As for the impact of associative on propositional processes, we argue that people usually base their evaluative judgments of an attitude object on their automatic affective reactions to this object (Gawronski & Bodenhausen, 2006). That is, the default mode of propositional reasoning is an affirmation of the propositional implication of an automatic affective reaction (see Gilbert, 1991). However, evaluative judgments can also be independent of automatic affective reactions when the propositional implications of these reactions are rejected as a valid basis for an evaluative judgment (Strack, 1992). Drawing on a central assumption of the APE Model (Gawronski & Bodenhausen, 2006), we argue that the primary determinant of perceived validity of a proposition—and thus of the propositional implication of an automatic affective reaction—is the consistency of this proposition with other propositions that are considered to be relevant for the respective judgment (Kruglanski, 1989; for a discussion of alternative determinants of perceived validity, see Briñol & Petty, 2004). In the case of evaluative judgments, such propositions may include nonevaluative propositions referring to general beliefs about the world or propositional evaluations of other attitude objects.[1] If the propositional implication of an automatic affective reaction is consistent with other relevant propositions, it may be considered valid and thus may serve as the basis for an evaluative judgment. If, however, the propositional implication of an automatic affective reaction is inconsistent with other relevant propositions, it may be considered invalid and thus may be rejected as a basis for an evaluative judgment. For example, the propositional implication of a negative affective reaction to a minority member (e.g., "I don't like this African-American person.") may be inconsistent with general beliefs about the world (e.g., "African Americans are a disadvantaged minority group.") and the propositional evaluation of another attitude object (e.g., "Negative evaluations of disadvantaged minority members are wrong."). In this case, the resulting inconsistency between the three propositions may lead to a rejection of the negative affective reaction as a valid basis for an evaluative judgment. However, the negative affective reaction may still serve as a basis for an evaluative judgment if one of the other inconsistent propositions is rejected (Gawronski, Peters, Brochu, & Strack, 2008).

The operating principles of the RIM (Strack & Deutsch, 2004) imply that propositional processes should influence associative evaluations under certain conditions. Specifically, propositional processes should influence associative evaluations when propositional reasoning leads to an affirmation of a given evaluation. However, propositional processes should leave associative evaluations unaffected when propositional reasoning leads to a negation of a given evaluation. The crucial assumption underlying this claim is that the validation process of affirming or negating a proposition implies an assignment of truth values, and thus cannot be performed associatively (Deutsch, Gawronski, & Strack, 2006). However, affirming or negating a given proposition may still activate the associative components of that proposition. Thus, affirming a propositional evaluation should directly activate its underlying associative evaluation (e.g., affirming the proposition "Old people are good drivers." activates *old people* and *good drivers*). However, negating a propositional evaluation should activate the underlying non-negated associative evaluation (e.g., negating the proposition "Old people are bad drivers." activates *old people* and *bad drivers*). Hence, negating a given proposition often leads to ironic or rebound effects on the associative level (e.g., Deutsch et al.; Gawronski, Deutsch, Mbirkou, Seibt, & Strack, 2008; Forehand & Perkins, 2005; for a review, see Wegner, 1994).[2]

The differential role of affirmation and negation can be illustrated with a study by Kawakami, Dovidio, Moll, Hermsen, and Russin (2000) on the reduction of automatic stereotyping. These researchers found that long-term training in the negation of social stereotypes resulted in lower levels of automatic stereotype activation. At a superficial level, this finding seems to be in contrast to the present assumptions implying that negation training should leave automatic stereotype activation unaffected. It is important to note, however, that Kawakami et al.'s negation training included two components: (a) a negation of stereotypes and (b) an affirmation of counterstereotypes. In one of their studies, for example, participants were presented with pictures of Black and White individuals and traits that were related either to the stereotype of Blacks or to the stereotype of Whites. Participants' task was to respond with a *No* key each time they saw a stereotype-congruent person-trait combination (e.g., a Black face with a stereotypically Black trait word) and to respond with a *Yes* key each time they saw stereotype-incongruent person-trait combination (e.g., a Black face with a stereotypically White trait word). Hence, it is not clear whether the resulting reduction in automatic stereotyping of Black people was due to the negation of the stereotype or to the affirmation of counterstereotype. Drawing on the considerations outlined above, we argue that Kawakami et al.'s findings are exclusively driven by the affirmation of the counterstereotype, rather than by the negation of the stereotype. This claim was recently confirmed by Gawronski, Deutsch et al. (2008), who found that only training in the affirmation of counterstereotypical information, but not training in the negation of stereotypical information, led to a reduction in automatic stereotype activation. In fact, negation of the stereotype even led to a significant increase in automatic stereotyping. This difference between affirmation versus negation is also consistent with research in other areas showing that deliberate attempts to suppress affective reactions (negation) usually leave these reactions unaffected, whereas attempts to attribute a different meaning to the response eliciting stimulus (affirmation) is indeed capable of modifying affective reactions (e.g., Butler, Egloff, Wilhelm, Smith, Erickson, & Gross, 2003; Gross, 1998).

Cognitive Elaboration

Cognitive elaboration has long been assumed to be of crucial importance in research on attitudes (Greenwald, 1968; Petty, Ostrom, & Brock, 1981). As with other models addressing the distinction between implicit and explicit attitude measures (e.g., Fazio & Olson, 2003; Wilson, Lindsey, & Schooler, 2000), our model implies a crucial role of cognitive elaboration for the relation between explicit and implicit attitude measures. Fazio's (1990) MODE model, for example, suggests that cognitive elaboration is a crucial determinant of the influence of automatic attitudes on behavior (see Chapter 2, this volume). Specifically, the MODE model posits that behavior is more likely to be influenced by automatic attitudes when either the motivation or the opportunity to deliberate is low. However, behavior should be less likely to be influenced by automatic attitudes when both the motivation and the opportunity to deliberate are high. Given that responses on a self-report measure simply reflect a particular kind of behavior (Fazio & Olson), the relation between explicit and implicit attitude measures is likely to be lower when either the motivation or the opportunity to deliberate is low. In contrast, correlations between the two kinds of measures are likely to be higher when both the motivation and the opportunity to deliberate are high (e.g., Florack, Scarabis, & Bless, 2001; Hofmann, Gawronski, Gschwendner, Le, & Schmitt, 2005; Koole, Dijksterhuis, & van Knippenberg, 2001).

We similarly posit that increased elaboration often reduces the correlation between explicit and implicit measures of attitudes. However, our model goes beyond the MODE model with regard to its assumptions about the underlying processes. According to the APE Model (Gawronski & Bodenhausen, 2006), cognitive elaboration primarily affects the complexity of propositional thinking by influencing how many judgment-relevant propositions are considered in addition to one's automatic affective reaction. More extensive elaboration generally implies considering a greater number of propositions about the attitude object. To the extent that any of these additional propositions is inconsistent with the automatic evaluative response, the extra elaboration will be likely to reduce the correlation between automatic affective reactions and evaluative judgments (Shiv & Nowlis, 2004).

It is important to note, however, that increased cognitive elaboration does not inevitably reduce the relation between explicit and implicit attitude measures. Drawing on earlier research on directional effects of cognitive elaboration (e.g., Judd & Lusk, 1984; Petty, Briñol, & Tormala, 2002), we argue that enhanced elaboration should reduce the relation between explicit and implicit attitude measures only if additionally considered propositions question the validity of one's automatic affective reaction as a basis for an evaluative judgment (Gawronski & Bodenhausen, 2006). However, if additionally considered propositions do not question the validity of one's automatic affective reaction, the relation between explicit and implicit attitude measures should be unaffected by cognitive elaboration. Moreover, if additionally considered propositions confirm the subjective validity of one's automatic affective reaction, the relation between explicit and implicit attitude measures should actually increase (rather than decrease) as a function of cognitive elaboration. For example, if increased cognitive elaboration identifies an additional proposition (e.g., "This African-American person behaved in a hostile manner.") that resolves the inconsistency between a propositionally transformed affective reaction (e.g., "I don't like this African-American person."), other nonevaluative propositions (e.g., "African Americans are a disadvantaged minority group."), and propositional evaluations of other attitude objects (e.g., "It is wrong to evaluate members of disadvantaged minority groups negatively."), the relation between explicit and implicit attitude measures should actually increase rather than decrease as a function of cognitive elaboration. In other words, whether the relation between explicit and implicit attitude measures increases or decreases as a function of cognitive elaboration does not depend on the amount of cognitive elaboration per se. Rather, it is a function of a consistency assessment regarding the momentarily considered set of propositions.

Cognitive Consistency

As already outlined above, cognitive consistency plays a crucial role in the propositional process of validating evaluations and beliefs. In fact, we argue that cognitive consistency is exclusively a concern of propositional reasoning (Gawronski & Bodenhausen, 2006; Gawronski & Strack, 2004). More precisely, consistency results from a propositional process of consistency assessment that is based on the assignment of truth values and the application of syllogistic rules and logical principles.[3] From a general perspective, two propositions are consistent with each other when both are regarded as true, and one does not imply the opposite of the other. In contrast, two propositions are inconsistent when both are regarded as true, and one follows from the opposite of the other (Festinger, 1957). Importantly, because (in)consistency between two propositions cannot even be defined without an assignment of truth values, inconsistency has to be resolved by means of propositional reasoning, that is, either by changing the truth value of one proposition or by finding an additional proposition that resolves the inconsistency (Gawronski & Bodenhausen, 2006). For example, if exposure to a minority member automatically activates negative associations, people may either reject the propositional implication of these associations because of its inconsistency with other accepted propositions (Gawronski, Peters et al., 2008), or they may find an additional proposition that resolves the inconsistency (e.g., "This African-American person was unfriendly."). Whereas the former process refers to what we described as negation of the propositional implications of an automatic affective reaction (Deutsch et al., 2006), the latter process has been described as *rationalization* (Festinger) or *justification* (Crandall & Eshleman, 2003).

Notwithstanding the propositional nature of cognitive consistency, it is important to note that associative processes can produce outcomes that have traditionally been described in terms of consistency principles. More precisely, spreading activation processes in associative networks often result in activation patterns that seem consistent from a logical perspective. For instance, if a Black person has a strong association between his or her representation of the self and the category *Black*, and an additional strong association between the category *Black* and *negative*, mere activation of the self should automatically activate "negative" by means of spreading activation. This spreading activation mechanism can certainly be described in propositional terms (i.e., "I am Black," "Black is bad," therefore, "I am bad."). However, this propositional description ignores that the underlying activation process is independent of whether the person considers these propositions as true or false. In other words, spreading activation processes can result in activation patterns that could be described as consistent from a propositional perspective. However, this does not necessarily imply that the process that gives raise to these activation patterns is itself propositional.

We argue that the distinction between associative processes of spreading activation and propositional processes of consistency assessment is crucial when it comes to understanding the convergence and divergence between explicit and implicit attitude measures. Whereas phenomena that have their roots in associative processes of spreading activation should be more likely to emerge on implicit rather than explicit attitude measures, phenomena that have their roots in propositional processes of consistency assessment should be more likely to emerge on explicit rather than implicit attitude measures. To be sure, the fact that a given phenomenon is due to associative processes does not imply that it cannot emerge on explicit attitude measures. In fact, spreading activation should lead to the same outcome on explicit attitude measures, unless associative evaluations are rejected as a valid basis for an evaluative judgment. Conversely, the fact that a given phenomenon is due to propositional processes does not imply that it cannot emerge on implicit attitude measures. Rather, propositional processes should lead to the same outcome on implicit attitude measures when they imply an affirmation of a given evaluation, but not when they imply a negation. Importantly, even when a given process leads to corresponding effects on explicit and implicit attitude measures, spreading activation and consistency assessment should be characterized by different patterns of mediation (Gawronski & Bodenhausen, 2006). That is, if a given phenomenon has its roots in associative processes of spreading activation, this phenomenon should be characterized by a direct effect on implicit attitude measures and an indirect effect on explicit attitude measures that is mediated by the effect on implicit attitude measures. In contrast, if a given phenomenon has its roots in propositional processes of consistency assessment, this phenomenon should be characterized by a direct effect on explicit attitude measures and an indirect effect on implicit attitude measures that is mediated by the effect on explicit attitude measures.

Empirical Evidence

So far, research on cognitive consistency employing implicit attitude measures focused on four different phenomena: balanced identities (Greenwald et al., 2002; Nosek, Banaji, & Greenwald, 2002; Rudman, Greenwald, & McGhee, 2001), cognitive dissonance arising from induced compliance (Gawronski & Strack, 2004), the spreading-of-alternatives effect (Gawronski, Bodenhausen, & Becker, 2007), and cognitive balance in attitude formation (Gawronski, Walther, & Blank, 2005). Drawing on the considerations outlined above, we argue that a sufficient understanding of these phenomena requires a focus on their underlying associative and propositional mechanisms: spreading activation and consistency assessment.

Balanced Identities

The first set of studies that applied the notion of cognitive consistency to implicit attitude measures was conducted under the framework of Greenwald et al.'s (2002) unified theory of attitudes, stereotypes, self-esteem, and self-concept (e.g., Greenwald et al., 2002; Nosek et al., 2002; Rudman et al., 2001). Consistent with the basic notion of Heider's (1958) balance theory, these studies showed that people's automatic evaluation of their ingroup, their automatic self-concept as a member of this group, and their automatic self-evaluation are generally related in a manner such that one construct is predicted by the interaction of the other two. In one study, for example, Greenwald et al. (2002) assessed female participants' automatic evaluation of the category woman, automatic evaluations of the self, and automatic associations between the self and the category *women* with three different IATs (Greenwald et al., 1998). Results showed that women's automatic self-evaluations were significantly related to the interaction of their automatic self-associations as female and their automatic evaluation of women. That is, the more women associated the category women with a positive (negative) evaluation, and the stronger they associated themselves with the category women, the more positive (negative) was their automatic self-evaluation. Interestingly, such patterns of balanced identities were generally obtained for implicit measures, whereas identities often showed imbalanced patterns on explicit measures.

Drawing on the distinction between associative and propositional processes, these findings can be explained in terms of spreading activation in associative memory. Specifically, the activation of a particular concept (e.g., self) can be sufficient to activate concepts that are chronically associated with this concept (e.g., ingroup category). As such, the valence of one concept may transfer associatively to the other. Importantly, this associative transfer of evaluations may be driven by processes of spreading activation without requiring any kind of higher-order propositional process. Hence, even though the relation between three concepts (e.g., self-ingroup association, ingroup evaluation, self-evaluation) could be translated into propositional format (e.g., "I am female," "Female is good," therefore, "I am good."), the process that gives raise to balanced identities seems to be independent of propositional reasoning. Moreover, balanced identities on explicit measures may result when people base their judgments on the propositional implications of their activated associations, thus directly reflecting the activation pattern obtained on the associative level. However, because the three propositions resulting from these associations may reflect only a limited portion of the many propositions that are considered for the corresponding judgments, the three components may sometimes be imbalanced on the propositional level even though they are balanced on the associative level (e.g., Greenwald et al., 2002). Importantly, such imbalanced identities on the propositional level may not represent a genuine logical inconsistency if the full set of momentarily considered propositions is taken into account. Rather, an imbalanced set of three propositions may still be consistent if there is an additional proposition that resolves the inconsistency between the three (Wellens & Thistlewaite, 1971; Wiest, 1965; for a review, see Insko, 1984). These assumptions imply that explicit and implicit measures may show dissociations, such that implicit measures are more likely to reflect balanced identities resulting from associative processes of spreading activation, whereas explicit measures reflect balanced identities only when processes of propositional reasoning do not lead to a rejection of the propositional implications of these associations.

Induced Compliance

Similar considerations were applied to cognitive dissonance arising from induced compliance by Gawronski and Strack (2004). Drawing on the distinction between associative and propositional processes, Gawronski and Strack claimed that both the cause of dissonance experiences and the process of dissonance reduction require a propositional representation of their elements. With regard to the causes of cognitive dissonance, Gawronski and Strack argued that cognitive inconsistency arises when two propositions are regarded as true, and one follows from the opposite of the other (Festinger, 1957). With regard to the process of dissonance reduction, Gawronski and Strack argued that cognitive inconsistency is resolved either by rejecting one of the inconsistent propositions as false or by finding an additional proposition that resolves the inconsistency (Kruglanski, 1989).

These assumptions have important implications for attitude change resulting from cognitive dissonance. If dissonance-related attitude changes are due to a rejection of a given evaluation because of its inconsistency with other propositions, cognitive dissonance can be expected to influence only explicitly assessed but not implicitly assessed attitudes. Moreover, given that evaluative judgments are typically based on associative evaluations unless the latter are rejected as a valid basis for an evaluative judgment, explicit and implicit attitude measures should be highly correlated when people can reduce their dissonance by an additional proposition that resolves the present inconsistency. However, explicit and implicit attitude measures should be uncorrelated when cognitive dissonance is reduced by a rejection of associative evaluations as a valid basis for an evaluative judgment.

To test these assumptions, Gawronski and Strack (2004) employed Festinger and Carlsmith's (1959) induced compliance paradigm. Participants wrote a counterattitudinal essay under conditions of either high or low situational pressure, and then completed an explicit and an implicit measure of attitudes toward the topic in question. Participants in a control condition completed the two measures without writing an essay. Replicating previous research on cognitive dissonance, explicitly assessed attitudes toward the initially counterattitudinal position were more favorable when situational pressure was low than when it was high. Most importantly, however, implicitly assessed attitudes were generally unaffected by dissonance manipulations. Moreover, explicit attitude measures were significantly related to implicit attitude measures under control conditions and when counterattitudinal behavior was elicited under high situational pressure, but not when situational pressure was low. These results were replicated in two studies using counterattitudinal essays in favor of a prohibition of alcoholic beverages (Experiment 1) and an increase of scholarships for Black students at the expense of funding for White students (Experiment 2). Taken together, these results are consistent with the assumption that cognitive dissonance following induced compliance is a propositional phenomenon, leading to dissonance-related attitude changes only for evaluative judgments but not for associative evaluations. Moreover, evaluative judgments seem to be based on associative evaluations unless the latter are rejected as a valid basis for these judgments, such as when cognitive dissonance is reduced by a deliberate rejection of associative evaluations.

Another finding that is consistent with Gawronski and Strack's (2004) assumptions was presented by Wilson et al. (2000). Also employing the induced compliance paradigm (Festinger & Carlsmith, 1959), Wilson et al. asked participants to write a counterattitudinal essay in favor of a tuition increase at participants' home university. Essays were written under either high or low perceived situational pressure. Orthogonal to this manipulation, half of the participants had to make their evaluative judgments under time pressure, whereas the remaining half had unlimited time to make their evaluative judgments. Results indicated that dissonance-related changes in evaluative judgments emerged only when participants had unlimited time to make their judgment. In this case, participants showed more positive attitudes toward a tuition increase when perceived situational pressure was low than when it was high. However, when participants were under time pressure, evaluative judgments did not differ as a function of perceived situational pressure. In this case, participants were strongly in opposition toward a tuition increase regardless of whether perceived situational pressure was high or low.

Wilson et al. (2000) interpreted these findings in terms of their dual attitudes model. Specifically, Wilson et al. argued that old attitudes are quite robust and thus are often not replaced by newly acquired attitudes. Hence, people often hold dual attitudes toward the same attitude object. Moreover, old attitudes are assumed to be activated automatically, whereas newly acquired attitudes are assumed to require a high amount of cognitive effort to be retrieved from memory. Thus, judgments and behavior should be influenced by new attitudes only when people have the motivation and cognitive capacity to retrieve their new attitudes from memory. However, if people lack either the motivation or the cognitive capacity to retrieve their new attitudes from memory, the old attitude may still have a significant impact on judgments and behavior.

It is important to note, however, that automatically activated evaluations have been shown to be quite malleable and sometimes are easier to change than deliberate evaluations (e.g., Karpinski & Hilton, 2001; Olson & Fazio, 2006; for reviews, see Blair, 2002; Gawronski & Bodenhausen, 2006). Thus, the assumption that implicit attitude measures reflect old representations that have not been replaced by newly acquired attitudes (e.g., Dovidio, Kawakami, & Beach, 2001; Greenwald & Banaji, 1995; Rudman, 2004; Wilson et al., 2000) seems questionable. As outlined above, we argue that explicitly and implicitly assessed attitudes should be understood in terms of their underlying processes (i.e., associative and propositional processes) rather than in terms of their robustness or relative age. Moreover, whether implicit or explicit attitude measures will be affected by a given factor may depend on which of the two processes is affected in the first place (Gawronski & Bodenhausen, 2006). For example, environmentally created associations (e.g., Karpinski & Hilton, 2001) or evaluative conditioning (e.g., Olson & Fazio, 2006) may directly influence the particular associations that are activated and thus may be more likely to change implicitly rather than explicitly assessed attitudes. Cognitive dissonance, in contrast, may lead to a rejection of a given evaluation because of its inconsistency with other propositions and thus may influence only explicitly but not implicitly assessed attitudes (e.g., Gawronski & Strack, 2004). Moreover, the relative complexity of propositional inferences may decrease as a function of time pressure (Hofmann et al., 2005; Koole et al., 2001), thereby increasing the likelihood that evaluative judgments will be based on associative evaluations. As such, Wilson et al.'s findings may point to the propositional nature of dissonance-related reasoning processes and the cognitive capacity required for these processes, rather than to the general robustness of old attitudes.

Spreading of Alternatives

When people have to make a decision between two equally attractive alternatives, they often evaluate the chosen alternative more positively than the rejected alternative after they have made their decision (Brehm, 1956). A common explanation for this spreading-of-alternatives effect is that people experience an uncomfortable feeling of postdecisional dissonance when they recognize that the rejected alternative might have been better than the chosen alternative (Brehm & Cohen, 1962). Hence, to reduce this uncomfortable feeling, people often emphasize (Brehm, 1956) or deliberately search for (Frey, 1986) positive characteristics of the chosen alternative and negative characteristics of the rejected alternative. This kind of selective information search, in turn, leads to more favorable evaluations of the chosen alternative and to less favorable evaluations of the rejected alternative.

Even though Gawronski and Strack (2004) tested their assumptions only for cognitive dissonance arising from induced compliance (Festinger & Carlsmith, 1959), their ideas can also be applied to postdecisional dissonance (Brehm, 1956). Specifically, one could argue that postdecisional dissonance arises when people recognize that the propositional implication of their decision (e.g., "I preferred alternative A over alternative B.") is inconsistent with the propositional implication of the attributes ascribed to the two alternatives (e.g., "Alternative B is better than alternative A."). Moreover, the proposed process of postdecisional dissonance reduction can also be regarded as propositional, because it involves a propositional attribution of positive and negative characteristics implying an evaluation that is consistent with the decision (i.e., "Alternative A is better than alternative B."). Depending on whether this process implies an affirmation (e.g., "Alternative A has a unique positive feature." or "Alternative B has a unique negative feature.") or a negation (e.g., "It is not true that alternative A has a unique negative feature." or "It is not true that alternative B has a unique positive feature."), the propositional process of dissonance reduction may or may not lead to corresponding changes in associative evaluations. Importantly, if postdecisional dissonance actually affects associative evaluations in a process of affirmation, this influence should be indirect rather than direct, such that changes in implicitly assessed attitudes should be mediated by changes in explicitly assessed attitudes. Even though these assumptions are speculative at this point, future research may provide evidence for the proposed direct, indirect, and nonexisting effects of postdecisional dissonance on explicit and implicit attitudes.

Drawing on the general notion of balanced identities (e.g., Greenwald et al., 2002; Nosek et al., 2002; Rudman et al., 2001), we argue that, in addition to the proposed propositional process of dissonance reduction, associative processes of spreading activation can lead to postdecisional changes in associative evaluations. The process that is responsible for such changes is associative self-anchoring. Associative self-anchoring can be understood as the formation of an association between an object and the self, leading to a subsequent transfer of already existing self-associations to the object (see Cadinu & Rothbart, 1996; Otten, 2003). Applied to the spreading-of-alternatives effect, choosing an object may create an association between the chosen object and the self, thus leading to a transfer of associative self-evaluations to the chosen object. Importantly, given that most people's self-evaluation is highly positive (Bosson, Swann, & Pennebaker, 2000; Greenwald & Farnham, 2000; Koole et al., 2001), this process of associative self-anchoring should lead to postdecisional changes in implicitly assessed attitudes without requiring the higher-order propositional processes implied by our analysis of dissonance reduction.

Evidence for these assumptions was provided in a series of studies by Gawronski et al. (2007). In a first study, participants were asked to decide which of two equally attractive pictures they would like to receive as a special gratification for their participation in the experiment. Immediately before and right after the decision, automatic evaluations of the two pictures were assessed with an affective priming task (Fazio et al., 1995). Consistent with the assumption that associative evaluations may be affected by participants' decision, implicitly assessed attitudes toward the chosen picture became more positive as a function of the decision, whereas implicitly assessed attitudes toward the rejected picture became more negative as a function of the decision. In order to test whether these effects are indeed related to the formation of self-object associations, participants in a second study were again asked to decide which of two equally attractive pictures they would like to receive as a special gratification for their participation in the experiment. In contrast to the implicit attitude measure in the first study, however, participants completed an implicit measure of self-picture associations. Consistent with the associative self-anchoring hypothesis, participants showed stronger associations between the chosen picture and the self after the decision. In contrast, associations between the rejected picture and the self became weaker after participants made their decision. A third study was designed to test the assumption that automatic self-evaluations associatively transfer to the chosen object. This study replicated the effects on automatic evaluations obtained in the first study. However, in contrast to the first study, this study additionally included a measure of automatic self-evaluations that was administered at the beginning of the experiment. Consistent with the assumption that postdecisional changes of implicitly assessed attitudes can be due to an associative transfer of implicit self-evaluations, participants who showed positive self-evaluations evaluated chosen pictures more positively after the decision. However, participants who exhibited negative self-evaluations evaluated chosen pictures more negatively after the decision. Finally, a fourth study was designed to rule out postdecisional dissonance as an alternative explanation for the obtained effects. In this study, self-object associations resulting from ownership were created by a random procedure rather than by participants' choice decision (see Beggan, 1992). Thus, if the obtained results are due to processes of associative self-anchoring, randomly determined ownership should be sufficient to change associative evaluations of owned objects and such evaluations should again depend on automatic self-evaluations. If, however, the obtained results are due to postdecisional dissonance, randomly determined ownership should leave associative evaluations of owned objects unaffected. Results provided clear evidence for the associative self-anchoring account, implying a change in associative evaluations of owned objects even when ownership was determined by a random procedure.

These findings have important implications for the interpretation of previous research on postdecisional attitude change. Lieberman, Ochsner, Gilbert, and Schacter (2001), for example, found that even amnesic participants exhibit postdecisional changes in explicitly assessed attitudes. In their study, participants showed postdecisional attitude changes even though they had no memory for their decision. Drawing on this finding, Lieberman et al. concluded that cognitive dissonance reduction does not require explicit memory for decisions (Brehm, 1956) or counterattitudinal behavior (Festinger & Carlsmith, 1959). This conclusion, however, is obviously in contrast with Gawronski and Strack's (2004) claim that both the causes of dissonance experiences and the process of dissonance reduction require a propositional representation of their elements. Gawronski et al.'s (2007) findings on associative self-anchoring help to resolve this inconsistency by suggesting that postdecisional attitude changes may occur even in the absence of cognitive dissonance. That is, postdecisional attitude changes exhibited by amnesic participants may be due to associative self-anchoring rather than cognitive dissonance, such that choice decisions influenced associative evaluations by a transfer of associative self-evaluations that were later used as a basis for evaluative judgments about the object. As this spreading activation process does not require explicit memory for the original decision, associative self-anchoring can explain why even amnesic participants exhibit postdecisional attitude change.

An important question related to Gawronski et al.'s (2007) results in the free choice paradigm is how they relate to Gawronski and Strack's (2004) findings in the induced compliance paradigm. Traditionally, judgmental phenomena in the induced compliance paradigm (Festinger

& Carlsmith, 1959) and the free choice paradigm (Brehm, 1956) have been assumed to derive from psychological mechanisms that are fundamentally similar, if not identical. This perspective stands in contrast to the results discussed in the present chapter, showing changes in implicit attitude measures as a result of free choice decisions (Gawronski et al., 2007), but not as a result of induced compliance (Gawronski & Strack, 2004). Drawing on the theoretical assumptions outlined above, we argue that the processes that lead to attitude change in the two paradigms are indeed identical (i.e., dissonance reduction, associative self-anchoring). However, attitude change at the implicit level may be moderated by contingent factors that either facilitate or inhibit the relative impact of these processes.

First, associative self-anchoring may be differentially effective in changing attitudes in the two paradigms. In the free choice paradigm, associative self-anchoring may create an association between the chosen object and the self, thus leading to an associative transfer of self-evaluations to the chosen object. This process should lead to a direct effect on implicit attitude measures, which may or may not lead to a corresponding indirect effect on explicit attitude measures. In the induced compliance paradigm, however, the relevant object (e.g., the boring task participants had to complete in Festinger and Carlsmith's 1959 study) may not become sufficiently "personal" for the formation of a new association between the attitude object and the self. Even though participants in this paradigm also make a "choice decision" to engage in counterattitudinal behavior, the choice decision refers to a behavior that stands in direct contrast to the original attitude. Hence, the decision to engage in counterattitudinal behavior may be insufficient to create a strong association between the attitude object and the self. For this reason, an associative transfer of self-evaluations seems unlikely in the induced compliance paradigm. This assumption implies that associative self-anchoring effects in the free choice paradigm should occur only when participants have to make a choice decision between two objects that are relatively attractive (e.g., a trip to Spain vs. a trip to Italy). However, associative self-anchoring effects should be substantially reduced when participants have to make a choice decision between two objects that are highly unattractive (e.g., going to jail for a year vs. paying a fine of $100,000).

Second, whereas cognitive dissonance arising from free choice decisions may result in either an affirmation or a negation focus, cognitive dissonance arising from induced compliance may be more likely to imply a negation rather than an affirmation focus. Specifically, participants in the free choice paradigm may either affirm (e.g., "Alternative A has a unique positive feature.") or negate (e.g., "It is not true that alternative A has a unique negative feature.") a particular evaluation to reduce postdecisional dissonance. Thus, depending on whether participants adopt an affirmation or a negation focus, the reduction of postdecisional dissonance may or may not lead to indirect changes in associative evaluations. This outcome, however, may again be different in the induced compliance paradigm. As counterattitudinal behavior—by definition—contradicts an already existing attitude, participants in the induced compliance paradigm may be more likely to negate this attitude rather than to affirm a new one. Thus, if participants in the free choice paradigm adopt an affirmation rather than a negation focus, postdecisional dissonance may lead to corresponding changes in explicit and implicit attitude measures, with changes on the implicit level being mediated by changes on the explicit level. In contrast, participants in the induced compliance paradigm may generally adopt a negation focus, thus leading to changes on explicit, but not implicit, attitude measures. Again, this interpretation implies that postdecisional dissonance should influence both explicitly and implicitly assessed attitudes, when participants have to make a choice decision between two objects that are relatively attractive (e.g., a trip to Spain vs. a trip to Italy). However, postdecisional dissonance should influence only explicitly, but not implicitly, assessed attitudes, when participants have to make a choice decision between two objects that are highly unattractive (e.g., going to jail for a year vs. paying a fine of $100,000).

Cognitive Balance

Another line of research employing implicit attitude measures to study principles of cognitive consistency is research on cognitive balance. According to Heider's (1958) original formulation of balance theory, people tend to like individuals who are liked by their friends, but they tend to dislike individuals who are disliked by their friends. People also tend to dislike individuals who are liked by people they personally dislike, but they tend to like individuals who are disliked by people they personally dislike (e.g., Aronson & Cope, 1968). According to Heider, a triad of interpersonal relations is balanced when it has either no or an even number of disliking relations; however, a triad of interpersonal relations is imbalanced when it has an odd number of disliking relations.

An interesting question is how the logic of cognitive balance may influence the formation of interpersonal attitudes. Drawing on the distinction between associative and propositional processes, balance-related inferences in interpersonal attitude formation can be assumed to involve higher-order propositional processes that determine the consistency between attitudes, as defined by balance-logic. Consider, for example, that you dislike a person named Paul, and that Paul dislikes a third person named John. From a mere associative perspective, your cognitive representation of John may include two negative associations: (a) John is associated with the quality of being disliked, and (b) John is associated with the disliked person Paul. Hence, simple processes of spreading activation in associative memory may lead to a negative evaluation of John on the associative level. This, however, should be different on the level of higher-order propositional processes. On this level, the logic of cognitive balance may be applied to the two negative associations, thus leading to a positive evaluative judgment about John because he is disliked by a negatively evaluated individual.

Notwithstanding these considerations, a sufficient understanding of how balance-logic may influence implicitly and explicitly assessed attitudes requires an additional consideration of the mutual interplay between the two processes. According to the RIM (Strack & Deutsch, 2004), propositional processes should influence associative evaluations when propositional reasoning leads to an affirmation of a given evaluation, but not when it implies a negation of an evaluation. This assumption has important implications for the influence of cognitive balance on explicit and implicit attitude measures. Previous research has shown that cognitive balance primarily affects the encoding of social information (e.g., Hummert, Crockett, & Kemper, 1990; Picek, Sherman, & Shiffrin, 1975). Importantly, such an impact on the encoding of social information implies an affirmation of a given evaluation, which should lead to an indirect effect on associative evaluations that is mediated by processes of propositional reasoning (see Gawronski & Bodenhausen, 2006). Specifically, a priori attitudes toward a given person may influence the interpretation of this person's sentiments about another individual, such that perceivers spontaneously interpret a positive (negative) sentiment exhibited by a positively evaluated source individual as positive (negative) information about the target, whereas a positive (negative) sentiment exhibited by a negatively evaluated source individual may be interpreted as negative (positive) information about the target. Thus, the available information may be stored in a manner that is already consistent with a balanced triad. Accordingly, a priori source attitudes, observed sentiments, and newly formed attitudes towards the targets may result in a balanced triad for both explicitly and implicitly assessed attitudes.

It is important to note, however, that such proactive, encoding-related influences are possible only if perceivers have an a priori positive or negative attitude toward the source before they learn about his or her sentiments. If perceivers form a positive or negative source attitude after they learn about this person's sentiments about a given target, encoding of these sentiments cannot differ as a function of a priori attitudes (see Srull & Wyer, 1980; Trope & Alfieri, 1997). In this case, the subsequent application of balance-logic implies a rejection (or negation) of the valence implied by the previously observed sentiment information (i.e., a given person is liked or disliked by someone else), thus leaving implicitly assessed attitudes unaffected. Moreover, the influence of cognitive balance on explicitly assessed attitudes should depend on whether or not people retroactively apply the logic of cognitive balance to the available information.

In a series of three studies, Gawronski et al. (2005) provided evidence that cognitive balance (a) proactively influences both explicitly and implicitly assessed attitudes via differences in the encoding of social information, and (b) has no retroactive influence on either explicitly or implicitly assessed attitudes. In a first study, participants formed either positive or negative attitudes toward several source individuals, and then learned that these source individuals either liked or disliked another set of neutral target individuals. Consistent with the assumption that cognitive balance can influence the encoding of social information, Gawronski et al. (2005) found balanced triads for both explicitly and implicitly assessed attitudes. Specifically, participants showed more positive attitudes toward targets who were liked rather than disliked by positive source individuals, but they showed more negative attitudes toward targets who were liked rather than disliked by negative source individuals. In a second study, Gawronski et al. (2005) used the same manipulation, the only difference being the order of information presentation. In this study, participants first learned whether a neutral source individual either liked or disliked a neutral target individual, and then formed a positive or negative attitude toward the source. In this case, the two kinds of information influenced target attitudes in an additive rather than interactive manner. That is, participants showed more positive attitudes toward targets who were liked rather than disliked, irrespective of whether the liking or disliking person was positive or negative. In addition, participants showed more positive attitudes toward targets who were associated with positive rather than negative source individuals, irrespective of whether the source individual liked or disliked the target (see also Hebl & Mannix, 2003; Walther, 2002).

Finally, in a third study, Gawronski et al. (2005) replicated these findings by manipulating source valence, observed sentiments, and order of information acquisition in a single study.

An important question related to these findings concerns their potential inconsistency with the available evidence on cognitive dissonance. As outlined above, Gawronski and Strack (2004) have shown that cognitive dissonance changes only explicitly but not implicitly assessed attitudes. However, cognitive balance has been shown to affect both explicitly and implicitly assessed attitudes, at least when participants first form an attitude about one person, and then learn about this person's sentiments about another individual (Gawronski et al., 2005). Given that both cognitive dissonance and balance-related inferences may reflect a propositionally rooted desire for cognitive consistency (Zajonc, 1960), one may expect cognitive balance to affect only explicit but not implicit attitudes. Drawing on the considerations outlined above, we argue that a crucial difference between the two lines of research is that dissonance-related attitude changes resulting from counterattitudinal behavior imply a rejection of an associative evaluation, whereas the obtained influence of cognitive balance on implicitly assessed attitudes reflects an affirmative influence on the encoding of social information. Whereas counterattitudinal behavior under conditions of low situational pressure led to a rejection of already existing associative evaluations, a priori attitudes toward a given source individual proactively influenced how this person's sentiments were encoded, and thus how this information was stored in associative memory. Most importantly, if the particular order of information acquisition in the balance paradigm implied a retroactive discounting of observed sentiments (Gawronski et al., 2005, Experiment 2), implicitly assessed attitudes were unaffected by cognitive balance, such as implicitly assessed attitudes have been shown to be unaffected by cognitive dissonance (Gawronski & Strack, 2004).

This interpretation, however, raises the new question of why consistency concerns did not affect explicitly assessed attitudes under rejection conditions—as was the case in Gawronski and Strack's (2004) research on cognitive dissonance. A possible explanation may be the independent encoding of source information (i.e., valence of the liking or disliking person) and message information (i.e., a person is liked or disliked by someone) under rejection conditions. Similar to the sleeper effect (for a review, see Kumkale & Albarracín, 2004), source valence and observed sentiments may be stored independently in memory when source valence is encoded after observed sentiments. In this case, observed sentiments may be discounted only if (a) both kinds of information are retrieved from memory, and (b) the two kinds of information can be related to one another. If both conditions are met, cognitive balance may indeed show an influence on explicitly assessed attitudes. Most importantly, such an influence should lead to the same dissociation Gawronski and Strack obtained for cognitive dissonance, such that cognitive balance affects only explicitly assessed attitudes, but not implicitly assessed attitudes. Future research may help to clarify the particular conditions under which cognitive balance influences explicitly assessed attitudes.

Final Discussion

The main goal of the present chapter is to provide an integrative review of research on cognitive consistency employing implicit attitude measures. This review is guided by a theoretical framework proposing that implicit and explicit attitude measures tap two distinct evaluative tendencies that have their roots in qualitatively different processes: associative and propositional processes (Gawronski & Bodenhausen, 2006; Strack & Deutsch, 2004). Specifically, we argue that a distinction between associative and propositional processes offers a deeper understanding of several phenomena commonly explained in terms of consistency theories, thus providing a new perspective on how cognitive consistency influences basic attitudinal processes. In addition, we posit that an application of consistency principles to research comparing explicit and implicit attitude measures can provide deeper insights into the distinct nature of their underlying evaluative processes, thus providing a better understanding of the conditions under which the two kinds of measures show converging or diverging effects.

Two Mechanisms

One of our major claims is that cognitive consistency is exclusively a concern of propositional reasoning. More precisely, we argue that (in)consistency between two propositions cannot even be defined without an assignment of truth values. Thus, cognitive inconsistency represents a propositional phenomenon that has to be resolved either by changing the truth value of one proposition or by finding an additional proposition that resolves the inconsistency (Gawronski & Bodenhausen,

2006; Kruglanski, 1989). Notwithstanding this propositional nature of cognitive consistency, it is important to note that associative processes often result in activation patterns that can be described as consistent from a logical perspective. However, the mere possibility of a propositional description does not necessarily imply that the process that gives rise to these activation patterns is itself propositional. Thus, the distinction between spreading activation and consistency assessment becomes crucial when it comes to understanding the convergence and divergence between explicit and implicit attitude measures. Whereas phenomena that have their roots in associative processes of spreading activation should be more likely to emerge on implicit rather than explicit attitude measures, phenomena that have their roots in propositional processes of consistency assessment should be more likely to emerge on explicit rather than implicit attitude measures. Moreover, even when a given process leads to corresponding effects on explicit and implicit attitude measures, spreading activation and consistency assessment should be characterized by different patterns of mediation (Gawronski & Bodenhausen, 2006). If a given phenomenon has its roots in associative processes of spreading activation, this phenomenon should be characterized by a direct effect on implicit attitude measures and an indirect effect on explicit attitude measures that is mediated by the effect on implicit attitude measures. In contrast, if a given phenomenon has its roots in propositional processes of consistency assessment, this phenomenon should be characterized by a direct effect on explicit attitude measures and an indirect effect on implicit attitude measures that is mediated by the effect on explicit attitude measures. Even though several of our assumptions regarding specific mediation patterns are still speculative at this point, future research may provide empirical support for these predictions.

Attitudinal Discrepancies

Even though the present chapter is primarily concerned with consistency *within* explicitly and implicitly assessed attitudes, the distinction *between* associative and propositional processes also has several implications for consistency between explicitly and implicitly assessed attitudes (e.g., Jordan, Spencer, Zanna, Hoshino-Browne, & Correll, 2003; Petty, Tormala, Briñol, & Jarvis, 2006; see also Briñol, Petty, & Wheeler, 2006). Previous research has shown that discrepancies between explicitly and implicitly assessed attitudes are often associated with particular behavioral patterns. For instance, Jordan et al.

(2003) found that individuals with high levels of explicitly assessed self-esteem and low levels of implicitly assessed self-esteem tend to show enhanced narcissism and defensive behaviors. In a similar vein, Petty et al. (2006) have shown that individuals with discrepancies between explicitly and implicitly assessed attitudes are more likely to engage in elaborate processing of attitude-relevant information. Drawing on the distinction between associative and propositional processes, we argue that discrepancies between explicitly and implicitly assessed attitudes predominantly reflect cases in which an automatic affective reaction is rejected as a valid basis for an evaluative judgment. If this rejection is motivationally driven, for example when a particular conclusion is set as the desired outcome of propositional reasoning (Gawronski & Bodenhausen, 2006), the resulting discrepancy may promote defensive behaviors to protect the desired conclusion (e.g., Jordan et al.). More-over, if the rejection is cognitively driven, for example when an infer-entially reached conclusion contradicts an automatic affective reaction (Gawronski & Bodenhausen, 2006), the resulting discrepancy may pro-mote elaborate information processing either to corroborate or to reas-sess the conclusion (e.g., Petty et al., 2006).

Methodological Issues

Throughout this chapter, we largely equated evaluative judgments resulting from propositional processes with responses on explicit mea-sures, and automatic affective reactions resulting from associative pro-cesses with performance on implicit measures. However, it is important to acknowledge that implicit attitude measures are not process-pure measures of automatically activated associations. For instance, Conrey, Sherman, Gawronski, Hugenberg, and Groom (2005) presented a mul-tinomial model (see Batchelder & Riefer, 1999) that is able to disentan-gle the contribution of four qualitatively different processes on implicit task performance: (a) automatic activation of associations, (b) discrim-inability of the stimulus, (c) success at overcoming automatic associa-tions, and (d) general guessing biases. Applied to the present question, such process dissociation models are a desirable way to disentangle the genuine contribution of associative processes from other nonassocia-tive processes when investigating the mutual interplay between asso-ciative evaluations and evaluative judgments.

Another important methodological issue concerns the interpretation of null effects. In the preceding sections, we discussed several cases in which a given factor should influence explicit but not implicit attitude measures, or implicit but not explicit attitude measures. Even though the interpretation of null effects poses several problems (e.g., lack of statistical power, beta-error), these problems can be circumvented by the prediction of specific patterns of correlations. For instance, with regard to Gawronski and Strack's (2004) finding that cognitive dissonance changed only explicitly but not implicitly assessed attitudes, one could object that reliability of the implicit measure may have been low, thus undermining significant effects on this measure. However, this interpretation can be ruled out on the basis of the predicted correlation pattern, such that explicit and implicit attitude measures were highly correlated when participants had a situational explanation for their counterattitudinal behavior as well as under control conditions, but not when participants did not have a situational explanation for their counterattitudinal behavior. Thus, even though some of the predictions outlined in this chapter imply null effects on either explicit or implicit attitude measures, it seems important to independently establish the validity of the respective measures, such as, for example, by means of predicted correlation patterns (e.g., Gawronski & Strack, 2004).

Finally, it is important to consider that the different lines of research reviewed in this chapter employed different kinds of implicit measures. Whereas research on balanced identities (Greenwald et al., 2002; Nosek et al., 2002; Rudman et al., 2001) and cognitive dissonance arising from induced compliance (Gawronski & Strack, 2004) primarily used the IAT as a measure of associative evaluations, research on the spreading-of-alternatives effect (Gawronski et al., 2007) and cognitive balance (Gawronski et al., 2005) employed affective priming tasks. As different kinds of implicit measures have been shown to differ in a number of important ways (e.g., Gawronski & Bodenhausen, 2005; Olson & Fazio, 2003), future research is needed to establish the generality of the obtained effects across different kinds of implicit measures.

Conclusion

Overall, we suggest that focusing on the processes that underlie implicit and explicit attitude measures (i.e., associative and propositional processes) may highlight important differences between phenomena that are commonly subsumed under the label *cognitive consistency*. In the present chapter, we identify two general mechanisms that can have different implications for explicitly and implicitly assessed attitudes: (a) associative processes of spreading activation, and (b) propositional processes of consistency assessment. As the two kinds of processes can lead to different effects on explicit and implicit attitude measures, it seems important to determine (a) which of the two processes is affected in the first place, and (b) whether changes in one kind of process lead to indirect changes in the other (Gawronski & Bodenhausen, 2006). These two questions can help to identify the particular conditions that lead to effects on implicit but not explicit attitude measures, effects on explicit but not implicit attitude measures, or corresponding effects on both implicit and explicit attitude measures. Thus, future research applying consistency principles to the study of explicitly and implicitly assessed attitudes might benefit from focusing on mediating processes and the mutual interplay between associative and propositional processes. Such a focus may help to achieve a deeper understanding of how exactly consistency principles affect basic attitudinal processes. In addition, it may provide further insights into the particular conditions under which explicit and implicit attitude measures show convergent or divergent effects.

References

Abelson, R. P., Aronson, E., McGuire, W. J., Newcomb, T. M., Rosenberg, M. J., & Tannenbaum, P. H. (Eds.). (1968). *Theories of cognitive consistency: A sourcebook*. Skokie, IL: Rand McNally.

Aronson, E., & Cope, V. (1968). My enemy's enemy is my friend. *Journal of Personality and Social Psychology, 8*, 8–12.

Batchelder, W. H., & Riefer, D. M. (1999). Theoretical and empirical review of multinomial process tree modeling. *Psychonomic Bulletin & Review, 6*, 57–86.

Beggan, J. K. (1992). On the social nature of nonsocial perception: The mere ownership effect. *Journal of Personality and Social Psychology, 62*, 229–237.

Blair, I. V. (2002). The malleability of automatic stereotypes and prejudice. *Personality and Social Psychology Review, 6*, 242–261.

Bosson, J. K., Swann, W. B., & Pennebaker, J. W. (2000). Stalking the perfect measure of implicit self-esteem: The blind men and the elephant revisited? *Journal of Personality and Social Psychology, 79*, 631–643.

Brehm, J. W. (1956). Postdecision changes in the desirability of alternatives. *Journal of Abnormal and Social Psychology, 52*, 384–389.

Brehm, J. W., & Cohen, A. R. (1962). *Explorations in cognitive dissonance*. New York: Wiley.

Briñol, P., & Petty, R. E. (2004). Self-validation processes: The role of thought confidence in persuasion. In G. Haddock & G. R. Maio (Eds.), *Contemporary perspectives on the psychology of attitudes* (pp. 205–226). London: Psychology Press.

Briñol, P., Petty, R. E., & Wheeler, S. C. (2006). Discrepancies between explicit and implicit self-concepts: Consequences for information processing. *Journal of Personality and Social Psychology, 91*, 154–170.

Butler, E. A., Egloff, B., Wilhelm, F. H., Smith, N. C., Erickson, E. A., & Gross, J. J. (2003). The social consequences of expressive suppression. *Emotion, 3*, 48–67.

Cadinu, M. R., & Rothbart, M. (1996). Self-anchoring and differentiation processes in the minimal group setting. *Journal of Personality and Social Psychology, 70*, 661–677.

Conrey, F. R., Sherman, J. W., Gawronski, B., Hugenberg, K., & Groom, C. (2005). Separating multiple processes in implicit social cognition: The Quad Model of implicit task performance. *Journal of Personality and Social Psychology, 89*, 469–487.

Crandall, C. S., & Eshleman, A. (2003). A justification-suppression model of the expression and experience of prejudice. *Psychological Bulletin, 129*, 414–446.

Deutsch, R., Gawronski, B., & Strack, F. (2006). At the boundaries of automaticity: Negation as reflective operation. *Journal of Personality and Social Psychology, 91*, 385–405.

Deutsch, R., & Strack, F. (2006). Duality models in social psychology: From dual processes to interacting systems. *Psychological Inquiry, 17*, 166–172.

Devine, P. G. (1989). Stereotypes and prejudice: Their automatic and controlled components. *Journal of Personality and Social Psychology, 56*, 5–18.

Dovidio, J. F., Kawakami, K., & Beach, K. R. (2001). Implicit and explicit attitudes: Examination of the relationship between measures of intergroup bias. In R. Brown & S. L. Gaertner (Eds.), *Blackwell handbook of social psychology: Vol. 4. Intergroup processes* (pp. 175–197). Malden, MA: Blackwell.

Eagly, A. H., & Chaiken, S. (1993). *The psychology of attitudes*. Fort Worth, TX: Harcourt Brace Jovanovich.

Fazio, R. H. (1990). Multiple processes by which attitudes guide behavior: The MODE model as an integrative framework. In M. Zanna (Ed.), *Advances in experimental social psychology* (Vol. 23, pp. 75–109). San Diego: Academic Press.

Fazio, R. H. (1995). Attitudes as object-evaluation associations: Determinants, consequences, and correlates of attitude accessibility. In R. E. Petty & J. A. Krosnick (Eds.), *Attitude strength* (pp. 247–282). Mahwah, NJ: Erlbaum.

Fazio, R. H., Jackson, J. R., Dunton, B. C., & Williams, C. J. (1995). Variability in automatic activation as an unobtrusive measure of racial attitudes: A bona fide pipeline? *Journal of Personality and Social Psychology, 69*, 1013–1027.

Fazio, R. H., & Olson, M. A. (2003). Implicit measures in social cognition research: Their meaning and use. *Annual Review of Psychology, 54*, 297–327.

Festinger, L. (1957). *A theory of cognitive dissonance*. Evanston, IL: Row Peterson.

Festinger, L., & Carlsmith, J. M. (1959). Cognitive consequences of forced compliance. *Journal of Abnormal and Social Psychology, 58*, 203–210.

Florack, A., Scarabis, M., & Bless, H. (2001). When do associations matter? The use of automatic associations towards ethnic groups in person judgments. *Journal of Experimental Social Psychology, 37*, 518–524.

Forehand, M. R., & Perkins, A. (2005). Implicit assimilation and explicit contrast: A set/reset model of response to celebrity voice-overs. *Journal of Consumer Research, 32*, 435–441.

Frey, D. (1986). Recent research on selective exposure to information. In L. Berkowitz (Ed.), *Advances in experimental social psychology* (Vol. 19, pp. 41–80). New York: Academic Press.

Gawronski, B., & Bodenhausen, G. V. (2005). Accessibility effects on implicit social cognition: The role of knowledge activation and retrieval experiences. *Journal of Personality and Social Psychology, 89*, 672–685.

Gawronski, B., & Bodenhausen, G. V. (2006). Associative and propositional processes in evaluation: An integrative review of explicit and implicit attitude change. *Psychological Bulletin, 132*, 692–731.

Gawronski, B., Bodenhausen, G. V., & Becker, A. P. (2007). I like it, because I like myself: Associative self-anchoring and post-decisional change of implicit evaluations. *Journal of Experimental Social Psychology, 43*, 221–232..

Gawronski, B., Deutsch, R., Mbirkou, S., Seibt, B., & Strack, F. (2008). When "just say no" is not enough: Affirmation versus negation training and the reduction of automatic stereotype activation. *Journal of Experimental Social Psychology, 44*, 370–377.

Gawronski, B., Peters, K. R., Brochu, P. M., & Strack, F. (2008). Understanding the relations between different forms of racial prejudice: A cognitive consistency perspective. *Personality and Social Psychology Bulletin, 34*, 648–665.

Gawronski, B., & Strack, F. (2004). On the propositional nature of cognitive consistency: Dissonance changes explicit, but not implicit attitudes. *Journal of Experimental Social Psychology, 40*, 535–542.

Gawronski, B., Walther, E., & Blank, H. (2005). Cognitive consistency and the formation of interpersonal attitudes: Cognitive balance affects the encoding of social information. *Journal of Experimental Social Psychology, 41*, 618–626.

Gilbert, D. T. (1991). How mental systems believe. *American Psychologist, 46*, 107–119.

Greenwald, A. G. (1968). Cognitive learning, cognitive response to persuasion, and attitude change. In A. G. Greenwald, T. C. Brock, & T. M. Ostrom (Eds.), *Psychological foundations of attitudes* (pp. 147–170). New York: Academic Press.

Greenwald, A. G., & Banaji, M. R. (1995). Implicit social cognition: Attitudes, self-esteem, and stereotypes. *Psychological Review, 102*, 4–27.

Greenwald, A. G., Banaji, M. R., Rudman, L. A., Farnham, S. D., Nosek, B. A., & Mellott, D. S. (2002). A unified theory of implicit attitudes, stereotypes, self-esteem, and self-concept. *Psychological Review, 109,* 3–25.

Greenwald, A. G., & Farnham, S. D. (2000). Using the Implicit Association Test to measure self-esteem and self-concept. *Journal of Personality and Social Psychology, 79,* 1022–1038.

Greenwald, A. G., McGhee, D. E., & Schwartz, J. K. L. (1998). Measuring individual differences in implicit cognition: The Implicit Association Test. *Journal of Personality and Social Psychology, 74,* 1464–1480.

Gross, J. J. (1998). Antecedent- and response-focused emotion regulation: Divergent consequences for experience, expression, and physiology. *Journal of Personality and Social Psychology, 74,* 224–237.

Harmon-Jones, E., & Mills, J. (Eds.). (1999). *Cognitive dissonance: Progress on a pivotal theory in social psychology.* Washington, DC: American Psychological Association.

Hebl, M. R., & Mannix, L. M. (2003). The weight of obesity in evaluating others: A mere proximity effect. *Personality and Social Psychology Bulletin, 29,* 28–38.

Heider, F. (1958). *The psychology of interpersonal relations.* New York: Wiley.

Hofmann, W., Gawronski, B., Gschwendner, T., Le, H., & Schmitt, M. (2005). A meta-analysis on the correlation between the Implicit Association Test and explicit self-report measure. *Personality and Social Psychology Bulletin, 31,* 1369–1385.

Hummert, M. L., Crockett, W. H., & Kemper, S. (1990). Processing mechanisms underlying use of the balance schema. *Journal of Personality and Social Psychology, 58,* 5–21.

Insko, C. A. (1984). Balance theory, the Jordan paradigm, and the Wiest tetrahedron. In L. Berkowitz (Ed.), *Advances in experimental social psychology* (Vol. 18, pp. 89–140). San Diego: Academic Press.

Jordan, C. H., Spencer, S. J., Zanna, M. P., Hoshino-Browne, E., & Correll, J. (2003). Secure and defensive high self-esteem. *Journal of Personality and Social Psychology 85,* 969–978.

Judd, C. M., & Lusk, C, M. (1984). Knowledge structures and evaluative judgments: Effects of structural variables on judgmental extremity. *Journal of Personality and Social Psychology, 46,* 1193–1207.

Kahneman, D. (2003). A perspective on judgment and choice: Mapping bounded rationality. *American Psychologist, 58,* 697–720.

Karpinski, A., & Hilton, J. L. (2001). Attitudes and the Implicit Association Test. *Journal of Personality and Social Psychology, 81,* 774–788.

Kawakami, K., Dovidio, J. F., Moll, J., Hermsen, S., & Russin, A. (2000). Just say no (to stereotyping): Effects of training in the negation of stereotypic associations on stereotypic activation. *Journal of Personality and Social Psychology, 78,* 871–888.

Koole, S. L., Dijksterhuis, A., & van Knippenberg, A. (2001). What's in a name: Implicit self-esteem and the automatic self. *Journal of Personality and Social Psychology, 80,* 669–685.

Kruglanski, A. W. (1989). *Lay epistemics and human knowledge: Cognitive and motivational bases.* New York: Plenum Press.

Kumkale, G. T., & Albarracín, D. (2004). The sleeper effect in persuasion: A meta-analytic review. *Psychological Bulletin, 130,* 143–172.

Lieberman, M. D., Gaunt, R., Gilbert, D. T., & Trope, Y. (2002). Reflection and reflexion: A social cognitive neuroscience approach to attributional inference. In M. P. Zanna (Ed.), *Advances in experimental social psychology* (Vol. 34, pp. 199–249). New York: Academic Press.

Lieberman, M. D., Ochsner, K. N., Gilbert, D. T., & Schacter, D. L. (2001). Do amnesics exhibit cognitive dissonance reduction? The role of explicit memory and attention in attitude change. *Psychological Science, 12,* 135–140.

Mayo, R., Schul, Y., & Burnstein, E. (2004). "I am not guilty" vs. "I am innocent": Successful negation may depend on the schema used for its encoding. *Journal of Experimental Social Psychology, 40,* 433–449.

Nosek, B. A., Banaji, M. R., & Greenwald, A. G. (2002). Math = male, me = female, therefore math ≠ me. *Journal of Personality and Social Psychology, 83,* 44–59.

Olson, M. A., & Fazio, R. H. (2003). Relations between implicit measures of prejudice: What are we measuring? *Psychological Science, 14,* 636–639.

Olson, M. A., & Fazio, R. H. (2006). Reducing automatically activated racial prejudice through implicit evaluative conditioning. *Personality and Social Psychology Bulletin, 32,* 421–433.

Olson, M. A., & Fazio, R. H. (in press). Implicit and explicit measures of attitudes: The perspective of the MODE model. In R. E. Petty, R. H. Fazio, & P. Briñol (Eds.), *Attitudes: Insights from the new implicit measures.* New York: Psychology Press.

Otten, S. (2003). "Me and us" or "us and them"? The self as a heuristic for defining minimal ingroups. *European Review of Social Psychology, 13,* 1–33.

Petty, R. E., Briñol, P., & Tormala, Z. L. (2002). Thought confidence as a determinant of persuasion: The self-validation hypothesis. *Journal of Personality and Social Psychology, 82,* 722–741.

Petty, R. E., Ostrom, T. M., & Brock, T. C. (Eds.) (1981). *Cognitive responses in persuasion.* Hillsdale, NJ: Erlbaum.

Petty, R. E., Tormala, Z. L., Briñol, P., & Jarvis, W. B. G. (2006). Implicit ambivalence from attitude change: An exploration of the PAST model. *Journal of Personality and Social Psychology, 90,* 21–41.

Picek, J. S., Sherman, S. J., & Shiffrin, R. M. (1975). Cognitive organization and coding of social structures. *Journal of Personality and Social Psychology, 31,* 758–768.

Rudman, L. A. (2004). Sources of implicit attitudes. *Current Directions in Psychological Science, 13,* 79–82.

Rudman, L. A., Greenwald, A. G., & McGhee, D. E. (2001). Implicit self-concept and evaluative implicit gender stereotypes: Self and ingroup share desirable traits. *Personality and Social Psychology Bulletin, 27,* 1164–1178.

Shiv, B., & Nowlis, S. M. (2004). The effect of distractions while tasting a food sample: The interplay of informational and affective components in subsequent choice. *Journal of Consumer Research, 31,* 599–608.

Sloman, S. A. (1996). The empirical case for two systems of reasoning. *Psychological Bulletin, 119,* 3–22.

Smith, E. R., & DeCoster, J. (2000). Dual-process models in social and cognitive psychology: Conceptual integration and links to underlying memory systems. *Personality and Social Psychology Review, 4,* 108–131.

Srull, T. K., & Wyer, R. S. (1980). Category accessibility and social perception: Some implications for the study of person memory and interpersonal judgments. *Journal of Personality and Social Psychology, 38,* 841–856.

Strack, F. (1992). The different routes to social judgments: Experiential versus informational strategies. In L. L. Martin & A. Tesser (Eds.), *The construction of social judgments* (pp. 249–275). Hillsdale, NJ: Erlbaum.

Strack, F., & Deutsch, R. (2004). Reflective and impulsive determinants of social behavior. *Personality and Social Psychology Review, 8,* 220–247.

Trope, Y., & Alfieri, T. (1997). Effortfulness and flexibility of dispositional judgment processes. *Journal of Personality and Social Psychology, 73,* 662–674.

Walther, E. (2002). Guilty by mere association: Evaluative conditioning and the spreading attitude effect. *Journal of Personality and Social Psychology, 82,* 919–934.

Wegner, D. M. (1994). Ironic processes of mental control. *Psychological Review, 101,* 34–52.

Wellens, A. R., & Thistlewaite, D. L. (1971). An analysis of two quantitative theories of cognitive balance. *Psychological Review, 78,* 141–150.

Wiest, N. M. (1965). A quantitative extension of Heider's theory of cognitive balance applied to interpersonal perception and self-esteem. *Psychological Monographs: General & Applied, 79,* 1–20.

Wilson, T. D., Lindsey, S., & Schooler, T. Y. (2000). A model of dual attitudes. *Psychological Review, 107,* 101–126.

Zajonc, R. B. (1960). The concepts of balance, congruity, and dissonance. *Public Opinion Quarterly, 24,* 280–296.

Endnotes

1 It is important to note that such other (evaluative or nonevaluative) propositions are also based on associations. The present model implies no independent storage of propositions in long-term memory (see also Deutsch & Strack, 2006).

2 An exception to this case is when the semantic content of the negated proposition is already stored independently in associative memory. This may be the case when the negated proposition has a specific referent (e.g., "no war" automatically activates "peace"; see Mayo, Schul, & Burnstein, 2004) or the negated proposition is used frequently in language (e.g., frequent use of "no problem" automatically activates positivity rather than negativity; see Deutsch et al., 2006).

3 The notion of logical consistency is intended to refer more broadly to subjective consistency resulting from any kind of inferential rule that is considered to be valid, rather than to strict logical consistency in terms of normative syllogistic rules.

5

Implicit Ambivalence
A Meta-Cognitive Approach

Richard E. Petty
Pablo Briñol

Introduction

Attitudes refer to people's general evaluations of issues, objects, and other people, including oneself. Do you like chocolate cake? Are you a fan of mystery novels? Are you a good or a bad person? For some people, attitudes are best described as univalent. That is, the attitude object is associated primarily with either positive or negative attributes. Other attitudes, in contrast, are best described as ambivalent. These attitudes are associated with both positive and negative attributes. When people are asked to report their attitudes on a traditional bipolar scale (e.g., –5 to +5), it is possible for people to claim the same overall evaluation even though one person is more ambivalent than another (Kaplan, 1972). For example, one person might rate his or her overall attitude toward a particular car as +2 because of a perceived awareness of a few moderately positive aspects of the car. Another person might rate the same car as +2 because he or she is aware of four very positive attributes of the car, but also two very negative attributes. Because the latter person recognizes both positive and negative aspects of the car, he or she is likely to describe his or her attitude as being at least somewhat ambivalent, mixed, or conflicted with respect to the car compared with the person whose attitude is one-sided (Thompson, Zanna & Griffin, 1995; Priester & Petty, 1996).

In this chapter, we argue that sometimes people can be ambivalent without recognizing it explicitly. We refer to this situation as one of *implicit ambivalence*. Implicit ambivalence occurs when people have conflicting evaluative reactions to some attitude object, but they do not label this conflict as ambivalence because they either are unaware of the evaluative conflict (e.g., being aware of their positive but not their negative reactions), or are aware of having both positive and negative reactions, but deny one reaction as representing their true response. Despite not labeling their reaction as ambivalent, we argue that implicit ambivalence is consequential. After first briefly reviewing some work on explicit ambivalence, we turn to understanding implicit ambivalence. We address issues such as how and why implicit ambivalence occurs, and what its consequences are.*

Explicit Ambivalence

Antecedents

At surprisingly regular intervals, researchers have argued for and presented data supporting the idea that attitudes can be based on separate positive and negative components (e.g., Cacioppo & Berntson, 1994; Chein, 1951; Edwards, 1946; Green & Goldfried, 1965; Kaplan, 1972; Katz, Wackenhut, & Hass, 1986; Klopfer & Madden, 1980; Priester & Petty, 1996; Scott, 1969; Thompson, Zanna, & Griffin, 1995). Although these components could be at the level of very specific attributes, traits, or emotions, there is growing support for the idea that some attitude objects are best characterized as linked to separable positive and negative reactions, perhaps linked to autonomous approach and avoidance systems (e.g., Cacioppo, Gardner, & Berntson, 1997).

The idea that attitude objects can be linked in memory to both positivity and negativity is critical for our approach to ambivalence, and thus it is worthwhile to review the available data. Perhaps the best evidence for this notion comes from two studies reported by de Liver, van der Pligt, and Wigboldus (2007). The goal of this research was to show that for ambivalent attitude objects, both positivity and negativity come to mind quickly. In one study, de Liver and colleagues first had participants generate the names of objects for which their attitudes were positive, negative, or ambivalent. Then, participants completed a single category Implicit Association Test (IAT; Karpinski & Steinman, 2006; Wigboldus, Holland, & van Knippenberg, 2004). In this task there were

---

* In addition to explicit versus implicit ambivalence, it would be possible to have implicit and explicit versions of other attitude strength concepts such as implicit versus explicit importance (see Petty & Krosnick, 1995, for a review of attitude strength indicators).

multiple trials. On certain (positive) trials they were instructed to press one computer key whenever the target attitude object (e.g., *chocolate*) or a positive word (e.g., *happiness*) appeared on their computer screen, and a different key whenever a negative word (e.g., *disgust*) appeared. On other (negative) trials, one computer key was associated with the target attitude object and negative words, whereas the other key was associated with positive words. As would be expected, when the target attitude objects were positive objects, people were faster to categorize them when they were associated with the positive rather than the negative key. When the target words were negative, the opposite was the case. Of most interest, when the target words were ambivalent, there was no difference in speed to the positive and negative trials. Notably, people were just as fast in responding to positive trials as when the target words were positive, and just as fast to negative trials as when the target words were negative. These data are consistent with the possibility that the target words spontaneously activated both positivity and negativity rather quickly.

In the second study, ambivalent attitudes were compared to neutral attitudes, positive attitudes, and negative attitudes. Whereas ambivalent attitudes should have strong positive and negative associations, as demonstrated in de Liver et al.'s first study (2007), neutral attitudes should have weak associations to positivity and negativity. All participants completed an evaluative priming measure (Fazio, Jackson, Dunton, & Williams, 1995) in which the typical priming procedure was reversed. That is, rather than evaluating positive or negative words after being primed by the target attitude object, in this procedure, positive (e.g., *perfect*), negative (e.g., *disgusting*), or neutral/baseline (e.g., *bbbbb*) primes were used and participants had to rate the subsequently presented target attitude object (e.g., chocolate) as positive or negative. As expected, for the positive and negative attitude objects, response time ratings were facilitated when the prime matched the valence of the object. That is, when primed with a positive word, they were faster to categorize a positive target object as good rather than bad compared to when the prime was a neutral word. And, when primed with a negative word, they were faster to categorize a negative word as bad rather than good compared to when the prime was a neutral word. For neutral attitude objects, no facilitation relative to baseline primes occurred. Of most interest, for ambivalent attitude objects, categorization was facilitated relative to the baseline trials for both positive and negative primes, suggesting once again that ambivalent attitude objects spontaneously elicited both positivity and negativity.

As mentioned earlier, when people have both positive and negative reactions to an attitude object, they typically recognize that their attitudes are ambivalent or mixed. Various formulas have been proposed to map the magnitude of positive versus negative reactions onto the subjective recognition of ambivalence (see Priester & Petty, 1996, for a review). Although it is possible to have exactly equivalent positivity and negativity, Priester and Petty noted that one valence is usually dominant, making the other conflicting. All ambivalence formulas recognize that the greater the number or magnitude of the conflicting reactions, the greater the report of ambivalence. Furthermore, Newby-Clark, McGregor, and Zanna (2002) found that having positive and negative reactions to an attitude object produces higher ratings of subjective ambivalence primarily when the positive and negative evaluations came to mind quickly and equally so. This held for both measured and manipulated accessibility of the positive and negative evaluations of an important attitude object (e.g., *abortion*).*

In sum, the available evidence suggests that although most attitude objects are probably associated with one dominant evaluative reaction (e.g., see Fazio, 1995; Chapter 2, this volume), some attitude objects—ambivalent ones—can be associated with very quick positive and negative reactions rather than one dominant evaluation. This is depicted in panel 2 of Figure 5.1 and can be compared with the univalent attitude structure depicted in panel 1. Furthermore, people who acknowledge both positive and negative aspects of an attitude object report being more mixed or ambivalent when asked, with greater ambivalence being reported as the magnitude and accessibility of the conflicting reactions increase.†

Consequences

Besides reporting being more mixed or two-sided, what are some of the consequences of holding attitudes with an ambivalent rather than a univalent structure? One consequence is that when reporting their

---

* In addition to the accessibility of the positive and negative associations (Newby-Clark et al., 2002), the confidence one has in these associations can also contribute to the experience of ambivalence. Thus, maximum ambivalence occurs when people feel confidence in both the positive and negative aspects of the object. Explicit ambivalence is reduced if the extent of confidence in the positive and negative attributes is highly discrepant (Briñol, Petty, DeMarree, & Priester, 2008).

† Other factors can increase reports of subjective ambivalence, such as the extent to which one's attitude disagrees with significant others (Priester & Petty, 2001), but this is not the focus of the current chapter.

1. Univalence

2. Explicit Ambivalence

3. Implicit Ambivalence (a)

4. Implicit Ambivalence (b)

FIGURE 5.1 Depiction of Univalence, Explicit Ambivalence, and Implicit Ambivalence from the perspective of the Meta-Cognitive Model (figure adapted from Petty, Briñol, & DeMarree, 2007).

attitudes on traditional bipolar scales, people tend to be slower to report attitudes that are ambivalent rather than univalent (Bargh, Chaiken, Govender, & Pratto, 1992; see also Costello, Rice, & Schoenfeld, 1974; Gilmore, 1982; Komorita & Bass, 1967; Tourangeau, Rasinski, Bradburn, & D'Andrade, 1989). This would be expected if ambivalent attitude objects spontaneously activate both positive and negative evaluative reactions (de Liver et al., 2007) that must be integrated in order to report an overall attitude.

Second, highly ambivalent attitudes (i.e., where positivity and negativity are equivalent) tend to be less extreme than univalent attitudes, as would be expected if positivity and negativity are combined in some manner when an overall attitude is reported. For this reason, Kaplan (1972) noted that with traditional bipolar attitude measures, it was often difficult to distinguish ambivalent attitudes from neutral ones. However, with unipolar measures (i.e., separate ratings of good and bad) and with the new implicit techniques assessing automatic positive and negative associations, ambivalence can be uncovered more easily.

One of the most studied consequences of ambivalent attitudes concerns their impact on information processing. In particular, there is suggestive evidence that ambivalent individuals engage in greater information processing aimed at resolving their ambivalence. For example, in one study (Jonas, Diehl, & Bromer, 1997), ambivalent individuals generated more thoughts in a thought-listing task on an ambivalent topic, and in another they took longer to integrate attributes into an overall impression than did unambivalent individuals, as if ambivalent people were deliberating about the attributes more (Van Harreveld, Van der Plight, De Vries, Wenneker, & Verhue, 2004).

Of most relevance to the research that we report in this chapter, ambivalent individuals have been shown to pay more attention to the information to which they are exposed, so long as that information might help to resolve the ambivalence. For example, in one study, Maio, Bell, and Esses (1996) measured participants' explicit ambivalence regarding the issue of immigration to Canada (i.e., the extent to which they endorsed both positive and negative aspects of the issue), and then exposed them to a message favoring immigration from Hong Kong to Canada that contained either strong or weak arguments. The degree to which participants processed the message information was assessed by examining the extent to which the quality of the arguments affected postmessage attitudes toward immigration (Petty, Wells, & Brock, 1976). When people are thinking carefully about information, they should be affected by the quality of the arguments a message contains (see Petty & Cacioppo, 1986). As hypothesized, Maio et al. found that individuals who had explicitly ambivalent attitudes toward immigration were more influenced by argument quality than were individuals low in ambivalence, suggesting that they engaged in enhanced scrutiny of the information.

The enhanced scrutiny is presumably aimed at resolving the ambivalence. Indeed, Clark, Wegener, and Fabrigar (2008) found that individuals who reported high levels of subjective ambivalence regarding an attitude object were especially likely to think about proattitudinal rather than counterattitudinal messages. That is, they were more interested in processing a message that was consistent with their dominant evaluative reaction rather than a conflicting one because the former message might more easily resolve the ambivalence.

The Experience of Ambivalence

Although it seems clear that people engage in greater processing when ambivalent, why do they do so? The obvious answer is to resolve the ambivalence, but why do people wish to resolve ambivalence? We already noted that when people endorse both positive and negative aspects of an attitude object, they report being ambivalent, mixed, and even conflicted. But is ambivalence sufficiently distressing and uncomfortable that people would be motivated to resolve it? In fact, some research has suggested that ambivalence is distressing and that processing is enhanced only when the ambivalence is seen as something bad rather than as something good (Bell & Esses, 2002).

The idea that holding inconsistent cognitions is uncomfortable and can thus produce enhanced information processing is most widely associated with Festinger's (1957) theory of cognitive dissonance. To the extent that people subscribe to beliefs that imply opposite things, dissonance theory holds that people will experience tension that they can resolve by changing one of the dissonant elements or generating new cognitions to resolve the inconsistency. Although there are many studies consistent with the dissonance framework (e.g., see Harmon-Jones & Mills, 1999, for a review), there are also numerous theoretical approaches suggesting that mere inconsistency alone need not produce tension. In some frameworks, for example, before inconsistency can lead to dissonance, the inconsistency must imply negative consequences (e.g., Cooper & Fazio, 1984) or must threaten self-integrity (Steele, 1988). Thus, according to various contemporary approaches to dissonance, holding evaluatively inconsistent beliefs about a non-self-relevant topic might not induce discomfort.

On the other hand, a few studies have suggested that attitudinal ambivalence is uncomfortable. In one study (Hass, Katz, Rizzo, Bailey, & Moore, 1992), for instance, it was found that with respect to racial attitudes, individuals who were ambivalent reported more negative feelings than nonambivalent respondents. In a more direct test of the idea that ambivalence is uncomfortable, Nordgren, van Harreveld, and van der Pligt (2006) found that similar to dissonance research (e.g., Cooper, Zanna, & Taves, 1978), people misattributed their ambivalence to a pill characterized as tension producing. In this study, participants first ingested a sugar pill that they were led to believe would cause them to feel relaxed or tense. Then, they were exposed to a message designed to induce ambivalence. The message was presented as a newspaper article that provided 11 positive and 11 negative consequences of genetically modified food. Following this, message recipients reported on the extent to which the issue of genetically modified food made them feel tense and anxious. As expected if ambivalence is associated with tension, participants told that the pill would make them feel calm reported significantly *more* tension than those told the pill would make them feel tense. Or viewed differently, when the pill was associated with tension, the discomfort presumably due to attitudinal ambivalence could be misattributed to the pill, thereby reducing tension with respect to the attitude issue.*

Implicit Ambivalence

Antecedents

We have seen that explicit ambivalence results from situations in which people consciously recognize both positive and negative aspects of some attitude object. Recognition of both positive and negative aspects of an object can produce discomfort, which motivates people to resolve the discrepancy, for example, by seeking out information that would help them to see the object as primarily positive or negative. To the extent that people are successful at this, the ambivalence is resolved at the explicit level and subjective feelings of being mixed or conflicted would be reduced or eliminated.

However, a person who has eliminated ambivalence at the explicit level might still be ambivalent at the implicit level. We have argued that implicit ambivalence occurs when people have both positive and negative associations to an attitude object, but one of these is not endorsed (Petty, Tormala, Briñol, & Jarvis, 2006). This situation is depicted in panels 3 and 4 of Figure 5.1. Why does this situation produce implicit, but not explicit, ambivalence? First, there is no explicit ambivalence because the person has rejected and does not endorse either the positive or the negative aspect of the attitude object. Explicit ambivalence requires people to recognize that some object has both positive and

---

* It is worth noting that the available research suggests that not all people are equally bothered by ambivalence. For example, some individuals have a greater need for consistency than others (Cialdini, Trost, & Newsome, 1995), and some cultures stress consistent selves whereas others favor more balanced (two-sided) selves (Kitayama & Markus, 1999). Furthermore, there are cultural differences such that inconsistency can be bothersome primarily because of intrapersonal or interpersonal factors (Kitayama, Snibbe, Markus, & Tomoko, 2004).

negative features. If one of the valences is not recognized or is denied, there is no reason to report any explicit ambivalence (see also Wilson, Lindsay, & Schooler, 2000).

There are several ways in which the attitude structures depicted in panels 3 and 4 of Figure 5.1 might come about. For example, we have already noted that people might have believed at one time that there were both good and bad features of an attitude object, but now they only agree with one side (i.e., they have resolved their ambivalence). In this situation people would not report any explicit ambivalence because it has presumably been resolved. Yet, at the structural level, the attitude object would still be linked to both positive and negative associations, one of which is no longer endorsed.

Alternatively, people might recognize that they used to endorse only one side of an issue, but now they have completely changed their minds and endorse the opposite side. That is, people sometimes recognize that their old attitude is different from their new one (cf. Ross & Conway, 1986). But would there be any explicit ambivalence resulting from the discrepancy between old and new attitudes? In some cases of attitude change, people might well experience some explicit conflict or tension between their old and new views. For example, people can be aware that their attitude toward smoking has changed from positive to negative, but when they find themselves automatically reaching for a pack of cigarettes, they might realize that their behavior contradicts their anti-smoking position and suggests an underlying ambivalence regarding cigarettes. This consciously recognized contradiction can cause explicit feelings of conflict. Such a situation is analogous to the conceptualization offered by Devine, Monteith, and colleagues with respect to racial prejudice. In a series of studies (e.g., Devine, Monteith, Zuwerink, & Elliot, 1991; Monteith, 1993; Monteith, Devine, & Zuwerink, 1993), they have argued that egalitarian individuals can recognize that they sometimes have spontaneous negative feelings toward Blacks or engage in prejudicial behavior. When this conflict is brought into consciousness, there is enhanced cognitive activity designed to prevent the prejudice (see also Petty, Fleming, & White, 1999).

However, we argue that sometimes when attitudes change, people do not recognize any ambivalence despite the fact that they are aware that their old and new attitudes conflict. For example, consider a student who had one pleasant date with another student only to discover subsequently that the person is a pedophile. The initial positive attitude turns to a negative one, but it seems unlikely that the person would report any ambivalence regarding the new negative attitude. Rather, the person might be quite confident in it. Or imagine that a corporate executive formed a very negative impression of a job candidate based on a job application only to find out that the application form was put in the wrong folder and, thus, the information was not appropriately attributed to that person. The correct application has very positive information. Here, a negative impression turns into a positive one, but there is no logical reason to be conflicted about the new impression. In this case also, there is no reason to report any explicit ambivalence.

To take a final example of how the attitude structures in panels 3 and 4 might come about, consider a person who recognizes that the media are full of negative depictions of various minority groups and even accept the idea that negative associations come to mind because of this. However, if the person only endorses positive aspects of these groups, and denies the validity of the negative information that comes to mind ("It's only a stereotype."), there is no reason to claim being ambivalent.

In each of these examples, people have both positive and negative associations to an attitude object, but one of these is rejected or negated. We argue that in such situations, people can experience implicit ambivalence, an ambivalence of which they are not aware, or at least they do not label it as such.* As should be apparent, our depiction of implicit ambivalence makes a number of assumptions about attitude structure that we have incorporated into a Meta-Cognitive Model (MCM) of attitudes (Petty, 2006; Petty & Briñol, 2006; see Petty, Briñol, & DeMarree, 2007, for an extended discussion). Before turning to the assessment and consequences of implicit ambivalence, we briefly review the MCM.

Meta-Cognitive Model of Attitudes

The MCM is a model of attitude structure that makes a number of assumptions about attitudes. First, in accord with what is probably the dominant view of attitudes as stored representations (e.g., Fazio, 1995; Fiske & Pavelchak, 1986) rather than as momentary constructions (e.g., Schwarz & Bohner, 2001; Wilson & Hodges, 1992), the MCM holds that attitude objects can be linked in memory to global evaluative associations, and these associations can vary in their accessibility (see Fazio,

---

* For expository purposes, we have described negation/acceptance tags as if they are all or none. More generally, people can hold their evaluations with varying degrees of confidence or certainty (see Gross, Holtz, & Miller, 1995; Petty, Briñol, & DeMarree, 2007). This means that if a person has strong positive and negative associations but one is only doubted rather than rejected completely, there can still be some degree of explicit ambivalence (see also footnote 2).

2007, for a review). There are many determinants of such accessibility, including the number of evaluative experiences a person has had with the attitude object and the recency of those experiences. Individual differences can also affect the accessibility of evaluations. For example, individuals high in their need to evaluate (Jarvis & Petty, 1996) tend to have stronger object-evaluation associations due to their chronic evaluative responding (Hermans, de Houwer, & Eelen, 2001).

Second, and more importantly, in concert with the idea that the positivity and negativity underlying attitudes can stem from separate systems (e.g., Cacioppo et al., 1997), the MCM holds that attitude objects can sometimes be linked in memory to evaluative associations of opposite valence. We have already reviewed evidence supporting this assumption (e.g., de Liver et al., 2007). Whether a positive or negative evaluation comes to mind first will depend on all of the various factors that can affect memory, including the context in which these associations developed. For example, if people have experienced positive reactions to African Americans in a sports context, but negative reactions in an urban setting, measures of association that include these contextual features should show different evaluations (Barden, Maddux, Petty, & Brewer, 2004; Wittenbrink, Judd, & Park, 2001). It is important to note, however, that not all attitude objects are expected to have an ambivalent structure. Rather, for many objects, one evaluation should be dominant and represent the integration of knowledge about the object (see top panel of Figure 5.1).

Third, the feature of the MCM that gives the model its name is the assumption that people can tag their evaluative associations as true or false, or held with varying degrees of confidence. In this way, the model builds on existing research on meta-cognition (Jost, Kruglanski, & Nelson, 1998; see Petty, Briñol, Tormala, & Wegener, 2007). The meta-cognitive associations in the MCM can be represented in various ways such as yes/no, confidence/doubt, true/false, accept/reject, and so forth.* Furthermore, these meta-cognitions can vary in the strength

---

* Affective validation is also possible wherein people's attitudes make them happy or sad, comforted or anxious. Though we focus on validity tags in this presentation, we also acknowledge that other tags might exist, and these tags could also exert an impact on attitudinal processes. For example, a person might tag a negative racial evaluation as "inappropriate to express" even though he or she might personally endorse the association. Validity tags are more likely to be stored, we think, because validity tends to be constant across contexts whereas other meta-cognitive features (e.g., appropriateness, diagnosticity, relevance) can vary from situation to situation (cf. Feldman & Lynch, 1988; Snyder, 1982).

of their association to the linked evaluation, and the strength of this association will determine the likelihood that the perceived validity of an evaluation will be retrieved along with the evaluation itself. Most notably, perhaps, the MCM goes beyond the idea that attitude validation is solely an on-line process (cf. Gawronski & Bodenhausen, 2006; Chapter 4, this volume) and contends that perceived validities, like the evaluations themselves, can be stored for later retrieval.

Although there is no definitive research on the storage of validity tags, some evidence consistent with this idea comes from research on the stability of belief certainty over time. For example, in one study, a manipulation of expressed agreement with one's judgment by another person (i.e., social consensus) produced the same increase in judgmental confidence whether that confidence was measured immediately or 48 hours later (Wells, Olson, & Charman, 2003). In other research, attitude certainty measured at one point in time was shown to predict certainty-related outcomes (i.e., resistance of attitudes to change) at a later time, even when certainty was not made salient at the second occasion (e.g., Bassili, 1996, Study 2). These results are consistent with the idea that confidence or validity information can reside in memory. Indeed, just as it is adaptive to have stored general evaluations that come to mind to help guide behavior (e.g., Fazio, 1995), it is useful to store whether the evaluations that come to mind are valid or not.*

Finally, the MCM concurs with research on cognitive negation that suggests that untagged evaluations are presumed to be true unless evidence against them is or has been generated. This proposal is analogous to Gilbert's suggestion (following the philosopher Spinoza over Descartes) that information initially held as true needs to be tagged as false to be disbelieved (Gilbert, 1991; Gilbert, Krull, & Malone, 1990; Gilbert, Tafarodi, & Malone, 1993). Only if the false tag is retrieved will a person who disbelieves an assertion recognize it as false. Otherwise, the

---

* The MCM does not specify exactly how evaluations and validities are stored in memory. That is, memory for evaluations and their validities can be conceptualized as part of a traditional semantic association network (e.g., Fiske & Pavelchak, 1986) or as linked patterns of activation in a connectionist model (e.g., Eiser, Fazio, Stafford, & Prescott, 2003). Either framework can accommodate the postulated linkages (stored associations) in the MCM (e.g., see van Overwalle & Siebler, 2005, for a connectionist model wherein attitude objects are linked to both positivity and negativity). More generally, just as factors that affect memory will influence whether and which evaluations are retrieved when exposed to the attitude object, so too will these same factors (e.g., rehearsal, context) determine if a validity tag is retrieved (e.g., Maddux, Barden, Brewer, & Petty, 2005).

person can misremember and act upon the assertion as if it were true. The accumulated research suggests that successful negation is quite difficult (e.g., Deutsch, Gawronski, & Strack, 2006). Indeed, overriding one's negated attitudes will require motivation and ability, at least in the early stages (Betsch, Haberstroh, Molter, & Glöckner, 2004).

People could attempt to invalidate or deny their evaluative associations for many reasons. For example, people might reject an evaluative association because they realize that it stems from the culture (e.g., media exposure) and not from personal beliefs (e.g., Devine, 1989). Or the association can represent the opinions of others that have been encoded (e.g., Han, Olson, & Fazio, 2006). In addition, the association can represent a previously accepted personal view that has more recently been discredited (e.g., Gregg, Seibt, & Banaji, 2006; Petty et al., 2006).* When the association and negation are presented at the same point in time (e.g., "John is not smart."), people can sometimes reverse the association (i.e., "not smart" becomes "stupid"; see Mayo, Schul, & Burnstein, 2004), but when the negation follows the association in time (e.g., "John is smart…WRONG!"), this is less likely.

Finally, prior research suggests that even when a person can consciously report that something is untrue when engaged in deliberative thinking (i.e., the negation is not lost from memory or has not decayed), the negation tag still might not be retrieved spontaneously. In one study, for example, Tybout, Calder, and Sternthal (1981) exposed people to a rumor about McDonald's hamburgers being made with worms. Even though participants reported that they believed the rumor to be false, this information had a negative impact on subsequent judgments of McDonald's compared to individuals who were not exposed to the rumor. Importantly, the effect of the false rumor was only apparent when people did not first think about McDonald's prior to responding. When they were asked a series of questions about McDonald's first (e.g., "Does McDonald's have indoor seating?"), the false rumor had no impact even though the questions were not specifically relevant to the rumor. This is consistent with the idea that with thought, information tagged as false will not be as impactful as when people respond spontaneously.

Note that if a negation tag is not retrieved spontaneously, then the person has both positive and negative associations to the attitude object and neither is negated, producing a state of ambivalence. Because

---

* When the negated evaluation is a prior attitude, we have referred to our approach as the PAST (Prior Attitudes are Still There) model (Petty & Jarvis, 1998; Petty et al., 2006). That is, the PAST model is a specialized case of the more general MCM.

this ambivalence is at the level of evaluative associations rather than endorsement, however, people would not recognize it. Yet could this implicit ambivalence be consequential? We conducted a series of studies to examine this question. We first describe some studies in which we attempted to identify individuals who were already likely experiencing implicit ambivalence with respect to some object of judgment. Then, in a second series of studies we aimed to experimentally create implicit ambivalence in the lab and examine its consequences.

Diagnosing Implicit Ambivalence With Discrepancies Between Implicit and Explicit Measures

According to the MCM, if a person's attitude structure is represented by one of the bottom two panels of Figure 5.1, then it is likely that automatic and deliberative attitude measures would show different evaluations. The reasons for this are quite straightforward. First, consider the attitude structure in panel 3 of Figure 5.1. According to this depiction, the individual has strong positive associations to smoking, but these are rejected. Perhaps the person used to enjoy smoking (i.e., smoking is associated with many likable events in the person's past) but the person now wants to quit. At the conscious level, the person rejects that there are any positive features of smoking and wishes to suppress any smoking urges. Furthermore, the person is completely convinced that smoking is bad, but this evaluation is not as strongly linked to the attitude object. What would automatic versus deliberative attitude measures with respect to smoking show for this person?

The MCM assumes that contemporary measures of automatic evaluation tap (though not perfectly) into evaluative associations without respect to validity tags. The impact of validity tags and validity processes more generally are revealed primarily on deliberative measures. There are several reasons for this. First, because a validity tag is a stored form of meta-cognition (i.e., a secondary cognition), it is not directly linked to the attitude object, but is instead linked to the evaluative association (the primary cognition), which is in turn linked to the attitude object. Because of this, validity tags will take more time to retrieve than evaluations, and the impact of these associations is less likely to be evident on automatic attitude measures. In addition, there are many circumstances where validity tags will not be as strongly linked to the evaluation as the evaluation is to the attitude object (e.g., because less thought was devoted to forming the validity association than the evaluation itself). However, as the strength of the link between an evaluation and the associated validity tag increases, the likelihood that it will be retrieved increases.

Thus, for the attitude structure in panel 3, an automatic attitude measure would likely reveal a relatively positive attitude because the attitude object is more strongly associated with good than bad. However, an explicit measure would more likely reveal a negative attitude because the validity tags are considered and the good associations are rejected. Thus, this person would have an implicit-explicit discrepancy, but would not likely report any experience of ambivalence because in the person's mind, smoking is only bad—the good aspects are rejected (unlike panel 2, in which both positive and negative aspects of smoking are endorsed). However, at the level of automatic associations, there is ambivalence. Panel 4 in Figure 5.1 presents the opposite scenario. Here the automatic attitude is likely to be negative, whereas the deliberative attitude will be relatively positive. Can situations of explicit-implicit discrepancy produce a state of implicit ambivalence in the absence of explicit ambivalence?

According to the MCM, implicit ambivalence is possible when there is a discrepancy in the valence of an attitude uncovered by a deliberative (explicit) versus automatic (implicit) measure. According to the MCM, the existence of an implicit-explicit discrepancy is consistent with an underlying attitude structure such as that depicted in panels 3 and 4 of Figure 5.1. In situations where people truly reject one of the evaluations with which an attitude object is associated in memory, implicit ambivalence should exist. The prediction of implicit ambivalence from the MCM stands in marked contrast to theories that assume that implicit and explicit measures tap into "dual attitudes" (see Wilson et al., 2000) that are stored in separate brain regions (see DeCoster, Banner, Smith, & Semin, 2006), stem from qualitatively different processes (see Rydell & McConnell, 2006; Rydell, McConnell, Mackie, & Strain, 2006), and operate in distinct situations (see Dovidio, Kawakami, Johnson, Johnson, & Howard, 1997; Chapter 6, this volume).

In the dual attitudes framework, the different evaluations tapped by implicit and explicit measures should not be jointly activated and are more like "two ships passing in the night" (Cohen & Reed, 2006, p. 9). The MCM suggests a more integrated relationship between the so-called dual attitudes in that both evaluations are linked to the same attitude object, but one evaluation is tagged as false or wrong. Because both evaluations are linked to the same attitude object, however, either or both can be activated at any point in time, depending on the strength of the linkage to the attitude object and the retrievability of the false tag (see Petty, Briñol, & DeMarree, 2007, for further comparison with the dual attitudes idea).*

If the more integrated MCM approach is correct, and implicit ambivalence exists, how can it be detected? Recall that people will not likely consciously label any discrepancy as ambivalence on an explicit self-report. Nevertheless, we suggest that such ambivalence can be detected in at least three ways. First, people with implicit-explicit discrepancies should show evidence of both positivity and negativity being linked to the attitude object on measures of automatic association, just as is the case with explicit ambivalence (de Liver et al., 2007). This is because automatic measures are not typically sensitive to the negations (Deutsch et al., 2006).

Second, people with such discrepancies, though they will not report explicit ambivalence, might show signs of tension or discomfort associated with the attitude object. In fact, in nonattitudinal domains, there is already some evidence that implicit-explicit discrepancies are associated with some negative outcomes. In one study, for instance, Zlenski and Larsen (2003) found that having incongruent explicit (i.e., self ratings) and implicit (measured by the Thematic Apperception Test, TAT; Proshansky, 1943) motive profiles was associated with reduced emotional well-being (see Briñol, Petty, & Wheeler, 2006, for a review).

Third, and perhaps most importantly, people with implicit-explicit discrepancies should behave as if they are ambivalent. As noted earlier, one behavioral concomitant of explicit ambivalence is that people engage in greater processing of information that might be helpful in resolving the ambivalence (e.g., Maio et al., 1996; Clark et al., in press). In our own research we examined whether people with implicit-explicit attitude discrepancies engaged in greater processing of information relevant to resolving ambivalence with respect to the target attitude object.

---

* Not all instances of implicit-explicit discrepancy should produce implicit ambivalence. That is, we recognize that these discrepancies can arise in more than one way. For example, a person might continue to like smoking but only feign an unfavorable attitude on an explicit measure for purposes of impression management (e.g., see Olson, Fazio, & Hermann, 2007, for supportive empirical evidence). In this case there would be no ambivalence because no conflict is present at the level of evaluative associations (i.e., there is only a good automatic association). Or, a person might have an initial automatic reaction to some attitude object ("That chocolate cake is yummy!") only to be followed by an opposite reaction upon reflection ("That cake will kill my diet.") that overrides the initial response. If the person sees both automatic and deliberative reactions as valid, this implicit-explicit discrepancy will cause explicit ambivalence, and the person should report being conflicted over whether or not to eat the cake.

Next, we review research on implicit-explicit attitude discrepancies with respect to two attitude objects: African Americans and the self.

Implicit-Explicit Discrepancies in the Domain of Racial Attitudes

Over the past decade, much research has accumulated suggesting that many White Americans report explicitly positive attitudes toward various minority groups such as African Americans, but score more negatively on measures of automatic evaluation (e.g., Greenwald, McGhee, & Schwartz, 1998). Although there could be many reasons for this (such as impression management), we suspect that in at least some cases, this situation represents implicit ambivalence. That is, people truly reject any negative stereotypes or evaluations that come to mind and endorse their positive reactions.* Is there any evidence that such discrepancies are associated with tension or enhanced information processing?

First, with respect to discomfort, although there is no definitive evidence that implicit-explicit discrepancies on racial attitudes produce tension, there is some suggestive evidence. In one relevant study, Olson and Fazio (2007) examined the discrepancies between a person's automatically activated attitude toward Blacks and their explicit attitude toward a particular Black individual. When these implicit and explicit evaluations were discrepant, regardless of the direction of discrepancy, people showed more discomfort-related nonverbal behavior (e.g., self-touching) when making a videotape about the Black target's qualities. However, because the explicit and implicit attitudes were assessed at different levels of specificity (i.e., attitudes toward Blacks in general on the implicit measure versus a specific Black individual on the explicit), the discomfort could have stemmed from a discrepancy between one's global and specific attitudes (e.g., see Woike & Baumgardner, 1993) rather than implicit-explicit discrepancies per se.

Do implicit-explicit discrepancies lead to enhanced information processing? There are now a number of studies suggesting that Whites will sometimes engage in greater processing of a persuasive message from a Black than a White source. In the first research on this topic, White and Harkins (1994) presented White participants with a persuasive message from a White or a Black source on the topic of senior comprehensive exams. The message contained either strong or weak arguments.

---

* This is to be distinguished from cases where individuals are truly ambivalent about minority group members (i.e., endorse both positive and negative aspects of the minority group; see Katz & Hass, 1988).

Across several replications, they consistently found that the impact of argument quality on attitudes was greater when the source was Black rather than White. But why?

In series of follow-up studies, Petty et al., (1999) suggested that this enhanced scrutiny might stem from a "watchdog motivation." That is, Whites might be processing messages from Blacks more than Whites in order to guard against possible prejudice toward Black sources. Petty et al. reasoned that if this were true, it should only be Whites who were low in prejudice who would show the enhanced scrutiny effect. To examine this, prejudice was assessed with several explicit measures (Katz & Hass, 1988; McConahay, Hardee, & Batts, 1981), and reactions to persuasive messages from Black and White sources were assessed. In several studies it was found that only Whites who were low in explicit prejudice processed messages more for Black than White sources. This enhanced scrutiny of Black sources by low-prejudiced individuals was replicated when the message was about a Black versus a White target individual rather than from a Black versus a White source (Fleming, Petty, & White, 2005).

In a more recent series of studies, we aimed to test a variation of the watchdog hypothesis based on the idea of implicit ambivalence. That is, Petty et al. (1999) suggested that people could be motivated to watch out for either their own prejudice or the possible prejudice of others. If people are motivated to watch out for their own prejudice, then it should be White individuals who are low in prejudice on an explicit measure, but high in prejudice on an implicit measure, who are most likely to show the watchdog effect (i.e., processing messages from Black sources or targets more carefully). If people are aware of their automatic negativity, then their watchdog motivation would be rather explicit (e.g., "I need to guard against these negative reactions that I don't want or don't believe."; see Devine et al., 1991; Monteith, 1993). However, even if these individuals are not aware of their automatic negativity, or deny it stems from racial associations, they might still process race-relevant messages due to the implicit ambivalence. Furthermore, our conceptualization of implicit ambivalence suggests that perhaps it will not only be people who are low in explicit prejudice and high in implicit prejudice who will process race-relevant messages more, but also individuals who are high in explicit prejudice and low in implicit prejudice. The reason is that these individuals would also experience some implicit ambivalence because their deliberative attitudes do not match their automatic evaluations.

To examine these issues, in an initial study (Briñol, Petty, & See, 2008), we assessed Ohio State University students' attitudes toward

African Americans using both automatic and deliberative measures. The automatic measure was an Implicit Association Test in which stereotypically Black names (e.g., *Tyrone, LaToya*) and White names (e.g., *Andrew, Katie*) were paired with good (e.g., *freedom, love*) and bad (e.g., *poison, disease*) terms (see Greenwald et al., 1998, for the scoring procedure and rationale). The explicit measure consisted of a series of anti-Black (e.g., "On the whole, Black people do not stress education or training.") and pro-Black (e.g., "It is surprising that Black people do as well as they do considering all of the obstacles they face.") statements to which participants were to rate their extent of agreement (see Katz & Hass, 1988 for the scoring procedure and rationale).

The explicit and implicit measures of attitudes were unrelated to each other. An index of explicit-implicit discrepancy was formed as the absolute value of the difference between the standardized explicit and implicit measures of racial attitudes. The discrepancy index considers where people fall within the distribution of participants in the study on the implicit versus explicit measures. A zero on the index indicates that the person's place in the distribution is exactly the same on the implicit and explicit measures (e.g., high in the distribution on both, low in the distribution on both, middling on both, and so forth). Discrepancies can be in either direction. That is, people can be higher in the sample distribution on the explicit measure than the implicit measure (a positive discrepancy) or they can be lower in the distribution on the explicit measure than the implicit measure (a negative discrepancy). As our key index of implicit-explicit discrepancy, we calculated the absolute value of the difference between the two standardized measures (see also Kehr, 2004). We also coded for the direction of discrepancy (i.e., implicit score more prejudiced than explicit or vice versa) to see if this mattered.

After completing the implicit and explicit measures of racial attitudes, all of the students were exposed to a message advocating a new program to hire African-American faculty at their university that was supported with either strong or weak arguments. As in past research, the strong arguments were designed to elicit favorable thoughts if people thought about them, whereas the weak arguments were designed to elicit mostly unfavorable thoughts (see Petty & Cacioppo, 1986). The strong arguments, among other things, mentioned that the new program would allow class sizes to be reduced and would allow a greater percentage of classes to be taught by faculty rather than graduate students. In contrast, the message with weak arguments stated that the new proposal was desirable because it would allow current professors to have more free time and that several parents wrote letters in support of the proposal.

Following exposure to the strong or weak message, students rated their attitudes toward the proposal on seven semantic differential scales (e.g., good-bad). Consistent with the idea that people with automatic-deliberative discrepancies would act as if they were ambivalent, discrepancy interacted with argument quality to predict attitudes toward the program. That is, as the discrepancy between attitudes assessed with implicit and explicit measures increased, attitudes were more affected by argument quality. Notably, the direction of the discrepancy did not further qualify the results. These results indicate that among those who were low in their explicit prejudice, it was primarily those who were high in implicit prejudice who engaged in greater scrutiny of a message about a program favoring Blacks. However, among those who were high in explicit prejudice, it was those who were low in implicit prejudice who engaged in the greatest scrutiny. The latter finding should be treated with caution, however, because on an absolute basis, there were far more people with discrepancies in one direction than the other. That is, more people were discrepant by having low explicit prejudice and high implicit prejudice than the reverse.

Implicit-Explicit Discrepancies in the Domain of Self-Esteem

Although our research on implicit-explicit discrepancies in the domain of racial attitudes is suggestive, discrepancies were unbalanced in that one kind of discrepancy was more common on an absolute basis than the other. Furthermore, racial attitudes are a domain where impression management might be operating. In particular, individuals who score low in explicit prejudice and high in implicit prejudice might be engaging in impression management, and they might process a race-relevant message for this reason rather than to resolve an evaluative discrepancy. Thus, it was desirable to replicate these results in another domain.

One area in which implicit-explicit discrepancies have been studied in some detail concerns the self. Thus, in another study we assessed self-esteem with both explicit and implicit measures. Implicit self-esteem typically has been defined as an evaluation of the self that occurs automatically and unintentionally, and can differ from one's more controlled and deliberative self-assessments (e.g., Farnham, Greenwald, & Banaji, 1999; Hetts & Pelham, 2001; Koole, Dijksterhuis, & van Knippenberg, 2001).

As was the case with racial attitudes, we hypothesized that discrepancies between implicit and explicit measures of self-esteem would be
associated with implicit ambivalence. Prior work has suggested that
such discrepancies are associated with numerous consequences (see
Chapter 9, this volume, for a review). Of most relevance for the current conceptualization, discrepancies between explicit and implicit
self-esteem scores have been associated with implicit but not explicit
self-doubt. Specifically, in one study (Briñol, Petty, & Wheeler, 2003),
we measured self-esteem with both an implicit and an explicit measure.
The automatic measure was an Implicit Association Test in which self
(e.g., *I, me*) and other (e.g., *they, them*) words were paired with good
(e.g., *freedom, love*) or bad (e.g., *poison, disease*) terms (see Greenwald &
Farnham, 2000). The explicit measure was the commonly used Rosenberg (1965) self-esteem inventory, on which participants rate their
extent of agreement with both proself (e.g., "On the whole, I am satisfied with myself.") and antiself (e.g., "At times, I think I am no good at
all.") statements. As in some other studies using these measures (e.g.,
Bosson, Swann, & Pennebaker, 2000; Hetts, Sakuma, & Pelham, 1999;
Karpinski, 2004; Kitayama & Uchida, 2003), the explicit and implicit
measures showed a small negative correlation. As we did in the racial
attitudes study, an index of explicit-implicit discrepancy was formed
by taking the absolute value of the difference between the standardized
explicit and implicit measures. The analyses also included a variable for
the direction of the discrepancy.

In addition to assessing self-esteem with implicit and explicit measures, we also assessed self-doubt with both explicit and implicit measures. The explicit measure asked participants to rate their extent of
self-doubt or confidence. The implicit measure was another IAT in
which self and other words were paired with confidence or doubt
terms. The key finding from this study was that as implicit-explicit discrepancy in self-esteem grew larger, participants had higher implicit
self-doubt. In contrast, the measure of explicit self-doubt was unrelated
to the discrepancy. This study therefore suggests that although individuals were not aware of any self-doubt associated with their implicit-
explicit discrepancies, people with such discrepancies were faster to
associate doubt words (or slower to associate confidence words) with
the self than people without such discrepancies. The direction of the
discrepancy made no difference.

In a second study on self-esteem (Briñol et al., 2006, Experiment 4),
we examined whether implicit-explicit self-esteem discrepancies would
predict processing of a self-relevant persuasive message. The message in

this study advocated increased consumption of vegetables and contained either strong or weak arguments. The strong message included arguments claiming that vegetables were more nutritious than vitamin supplements and that eating vegetables would increase energy and grades. In contrast, the weak arguments advocated eating vegetables because they were becoming more popular for special occasions such as weddings and looked very attractive on the plates when served. In addition to argument quality, we also varied the ostensible discrepancy-relatedness of the message information by framing the message on vegetables as either related or unrelated to the self. In the unrelated condition, the message was described simply as a message about vegetables that was based on a recent newspaper article. In the self-relevant condition, the message was described as relevant to the participant's self-concept and the way that they get along in the world. In all cases, participants received a message advocating greater vegetable consumption.

If implicit-explicit self-esteem discrepancies enhance information processing when the message is relevant to the discrepancy, then argument quality should have a larger impact on attitudes for participants with large than small discrepancies, but only when the message is framed as related to the discrepancy (i.e., when the message is framed as relevant to the self-concept). The expected three-way Discrepancy × Argument quality × Message frame interaction on attitudes was exactly what we observed (see Figure 5.2). As can be seen in the top panel of Figure 5.2, when the message was framed as relevant to the discrepancy (i.e., the self), increased discrepancy in explicit versus implicit self-esteem was associated with greater argument quality effects, a sign of enhanced information processing. Also, as can be seen in the bottom panel of Figure 5.2, when the message was framed as irrelevant to the discrepancy, message scrutiny was low overall and not related to the extent of discrepancy.

Creating Implicit Ambivalence by Changing Attitudes

In the prior section we reviewed studies showing that when people had large discrepancies between their implicit and explicit racial and self attitudes, they engaged in greater processing of information relevant to the attitude issue compared to when discrepancies were small. In addition to examining discrepancies in racial and self attitudes, we have

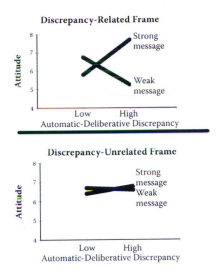

FIGURE 5.2 Interaction of Frame, Implicit-Explicit Self-Esteem Discrepancy, and Argument Quality on Attitudes (data from Briñol, Petty, & Wheeler, 2006, Experiment 4).

also investigated discrepancies in other individual differences assessed with both explicit and implicit measures. For example, in one study (Briñol et al., 2006, Experiment 1) we showed that discrepancies in explicit and implicit shyness (Asendorpf, Banse, & Mücke, 2002) were associated with enhanced processing of a persuasive message on the topic of shyness. Similarly, discrepancies in explicit and implicit need to evaluate (Jarvis & Petty, 1996) were associated with increased processing of a message framed as opinion relevant (Briñol et al., 2006, Experiment 2). Because shyness and need to evaluate are plausibly less subject to impression management concerns than are racial and self attitudes, this suggests that it is the discrepancies that are responsible for the enhanced information processing rather than a concern about being caught in one's deception, or conflict stemming from social desirability concerns.*

---

* If implicit-explicit discrepancies do not stem from impression management concerns, from where do they come? One source would be reactions to the self from others. For example, a person might have a self-conception of being very sociable (resulting from a comparison to one's own immediate family members), but be seen as quite introverted by friends (who are making comparisons to their other acquaintances). If other people keep saying you are shy, but this makes little sense to you, an implicit association between the self and shy could develop, leading to an implicit-explicit discrepancy.

Alternatively, a remaining concern with our studies is that because they all used the IAT to assess automatic attitudes, perhaps the results were obtained because the IAT is tapping into consciously held normative beliefs rather than personal beliefs (e.g., see Olson & Fazio, 2004; Karpinski & Hilton, 2001), and the ambivalence we are tapping is interpersonal in nature: between recognized social norms and personal views. Prior research has shown that even if one's own attitudes are internally consistent, conscious ambivalence can be experienced if one's attitudes conflict with the perceived views of significant others (see Priester & Petty, 2001). However, we do not think this explanation is plausible for the data we reviewed for two reasons. First, prior research on interpersonal ambivalence suggests that people can report this type of conflict as easily as intrapersonal ambivalence. Yet participants in our studies did not report such conflict. Thus, we do not think that the ambivalence consequences we observed stem from a conscious perception of being different from social norms or others' expectations for us. Second, the fact that the results we observed for discrepancy were not moderated by direction of discrepancy is telling. That is, if social norms were operating, they should largely be in one direction, and thus the ambivalence results should occur when personal attitudes are in conflict with the direction of the social norm. Yet discrepancies in both directions produced equivalent levels of ambivalent responding.

Nevertheless, one possible criticism of all of the studies that we have reviewed on implicit ambivalence so far is that they rely on correlational designs. Thus, from these studies all we can say confidently is that the discrepancies we measured were associated with increased information processing of a discrepancy-relevant message. Even more compelling evidence for the implicit ambivalence idea would come from research that manipulated rather than measured implicit ambivalence.

Recall from our prior discussion of the Meta-Cognitive Model of attitudes that situations in which a person's attitude changes from one valence to another can set up the conditions for implicit ambivalence. As depicted in panels 3 and 4 of Figure 5.1, if a person used to have one attitude (positive or negative), but rejects this attitude in favor of an attitude of the opposite valence, ambivalence exists at the level of evaluative association. This implicit ambivalence should be most evident when people do not have the motivation or ability to retrieve the invalidity information associated with the rejected evaluation. When people are conscious of the fact that their attitudes have genuinely changed from what they were originally, and thus one evaluation is rejected (as

when responding to a deliberative measure), they should report no feelings of ambivalence.*

In a series of studies we examined whether changing a person's
attitude from one valence to another would produce implicit ambivalence. In this research we first created attitudes of one valence, and then
changed them to be of another valence. Following change, we examined whether people acted in an ambivalent manner even though they
were not expected to report any explicit ambivalence.

In the initial study in this line of work (Petty et al., 2006, Experiment
1), we first wanted to examine whether changing attitudes from one
valence to another would leave both evaluations associated with the
attitude object on a measure of automatic association. On an explicit
measure, only the endorsed evaluation should be reported. Most prior
models of attitude change (e.g., Anderson, 1971) assume that when attitudes change, the old attitude either disappears or is incorporated into
the new one. Thus, the old attitude has no separate representation. Dual
attitudes models (e.g., Wilson et al., 2000) allow for separate representation of old and new attitudes, but these are assumed to be stored separately in different areas of the brain (e.g., see DeCoster et al., 2006), to
operate in different situations (Dovidio et al., 1997), and not to interact
with each other. However, if the more integrated MCM depiction of old
and new attitudes is correct, then both old and new attitudes should be
capable of joint activation when the invalidity of the old attitude is not
considered, such as when responding under time pressure.

To examine this idea, we first created positive or negative attitudes
toward a previously unfamiliar target person and then changed these
attitudes to a different valence or not. To create the initial attitudes, we
used a classical conditioning procedure in which a picture of the target
individual (labeled *Eddie* or *Phil*) was paired with either very positive
(e.g., puppies) or very negative (e.g., autopsy) photographs. This conditioning manipulation was effective in modifying both automatic (evaluative priming; Fazio, et al., 1995) and deliberative (semantic differential; Osgood, Suci, & Tannenbaum, 1957) evaluations of the person.

Following the creation of an initial attitude, we aimed to change
the valence of the attitude or not. In order to do this, participants next

---

* In the domain of attitude change, the conflict need not be between an invalidated old
  opinion and a validated new one. Rather, people might change their attitudes only to
  learn that the new attitude is based on faulty information and that the old attitude is
  correct (as in the sleeper effect paradigm; see Kumkale & Albarracin, 2004; Priester,
  Wegener, Petty, & Fabrigar, 1999). This too will set up a situation of implicit ambivalence (see Petty, Briñol, & DeMarree, 2007, for further discussion).

received information about the opinions of the target person on several important issues (e.g., abortion, capital punishment, religion) that would make the person appear either very likable (i.e., had similar attitudes to the participant) or dislikable (i.e., had dissimilar attitudes to the participant; see Byrne, 1961). In some conditions, this information reinforced the initial impression (i.e., no attitude change), and in other conditions, this information contradicted the initial impression (i.e., attitude change).

Our results indicated that in the reinforcement (no attitude change) conditions, both the deliberative and automatic measures of attitudes showed the same pattern of results. That is, participants were more positive toward the similar person who was conditioned positively than to the dissimilar person who was conditioned negatively. However, in the incongruent (attitude change) conditions, the automatic and deliberative measures diverged such that attitudes were more sensitive to the contradictory similarity information about the target on the deliberative than on the automatic measure. In this research, the deliberative measure reflected the fact that the old attitude was rejected, whereas the automatic measure reflected fast association of the target person to both the old and the new evaluations. This state of affairs represents what might be called the normal attitude-change situation, in which people reject their previous attitude and accept a new one. The explicit measure tracks this change quite well, but the implicit measure lags behind because of its relative insensitivity to the negation (see also Gregg et al., 2006).

Thus, when attitudes were not changed in valence from the conditioning to the similarity induction, automatic attitudes corresponded with deliberative ones. However, when attitudes were changed in valence from the conditioning to the similarity procedure, the automatic attitude assessment reflected old as well as new attitudes. To unpack the findings on the evaluative priming (implicit) measure, we conducted an analysis to determine whether participants in the attitude-change condition were relatively fast to respond to both positive and negative stimuli (indicating ambivalence), or relatively slow to respond to both positive and negative stimuli (which could indicate an absence of attitudes or neutrality). As depicted in the top panel of Figure 5.3, individuals in the no-change conditions were relatively fast to respond to positive stimuli when primed with similar (likable) targets and to negative stimuli when primed with dissimilar (dislikable) targets, suggesting strong associations to positivity and negativity in the appropriate conditions. Furthermore, individuals in the no-change conditions

No Attitude Change

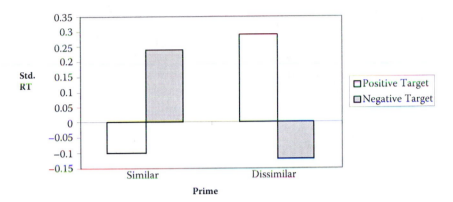

Attitude Change

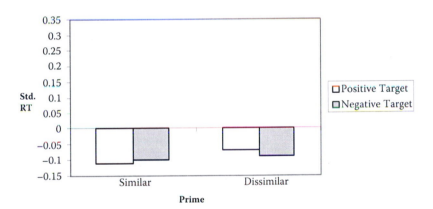

FIGURE 5.3 Standardized response times in Study 1 as a function of whether initial attitudes did not change (top panel) or changed (bottom panel) from the conditioning to the similarity induction. Lower values indicate faster response times, or stronger associations (data from Petty, Tormala, Briñol, & Jarvis, 2006).

were relatively slow to respond to negative stimuli when primed with similar (likable) targets and to positive stimuli when primed with dissimilar (dislikable) targets. This suggests the absence or weakness of these links.

As depicted in the bottom panel of Figure 5.3, however, participants in the conditions where attitudes were changed in valence were relatively fast to respond to both positive and negative stimuli regardless of similarity of the target. In fact, participants in the attitude-change conditions (which did not differ from each other) were just as fast as the two fast no-change groups, and significantly faster than the two slow no-change groups. Overall, then, the data suggested that participants who experienced attitude change responded relatively quickly to both positive and negative stimuli, consistent with the notion of implicit ambivalence. Conceptually, this is the same pattern as observed when people consciously endorse both positive and negative aspects of the attitude object (see de Liver et al., 2007).

Having demonstrated that people who have rejected one evaluation but accepted another respond in an ambivalent like manner on an implicit evaluation task, our next step was to see if people who have changed their attitudes behave in a more ambivalent-like manner than people who have exactly the same explicit attitude currently, but always felt this way. To examine this, we conducted a study (Petty et al., 2006, Experiment 3) using the procedure just described in which we first classically conditioned participants to like or dislike a target individual. Then, the participants received information about the target individual's attitudes on several important topics. The attitudinal information was designed to get the person to either like or dislike the target by having the target agree or disagree with the participant. As just reviewed, in some conditions, this information was in the same direction as the conditioning manipulation so that no attitude change would occur, and in other conditions the information was opposite in valence to the conditioning. In the latter situation, we showed in the earlier study that individuals rejected their initial evaluations based on conditioning and adopted new evaluations based on the similarity information.

However, rather than measuring automatic and deliberative attitudes following attitude change as described earlier, in this study participants were told that the target person was a candidate for a job at their university. To evaluate the candidate, they were provided with either a strong or a weak resumé to examine. The strong resumé was very impressive. For example, the candidate was said to have won several national honors and awards, edited two books, and had exceptional teaching ratings. In contrast, the weak resumé noted that the candidate had yet to receive his Ph.D., had written two book chapters, and had only average teaching ratings. Of most interest was how much scrutiny the candidate's resumé received in making evaluations of him. The key result, depicted in the top panel of Figure 5.4, was that attitudes toward the target as a job candidate were more influenced by resumé quality in the condition where attitudes were changed than when attitudes toward the candidate

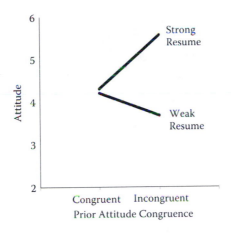

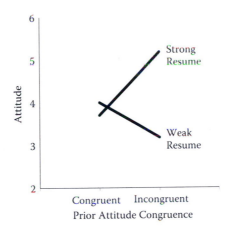

FIGURE 5.4 Top panel: Interaction on attitudes between Congruency (Attitude Change or Not) and Argument Quality (Petty et al., 2006, Study 3). Bottom panel: Interaction on attitudes between Congruency (Attitude Change or Not) and Argument Quality (Petty, Study 4).

had not been changed. That is, when attitudes were changed, people engaged in greater information processing as if they were attempting to resolve some underlying ambivalence regarding the candidate.

In a conceptual replication of this study (Petty et al., 2006, Experiment 4), we wanted to change attitudes in a very different way. In the study just described, attitudes were created initially with a procedure based on affective associations, whereas the change manipulation involved providing cognitive information. Thus, it could be argued that ambivalence depended in part on some type of affective-cognitive inconsistency. To demonstrate that implicit ambivalence need not involve affective-cognitive conflict (possibly stemming from separate affective and cognitive systems or evaluations stored in separate emotional versus cognitive areas of the brain), we used a different procedure. In this study, attitudes toward the target individuals, Eddie or Phil, were first created using the attitude similarity induction described previously. Then, half of the participants were told that due to a computer mistake, the information about Eddie and Phil had been switched. For the individuals in this attitude-change condition, then, if Eddie had been liked because he was similar and Phil disliked because he was dissimilar, these evaluations would need to be reversed. In the no-attitude-change condition, the computer did not make any mistakes, and the original evaluations thus held.

After attitudes were formed and then changed or not, participants were told that the target individual was a job candidate at their university and they were presented with either the strong or weak resumé from the prior study. Following this, they rated how good a candidate they thought the target person would be for the open faculty position. As was the case in the prior study, participants whose attitudes toward the candidate were recently changed (i.e., reversed) were more influenced by the quality of the resumé than participants whose attitudes did not change (see bottom panel of Figure 5.3). That is, people who had recently associated both positive and negative information with the target person (even though one of these was now negated) acted as if they were ambivalent.

In the studies just described, the topic of the message that participants processed more when experiencing implicit ambivalence was always of high potential personal relevance (i.e., selecting a candidate for a job at their university). The same is true of the studies described earlier on implicit-explicit discrepancies (e.g., evaluating a new program for their university to hire more African-American professors). What if the implicit ambivalence involved a target of no personal consequence? We hypothesized that if the message had few personal implications, people would not be as motivated to resolve the ambivalence.

To examine this, Maimaran, Wheeler, Briñol, and Petty (2008) first had participants develop positive attitudes toward one foster care program and negative attitudes toward another ("Rhode Island" versus "State Mountain"). The positive attitude was based on positive information provided (e.g., workers in the program report high levels of satisfaction), whereas the negative attitude was based on negative information (e.g., the program was involved in an accounting scandal). Immediately following the initial information about the programs, participants were exposed to the attitude-change manipulation or not. As in the prior study, participants in the attitude-change condition were led to believe that the information they had just received about the two foster care programs had been accidentally transposed, and thus needed to be reversed in order to be accurate. Participants in the no-change condition did not receive this information. At this point of the experiment, participants who had to change their attitudes to be correct had the same degree of liking or disliking for the programs as participants who were not told of the computer error.

To test the information processing implications of having a changed attitude, participants were randomly assigned to receive strong or weak arguments in favor of the target foster care program. The gist of an example strong argument in favor of the advocated program was that brothers and sisters are an additional source of love and support for the social development of the child. In contrast, the gist of an example weak argument in favor of the program was that the program recognizes that children need other children to fight with, and brothers and sisters provide an ideal opportunity for this to occur (see Petty, Schumann, Richman, & Strathman, 1993). Of most importance, in this study the personal relevance of the information was also varied (Petty & Cacioppo, 1979). Participants in the high-relevance condition were told that the proposed foster care program was being considered for implementation in their own city in the next few weeks, and that students at their university would be able to get credits by taking part in this program (e.g., tutoring the foster children). Participants in the low-relevance conditions did not receive any information about when or where the program would be implemented, nor about their possibilities to participate. However, the titles of the programs made the likelihood of participation seem remote. Following exposure to the information, all participants rated their attitudes regarding the program on several semantic differential scales.

The key result of this study was an interaction between the attitude-change manipulation, argument quality, and personal relevance on attitudes toward the foster care program. Specifically, the interaction resulted from the fact that when personal relevance was low, whether people had changed their attitudes or not had little impact on information processing. However, when personal relevance was high, the results of the prior two studies were apparent. People whose attitudes had changed, and presumably experienced implicit ambivalence, showed a greater impact of argument quality on their evaluations of the foster care program than those whose attitudes had not been changed.

Our three studies on attitude change have clearly shown that people whose attitudes have changed are more likely to engage in careful processing of information about the attitude object, at least if that object has some personal relevance. Notably, in each of the paradigms we also checked to see if people reported feeling any explicit ambivalence when their attitudes had changed, but they did not. Thus, by the standard criteria used in attitude-change studies, the changed attitudes seemed identical in valence and strength to the attitudes that were not changed. Nevertheless, we found that people whose attitudes had changed still acted as if they were ambivalent. According to the MCM, this is because when attitudes change from one valence to another, both evaluations are still associated with the attitude object. People do not report any ambivalence on an explicit measure because one of the evaluations is rejected. However, the implicit ambivalence is presumably uncomfortable and leads to enhanced information processing.

To provide more direct evidence regarding implicit ambivalence, in another study in this line of work (Petty et al., 2006, Study 2) we attempted to assess implicit ambivalence with an implicit measure. In this study we used the paradigm in which attitudes toward a target individual were first created using the similarity procedure, and then changed or not by telling the participants about a computer error. Following this, participants received an explicit measure asking about any doubts or conflicts they had regarding the target person as well as an implicit measure of doubt. The implicit measure was an IAT in which the categories were the target person's name versus other names and confidence versus doubt words (e.g., *certain, sure, confident* versus *hesitant, conflicted, ambiguous*). Consistent with the idea that explicit attitude change can produce implicit ambivalence (due to conflict between old rejected evaluations and newly accepted ones), participants whose attitudes were changed did not report any more explicit doubt about the target individual, but they did show more doubt associated with the target name on an IAT compared to when attitudes were not changed.

Conclusion

In this chapter we have reviewed research on a phenomenon we have called implicit ambivalence (Petty et al., 2006). We refer to this ambivalence as implicit for two reasons. First, people do not have to deliberate on the discrepancy for ambivalence to be manifest. Indeed, deliberation would lead people to think that there is no discrepancy because one evaluation is rejected. In that sense, the ambivalence is relatively automatic and manifests itself primarily when people do not think carefully about their attitude prior to responding.

Second, people do not seem to be aware of the ambivalence, or at least do not appear to label it as such. We are not arguing that people are necessarily unaware of the discrepant automatic evaluation itself. That is, people could be very aware that a reaction opposite to the wanted one comes to mind when they think about the attitude object. However, this reaction is not attributed to one's current personal opinion. Rather, people might assume that it stems from a past attitude or from cultural associations (e.g., the media) that they reject. Or, in some instances, they might be aware of the reaction and be completely confused as to its origin. Epstein (2003) provided an example of a young man who consciously believes that he loves his partner, but always finds himself making excuses to avoid marriage. Because an opposite reaction to the consciously desired one keeps occurring and the person cannot explain it, feelings of discomfort are likely to develop, and the person in Epstein's example eventually decides to seek therapy. Seeking therapy is one way to obtain additional information and thereby resolve the implicit conflict.

The idea of implicit ambivalence stems from our Meta-Cognitive Model of attitudes. In brief, the MCM offers an integrated attitude representation in which attitude objects can be linked to both positive and negative evaluations. Viewing the attitude representation as an integrated unit rather than as separate representations activated in different situations (as advanced by some dual attitudes models) allows for joint activation of positivity and negativity in any given situation where the attitude object is encountered (assuming people have both positive and negative associations). As depicted in Figure 5.1, the possession of both positive and negative associations can lead to explicit ambivalence when both evaluations are endorsed, or to implicit ambivalence when one evaluation is accepted and the other is rejected (see Figure 5.1). Both kinds of ambivalence are uncomfortable and can have similar consequences (e.g., enhanced information processing).

In the research reviewed, we first showed that the extent of discrepancy between one's automatic evaluations and one's more deliberative ones could index the extent of implicit ambivalence. In particular, we demonstrated that implicit-explicit discrepancies regarding racial and self attitudes predicted the extent of processing of information regarding racial and self-relevant messages. We also showed that implicit-explicit discrepancies were associated with implicit but not explicit self-doubt. In a second series of studies, we showed that changing attitudes from one valence to another produced three consequences. First, changing attitudes from one valence to another on an explicit measure led the attitude object to be associated with both positive and negative evaluations on an automatic measure. Second, changed attitudes were associated with greater information processing than were unchanged attitudes of the same valence. Third, even though people did not report any more explicit ambivalence regarding their changed attitudes, the attitude object itself was associated with more implicit doubt.*

Because people seem motivated to process information when they have an explicit-implicit conflict, in an attempt to resolve the ambivalence, it could be argued that the attitude structures we depict in the bottom two panels of Figure 5.2 might be rather unstable and temporary. That is, as people process more information and solidify the dominant evaluation, making it highly accessible, the attitude structure might for all practical purposes become one in which there is just one dominant evaluative association. On the other hand, if people are continually exposed to information in the media and elsewhere involving the rejected association, the bivalent evaluative structure might be persistent. That is, even if people continually counterargue the opposite side and deny its validity, the negated evaluative association itself could strengthen. For example, whenever people attempt to negate a statement (e.g., Gawronski, Deutsch, Mbirkou, Seibt, & Strack, 2008), deny their attitude (e.g., Maio & Olson, 1995), or suppress a thought (e.g., Wegner, 1989), they appear to make the original statement, attitude, and thought more accessible. Thus, implicit ambivalence and the attitude structure depicted by the MCM might be more common than realized.

References

Anderson, N. H. (1971). Integration theory and attitude change. *Psychological Review, 78,* 171–206.

Asendorpf, J. B., Banse, R., & Mücke, D. (2002). Double dissociation between implicit and explicit personality self-concept: The case of shy behavior. *Journal of Personality and Social Psychology, 83,* 380–393.

Barden, J., Maddux, W. W., Petty, R. E., & Brewer, M. B. (2004). Contextual moderation of racial bias: The impact of social roles on controlled and automatically activated attitudes. *Journal of Personality and Social Psychology, 87,* 5–22.

---

* Notably, just as all individuals might not be equally troubled by explicit ambivalence (see Cialdini et al., 1995; Kitayama & Markus, 1999), so too might there be personality and cultural differences in the experience and impact of implicit ambivalence.

Bargh, J. A., Chaiken, S., Govender, R., & Pratto, F. (1992). The generality of the automatic attitude activation effect. *Journal of Personality and Social Psychology, 62*, 893–912.

Bassili, J. N. (1996) Meta-judgmental versus operative indices of psychological properties: The case of measures of attitude strength. *Journal of Personality and Social Psychology, 71*, 637–653.

Bell, D. W., & Esses, V. (2002). Ambivalence and response amplification: A motivational perspective. *Personality and Social Psychology Bulletin, 28*, 1143–1152.

Betsch, T., Haberstroh, S., Molter, B., & Glöckner, A. (2004). Oops, I did it again—relapse errors in routinized decision making. *Organizational Behavior and Human Decision Processes, 93*, 62–74.

Bosson, J. K., Swann, W. B., Jr., & Pennebaker, J. W. (2000). Stalking the perfect measure of implicit self-esteem: The blind men and the elephant revisited? *Journal of Personality and Social Psychology, 79*, 631–643.

Briñol, P., Petty, R. E., DeMarree, K., & Priester, J. R. (2008). *Subjective ambivalence: A self-validation analysis.* Unpublished manuscript, Ohio State University.

Briñol, P., Petty, R. E., & See, Y. H. M. (2008). *Implicit-explicit discrepancies in racial attitudes predict race-relevant information processing.* Unpublished manuscript, Ohio State University.

Briñol, P., Petty, R. E., & Wheeler, S. C. (2003, May). *Implicit ambivalence: Implications for attitude change.* Paper presented at the Attitudinal Incongruence and Information Processing Symposium. Amsterdam, Netherlands.

Briñol, P., Petty, R. E., & Wheeler, S. C. (2006). Discrepancies between explicit and implicit self-concepts: Consequences for information processing. *Journal of Personality and Social Psychology, 91* (1), 154–170.

Byrne, D. (1961). Interpersonal attraction and attitude similarity. *Journal of Abnormal and Social Psychology, 62*, 713–715.

Cacioppo, J. T., & Berntson, G. (1994). Relationship between attitudes and evaluative space: A critical review, with emphasis on the separability of positive and negative substrates. *Psychological Bulletin, 115*, 401–423.

Cacioppo, J. T., Gardner, W. L., & Berntson, G. G. (1997). Beyond bipolar conceptualizations and measures: The case of attitudes and evaluative space. *Personality and Social Psychology Review, 1*, 3–25.

Chein, I. (1951). Notes on a framework for the measurement of discrimination and prejudice. In M. Jahoda, M. Deutsch, & S. W. Cook (Ed.), *Research methods in social relations with especial reference to prejudice.* New York: The Dryden Press.

Cialdini, R. B., Trost, M. R., & Newsome, J. T. (1995). Preference for consistency: The development of a valid measure and the discovery of surprising behavioral implications. *Journal of Personality and Social Psychology, 69*, 318–328.

Clark, J., Wegener, D. T., & Fabrigar, L. R. (2008). Attitudinal ambivalence and message based processing: Motivated processing of proattitudinal information and avoidance of counterattitudinal information. *Personality and Social Psychology Bulletin, 34,* 565–577.

Cohen, J. B., & Reed, A. (2006). A multiple pathway anchoring and adjustment (MPAA) model of attitude generation and reinforcement. *Journal of Consumer Research, 33,* 1–15.

Cooper, J., & Fazio, R. H. (1984). A new look at dissonance theory. In L. Berkowitz (Ed.), *Advances in experimental social psychology* (Vol. 17, pp. 229–266). New York: Academic Press.

Cooper, J., Zanna, M. P., & Taves, P. A. (1978). Arousal as a necessary condition for attitude change following induced compliance. *Journal of Personality and Social Psychology, 36,* 1101–1106.

Costello, R. M., Rice, D. P., & Schoenfeld, L. S. (1974). Attitudinal ambivalence with alcoholic respondents. *Journal of Consulting and Clinical Psychology, 42,* 303–304.

DeCoster, J., Banner, M. J.; Smith, E. R., & Semin, G. R. (2006). On the inexplicability of the implicit: Differences in the information provided by implicit and explicit tests. *Social Cognition, 24,* 5–21.

de Liver, Y., van der Pligt, J., & Wigboldus, D. (2007). Positive and negative associations underlying ambivalent attitudes. *Journal of Experimental Social Psychology, 43,* 319–326.

Deutsch, R., Gawronski, B., & Strack, F. (2006). At the boundaries of automaticity: Negation as reflective operation. *Journal of Personality and Social Psychology, 91,* 385–405.

Devine, P. G. (1989). Stereotypes and prejudice: their automatic and controlled components. *Journal of Personality and Social Psychology, 56,* 5–18.

Devine, P. G., Monteith, M. J., Zuwerink, J. R., & Elliot, A. J. (1991). Prejudice with and without compunction. *Journal of Personality and Social Psychology, 60,* 817–830.

Dovidio, J., Kawakami, K., Johnson, C., Johnson, B., & Howard, A. (1997). On the nature of prejudice: Automatic and controlled processes. *Journal of Experimental Social Psychology, 33,* 510–540.

Dovidio, J. F., Kawakami, K., Smoak, N., & Gaertner, S. L. (in press). The nature of contemporary racial prejudice: Insight from implicit and explicit measures of attitudes. In R. E. Petty, R. H. Fazio, & P. Briñol (Eds.), *Attitudes: Insights from the new implicit measures.* New York: Psychology Press.

Dunton, B. C., & Fazio. R. H. (1997). An individual difference measure of motivation to control prejudiced reactions. *Personality and Social Psychology Bulletin, 15,* 543–538.

Edwards, A. L. (1946). A critique of "neutral" items in attitude scales constructed by the method of equal appearing intervals. *Psychological Review, 53,* 159–169.

Eiser, J. R., Fazio, R. H., Stafford, T., & Prescott, T. J. (2003). Connectionist simulation of attitude learning: Asymmetries in the acquisition of positive and negative evaluations. *Personality and Social Psychology Bulletin, 29*, 1221–1235.

Epstein, S. (2003). Cognitive-experiential self-theory of personality. In T. Millon & M. J. Lerner (Eds.), *Handbook of psychology* (Vol. 5, pp. 159–184). Hoboken, NJ: John Wiley & Sons.

Farnham, S. D., Greenwald, A. G., & Banaji, M. R. (1999). Implicit self-esteem. In D. Abrams & M. A. Hogg (Eds.), *Social identity and social cognition* (pp. 230–248). Oxford, England: Blackwell.

Fazio, R. H. (1995). Attitudes as object-evaluation associations: Determinants, consequences, and correlates of attitude accessibility. In R. E. Petty & J. A. Krosnick (Eds.), *Attitude strength: Antecedents and consequences* (pp. 247–283). Hillsdale, NJ: Erlbaum.

Fazio, R. H. (2007). Attitudes as object-evaluation associations of varying strength. *Social Cognition, 25*, 664–703.

Fazio, R. H., Jackson, J. R., Dunton, B. C., & Williams, C. J. (1995). Variability in automatic activation as an unobtrusive measure of racial attitudes: A bona fide pipeline? *Journal of Personality and Social Psychology, 69*, 1013–1027.

Feldman, J. M., & Lynch, J. G. (1988). Self-generated validity and other effects of measurement on belief, attitude, intention, and behavior. *Journal of Applied Psychology, 73*, 421–435.

Festinger, L. (1957). *A theory of cognitive dissonance.* Oxford, England: Row, Peterson.

Fiske, S. T., & Pavelchak, M. A. (1986). Category-based versus piecemeal-based affective responses: Developments in schema driven affect. In R. M. Sorrentino & E. T. Higgins (Eds.), *Handbook of motivation and cognition: Foundations of social behavior* (pp. 167–203). New York: Guilford Press.

Fleming, M. A., Petty, R. E., & White, P. H. (2005). Stigmatized targets and evaluation: Prejudice as a determinant of attribute scrutiny and polarization. *Personality and Social Psychology Bulletin, 31*, 496–507.

Gawronski, B., & Bodenhausen, G. V. (2006). Associative and prepositional processes in evaluation: An integrative review of implicit and explicit attitude change. *Psychological Bulletin, 132*, 692–731.

Gawronski, B., Deutsch, R. M., Mbirkou, S., Seibt, B., & Strack, F. (in press). When "just say no" is not enough: Affirmation versus negation training and the reduction of automatic stereotype activation. *Journal of Experimental Social Psychology, 44*, 370–377.

Gawronski, B., Strack, F., & Bodenhausen, G. V. (in press). Attitudes and cognitive consistency: The role of associative and propositional processes. In R. E. Petty, R. H. Fazio, & P. Briñol (Eds.), *Attitudes: Insights from the new implicit measures.* New York: Psychology Press.

Gilbert, D. T. (1991). How mental systems believe. *American Psychologist, 46,* 107–119.

Gilbert, D. T., Krull, D. S., & Malone, P. S. (1990). Unbelieving the unbelievable: Some problems in the rejection of false information. *Journal of Personality and Social Psychology, 59,* 601–613.

Gilbert, D. T., Tafarodi, R. W., & Malone, P. S. (1993). You can't not believe everything you read. *Journal of Personality and Social Psychology, 65,* 221–233.

Green, R. F., & Goldfried, M. R. (1965). On the bipolarity of semantic space. *Psychological Monographs: General and Applied, 79,* 1–31.

Greenwald, A. G., & Banaji, M. (1995). Implicit social cognition: Attitudes, self-esteem, and stereotypes. *Psychological Review, 102,* 4–27.

Greenwald, A. G., & Farnham, S. D. (2000). Using the Implicit Association Test to measure self-esteem and self-concept. *Journal of Personality and Social Psychology, 79,* 1022–1038.

Greenwald, A. G., McGhee, D. E., & Schwartz, J. L. K. (1998). Measuring individual differences in implicit cognition: The Implicit Association Test. *Journal of Personality and Social Psychology, 74,* 1464–1480.

Gregg, A. P., Seibt, B, & Banaji, M. R. (2006). Easier done than undone: Asymmetry in the malleability of implicit preferences. *Journal of Personality and Social Psychology, 90,* 1–20.

Gross, S. R., Holtz, R., & Miller, N. (1995). Attitude certainty. In R. E. Petty & J. A. Krosnick (Eds.), *Attitude strength: Antecedents and consequences* (pp. 215–245). Hillsdale, NJ: Lawrence Erlbaum Associates.

Han, H. A., Olson, M. A., & Fazio, R. H. (2006). The influence of experimentally created extrapersonal associations on the Implicit Association Test. *Journal of Experimental Social Psychology, 42,* 259–272

Harmon-Jones, E., & Mills, J. (Eds.). (1999). *Cognitive dissonance: Progress on a pivotal theory in social psychology.* Washington, DC: American Psychological Association.

Hass, R. G., Katz, I., Rizzo, N., Bailey, J., & Moore, J. (1992). When racial ambivalence evokes negative affect using a disguised measure of feelings. *Personality and Social Psychology Bulletin, 18,* 786–797.

Hermans, D., de Houwer, J., & Eelen, P. (2001). A time analysis of the affective priming effect. *Cognition and Emotion, 15,* 143–165.

Hetts, J. J., & Pelham, B. W. (2001). A case for the nonconscious self-concept. In G. B. Moskowitz (Ed.), *Cognitive social psychology: The Princeton Symposium on the legacy and future of social cognition* (pp. 105–123). Washington, DC: American Psychological Association.

Hetts, J. J., Sakuma, M., & Pelham, B. W. (1999). Two roads to positive regard: Implicit and explicit self-evaluation and culture. *Journal of Experimental Social Psychology, 35,* 512–559.

Hovland, C. I., Janis, I. L., & Kelley, H. H. (1953). *Communication and persuasion: Psychological studies of opinion change.* New Haven, CT: Yale University Press.

Jarvis, W. B. G., & Petty, R. E. (1996). The need to evaluate. *Journal of Personality and Social Psychology, 70*, 172–194.

Jonas, K., Diehl, M., & Bromer, P. (1997). Effects of attitudinal ambivalence on information processing and attitude-intention consistency. *Journal of Experimental Social Psychology, 33*, 190–210.

Jordan, C. H., Logel, C. E. R., Spencer, S. J., Zanna, M. P., & Whitfield, M. L. (in press). The heterogeneity of self-esteem: Exploring the interplay between implicit and explicit self-esteem. In R. E. Petty, R. H. Fazio, & P. Briñol (Eds.), *Attitudes: Insights from the new implicit measures*. New York: Psychology Press.

Jost, J. T., Kruglanski, A. W., & Nelson, T. O. (1998). Social meta-cognition: An expansionist review. *Personality and Social Psychology Review, 2*, 137–154.

Kaplan, K. J. (1972). On the ambivalence-indifference problem in attitude theory and measurement: A suggested modification of the semantic differential technique. *Psychological Bulletin, 77*, 361–372.

Karpinski, A. (2004). Measuring self-esteem using the Implicit Association Test: The role of the other. *Personality and Social Psychology Bulletin, 30*, 22–34.

Karpinski, A., & Hilton, J. L. (2001). Attitudes and the Implicit Association Test. *Journal of Personality and Social Psychology, 81*, 774–788.

Karpinski, A., & Steinman, R. B. (2006). The single category Implicit Association Test as a measure of implicit social cognition. *Journal of Personality and Social Psychology, 91*, 16–32.

Katz, I., & Hass, R. G. (1988). Racial ambivalence and American value conflict: Correlational and priming studies of dual cognitive structures. *Journal of Personality and Social Psychology, 55*, 893–905.

Katz, I., Wackenhut, J., & Hass, R. G. (1986). Racial ambivalence, value duality, and behavior. In J. F. Dovidio & S. L. Gaertner (Ed.), *Prejudice, discrimination, and racism* (pp. 35–59). San Diego: Academic Press.

Kehr, H. M. (2004). Implicit/explicit motive discrepancies and volitional depletion among managers. *Personality and Social Psychology Bulletin, 30*, 315–327.

Kitayama, S., & Markus, H. R. (1999). The yin and yang of the Japanese self: The cultural psychology of personality coherence. In D. Cervone & Y. Shoda (Eds.), *The coherence of personality: Social-cognitive bases of consistency, variability, and organization* (pp. 242–302). New York: Guilford Press.

Kitayama, S., Snibbe, A. C., Markus, H. R., & Tomoko, S. (2004). Is there any free choice? Self and dissonance in two cultures. *Psychological Science, 15*, 527–533.

Kitayama, S., & Uchida, Y. (2003). Explicit self-criticism and implicit self-regard: Evaluating self and friend in two cultures. *Journal of Experimental Social Psychology, 39*, 476–482.

Klopfer, F. J., & Madden, T. M. (1980). The middlemost choice on attitude items: Ambivalence, neutrality, or uncertainty? *Personality and Social Psychology Bulletin, 6*, 97–101.

Komorita, S. S., & Bass, A. R. (1967). Attitude differentiation and evaluative scales of the semantic differential. *Journal of Personality and Social Psychology, 6*, 241–244.

Koole, S. L., Dijksterhuis, A., & van Knippenberg, A. (2001). What's in a name? Implicit self-esteem and the automatic self. *Journal of Personality and Social Psychology, 80*, 669–685.

Kumkale, G. T., & Albarracín, D. (2004). The sleeper effect in persuasion: A meta-analytic review. *Psychological Bulletin, 130*, 143–172.

Maddux, W. W., Barden, J., Brewer, M. B., & Petty, R. E. (2005). Saying no to negativity: The effects of context and motivation to control prejudice on automatic evaluative responses. *Journal of Experimental Social Psychology, 41*, 19–35.

Maimaran, M., Wheeler, S. C., Briñol, P., & Petty, R. E. (2008). *Personal relevance moderates the impact of implicit-explicit discrepancies on information processing.* Unpublished manuscript.

Maio, G. R., Bell, D. W., & Esses, V. M. (1996). Ambivalence in persuasion: The processing of messages about immigrant groups. *Journal of Experimental Social Psychology, 32*, 513–536.

Maio, G. R., & Olson, J. M. (1995). The effect of attitude dissimulation on attitude accessibility. *Social Cognition, 13*, 127–144.

Mayo, R., Schul, Y., & Burnstein, E. (2004). "I am not guilty" versus "I am innocent": Successful negation may depend on the schema used for its encoding. *Journal of Experimental Social Psychology, 40*, 433–449.

McConahay, J. B., Hardee, B. B., & Batts, V. (1981). Has racism declined in America? It depends upon who's asking and what is asked. *Journal of Conflict Resolution, 25*, 563–579.

Monteith, M. J. (1993). Self-regulation of prejudiced responses: Implications for progress in prejudice reduction effects. *Journal of Personality and Social Psychology, 65*, 469–485.

Monteith, M. J., Devine, P. G., & Zuwerink, J. R. (1993). Self-directed versus other directed affect as a consequence of prejudice-related discrepancies. *Journal of Personality and Social Psychology, 64*, 198–210.

Newby-Clark, I. R., McGregor, I., & Zanna, M. P. (2002). Thinking and caring about cognitive inconsistency: When and for whom does attitudinal ambivalence feel uncomfortable? *Journal of Personality and Social Psychology, 82*, 157–166.

Nordgren, L. F., van Harreveld, F., & van der Pligt, J. (2006). Ambivalence, discomfort, and motivated information processing. *Journal of Experimental Social Psychology, 42*, 252–258.

Nosek, B. A. (2005). Moderators of the relationship between implicit and explicit evaluation. *Journal of Experimental Psychology: General, 134*, 565–584.

Olson, M. A., & Fazio, R. H. (2004). Reducing the influence of extra-personal associations on the Implicit Association Test: Personalizing the IAT. *Journal of Personality and Social Psychology, 86,* 653–667.

Olson, M. A., & Fazio, R. H. (2007). Discordant evaluations of Blacks affect nonverbal behavior. *Personality and Social Psychology Bulletin, 33,* 1214–1224.

Olson, M. A., Fazio, R. H., & Hermann, A. D. (2007). Reporting tendencies underlie discrepancies between implicit and explicit measures of self-esteem. *Psychological Science, 18,* 287–291.

Olson, M. A., & Fazio, R. H. (in press). Implicit and explicit measures of attitudes: The perspective of the MODE model. In R. E. Petty, R. H. Fazio, & P. Briñol (Eds.), *Attitudes: Insights from the new implicit measures.* New York: Psychology Press.

Osgood, C. E., Suci, G. J., & Tanenbaum, P. H. (1957). *The measurement of meaning.* Urbana: University of Illinois Press.

Petty, R. E. (2006). A metacognitive model of attitudes. *Journal of Consumer Research, 33,* 22–24.

Petty, R. E., & Briñol, P. (2006). A meta-cognitive approach to "implicit" and "explicit" evaluations: Comment on Gawronski and Bodenhausen (2006). *Psychological Bulletin, 132,* 740–744.

Petty, R. E., Briñol, P., & DeMarree, K. (2007). The Meta-Cognitive Model (MCM) of attitudes. Implications for attitude measurement, change, and strength. *Social Cognition, 25,* 657–686.

Petty, R. E., Briñol, P., & Tormala, Z. L. (2002). Thought confidence as a determinant of persuasion: The self-validation hypothesis. *Journal of Personality and Social Psychology, 82,* 722–741.

Petty, R. E., Briñol, P., Tormala, Z. L., & Wegener, D. T. (2007). The role of meta-cognition in social judgment. In E. T. Higgins & A. W. Kruglanski (Eds.), *Social psychology: Handbook of basic principles* (2nd ed.). New York: Guilford Press.

Petty, R. E., & Cacioppo, J. T. (1979). Issue involvement can increase or decrease persuasion by enhancing message-relevant cognitive responses. *Journal of Personality and Social Psychology, 37,* 1915–1926.

Petty, R. E., & Cacioppo, J. T. (1986). *Communication and persuasion: Central and peripheral routes to attitude change.* New York: Springer-Verlag.

Petty, R. E., Fleming, M. A., & White, P. (1999). Stigmatized sources and persuasion: Prejudice as a determinant of argument scrutiny. *Journal of Personality and Social Psychology, 76,* 19–34.

Petty, R. E., & Jarvis, W. B. G. (1998, October). *What happens to the old attitude when attitudes change?* Paper presented at the annual meeting of the Society for Experimental Social Psychology, Lexington, KY.

Petty, R. E., & Krosnick, J. A. (Eds.). (1995). *Attitude strength: Antecedents and consequences.* Hillsdale, NJ: Lawrence Erlbaum Associates.

Petty, R. E., Schumann, D. W., Richman, S. A., & Strathman, A. J. (1993). Positive mood and persuasion: Different roles for affect under high and low elaboration conditions. *Journal of Personality and Social Psychology, 64,* 5–20.

Petty, R. E., Tormala, Z. L., Briñol, P., & Jarvis, W. B. G. (2006). Implicit ambivalence from attitude change: An exploration of the PAST model. *Journal of Personality and Social Psychology, 90,* 21–41.

Petty, R. E., Wells, G. L., & Brock, T. C. (1976). Distraction can enhance or reduce yielding to propaganda: Thought disruption versus effort justification. *Journal of Personality and Social Psychology, 34,* 874–884.

Priester, J. R., & Petty, R. E. (1996). The gradual threshold model of ambivalence: Relating the positive and negative bases of attitudes to subjective ambivalence. *Journal of Personality and Social Psychology, 71,* 431–449.

Priester, J. R., & Petty, R. E. (2001). Extending the bases of subjective attitudinal ambivalence: Interpersonal and intrapersonal antecedents of evaluative tension. *Journal of Personality and Social Psychology, 80,* 19–34.

Priester, J. R., Wegener, D., Petty, R. E., & Fabrigar, L. (1999). Examining the psychological processes underlying the sleeper effect: The Elaboration Likelihood Model explanation. *Media Psychology, 1,* 27–48.

Proshansky, H. M. (1943). A projective method for the study of attitudes. *Journal of Abnormal and Social Psychology, 38,* 393–395.

Ross, M., & Conway, M. (1986). Remembering one's own past: The construction of personal histories. In R. M. Sorrentino & E. T. Higgins (Eds.), *Handbook of motivation and cognition: Foundations of social behavior* (pp. 122–144). New York: Guilford Press.

Rydell, R. J., & McConnell, A. R. (2006). Understanding implicit and explicit attitude change: A systems of reasoning analysis. *Journal of Personality and Social Psychology, 91,* 995–1008.

Rydell, R. J., McConnell, A. R., Mackie, D. M., & Strain, L. M. (2006). Of two minds: Forming and changing valence-inconsistent implicit and explicit attitudes. *Psychological Science, 17,* 954–958.

Schwarz, N., & Bohner, G. (2001). The construction of attitudes. In A. Tesser & N. Schwarz (Eds.), *Blackwell handbook of social psychology: Intraindividual processes* (pp. 436–457). Malden, MA: Blackwell Publishers.

Scott, W. A. (1969). Structure of natural cognitions. *Journal of Personality and Social Psychology, 12,* 261–278.

Snyder, M. (1982). When believing means doing: Creating links between attitudes and behavior. In M. P. Zanna, E. T. Higgins, & C. P. Hermann (Eds.), *Consistency in social behavior: The Ontario Symposium* (Vol. 2, pp. 105–130). Hillsdale, NJ: Erlbaum.

Steele, C. M. (1988). The psychology of self-affirmation: Sustaining the integrity of the self. *Advances in Experimental Social Psychology, 21,* 261–302.

Thompson, M. M., Zanna, M. P., & Griffin, D. W. (1995). Let's not be indifferent about (attitudinal) ambivalence. In R. E. Petty & J. A. Krosnick (Eds.), *Attitude strength: Antecedents and consequences.* Hillsdale, N.J.: Erlbaum.

Tourangeau, R., Rasinski, K. A., Bradburn, N., & D'Andrade, R. (1989). Carryover effects in attitude surveys. *Public Opinion Quarterly, 53,* 495–524.

Tybout, A. M., Calder, B. J., & Sternthal, B. J. (1981). Using information processing theory to design marketing strategies. *Journal of Marketing Research, 28,* 73–79.

van Harreveld, F., van der Pligt, J., De Vries, N. K., Wenneker, C., & Verhue, D. (2004). Ambivalence and information integration in attitudinal judgment. *British Journal of Social Psychology, 43,* 431–447.

van Overwalle, F., & Siebler, F. (2005). A connectionist model of attitude formation and change. *Personality and Social Psychology Review, 9,* 231–274.

Wegner, D. M. (1989). *White bears and other unwanted thoughts.* New York: Viking Press.

Wells, G. L., Olson, E. A., & Charman, S. D. (2003). Distorted retrospective eyewitness reports as functions of feedback and delay. *Journal of Experimental Psychology: Applied, 9,* 42–52.

White, P., & Harkins, S. G. (1994). Race of source effects in the elaboration likelihood model. *Journal of Personality and Social Psychology, 67,* 790–807.

Wigboldus, D. H. J., Holland, R. W., & van Knippenberg, A. (2004). *Single target implicit associations.* Unpublished manuscript.

Wilson, T. D., & Hodges, S. D. (1992). Attitudes as temporary constructions. In L. L. Martin & A. Tesser (Eds.), *The construction of social judgments* (pp. 37–65). Hillsdale, NJ: Lawrence Erlbaum Associates.

Wilson, T. D., Lindsey, S., & Schooler, T. Y. (2000). A model of dual attitudes. *Psychological Review, 107,* 101–126.

Wittenbrink, B., Judd, C. M., & Park, B. (2001). Spontaneous prejudice in context: Variability in automatically activated attitudes. *Journal of Personality & Social Psychology, 81,* 815–827.

Woike, B. A., & Baumgardner, A. H. (1993). Global-specific incongruencies in self-worth and the search for self-knowledge. *Personality and Social Psychology Bulletin, 19,* 290–295.

Zelenski, J. M., & Larsen, R. J. (2003, February). *The importance of knowing what we want: How implicit and explicit motives interact to predict well-being.* Paper presented at the Society for Personality and Social Psychology, Los Angeles.

Section III

Prejudice

6

The Nature of Contemporary Racial Prejudice

Insight from Implicit and Explicit Measures of Attitudes

John F. Dovidio
Kerry Kawakami
Natalie Smoak
Samuel L. Gaertner

Prejudice and Intergroup Attitudes

Prejudice is commonly defined as a negative attitude toward a social group or a person perceived to be a member of that group (Dovidio, Brigham, Johnson, & Gaertner, 1996). Like other attitudes, prejudice subjectively organizes people's environment and orients them to objects and people within it. Prejudice also serves other functions, such as enhancing self-esteem (Fein & Spencer, 1997) and materially or symbolically maintaining or improving group status (Sherif & Sherif, 1969; Tajfel & Turner, 1979). Although prejudice can be expressed blatantly and translate directly into discrimination (Allport, 1954; Crandall & Eshleman, 2003), it is often expressed in subtle and indirect ways (Gaertner & Dovidio, 1986; Pettigrew & Meertens, 1995). The main goal of this chapter is to examine the nature of contemporary prejudice, considering explicit and implicit expressions of these attitudes. In exploring the dynamics of explicit and implicit attitude measures, the primary focus will be on Whites' prejudice toward Blacks.

The central thesis of the current chapter is that implicit measures can serve as useful tools for understanding racial discrimination, permitting predictions that are often unattainable using explicit measures alone. In this chapter, we first review different conceptions of racial prejudice. Several theories of contemporary racial prejudice converge on the proposition that Whites' attitudes may be characterized by both positive conscious orientations toward Blacks and racial equality and by negative unconscious evaluations and beliefs. By unconscious we mean that these evaluations and beliefs are automatically activated and occur without full awareness upon exposure to a Black person. Thus, we explore recent evidence, using both implicit and explicit measures, of Whites' prejudice toward Blacks, and consider the importance of these findings for current theories of prejudice and racism. In subsequent sections, we examine the relationship between implicit and explicit measures of racial attitudes and then between each of these measures of attitudes and race-related behavior. We consider alternative perspectives of attitudes—specifically single attitude and dual attitudes models—throughout the chapter, identifying how each or both can accommodate the existing data. Finally, we discuss future directions for theoretical development and consider the implications of different theoretical perspectives and our analysis for understanding and changing Whites' attitudes and behavior toward Blacks.

The Nature of Prejudice

Much of the psychological research on prejudice from the 1920s through the 1950s portrayed prejudice as a psychopathology (Dovidio, 2001). Prejudice was viewed as a type of "social cancer." For example, stimulated politically by the Nazis' rise to power in Germany, historically by the Holocaust, and intellectually by the classic work on the authoritarian personality (Adorno, Frenkel-Brunswik, Levinson, & Sanford, 1950), psychologists of the 1950s typically viewed prejudice and other forms of racial and ethnic bias as dangerous aberrations from normal thinking. One implication of this perspective was that it focused on changing and constraining the attitudes of this "abnormal" minority as the primary way to combat prejudice.

While acknowledging the contribution of authoritarianism and other abnormal psychological influences (e.g., such as low self-esteem; Allport, 1954; Fein & Spencer, 1997), scholars have more recently begun to recognize that racial bias can also be rooted in normal psychological processes and woven into the basic fabric of American society (Dovidio & Gaertner, 2004; Gaertner & Dovidio, 1986). These processes involve both individual factors, such as cognitive (Fiske, 2005) and motivational (Sidanius & Pratto, 1999) biases and socialization (Devine, 1989), as well as intergroup functions, such as acquiring material advantage (Sherif & Sherif, 1969) and status (Bobo, 1999).

Basic values of fairness and equality, which characterize a broad range of cultures including the United States (Schuman, Steeh, Bobo, & Krysan, 1997), often inhibit the direct expression of prejudice. Although these values are applied differentially to various groups (e.g., Blacks, homosexuals), the vast majority of White Americans today believe that prejudice and discrimination are generally wrong, and they indicate strong support for social and political equality (Bobo, 2001). This existence of both almost unavoidable racial biases and conscious adherence to nondiscriminatory principles forms the basis for contemporary theories of prejudice.

Specifically, we have proposed (Dovidio & Gaertner, 2004; Gaertner & Dovidio, 1986) that because of these conflicting psychological and social forces, contemporary racial prejudice is more complex and expressed more subtly than traditional prejudice. Our work has focused on one form of intergroup bias, *aversive racism* (Kovel, 1970). In contrast to "old-fashioned" racism, which is blatant, aversive racism represents a subtle, often unintentional form of bias that characterizes many White Americans who possess strong egalitarian values and who believe that they are nonprejudiced. Because of the central role that racial politics has played in the history of the United States, this research has focused on the attitudes of Whites toward Blacks. Nevertheless, we note that many of the findings and principles we discuss extend to biases toward other groups, such as Latinos (Dovidio, Gaertner, Anastasio, & Sanitioso, 1992) and homosexuals (Hebl, Foster, Mannix, & Dovidio, 2002).

One critical aspect of aversive racism is the conflict between the denial of personal prejudice and underlying unconscious negative feelings and beliefs. Because of current cultural values and their genuine desire to conform to egalitarian ideals, most Whites have strong convictions concerning fairness, justice, and racial equality. However, at the same time, a range of normal cognitive, motivational, and sociocultural processes promote intergroup biases, and as a consequence, Whites are also likely to develop negative feelings toward or beliefs about Blacks. These biases develop through fundamental, cognitive processes (e.g., social categorization; Hamilton & Trolier, 1986), motivational processes (related to achieving greater group status; Tajfel & Turner, 1979; Sidanius & Pratto, 1999), and socialization processes (e.g., the cultural transmission of stereotypes; Devine, 1989). Because these processes are so basic to social functioning, it is difficult for Whites to avoid developing these negative feelings and beliefs.

Moreover, the framework assumes that, because these negative feelings and beliefs are incompatible with their central egalitarian value, aversive racists deny their existence, and ultimately become unaware of the influence of these unacknowledged negative feelings and beliefs on their behavior. In this respect, the aversive racism framework is conceptually aligned with Wilson, Lindsey, and Schooler's (2000) dual attitudes framework and with Katz, Hass, and colleagues' research on racial ambivalence (e.g., Katz, Wackenhut, & Hass, 1986). Specifically, Wilson et al. proposed that people can "have more than one evaluation of the same object, one of which is more accessible than the other" (p. 101). Katz et al. further argued that these evaluations, particularly in the case of racial attitudes, can be conflicted, with different components manifested in different situations. The existence of negative racial feelings and beliefs, which involve basic cognitive and motivational processes, coupled with a simultaneous desire to be nonprejudiced, represents a basic duality of attitudes for aversive racists.

We have hypothesized that despite aversive racists' negative feelings, they will not discriminate directly and openly in ways that can be attributed to racism. However, when their behavior can be justified on the basis of some factor other than race (e.g., questionable qualifications for a position), aversive racists may regularly engage in discrimination while still maintaining a nonprejudiced self-image. Furthermore, we have found consistent support for the basic proposition of the aversive racism framework that contemporary biases are expressed in subtle rather than in blatant ways across a broad range of situations (Dovidio & Gaertner, 2004; Gaertner & Dovidio, 1986). For example, when White bystanders are the only witnesses to an emergency situation, thus bearing all of the responsibility for helping, they do not discriminate in their helping for Black or White victims. However, when Whites believe that other witnesses are present and they can rationalize their inactivity by assuming that someone else will intervene, they help Black victims much less frequently than White victims (Gaertner & Dovidio, 1977). A recent meta-analysis by Saucier, Miller, and Doucet (2005) of 31 experiments examining Whites' helping behavior over the past 40 years found that, consistent with the aversive racism framework, "less help was offered to Blacks relative to Whites when helpers had more attributional cues available for rationalizing the failure to help with reasons having nothing to do with race" (p. 10).

Furthermore, we have found in a series of studies that Whites will not discriminate in hiring when Black applicants are clearly qualified for the position, but they will discriminate against Blacks when candidates are only moderately qualified (Dovidio & Gaertner, 2000) or when candidates have a mixture of both strong and weak credentials (Hodson, Dovidio, & Gaertner, 2002). One reason for this discrimination was that when candidates had a mixture of strong and weak credentials, Whites placed more emphasis on the weaker aspects of the record for Black applicants and on the stronger aspects for White applicants (Hodson et al.). Additionally, people may often shift their emphasis of the importance of different types of credentials in ways that permit discrimination while maintaining a belief in the objective basis of the decision (Uhlmann & Cohen, 2005). Although it is expressed more subtly, the consequences of these types of strategies and biases (e.g., restricted economic opportunity) may be as significant for people of color and as pernicious as those of the traditional overt form of discrimination.

We note that other forms of contemporary racial biases, such as *modern racism* (McConahay, 1986) and *symbolic racism* (Sears, Henry, & Kosterman, 2000), also hypothesize a conflict between the denial of personal prejudice and underlying unconscious negative feelings and beliefs. However, whereas modern and symbolic racism theories focus on the ideology and actions of conservatives, the aversive racism framework emphasizes biases among people who are politically liberal and who openly endorse nonprejudiced beliefs, but whose unconscious negative feelings get expressed in subtle, indirect, and rationalizable ways (Gaertner & Dovidio, 1986). For example, research by Nail, Harton, and Decker (2003, Studies 1 and 2) revealed that in a context in which race was very salient, politically liberal participants responded more leniently toward a Black than a White defendant in a legal scenario, whereas politically conservative respondents responded more leniently toward the White person. In further support of the aversive racism framework, Nail et al. (Study 3) found that only liberals displayed greater physiological arousal when touched by a Black as compared to a White person, which Nail et al. argued reflected the intrapsychic conflict associated with aversive racism.

In general, contemporary theories of racial prejudice share the assumption that Whites may simultaneously hold egalitarian attitudes about Blacks while also harboring negative racial feelings. However, because of heightened awareness and sensitivity to race, it has been increasingly difficult to assess these hypothesized negative attitudes through self-report measures (Fazio, Jackson, Dunton, & Williams, 1995). Thus, research in this area began to explore a range of nonreactive measures of racial attitudes (Dovidio & Fazio, 1992), and theoretical perspectives correspondingly evolved. For instance, although the aversive racism framework has its historical roots in psychodynamic principles (see Kovel, 1970), recent treatments (e.g., Dovidio, Kawakami, Johnson, Johnson, & Howard, 1997; Dovidio & Gaertner, 2004) have reconceptualized it in terms of dual attitudes, one explicit and egalitarian and the other implicit and negative. In the next section, we examine evidence for the activation of implicit negative racial attitudes of Whites toward Blacks.

Implicit Measures of Attitudes

Attitudes do not have to be consciously accessible to produce evaluative reactions. The mere presence of the attitude object is often sufficient to activate the associated attitude automatically (Chen & Bargh, 1997). In contrast to explicit processes, which are conscious, deliberative, and controllable, these types of implicit processes involve a lack of awareness and are unintentionally activated (Greenwald & Banaji, 1995). Whereas explicit measures of prejudice typically utilize self-reports, implicit measures utilize a variety of techniques, including psychophysiological measures; brain activity, as indicated by functional magnetic resonance imaging (fMRI); and a range of indirect self-report responses, such as word fragment completions, linguistic cues, attributions, and explanations (for a review, see Fazio & Olson, 2003). Measures involving response latencies, however, represent the most widely used strategies to assess implicit prejudice. One type of response latency measure involves priming people, subliminally (Dovidio et al., 1997; Wittenbrink, Judd, & Park, 1997) or supraliminally (Fazio et al., 1995), with a word, symbol, or photograph representing a social category (e.g., Blacks or Whites) and asking respondents to make a decision about a positively or negatively valenced word. The basic assumption is that shorter latencies reflect greater association between the social category and the positive or negative evaluation in memory. Other popular implicit measurement techniques utilizing response latencies are the Implicit Association Test (IAT; Greenwald, McGhee, & Schwartz, 1998) and the Go/No-Go Association Task (GNAT; Nosek & Banaji, 2001). The general assumption underlying these tests is that people respond more quickly to stimuli with compatible than incompatible evaluations (e.g., negative category and negative words vs. negative category and positive words).

The early work on implicit cognition, attitudes, and prejudice was devoted to establishing the existence of social processes that occur outside of awareness (Bargh & Pietromonaco, 1982), demonstrating their robustness (Bargh, 1999), and illustrating their operation in the area of prejudice (Dovidio, Evans, & Tyler, 1986; Gaertner & McLaughlin, 1983). The value of examining implicit measures of attitudes (and stereotypes) is now widely acknowledged (Blair, 2001; Fazio & Olson, 2003). For example, Nosek, Banaji, and Greenwald (2002a) analyzed website responses, from October 1998 through April 2000, of over 100,000 Whites ($N = 103,316$) on a race IAT task using faces as stimuli. Overall, White respondents showed a significant preference for Whites over Blacks (Cohen $d = 0.83$) on this implicit measure, with this effect being stronger than for an explicit measure of race preference for the same respondents (Cohen $d = 0.59$). Although Black respondents ($N = 17,510$) showed a substantial preference for Blacks over Whites (Cohen $d = -0.80$) on the explicit measure, they exhibited a significant preference for Whites over Blacks (Cohen $d = 0.16$; cf. Livingston, 2002) on the implicit measure. This study also provided evidence for other types of social biases. For instance, a significant preference for young over the elderly ($N = 68,144$; Cohen $d = 0.99$) was stronger for the implicit measure (IAT responses) than for an explicit measure of bias on a self-report scale (Cohen $d = 0.51$).

Whereas previous research has provided strong support for the existence and robustness of prejudices that can be automatically activated without full awareness, recent research has shifted its focus to a second generation of questions: (a) Theoretically, how are implicit and explicit measures of attitudes related? (b) Empirically, what is the relationship between implicit and explicit measures of attitudes? (c) How do implicit and explicit measures of attitudes predict behavior? In the remainder of this chapter, we explore these three questions, with the main focus on the last issue.

Theoretical Relationship between Implicit and Explicit Measures of Attitudes

Most researchers investigating automatically activated attitudes now assume that these attitudes are developed through repeated exposure and association between attitude objects and positively or negatively valenced responses (Olson & Fazio, 2001). They are habits of mind that become internalized with practice and are activated spontaneously upon presentation of the attitude object. What is more controversial, however, is the nature of the theoretical relationship between implicit and explicit measures of attitudes. Perhaps because of the initial emphasis on implicit responses as nonreactive measures, much of the earlier research in this area focused on developing reliable techniques for assessing implicit measures of attitudes. In their comprehensive review of the literature, Fazio and Olson (2003) wrote, "Where's the theory? Despite incredible activity, research concerning implicit measures has been surprisingly atheoretical. It largely has been a methodological, empirically driven enterprise" (p. 301).

With regard to current theoretical developments in this area, there are several potentially competing conceptualizations of implicit attitudes in the literature. Although some researchers question whether implicit measures of attitudes represent attitudes at all or are simply cultural associations (Karpinski & Hilton, 2001), others have argued that they reflect essentially a single attitude measured at different points in the process of expression, with social desirability concerns more strongly shaping overt expressions (Fazio et al., 1995). This position is compatible with the fundamental distinction between activation and application (Gilbert & Hixon, 1991). Whereas stereotype activation represents the accessibility of information stored in memory and is determined by the fit of a stimulus with a pre-existing category of stimuli, stereotype application refers to using stereotypes in perceptual or evaluative operations and is shaped by influences within the context of expression (e.g., social norms).

Other scholars, however, consider implicit and explicit measures of attitudes as indicating different components of a system of dual attitudes. Wilson et al. (2000), for example, described an alternative model of attitudes representing different evaluations of the same object. Specifically, they hypothesized that people may have "different evaluations of the same attitude object, one of which is an automatic, implicit attitude and the other of which is an explicit attitude" (p. 102). They further proposed that although explicit and implicit components of dual attitudes can be acquired in either order or simultaneously, they commonly arise developmentally. According to this perspective, when attitude change occurs, the original attitude is not replaced, but rather it is stored in memory and becomes implicit, whereas the newer attitude is conscious and explicit (see also Chapter 5, this volume). In general, explicit attitudes can change and evolve relatively easily, whereas implicit processes, because they are rooted in overlearning and habitual reactions, are much more difficult to alter. As we noted earlier, the dual attitudes framework of Wilson et al. is somewhat more compatible with the aversive racism framework (see Dovidio & Gaertner, 2004) than is conceptualization of implicit and explicit measures of racial bias representing a single attitude measured in two different contexts (Fazio et al., 1995). Nevertheless, the empirical implications of these different theoretical positions are often similar.

Whether implicit and explicit measures of racial bias are conceived to be different phenomena (cultural associations rather than a personal attitude; Karpinski & Hilton, 2001), expressions of the same attitude but at different levels (Fazio et al., 1995), or different types of attitudes (Greenwald, Banaji, Rudman, Farnham, Nosek, & Mellott, 2002; Wilson et al., 2000), each of these positions suggests the possibility that implicit measures and explicit measures may not be highly correlated (Nosek, Banaji, & Greenwald, 2002b). As Gilbert and Hixon (1991) argued, automatic activation "does not mandate such use, nor does it determine the precise nature of its use. It is possible for activated information to exert no effect on subsequent judgments or to have a variety of different effects" (p. 512). However, when these positions have different implications, we will highlight the difference and the relevant evidence. As such, we briefly consider the empirical relationship between implicit and explicit measures in the next section.

Empirical Relationship between Implicit and Explicit Measures of Social Attitudes

The relationship between implicit and explicit measures of attitudes has been explored in two meta-analytic reviews within the past seven years. These reviews reflected alternative strategies. Dovidio, Kawakami, and Beach (2001) focused on the correlation between a range of different implicit measures (including the physiological measure of galvanic skin response, GSR, as well as response latency measures) and explicit measures of attitudes in a specific and socially sensitive area, Whites' racial attitudes toward Blacks. Their meta-analysis was based on 27 tests involving 1,562 participants. Overall, there was a significant, $p < .001$, but modest positive direct relationship, mean $r = .24$. Hofmann, Gawronski, Geschwender, Le, and Schmitt (2005), alternatively, focused on one specific technique for measuring implicit responses, the IAT (Greenwald et al., 1998), but examined responses in a range of different domains. Nevertheless, based on 126 tests involving 12,289 participants, the overall correlation between implicit and explicit measures was .24, an effect size similar to what Dovidio et al. found.

Importantly, findings related to the relationship between implicit and explicit measures of attitudes generally show higher correlations for less socially sensitive domains (see also Dovidio & Fazio, 1992). For instance, Hofmann et al. (2005) found that the mean r was .34 for consumer attitudes but .25 for group attitudes. Similarly, based on the responses of 6,836 participants who performed IAT tasks for 57 different attitude objects, Nosek (2005) found an overall correlation between implicit and explicit measures of .36. This relationship, however, was moderated by self-presentational concerns, with a lower correlation for domains in which self-presentational concerns were higher.

The single attitude perspective on implicit and explicit measures suggests that the weaker correspondence between explicit and implicit measures in socially sensitive areas occurs because participants strategically alter their explicit expressions of prejudice to appear less biased than they actually are. Supportive of this interpretation, Nier (2005) found that when participants believed that their "true" attitudes could be assessed by a computer task, they appeared more prejudiced on an explicit measure (but not an implicit measure), and the correlation between the explicit and implicit measure ($r = .51$) was stronger than when they thought that the computer task was an inaccurate measure ($r = .18$) or when they received no information about the accuracy of the computer task ($r = .14$).

Although the moderating influence of self-presentational concerns on the relationship between implicit and explicit measures suggests the possibility that many participants are strategically and consciously altering their responses on controllable, explicit measures, these findings do not necessarily refute the possibility that some participants genuinely believe they are not prejudiced and thus do not alter their explicit expression of their attitudes. In addition, this pattern of findings does not imply that explicit responses are less valid than implicit measures of attitudes in predicting behavior. However, the issue of the predictive validity of both measures of attitudes has both theoretical and practical implications, and therefore is discussed in detail in the next section.

The Relationship of Implicit and Explicit Measures to Behavior

The dual attitudes and single attitude perspectives on implicit and explicit measures, although fundamentally different in many respects, often make similar predictions about the ways implicit and explicit measures predict behavior. They both suggest that a key factor in the relative validity of implicit and explicit measures for predicting behavior is the context in which the behavior occurs and the type of behavior being examined (see also Dovidio et al., 1997, 2001). From the single attitude perspective, Fazio's (1990) MODE model indicates that whereas implicit measures will better predict spontaneous behaviors, explicit measures will better predict deliberative behaviors, including those in situations in which social desirability factors are salient (Fazio & Olson, 2003). The name *MODE* refers to motivation and opportunity as determinants of the processing mode by which behavioral decisions are made (Fazio). The MODE model suggests that behavioral decisions may involve conscious deliberation or occur as spontaneous, unconscious reactions to an attitude object or issue. When people have the opportunity (e.g., sufficient time) and motivation (e.g., concerns about the evaluation) to assess the consequences of various actions, explicit measures primarily relate to responses and behaviors. When the opportunity is not permitted (e.g., because of time pressure) or motivation is absent (e.g., because the task is unimportant), implicit measures of attitudes are more strongly predictive. Thus the relative relationship of implicit and explicit to behavior is a function of the context in which the attitudinal object appears, the motivation and opportunity to engage in deliberative processes, and the nature of the behavioral response.

In their model of dual attitudes, Wilson et al. (2000) similarly identified how and when implicit measures and explicit measures, assumed to represent different attitudes, relate to behavior. Specifically, they proposed that "when dual attitudes exist, the implicit attitude is activated automatically, whereas the explicit one requires more capacity and motivation to retrieve from memory" (p. 104). Accordingly, the relative influence of explicit and implicit attitudes depends upon the type of response that is made. Explicit attitudes shape deliberative, well-considered responses in which the costs and benefits of various courses of action are weighed. Implicit attitudes influence "uncontrollable responses (e.g., some nonverbal behaviors) or responses that people do not view as an expression of their attitude and thus do not attempt to control" (p. 104). Thus, Wilson et al.'s position also indicates that implicit measures of prejudice will better predict spontaneous interracial behavior, whereas explicit measures will better predict deliberative, controllable responses.

The evidence in the area of racial prejudice, in particular, and social attitudes, in general, is largely consistent with the propositions of Fazio

(1990), Wilson et al. (2000), and Dovidio et al. (1997, 2001). That is, overt expressions of racial bias and discrimination are related to explicit measures of racial attitudes when there is time for deliberation or when people are motivated and have the ability to respond in ways consistent with the orientation reflected in their explicit measure of their attitudes. Consistent with this proposition, a meta-analysis by Dovidio et al. (1996) revealed that traditional explicit measures of Whites' prejudice significantly predicted overt discrimination toward Blacks, mean $r = .32$. In contrast, implicit measures were assumed to predict negative intergroup behavior when responses were spontaneous, occurring without full awareness or in the absence of strong motivations for control.

Studies examining the predictive validity of implicit measures of prejudice that have included both implicit and explicit measures of attitudes and relatively spontaneous and deliberative dependent behaviors further support this theorizing. For instance, Fazio et al. (1995) showed that direct ratings related to the legitimacy of the Rodney King verdict and the illegitimacy of the anger of the Black community were correlated mainly with explicit measures of prejudice such as self-reported attitudes and not with implicit measures of prejudice such as response latencies. However, the implicit measure of prejudice correlated more highly than the explicit measure with the relative responsibility ascribed to Blacks and Whites for the tension and violence that ensued after the verdict as well as perceptions of participant friendliness by a Black interviewer. These latter behaviors related to the implicit measure of prejudice because they were presumably more subtle and indirect manifestations of racial bias. Dovidio et al. (1997, Study 2) similarly found that whereas an explicit measure of prejudice predicted deliberative expressions of bias such as the perceived guilt of a Black defendant in a jury decision-making task, an implicit measure of prejudice primarily predicted less deliberative expressions of bias such as completions of letter sequences with more negative words under time pressure. Son Hing, Chung-Yan, Hamilton, and Zanna (2008) also showed that an implicit measure of prejudice was a better predictor of racial bias in hiring (toward Asian job applicants in Canada) than an explicit measure when a decision not to hire the person could be readily justified on the basis of some factor other than race (i.e., a weakness in the applicant's credentials).

Dovidio et al. (1997, Study 3) pursued this line of research by examining the predictive validity of explicit and implicit measures of prejudice on overt evaluations of a Black partner and on more spontaneous, less controllable, nonverbal behavior such as eye contact and blinking. Although nonverbal behavior can be controlled to some extent, nonverbal signals are frequently emitted without awareness or intention (DePaulo & Friedman, 1998). As Fazio et al. (1995) proposed, "Nonverbal behavior, in particular, may be subject to 'leakage' of negativity that a person is experiencing, despite the individual's effort to behave in a nonprejudiced manner" (p. 1026). Whereas higher levels of visual contact (i.e., time spent looking at another person) reflect greater attraction, intimacy, and respect, higher rates of blinking reflect more negative arousal and tension.

As hypothesized, although the explicit measure of prejudice predicted less favorable evaluations of a Black relative to a White interviewer by White participants ($r = .37$), implicit prejudice did not predict these evaluations ($r = .02$). In contrast, although the implicit measure of racial prejudice predicted higher rates of blinking ($r = .43$) and less visual contact ($r = -.40$) with the Black relative to the White interviewer, the explicit measure of prejudice predicted neither of these behaviors ($rs = .02, -.04$). Subsequent work by McConnell and Leibold (2001) has revealed that an implicit measure of prejudice, the IAT, predicted a range of nonverbal behaviors in Whites' interactions with Blacks, but an explicit self-report measure of prejudice did not. In terms of another domain of prejudice, Bessenoff and Sherman (2000) found that implicit antifat prejudice on a lexical decision task, but not explicit antifat attitudes, predicted how far participants sat from an overweight woman. Together these results suggest that implicit rather than explicit measures of prejudice are generally better predictors of subtle nonverbal manifestations of bias.

Implicit measures have also been found to be better predictors of biases in perceptions of others than are explicit measures of prejudice. For example, Hugenberg and Bodenhausen (2004) hypothesized that because implicit measures of prejudice "may be better than explicit measures in capturing the aspects of prejudiced attitudes that are most relevant in the parsing of nonverbal displays" (p. 342), they may be a better predictor of stereotypic responses in situations in which the appropriateness of decisions are not clear-cut. Consistent with their hypothesis and aversive racism theorizing (Gaertner & Dovidio, 1986), an implicit measure of racial prejudice, but not an explicit measure, was related to the extent that Whites categorized a racially ambiguous person who displayed an angry expression as Black. Neither measure predicted the racial categorization with happy expressions. In addition, in another set of studies, Hugenberg and Bodenhausen (2003) found that an implicit measure of prejudice, but not an explicit measure of prejudice, predicted the readiness of Whites to interpret a facial expression of a Black person as indicating anger. Taken together, these studies indicate that implicit measures of prejudice, relative to explicit measures, are stronger and more consistent predictors not only of spontaneous ways in which Whites behave nonverbally toward Blacks but also of perceptions of the nonverbal displays of Blacks by Whites. In contrast, the expression of negative verbal expressions, which is under greater personal control and intention, tends to be more highly related to explicit measures of prejudice than to implicit measures of prejudice (Rudman, Ashmore, & Gary, 1999).

These findings of different expressions of favorability of Whites in their spontaneous and deliberative behaviors can produce fundamental miscommunication between Blacks and Whites in interracial interaction. From the dual attitudes perspective, aversive racists' explicit egalitarian attitudes may motivate favorable deliberative action (such as positive verbal expressions), but negative implicit attitudes may simultaneously produce undermining negative nonverbal behaviors. From the single attitude position, Whites who are strategically trying to alter their behavior to appear nonprejudiced may be successful at controlling their most overt behaviors but not their spontaneous behaviors. Both of these views suggest that to the extent that most Whites harbor racial biases, as hypothesized by the aversive racism framework, they will display conflicting signals about their feelings and beliefs toward Blacks in interracial interactions.

In addition, Whites and Blacks are likely to be differentially sensitive to the controllable and spontaneous actions demonstrated by Whites during interracial interactions. Whereas Whites can monitor and control their more overt and deliberative behaviors, they are less able to monitor spontaneous behaviors. As a consequence, Whites' beliefs about how they are behaving may be based primarily on their more overt behaviors such as the verbal content of their interaction with Blacks, and not on less deliberative behaviors such as their nonverbal actions. In contrast to the perspective of Whites, the perspective of Black partners in these interracial interactions allows them to attend to both the spontaneous nonverbal and the deliberative verbal behaviors of Whites. To the extent that the Black partners attend to both Whites' nonverbal behaviors and their verbal behaviors, Blacks are likely to form more negative impressions of the encounter and be less satisfied with the interaction than are Whites.

Consistent with these hypothesized processes, we (Dovidio, Kawakami, & Gaertner, 2002) found that White participants' explicit, self-reported measures of racial attitudes predicted their verbal friendliness toward Black relative to White partners, which in turn was related to how Whites perceived their own behavior during the interaction. However, an implicit response latency measure of racial attitudes independently predicted bias in White participants' nonverbal behaviors. As expected, Whites' nonverbal behaviors did not relate to their self-impressions of bias in the situation. In contrast, Blacks appeared to base their impressions of the friendliness of their White interaction partner on not only the partner's verbal behaviors but also his or her nonverbal behavior. As a consequence, Blacks had more negative impressions of the friendliness of Whites than Whites themselves, and the impressions of White and Black interactants in the same session were essentially uncorrelated. Because of this differing reliance on more deliberative or spontaneous behaviors as a source of information, Whites and Blacks left the same interaction with very different impressions.

Although this example suggests that Whites' underlying prejudice can exert a pervasive negative influence on interracial interactions, recent findings also demonstrate that these consequences are not inevitable. For example, Dasgupta and Rivera (2006) found that whereas nonverbal behaviors are typically spontaneous, they can still be controlled, particularly when, as described in the MODE model, people are highly motivated and able. Specifically, they found that the relationship between an implicit measure of prejudice (an IAT) against gay men and the favorability of spontaneous behaviors (smiling, eye contact, posture, interest, comfort, and friendliness, as coded by observers) during an interaction with a gay man can be moderated by the nature of participants' values about gender roles and gender identity, and the participants' skill in controlling their behavior. Although the implicit measure of prejudice generally predicted more negative interpersonal responses to a gay relative than to a heterosexual man, this was not the case when participants had a strong acceptance of nontraditional values or were highly skilled at controlling their behavior.

Research by Fazio and his colleagues has also produced evidence of the moderating role of motivation in controlling implicit processes (Dunton & Fazio, 1997). In particular, a participant's concern with acting prejudiced, as measured on a subscale of the Motivation to Control Prejudiced Reactions scale, moderated the relationship of implicit prejudice on Whites' evaluations of "the typical male Black undergraduate" (Dunton & Fazio) and anticipated comfort while interacting with a Black person (Towles-Schwen & Fazio, 2003). Although in these studies measures of implicit prejudice were directly related to more negative evaluations of the typical Black male undergraduate and greater anticipated discomfort among those low in concern with acting prejudiced, this relationship was not evident among those high on this concern. In another study (Olson & Fazio, 2004), greater prejudice on an implicit measure predicted more negative impressions of a Black person compared to a comparable White person for Whites low in restraint to avoid dispute, a subscale of the Motivation to Control Prejudiced Reactions scale. Alternatively, Whites high in restraint to avoid dispute displayed the opposite relationship, suggesting an "overcorrection" of bias. Other research, however, reveals that implicit measures of prejudice and motivation can independently relate to interracial responses. For example, Fazio and Hilden (2001) demonstrated that people with lower levels of prejudice on an implicit measure and higher levels of self-reported motivation to control prejudice experienced greater guilt after being exposed to a television commercial that led them to make an erroneous negative inference about Blacks.

In summary, the pattern of results across various measures of implicit and explicit prejudice and across various domains of prejudice suggests three general conclusions: (a) Implicit measures of prejudice typically predict spontaneous expressions of bias and do so better than explicit measures of prejudice; (b) Explicit measures of prejudice are better predictors of deliberative than of spontaneous behavior, and they are typically better predictors of deliberative behavior than are implicit measures of prejudice; and (c) With sufficient opportunity, motivation, and ability, explicit measures of attitudes are often better predictors than are implicit measures of actions overall. The results in support of the last conclusion are directly supportive of the tenets of Fazio's (1990) MODE model (see also Fazio & Olson, 2003; Strack & Deutsch, 2004).

These conclusions are also compatible with the basic findings of the research on subtle, contemporary forms of prejudice, such as aversive racism. As reviewed earlier, research in this area provides strong evidence that overt discrimination against Blacks is less likely to occur when Whites can monitor and control their actions and appropriate behavior is more clearly defined in the context. In contrast, Whites will tend to express bias when they are unaware that their actions are discriminatory or when non-race-related justifications for their actions are available, potentially relaxing their motivation to control prejudice. Despite the general convergence of findings, we caution that future work needs to consider more fully the different dimensions that can characterize interracial behaviors and map them more directly onto their potential relationships with implicit and explicit measures of attitudes. In the final section, we consider some other productive possible directions for future research.

Future Directions

Beyond its practical implications for providing a new perspective on the dynamics of race relations, understanding the relationship between explicit and implicit measures of attitudes and behavior in different contexts can also suggest new theoretical insights into the nature of prejudice and its expression. Perhaps one of the most relevant theoretical issues is the debate between single attitude and dual attitudes perspectives, in general, and their relationship to racial prejudice, in particular. We have pointed out that much of the evidence about the relationship between implicit and explicit measures of prejudice can be interpreted within either framework. The finding that people systematically alter their explicit expressions of prejudice, but not their responses on an implicit measure, when they believe that their true attitude is known (Nier, 2005), however, is specifically supportive of the single attitude view (see also Fazio et al., 1995). That is, the change in the explicit measure to conform to the implicit measures suggests that people were strategically altering their true attitude to manage others' impressions of them.

Nevertheless, the fact that some Whites alter their explicit expression of racial attitudes because of social evaluative pressures does not automatically negate the possibility that some other Whites may possess dual attitudes toward Blacks, one representing their explicit egalitarian standards and the other reflecting negative feelings and beliefs outside of normal conscious awareness. In particular, if these people possess dual attitudes, they might appear prejudiced on an implicit measure but will be seen as nonprejudiced on explicit measures regardless of whether they believe their true attitude will be revealed by some other means, such as a bogus pipeline technique (Sigall & Page, 1971; Roese & Jamieson, 1993). Consistent with this latter view, Katz and Hass (1988) found that people hypothesized to have racially ambivalent attitudes independently activated positive and negative components of their attitudes with different priming stimuli.

Whether Whites attempt to disguise their true underlying prejudice or genuinely have both positive conscious and negative unconscious attitudes toward Blacks may have the same consequences in some contexts but may produce divergent actions in other situations. For example, Whites whose nonprejudiced response on an explicit measure reflects a self-presentation strategy more than an authentic belief may be more likely to behave in a racially biased manner when they cannot be personally identified, because there is no need to manage others' impressions in this context.

Other promising areas of future research involve the relationship of motivated processes, such as the desire to appear or to actually be non-prejudiced, on the automatic activation of racial attitudes. In particular, recent findings that people can inhibit even relatively spontaneous expressions of bias (e.g., nonverbal behavior) suggests the possibility that they may also be able to inhibit the activation of negative racial attitudes and stereotypes even when these processes are considered to be automatic. There is a growing literature that demonstrates that although exposure to a social category or a member of that group typically activates negative attitudes and stereotypes, as reflected in implicit measures, this activation can often be prevented by changing the perspective and expectations of perceivers (e.g., by instructing people to imagine positive exemplars or counterstereotypic members of the group; see Blair, 2002, for a review) or even inhibited once activated (John, Agocha, & Dovidio, 2006).

From a single attitude perspective, these findings relate to how contextual features can determine whether an attitude is activated. From a dual attitudes view, implicit and explicit measures may be tapping different and distinct attitudes. Although these attitudes may operate independently in many circumstances, with one being more relevant and dominant in a given situation, the dual attitudes are also potentially interactive (see also Nosek, 2005). Indeed, recent research from cognitive neuroscience is consistent with an interactive components view. Structurally, there are neural pathways through which the prefrontal cortex, which is associated with action control, can inhibit amygdala activation, which is related to many basic affective reactions (Grace & Rosenkranz, 2002). Amygdala activation has been associated with implicit racial bias (Phelps et al., 2000). Although research in social neuroscience has not directly demonstrated the operation of a direct inhibiting pathway, it has revealed that "explicit and implicit evaluations involve somewhat different neural circuits" (Cunningham, Raye, & Johnson, 2004, p. 1717). In particular, Cunningham, Raye et al. found that the mere exposure to an attitude object elicited amygdala activation, which was correlated with the emotional intensity of evaluative response. When the task involved explicit evaluation, however, activation occurred primarily in the areas in the frontal cortex rather than in the amygdala.

Cunningham, Johnson, Raye, Getenby, Gore, & Banaji (2004) found converging evidence in their investigation of responses to Black and White faces by White participants. When the faces were presented subliminally (30 ms), amygdala activation was stronger for Black than for White faces, and this effect was stronger among participants who showed higher levels of implicit racial prejudice on an IAT. The correlation between IAT responses and amygdala activation was .79. Phelps et al. (2000) similarly found a substantial correlation ($r = .56$) between IAT responses and amygdala activation, but not between self-reported prejudice and activation ($r = -.05$). Notably, the Cunningham, Johnson et al. (2004) study also showed that when the photographs of faces were presented supraliminally under controlled processing conditions (525 ms), frontal activation also occurred. Consistent with the idea that Whites are consciously motivated to be nonprejudiced and that this motivation can, with sufficient time, inhibit responses associated with implicit prejudice, the degree of this activation was correlated with weaker amygdala activation for Black than White faces. The authors (Cunningham, Johnson et al., 2004; see also Cunningham, Johnson, Gatenby, Gore, & Banaji, 2003) interpreted these findings as reflecting the ambivalence of Whites' attitudes toward Blacks, a conclusion consistent with the basic premises of the aversive racism framework (Dovidio & Gaertner, 2004; Gaertner & Dovidio, 1986). We note that behavioral evidence for the interaction of conscious and unconscious social attitudes is still tenuous, but we believe that these findings from social cognitive neuroscience suggest productive avenues for future inquiry.

A better understanding of the relationship between conscious and unconscious processes and behavior can also help guide the development of effective interventions to combat contemporary forms of prejudice. Approaches for dealing with the traditional, blatant form of prejudice are generally less effective for combating the consequences of contemporary forms of prejudice. If certain groups of Whites already consciously endorse egalitarian, nonprejudiced views; disavow traditional stereotypes; and are motivated to inhibit their biases, strategies aimed at changing overt biases may not be effective. Both the single attitude and dual attitudes perspectives suggest that it is essential to address the activation of negative attitudes and stereotypes.

The inhibition of bias among Whites typically requires a deliberate expenditure of cognitive effort associated with the activation of areas of the brain associated with executive function and conscious control (Amodio, Harmon-Jones, Devine, Curtin, Hartley, & Covert, 2004; Bartholow, Dickter, & Sestir, 2006; Richeson et al., 2003) and can result in the depletion of cognitive resources (Richeson & Shelton, 2003; Richeson & Trawalter, 2005). However, with repeated experience or practice, it may be possible to automatically inhibit biases related to unwanted prejudices (Glaser & Kihlstrom, 2005; Gollwitzer & Bargh, 2005). For instance, Phelps et al. (2000, Experiment 2) found that White participants did not show amygdala activation in response to pictures of familiar and well-liked Blacks. Supportive of this possibility, we demonstrated that the automatic activation of racial stereotypes and implicit racial prejudice can be eliminated through repeated practice in developing incompatible associations (Kawakami, Dovidio, Moll, Hermsen, & Russin, 2000; Kawakami, Dovidio, & van Kamp, 2005, in press; Kawakami, Phills, Steele, & Dovidio, in press). As Monteith, Sherman, and Devine (1998) noted, "Practice makes perfect" (p. 71). Like any other mental process, responding in new ways to social stimuli can become proceduralized and relatively automatic.

From either a single attitude or dual attitudes perspective, however, it is important to understand further the processes by which practice in developing new associations that are incompatible with automatically activated biases, and which may be more aligned with explicitly expressed attitudes, inhibit the activation of prejudice (see Gawronski & Bodenhausen, 2006). In particular, the development of new, incompatible associations may directly inhibit or weaken the activation of the originally biased associations or, alternatively, may be creating a more dominant associative link that becomes activated by exposure to the group. Whereas the former interpretation implies the elimination of the original attitude, the latter explanation suggests that the original implicit association remains intact, but it is subordinated to the newer, stronger set of associations (see Deutsch, Gawronski, & Strack, 2006). This process is consistent with the description of Wilson et al. (2000) of the formation of dual attitudes.

Conclusion

In conclusion, recent research related to implicit measures has provided important insights into the nature and expression of contemporary racial prejudice of Whites toward Blacks and to understanding the nature of prejudice. Whereas previous research and theory postulated the existence of separate conscious and unconscious components of racial attitudes (Dovidio & Gaertner, 2004), these theorists struggled to find ways to measure the latter component that were not strongly constrained by historical and social context (McConahay, 1986). The introduction of techniques for assessing attitudes with implicit measures has permitted researchers to distinguish reliably between Whites who appear nonprejudiced on explicit measures and who do not exhibit prejudice on implicit measures (i.e., nonprejudiced Whites) and those who appear nonprejudiced on explicit measures but who seem prejudiced on implicit measures. As we noted earlier, with greater methodological refinement it may be possible to distinguish those who are skillful at strategically masking their bias from those who genuinely endorsed egalitarian attitudes (i.e., aversive racists).

Practically, this development improves researchers' ability to predict how and when individual Whites may respond to racially relevant situations (Son Hing, Li, & Zanna, 2002) and focuses research on the consideration of different dimensions that may underlie both spontaneous and deliberative interracial behaviors. Understanding these processes can help explain the dynamics of distrust and suspicion that characterize contemporary race relations in North America (Crocker, Luhtanen, Broadnax, & Blaine, 1999) and highlight the value of implicit measures for providing insight into the significant and potentially lethal (Correll, Park, & Judd, 2002) consequences of biases that cannot be detected with explicit measures.

References

Adorno, T. W., Frenkel-Brunswik, E., Levinson, D. J., & Sanford, R. N. (1950). *The authoritarian personality.* New York: Harper.

Allport, G. W. (1954). *The nature of prejudice.* New York: Addison-Wesley.

Amodio, D. M., Harmon-Jones, E., Devine, P. G., Curtin, J. J., Hartley, S. L., & Covert, A. E. (2004). Neural signals for the detection of unintentional race bias. *Psychological Science, 15,* 88–93.

Bargh, J. A. (1999). The cognitive monster: The case against the controllability of automatic stereotype effects. In S. Chaiken & Y. Trope (Eds.), *Dual-process theories in social psychology* (pp. 361–382). New York: Guilford Press.

Bargh, J. A., & Pietromonaco, P. (1982). Automatic information processing and social perception: The influence of trait information presented outside of awareness on impression formation. *Journal of Personality and Social Psychology, 43,* 437–449.

Bartholow, B. D., Dickter, C. L., & Sestir, M. A. (2006). Stereotype activation and control of race bias: Cognitive control and its impairment by alcohol. *Journal of Personality and Social Psychology, 90,* 272–287.

Bessenoff, G. R., & Sherman, J. W. (2000). Automatic and controlled components of prejudice toward fat people: Evaluation versus stereotype activation. *Social Cognition, 18,* 329–353.

Blair, I. V. (2001). Implicit stereotypes and prejudice. In G. B. Moskowitz (Ed.), *Cognitive social psychology: The Princeton Symposium on the legacy and future of social cognition* (pp. 359–374). Mahwah, NJ: Erlbaum.

Blair, I. V. (2002). The malleability of automatic stereotypes and prejudice. *Personality and Social Psychology Review, 6*, 242–261.

Bobo, L. (1999). Prejudice as group position: Micro-foundations of a sociological approach to racism and race relations. *Journal of Social Issues, 55*(3), 445–472.

Bobo, L. (2001). Racial attitudes and relations at the close of the twentieth century. In N. J. Smelser, W. J. Wilson, & F. Mitchell, F. (Eds.), *Racial trends and their consequences* (Vol. 1, pp. 264–301). Washington, DC: National Academy Press.

Chen, M., & Bargh, J. (1997). Nonconscious behavioral confirmation processes: The self-fulfilling consequences of automatic stereotype activation. *Journal of Experimental Social Psychology, 33*, 541–560.

Correll, J., Park, B., & Judd, C. M. (2002). The police officer's dilemma: Using ethnicity to disambiguate potentially threatening individuals. *Journal of Personality and Social Psychology, 86*, 1314–1329.

Crandall, C. S., & Eshleman, A. (2003). A justification-suppression model of the expression and experience of prejudice. *Psychological Bulletin, 129*, 414–446.

Crocker, J., Luhtanen, R., Broadnax, S., & Blaine, B. E. (1999). Belief in U.S. government conspiracies against Blacks among Black and White college students: Powerlessness or system blame? *Personality and Social Psychology Bulletin, 25*, 941–953.

Cunningham, W. A., Johnson, M. K., Gatenby, J. C., Gore, J. C., & Banaji, M. R. (2003). Neural components of social evaluation. *Journal of Personality and Social Psychology, 85*, 639–649.

Cunningham, W. A., Johnson, M. K., Raye, C. L., Getenby, J. C., Gore, J. J., & Banaji, M. R. (2004). Separable neural components in the processing of Black and White faces. *Psychological Science, 15*, 806–813.

Cunningham, W. A., Raye, C. L., & Johnson, M. K. (2004). Implicit and explicit evaluation: fMRI correlates of valence, emotional intensity, and control in the processing of attitudes. *Journal of Cognitive Neuroscience, 16*, 1717–1729.

Dasgupta, N., & Rivera, L. M. (2006). From automatic anti-gay prejudice to behavior: The moderating role of conscious beliefs about gender and behavioral control. *Journal of Personality and Social Psychology, 91*, 268–280.

DePaulo, B. M., & Friedman, H. S. (1998). Nonverbal communication. In D. T. Gilbert, S. T. Fiske, & L. Gardner (Eds.), *The handbook of social psychology* (Vol. 2, 4th ed., pp. 3–40). New York: McGraw-Hill.

Deutsch, R., Gawronski, B., & Strack, F. (2006). At the boundaries of automaticity: Negation as a reflective operation. *Journal of Personality and Social Psychology, 91*, 385–405.

Devine, P. G. (1989). Stereotypes and prejudice: The automatic and controlled components. *Journal of Personality and Social Psychology, 56*, 5–18.

Dovidio, J. F. (2001). On the nature of contemporary prejudice: The third wave. *Journal of Social Issues, 57,* 829–849.

Dovidio, J. F., Brigham, J. C., Johnson, B. T., & Gaertner, S. L. (1996). Stereotyping, prejudice, and discrimination: Another look. In C. N. Macrae, M. Hewstone, & C. Stangor (Eds.), *Foundations of stereotypes and stereotyping* (pp. 276–319). New York: Guilford Press.

Dovidio, J. F., Evans, N., & Tyler, R. B. (1986). Racial stereotypes: The contents of their cognitive representations. *Journal of Experimental Social Psychology, 22,* 22–37.

Dovidio, J. F., & Fazio, R. H. (1992). New technologies for the direct and indirect assessment of attitudes. In J. Tanur (Ed.), *Questions about survey questions: Meaning, memory, attitudes, and social interaction* (pp. 204–237). New York: Russell Sage Foundation.

Dovidio, J. F., & Gaertner, S. L. (2000). Aversive racism and selection decisions: 1989 and 1999. *Psychological Science, 11,* 319–323.

Dovidio, J. F., & Gaertner, S. L. (2004). Aversive racism. In M. P. Zanna (Ed.), *Advances in experimental social psychology* (Vol. 36, pp. 1–51). San Diego: Academic Press.

Dovidio, J. F., Gaertner, S. L., Anastasio, P. A., & Sanitioso, R. (1992). Cognitive and motivational bases of bias: The implications of aversive racism for attitudes toward Hispanics. In S. Knouse, P. Rosenfeld, & A. Culbertson (Eds.), *Hispanics in the workplace* (pp. 75–106). Newbury Park, CA: Sage.

Dovidio, J., Kawakami, K., & Beach, K. (2001). Implicit and explicit attitudes: Examination of the relationship between measures of intergroup bias. In R. Brown & S. L. Gaertner (Eds.), *Blackwell handbook of social psychology: Vol. 4. Intergroup relations* (pp. 175–197). Oxford, England: Blackwell.

Dovidio, J. F., Kawakami, K., & Gaertner, S. L. (2002). Implicit and explicit prejudice and interracial interaction. *Journal of Personality and Social Psychology, 82,* 62–68.

Dovidio, J., Kawakami, K., Johnson, C., Johnson, B., & Howard, A. (1997). On the nature of prejudice: Automatic and controlled processes. *Journal of Experimental Social Psychology, 33,* 510–540.

Dunton, B. C., & Fazio, R. H. (1997). An individual difference measure of motivation to control prejudiced reactions. *Personality and Social Psychology Bulletin, 23,* 316–326.

Fazio, R. H. (1990). Multiple processes by which attitudes guide behavior: The MODE Model as an integrative framework. In M. P. Zanna (Ed.), *Advances in experimental social psychology* (Vol. 23, pp. 75–109). Orlando, FL: Academic Press.

Fazio, R. H., & Hilden, L. E. (2001). Emotional reactions to a seemingly prejudiced response: The role of automatically activated racial attitudes and motivation to control prejudiced reactions. *Personality and Social Psychology Bulletin, 27,* 538–549.

Fazio, R. H., Jackson, J. R., Dunton, B. C., & Williams, C. J. (1995). Variability in automatic activation as an unobtrusive measure of racial attitudes: A bona fide pipeline? *Journal of Personality and Social Psychology, 69*, 1013–1027.

Fazio, R. H., & Olson, M. A. (2003). Implicit measures in social cognition research: Their meaning and uses. *Annual Review of Psychology, 54*, 297–327.

Fein, S., & Spencer, S. J. (1997). Prejudice as self-image maintenance: Affirming the self through derogating others. *Journal of Personality and Social Psychology, 73*, 31–44.

Fiske, S. T. (2005). Social cognition and the normality of prejudgment. In J. F. Dovidio, P. Glick, & L. A. Rudman (Eds.), *On the nature of prejudice: Fifty years after Allport* (pp. 36–53). Malden, MA: Blackwell.

Gaertner, S. L., & Dovidio, J. F. (1977). The subtlety of White racism, arousal, and helping behavior. *Journal of Personality and Social Psychology, 35*, 691–707.

Gaertner, S. L., & Dovidio, J. F. (1986). The aversive form of racism. In J. F. Dovidio & S. L. Gaertner (Eds.), *Prejudice, discrimination, and racism* (pp. 61–89). Orlando, FL: Academic Press.

Gaertner, S. L., & McLaughlin, J. P. (1983). Racial stereotypes: Associations and ascriptions of positive and negative characteristics. *Social Psychology Quarterly, 46*, 23–30.

Gawronski, B., & Bodenhausen, G. V. (2006). Associative and propositional processes in evaluation: An integrative review of implicit and explicit attitude change. *Psychological Bulletin, 132*, 265–286.

Gilbert, D. T., & Hixon, J. G. (1991). The trouble of thinking: Activation and application to stereotypic beliefs. *Journal of Personality and Social Psychology, 60*, 509–517.

Glaser, J., & Kihlstrom, J. F. (2005). Compensatory automaticity: Unconscious volition is not an oxymoron. In R. R. Hassin, J. S. Uleman, & J. A. Bargh (Eds.), *The new unconscious* (pp. 171–195). New York: Oxford University Press.

Gollwitzer, P. M., & Bargh, J. A. (2005). Automaticity in goal pursuit. In A. J. Elliot & C. S. Dweck (Eds.), *Handbook of competence and motivation* (pp. 624–646). New York: Guilford Press.

Grace, A. A., & Rosenkranz, J. A. (2002). Regulation of conditioned responses of basolateral amygdala neurons. *Physiology and Behavior, 77*, 489–493.

Greenwald, A. G., & Banaji, M. (1995). Implicit social cognition: Attitudes, self-esteem, and stereotypes. *Psychological Review, 102*, 4–27.

Greenwald, A. G., Banaji, M. R., Rudman, L. A., Farnham, S. D., Nosek, B. A., & Mellott, D. S. (2002). A unified theory of implicit attitudes, stereotypes, self-esteem, and self-concept. *Psychological Review, 109*, 3–25.

Greenwald, A. G., McGhee, D., & Schwartz, J. (1998). Measuring individual differences in implicit cognition: The implicit association test. *Journal of Personality and Social Psychology, 74*, 1464–1480.

Hamilton, D. L., & Trolier, T. K. (1986). Stereotypes and stereotyping: An overview of the cognitive approach. In J. F. Dovidio & S. L. Gaertner (Eds.), *Prejudice, discrimination, and racism* (pp. 127–163). Orlando, FL: Academic Press.

Hebl, M. R., Foster, J. B., Mannix, L. M., & Dovidio, J. F. (2002). Formal and interpersonal discrimination. A field study of bias toward homosexual applicants. *Personality and Social Psychology Bulletin, 28*, 815–825.

Hodson, G., Dovidio, J. F., & Gaertner, S. L. (2002). Processes in racial discrimination: Differential weighting of conflicting information. *Personality and Social Psychology Bulletin, 28*, 460–471.

Hofmann, W., Gawronski, B., Gschwendner, T., Le, H., & Schmitt, M. (2005). A meta-analysis on the correlation between the Implicit Association Test and explicit self-report measures. *Personality and Social Psychology Bulletin, 31*, 1369–1385.

Hugenberg, K., & Bodenhausen, G. V. (2003). Facing prejudice: Implicit prejudice and the perception of facial threat. *Psychological Science, 14*, 640–643.

Hugenberg, K., & Bodenhausen, G. V. (2004). Ambiguity in social categorization: The role of prejudice and facial affect in race categorization. *Psychological Science, 15*, 342–345.

John, M. S., Agocha, V. B., & Dovidio, J. F. (2006, May). *Putting the brakes on stereotype activation: Undermining racial categorization.* Poster presented at the annual meeting of the American Psychological Society, New York.

Karpinski, A., & Hilton, J. L. (2001). Attitudes and the Implicit Association Test. *Journal of Personality and Social Psychology, 81*, 774–788.

Katz, I., & Hass, R. G. (1988). Racial ambivalence and American value conflict: Correlational and priming studies of dual cognitive structures. *Journal of Personality and Social Psychology, 55*, 893–905.

Katz, I., Wackenhut, J., & Hass, R. G. (1986). Racial ambivalence, value duality, and behavior. In J. F. Dovidio & S. L. Gaertner (Eds.), *Prejudice, discrimination, and racism* (pp. 35–59). Orlando, FL: Academic Press.

Kawakami, K, Dovidio, J. F., Moll, J., Hermsen, S., & Russin, A. (2000). Just say no (to stereotyping): Effects of training in trait negation on stereotype activation. *Journal of Personality and Social Psychology, 78*, 871–888.

Kawakami, K., Dovidio, J.F., & van Kamp, S. (2005). Kicking the habit: Effects of nonstereotypic association training on the application of stereotypes. *Journal of Experimental Social Psychology, 41*, 68–75.

Kawakami, K., Dovidio, J. F., & van Kamp, S. (in press). The impact of naïve theories related to strategies to reduce biases and correction processes on the application of stereotypes. *Group Processes and Intergroup Relations.*

Kawakami, K., Phills, C., Steele, J., & Dovidio, J. F. (in press). (Close) Distance makes the heart grow fonder: Improving implicit racial attitudes and interracial interactions through approach behaviors. *Journal of Personality and Social Psychology.*

Kovel, J. (1970). *White racism: A psychohistory.* New York: Pantheon.

Lepore, L., & Brown, R. (1997). Category and stereotype activation: Is prejudice inevitable? *Journal of Personality and Social Psychology, 72,* 275–287.

Livingston, R. W. (2002). The role of perceived negativity in the moderation of African-Americans' implicit and explicit racial attitudes. *Journal of Experimental Social Psychology, 38,* 405–413.

McConahay, J. B. (1986). Modern racism, ambivalence, and the modern racism scale. In J. F. Dovidio & S. L. Gaertner (Eds.), *Prejudice, discrimination, and racism* (pp. 91–125). Orlando, FL: Academic Press.

McConnell, A. R., & Leibold, J. M. (2001). Relations among the Implicit Association Test, discriminatory behavior, and explicit measures of racial attitudes. *Journal of Experimental Social Psychology, 37,* 435–442.

Monteith, M. J., Sherman, J., & Devine, P. G. (1998). Suppression as a stereotype control strategy. *Personality and Social Psychology Review, 1,* 63–82.

Nail, P. R., Harton, H. C., & Decker, B. P. (2003) Political orientation and modern versus aversive racism: Tests of Dovidio and Gaertner's (1998) Integrated Model. *Journal of Personality and Social Psychology, 84,* 754–770.

Nier, J. A. (2005). How dissociated are implicit and explicit racial attitudes? A bogus pipeline approach. *Group Processes and Intergroup Relations, 8,* 39–52.

Nosek, B. A. (2005). Moderators of the relationship between implicit and explicit evaluation. *Journal of Experimental Psychology: General, 134,* 565–584.

Nosek, B. A., & Banaji, M. R. (2001). The Go/No-Go Association Task. *Social Cognition, 19,* 625–666.

Nosek, B. A., Banaji, M. R., & Greenwald, A. G. (2002a). Harvesting implicit group attitudes and beliefs from a demonstration website. *Group Dynamics: Theory, Research, and Practice, 6,* 101–115.

Nosek, B. A., Banaji, M. R., & Greenwald, A. G. (2002b). Math = male, me = female, therefore math ≠ me. Journal of Personality and Social Psychology, 83, 44–59.

Olson, M. A., & Fazio, R. H. (2001). Implicit attitude formation through classical conditioning. *Psychological Science, 12,* 413–417.

Olson, M. A., & Fazio, R. H. (2004). Trait inferences as a function of automatically activated racial attitudes and motivation to control prejudiced reactions. *Basic and Applied Social Psychology, 26,* 1–11.

Pettigrew, T. F., & Meertens, R. W. (1995). Subtle and blatant prejudice in Western Europe. *European Journal of Social Psychology, 25,* 57–76.

Petty, R. E., & Briñol, P. (in press). Implicit ambivalence: A meta-cognitive approach. In R. E. Petty, R. H. Fazio, & P. Briñol (Eds.), *Attitudes: Insights from the new implicit measures.* Hillsdale, NJ: Erlbaum.

Phelps, E. A., O'Conner, K. J., Cunningham, A. A., Funayama, E. S., Gatenby, J. C., Gore, J. C., & Banaji, M. R. (2000). Performance on indirect measures of race evaluation predicts amygdala activation. *Journal of Cognitive Neuroscience, 12*, 729–738.

Richeson, J. A., Baird, A. A., Gordon, H. L., Heatherton, T. F., Wyland, C. L., Trawalter, S., & Shelton, J. N. (2003). An fMRI investigation of the impact of interracial contact on executive function. *Nature Neuroscience, 6*, 1323–1328.

Richeson, J. A., & Shelton, J. N. (2003). When prejudice does not pay: Effects of interracial contact on executive function. *Psychological Science, 14*, 287–290.

Richeson, J. A., & Trawalter, S. (2005). Why do interracial interactions impair executive function? A resource depletion account. *Journal of Personality and Social Psychology, 88*, 934–947.

Roese N. J., & Jamieson, D. W. (1993). Twenty years of bogus pipeline research: A critical review and meta-analysis. *Psychological Bulletin, 114*, 363–375.

Rudman, L. A., Ashmore, R. D., & Gary, M. (1999). *Implicit and explicit prejudice and stereotypes: A continuum model of intergroup orientation assessment.* Unpublished data, Rutgers University, Piscataway, NJ.

Rudman, L. A., & Lee, M. R. (2002). Implicit and explicit consequences of exposure to violent and misogynous rap music. *Group Processes and Intergroup Relations, 5*, 133–150.

Saucier, D. A., Miller, C. T., & Doucet, N. (2005). Differences in helping Whites and Blacks: A meta-analysis. *Personality and Social Psychology Review, 9*, 2–16.

Schacter, D. L. (1990). Introduction to "Implicit memory: Multiple perspectives." *Bulletin of the Psychonomic Society, 28*, 338–340.

Schuman, H., Steeh, C., Bobo, L., & Krysan, M. (1997). *Racial attitudes in America: Trends and interpretations.* Cambridge, MA: Harvard University Press.

Sears, D. O., Henry, P. J., & Kosterman, R. (2000). Egalitarian values and contemporary racial politics. In D. O. Sears, J. Sidanius, & L. Bobo (Eds.), *Racialized politics: The debate about racism in America* (pp. 75–117). Chicago: University of Chicago Press.

Sherif, M., & Sherif, C. W. (1969). *Social psychology.* New York: Harper & Row.

Sidanius, J., & Pratto, F. (1999). *Social dominance: An intergroup theory of social hierarchy and oppression.* New York: Cambridge University Press.

Sigall, H., & Page, R. (1971). Current stereotypes: A little fading, a little faking. *Journal of Personality and Social Psychology, 18*, 247–255.

Son Hing, L. S., Li, W., & Zanna, M. P. (2002). Inducing hypocrisy to reduce prejudicial responses among aversive racists. *Journal of Experimental Social Psychology, 38*, 71–78.

Son Hing, L. S., Chung-Yan, G. A., Hamilton, L. K., & Zanna, M. P. (2008). A two-dimensional model that employs explicit and implicit attitudes to characterize prejudice. *Journal of Personality and Social Psychology, 94*, 971–987.

Strack, F., & Deutsch, R. (2004). Reflective and impulsive determinants of social behavior. *Personality and Social Psychology Review, 8,* 220–247.

Tajfel, H., & Turner, J. C. (1979). An integrative theory of intergroup conflict. In W. G. Austin & S. Worchel (Eds.), *The social psychology of intergroup relations* (pp. 33–48). Monterey, CA: Brooks/Cole.

Towles-Schwen. T., & Fazio, R. H. (2003). Choosing social situations: The relation between automatically activated racial attitudes and anticipated comfort interacting with African Americans. *Personality and Social Psychology Bulletin, 29,* 172–180.

Uhlmann, E. L., & Cohen, G. L. (2005). Constructed criterion: Redefining merit to justify discrimination. *Psychological Science, 16,* 474–480.

Webb, E. J., Campbell, D. T., Schwartz, R. D., & Sechrest, L. (1966). *Unobtrusive measures: Nonreactive research on the social sciences.* Chicago: Rand McNally.

Wilson, T. D., Lindsey, S., & Schooler, T. Y. (2000). A model of dual attitudes. *Psychological Review, 107,* 101–126.

Wittenbrink, B., Judd, C. M., & Park, B. (1997). Evidence for racial prejudice at the implicit level and its relationship with questionnaire measures. *Journal of Personality and Social Psychology, 72,* 262–274.

7

On the Interpersonal Functions of Implicit Stereotyping and Evaluative Race Bias

Insights from Social Neuroscience

David M. Amodio
Patricia G. Devine

Introduction

How many times have you been treated inappropriately because of the way you look? One of us—a woman—has been mistaken as a secretary when standing in the main office of her department on more than one occasion. The other—a man—cannot remember a single instance of this occurring during his years in the same department. Most likely, this is an example of an implicit inference based on gender. The tendency for people to mistake a woman, but not a man, as a secretary is an example of implicit stereotyping, because secretary positions are often associated with females in American society. The implicit nature of the bias suggests that it comes to mind automatically and can have unintentional and often subconscious influences on judgments and behaviors. In this case, the female professor might have been asked for directions to the Xerox machine. This example may appear relatively benign, however, when compared with more pernicious examples in recent history of innocent Arab-Americans being mistaken as terrorists and African-American men mistaken as criminals. At their worst, implicit racial biases can lead to wrongful indictments and executions.

Why do humans possess implicit racial biases? Most people agree that prejudice is a maladaptive form of human behavior. But if it is maladaptive, why does it persist—thrive, even—in modern human societies? The overarching thesis of this chapter is that at some level, the mechanisms that give rise to implicit stereotypes and implicit evaluative racial biases (e.g., prejudiced attitudes and emotions) serve adaptive functions. We contend that an understanding of how implicit biases relate to adaptive functions is essential for designing strategies to combat racial prejudice. However, not much is known regarding the function of implicit race bias. Much of the extant research on race bias focuses on questions of *what*: What is implicit race bias? How can the construct of implicit bias be identified and measured? Much less work has addressed *why* questions, which pertain to the function of implicit biases (Allport, 1954; Jost, Pelham, & Carvallo, 2002; Hardin & Higgins, 1996; Macrae, Milne, & Bodenhausen, 1994; Macrae, Stangor, & Milne, 1994). In this chapter, we describe one way in which our research has begun to address the function of implicit bias—the *why* question—through a consideration of the neurocognitive mechanisms believed to underlie different forms of implicit racial bias.

When discussing the function of implicit race bias, it is useful to consider the history of the construct. How were implicit biases first conceived? What are the psychological mechanisms that underlie implicit stereotyping and evaluative race bias? What might these mechanisms tell us about function? In what follows, we provide a brief review of some of the major developments in implicit bias research addressing issues of stereotyping and prejudice. Our purpose in doing so is to highlight not only the developments but also what we perceive to be the limitations in the extant literature. This review, then, serves as a springboard for suggesting a theoretical framework for understanding how implicit biases, both stereotyping and evaluative, serve a function in orchestrating interpersonal behavior.

A Brief History of Implicit Race Bias

Early work in the study of stereotyping and prejudice focused largely on the content of ethnic and racial stereotypes and the attitudes that people could readily express on self-report measures. Considering stereotypes, for example, Lippman (1922) wrote about them as "pictures in our heads," and empirical research was directed at assessing these pictures, or more aptly, the content of stereotypes (e.g., Katz & Braly, 1933). Specifically, participants were asked in a very straightforward manner to identify the traits that they believed characterized various ethnic and racial groups. Other work focused on the development of measures to assess prejudiced attitudes. For example, Woodmansee and Cook (1967) developed a series of Likert-type items to assess the factors underlying racial attitudes (e.g., derogatory beliefs, ease in interracial contact, acceptance in close relationships). Similarly, Bogardus (1925) asked respondents to report how close they would allow members of stigmatized groups to themselves and members of their ingroup (e.g., allow into one's country, city, local neighborhood, home, or family). The assumption was that a preference for greater interpersonal distance was indicative of less favorable attitudes toward members of the group. This line of inquiry, strongly influenced by classic attitude theory, had the ultimate goals of predicting behavior (e.g., discrimination) and attitude change (e.g., reducing prejudice).

It was soon apparent, however, that as social norms discouraging prejudice became increasingly salient, such straightforward approaches to the measurement of stereotype content and prejudice were problematic. For example, subsequent research suggested that the content of stereotypes reported by participants using the adjective checklist method had changed, yet the meaning of the change was unclear (Devine & Elliot, 1995; Gilbert, 1951; Karlins, Coffman, & Walters, 1969). Had the stereotypes faded? Or had the content of the stereotypes changed? Or, as a third possibility, had people simply become less willing to express stereotypic (particularly negative) views of others? In the same time frame, it also became evident that self-reported measures of prejudice did not reliably predict behavior. In a review of this literature, Crosby, Bromley, and Saxe (1980) showed that people's behavior often revealed more prejudice than would be expected based on subjects' self-reported attitudes. Their review led them to conclude that "Whites today are, in fact, more prejudiced than they are wont to admit" (p. 556). Indeed, throughout the field there was a growing uneasiness with self-reports.

In the intergroup context, the specific concern was that self-reports, be they of stereotypes or prejudice, could be biased by social desirability demands created by the newly emerging social context that favored egalitarianism and discouraged overt prejudice. As a result, self-reports were often held in suspicion, and many researchers began to search for measures of stereotyping and prejudice that would circumvent such response biases in the hopes of identifying more accurate predictors of intergroup behavior (McConahay, Hardee, & Batts, 1981; Sigall & Page, 1971). Theoretical efforts shifted to trying to understand the nature of dissociation between what people said about their attitudes and what they did in terms of their behavior. If attitudes had become more tolerant over time, what was driving the dissociation between word and deed? The central idea emerging from these efforts, though varying in some details, was that despite changes at an explicit or conscious personal level, biases remained at an implicit or unconscious level (e.g., Devine, 1989; Dovidio & Gaertner, 1986; McConahay, 1986). In addition, whereas explicit responses are easy to control and lend themselves well to strategic self-presentation, measures of implicit responses were viewed as useful, and perhaps more valid, precisely because they lacked these characteristics. In recent years, students of stereotyping and prejudice have become consumed with the study of implicit forms of bias and what they may reveal about the nature of intergroup attitudes and stereotypes.

Early Approaches to the Study of Implicit Race Bias

Early work on implicit forms of bias fell into two general approaches. The first, heavily influenced by then recent advances in cognitive psychology and associative network models of memory, focused on the development of response latency-based measures of the content of stereotypes (e.g., Dovidio, Evans, & Tyler, 1986; Gaertner & McLaughlin, 1983). Using sequential priming methods, the objective was to assess the contents of stereotypes by how quickly participants could make judgments of stereotypic words (e.g., *lazy, musical*) following social group labels (e.g., Blacks, Whites). By requiring respondents to respond quickly, it was presumed that the response latencies were uncontaminated by strategic processes and, hence, would reveal the "true" content of stereotypes. In these studies, the primary focus was to develop alternatives to self-report, and relatively little attention was given to explicit biases or the prediction of behavior. It is notable that although the term *implicit* usually refers to a construct, the behavioral reaction-time measures often used to assess implicit bias are themselves often called *implicit measures*. Caution is warranted with this usage, because the tendency to refer to reaction-time and self-report measures as implicit measures and explicit measures, respectively, may lead to a confounding of method with process.

The second general approach reflected in the then-emerging models of prejudice and prejudice reduction focused less on the measurement of implicit biases and more on the nature and implications of implicit biases vis-à-vis explicit biases. The central questions concerned the types of behavioral responses that both implicit and explicit biases would predict, as well as the situational factors that might moderate these predictions. As such, in the prediction of behavior, implicit measures were not viewed as alternatives to or better than explicit measures. Rather, theorists recognized that explicit and implicit aspects of bias each told incomplete yet complementary parts of the story, such that both must be considered to understand intergroup behavior. According to some formulations, for example, prejudice had not truly been reduced but rather had been driven "underground," resurfacing to influence behavior only under particular circumstances, such as when social norms for appropriate conduct were not obvious (e.g., Dovidio & Gaertner, 1986). Other formulations held that despite the rejection of prejudice at the conscious, explicit level, biases that remained at the implicit level could affect behavior under circumstances that precluded deliberative responding (e.g., Devine, 1989). Thus, the major conceptual focus was on why people might have implicit biases (e.g., where did they come from and what function do they serve) and when each type of bias would predict behavior.

Subsequent research refined measurement of implicit biases but maintained a focus on predicting behavior. For example, Fazio, Jackson, Dunton, & Williams (1995) developed a sequential priming measure of implicit evaluative race bias and showed, consistent with Devine's analysis (1989), that implicit biases and explicit biases were theoretically independent and predicted different types of responses. Whereas implicit biases predicted subtle forms of discrimination (e.g., less friendly behavior toward a Black research assistant), explicit biases predicted more thoughtful and deliberative responses (e.g., judgment about the Rodney King verdict). Conceptually similar findings were obtained by Dovidio and colleagues (e.g., Dovidio, Kawakami, & Gaertner, 2002; Dovidio, Kawakami, Johnson, Johnson, & Howard, 1997) and by McConnell and Leibold (2001; see also Chapter 2 and Chapter 6, this volume). That is, these researchers found that measures of implicit but not explicit prejudice predicted negative nonverbal responses toward Black interaction partners. Broadly speaking, the focus on the prediction of behavior taken by these approaches reflected an inherently functional perspective.

A Shift in Focus: From Function to Description

While several advances were being made in understanding how implicit biases function in concert with explicit processes to produce behavior, interest in developing new implicit measures never waned. Indeed, over the past 10 years, issues of measurement and description appear to have taken center stage in the study of implicit biases (Fazio & Olson, 2003; Greenwald, McGhee, & Schwartz, 1998; Judd, Blair, & Chapleau, 2004; Payne, Cheng, Govorun, & Stewart, 2005; Chapter 15 and Chapter 14, this volume). Issues related to the measurement of implicit bias are quite interesting in their own right. As was true with the early measurement research, the goal was to develop measures of implicit biases that would bypass strategic self-presentation. This goal led to several clever behavioral and physiological methods for assessing racial biases (e.g., Amodio, Harmon-Jones, & Devine, 2003; Chapter 16, this volume; Fazio et al., 1995; Greenwald et al.; Vanman, Paul, Ito, & Miller, 1997). Initial research using these methods was descriptive: The primary finding of interest was that a racial bias could be revealed on so-called implicit measures. To further demonstrate the efficacy of such measures, they were often compared with explicit reports of attitudes, with most studies reporting little correspondence between the two types of measures (i.e., low correlations; but see Cunningham, Preacher, & Banaji, 2001). In response, a great deal of effort has focused on factors that affect the magnitude of the implicit–explicit correspondence (see Hofmann, Gawronski, Gschwendner, Le, & Schmitt, 2005, for a recent meta-analysis).

Initially, the lack of relationship between implicit and explicit responses served to corroborate the notion that they reflect independent automatic and controlled processes, respectively (Devine, 1989). Nevertheless, the lack of relationship between responses on implicit and explicit measures puzzled many researchers, leading some to suggest that one form of response should be the "true" response (Banaji, 2001; Fazio et al., 1995; but see Payne, 2005; Wilson, Lindsey, & Schooler, 2000). Consequently, much research has sought to understand how, and under what conditions, implicit and explicit forms of bias might be related. The focus on implicit–explicit correspondence has, by and large, led to an emphasis on explicit measures of attitudes and beliefs as the primary outcome measure in research studies, moving away from the emphasis on predicting expressions of bias in behavior. In light of past theory and research regarding dual-processes systems in intergroup bias, as well as significant evidence for multiple memory systems from the neuroscience literature (Poldrack & Foerde, 2008), it is curious that so much effort has been devoted to finding a relationship between responses believed to arise from independent systems (but see Kruglanski, Erbs, Pierro, Mannetti, & Chun, 2006, for a single-system view). It is also notable that the shift in focus to examining implicit–explicit correspondences rather than the effect of implicit bias on behavior has influenced the way researchers design and use their measures of implicit race bias. That is, researchers have begun to design their implicit bias measures to be better predictors of explicit responses rather than behavioral expressions of prejudice. For example, the recommended scoring algorithm for the most widely used measure of implicit bias, the Implicit Association Test (IAT), was calibrated according to its ability to predict individuals' self-reported explicit attitudes, but not their behavior (Greenwald, Nosek, & Banaji, 2003). We suspect that this detour from the original question—how implicit and explicit responses interact to produce behavior—has served to limit advances in the understanding of how implicit biases influence social behavior.

A second obstacle to understanding the function of implicit race bias is that extant theoretical models of implicit evaluation and stereotyping may be limited in some important ways. That is, social cognitive models of implicit race bias have focused primarily on information processing aspects of implicit bias, such as the issues of automaticity and control and categorical processing. The mechanisms through which implicit biases interface with behavior have received substantially less attention. If the primary function of implicit processes is to orchestrate behavioral responses, as originally proposed (e.g., Devine, 1989; Fazio et al., 1995), a focus on the pathways through which they affect behavior is critical. In the next section of this chapter, we turn our attention to this issue. In addressing the theoretical mechanisms of implicit bias, we consider neuroscience evidence suggesting distinct neurocognitive mechanisms underlying implicit stereotyping and evaluation that interface with behavioral responses in different ways, and then use this social neuroscience framework as a basis for discussing function.

Beyond Implicit–Explicit Correspondences: A Theoretical Framework for Relating Implicit Stereotyping and Evaluative Race Bias to Behavior

In our view, an impediment to understanding the function of implicit biases is that current theoretical models were not designed to account for multiple modes of implicit processing. That is, most social psychological models of racial bias assume that both prejudiced attitudes and stereotypic beliefs reflect semantic associations within a network of long-term memory, a view largely influenced by the cognitive approach to social psychology from which modern interest in implicit race bias has developed (Bodenhausen, Macrae, & Sherman, 1999; Devine, 1989; Dovidio et al., 1986; Fazio et al., 1995; Gaertner & McLaughlin, 1983; for reviews, see Hamilton & Sherman, 1994; Hamilton & Trolier, 1986; Sherman, 1996). According to these models, stereotypes represent associations in long-term memory between a social group (e.g., African Americans) and a trait attribute (e.g., the stereotype *lazy*). Prejudices toward social groups have been conceived in two slightly different ways according to the social cognition approach. Some theorists have conceived of prejudice as the net valence of these conceptual links (as discussed in Park & Judd, 2005). Others have posited that prejudice reflects the association between a mental representation of a social group (e.g., African Americans) and an evaluative description or category (e.g., *negative* or *unpleasant*; Fazio et al.; Greenwald et al., 1998). Racial associations are considered implicit when they become activated quickly through spreading activation along semantically related informational nodes, without intention and without conscious awareness of their activation (Bargh, 1994; Greenwald & Banaji, 1995). This "semantic network" model of implicit social cognition has provided a sufficient explanation for basic priming effects on judgments and behaviors and of implicit associations observed in reaction-time measures of implicit bias.

Although the semantic network model of implicit race bias has been enormously useful in explaining a wide range of phenomena, this theoretical explanation is limited in a few important respects. First, it assumes that implicit stereotyping and evaluative bias adhere to the same processing dynamics. That is, the semantic network view assumes that stereotypic and evaluative associations are learned, activated, changed, and controlled in the same manner. However, previous research suggests this might not be the case, such that evaluative forms of implicit bias are primarily driven by affective processes rather than semantic associations (e.g., Amodio, Harmon-Jones, et al., 2003; Phelps et al., 2000). Thus, the prevalent view in social cognition that implicit bias reflects a single underlying process does not correspond well to recent advances in the neuroscience literature elucidating multiple mechanisms underlying different forms of memory (e.g., episodic, procedural, affective, and semantic). Findings from this literature indicate that different forms of memory are often supported by different underlying neural structures (or networks of structures; Knowlton & Squire, 1994; Squire & Zola, 1996). Importantly, the neuroscience literature suggests that the dynamics of different forms of memory can vary considerably. For example, affective versus semantic associations may be learned, modulated, and unlearned through very different processes, and therefore it may be important to measure and conceive of affective and semantic associations independently. Finally, a third limitation of the semantic network explanation is that it is generally silent regarding the expression of implicit stereotypes and evaluative biases in behavior. That is, it has focused more on information processing characteristics and less on the interface with behavior. Given our previous suggestion that alternative neurocognitive systems may underlie implicit stereotyping versus evaluation, it is possible that these two forms of implicit bias are expressed through somewhat different sets of behavioral channels.

Does Implicit Evaluative Race Bias Fit with the Semantic Processing Model of Bias?

In considering the limitations of the semantic network explanation of implicit evaluation, our early collaborations raised questions of whether implicit evaluation is more accurately characterized as a semantic categorization according to positive/negative valence or a basic-level affective association (e.g., as in classical conditioning). Advances in the understanding of affective systems suggested that the amygdala, a neural structure comprising a set of nuclei in the medial temporal lobes, was critical for the acquisition of affective associations, as well as for affective responses to threatening stimuli, as determined by animal research (Davis, 1992; LeDoux, 1992), human lesion studies (Bechara, Tranel, Damasio, Adolphs, Rockland, & Damasio, 1995), functional neuroimaging (Breiter et al., 1996; Morris et al., 1996), and startle eyeblink research (Lang, Bradley, & Cuthbert, 1990) of normal humans. This body of work naturally led some prejudice researchers to ask whether these mechanisms might underlie implicit evaluative bias.

To examine whether implicit evaluative bias was related to basic-level affective systems, we used startle-eyeblink methodology to test whether exposure to Black faces would elicit greater amygdala activity, compared with exposure to White faces (Amodio, Harmon-Jones, et al., 2003). Although cognitive neuroscientists had previously reported data suggestive of a role for the amygdala in implicit race bias (Hart, Whalen, Shin, McInerney, Fischer, & Rauch, 2000; Phelps et al., 2000), the functional magnetic resonance imaging (fMRI) methods used by these researchers were unable to determine whether amygdala activity was associated with the initial activation or later modulation of implicit bias. This is because these early studies used blocked (vs. event-related) designs that were sensitive to sustained, tonic changes in amygdala activity, but not to phasic, event-related changes associated with the automatic response to a face. Neither of these previous studies found a main-effect difference in amygdala activity to Black faces versus White faces, but both indicated a potential relationship between the amygdala and race bias. Phelps et al. found that the degree of amygdala activity to Black versus White faces was significantly correlated with participants' scores on the IAT. Hart et al. found that the typically observed amygdala response to face presentations habituated more quickly for White faces than for Black faces.

Given the concern that fMRI is generally insensitive to the rapid activation associated with automatic race bias, we used the startle-eyeblink method of assessing amygdala activity related to implicit racial bias. The startle-eyeblink method permits temporally precise measurement of an affective response that is known to be modulated by changes in amygdala activity (see Lang et al., 1990, for a review), and therefore it can assess amygdala activity within the time frame of an automatic response. Results from our study suggested that, overall, amygdala activity was greater while participants viewed faces of Black people compared with White people (Amodio, Harmon-Jones, et al., 2003). Moreover, we found that startle-eyeblink responses varied as a function of participants' internal and external motivations to respond without prejudice in a pattern that replicated previously observed individual differences on measures of implicit evaluation (Devine et al., 2002) but not implicit stereotyping (Amodio, Stahlhut, & Devine, 2003). This pattern of results, combined with previous (Hart et al., 2000; Phelps et al., 2000) and subsequent (Cunningham, Johnson, Raye, Gatenby, Gore, & Banaji, 2004; Wheeler & Fiske, 2005) findings, suggested that implicit evaluative race bias may be best described as reflecting an affectively driven process rather than a semantic categorization made on the basis of valence (although this characterization does not preclude a semantic component playing a role in implicit evaluation). In interpreting our findings, we noted that by associating implicit evaluation with amygdala activation, researchers could then access the large body of knowledge regarding the dynamics of amygdala-based learning and memory to better understand how implicit evaluative race bias is learned, expressed, controlled, and potentially extinguished.

These initial studies of the role of the amygdala suggested that a clearer understanding of the mechanisms of implicit race bias might require a closer look at the underlying neurocognitive systems for learning and memory. To this end, we will next introduce a neurocognitive framework for understanding the constructs of implicit stereotyping and evaluation and their interface with behavior, and then suggest that this framework provides important clues for understanding the functions of implicit racial biases. As a first step, we highlight the distinction between implicit stereotyping and implicit evaluative race bias that is suggested by the cognitive neuroscience literature on memory and describe how this distinction may be critical for understanding how implicit processes affect behavior.

Cognitive Neuroscience of Memory

Interest in the potential dissociation between underlying systems for learning and memory dates back to the famous case study of HM, who, after surgical removal of the medial temporal lobes as treatment for epilepsy, was observed to have severe anterograde amnesia (Scoville & Milner, 1957). That is, HM was unable to form new episodic memories. Yet he retained previously established episodic memories (e.g., for people, places, and events encountered before surgery) and semantic knowledge, and could still form new long-term procedural (e.g., *motor*) memories, even while having no explicit memory for the learning episodes. From HM's case, researchers inferred that the hippocampus and surrounding medial temporal cortical structures supported a rather specific memory function—that of acquiring and consolidating new episodic memories. Subsequent research on neuropsychological patients and, more recently, neuroimaging research on normal subjects has focused on disentangling the multiple aspects of memory function and identifying their respective neural substrates.

Since the case of HM, cognitive psychologists and neuroscientists have made great strides in unpacking the complex subprocesses of memory. We suggest that a consideration of this literature may prove extremely useful for elucidating a host of social cognitive constructs, including implicit stereotyping and evaluative bias, which we focus on here. Figure 7.1 illustrates a common taxonomy of memory systems that are distinguishable on the basis of both their function and associated neuroanatomy. An initial distinction in this taxonomy, which represents

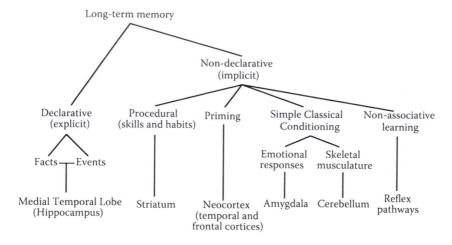

FIGURE 7.1 Diagram of independent memory systems and their putative neural substrates (adapted from Squire & Knowlton, 1994).

the convergence of several years of research across many laboratories, is between explicit and implicit memory. This distinction reveals that there are different forms of implicit memory, each localized to different neuroanatomical structures. This multisystem framework stands in contrast to long-standing popular conceptions in social psychology of two relatively homogeneous systems (e.g., implicit vs. explicit, automatic vs. controlled, associative vs. rule-based; e.g., Devine, 1989; Greenwald & Banaji, 1995; Smith & DeCoster, 2000). Indeed, interest in implicit forms of memory in social psychology is a relatively recent development, and few, if any, programs of social psychological research distinguish between various forms of implicit memory. Thus, there remains much to be gained from considering the roles of different components of memory in social processes. For the present concerns regarding the function of implicit race bias, Figure 7.1 illustrates a distinction between mechanisms for emotional classical conditioning versus semantic priming, which we have argued correspond largely with implicit evaluative race bias versus implicit stereotyping (Amodio & Devine, in press; Amodio et al., 2003). Here, we describe each in some detail:

Classical conditioning. Since Pavlov's (1927) famous observations, hundreds of studies have investigated the mechanisms of classical conditioning, a form of implicit affective memory (LeDoux, 2000). In particular, *fear conditioning*—associating an aversive unconditioned stimulus (US), such as an electrical shock, with a neutral conditioned stimulus (CS)—has been observed in hundreds of studies involving both animals (Davis, 1992) and humans (e.g., Adolphs, Tranel, Damasio, & Damasio, 1995; Phelps & LeDoux, 2005). A key feature of classical conditioning is that it is acquired rapidly, often after a single US-CS pairing (LeDoux, 1996). Extinction occurs only after repeated exposure to the CS in a safe (neutral or appetitive) context, and recent theorizing suggests extinction involves a role of the medial prefrontal cortex (mPFC; Sotres-Bayon, Cain, & LeDoux, 2006). However, extinction occurs very slowly, if at all (Gale et al., 2004), and exposure to previously extinguished US-CS pairs results in rapid and stronger "reconditioning" (Bouton, 1994). Hence, classical fear conditioning is an extremely tenacious form of implicit memory. Other forms of conditioning, such as Pavlovian reward conditioning, may follow a somewhat different pattern of extinction. Nevertheless, given that implicit racial biases tend to be negative in nature, and not rewarding, reward conditioning is not as relevant to the present theoretical analysis.

Neuroanatomical studies have established that classical fear conditioning is primarily dependent on the amygdala, as described above (Fendt & Fanselow, 1999; LeDoux, 1992). The amygdala is part of a set of "rapid response" structures activated and expressed within milliseconds of a potentially threatening event (Whalen, 1998), such that sensory information is relayed by the thalamus via a single synapse to the amygdala for initial processing while slower, more elaborative processing continues throughout the cortex. This "quick-and-dirty" quality makes fear conditioning an extraordinary mechanism for survival but, at the same time, relatively resistant to change and prone to generalization. In animals with less-developed neocortices, the amygdala is a primary mechanism for orchestrating adaptive behavior, such as basic approach/withdrawal responses. The amygdala and its associated subcortical structures accomplish this function through its strong connections to systems for initiating and monitoring behavior, including brainstem structures, the thalamus, hypothalamus, basal ganglia, and mPFC (Davis & Whalen, 2001).

Semantic priming. Semantic (or *conceptual*) priming refers to the facilitated processing of symbolic representations (see Gabrieli, 1998 for a review; Logan, 1990; Roediger & McDermott, 1993). Semantic associations of abstract concepts are believed to be represented in a parallel-distributed semantic network associated with higher-level cognition (McClelland & Rumelhart, 1985). The learning dynamics of conceptual priming are different from those of classical conditioning. Whereas affective conditioning may occur in a single trial, implicit semantic associations are learned across repeated stimulus pairings in a probabilistic fashion (Poldrack, Selco, Field, & Cohen, 1999; Reber & Squire, 1994; Shiffrin, 2003).

Neuroimaging studies consistently link semantic priming effects with distributed regions of neocortex (Squire & Zola, 1996), including regions of left dorsolateral prefrontal cortex (DLPFC, e.g., Blaxton, Bookheimer, Zeffiro, Figlozzi, Gaillard, & Theodore, 1996; Demb, Desmond, Wagner, Vaidya, Glover, & Gabrieli, 1995; Raichle et al., 1994; Wagner, Gabrieli, & Verfaellie, 1997) and temporal cortex (Rissman, Eliassen, & Blumstein, 2003; Schacter & Buckner, 1998; Squire, 1992). Importantly, classical conditioning and semantic priming are associated with different neural substrates, and research has demonstrated dissociations of classical fear conditioning and forms of semantic memory in brain-lesion patients (Bechara et al., 1995; LaBar, LeDoux, Spencer, & Phelps, 1995)

Unlike the amygdala, which is richly connected to neural regions that regulate one's autonomic and rapid behavioral responses to a threat, neocortical substrates of semantic priming appear to have more distal connections to basic reactive systems. Rather, the distributed nature of semantic priming effects in the neocortex suggests primary links to the higher-order processes of social cognition, self-reflection, and theory of mind (Amodio, Kubota, Harmon-Jones, & Devine, 2006; Frith & Frith, 1999; Kelley, Macrae, Wyland, Caglar, Inati, & Heatherton, 2002; Mitchell, Banaji, & Macrae, 2005; Ochsner et al., 2005; Saxe & Kanwisher, 2005; Yonelinas, 2002). Compared with classical fear conditioning, semantic priming is likely to have stronger influences on cognitive aspects of social judgment and decision-making and on approach-related action plans. In addition, this pattern of neural connectivity suggests that semantic priming should have greater influence on behaviors requiring more elaborate cognition than the conditioned fear response (Amodio & Frith, 2006). Thus, it appears that affective and semantic memory systems may have somewhat distinct effects on behavior, although it is important to note that these systems are coordinated and typically function in concert, appearing blended in outward verbal and behavioral responses.

Evidence for a Dissociation Between Implicit Stereotyping and Evaluative Race Bias

Given the precedence for distinct mechanisms underlying implicit affective versus semantic associations in the cognitive neuroscience literature, might this distinction correspond to implicit stereotyping and evaluative racial bias? Indeed, several past studies have featured measures that may be characterized as assessing either implicit stereotyping (e.g., Lepore & Brown, 1997; Spencer, Fein, Wolfe, Fong, & Dunn, 1998) or implicit evaluation (e.g., Amodio et al., 2003; see also Dovidio et al., 1997; Fazio et al., 1995; Greenwald et al., 1998 for relevant research on evaluation), or some combination of stereotyping and affect/evaluation (e.g., Dovidio et al., 1986; Kawakami, Dion, & Dovidio, 1998; Rudman, Ashmore, & Gary, 2001; Wittenbrink, Judd, & Park, 1997, 2001). The use of such measures suggests that both are valid constructs that have been studied somewhat independently, and that both forms of implicit bias are prevalent among White Americans, such that African Americans are typically associated with negative concepts and with the culturally defined stereotype content (Blair, 2001).

However, a survey of the implicit race bias literature reveals that very few studies have directly examined the *relation* between affective and cognitive aspects of implicit bias, and none have sought to obtain truly independent measures of implicit stereotyping versus evaluative bias. For example, although some research has made conceptual distinctions between evaluative and stereotyping components of implicit bias (e.g., Dovidio et al., 1986; Wittenbrink et al., 1997), the measures of implicit bias used in these studies did not permit the independent assessment of these two components. Similarly, theoretical distinctions between implicit stereotyping and evaluative race bias have been made in previous reviews (e.g., Fiske, 1998; Greenwald & Banaji, 1995; Greenwald, Banaji, Rudman, Farnham, Nosek, & Mellott, 2002), but such distinctions were not grounded in theorizing that directly addressed the relation between underlying cognitive and affective mechanisms. Granted, most expressions of race bias reflect a combination of affective and cognitive processes, and the most commonly reported African-American stereotypes are negative in valence (e.g., *unintelligent, hostile, poor, lazy,* and *dishonest*; Devine & Elliot, 1995). But despite the common concurrence of negative valence and stereotypic content of stigmatized groups, the cognitive neuroscience literature of memory suggests that underlying distinctions between affective and cognitive components may be very important for understanding mechanisms of implicit race biases and their effects on behavior.

As an initial step toward understanding how implicit stereotyping and evaluative bias may serve different functions in social behavior, we tested the hypothesis derived from findings in neuroscience that independent measures of implicit evaluative bias and stereotyping should be conceptually independent (Amodio & Devine, 2006). A major challenge in this research was to find measures of implicit responses capable of disentangling the effects of stereotyping and evaluation, given that stereotypes and evaluations are typically congruent in expressions of bias. Our strategy was to use two different Implicit Association Tests to separately assess implicit evaluation and stereotyping (Greenwald et al., 1998). To measure implicit evaluative race bias, we used the typical version of the IAT in which participants categorize faces according to race (Black vs. White) and words according to valence (pleasant vs. unpleasant). Importantly, the words included in this IAT were unrelated to stereotypes of either African Americans or White Americans (e.g., *love, sunshine, evil, cancer*).

To measure implicit stereotyping, we needed to use a version of the IAT in which participants could categorize words representing common African-American stereotypes in a way that did not involve evaluation. We designed a new version of the IAT that focused on two of the most common stereotypes ascribed to African Americans: *(un)intelligent* and *athletic* (Devine & Elliot, 1995). In keeping with the previously established design of the IAT, it was critical that words associated with intelligence and athleticism could be categorized along a single dimension. In our stereotyping IAT, we capitalized on a common colloquial dichotomy between "mental" and "physical." That is, intelligence words (e.g., *college*) were categorized as mental and athletic words (e.g., *basketball*) were categorized as physical. It is notable that words used in this IAT included other widely cited stereotypic constructs, including motivated (vs. lazy) and rhythmic. Stimulus words were pretested and chosen so that mental words were more strongly associated with White (vs. African) Americans, whereas physical words were more strongly associated with African (vs. White) Americans. Both sets of words were rated as being positive in valence, and therefore categorizations of the two groups of words could not be made on the basis of affective or evaluative associations. Participants in three separate studies completed both IATs in counterbalanced order, and responses were scored using the "improved" algorithm (Greenwald et al., 2003). Across studies, participants exhibited significant IAT effects on both measures, indicating associations between African Americans and both negative (vs. positive) evaluations and athletic (vs. intelligent) stereotypes, relative to White Americans. Importantly, however, across three studies, participants' levels of implicit stereotyping and evaluation were not correlated, consistent with the hypothesis that implicit evaluative bias and implicit stereotyping reflect conceptually independent underlying mechanisms.

Although it is possible the lack of correlation was observed because the stereotyping IAT measured a very specific subset of stereotypes, the fact that the target words included in the stereotyping IAT represented a range of the most-often-cited stereotypes of African Americans (intelligence, laziness, athleticism, rhythmicity/musicality; Devine & Elliot) renders this alternative explanation to be unlikely.

Considering the Functions of Implicit Stereotyping and Evaluative Race Bias

What does evidence for separate systems for affective versus semantic associations tell us about the function of implicit bias? From the functional perspective in behavioral neuroscience, the amygdala provides a critical mechanism for detecting whether a stimulus is safe. When threat is detected, the amygdala has the ability to interrupt ongoing deliberative behavior in order to orchestrate a fight-or-flight response. Much less is known regarding the function of implicit semantic memory because past work on this form of memory has focused primarily on its information processing characteristics. However, the research reviewed above suggests that it functions to enhance the efficiency of judgment and decision-making processes in light of previous experiences, to facilitate goal-directed action (e.g., Norris, 2006; Shiffrin, 2003). Importantly, it appears that implicit affective and semantic memory systems serve qualitatively different adaptive functions. Might this distinction in function correspond to the distinction between implicit stereotyping and evaluation?

Functional Accounts of Affective versus Cognitive Processes in the Context of Race Bias

Relatively little theorizing in social psychology has focused on the independent functions of implicit stereotyping and evaluative bias. It is notable that several theorists have proposed ways that implicit stereotyping may affect other aspects of cognition (e.g., as resource-saving devices, as means of legitimizing prejudices, or as relational guides; Hardin & Higgins, 1996; Jost et al., 2002; Macrae, Stangor, & Milne,

1994), yet few if any have addressed the mechanisms through which implicit stereotypes influence such processes. Research by Dovidio and his colleagues (Dovidio, Brigham, Johnson, & Gaertner, 1996; Dovidio, Esses, Beach, & Gaertner, 2004) has applied functional accounts of attitudes to begin to address functions of affective versus cognitive forms of explicit race bias. Millar and Tesser (1986, 1989) introduced the argument that cognitive and affective processes, broadly conceived, provide different functions in promoting adaptive behavior. They conceptualized their proposal in the context of attitudes, but their ideas translate easily to issues of prejudice and stereotyping. Millar and Tesser proposed that cognitive processes serve primarily to orchestrate instrumental behaviors (e.g., forming and acting on judgments and goals), whereas affective/evaluative processes serve primarily to orchestrate consumatory behaviors (e.g., appetitive or aversive behaviors). This perspective is consistent with the functional account of affective versus semantic memory systems described in the neuroscience literature.

Dovidio and his colleagues (Dovidio et al., 1996, 2004; Esses & Dovidio, 2002; see also Stangor, Sullivan, & Ford, 1991) applied the reasoning of Millar and Tesser (1986) to issues of prejudice and stereotyping. Dovidio et al. (1996) proposed that greater correspondences between assessments of race bias and behavior may be attained when the match between the affective versus cognitive nature of measures of race bias and behavior is taken into account. In a meta-analysis focusing on explicit forms of stereotyping and prejudice, Dovidio et al. (2004) found that affect-based self-report measures of race bias tended to predict basic affective and approach/avoidance responses (e.g., nonverbal behaviors and affective responses) toward African Americans, whereas cognition-based self-report measures of race bias tended to predict the endorsement of stereotypes and support for policies that disadvantage African Americans. This pattern of findings supported the idea that affective versus cognitive aspects of explicit racial bias may serve alternative functions in organizing intergroup behavior.

Dovidio et al.'s meta-analysis focused on explicit measures of race bias, yet extant findings from the implicit race bias literature are generally consistent with their conclusions (e.g., Ashburn-Nardo, Knowles, & Monteith, 2003; Dovidio et al., 2002, 1997; Fazio et al., 1995; McConnell & Leibold, 2001; Sekaquaptewa, Espinoza, Thompson, Vargas, & von Hippel, 2003; Wilson et al., 2000). As described above, implicit evaluative bias, which is typically negative in valence, has been shown to predict less friendly behavior toward a Black experimenter and less comfortable interracial interactions (Dovidio et al., 2002, 1997; Fazio et al.; McConnell & Leibold). By contrast, research has not examined the unique effects of implicit stereotyping on behavior. However, some research suggests that implicit activation of stereotypes (e.g., through subliminal priming) can lead to race-biased trait judgments of members of stigmatized racial groups (Devine, 1989; Gilbert & Hixon, 1991). What does this pattern reveal about the function of implicit bias? As suggested by the neuroscience literature, this pattern may indicate that implicit evaluations function to prepare one to respond behaviorally to a potential threat, whereas implicit stereotypes function to bias judgment and decision-making. However, this conclusion requires evidence that implicit evaluative race bias and stereotyping have unique and dissociable effects on behavior.

Evidence for Dissociable Effects of Implicit Stereotyping and Evaluative Bias on Behavior

On the basis of theorizing in social psychology (Dovidio et al., 1996, 2004; Millar & Tesser, 1986, 1989) and in behavioral neuroscience, we designed a set of studies to provide direct evidence that implicit evaluation and stereotyping have unique and dissociable effects on behavior (Amodio & Devine, 2006). The neuroscience literature suggests that amygdala-based memory processes interface strongly with basic-level behavioral systems (Davis, 1992), such as those that orchestrate approach/withdrawal behaviors and affective dispositions (Adolphs, 2003; Adolphs, Tranel, & Damasio, 1998). On the other hand, semantic memory systems appear to have fewer links to these basic-level behavioral systems, but rather are strongly connected to regions associated with person knowledge and social cognition (Frith & Frith, 2003; Rissman et al., 2003; Saxe, Carey, & Kanwisher, 2004) and, therefore, should play a larger role in judgments and decision-making, including the formation of interpersonal impressions (Amodio & Frith, 2006; Sherman & Klein, 1994). Therefore, we designed two studies to test the hypothesis that implicit evaluative bias should uniquely predict consumatory responses (e.g., behavioral approach vs. withdrawal), whereas implicit stereotyping should uniquely predict instrumental responses (e.g., forming trait impressions).

The first study was introduced to participants as examining their ability to form accurate inferences about a person's personality based on a writing sample. White participants in this study read an essay written by a student at a local area college. All participants read the same essay, which was somewhat poorly written, and were provided with a form listing demographic information indicating that the writer was male, 19 years old, and African American. After reading the essay, participants rated the general quality of the essay, and then rated their impression of the writer's personality traits and the extent to which they thought that the writer is someone they would be friends with. Lastly, participants completed the two IATs designed to measure implicit evaluative bias and stereotyping, as described above. Results indicated that higher implicit stereotyping scores predicted greater endorsement of stereotypical African-American personality traits, but not traits unaffiliated with African Americans. Implicit evaluation scores did not predict either class of trait ratings. By contrast, higher implicit evaluation scores predicted lower expectations that one would befriend the African-American writer, whereas implicit stereotyping scores were unrelated to expectations of friendship. These results supported our hypotheses regarding the unique behavioral effects of implicit stereotyping and evaluative bias and were consistent with the notion that implicit stereotyping and evaluation serve different functions in orchestrating intergroup behavior. However, a limitation of this study was that the outcome measures concerned relatively hypothetical situations of judging personality or forming a friendship, but did not assess actual behavioral responses. We therefore conducted a second study to replicate the basic finding in a more ecologically valid setting.

The second study was conducted in two ostensibly unrelated sessions. In the first session, participants completed the two IAT measures of implicit stereotyping and evaluative bias and were dismissed. A few weeks later, these participants were recruited to participate in the second session, in which they were led to believe they would interact with another participant (who happened to be African American) in an experiment involving cooperation. Participants were told that they and their partner would complete a set of tests assessing academic (math and verbal skills) and nonacademic (sports and popular culture) knowledge with the goal of achieving the highest possible combined score compared with other participants in the study. Participants were told that before meeting their partner, they would rate how well they expected themselves and their partner to perform on the different tests. Then they would meet their partner in another room to complete the tests. After they completed the initial ratings of expected performance, participants were led out into the hallway to wait for the test portion of the experiment. In the hallway, a row of eight chairs were lined up against the wall, with a jacket and backpack resting on the nearest chair. The experimenter explained that the partner had gone to the restroom and left his belongings (i.e., the jacket and backpack) on the chair. The participant was asked to have a seat until the partner returned. The seating distance chosen by the participant was surreptitiously recorded by the experimenter. Consistent with hypotheses, higher implicit stereotyping scores uniquely predicted expectations that the African-American partner would perform more poorly on the academic tasks, relative to the nonacademic tasks, whereas implicit evaluative bias scores were unrelated to these judgments. By contrast, implicit evaluation scores uniquely predicted the distance participants sat from the partner's coat and backpack in the row of chairs, such that participants with higher implicit evaluative race bias scores sat farther away. Implicit stereotyping scores were unrelated to seating distance. These results conceptually replicated the findings from the first study and, together, extended the finding that implicit stereotyping and evaluative bias reflect independent underlying mechanisms by demonstrating that they uniquely predict different discriminatory outcomes.

On the Functions of Implicit Evaluative Race Bias and Stereotyping

When we consider the constructs of implicit evaluative bias and stereotyping in terms of their broader underlying mechanisms and neural substrates, a clearer picture of their functions emerges. An important step in addressing questions about function requires that we distinguish between implicit stereotyping and implicit evaluation. Table 7.1 summarizes the key differences between implicit evaluative race bias and implicit stereotyping suggested by our review. Implicit evaluative race bias functions to alert us to a potential threat and to initiate behavior designed to either evade or confront the threat, and this response is typically manifested in increased interpersonal distance from the target of prejudice and feelings of anxiety.

Implicit stereotyping, on the other hand, functions to inform judgment and decision-making and the formation of goals, which serve to guide goal-directed action. In this way, implicit stereotypes can bias the types of impressions one may form of a member of a stigmatized group, or influence the way we might balance the pros and cons of a job applicant.

TABLE 7.1 Comparison of Features Associated with Implicit Evaluative Race Bias and Implicit Stereotyping

Implicit Evaluative Race Bias

Definition: Association between symbolic representation of stigmatized group member and affective response

Underlying mechanism: Classical conditioning

Likely neural substrate: The amygdala; related subcortical structures

Function: To detect potential threat and orchestrate rapid behavioral response to threat

Implicit Stereotyping

Definition: Associations between symbolic representations of stigmatized group member and semantic concepts (e.g., traits)

Semantic memory (e.g., conceptual priming)

Likely neural substrate: Distributed regions of neocortex; primarily temporal and posterior prefrontal cortex

Function: To facilitate information processing of a stimulus on the basis of previously learned information, as when forming impressions and making decisions, in order to serve goal-directed action.

A major goal of future research will be to determine just how mechanisms of implicit stereotyping and evaluative race bias interface. Clearly, implicit semantic and affective associations function in concert to direct behavior. Implicit racial evaluations and stereotypes are typically congruent, in that most stereotypic attributes of African Americans, for example, are negative. Similarly, recent findings from cognitive neuroscience and the nascent field of neuroeconomics suggest that implicit emotional responses linked to classical conditioning systems have biasing effects on judgment and decision-making, suggesting an interface between affective and semantic processes (De Martino, Kumaran, Seymour, & Dolan, 2006; Walter, Abler, Ciaramidaro, & Erk, 2005). In addition, appraisal theorists have long argued that semantic concepts provide labels for undifferentiated affective responses (e.g., Schachter & Singer, 1962; Schwarz & Clore, 1983). Although the neuroscience literature suggests that cognitive appraisal is not necessary for adaptive affect-driven behavior, such appraisals likely serve to modulate the impact of an affective response on cognitive processing. These possibilities reflect perennial questions about the interface of cognition and emotion. Addressing these classic questions within the context of implicit stereotyping and evaluative race bias may provide some fresh insights.

Implications of the Functional Analysis of Implicit Race Bias

Identifying the interpersonal functions of implicit evaluative race bias and stereotyping is the first step in designing strategies for reducing the effects of implicit bias on intergroup behavior. The next step is to apply what we know about function to better understand the situational moderators of implicit bias. For example, our social neuroscience analysis of implicit evaluative bias suggests that it functions to signal threat, in the case of an aversive cue, to prepare oneself for flight or flight. Thus, it is likely that the effects of implicit evaluative bias would be enhanced in anxiety-provoking situations (Lambert, Payne, Shaffer, Jacoby, Chasteen, & Khan, 2003). According to our theoretical analysis, implicit stereotyping should be less affected by feelings of anxiety. By contrast, implicit stereotypes appear to affect more cognitive aspects of judgment and decision-making, and thus their influence may be more susceptible to the effects of cognitive load than implicit evaluation. Future research will be needed to test these possibilities. Once researchers understand how different situational moderators have differential effects on the activation of implicit evaluative versus stereotyping biases, greater care can be taken to control and monitor situations in order to mitigate the effects of implicit bias on behavior.

Our social neuroscience analysis also leads us to predict that implicit evaluative bias may be more difficult to change than implicit stereotypes, given that that the putative classical conditioning mechanism underlying implicit evaluative bias is more tenacious and comprises a more than basic and highly entrained survival mechanism semantic priming. If implicit affective and semantic associations extinguish via different mechanisms, then implicit race bias reduction will be most successful when interventions target implicit stereotyping and implicit evaluative biases independently, a tack that echoes previous theorizing of explicit attitude change by Edwards (1990). The extant literature, however, does not permit a direct examination of this hypothesis, as most of the work has addressed reductions in implicit evaluative race bias or a mixture of implicit evaluation and stereotyping (see Kawakami, Dovidio, Moll, Hermsen, & Russin, 2000, for a focus on reducing implicit race stereotypes). Moreover, examination of the extant literature on reducing implicit evaluation has yielded mixed results and ultimately leads to more questions than answers concerning the mutability of implicit evaluative race bias.

Notably, however, some studies have produced reductions in the expression of implicit evaluative bias that in some cases have been relatively long-lasting (e.g., 24 hours). Reduction in evaluative implicit race bias has been observed, for example, after exposure to admired Blacks (Dasgupta & Greenwald, 2001), interaction with a nonprototypic Black (e.g., a Black experimenter; Lowery, Hardin, & Sinclair, 2001), rapid presentation of counterattitudinal information (Olson & Fazio, 2006; Rydell & McConnell, 2006), and surreptitiously adopting a smiling pose while observing pictures of Black individuals (Ito, Chiao, Devine, Lorig, & Cacioppo, 2006). However, questions remain regarding the specific processes by which implicit bias was reduced. Furthermore, it is not clear whether changes in responses on implicit measures in these studies reflect a change in the underlying associations or an increase in some aspect of regulation. Future research will need to sort out these issues. We hope that researchers will find the social neuroscience approach to be useful in addressing these questions, as it provides access to the large behavioral neuroscience literature concerning the different dynamics of acquisition and extinction associated with classical conditioning versus conceptual priming components of implicit associations.

Conclusion

The common theme running through chapters in this volume concerns the insights that may be gleaned from research on implicit measures about attitudes, such as their underlying representations and the pathways through which they relate to behavior. The area of stereotyping and prejudice has proven to be a rich context for exploring these issues. Just as early work suggested that there are great benefits to be gained by distinguishing between explicit and implicit forms of bias, we argue that similar benefits may be gained by distinguishing between stereotyping and evaluative forms of race bias. Furthermore, by expanding our analysis to include perspectives from the neuroscience literature, we are discovering that these distinct forms of implicit race bias, which our research suggests function to orchestrate different behavioral outcomes, are anchored in different neuroanatomical structures that give rise to independent processes. This integrative social neuroscience analysis has the potential to provide a more complete understanding of the origins of implicit racial biases and the challenges associated with reducing them.

References

Adolphs, R. (2003). Cognitive neuroscience of human social behaviour. *Nature Reviews Neuroscience, 4,* 165–178.

Adolphs, R., Tranel, D., & Damasio, A. R. (1998). The human amygdala in social judgment. *Nature, 393,* 470–474.

Adolphs, R., Tranel, D., Damasio, H., & Damasio, A. R. (1995). Fear and the human amygdala. *Journal of Neuroscience, 15,* 5879–5891.

Allport, G. W. (1954). *The nature of prejudice.* New York: Addison-Wesley.

Amodio, D. M., & Devine, P. G. (2006). Stereotyping and evaluation in implicit race bias: Evidence for independent constructs and unique effects on behavior. *Journal of Personality and Social Psychology, 91,* 652–661.

Amodio, D. M., & Frith, C. D. (2006). Meeting of minds: The medial frontal cortex and social cognition. *Nature Reviews Neuroscience, 7,* 268–277.

Amodio, D. M., Harmon-Jones, E., & Devine, P. G. (2003). Individual differences in the activation and control of affective race bias as assessed by startle eyeblink response and self-report. *Journal of Personality and Social Psychology, 84,* 738–753.

Amodio, D. M., Kubota, J. T., Harmon-Jones, E., & Devine, P. G. (2006). Alternative mechanisms for regulating racial responses according to internal vs. external cues. *Social Cognitive and Affective Neuroscience, 1,* 26–36.

Amodio, D. M., Stahlhut, C., & Devine, P. G. (2003). *Strategic concealment of race bias.* Unpublished manuscript.

Ashburn-Nardo, L., Knowles, M. L., & Monteith, M. J. (2003). Black Americans' implicit racial associations and their implications for intergroup judgment. *Social Cognition, 21,* 61–87.

Banaji, M. R. (2001). Implicit attitudes can be measured. In H. L. Roediger, J. S. Nairne, I. Neath, & A. Surprenant (Eds.), *The nature of remembering: Essays in honor of Robert G. Crowder* (pp. 117–150). Washington, DC: American Psychological Association.

Bargh, J. A. (Ed.). (1994). *The four horsemen of automaticity: Awareness, intention, efficiency, and control in social cognition.* Hillsdale, NJ: Lawrence Erlbaum Associates.

Bechara, A., Tranel, D., Damasio, H., Adolphs, R., Rockland, C., and Damasio, A. R. (1995). Double dissociation of conditioning and declarative knowledge relative to the amygdala and hippocampus in humans. *Science, 269,* 1115–1118.

Blair, I. (2001). Implicit stereotypes and prejudice. In G. Moskowitz (Ed.), *Cognitive social psychology: On the tenure and future of social cognition* (pp. 359–374). Mahwah, NJ: Erlbaum.

Blaxton, T. A., Bookheimer, S. Y., Zeffiro, T. A., Figlozzi, C. M., Gaillard, W. D., & Theodore, W. H. (1996). Functional mapping of human memory using PET: Comparisons of conceptual and perceptual tasks. *Canadian Journal of Experimental Psychology, 50,* 42–56.

Bodenhausen, G. V., Macrae, C. N., & Sherman, J. S. (1999). On the dialectics of discrimination: Dual processes in social stereotyping. In S. Chaiken & Y. Trope (Eds.), *Dual-process theories in social psychology* (pp. 271–290). New York: Guilford Press.

Bogardus, E. S. (1925). Measuring social distance. *Journal of Applied Sociology, 2*, 299–308.

Bouton, M. E. (1994). Conditioning, remembering, and forgetting. *Journal of Experimental Psychology: Animal Behavior Processes, 20*, 219–231.

Breiter, H. C., Rauch, S. L., Kwong, K. K., Baker, J. R., Weisskoff, R. M., Kennedy, D. N., Kendrick, A. D., Davis, T. L., Jiang, A., Cohen, M. S., Stern, C. E., Belliveau, J. W., Baer, L., O'Sullivan, R. L., Savage, C. R., Jenike, M. A., Rosen, B. R. (1996). Functional magnetic resonance imaging of symptom provocation in obsessive-compulsive disorder. *Archives of General Psychiatry, 53*, 595–606.

Crosby, F., Bromley, S., & Saxe, L. (1980). Recent unobtrusive studies of Black and White discrimination and prejudice: A literature review. *Psychological Bulletin, 87*, 546–563.

Cunningham, W. A., Johnson, M. K., Raye, C. L., Gatenby, J. C., Gore, J. C., & Banaji, M. R. (2004). Separable neural components in the processing of Black and White faces. *Psychological Science, 15*, 806–813.

Cunningham, W. A., Preacher, K. J., & Banaji, M. R. (2001). Implicit attitude measures: Consistency, stability, and convergent validity. *Psychological Science, 12*, 163–170.

Dasgupta, N., & Greenwald, A. G. (2001). On the malleability of automatic attitudes: Combating automatic prejudice with images of admired and disliked individuals. *Journal of Personality and Social Psychology, 81*, 800–814.

Davis, M. (1992). The role of the amygdala in fear and anxiety. *Annual Review of Neuroscience, 15*, 353–375.

Davis, M., & Whalen, P. J. (2001). The amygdala: Vigilance and emotion. *Molecular Psychiatry, 6*, 13–34.

De Martino, B., Kumaran, D., Seymour, B., & Dolan, R. J. (2006). Frames, biases, and rational decision-making in the human brain. *Science, 313*, 684–687.

Demb, J. B., Desmond, J. E., Wagner, A. D., Vaidya, C. J., Glover, G. H., & Gabrieli, J. D. E. (1995). Semantic encoding and retrieval in the left inferior prefrontal cortex: A functional MRI study of task difficulty and process specificity. *Journal of Neuroscience, 15*, 5870–5878.

Devine, P. G. (1989). Prejudice and stereotypes: Their automatic and controlled components. *Journal of Personality and Social Psychology, 56*, 5–18.

Devine, P. G., & Elliot, A. J. (1995). Are racial stereotypes really fading? The Princeton Trilogy revisited. *Personality and Social Psychology Bulletin, 21*, 1139–1150.

Devine, P. G., Plant, E. A., Amodio, D. M., Harmon-Jones, E, & Vance, S. L. (2002). The regulation of explicit and implicit race bias: The role of motivations to respond without prejudice. *Journal of Personality and Social Psychology, 82*, 835–848.

Dovidio, J. F., Brigham, J. C., Johnson, B. T., & Gaertner, S. L. (1996). Stereotyping, prejudice and discrimination: Another look. In C. N. McCrae, C. Stangor, & M. Hewstone (Eds.), *Stereotypes and stereotyping* (pp. 276–319). New York: Guilford Press.

Dovidio, J. F., Esses, V. M., Beach, K. R., & Gaertner, S. L. (2004). The role of affect in determining intergroup behavior: The case of willingness to engage in intergroup affect. In D. M. Mackie & E. R. Smith (Eds.), *From prejudice to intergroup emotions: Differentiated reactions to social groups* (pp. 153–171). Philadelphia: Psychology Press.

Dovidio, J. F., Evans, N., & Tyler, R. B. (1986). Racial stereotypes: The contents of their cognitive representations. *Journal of Experimental Social Psychology, 22*, 22–37.

Dovidio, J. F., & Gaertner, S. L. (Eds.). (1986). *Prejudice, discrimination, and racism.* San Diego: Academic Press.

Dovidio, J. F., Kawakami, K., & Gaertner, S. L. (2002). Implicit and explicit prejudice and interracial interaction. *Journal of Personality and Social Psychology, 82*, 62–68.

Dovidio, J. F., Kawakami, K., Johnson, C., Johnson, B., & Howard, A. (1997). On the nature of prejudice: Automatic and controlled processes. *Journal of Experimental Social Psychology, 33*, 510–540.

Dovidio, J. F., Kawakami, K., Smoak, N., & Gaertner, S. L. (in press). The nature of contemporary racial prejudice: Insight from implicit and explicit measures of attitudes. In R. E. Petty, R. H. Fazio, & P. Briñol (Eds.), *Attitudes: Insights from the new implicit measures.* Hillsdale, NJ: Erlbaum.

Edwards, K. (1990). The interplay of affect and cognition in attitude formation and change. *Journal of Personality and Social Psychology, 59*, 202–216.

Esses, V. M., & Dovidio, J. F. (2002). The role of emotions in determining willingness to engage in intergroup contact. *Personality and Social Psychology Bulletin, 28*, 1202–1214.

Fazio, R. H., Jackson, J. R., Dunton, B. C., & Williams, C. J. (1995). Variability in automatic activation as an unobtrusive measure of racial attitudes: A bona fide pipeline? *Journal of Personality and Social Psychology, 69*, 1013–1027.

Fazio, R. H., & Olson, M. A. (2003). Implicit measures in social cognition research: Their meaning and uses. *Annual Review of Psychology, 54*, 297–327.

Fendt, M., & Fanselow, M. S. (1999). The neuroanatomical and neurochemical basis of conditioned fear. *Neuroscience & Biobehavioral Reviews, 23*, 743–760.

Fiske, S. T. (Ed.). (1998). *Stereotyping, prejudice, and discrimination.* New York: McGraw-Hill.

Frith, C. D., & Frith, U. (1999). Interacting minds—A biological basis. *Science, 286,* 1692–1695.

Frith, U., & Frith, C. D. (2003). Development and neurophysiology of mentalizing. *Philosophical Transactions of the Royal Society of London Series B—Biological Sciences, 358,* 459–473.

Gabrieli, J. D. E. (1998). Cognitive neuroscience of human memory. *Annual Review of Psychology, 49,* 87–115.

Gaertner, S. L., & McLaughlin, J. P. (1983). Racial stereotypes: Associations and ascriptions of positive and negative characteristics. *Social Psychology Quarterly, 46,* 23–30.

Gale, G. D., Anagnostaras, S. G., Godsil, B. P., Mitchell, S., Nozawa, T., Sage, J. R., Wiltgen, B., & Fanselow, M. S. (2004). Role of the basolateral amygdala in the storage of fear memories across the adult lifetime of rats. *Journal of Neuroscience, 24,* 3810–3815.

Gilbert, D. T., & Hixon, J. G. (1991). The trouble of thinking: Activation and application of stereotypic beliefs. *Journal of Personality and Social Psychology, 60,* 509–517.

Gilbert, G. M. (1951). Stereotype persistence and change among college students. *Journal of Abnormal & Social Psychology, 46,* 245–254.

Greenwald, A. G., & Banaji, M. R. (1995). Implicit social cognition: Attitudes, self-esteem, and stereotypes. *Psychological Review, 102,* 4–27.

Greenwald, A. G., Banaji, M. R., Rudman, L. A., Farnham, S. D., Nosek, B. A., & Mellott, D. S. (2002). A unified theory of implicit attitudes, stereotypes, self-esteem, and self-concept. *Psychological Review, 109,* 3–25.

Greenwald, A. G., McGhee, D. E., & Schwartz, J. L. K. (1998). Measuring individual differences in implicit cognition: The implicit association test. *Journal of Personality and Social Psychology, 74,* 1464–1480.

Greenwald, A. G., Nosek, B. A., & Banaji, M. R. (2003). Understanding and using the Implicit Association Test: I. An improved scoring algorithm. *Journal of Personality and Social Psychology, 85,* 197–216.

Gregg, A. P., Seibt, B., & Banaji, M. R. (2006). Easier done than undone: Asymmetry in the malleability of implicit preferences. *Journal of Personality and Social Psychology, 90,* 1–20.

Hamilton, D. L., & Sherman, J. W. (1994). Stereotypes. In J. R. S. Wyer & T. K. Srull (Eds.), *Handbook of social cognition* (2nd ed., Vol. 2, pp. 1–68). Hillsdale, NJ: Erlbaum.

Hamilton, D. L., & Trolier, T. K. (Eds.). (1986). *Stereotypes and stereotyping: An overview of the cognitive approach.* San Diego: Academic Press.

Hardin, C. D., & Higgins E. T. (1996). Shared reality: How social verification makes the subjective objective. R. M. Sorrentino & E. T. Higgins (Eds.), *Handbook of motivation and cognition: Vol. 3. The interpersonal context* (pp. 28–84). New York: Guilford Press.

Hart, A. J., Whalen, P. J., Shin, L. M., McInerney, S. C., Fischer, H. K., & Rauch, S. L. (2000). Differential response in the human amygdala to racial outgroup vs. ingroup face stimuli. *NeuroReport: For Rapid Communication of Neuroscience Research, 11,* 2351–2355.

Hofmann, W., Gawronski, B., Gschwendner, T., Le, H., & Schmitt, M. (2005). A meta-analysis on the correlation between the Implicit Association Test and explicit self-report measures. *Personality and Social Psychology Bulletin, 31,* 1369–1385.

Ito, T. A., Chiao, K. W., Devine, P. G., Lorig, T. S., & Cacioppo, J. T. (2006). The influence of facial feedback on race bias. *Psychological Science, 17,* 256–261.

Jost, J. T., Pelham, B. W., & Carvallo, M. (2002). Non-conscious forms of system justification: Cognitive, affective, and behavioral preferences for higher status groups. *Journal of Experimental Social Psychology, 38,* 586–602.

Judd, C. M., Blair, I. V., & Chapleau, K. M. (2004). Automatic stereotypes vs. automatic prejudice: Sorting out the possibilities in the Payne (2001) weapon paradigm. *Journal of Experimental Social Psychology, 40,* 75–81.

Karlins, M., Coffman, T. L., & Walters, G. (1969). On the fading of social stereotypes: Studies in three generations of college students. *Journal of Personality and Social Psychology, 13,* 1–16.

Katz, D., & Braly, K. (1933). Racial stereotypes of one hundred college students. *Journal of Abnormal and Social Psychology, 28,* 280–290.

Kawakami, K., Dion, K. L., & Dovidio, J. F. (1998). Racial prejudice and stereotype activation. *Personality and Social Psychology Bulletin, 24,* 407–416.

Kawakami, K., Dovidio, J. F., Moll, J., Hermsen, S., & Russin, A. (2000). Just say no (to stereotyping): Effects of training in the negation of stereotypic associations on stereotype activation. *Journal of Personality and Social Psychology, 78,* 871–888.

Kelley, W. M., Macrae, C. N., Wyland, C. L., Caglar, S., Inati, S., & Heatherton, T. F. (2002). Finding the self? An event-related fMRI study. *Journal of Cognitive Neuroscience, 14,* 785–794.

Knowlton, B. J., & Squire, L. R. (1994). The information acquired during artificial grammar learning. *Journal of Experimental Psychology: Learning, Memory, and Cognition, 20,* 79–91.

Kruglanski, A. W., Erbs, H. P., Pierro, A., Mannetti, L., Chun W. Y. (2006). On Parametric Continuities in the World of Binary Either Ors. *Psychological Inquiry, 17,* 153–165.

LaBar, K. S., LeDoux, J. E., Spencer, D. D., & Phelps, E. A. (1995). Impaired fear conditioning following unilateral temporal lobectomy in humans. *Journal of Neuroscience, 15,* 6846–6855.

Lambert, A. J., Payne, B. K., Shaffer, L. M., Jacoby, L. L., Chasteen, A., & Khan, S. (2003). Stereotypes as dominant responses: On the "social facilitation" of prejudice in anticipated public contexts. *Journal of Personality and Social Psychology, 84,* 277–295.

Lang, P. J., Bradley, M. M., & Cuthbert, B. N. (1990). Emotion, attention, and the startle reflex. *Psychological Review, 97,* 377–395.

LeDoux, J. E. (1992). Emotion and the amygdala. In J. P. Aggleton (Ed.), *The amygdala: Neurobiological aspects of emotion, memory, and mental dysfunction* (pp. 339–351). New York: Wiley-Liss.

LeDoux, J. E. (1996). *The emotional brain: The mysterious underpinnings of emotional life.* New York: Simon & Schuster.

LeDoux, J. E. (2000). Emotion circuits in the brain. *Annual Review of Neuroscience, 23,* 155–184.

Lepore, L., & Brown, R. (1997). Category and stereotype activation: Is prejudice inevitable? *Journal of Personality and Social Psychology, 72,* 275–287.

Lippman, W. (1922). *Public opinion.* New York: Macmillan.

Logan, G. D. (1990). Repetition priming and automaticity: Common underlying mechanisms? *Cognitive Psychology, 22,* 1–35.

Lowery, B. S., Hardin, C. D., & Sinclair, S. (2001). Social influence effects on automatic racial prejudice. *Journal of Personality and Social Psychology, 81,* 842–855.

Macrae, C. N., Milne, A. B., & Bodenhausen, G. V. (1994). Stereotypes as energy-saving devices: A peek inside the cognitive toolbox. *Journal of Personality and Social Psychology, 66,* 37–47.

Macrae, C. N., Stangor, C., & Milne, A. B. (1994). Activating social stereotypes: A functional analysis. *Journal of Experimental Social Psychology, 30,* 370–389.

McClelland, J. L., & Rumelhart, D. E. (1985). Distributed memory and the representation of general and specific information. *Journal of Experimental Psychology: General, 114,* 159–188.

McConahay, J. B. (1986). Modern racism, ambivalence, and the modern racism scale. In J. F. Dovidio & S. L. Gaertner (Eds.), *Prejudice, discrimination, and racism* (pp. 91–125). Orlando, FL: Academic Press.

McConahay, J. B., Hardee, B. B., & Batts, V. (1981). Has racism declined in America? It depends upon who is asking and what is asked. *Journal of Conflict Resolution, 25,* 563–579.

McConnell, A. R., & Leibold, J. M. (2001). Relations among the Implicit Association Test, discriminatory behavior, and explicit measures of racial attitudes. *Journal of Experimental Social Psychology, 37,* 435–442.

Millar, M. G., & Tesser, A. (1986). Effects of affective and cognitive focus on the attitude-behavior relation. *Journal of Personality and Social Psychology, 51,* 270–276.

Millar, M. G., & Tesser, A. (1989). The effects of affective-cognitive consistency and thought on the attitude behavior relation. *Journal of Experimental Social Psychology, 25,* 189–202.

Mitchell, J. P., Banaji, M. R., & Macrae, C. N. (2005). The link between social cognition and self-referential thought in the medial prefrontal cortex. *Journal of Cognitive Neuroscience, 17,* 1306–1315.

Morris, J. S., Frith, C. D., Perrett, D. I., Rowland, D., Young, A. W., Calder, A. J., & Dolan, A. J. (1996). A differential neural response in the human amygdala to fearful and happy facial expressions. *Nature, 383,* 812–815.

Nisbett, R. E., & Wilson, T. D. (1977). Telling more than we can know: Verbal reports on mental processes. *Psychological Review, 84,* 231–259.

Norris, D. (2006). The Bayesian reader: Explaining word recognition as an optimal Bayesian decision process. *Psychological Review, 113,* 327–357.

Ochsner, K. N., Beer, J. S., Robertson, E. R., Cooper, J. C., Gabrieli, J. D. E., Kihlstrom, J. F., & D'Esposito, M. (2005). The neural correlates of direct and reflected self-knowledge. *Neuroimage, 28,* 797–814.

Olson, M. A., & Fazio, R. H. (2001). Implicit attitude formation through classical conditioning. *Psychological Science, 12,* 413–417.

Olson, M. A., & Fazio, R. H. (2006). Reducing automatically activated racial prejudice through implicit evaluative conditioning. *Personality and Social Psychology Bulletin, 32,* 421–433.

Olsson, A., Ebert, J. P., Banaji, M. R., & Phelps, E. A. (2005). The role of social groups in the persistence of learned fear. *Science, 309,* 785–787.

Olson, M. A., & Fazio, R. H. (in press). Implicit and explicit measures of attitudes: The perspective of the MODE model. In R. E. Petty, R. H. Fazio, & P. Briñol (Eds.), *Attitudes: Insights from the new implicit measures.* Hillsdale, NJ: Erlbaum.

Park, B., & Judd, C. M. (2005). Rethinking the link between categorization and prejudice within the social cognition perspective. *Personality and Social Psychology Review, 9,* 108–130.

Pavlov, I. (1927). *Conditioned reflexes.* New York: Oxford University Press.

Payne, B. K. (2005). Conceptualizing control in social cognition: How executive functioning modulates the expression of automatic stereotyping. *Journal of Personality and Social Psychology, 89,* 488–503.

Payne, B. K., Cheng, C. M., Govorun, O., & Stewart, B. D. (2005). An inkblot for attitudes: Affect misattribution as implicit measurement. *Journal of Personality and Social Psychology, 89,* 277–293.

Phelps, E. A., & LeDoux, J. E. (2005). Contributions of the amygdala to emotion processing: from animal models to human behavior. *Neuron, 48,* 175–187.

Phelps, E. A., O'Connor, K. J., Cunningham, W. A., Funayama, E. S., Gatenby, J. C., Gore, J. C., & Banaji, M. R. (2000). Performance on indirect measures of race evaluation predicts amygdala activation. *Journal of Cognitive Neuroscience, 12,* 729–738.

Poldrack, R.A., & Foerde, K. (2007). Category learning and the memory systems debate. *Neuroscience and Biobehavioral Reviews, 32,* 197–205.

Poldrack, R. A., Selco, S. L., Field, J. E., & Cohen, N. J. (1999). The relationship between skill learning and repetition priming: Experimental and computational analyses. *Journal of Experimental Psychology: Learning, Memory, and Cognition, 25,* 208–235.

Raichle, M. E., Fiez, J. A., Videen, T. O., MacLeod, A.-M. K., Pardo, J. V., Fox, P. T., & Petersen, S. E. (1994). Practice-related changes in human brain functional anatomy during nonmotor learning. *Cerebral Cortex, 4,* 8–26.

Reber, P. J., & Squire, L. R. (1994). Parallel brain systems for learning with and without awareness. *Learning & Memory, 1,* 217–229.

Rissman, J., Eliassen, J. C., & Blumstein, S. E. (2003). An event-related fMRI investigation of implicit semantic priming. *Journal of Cognitive Neuroscience, 15,* 1160–1175.

Roediger, H. L., & McDermott, K. B. (1993). Implicit memory in normal human subjects. In F. Boller & J. Grafman (Eds.), *Handbook of neuropsychology* (Vol. 8, pp. 63–131). Amsterdam: Elsevier.

Rudman, L. A., Ashmore, R. D., & Gary, M. L. (2001). "Unlearning" automatic biases: The malleability of implicit prejudice and stereotypes. *Journal of Personality and Social Psychology, 81,* 856–868.

Rydell, R. J., & McConnell, A. R. (2006). Understanding implicit and explicit attitude change: A system of reasoning analysis. *Journal of Personality and Social Psychology, 91,* 995–1008.

Saxe, R., Carey, S., & Kanwisher, N. (2004). Understanding other minds: Linking developmental psychology and functional neuroimaging. *Annual Review of Psychology, 55,* 87–124.

Saxe, R., & Kanwisher, N. (Eds.). (2005). *People thinking about thinking people: The role of the temporo-parietal junction in "Theory of Mind."* New York: Psychology Press.

Schachter, S., & Singer, J. (1962). Cognitive, social, and physiological determinants of emotional state. *Psychological Review, 69,* 379–399.

Schacter, D. L., & Buckner, R. L. (1998). On the relations among priming, conscious recollection, and intentional retrieval: Evidence from neuroimaging research. *Neurobiology of Learning and Memory, 70,* 284–303.

Schwarz, N., & Clore, G. L. (1983). Mood, misattribution, and judgments of well-being: Informative and directive functions of affective states. *Journal of Personality and Social Psychology, 45,* 513–523.

Scoville WB, Milner B. 1957. Loss of recent memory after bilateral hippocampal lesions. *Journal of Neurology, Neurosurgery, & Psychiatry, 20,* 11–21.

Sekaquaptewa, D., Espinoza, P., Thompson, M., Vargas, P., & von Hippel, W. (2003). Stereotypic explanatory bias: Implicit stereotyping as a predictor of discrimination. *Journal of Experimental Social Psychology, 39,* 75–82.

Sherman, J. W. (1996). Development and mental representation of stereotypes. *Journal of Personality and Social Psychology, 70,* 1126–1141.

Sherman, J. W., & Klein, S. B. (1994). Development and representation of personality impressions. *Journal of Personality and Social Psychology, 67,* 972–983.

Shiffrin, R. M. (2003). Modeling memory and perception. *Cognitive Science, 27,* 341–378.

Sigall, H., & Page, R. (1971). Current stereotypes: A little fading, a little faking. *Journal of Personality and Social Psychology*, Vol. 18, 247–255.

Smith, E. R., & DeCoster, J. (2000). Dual-process models in social and cognitive psychology: Conceptual integration and links to underlying memory systems. *Personality and Social Psychology Review, 4*, 108–131.

Sotres-Bayon, F., Cain, C. K., & LeDoux, J. E. (2006). Brain mechanisms of fear extinction: Historical perspectives on the contribution of prefrontal cortex. *Biological Psychiatry, 60*, 329–336.

Spencer, S. J., Fein, S., Wolfe, C. T., Fong, C., & Dunn, M. A. (1998). Automatic activation of stereotypes: The role of self-image threat. *Personality and Social Psychology Bulletin, 24*, 1139–1152.

Squire, L. R. (1992). Memory and the hippocampus: A synthesis from findings with rats, monkeys, and humans. *Psychological Review, 99*, 195–231.

Squire, L. R., & Knowlton, B. J. (Eds.). (1994). *The organization of memory*. Reading, MA: Addison-Wesley/Addison-Wesley Longman.

Squire, L. R., & Zola, S. M. (1996). Ischemic brain damage and memory impairment: A commentary. *Hippocampus, 6*, 546–552.

Stangor, C., Sullivan, L. A., & Ford, T. E. (1991). Affective and cognitive determinants of prejudice. *Social Cognition, 9*, 359–380.

Vanman, E. J., Paul, B. Y., Ito, T. A., & Miller, N. (1997). The modern face of prejudice and structural features that moderate the effect of cooperation on affect. *Journal of Personality and Social Psychology, 73*, 941–959.

Wagner, A. D., Gabrieli, J. D. E., & Verfaellie, M. (1997). Dissociations between familiarity processes in explicit recognition and implicit perceptual memory. *Journal of Experimental Psychology: Learning, Memory, and Cognition, 23*, 305–323.

Walter, H., Abler, B., Ciaramidaro, A., & Erk, S. (2005). Motivating forces of human actions. Neuroimaging reward and social interaction. *Brain Research Bulletin, 67*, 368–381.

Whalen, P. J. (1998). Fear, vigilance, and ambiguity: Initial neuroimaging studies of the human amygdala. *Current Directions in Psychological Science, 7*, 177–188.

Wheeler, M. E., & Fiske, S. T. (2005). Controlling racial prejudice: Social-cognitive goals affect amygdala and stereotype activation. *Psychological Science, 16*, 56–63.

Wilson, T. D., Lindsey, S., & Schooler, T. Y. (2000). A model of dual attitudes. *Psychological Review, 107*, 101–126.

Wittenbrink, B., Judd, C. M., & Park, B. (1997). Evidence for racial prejudice at the implicit level and its relationship with questionnaire measures. *Journal of Personality and Social Psychology, 72*, 262–274.

Wittenbrink, B., Judd, C. M., & Park, B. (2001). Evaluative versus conceptual judgments in automatic stereotyping and prejudice. *Journal of Experimental Social Psychology, 37*, 244–252.

Woodmansee, J. J., & Cook, S. W. (1967). Dimensions of verbal racial attitudes: Their identification and measurement. *Journal of Personality and Social Psychology, 7*, 240–250.

Yonelinas, A. P. (2002). The nature of recollection and familiarity: A review of 30 years of research. *Journal of Memory and Language, 46*, 441–517.

Zinner, L. R., Harmon-Jones, E., Devine, P. G., & Amodio, D. M. (2003). Prejudice level and aversive conditioning to Black and White faces [Abstract]. *Psychophysiology, 40*, S92.

Section IV

Self-Esteem

8

Digging for the Real Attitude[*]
Lessons from Research on Implicit and Explicit Self-Esteem

Ap Dijksterhuis
Luuk W. Albers
Karin C.A. Bongers

Introduction

It has been argued that attitude formation and attitude expression are more reminiscent of architecture than of archeology. Rather than uncovering true, deeper beliefs and values, people's attitudinal expressions are the result of often distorted, temporary constructions created on the spot (Bettman, Luce, & Payne, 1998; see also Dijksterhuis & Nordgren, 2006). Researchers administer questionnaires aimed at measuring how people think about themselves, about George W. Bush, or about chocolate chip cookies, and how people construct what we call *attitudes*. Just as there is nothing wrong with architecture, there is nothing inherently wrong with measuring attitudes with questions, that is, *explicitly*. Usually, the goal behind measuring attitudes is to predict behavior, and indeed, explicitly measured attitudes often do: We are fairly positive about ourselves, helping us to navigate life reasonably well; we vote against George W. Bush; and we eat way too many chocolate chip cookies.

Still, there is something about this practice that makes it somewhat unsatisfactory. If an old manuscript suggests an undiscovered tomb in the Egyptian desert, we send archeologists to find it, rather than ask architects to re-create the tomb on the basis of some vague descriptions. Have you ever been in a museum, staring in awe at some beautiful piece of old art, only then to discover (by reading the brochure that

[*] This research was supported by NWO-Vernieuwingsimpuls 016.025.030.

was handed to you at the entrance) that you are looking at a replica? The real statue created by Michelangelo is in an area inaccessible to the public, and you are looking at a copy made in 1987 in some Florentine factory. Even in such cases, when a replica looks exactly like the original, looking at it just does not feel quite right. It is nothing more than a minor nuisance, and it certainly does not spoil your entire day, but you would prefer to see the real thing.

One way to look at explicitly measured attitudes is to assume that what one measures is all there is. Explicitly measured attitudes are what they are, and there are no such things as underlying, "real" attitudes. This is unsatisfactory, of course, as we know enough about unconscious affective and cognitive processes to assume that a 7 on a 9-point Likert scale about chocolate chip cookies is not just something hovering in the air. It must come from somewhere, somehow. It may be the result of a construction process, but we hope it is, at least to some extent, influenced by deeper psychological forces. Hence, an alternative viewpoint that is more realistic (and much more exciting) is to assume that there are such things as "real" attitudes and that what we assess with attitude measures is at least in part based on this real thing. Sure, due to poor construction we routinely end up with very poor replicas, indeed much more reminiscent of the work of architects working on the basis of vague descriptions than of contemporary Florentine artists who can make a detailed copy of the Michelangelo statue. After all, when we answer a questionnaire we often have not much to work with other than perhaps some vague hints, such as subtle affective reactions or old memories of past behavior. Still, somewhere in that Egyptian desert is the real thing we are looking for. Some process sparked by our millions of brain cells represents that real attitude.

The observation that attitudes are more the result of architecture than of archeology was made before psychologists started to develop *implicit* attitude measures. In our view, the creation and development of implicit measures is of paramount importance, because it fundamentally changes the way we think (at least it should) about attitudes. In the present chapter, we will argue that implicit attitude measurement is not just another style of architecture. Instead, we will review evidence (and present some new evidence) strongly suggesting that implicit measurement reflects archeology: amateur archeology with limited equipment, perhaps, but archeology.

In this chapter, we focus on arguably the most important attitude we have: self-esteem, or the attitude toward the self. However, our hope is that our thinking is generalizable to attitudes in general. Most of this chapter deals with research on the relation between three protagonists: explicitly measured self-esteem, implicitly measured self-esteem, and what we until now called "the real thing." We start out by defining what we conceive of as this hypothesized "real" attitude and by proposing three hypotheses concerning the relationship between explicit and implicit self-esteem. We then discuss relevant research with the aim to differentiate between these hypotheses and to decide which of the three is the most plausible. Before we end with some conclusions, we present an experiment that we recently conducted.

Three Alternative Hypotheses on the Relation Between Explicit and Implicit Self-Esteem

A chapter that features the term "the real thing" too often runs the risk of alienating a scientific audience (but perhaps attracting people from the music industry!), so a definition is in order. The "real" attitude, we propose, is the evaluative "tone" that is automatically activated upon the perception of the attitude object (Bargh, Chaiken, Govender, & Pratto, 1992; Fazio, Sanbonmatsu, Powell, & Kardes, 1986). With more multifaceted or important attitude objects, it is perhaps more appropriate (see, e.g., Cacioppo, Crites, Berntson, & Coles, 1993) to define the attitude as the sum of the various evaluative tones that are automatically activated. It is a proposed underlying construct constituting the core of the attitude, sitting there waiting to be excavated. It is itself undisturbed by biasing processes that occur when the attitude is measured or verbalized, but at the same time it feeds such processes. From now on, we call it the *core attitude* or *core self-esteem* (see also Dijksterhuis, 2004).

What is the relation between this core attitude and implicitly and explicitly measured attitudes? Or, to turn to self-esteem, is there one core self-esteem that is related to both measures of implicit and explicit self-esteem? And if so, how are they related? Let us briefly discuss three possible hypotheses pertaining to this relation.

1. *The independence hypothesis.* According to this hypothesis, implicit and explicit self-esteem are independent constructs. They happen to partly share their name, they happen to be about the same object, but they are unrelated. Both implicitly measured self-esteem and explicitly measured self-esteem are based on their own underlying core construct. Implicit self-esteem could be based on the automatically activated evaluative tone, whereas explicit self-esteem could be

based on the evaluative tone that becomes apparent only when one explicitly or consciously reflects on the self.

2. *The equal relationship hypothesis.* This hypothesis states that implicit and explicit self-esteem are related because they are both related to the same core attitude, the one defined above. They are simply different manifestations of this core. In addition, the two manifestations do not differ as to how well they represent that core. They measure a different aspect, but generally do so equally well.

3. *The hierarchy hypothesis.* This hypothesis also assumes that implicit and explicit self-esteem are related because they are both related to the same core. However, here implicit measures of self-esteem better represent core self-esteem than explicit measures of self-esteem. That is, implicit self-esteem digs deeper and more closely approaches the hidden Egyptian tomb. This hypothesis also implies that what we measure explicitly is partly based on (and can be partly predicted by) what we find when we measure implicitly.*

In what follows, we will make a (stepwise) comparison between the plausibility of the hypotheses by reviewing evidence. We will start with comparing the independence hypothesis with the remaining two, the equal relationship hypothesis and the hierarchy hypothesis, whereby no distinction will be made between latter two yet.

Before we move on, it should be noted that although we only review evidence on self-esteem, the three hypotheses encompass possible relations between implicit and explicit measures of attitudes in general.

---

* One could raise the reverse hierarchy hypothesis, namely that explicit self-esteem is closer to the core than implicit self-esteem. However, such a hypothesis is at odds with so much psychological knowledge that it cannot be seriously defended. Conscious processes are by necessity preceded by unconscious processes (at least when one maintains that consciousness resides in the brain). Hence, one cannot be conscious of an attitude ("I really like chocolate chip cookies.") without preceding unconscious attitudinal processes (such as positive affective reactions upon the perception of chocolate chip cookies). One way out would be to say that attitudes are only attitudes when they are conscious and that the core is to be found in consciousness. Such a conceptualization is possible, but it would have some undesirable consequences, the least problematic being that the current chapter would be superfluous (as implicit attitudes would not exist). However, it would also render the attitude concept rather limp as we are not that often consciously aware of our attitudes, except perhaps during communication. Of course, we are very often aware of attitude objects ("Ah, cookies!") but not of the attitude. In addition, the reverse hierarchy hypothesis would severely constrain the number of cases where attitudes can predict behavior, because even if we are consciously aware of an attitude, this very often happens only after we act (such as when one mindlessly reaches for chocolate chip cookies, and only then thinks, "I'm fond of them!").

Indeed, versions of both the independence hypothesis and the equal relationship hypothesis shine through in work on racial attitudes (i.e., prejudice; Dovidio, Kawakami, Johnson, Johnson, & Howard, 1997). Likewise, the hierarchy hypothesis is in part based on, and fully in line with, the work by Fazio and colleagues on the MODE model (see, e.g., Fazio, 1990; Chapter 2, this volume). The MODE model also views an attitude as a "core" that can be automatically activated, whereby implicit measures are more proximal indicators of these automatically activated attitudes than more downstream explicit measures.

Are Implicit and Explicit Self-Esteem Related?

If we find evidence for the notion that implicit and explicit self-esteem are related, this implies that both the equal relationship hypothesis and hierarchy hypothesis are more plausible than the independence hypothesis. In our view, there are currently three relevant sets of research findings. First, quite a number of researchers have directly investigated the relation between implicit and explicit self-esteem by assessing correlations between the two. A second fruitful avenue is to investigate whether the same specific levels of implicit and explicit self-esteem have the same or comparable consequences for other psychological processes. A third way to shed light on the relationship between implicit and explicit self-esteem is to see if there are experimental manipulations that affect both implicit and explicit self-esteem in comparable ways.

Are implicit and explicit self-esteem correlated? The answer is "sort of." Some researchers did not find correlations (Baccus, Baldwin, & Packer, 2004; Bosson, Swann, & Pennebaker, 2000; Jordan, Spencer, Zanna, Hoshino-Browne, & Correll, 2003; Spalding & Hardin, 1999), others did find significant correlations (DeHart, Pelham, & Tennen, 2006; Greenwald & Farnham, 2000), yet others found significant correlations in some experimental conditions or in some samples and not in others (Jones, Pelham, Mirenberg, & Hetts, 2002; Koole, Dijksterhuis, & van Knippenberg, 2001; Pelham, Koole, Hardin, Hetts, Seah, & DeHart, 2005). Various people have concluded that implicit and explicit self-esteem correlate "weakly at best." There is no arguing with that conclusion, and on the basis of the current state of affairs we cannot say much about the plausibility of the independence hypothesis. Rejecting the independence hypothesis would have required more consistent correlations between explicit and implicit self-esteem. On the other hand, given that some researchers did find significant correlations, the data cannot be interpreted as support for the independence hypothesis either.

It may be noted that the generally low correlations between measures of implicit and explicit self-esteem are at least in part caused by the fact that implicit measures are still in a developing stage. Their reliability is often low (Bosson et al. 2000), and it is not fully understood yet what exactly drives the effects of some of the implicit measures. Recently, various researchers have proposed improvements to various measures of implicit self-esteem. Both Karpinski (2004) and Albers, Dijksterhuis, and Rotteveel (in press) suggested improvements to implicit measures of self-esteem that will likely result in more meaningful correlations between implicit and explicit measures of self-esteem. Wentura, Kulfanek, and Greve (2005) even proposed an interesting new measure that alleviates some problems of other measures. Such initiatives to strengthen implicit measures of self-esteem give rise to optimism, and it is likely that researchers will obtain higher and more consistent correlations between implicit and explicit self-esteem in the future.

Do implicit and explicit self-esteem have comparable consequences? Explicit self-esteem is known to be predictive of many things, but arguably the best-known fact is that it is related to how people cope with negative experiences: High levels of explicit self-esteem help people cope with negative feedback or negative experiences in general. High explicit self-esteem forms a "buffer" against stress and experiences of failure (see, e.g., Dodgson & Wood, 1998; Shrauger & Rosenberg, 1970; Steele, 1988). For instance, it has been observed that people with low explicit self-esteem exhibit stronger emotional reactions after failure than people with high explicit self-esteem (Brown & Dutton, 1995) and that people with low explicit self-esteem demonstrate impaired motivation after failure, whereas individuals with high self-esteem generally do not (e.g., Di Paula & Campbell, 2002; Shrauger & Rosenberg).

After only a few years of research on implicit self-esteem, we can safely conclude that implicit self-esteem has comparable consequences indeed. Spalding and Hardin (1999) demonstrated that low implicit self-esteem individuals show more anxiety during a confronting interview than high implicit self-esteem individuals. Greenwald and Farnham (2000) showed that implicit self-esteem is negatively related to motivation after failure such that people with low self-esteem show a stronger decrease in motivation than people with high self-esteem. Baccus et al., (2004) demonstrated that people with high implicit self-esteem show less aggression after an insult than people with lower implicit self-esteem.

Finally, Dijksterhuis (2004) showed that people with high implicit self-esteem show no changes in mood after negative feedback, whereas people with lower implicit self-esteem report a more negative mood after negative feedback. Indeed, high implicit self-esteem is a buffer against negative experiences, just as high explicit self-esteem is. These findings strongly suggest that implicit and explicit self-esteem are to some extent related, rendering the independence hypothesis less plausible.

Do (some) experimental manipulations have the same effects on implicit and explicit self-esteem? Currently, there are two areas of research that indeed suggest this to be the case. First, threats to the self have been known to decrease explicit self-esteem. For instance, both Dutton and Brown (1997) and Heatherton and Polivy (1991) found that people report lower explicit self-esteem after negative intelligence feedback. In recent years, various researchers have reported comparable consequences of threats to the self on implicit self-esteem. Jones et al., (2002) asked participants to write about a negative aspect of their personality and demonstrated that this lowered implicit self-esteem. In addition, Dijksterhuis (2004) gave participants (bogus) negative intelligence feedback and found that it lowered participants' score on an implicit measure of self-esteem. It is also known that people engage in self-affirming behavior in order to repair "dents" in their self-esteem. And again, engaging in self-affirmation after threat has been shown to restore both explicit (Steele, Spencer, & Lynch, 1993) as well as implicit self-esteem (Koole, Smeets, van Knippenberg, & Dijksterhuis, 1999).

Second, it has been demonstrated that both explicit self-esteem and implicit self-esteem can be changed by evaluative conditioning (Baccus et al., 2004; Dijksterhuis, 2004; Riketta & Dauenheimer, 2003). Evaluative conditioning (see De Houwer, Thomas, & Baeyens, 2001, for a review) is a technique in which is an attitude object (the conditioned stimulus, or CS [plural CSi]) is repeatedly paired with either a positive or a negative stimulus (the unconditioned stimulus, or US [plural USi]). After a number of pairings, the CS takes on the valence of the USi. In our view, evaluative conditioning is fascinating because it changes an attitude at its core. Earlier, we defined the core attitude as the evaluative tone (or tones) that becomes automatically activated upon the perception of the attitude object. And it is this evaluative tone that evaluative conditioning works on directly.

The procedures used by the different researchers differed only subtly. Baccus et al. (2004) presented participants with self-relevant words (such as their own names) on a computer screen, and in the experimental condition the words were followed by smiling faces. In a control condition, self-relevant words were randomly paired with smiling, frowning, and neutral faces. Dijksterhuis (2004) presented participants repeatedly with the word *I* in the experimental condition followed by positive adjectives. In the control condition, neutral adjectives followed the word I. In some of the experiments, all this information was presented subliminally. Riketta and Dauenheimer (2003) followed almost exactly the same procedure, except that whereas in the experiments by Dijksterhuis the adjectives immediately followed the word I, in the Riketta and Dauenheimer experiments the word I and the positive adjectives were presented simultaneously. Both Baccus et al. (2004) and Dijksterhuis (2004) assessed implicit self-esteem after the evaluative conditioning procedure, whereas Riketta and Dauenheimer measured self-esteem explicitly. Crucially, in all sets of studies it was found that evaluative conditioning increased self-esteem.*

Where does this leave things? Although the findings on correlations between implicit and explicit self-esteem are inconclusive, other evidence is not. First, high (and low) implicit and explicit self-esteem have comparable consequences for how people deal with negative experiences. Second, various experimental manipulations (threat to the self, evaluative conditioning) have the same effect on implicit as on explicit self-esteem. In our view, this makes the independence hypothesis untenable. There is some sort of relation between implicit and explicit self-esteem. Put differently, they must, at least to some extent, represent the same underlying core.

Is Implicit Self-Esteem Closer to the Core than Explicit Self-Esteem?

Now that we have rejected the independence hypothesis, we can begin to analyze which of the two remaining hypotheses is the most plausible. Is the equal relationship hypothesis, whereby (measures of) explicit and implicit self-esteem represent the underlying core attitude equally well (or equally poorly), the best descriptor of the current state of affairs? Or are the relevant findings better described by the hierarchy hypothesis, stating that implicit measures of self-esteem represents core self-esteem better?

---

* It should be noted that we take the liberty here to interpret the Riketta and Dauenheimer findings in terms of evaluative conditioning. The authors themselves favored a different explanation for their findings.

In order for the hierarchy hypothesis to trump over the equal relationship hypothesis, it has to be proven that explicit self-esteem is more
dissociated from the core attitude than implicit self-esteem. If this is
true, it should be possible to demonstrate why this dissociation is indeed
more pronounced. As our opening lines suggested, explicit attitudes
are often active constructions, more reminiscent of architecture than of
archeology. A prediction one can derive from the conceptualization of
explicit self-esteem as a construction process is that, because constructive processes are easier to change than underlying representations,
explicit self-esteem must be easier to change than implicit self-esteem.
Another way to differentiate between the two hypotheses is to examine
the construction process itself. Is there evidence for the architectural
aspect of explicit self-esteem? Can we find evidence for biasing psychological forces that leads explicit self-esteem away from its underlying
core? In what follows, we first look at the changeability of explicit and
implicit self-esteem. Later, we examine the evidence for the notion that
explicit self-esteem is a construction partly based on biasing processes
that are not related to the core attitude.

Is explicit self-esteem easier to change than implicit self-esteem? We
already discussed evidence that shows that both implicit and explicit
self-esteem can be changed, at least for a brief period of time, by various experimental manipulations. However, what can we say about more
enduring changes as a result of major life events?

There is indeed some evidence for a greater flexibility of explicit self-
esteem. Hetts and Pelham (2003) found people whose birthday was
overlooked reported low implicit self-esteem, whereas their explicit
self-esteem was on a normal level. One could assume that when one's
birthday is overlooked, this initially has negative consequences for both
implicit and explicit self-esteem. However, due to the assumed nature of
explicit self-esteem as more of an active construction process, explicit
self-esteem can be easier brought to more normal levels than implicit
self-esteem. Although we concede that this interpretation of the findings of Hetts and Pelham is somewhat speculative, other research
from Hetts, Pelham, and colleagues more firmly support the hierarchy
hypothesis. Hetts, Sakuma, and Pelham (1999) assessed implicit and
explicit self-esteem among Asian-Americans who immigrated relatively recently. They reasoned that such major life events would affect
both explicit and implicit self-esteem, but that it is more likely, due to
the nature of explicit self-esteem measures, that explicit self-esteem
changes more quickly than implicit self-esteem. This is exactly what
they found. Whereas recent immigrants still demonstrated low implicit

self-esteem, their explicit self-esteem soon appeared to be back to normal levels. Fully in line with the hierarchy hypothesis, they concluded that conscious constructions are more malleable than "deeper" unconscious representations (see also DeHart et al., 2006).

Is explicit self-esteem a construction process? One could argue that explicit self-esteem must largely be a construction process, simply because people do not have much conscious access to deeper, unconscious processes. Following Nisbett and Wilson (1997) one could reasonably assume that explicit self-esteem (or explicit measures in general) relies on introspective processes to an extent that is unwarranted and perhaps even unrealistic. We simply do not know how we truly feel about ourselves, so we have no choice but to engage in construction. We are architects working with poor and vague instructions.

Pelham et al. (2005) recently reported evidence supporting this idea. They reasoned that some people may have better access to how they truly feel about themselves than others. Now the better people have access to core self-esteem, the less need there is for construction. That means that, assuming implicit self-esteem reflects core self-esteem better than explicit self-esteem, implicit self-esteem and explicit self-esteem should correlate higher among people who have better access to their core self-esteem. Pelham et al. reasoned this could well mean that gender moderates the correlation between implicit and explicit self-esteem. After all, aren't women generally better at accessing their deeper feelings than men? Socialization processes make women trust their feelings and intuitions more (Pacini & Epstein, 1999), and we know that women are generally better than men in expressing their emotions (e.g., Lakoff, 1990). Pelham et al. compared six samples from three different countries and indeed confirmed their prediction. Among men, explicit and implicit self-esteem did not correlate in any of the samples, whereas significant correlations were found in all samples for women (ranging in size from .11 to .51).

Other evidence for explicit self-esteem as a construction comes from studies suggesting that explicit self-esteem assesses factors other than the core attitude toward the self. For example, various researchers have found that explicit self-esteem correlates significantly with style of self-presentation, impression management, and self-deception (Greenwald & Farnham, 2000; Jordan et al., 2003; Raskin, Novacek, & Hogan, 1991). These findings support the hierarchy hypothesis. Explicit self-esteem may be assessing a mixture of core self-esteem and various essentially unrelated motives. The finding that explicit self-esteem is correlated with self-deception is especially interesting. The higher one's explicit self-esteem, the greater the possibility that people's construction work reflects an attempt to fool oneself.

If one is willing to assume that motivated construction takes effort, one can derive a straightforward prediction from the notion that explicit self-esteem correlates with various motives. Obviously, the people whose explicit self-esteem does not reflect core self-esteem are the ones who have to engage in effortful strategies to maintain this inconsistency. Specifically, people with high explicit self-esteem but low implicit self-esteem are the true construction workers. They engage in self-presentation and self-deception; thus, they expend the most effort. Conversely, given that implicit self-esteem represents this core attitude quite well, people with comparable explicit self-esteem and implicit self-esteem (both high or both low) do not engage in much construction and, hence, do not expend much effort.

There is indeed some evidence that maintaining high self-esteem in the face of negative experiences requires work. People have to "explain things away," for instance by changing the way they interpret experiences or by making self-serving attributions (e.g., Crocker & Major, 1989; Pelham, DeHart, & Carvallo, 2003). Importantly, however, there is evidence that this is especially true for people who want to maintain high explicit self-esteem in the face of low implicit self-esteem (Bosson, Brown, Ziegler-Hill, and Swann, 2003; Jordan et al. 2003; McGregor & Marigold, 2003; see also Chapter 9, this volume).

Bosson et al. (2003) investigated two groups of participants. They compared both people with high explicit and implicit self-esteem and people with high explicit but low implicit self-esteem (often called *fragile* or *defensive self-esteem*; see, e.g., Kernis, 2003). They found that people with low implicit self-esteem engaged more in unrealistic optimism. In addition, they found evidence that supports the notion that high explicit self-esteem can be related to self-deception. Participants were presented with four personality profiles about themselves ranging from highly unflattering to highly flattering. They were then asked to rate the accuracy of each of the profiles (that were allegedly written by clinical psychology students), and as it turned out, participants with low implicit and high explicit self-esteem rated the very flattering profile as more descriptive of themselves than participants with both high explicit and implicit self-esteem. The different profiles are given in the appendix to the Bosson et al. article, and this makes the data even more interesting, as the flattering profile is indeed rather extreme, including the phrase "knows that affection and admiration from others are well-deserved" (p. 183).

Jordan et al. (2003) distinguished between the same two groups: people whose explicit and implicit self-esteem are high versus people whose explicit self-esteem is high, while their implicit self-esteem is low. They first established that people with low implicit self-esteem showed more narcissistic behavior. In later experiments, they obtained more direct evidence for the idea that maintaining high explicit self-esteem based on low implicit self-esteem takes effort. They demonstrated that individuals with high explicit but low implicit self-esteem showed much more defensive behavior. They engaged more in ingroup bias, they demonstrated more prejudice when threatened, and they put more effort in dissonance reduction.

McGregor and Marigold (2003) investigated effects of personal uncertainty on "compensatory conviction." *Conviction* refers to the extremity and certainty of important personal attitudes, and *compensatory conviction* is the tendency to increase the extremity of such attitudes and the commitment with which such attitudes are held. People under uncertainty generally show compensatory conviction, but McGregor and Marigold showed that this is especially true for people with low implicit and high explicit self-esteem. That is, relative to people with both high implicit and explicit self-esteem, people with low implicit and high explicit self-esteem engaged in more compensatory conviction regarding such moral topics as the death penalty or abortion.

The work by Jordan and colleagues (Chapter 9, this volume) on people with low implicit and high explicit self-esteem is consistent with our reasoning. Moreover, their analysis sheds some more light on why people with low implicit and high explicit self-esteem have to engage in defensive effort. Jordan et al. reason that implicit self-esteem is not so much unconscious as it is preconscious. Sometimes, especially in the face of threats, people become aware of their (low level of) implicit self-esteem. This fleeting awareness is assumed to be aversive among people with low implicit and high explicit self-esteem, leading to what they call "nagging doubts." These nagging doubts, in turn, will motivate defensive effort. Jordan et al. present some interesting first evidence for their reasoning in this volume.

To conclude, the research on people with high explicit and low implicit self-esteem clearly shows that maintaining high explicit self-esteem when implicit self-esteem is low is, at least sometimes, hard work—construction work. In general, the evidence for explicit self-esteem as a construction process with many inherent biases is strong, rendering the hierarchy hypothesis more plausible than the equal relation hypothesis.

Finding Support for the Hierarchy Hypothesis

With the hierarchy hypothesis coming out as the most plausible, in the last part of this chapter we try to corroborate the hierarchy hypothesis by discussing (and to some extent testing) the support for a few hypotheses derived from the hierarchy hypothesis. The first hypothesis following from the hierarchy hypothesis is that there should be an asymmetry in frequency of occurrence of different combinations of implicit and explicit self-esteem. That is, we can predict that the combination high explicit/low implicit self-esteem is more common than the combination low explicit/high implicit self-esteem. The second hypothesis pertains to the fact that, if we assume explicit self-esteem is a construction, variations in the degree to which people engage in active construction should affect the relation between implicit and explicit self-esteem. That is, we expect implicit and explicit self-esteem to correlate higher when there is less construction. Both hypotheses will be further discussed, starting with the asymmetry hypothesis.

Is there an asymmetry? First, let us make the rather safe assumption that the construction process underlying explicit self-esteem biases explicit self-esteem more often in a positive rather than in a negative fashion. After all, people are known to be motivated to see themselves (and have others see them) in a positive light. This was already suggested earlier by the finding that explicit self-esteem is correlated with self-presentation style, self-deception, and impression management (Greenwald & Farnham, 2000; Jordan et al., 2003; Raskin et al., 1991). It may certainly be the case that people strategically report low explicit self-esteem (perhaps because they want to come across as modest), but this is likely to be relatively rare.

If this reasoning is correct we should be able to witness the following asymmetry: For people with incongruent implicit and explicit self-esteem (i.e., one is high, the other low), the combination low implicit/high explicit self-esteem should occur much more often, or among many more people, than the combination high implicit/low explicit self-esteem. People with high implicit self-esteem are seldom motivated to report low explicit self-esteem, whereas low implicit self-esteem individuals may often report relatively high explicit self-esteem (even if, as we have seen, it is often hard work). Now is there such an asymmetry?

One problem is that whether one finds support for this asymmetry or not depends on where one draws the line. When do we categorize implicit self-esteem and explicit self-esteem as truly low or truly high?

The evidence for the hypothesized asymmetry is, up to this point, only suggestive. First, various people have made the same prediction (Epstein, 1983; O'Brien & Epstein, 1988; Kernis, 2003). Others have argued that the combination of high implicit/low explicit self-esteem is indeed uncommon in Western cultures but not in Asian cultures (see Kitayama & Uchida, 2003, for a brief review). Kitayama and Uchida reported that the combination of high implicit/low explicit self-esteem can be found among Western participants but only (or at least mostly) under highly specified measuring circumstances. Concretely, Western participants only showed the high implicit/low explicit self-esteem com-bination in the context of close, interdependent relations. Perhaps also telling is the fact that the combination low implicit/high explicit has been named—as defensive or fragile self-esteem—and its consequences have been investigated by an increasing number of research groups (e.g., Bosson et al., 2003; Jordan et al., 2003; Kernis; McGregor & Marigold, 2003), whereas the combination of high implicit/low explicit self-esteem has received relatively little attention (for exceptions, see Chapter 9, this volume; Kitayama & Uchida). Still, we concede that research is needed to more strongly corroborate this hypothesized asymmetry.

Variations in construction and the relation between implicit and explicit self-esteem. The second hypothesis derived from the hierar-chy hypothesis is much easier to test. If explicit self-esteem is partly a construction process guiding people away from core self-esteem and, therefore, also from implicit self-esteem, it means that the less con-struction there is, the more explicit self-esteem should correlate with implicit self-esteem. After all, the less construction there is, the better explicit self-esteem should represent core self-esteem.

Koole et al. (2001) have reported supportive evidence for this hypoth-esis. In one experiment, they first assessed people's implicit self-esteem. Later they measured explicit self-esteem and they measured the time it took participants to complete the explicit self-esteem items. They hypothesized that the longer people would take to complete the mea-sure of explicit self-esteem, the more they engaged in active construc-tion. By measuring response times they assessed natural variations in people's degree of construction. They then divided the participants in two groups: fast responders and slow responders. In support of the hier-archy hypothesis, for fast responders the correlation between explicit and implicit self-esteem was high (.51), whereas for slow responders there was no correlation at all (−.06). In sum, the less people engaged in active construction during assessment of explicit self-esteem, the more explicit self-esteem correlated with implicit self-esteem.

In another experiment, Koole et al. (2001) manipulated rather than measured construction. Again, they first measured participants' implicit self-esteem. Subsequently, explicit self-esteem was assessed and this was done either under cognitive load or not. Obviously, cognitive load prevents people from engaging in too much active construction, and the experimenters predicted that explicit self-esteem would correlate with implicit self-esteem under load, but not necessarily under normal conditions. Indeed, this is what they found. The correlation between explicit and implicit self-esteem was high under load (.48) and absent under normal conditions (–.15). This fully supports the hierarchy hypothesis.

Further Support for the Hierarchy Hypothesis: An Experiment

The experiment we report here extends the experiments reported by Koole et al. (2001). Again, we tried to manipulate the extent to which participants would engage in active construction processes biasing explicit self-esteem away from core self-esteem. Before participants completed measures of implicit and explicit self-esteem, we subliminally primed half of our participants with the goal to be honest. This was done under the guise of a lexical decision task whereby experimental participants were subliminally presented with words such as *honest*, *sincere*, and *true*. Control participants were not presented with words related to honesty. We then measured implicit self-esteem by name-letter preferences and explicit self-esteem with Heatherton and Polivy's (1991) State Self-Esteem Scale (SSES).* We tested three hypotheses.

Hypothesis 1. The first hypothesis is the most important and the most straightforward. Assuming that explicit self-esteem is in part the result of a construction process biasing the view of the self in a positive way, the goal to be honest should lead people to engage in this biased construction to a lesser extent. The goal to be honest should lead reported explicit self-esteem to be more strongly related to core self-esteem and, therefore, to implicit self-esteem. This means that the correlation between the measures of implicit self-esteem and explicit self-esteem should be higher for people with a primed honesty goal than for control participants.

---

* The order in which implicit self-esteem and explicit self-esteem were administered was counterbalanced. Order did not affect the results.

Hypothesis 2. The advantage of the SSES is that explicit self-esteem is divided into three subscales: appearance self-esteem, performance self-esteem, and social self-esteem. Hypothesis 2 pertains to these subscales. One could argue that the extent to which people can positively construct self-esteem differs for the different subscales. After all, reality constraints differ between the different domains they represent. Appearance self-esteem is probably the hardest to strategically bias in a positive way. We can maintain that our attractiveness is on par with that of Brad Pitt or Jennifer Lopez, but it does not make sense. It's a form of absurd self-deception and we know it. A mild form of self-deception is likely to be easier in the domain of performance self-esteem. The truth is still to some extent objective, but at least one can easily switch between different domains ("Yes, I lost a game of Trivial Pursuit against friends, but I had an A+ for Intro Social Psychology!"). Social self-esteem is, with the exception of extreme cases perhaps, likely the easiest one to steer toward rosiness. One can think about many different relationships, and it is often possible to flexibly interpret social behavior ("His insult was not personal, he must have been in an awful mood."). If this reasoning is valid, this would mean that, for people without an honesty goal, appearance self-esteem correlates highest with implicit self-esteem, whereas social self-esteem correlates lowest with implicit self-esteem. For participants with an honesty goal, these differences should disappear.

Hypothesis 3. Assuming that explicit self-esteem, although partly constructed, does to some extent represent core self-esteem, this should also be true for the three subscales. If participants primed with honesty engage less in construction, their self-esteem should better reflect core self-esteem (as reflected in Hypothesis 1). As this should be true for all subscales, it follows that the different subscales should "converge" toward core self-esteem and, therefore, also to each other. Hence, the correlations between the subscales should be higher among people primed with honesty.

In total, 71 undergraduate students participated in the experiment, 37 in the control condition, 34 in the honesty-prime condition. The correlations pertaining to the hypotheses are listed in Table 8.1. As can be seen, Hypothesis 1 was supported, although the difference just failed to reach significance. As predicted, we found a high correlation between explicit and implicit self-esteem after honesty priming, and no such correlation for control participants. Hypothesis 2 also received support in that, for control participants, the correlation between implicit self-esteem and appearance self-esteem was highest, whereas the cor-

TABLE 8.1 Correlations Between Implicit and Explicit Self-Esteem (and Its Subscales) and Between the Subscales As a Function of Condition

	Honesty	Control	Difference (p – one-tailed)
Correlations with Implicit SE			
Overall explicit SE	.54*	.21	< .06
Appearance	.41*	.33*	ns
Performance	.45*	.16	< .09
Social	.48*	.05	< .03
Correlations among Subscales			
Appearance–Performance	.63*	.51*	ns
Appearance–Social	.70*	.42*	< .02
Performance–Social	.77*	.68*	ns

* *p* = < .05

relation between implicit self-esteem and social self-esteem was lowest. The honesty prime significantly increased the correlation between implicit self-esteem and social self-esteem and between implicit self-esteem and performance self-esteem (although this latter effect was marginally significant), whereas the honesty prime did not affect the correlation between implicit self-esteem and appearance self-esteem. Finally, Hypothesis 3 also received support. Correlations between subscales were generally higher under honesty conditions than under control conditions, with one of them reaching conventional levels of significance. As predicted, the different subscales converged because the honesty prime decreased the amount of construction work.

In sum, although some of the evidence was statistically somewhat weak, the results support the hierarchy hypothesis. The effects of priming of the honesty goal were exactly as predicted.

Conclusion

To conclude, the hierarchy hypothesis best describes the relation between implicit and explicit self-esteem. Both explicit and implicit self-esteem are, in part, based on the same underlying construct: what we called core self-esteem. However, due to the fact that explicit self-esteem is often the consequence of active and biased construction processes, it represents core self-esteem less well than implicit self-esteem. Furthermore, as implicit self-esteem represents core self-esteem better, explicit self-esteem can be partly predicted by implicit self-esteem. In addition, it was shown (in line with Koole et al., 2001) that the correlation between explicit and implicit self-esteem can be increased by interfering with the active construction process that explicit self-esteem is partly based on.

Before ending, we would like to remark that we do not see implicit self-esteem as an infinitely better construct than explicit self-esteem. In addition, we certainly do not argue that we should stop using the latter. Such a claim would clearly be unwarranted. The relation between explicit and implicit self-esteem is often so weak that it clearly pays off to investigate both and to scrutinize combinations of consistent and inconsistent combinations, as interesting recent research clearly shows. Another reason for not solely relying on implicit self-esteem is the fact that measures of implicit self-esteem are in a sense still in a developing stage. For some measures, the underlying processes driving its effects are not fully understood. Although some important improvements have been proposed recently (Albers et al., in press; Karpinski, 2004; Wentura et al., 2005), there is still quite some work to be done to optimize implicit measurement.

However, we do want to maintain that explicit self-esteem is a less pure form of self-esteem. In addition to being less pure, though, it is also more rich and multifaceted. It is, in part, construction rather than excavation work. It only weakly reflects core self-esteem, and it is affected by self-deception, impression management, and self-presentation style. However, this inherent richness is not in itself problematic; after all, explicit self-esteem predicts quite a number of psychological processes very well.

To recapitulate, both explicit and implicit self-esteem clearly have their value, also in an Egyptian desert. Measuring explicit self-esteem may be architecture, but it is pretty good architecture with means we are familiar with. Measuring implicit self-esteem, on the other hand, is sincere archeology, but with equipment that still leaves things to be desired.

References

Albers, L. W., Dijksterhuis, A., & Rotteveel, M. (in press). Towards optimizing the name letter test as a measure of implicit self-esteem. *Self and Identity*.

Baccus, J. R., Baldwin, M. W., & Packer, D.J. (2004). Increasing implicit self-esteem through classical conditioning. *Psychological Science, 15,* 498–502.

Bargh, J. A., Chaiken, S., Govender, R., & Pratto, F. (1992). The generality of the automatic evaluation effect. *Journal of Personality and Social Psychology, 62,* 893–912.

Bettman, J. R., Luce, M. F., & Payne, J.W. (1998). Constructive consumer choice processes. *Journal of Consumer Research, 25,* 187–217.

Bosson, J. K., Brown, R. P., Zeigler-Hill, V., & Swann, W. B. (2003). Self-enhancement tendencies among people with high explicit self-esteem: The moderating role of implicit self-esteem. *Self and Identity, 2,* 169–187.

Bosson, J. K., Swann, W. B., Jr., & Pennebaker, J. W. (2000). Stalking the perfect measure of implicit self-esteem: The blind men and the elephant revisited. *Journal of Personality and Social Psychology, 79,* 631–643.

Brown, J. D., & Dutton, K. A. (1995). The thrill of victory, the complexity of defeat: Self-esteem and people's emotional reactions to success and failure. *Journal of Personality and Social Psychology, 68,* 712–722.

Cacioppo, J. T., Crites, S. L., Jr., Berntson, G. G., & Coles, M. G. H. (1993). If attitudes affect how stimuli are processed, should they not affect the event-related brain potential? *Psychological Science, 4,* 108–112.

Crocker, J., & Major, B. (1989). Social stigma and self-esteem: The self-protective properties of stigma. *Psychological Review, 96,* 608–630.

DeHart, T., Pelham, B. W., & Tennen, H. (2006). What lies beneath: Parenting style and implicit self-esteem. *Journal of Experimental Social Psychology, 42,* 1–17.

De Houwer, J., Thomas, S., & Baeyens, F. (2001). Associative learning of likes and dislikes: A review of 25 years of research on human evaluative conditioning. *Psychological Bulletin, 127,* 853–869.

Dijksterhuis, A. (2004). I like myself but I don't know why: Enhancing implicit self-esteem by subliminal evaluative conditioning. *Journal of Personality and Social Psychology, 86,* 345–355.

Dijksterhuis, A., & Nordgren, L. F. (2006). A theory of unconscious thought. *Perspectives on Psychological Science, 1,* 95–109.

Di Paula, A., & Campbell, J. D. (2002). Self-esteem and persistence in the face of failure. *Journal of Personality and Social Psychology, 83,* 711–723.

Dodgson, P. G., & Wood, J. V. (1998). Self-esteem and the cognitive accessibility of strength and weaknesses after failure. *Journal of Personality and Social Psychology, 75,* 178–197.

Dovidio, J. F., Kawakami, K., Johnson, C., Johnson, B., & Howard, A. (1997). On the nature of prejudice: Automatic and controlled processes. *Journal of Experimental Social Psychology, 33,* 510–540.

Dutton, K. A., & Brown, J. D. (1997). Global self-esteem and specific self-views as determinants of people's reactions to success. *Journal of Personality and Social Psychology, 73,* 139–148.

Epstein, S. (1983). The unconscious, the preconscious, and the self-concept. In J. Suls & A. Greenwald (Eds.), *Psychological perspectives on the self* (Vol. 2, pp. 219–247). Hillsdale, NJ. Lawrence Erlbaum.

Fazio, R. H. (1990). Multiple processes by which attitudes guide behavior: The MODE model as an integrative framework. In M. P. Zanna (Ed.), *Advances in experimental social psychology* (Vol. 23, pp. 75–109). New York: Academic Press.

Fazio, R. H., Sanbonmatsu, D. M., Powell, M. C., & Kardes, F. R. (1986). On the automatic activation of attitudes. *Journal of Personality and Social Psychology, 50*, 229–238.

Greenwald, A. G., & Farnham, S. D. (2000). Using the Implicit Association Test to measure self-esteem and self-concept. *Journal of Personality and Social Psychology, 79*, 1022–1038.

Heatherton, T. F., & Polivy, J. (1991). Development and validation of a scale for measuring state self-esteem. *Journal of Personality and Social Psychology, 60*, 895–910.

Hetts, J. J., & Pelham, B. W. (2001). A case for the nonconscious self-concept. In G. B. Moskowitz (Ed.), *Cognitive social psychology: The Princeton Symposium on the legacy and future of social cognition* (pp. 105–124). Mahwah, NJ: Erlbaum.

Hetts, J. J., & Pelham, B. W. (2003). *The ghosts of Christmas past: Reflected appraisals and the perils of near Christmas birthdays*. Manuscript in preparation.

Hetts, J. J., Sakuma, M., & Pelham, B. W. (1999). Two roads to positive regard: Implicit and explicit self-evaluations and culture. *Journal of Experimental Social Psychology, 35*, 512–559.

Jones, J. T., Pelham, B. W., Mirenberg, M. C., & Hetts, J. J. (2002). Name-letter preferences are not merely mere exposure: Implicit egotism as self-regulation. *Journal of Experimental Social Psychology, 38*, 170–177.

Jordan, C. H., Logel, C., Spencer, S. J., Zanna, M. P., & Whitfield, M. L. (in press). The heterogeneity of self esteem: Exploring the interplay between implicit and explicit self-esteem In R. E. Petty, R. H. Fazio, & P. Briñol (Eds.), *Attitudes: Insights from the new implicit measures*. Hillsdale, NJ: Erlbaum.

Jordan, C. H., Spencer, S. J., Zanna, M. P., Hoshino-Browne, E., & Correll, J. (2003). Secure and defensive high self-esteem. *Journal of Personality and Social Psychology, 85*, 969–978.

Karpinski, A. (2004). Measuring self-esteem using the implicit self-association test: The role of the other. *Personality and Social Psychology Bulletin, 30*, 22–34.

Kernis, M. H. (2003). Towards a conceptualization of optimal self-esteem. *Psychological Inquiry, 14*, 1–26.

Kitayama, S., & Uchida, Y. (2003). Explicit self-criticism and implicit self-regard: Evaluating self and friend in two cultures. *Journal of Experimental Social Psychology, 39*, 476–482.

Koole, S. L., Dijksterhuis, A., & van Knippenberg, A. (2001). What's in a name: Implicit self-esteem and the automatic self. *Journal of Personality and Social Psychology, 80,* 669–685.

Koole, S. L., & Pelham, B. W. (2003). On the nature of implicit self-esteem: The case of the name-letter effect. In S. Spencer & M. P. Zanna (Eds.), *Ontario Symposium on personality and social psychology* (Vol. 7), Mahwah, NJ: Erlbaum. pp. 93–116.

Koole, S. L., Smeets, K., van Knippenberg, A., & Dijksterhuis, A. (1999). The cessation of rumination through self-affirmation. *Journal of Personality and Social Psychology, 77,* 111–125.

Lakoff, R. T. (1990). *Talking power: The politics of language.* New York: Basic Books.

McFarlin, D. B., Baumeister, R. F., & Blascovich, J. (1984). On knowing when to quit: Task failure, self-esteem, advice, and nonproductive persistence. *Journal of Personality, 52,* 138–155.

McGregor, I., & Marigold, D. C. (2003). Defensive zeal and the uncertain self: What makes you so sure? *Journal of Personality and Social Psychology, 85,* 838–852.

Nisbett, R. E., & Wilson, T. D. (1997). Telling more than we can know: Verbal reports on mental processes. *Psychological Review, 84,* 231–259.

O'Brien, E. J., & Epstein, S. (1988). *The multidimensional self-esteem inventory.* Odessa, FL: Houghton Mifflin.

Olson, M. A., & Fazio, R. H. (in press). Implicit and explicit measures of attitudes: The perspective of the MODE model. In R. E. Petty, R. H. Fazio, & P. Briñol (Eds.), *Attitudes: Insights from the new implicit measures.* Hillsdale, NJ: Erlbaum.

Pacini, R., & Epstein, S. (1999). The relation of rational and experiential information processing styles to personality, basic beliefs, and the rational-bias phenomenon. *Journal of Personality and Social Psychology, 76,* 972–987.

Pelham, B. W., DeHart, T., & Carvallo, M. (2003). *Implicit effects of stigmatizing names.* Unpublished manuscript, State University of New York at Buffalo.

Pelham, B. W., Koole, S. L., Hardin, C. D., Hetts, J. J., Seah, E., & DeHart, T. (2005). Gender moderates the relation between implicit and explicit self-esteem. *Journal of Experimental Social Psychology, 41,* 84–89.

Raskin, R., Novacek, J., & Hogan, R. (1991). Narcissism, self-esteem, and defensive self-enhancement. *Journal of Personality, 59,* 19–38.

Riketta, M., & Dauenheimer, D. (2003). Manipulating self-esteem with subliminally presented words. *European Journal of Social Psychology, 33,* 679–699.

Shrauger, J. S., & Rosenberg, S. E. (1970). Self-esteem and the effects of success and failure feedback on performance. *Journal of Personality, 38,* 404–417.

Spalding, L. R., & Hardin, C. D. (1999). Unconscious unease and self-handicapping: Behavioral consequences of individual differences in implicit
and explicit self-esteem. *Psychological Science, 10*, 535–539.

Steele, C. M. (1988). The psychology of self-affirmation: Sustaining the integrity of the self. In L. Berkowitz (Ed.), *Advances in experimental social
psychology* (Vol. 21, pp. 261–302). New York: Academic Press.

Steele, C. M., Spencer, S. J., & Lynch, M. (1993). Self-image and dissonance:
The role of affirmational resources. *Journal of Personality and Social Psychology, 64*, 885–896.

Wentura, D., Kulfanek, M., & Greve, W. (2005). Masked affective priming by
name letters: Evidence for a correspondence of explicit and implicit self-
esteem. *Journal of Experimental Social Psychology, 41*, 654–663.

9

The Heterogeneity of Self-Esteem
Exploring the Interplay between Implicit and Explicit Self-Esteem

Christian H. Jordan
Christine Logel
Steven J. Spencer
Mark P. Zanna
Mervyn L. Whitfield

Self-esteem: An erroneous appraisement.

Ambrose Bierce, *The Devil's Dictionary*

Introduction

One opinion, apparent in many popular books and websites dealing with self-esteem, is that some people who report having high self-esteem are actually deluding themselves. Some people—typically characterized as bullies, narcissists, or egotists—may claim to have high self-esteem, but their arrogant behavior is taken instead as a sign of low self-esteem or a "lack of authentic self-esteem" (Reasoner, 2005). A similar logic has occasionally figured into scholarly research as well (e.g., Jankowski, 1991; Olweus, 1994; see Baumeister, Smart, & Boden, 1996), but it is difficult to justify empirically. It is difficult to conclude, for example, that violent gang members and murderers have low self-esteem when they report feeling good about themselves (Baumeister et al.). What people say about themselves, however, may be only one part of the story. People may also possess less conscious self-feelings that can contradict their deliberate self-views, with implications for their self-relevant thoughts, motives, and behavior. This possibility is the focus of the present chapter. We review evidence that people hold distinct self-evaluations at conscious and nonconscious levels, and that the interplay between these evaluations defines unique psychological states within individuals.

Accumulating evidence suggests that high self-esteem is heterogeneous; that is, that not all people with high self-esteem are psychologically equivalent. Two individuals who report having equally high levels of self-esteem may differ dramatically in the extent to which their self-esteem is secure and confidently held as opposed to fragile and easily upset (see Kernis, 2003; Kernis & Paradise, 2002). One conclusion of a recent review of the self-esteem literature was that high self-esteem, as it is normally conceptualized and measured, describes a mixed group of people (Baumeister, Campbell, Kreuger, & Vohs, 2003). Indeed, high self-esteem has been variously associated with both prosocial and antisocial behaviors. Adolescents with relatively high self-esteem, for example, are not only more likely to stand up for others against bullies, but are also more likely to be bullies themselves (Salmivalli, Kaukiainen, Kaistaniemi, & Lagerspetz, 1999; see Baumeister et al.).

Such observations have led several theorists to suggest that self-esteem research must move beyond a focus on levels of self-esteem to consider additional factors that can affect the quality of self-esteem (e.g., Crocker & Park, 2004; Crocker & Wolfe, 2001; Deci & Ryan, 1995; Epstein & Morling, 1995; Kernis, 2003; Kernis & Paradise, 2002; Kernis & Waschull, 1995). Factors such as self-esteem stability (e.g., Kernis & Waschull), contingencies of self-worth (e.g., Crocker & Wolfe; Deci & Ryan), and need for approval (e.g., Lobel & Teiber, 1994; Schneider & Turkat, 1975) have thus offered increased fidelity to self-esteem research. Our focus dovetails neatly with these approaches but differs somewhat too. Consistent with the possibility that high self-esteem sometimes masks insecurities and self-doubts, we focus on people's nonconscious self-evaluations, or implicit self-esteem, in combination with their explicit reports of self-esteem (Epstein & Morling; Kernis & Paradise).

Implicit Self-Esteem

As the work described throughout the present volume attests, many attitudes and evaluations can be activated automatically—that is, without conscious effort or guidance (e.g., Bargh, Chaiken, Raymond, & Hymes, 1996; Fazio, Sanbonmatsus, Powell, & Kardes, 1986). Evidence suggests that this is true of self-attitudes as well. Roughly a decade ago, theorists began suggesting that there might be an automatic, and even implicit, component of self-esteem (e.g., Greenwald & Banaji, 1995; Epstein & Morling, 1995). A flurry of research followed, often progressing in fits and starts. Thus, early efforts, focused on developing sound implicit measures of self-esteem, were met with persistent difficulties that have not yet been fully resolved (e.g., Bosson, Swann, & Pennebaker, 2000; Jordan, Spencer, & Zanna, 2003). Nevertheless, several implicit measures of self-esteem do now exist and have revealed intriguing insights into self-relevant behavior.

Many theorists believe that at least some implicit measures of self-esteem tap into a distinct implicit construct. This construct, implicit self-esteem, is generally defined as efficient evaluations of the self that exist largely outside of awareness (e.g., Epstein & Morling, 1995; Farnham, Greenwald, & Banaji, 1999; Greenwald & Banaji, 1995; Koole & Pelham, 2003). It is thus measured indirectly, often by reaction time measures that are difficult to control, such as the Implicit Association Test (IAT; Greenwald & Farnham, 2001; Greenwald, McGhee, & Schwartz, 1998). In contrast, explicit self-esteem represents people's deliberately reasoned and conscious self-evaluations, and so is measured more directly by standard self-report scales. An intriguing aspect of implicit and explicit measures of self-esteem is that they are largely independent of each other (Bosson et al., 2000; Farnham et al., 1999; Jordan, Spencer, & Zanna, 2003). Thus, knowing a person's reported level of self-esteem reveals almost nothing about his or her implicitly measured self-esteem. Someone who reports having high self-esteem, for example, could demonstrate quite negative self-evaluations on implicit measures.

The fact that implicit measures of self-esteem can contradict direct self-reports was taken as strong evidence that implicit measures circumvent response biases (e.g., Farnham et al., 1999; Greenwald & Farnham, 2001). Accordingly, it was initially suggested that implicit measures capture self-esteem more clearly than do explicit measures; that is, implicit measures were thought to capture the same underlying self-attitudes as explicit measures, but with greater fidelity. Although implicit measures undoubtedly do bypass many self-presentational tendencies, this fact probably does not account entirely for the near-zero correlations regularly observed between implicit and explicit measures of self-esteem. In addition, whereas it is easy to appreciate why some people might report having higher self-esteem than they actually feel, it is less clear why many people might report having lower self-esteem than they feel. Given the independence of implicit and explicit measures of self-esteem, however, both patterns of discrepancy are equally common (cf. Epstein & Morling, 1995). That is, on a relative basis, some individuals are higher in explicit than implicit self-esteem, whereas others are lower in explicit than implicit self-esteem—although, in general, individuals in Western cultures report fairly high levels of explicit self-esteem on standard scales (Baumeister, Tice, & Hutton, 1989; Heine, Lehman, Markus, & Kitayama, 1999).

It thus seems reasonable to conclude, at least tentatively, that implicit and explicit measures of self-esteem tap distinct psychological constructs, which we refer to as implicit and explicit self-esteem (cf. Fazio & Olson, 2003). Consistent with this possibility, implicit measures of self-esteem have been shown to predict different responses than explicit measures of self-esteem. Implicit self-esteem has thus predicted cognitive and affective responses to performance feedback (Greenwald & Farnham, 2001) and perseverance in the face of failure (Jordan, Spencer, & Zanna, 2003). These findings emerged while statistically controlling for the influence of explicit self-esteem, and in fact, in these studies, explicit measures of self-esteem did not predict these reactions. Moreover, implicit and explicit measures of self-esteem can each predict distinct psychological responses in a *double dissociation* pattern (see Asendorpf, Banse, & Mucke, 2002). In one study, explicit self-esteem predicted reports of anxiety in anticipation of a revealing personal interview, whereas implicit self-esteem did not (Spalding & Hardin, 1999). In contrast, implicit self-esteem predicted less controllable, nonverbal indicators of anxiety, whereas explicit self-esteem did not.

A guiding framework in our research has thus been that implicit and explicit measures of self-esteem capture distinct self-evaluations that operate within separate, though interacting, psychological systems (e.g., Epstein & Morling, 1995; Smith & DeCoster, 2000; Wilson, Lindsey, & Schooler, 2000). In this sense, we take a broader view of implicit self-esteem than defining it simply in terms of being nonconscious. A number of theorists have suggested that humans have evolved two largely independent cognitive systems (see, e.g., Sloman, 1996; Smith & DeCoster; Smolensky, 1988; Strack & Deutsch, 2004). One system is conscious; it is also verbal, deliberative, effortful, and rule-based. The other system is preconscious; it is also preverbal, unintentional, efficient, and associative in nature. The former system is thought to operate primarily through controlled processes, whereas the latter is thought to operate primarily through automatic processes. For our purposes, the important implication of these models is that people can hold two distinct self-evaluations simultaneously—one that is preconscious and associative in nature and another that is conscious and deliberately reasoned.

Thus, beyond being simply nonconscious, we conceptualize implicit self-esteem as also being associative and automatic, in the sense of being activated efficiently and unintentionally by self-relevant stimuli. Explicit self-esteem, on the other hand, is clearly conscious, but it is also deliberative and controlled, and so can be affected to a greater extent by purposeful reasoning. Using this framework as our guiding theoretical backdrop, we have thus explored how interactions between implicit and explicit self-esteem predict self-relevant motives and behavior. It is worth noting, however, that a strict dual attitudes framework is not necessary for deriving our predictions. Our hypotheses, and findings, are compatible with models that posit more integrated attitude representations, such as the MODE model (Fazio & Towles-Schwen, 1999; Chapter 2, this volume) or the Meta-Cognitive Model (MCM) of attitudes (Petty & Briñol, 2006; Chapter 5, this volume).

In fact, our views diverge from a number of dual attitudes perspectives in that we do not claim that implicit attitudes are unconscious. We suggest, rather, that they are preconscious; that people are aware of their implicit (or associative) evaluations, but not the cognitive processes that produce them. Under this view, people can be aware of both implicit and explicit attitudes. This suggestion is consistent with the MODE and MCM, as well as some dual systems models of information processing (e.g., Sloman, 1996; Smolensky, 1988). Thus, people may experience both implicit and explicit attitudes, but they may do so in different ways. Subjectively, people may feel that they can identify propositional reasons for their explicit attitudes. Implicit attitudes, in contrast, may subjectively just "pop" into one's head. Because of this, people may experience implicit attitudes as gut feelings or intuitions (Jordan, Whitfield, & Zeigler-Hill, 2007; see also Hinton 1990; Hogarth, 2001; Lieberman, 2000). Thus people may become simultaneously aware of explicit and implicit attitudes. When the two are discrepant, such awareness may create a state of psychological discomfort that people are motivated to reduce (see Jordan, Spencer, & Zanna, 2003; Petty & Briñol, 2006).

Overview

The majority of our work to date has focused on individuals with high explicit self-esteem. In this chapter, we thus begin by reviewing evidence that, among such individuals, those with relatively low implicit self-esteem are most characteristically defensive. That is, when their positive self-views are challenged, individuals with high explicit but low implicit self-esteem react defensively, in a variety of ways, more so than do individuals with high explicit and high implicit self-esteem.

We then turn to preliminary evidence for why the combination of high explicit with low implicit self-esteem motivates defensiveness. As noted above, we believe that implicit and explicit self-esteem can enter awareness simultaneously. Because implicit self-esteem is associative, we believe that self-relevant stimuli can activate it, potentially bringing it into consciousness (see, e.g., Cheng, Govorund, & Chartrand, 2006). We conceptualize individuals with low implicit self-esteem, for example, as having strong associations between their self-concepts and negative evaluations. Thus, when such individuals receive performance feedback—whether it is success or failure feedback—because it implicates the self, it will associatively activate negative self-feelings and negative self-views. Furthermore, for individuals with discrepant implicit and explicit self-esteem, if implicit self-esteem enters awareness simultaneously with explicit self-esteem (as is likely to happen in evaluative situations), this creates cognitive inconsistency. Such inconsistency will in turn create an uncomfortable state of arousal, akin to cognitive dissonance, that people are motivated to reduce (see also Briñol, Petty, & Wheeler, 2006). We argue that individuals with high explicit but low implicit self-esteem will be strongly motivated to resolve such inconsistency in favor of their positive explicit self-views. This may help to account for their characteristically defensive tendencies.

Finally, we explore how implicit self-esteem can affect the psychology of individuals with low explicit self-esteem. We examine recent research on how implicit self-esteem can influence reactions to success. Within our framework, success, as a self-relevant event, should activate implicit self-esteem and bring it into awareness. For individuals with low explicit but high implicit self-esteem, this will create an uncomfortable state of cognitive inconsistency that they are motivated to reduce. However, the associative activation of high implicit self-esteem may also provide them with a *glimmer of hope*, as they become aware of positive self-feelings and positive self-views. Such experiences may allow them to sometimes resolve their cognitive inconsistencies in a positive direction following success. We thus believe that individuals with low explicit but high implicit self-esteem will be able to psychologically benefit from success in ways that individuals who are low in both explicit and implicit self-esteem cannot. In fact, success may ironically make these latter individuals feel worse, as it activates their low implicit self-esteem.

Types of High Self-Esteem

Our initial work in this area focused on the possibility that individuals with high explicit but low implicit self-esteem are more defensive than those with high explicit and high implicit self-esteem. As noted previously, it has been widely suggested that high self-esteem is heterogeneous. Kernis and his colleagues have outlined two contrasting forms that high self-esteem can assume (e.g., Kernis, 2003; Kernis & Paradise, 2002; Kernis & Waschull, 1995). Whereas some individuals appear to have positive self-views that are secure and confidently held, others appear to have positive self-views that are fragile and vulnerable to threat. These latter individuals are believed to engage in a wide variety of defensive and self-enhancing behaviors, often at the expense of others in their social environments. Kernis and his colleagues have, in fact, amassed a wide array of evidence that stability of self-esteem is one means by which secure and fragile (or defensive) self-esteem can be differentiated. High self-esteem individuals who have stable self-views appear to be relatively secure, whereas those with unstable self-views appear to be relatively defensive and easily threatened. A complementary means of distinguishing secure from defensive high self-esteem may be to consider people's levels of implicit self-esteem (see Epstein & Morling, 1995; Kernis & Paradise; for consideration of how these different approaches may relate to each other, see Jordan, Spencer, & Zanna, 2003; Kernis & Paradise).

A number of theorists suggest that some individuals who report having high self-esteem are actually insecure at less conscious levels. An early proponent of this view, Coopersmith (1959), suggested that some individuals report highly positive self-views in order to protect the self from conscious recognition of low status. Similarly, it has been suggested that narcissists' grandiose self-views conceal an unacknowledged base of self-doubt and self-loathing (e.g., Kohut, 1971; Morf & Rhodewalt, 2001). Framed in contemporary social cognitive terms, these theoretical accounts suggest that narcissists and other defensive individuals have high explicit but low implicit self-esteem (see also Epstein & Morling, 1995). We believe it is precisely this combination of explicit and implicit self-esteem that often motivates defensiveness. In an early study, we explored directly whether the correspondence between explicit and implicit self-esteem predicts narcissism.

Narcissism. The design of this study was straightforward (Jordan, Spencer, Zanna et al., 2003, Study 1). We first measured participants' implicit self-esteem, using an IAT measure. The IAT is a response-mapping procedure for which participants categorize words presented on a computer screen as quickly and accurately as possible. In this particular IAT, participants distinguished pleasant and unpleasant words as well as self and not-self words. During the critical blocks of the task, participants made both discriminations on alternate trials using only a single set of response keys. In one critical block, self and unpleasant shared a response, whereas not-self and pleasant shared another response. This combination of responses should make the task relatively difficult for people with high implicit self-esteem, because they do not naturally associate the self with negative feelings. They should thus respond relatively slowly during this block of trials. In the other critical block, self and pleasant share a response. This combination should make the task relatively easy for people with high implicit self-esteem, and so their responses should be faster during this block. This facilitation effect serves as an index of implicit self-esteem. In addition to the IAT, participants also completed a standard self-report measure of explicit self-esteem, the Rosenberg (1965) Self-Esteem Scale (RSES), and a measure of narcissism intended for use in subclinical populations, the Narcissistic Personality Inventory (Raskin & Hall, 1988).

Consistent with our predictions, participants who had high explicit but low implicit self-esteem showed the highest levels of narcissism overall.* In contrast, participants with high explicit and high implicit self-esteem showed significantly less narcissism—in fact, they showed levels of narcissism comparable to individuals with low explicit self-esteem. It is worth noting that similar findings have been reported by other researchers, often using different measures of implicit self-esteem. Brown and Bosson (2001) report that they observed the same interaction using a name-letter preference measure of implicit self-esteem. More recently, Zeigler-Hill (2008) replicated this interaction using both an IAT measure and a paper-and-pencil priming measure

---

* In our research, including this particular study, we maintain explicit and implicit self-esteem as continuous measures, which we analyze with multiple regression. Thus, when we refer to individuals who are high in explicit but low in implicit self-esteem, for example, these are relative designations within a specific sample. That is, we are referring to individuals who are relatively high in explicit self-esteem and relatively low in implicit self-esteem, based on predicted values derived through multiple regression analyses. Different "types" of individuals, in this way, are conventionally represented by predicted values at one standard deviation above or below the mean of relevant variables (following Cohen & Cohen, 1983).

of implicit self-esteem (the Implicit Self-Evaluation Survey; Pelham & Hetts, 1999).

These findings are noteworthy because they support theoretical accounts of narcissism that suggest that narcissists actually harbor negative self-feelings (e.g., Kohut, 1971; Morf & Rhodewalt, 2001). Although this has been a common theme in the narcissism literature for decades, this is the first empirical evidence we are aware of to support this possibility. Furthermore, because narcissism is closely related to individual differences in defensiveness (e.g., Paulhus, 1998; Raskin, Novacek, & Hogan, 1991), these findings suggest that individuals with high explicit but low implicit self-esteem are particularly defensive. We explored this possibility further by examining whether implicit and explicit self-esteem predict defensive responses.

Cognitive dissonance reduction. Cognitive dissonance is an aversive state that arises when people hold two or more inconsistent cognitions simultaneously. Early theorizing suggested that dissonance often arises from inconsistent thoughts that threaten one's positive self-views (e.g., "I am a smoker." and "Smoking jeopardizes my health."; Aronson, 1968; Aronson & Carlsmith, 1962). Indeed, Steele (1988) suggested that dissonance arises from a threat to one's global sense of self-integrity (i.e., one's sense of being a moral and competent person) and that dissonance reduction is one means by which this threat can be neutralized. Although inconsistent cognitions normally provoke rationalizations and attitude change, Steele and his colleagues showed that these reactions do not occur if people are otherwise affirmed—obviating the need to protect self-views (e.g., Steele & Lui, 1983; Steele, Spencer, & Lynch, 1993). It thus seems likely that dissonance reduction serves a defensive purpose. Hence, we expected that individuals with high explicit but low implicit self-esteem would be particularly likely to rationalize their decisions in the form of dissonance reduction (Jordan, Spencer, Zanna et al., 2003, Study 3). To explore this possibility, we used the classic free-choice dissonance paradigm (employing materials originally developed by Hoshino-Browne, Zanna, Spencer, & Zanna, 2004).

Prior to the study, we measured participants' explicit self-esteem with the RSES and their implicit self-esteem with the IAT. Participants were informed that the study dealt with consumer attitudes and was being conducted in cooperation with the proprietors of a new Chinese food restaurant. The proprietors were purportedly interested in learning more about students' meal preferences. Participants were presented with a list of 25 entrées and asked to select the 10 they found most appealing. They then rank ordered these 10 entrées in terms of their preferences and rated how appealing each entrée was to them. Shortly after, participants were unexpectedly presented with coupons for their fifth- and sixth-ranked entrées and told that they could have one coupon as thanks for participating. After they made their decisions, participants were asked to rate the same entrées again. This time, the entrées were presented with elaborate descriptions, in order to give participants grounds to revise their original ratings.

Because the two entrées participants chose between were similarly appealing to them (a fact confirmed by their initial ratings), their decisions were relatively difficult and thus likely to cause cognitive dissonance. Participants faced the possibility of later regretting their decisions, hence threatening their positive views of themselves as being competent decision makers. This threat could be resolved by rationalizing their decisions. Overall, we found that participants did increase their ratings of their chosen alternatives and decreased their ratings of their rejected alternatives, a form of dissonance reduction known as the *spread of alternatives*. Of greater interest, however, was that this response was most pronounced for individuals with high explicit but low implicit self-esteem—significantly more so than for individuals with any other combination of implicit and explicit self-esteem. Consistent with our predictions, then, individuals with high explicit but low implicit self-esteem appeared to be particularly defensive. In order to test this possibility further, we examined a different self-enhancing response, namely ingroup bias (Jordan, Spencer, Zanna et al., 2003, Study 2).

Ingroup bias. Social identity theory suggests that an important part of people's identities derives from the social groups to which they belong (e.g., Tajfel, 1981; Tajfel & Turner, 1979). Accordingly, people can enhance their sense of personal self-esteem by making their ingroups appear superior to contrasting outgroups—either by derogating those outgroups or by favoring ingroups. People do, in fact, show a robust tendency to favor ingroups over outgroups, even when the groups in question are novel and were established on the basis of purely arbitrary criteria (such as coin flips). Moreover, engaging in ingroup bias does tend to enhance people's state self-esteem (Rubin & Hewstone, 1998). We thus expected that people with high explicit but low implicit self-esteem would favor their ingroups to a greater extent than people with high explicit and high implicit self-esteem. To explore this possibility, we employed the minimal group paradigm.

To begin, participants estimated the numbers of dots that appeared in a series of arrays presented to them via computer. They were subsequently informed that they had a strong tendency to either over- or underestimate dots. This established two novel groups (i.e., over- and underestimators) that served as an ingroup and an outgroup for each participant. Participants were then asked to allocate points to other participants in the study, who were identified only by their ingroup or outgroup status. These points would ostensibly be used in a lottery to determine the winner of a monetary prize at the end of the study. Points were allocated through Tajfel's matrices (Tajfel, 1981), which require participants, under specific constraints, to award points simultaneously to an ingroup member and an outgroup member. The extent to which participants allocated more points to ingroup members than to outgroups members served as our measure of ingroup bias. Participants' implicit and explicit self-esteem were again measured with the IAT and RSES, respectively.

Consistent with our predictions, we found that the interaction between implicit and explicit self-esteem predicted ingroup bias. Implicit self-esteem was not related to ingroup bias among low explicit self-esteem individuals. Implicit self-esteem and ingroup bias were, however, negatively related among high explicit self-esteem individuals. Among such individuals, those with low implicit self-esteem showed significantly more ingroup bias than those with high implicit self-esteem. In fact, individuals with high explicit but low implicit self-esteem showed the most ingroup bias overall, whereas those with high explicit and high implicit self-esteem showed the least. These results thus provide further evidence that individuals with high explicit but low implicit self-esteem are relatively defensive, whereas those with high explicit and high implicit self-esteem are relatively secure.

Ethnic discrimination. Our ingroup bias findings might also suggest that individuals with high explicit but low implicit self-esteem are likely to discriminate against existing outgroups. Because the minimal group paradigm was designed to rule out ongoing prejudices as a cause of bias, however, we cannot extrapolate directly from our findings to discrimination in general. Nevertheless, discrimination can sometimes serve a defensive function. Fein and Spencer (1997) found that people used negative stereotypes in their judgments of outgroup members more when they had recently suffered a failure. Moreover, to the extent that people did so, their state self-esteem was enhanced. Other evidence suggests that positive self-views are related to prejudice and discrimination. Contrary to popular opinion, people with high self-esteem express more racist attitudes than those with low self-esteem (Emler, 2001), and they sometimes discriminate more against extant outgroups

(Crocker, Thompson, McGraw, & Ingerman, 1987). We thus sought to explore whether this relation holds primarily for individuals with high explicit but low implicit self-esteem.

We recruited participants for a study of perceptions of student offenders (Jordan et al., 2005, Study 1). We first preselected individuals with high explicit self-esteem—only those individuals who scored in the top third of the RSES distribution were invited. We then measured their implicit self-esteem with the IAT. Next, participants completed a supposed measure of verbal intelligence, derived from entrance exams for graduate and professional schools (following Fein & Spencer, 1997). The test was designed to be extremely difficult, and all participants received negative feedback—they were told that they scored between the 32nd and 56th percentiles on all sections of the exam. This served to threaten participants' positive self-views. All of our participants thus had high explicit self-esteem and were under self-threat.

Participants were then presented with three scenarios, each describing a case of student misconduct that had ostensibly appeared before the university's disciplinary committee. The first two cases dealt with vandalism and drug use. The third was the focal case and described a student who started a fistfight outside a campus bar. For this case, half of the participants read about a student named John Proudfoot, whereas the remaining half read about John Pride. This manipulation was intended to convey that the student was or was not Native Canadian in ethnicity. In this target case, the student offender is asleep on a couch outside a campus bar, late on a Friday night. It is unclear whether he has been drinking. A group of students, exiting the bar, disturbs him and they exchange words. Eventually, one student calls John an "asshole," and he responds by punching that student twice in the face. John is thus guilty of physical aggression but has also been clearly provoked. Participants were asked to indicate the severity of punishment that John deserved. They indicated whether he should be forced to take an anger management class, recommended the subjective severity of punishment he deserved, and selected an objective punishment from a list of punishments of escalating severity. These three ratings were combined into a single index of the severity of recommended punishment.

Among our threatened high self-esteem participants, we expected that those with low implicit self-esteem would discriminate more on the basis of ethnicity. This is precisely what we found. Participants with high explicit but low implicit self-esteem recommended a more severe punishment for John Proudfoot than John Pride. Participants with high explicit and high implicit self-esteem, although they were under threat, showed a nonsignificant tendency in the opposite direction. Moreover, we replicated this study with participants from the full range of explicit self-esteem (Jordan et al., 2005, Study 2). Among high explicit self-esteem individuals, we again found the same pattern of results. This pattern, however, was not apparent for individuals with moderate or low explicit self-esteem. These findings thus suggest that individuals with high explicit but low implicit self-esteem may be particularly likely to use discrimination as a means of protecting the self.

Other evidence. Independent evidence also converges on the conclusion that individuals with high explicit but low implicit self-esteem are more defensive than those who are high in both forms of self-esteem. Bosson, Brown, Zeigler-Hill, and Swann (2003) examined self-enhancing tendencies in relation to explicit and implicit self-esteem, as measured by a name-letter preference measure. Among individuals with high explicit self-esteem, they found that those with relatively low implicit self-esteem showed more unrealistic optimism about their futures and more strongly endorsed a highly flattering personality profile as self-descriptive (Study 1). They also reported that they viewed their current selves as being closer to their ideals (i.e., they showed smaller actual-ideal self-discrepancies; Study 2). In addition, McGregor and his colleagues (McGregor & Marigold, 2003; McGregor, Nail, Marigold, & Kang, 2005), using an IAT measure of implicit self-esteem, found that individuals with high explicit but low implicit self-esteem respond to threat by defensively hardening their attitudes (i.e., by holding their attitudes with greater conviction and perceiving greater social consensus for them). Individuals with high explicit and high implicit self-esteem did not show these responses to threat, nor did any individuals with low explicit self-esteem.

Why Defensiveness? The Case for Nagging Doubts

Considerable evidence thus supports the idea that individuals with high explicit but low implicit self-esteem are more defensive than those with high explicit and high implicit self-esteem. But what is it about the combination of high explicit and low implicit self-esteem that motivates defensiveness? We contend that implicit self-esteem, although generally existing outside of awareness, can be experienced consciously (see Jordan, Spencer, & Zanna, 2003; Spencer, Jordan, Logel, & Zanna, 2005).

Though most definitions of implicit self-esteem suggest that it is unconscious, existing wholly outside of awareness, as noted previously, we
believe that it is actually preconscious. We conceptualize implicit self-
esteem as strong associations between the self and positive or negative
evaluations. Self-relevant stimuli, by activating the self-concept, may
thus lead associatively to the activation of positive or negative self-feelings and self-views, consistent with one's level of implicit self-esteem.
People may thus become conscious of their implicit self-esteem if self-
relevant stimuli activate their associated evaluations enough for them
to reach consciousness. This may be particularly likely when people
receive, or even expect to receive, positive or negative evaluations.

Thus, when a student does poorly on an exam, for instance, she may
experience feelings that are consistent with her level of implicit self-
esteem. Certainly, this failure will be generally disappointing, as it
frustrates her goal of doing well academically. Additionally, however,
the self-relevant nature of this feedback may also activate the positive or negative evaluations that are automatically associated with her
self-concept and bring them into awareness. For individuals with congruent implicit and explicit self-esteem, such experiences of implicit
self-esteem will be largely inconsequential, as they merely reinforce
what these individuals otherwise believe about themselves. In contrast,
awareness of implicit self-esteem is likely to be experienced as aversive
for individuals with high explicit but low implicit self-esteem. They may
experience what we have called *nagging doubts* about their competence
and worth. Such nagging doubts are likely to motivate defensive efforts
to deny implicitly negative self-views and confirm explicitly positive
self-views. We have recently begun exploring this possibility.

To find evidence of nagging doubts among individuals with high
explicit but low implicit self-esteem, we faced a real challenge. Such individuals, considering their defensive tendencies, are unlikely to admit
openly to experiencing any self-doubts. Because implicit self-esteem,
moreover, may be experienced as intuitive self-evaluations, or gut feelings about the self that, to the individuals involved, do not seem to be
supported by well-thought-out reasons (Jordan et al., 2006), negative
implicit self-views may be subjectively experienced as less valid than
positive explicit self-views. In the terms of the Meta-Cognitive Model of
attitudes (Petty, Briñol, & DeMarree, 2007), defensive individuals may
often, for both motivated and epistemic reasons, tag their implicit self-
views as invalid. They may thus strive to deny their implicit self-esteem,
particularly when they feel threatened. Thus, rather than exposing
participants to failure and then soliciting their self-views, we initially

took a different approach—we exposed participants to success. Because implicit self-esteem represents automatic associations to the self, any self-relevant, evaluative experience can potentially bring implicit self-esteem into awareness. When this happens, people may then explicitly report more positive or negative self-views, depending on their levels of implicit self-esteem. Thus success, somewhat ironically, may cause nagging doubts in defensive individuals. Success, moreover, may be more likely than failure to leave such individuals with their guards down, so to speak, making it easier to find evidence of nagging doubts.

In a recent study testing these ideas, we first measured participants' explicit and implicit self-esteem using the RSES and the IAT. We then manipulated perceptions of success: Half of the participants completed an ostensible intelligence test and received highly positive feedback on their performance; the remaining participants read the test and received no feedback. All participants then rated the extent to which positive and negative trait words were self-descriptive (e.g., *likeable, inadequate*). However, in order to prevent participants from responding defensively, they were given only 1 second to respond to each of the target words. We reasoned that if we restricted the time with which participants were allowed to consider their responses, they would be less able to override their nagging doubts. Consistent with our predictions, but counterintuitively, participants with high explicit but low implicit self-esteem rated positive traits as less self-descriptive and negative traits as more self-descriptive following success, relative to when they were not evaluated. Participants who were high in both explicit and implicit self-esteem tended to show the opposite pattern, becoming more positive in their self-descriptions after success. A second study, using the same success manipulation but different trait words, produced comparable results.

We were encouraged by the results we observed in response to success. Because we believe that nagging doubts can be a proximal cause of defensiveness, however, we sought further evidence that they may also follow failure, which more commonly arouses defenses. We predicted that failure would associatively activate negative self-views for individuals with low implicit self-esteem. In principle, the speeded self-rating task described above could demonstrate this response. However, that measure is quite direct in measuring self-views, and we thought that the strong defensive tendencies aroused by failure might make it difficult to find evidence of nagging doubts with that particular measure, even with fast responses. Instead, we employed an indirect measure of self-assurance—self-serving prototypes of success (e.g., Dunning, Perie, & Story, 1991; Epley & Dunning, 2000).

People often define social concepts in self-serving ways. Thus, they may rate their personal attributes as more central to being a good leader than attributes they do not possess, the implication being that they have what it takes to be a good leader. This tendency, moreover, is more common among individuals with high explicit self-esteem (Beauregard & Dunning, 1998). Note, however, that these are indirect ratings of self-assurance. Because the implications of such ratings for the self are not obvious, they might not be distorted by defensiveness. We thus predicted that individuals with high explicit but low implicit self-esteem would actually show less self-assurance on this measure following failure. That is, if failure associatively activates negative self-views for individuals with low implicit self-esteem, such self-views may undercut their self-serving prototypes of success, despite their normally defensive tendencies. Put differently, this indirect measure of self-assurance might show evidence of nagging doubts following failure.

As in previous studies, we measured participants' implicit and explicit self-esteem with the IAT and RSES. We then asked half of our participants to recall a significant personal failure. They were asked to write in detail about this experience, indicating why it was significant to them and who else knew about their failure. The remaining participants, in the control condition, wrote instead about their typical morning routine. Following this threat manipulation, participants rated themselves on a number of traits that were fairly neutral in terms of their social desirability (e.g., *talkative, practical, disorganized, cooperative*). They then rated the extent to which these same traits contribute to being a good leader. From these two sets of ratings, we calculated a correlation coefficient for each participant, representing the degree of correspondence between their self- and leader ratings. We took this correlation as an indicator of self-assurance, or the extent to which participants saw their own traits as contributing to being a good leader (following Dunning et al., 1991).

Overall, we found that participants with high explicit self-esteem showed more self-serving definitions of leadership ability (conceptually replicating Beauregard & Dunning, 1998). This was the only effect apparent in the control condition. In contrast, after participants had described a personal failure, the interaction between implicit and explicit self-esteem predicted self-assurance. Individuals with high explicit but low implicit self-esteem, consistent with our predictions, showed less self-assurance after failure—relative to their counterparts in the control condition, these individuals showed less correspondence between their self and leader ratings. In contrast, those with high explicit and high implicit self-esteem showed somewhat more self-assurance, consistent with the idea that failure activated their implicit self-esteem, bringing positive self-views automatically into awareness (cf. Dodgson & Wood, 1998). This study thus suggests that failure can activate implicit self-esteem. For individuals with high explicit but low implicit self-esteem, failure undermined their self-assurance, perhaps reflecting the impact of nagging doubts.

An additional study provided convergent evidence that failure can bring implicit self-esteem into awareness. Some evidence suggested that people may experience discrepancies between implicit and explicit self-esteem as a kind of ambivalence (Briñol et al., 2006, Study 4). Consistent with this possibility, we believe that simultaneous awareness of implicit and explicit self-esteem may create an aversive state of cognitive inconsistency similar to cognitive dissonance. That is, as implicit self-esteem is activated by failure, as an evaluative event, it should make inconsistent self-views simultaneously accessible to these individuals and so may arouse in them the same discomfort that is generally associated with cognitive inconsistency. Elliot and Devine (1994) demonstrated that cognitive dissonance is subjectively experienced as psychological discomfort, which is alleviated through dissonance reduction. If failure brings implicit self-esteem into awareness, even though defensive individuals might not admit openly to experiencing self-doubts, they might report heightened experiences of discomfort and negative affect. We thus had participants again write about a significant personal failure or a mundane routine. We then had them complete a mood measure, including the "dissonance thermometer" items developed by Elliot and Devine.

We found that, following failure, participants with discrepant implicit and explicit self-esteem tended to report more negative affect. Consistent with our reasoning, this effect occurred for individuals with either direction of discrepancy (i.e., high explicit but low implicit self-esteem, or low explicit but high implicit self-esteem). Importantly, this same pattern was significant for the dissonance thermometer items. Following failure, individuals with discrepant self-esteem showed greater psychological discomfort than those in the control condition. Specifically, they showed the same kind of discomfort that has been linked to cognitive inconsistency. This suggests that failure may bring implicit self-esteem into awareness, causing discomfort for individuals whose implicit self-esteem contradicts their explicit self-views.

Notably, we also included within the mood measure three items that reflect negative self-directed feelings. Specifically, participants indicated how "angry at self," "disgusted with self," and "dissatisfied with self" they felt. On these items, as with psychological discomfort, participants with discrepant implicit and explicit self-esteem reported more negative self-directed feelings after recalling a personal failure. This is perhaps the most direct evidence so far demonstrating that individuals with high explicit but low implicit self-esteem feel negatively toward themselves after failure, more so than individuals with high explicit and high implicit self-esteem. Note, however, that these ratings do not necessarily reflect devaluation of the self. Rather, they focus on frustration and perhaps disappointment with oneself. Defensive individuals may, in effect, be saying, "I know I'm capable of better than that." Nevertheless, following failure, such individuals clearly experienced heightened discomfort and negative self-directed feelings.

A number of findings thus converge on the possibility that implicit self-esteem is preconscious and may cause nagging doubts in individuals with high explicit but low implicit self-esteem. This evidence is, perhaps of necessity, indirect. As noted, defensive individuals will not readily admit to experiencing self-doubts. Nevertheless, following success, their self-evaluations suggested that they experienced more negative self-views—at least when they were made rapidly. In addition, after recalling a significant personal failure, individuals with high explicit but low implicit self-esteem showed less self-assurance, in that they were less likely to rate their personal attributes as central to leadership ability. Finally, after recalling a failure, individuals with discrepant implicit and explicit self-esteem reported more negative affect, more psychological discomfort, and more negative self-directed feelings, consistent with the idea that failure made implicit and explicit self-esteem simultaneously accessible to them. Taken together, these findings suggest that evaluative experiences may associatively activate implicit self-esteem, causing nagging doubts in individuals with high explicit but low implicit self-esteem. Such nagging doubts, moreover, may motivate defensiveness, although this latter conclusion awaits further research.

Types of Low Self-Esteem: A Glimmer of Hope

Most of our research so far has focused on individuals with high explicit self-esteem. Nevertheless, we believe that implicit self-esteem also affects the psychology of individuals with low explicit self-esteem. As noted above, we found that failure caused greater psychological discomfort in individuals with discrepant self-esteem, including those with low explicit but high implicit self-esteem. This finding might seem a bit counterintuitive. Awareness of high implicit self-esteem among individuals with low explicit self-esteem might be expected to be generally pleasant. However, such awareness also highlights a cognitive inconsistency that can cause discomfort. Individuals with low explicit but high implicit self-esteem should thus be motivated to resolve this inconsistency—just as are their counterparts with defensive high self-esteem. Unlike defensive individuals, however, those with low explicit but high implicit self-esteem may often strive to resolve such discrepancies in the direction of their implicit self-feelings, especially when implicit self-esteem has been brought into awareness by success or positive feedback. Among individuals with low explicit self-esteem, those with relatively high implicit self-esteem may thus more readily accept positive information and so may benefit more from success. We have recently begun exploring this possibility.

It has generally been taken for granted that failure makes individuals with low explicit self-esteem feel worse about themselves, but that positive feedback and success gives such individuals a self-esteem boost (e.g., Brown & Dutton, 1995; Shrauger & Rosenberg, 1970). Studies on which this conclusion is based have typically shown that low self-esteem individuals feel better about themselves after positive feedback than after negative feedback. Without a neutral control to compare these findings against, however, it is unclear whether positive feedback actually raises self-esteem beyond baseline levels. In fact, it is even possible that positive feedback induces a mild threat, depressing self-views somewhat below baseline. Surprisingly, studies that compare positive feedback to a neutral condition may support this latter possibility—positive feedback may not be entirely favorable for individuals with low self-esteem.

Murray, Holmes, MacDonald, and Ellsworth (1998) told some participants that they possess desirable relationship qualities (Study 3) or gave them positive feedback on an intellectual test (Study 4). They found that individuals with low explicit self-esteem actually reported more relationship insecurities under these conditions than they did when they received no feedback. Similarly, Wood, Heimpel, Newby-Clark, and Ross (2005) found in two recent studies that low explicit self-esteem individuals reported greater anxiety after receiving positive feedback on an intelligence test, relative to a neutral control condition. Moreover, Logel, Spencer, Wood, and Holmes (2004) found that low self-esteem individuals who were led to believe they had excelled on an intelligence test were actually more concerned about the positive regard of their friends and family, as compared to a baseline condition. This was not true for high self-esteem individuals. Although such findings may be surprising, they are not wholly inconsistent with current theory.

Low self-esteem individuals tend to be self-protective; that is, they are motivated to avoid situations that could cause failure, embarrassment, or humiliation (Baumeister et al., 1989). They may thus believe that if they accept positive feedback, they will eventually feel worse about themselves if they fail to maintain the same level of achievement. Similarly, Swann and his colleagues suggested that low self-esteem individuals are motivated to self-verify, often striving to maintain their negative self-views (see Swann, 1992). According to this view, low self-esteem individuals may be threatened by positive feedback for pragmatic reasons, because they believe that others could develop unrealistically positive expectations for them, which will ultimately cause disappointment. Although low self-esteem individuals associate success with acceptance and failure with rejection (Baldwin & Sinclair, 1996), they may fear that one success only opens the door to future failure and rejection.

Research and theory thus suggest that success can be detrimental to low self-esteem individuals. But is this true of all low self-esteem individuals? As we suggested earlier, individuals with low explicit but high implicit self-esteem may benefit more from success and positive evaluations than do individuals with low explicit and low implicit self-esteem. Indeed, it may be only these latter individuals who suffer in the face of success. This prediction follows directly from the possibility that success, as a self-relevant event, will associatively activate implicit self-esteem and bring it into awareness. Logel, Spencer, Wood et al. (2006) tested this possibility directly. They measured participants' implicit and explicit self-esteem with the IAT and RSES. Half of their participants then completed an alleged test of intelligence and were told that they did extremely well; the remaining half simply read the test and received no performance feedback. This served to manipulate success relative to a neutral baseline.

Across a variety of measures, Logel, Spencer, Wood et al. (2008) found that participants with both low explicit and low implicit self-esteem fared worse after success. Such individuals were more concerned about the regard of their friends and family, reported feeling more anxious, and perhaps most intriguingly, reported lower state self-esteem after experiencing success. They also worried about meeting others' expectations in the future, perhaps reflecting their self-protective concerns that success would only lead to future failure. In contrast, individuals with low explicit but high implicit self-esteem responded more positively to success. They showed no detrimental reactions and actually reported more confidence in significant others' regard and higher state self-esteem. These results give an important qualification to past findings of the negative impact of success (e.g., Murray et al., 1998; Wood et al., 2005); it seems that not all low explicit self-esteem individuals fare worse after success. In fact, individuals with low explicit but high implicit self-esteem may instead experience a glimmer of hope as they benefit from the same successes that those with low explicit and low implicit self-esteem find distressing (see also Spencer et al., 2005).

Further evidence suggests that high implicit self-esteem combined with success may improve the long-term prognosis of individuals with low explicit self-esteem. We followed a large number of university students over the course of an academic term (Logel, Spencer, Zanna, Jordan, & Sadler, 2008). Participants completed online surveys every 2 weeks for 10 weeks, including various measures of self-views and subjective well-being. We conducted analyses to see whether initial levels of implicit and explicit self-esteem could predict changes in well-being 2 weeks after midterms, as a function of midterm performance. When participants did well on their midterms, those with low explicit but high implicit self-esteem reported less stress in their personal relationships, controlling for initial levels of relationship stressors. In contrast, participants with low explicit and low implicit self-esteem reported more relationship stress. Similarly, among low explicit self-esteem individuals who did well on their midterms, those with high implicit self-esteem reported significantly less depression, whereas those with low implicit self-esteem reported being more depressed. Perhaps most strikingly, when low explicit self-esteem individuals did well on their midterms, those with high implicit self-esteem actually showed higher trait self-esteem 2 weeks later. Those with low implicit self-esteem, in contrast, showed still lower trait self-esteem.

Convergent short-term and long-term findings thus strongly suggest that implicit self-esteem moderates how low explicit self-esteem individuals respond to success (Logel, Spencer, Wood et al., 2008; Logel, Spencer, Zanna et al., 2008). Whereas those with low implicit self-esteem appear to react negatively and suffer in response to success, those with high implicit self-esteem may actually benefit from it. We have dubbed this latter reaction a glimmer of hope, to contrast it with the nagging doubts of defensive individuals (Spencer et al., 2005). It should be noted, however, that high implicit self-esteem might not always be beneficial to those with low explicit self-esteem. Although some theorists have suggested that high implicit self-esteem acts as a buffer against threat (e.g., Dijksterhuis, 2004), it is possible that those with low explicit but high implicit self-esteem will sometimes react more negatively to failure. As failure brings high implicit self-esteem into awareness for these individuals, it should create an uncomfortable inconsistency that they are motivated to reduce. In the face of failure, as opposed to success, however, they may be unable to benefit from the glimmer of hope that high implicit self-esteem gives them and may instead resolve this inconsistency in the direction of their low explicit self-esteem. Thus, current evidence suggests that individuals with low explicit but high implicit self-esteem are capable of capitalizing on success. Precisely how they handle failure, however, is currently unclear. We expect that, at least sometimes, they will be more vulnerable to failure and have more volatile self-views (Logel, Spencer, Wood et al.).

Conclusion

Implicit self-esteem has proven useful in exploring the heterogeneity of self-esteem. Convergent evidence suggests that, among individuals with high explicit self-esteem, those with relatively low implicit self-esteem are more defensive (e.g., Bosson et al., 2003; Jordan et al., 2005; Jordan, Spencer, Zanna et al., 2003). Such defensiveness, moreover, may be motivated by nagging doubts—occasional awareness of low implicit self-esteem, which may threaten positive self-views. Indeed, when faced with evaluative feedback, even success, individuals with high explicit but low implicit self-esteem showed evidence of more negative self-views and diminished self-assurance. In addition, implicit self-esteem appears to play an important role in the psychology of low self-esteem. Preliminary evidence suggests that among individuals with low explicit self-esteem, those with relatively high implicit self-esteem benefit more from success (Logel, Spencer, Wood et al., 2008; Logel, Spencer, Zanna et al., 2008). People with low explicit but high implicit self-esteem may thus experience a glimmer of hope in response to positive evaluations. These results are certainly encouraging, but some conceptual issues remain.

Throughout this chapter, we have treated evidence stemming from different implicit measures of self-esteem equivalently. This has simplified our discussion, but it must be acknowledged that different implicit measures of self-esteem do not correlate with each other (e.g., Bosson et al., 2000; Jordan, Spencer, & Zanna, 2003). Thus, speaking as though these measures represent a common underlying construct may be somewhat misleading. This problem appears to be endemic to research on implicit constructs in general. Different measures of implicit memory, for example, often do not correlate with each other (Buchner & Wippich, 2000; Perruchet & Baveux, 1989; see DeHart, Pelham, & Tennen, 2006, for further discussion of this point).

Nevertheless, as we have seen, different implicit measures of self-esteem sometimes converge in showing the same patterns of association with other variables. Thus, the IAT and name-letter preference measures both suggest that people with high explicit but low implicit self-esteem are characteristically defensive (e.g., Bosson et al., 2003; Jordan, Spencer, Zanna et al., 2003). The IAT, name-letter preferences, and an evaluative priming measure of implicit self-esteem all appear to suggest that individuals with high explicit but low implicit self-esteem are narcissistic (Brown & Bosson, 2001; Jordan, Spencer, Zanna et al., 2003; Zeigler-Hill, 2008; see Dijksterhuis, 2004, for an additional example of such convergence). Findings such as these may suggest that different implicit measures of self-esteem, despite their lack of mutual correlation, actually do tap different aspects of the same underlying construct. This issue, however, needs further clarification.

Another conceptual issue concerns the stability of implicit self-esteem. It has been commonly assumed that implicit self-esteem develops early and is resistant to change (e.g., Greenwald & Banaji, 1995; Koole, Dijksterhuis, & van Knippenberg, 2001). Similar arguments have been made with respect to implicit attitudes more generally (e.g., Smith & DeCoster, 2000; Wilson et al., 2000). Such theories reflect, in part, prevailing assumptions about automatic processes. It is commonly believed that automatic processes represent deeply engrained, habitualized responses that are slow to change. This is, in fact, a defining feature of the associative memory system proposed by Smith and DeCoster, which operates primarily through automatic processes (see also Strack & Deutsch, 2004). By this view, a slowly evolving, stable system of automatic associations is one element of an adaptive cognitive architecture. Consistent with the idea that implicit self-esteem is stable, some recent research suggests that it may have origins in early parent-child interactions (DeHart et al., 2006; see also Rudman, 2004).

On the other hand, other evidence also suggests that implicit self-esteem is malleable. Classical conditioning procedures, in which self-relevant stimuli are paired repeatedly with positive stimuli, enhance implicit self-esteem (Baccus, Baldwin, & Packer, 2004; Dijksterhuis, 2004). This occurs even when the stimuli are subliminally presented.

Although such findings reaffirm the idea that implicit self-esteem is associative and automatic, they also, somewhat ironically, suggest that implicit self-esteem is easy to change. Other evidence suggests that threat can affect implicit self-esteem (Jones, Pelham, Mirenberg, & Hetts, 2002) and that daily negative events are associated with fluctuations in implicit self-esteem for at least some people (DeHart & Pelham, 2007). Thus evidence suggests that implicit self-esteem is both stable and malleable. This might suggest that people have a relatively stable, average level of implicit self-esteem around which their implicit self-esteem fluctuates (see DeHart & Pelham, 2007; Hetts & Pelham, 2001). Thus, situational factors may occasionally deflect implicit self-esteem, but it is likely to return to a solid baseline level.

Such considerations have implications for research on the heterogeneity of self-esteem. The degree of correspondence between people's implicit and explicit self-esteem will be only as stable as are implicit and explicit self-esteem themselves. If implicit self-esteem is malleable, then secure individuals, with generally high explicit and implicit self-esteem, for example, may behave defensively if their implicit self-esteem is acutely lowered. Interestingly, recent research suggests that acute changes to implicit self-esteem may affect defensive responses. Kernis, Abend, Goldman, Shrira, Paradise, and Hampton (2005) subliminally primed positive or negative associations with the self. When these primes were discrepant from participants' explicit self-views (e.g., high explicit self-esteem individuals received negative primes), those participants were more self-promoting and more derogatory in their ratings of an outgroup member. It thus seems that situationally induced discrepancies between implicit and explicit self-esteem may mimic chronic discrepancies. It would thus be instructive to determine how long such priming effects last and whether chronic levels of implicit self-esteem moderate such effects.

Certainly additional questions remain. Indeed, much of the work in this area can still be considered preliminary. It thus remains unclear whether implicit self-esteem, so called, is actually best characterized as unconscious, preconscious, or even conscious (see Jordan, Logel, Spencer, & Zanna, 2006, for more in-depth consideration of this issue). Consequently, it remains unclear precisely why low implicit self-esteem motivates defensiveness among high explicit self-esteem individuals— although our recent research is starting to make a case that nagging doubts play a role. It is similarly unclear why high implicit self-esteem allows individuals with low explicit self-esteem to benefit from success. Such issues notwithstanding, it is clear that implicit self-esteem plays a role in defining the heterogeneity of self-esteem. The interplay between implicit and explicit measures of self-esteem appears to define unique psychological states within individuals. Additional research will surely clarify these states further. For now, the most important thing to recognize may be that what people say about themselves really is only one part of the story.

References

Aronson, E. (1968). Dissonance theory: Progress and problems. In R. Abelson, E. Aronson, W. McGuire, T. Newcomb, M. Rosenberg, & P. Tannenbaum (Eds.), *Theories of cognitive consistency: A sourcebook* (pp. 5–27). Chicago: Rand McNally.

Aronson, E., & Carlsmith, J. M. (1962). Performance expectancy as a determinant of actual performance. *Journal of Abnormal and Social Psychology, 68*, 986–996.

Asendorpf, J. B., Banse, R., & Mucke, D. (2002). Double dissociation between implicit and explicit personality self-concept: The case of shy behavior. *Journal of Personality and Social Psychology, 83*, 380–393.

Baccus, J. R., Baldwin, M. W., & Packer, D. J. (2004). Increasing implicit self-esteem through classical conditioning. *Psychological Science, 15*, 498–502.

Baldwin, M. W., & Sinclair, L. (1996). Self-esteem and "if...then" contingencies of interpersonal acceptance. *Journal of Personality and Social Psychology, 71*, 1130–1141.

Bargh, J. A., Chaiken, S., Raymond, P., & Hymes, C. (1996). The automatic evaluation effect: Unconditional automatic attitude activation with a pronunciation task. *Journal of Experimental Social Psychology, 32*, 104–128.

Baumeister, R. F., Campbell, J. D., Krueger, J. I., & Vohs, K. D. (2003). Does high self-esteem cause better performance, interpersonal success, happiness, or healthier lifestyles? *Psychological Science in the Public Interest, 4*, 1–44.

Baumeister, R. F., Smart, L., & Boden, J. M. (1996). Relation of threatened egotism to violence and aggression: The dark side of high self-esteem. *Psychological Review, 103*, 5–33.

Baumeister, R. F., Tice, D. M., & Hutton, D. G. (1989). Self-presentation motivations and personality differences in self-esteem. *Journal of Personality, 57*, 547–579.

Beauregard, K. S., & Dunning, D. (1998). Turning up the contrast: Self-enhancement motives prompt egocentric contrast effects in social judgments. *Journal of Personality and Social Psychology, 74*, 606–621.

Bosson, J. K., Brown, R. P., Zeigler-Hill, V., & Swann, W. B. (2003). Self-enhancement tendencies among people with high explicit self-esteem: The moderating role of implicit self-esteem. *Self and Identity, 2*, 169–187.

Bosson, J. K., Swann, W. B., & Pennebaker, J. W. (2000). Stalking the perfect measure of implicit self-esteem: The blind men and the elephant revisited? *Journal of Personality and Social Psychology, 79*, 631–643.

Briñol, P., Petty, R. E., & Wheeler, S. C. (2006). Discrepancies between explicit and implicit self-concepts: Consequences for information processing. *Journal of Personality and Social Psychology, 91*, 154–170.

Brown, R. P., & Bosson, J. K. (2001). Narcissus meets Sisyphus: Self-love, self-loathing, and the never-ending pursuit of self-worth. *Psychological Inquiry, 12*, 210–213.

Brown, J. D., & Dutton, K. A. (1995). The thrill of victory, the complexity of defeat: Self-esteem and people's emotional reactions to success and failure. *Journal of Personality and Social Psychology, 68*, 712–722.

Buchner, A., & Wippich, W. (2000). On the reliability of implicit and explicit memory measures. *Cognitive Psychology, 40*, 227–259.

Cheng, C. M., Govorun, O., & Chartrand, T. L. (2006, January). *Mirror, mirror on the wall…: Implicit self-esteem predicts mood following self-awareness.* Paper presented at the annual meeting of the Society for Personality and Social Psychology, Palm Springs, CA.

Cohen, J., & Cohen, P. (1983). *Applied multiple regression/correlation analyses for the behavioral sciences* (1st ed.). Hillsdale, NJ: Lawrence Erlbaum.

Coopersmith, S. (1959). A method for determining types of self-esteem. *Journal of Abnormal and Social Psychology, 59*, 87–94.

Crocker, J., & Park, L. E. (2004). The costly pursuit of self-esteem. *Psychological Bulletin, 130*, 392–414.

Crocker, J., Thompson, L., McGraw, K., & Ingerman, C. (1987). Downward comparison, prejudice, and evaluations of others: Effects of self-esteem and threat. *Journal of Personality and Social Psychology, 60*, 218–228.

Crocker, J., & Wolfe, C. T. (2001). Contingencies of self-worth. *Psychological Review, 108*, 593–623.

Deci, E. L., & Ryan, R. M. (1995). Human autonomy: The basis for true self-esteem. In M. H. Kernis (Ed.), *Efficacy, agency, and self-esteem* (pp. 31–49). New York: Plenum Press.

DeHart, T., & Pelham, B. W. (2007). Fluctuations in state implicit self-esteem in response to daily negative events. *Journal of Experimental Social Psychology, 42*, 157–165.

DeHart, T., Pelham, B. W., & Tennen, H. (2006). What lies beneath: Parenting style and implicit self-esteem. *Journal of Experimental Social Psychology, 42*, 1–17.

Dijksterhuis, A. (2004). I like myself but I don't know why: Enhancing implicit self-esteem by subliminal evaluative conditioning. *Journal of Personality and Social Psychology, 86*, 345–355.

Dodgson, P. G., & Wood, J. V. (1998). Self-esteem and the cognitive accessibility of strengths and weaknesses after failure. *Journal of Personality and Social Psychology, 75,* 178–197.

Dunning, D., Perie, M., & Story, A. L. (1991). Self-serving stereotypes of social categories. *Journal of Personality and Social Psychology, 61,* 957–968.

Elliot, A. J., & Devine, P. G. (1994). On the motivational nature of cognitive dissonance: Dissonance as psychological discomfort. *Journal of Personality and Social Psychology, 67,* 382–394.

Emler, N. (2001). *Self-esteem: The costs and causes of low self-worth.* York, PA: York Publishing Services for the Joseph Rowntree Foundation.

Epley, N., & Dunning, D. (2000). Feeling "holier than thou": Are self-serving assessments produced by errors in self- or social prediction? *Journal of Personality and Social Psychology, 79,* 861–875.

Epstein, S., & Morling, B. (1995). Is the self motivated to do more than enhance and/or verify itself? In M. Kernis (Ed.), *Efficacy, agency, and self-esteem* (pp. 9–29). New York: Plenum Press.

Farnham, S. D., Greenwald, A. G., & Banaji, M. R. (1999). Implicit self-esteem. In D. Abrams & M. A. Hogg (Eds.), *Social identity and social cognition* (pp. 230–248). Oxford, England: Blackwell.

Fazio, R. H., Sanbonmatsu, D. M., Powell, M. C., & Kardes, F. R. (1986). On the automatic activation of attitudes. *Journal of Personality and Social Psychology, 50,* 229–238.

Fazio, R. H., & Towles-Schwen, T. (1999). The MODE model of attitude-behavior processes. In S. Chaiken & Y. Trope (Eds.), *Dual-process theories in social psychology* (pp. 97–116). New York: Guilford Press.

Fein, S., & Spencer, S. J. (1997). Prejudice as self-image maintenance: Affirming the self through derogating others. *Journal of Personality and Social Psychology, 73,* 31–44.

Greenwald, A. G., & Banaji, M. R. (1995). Implicit social cognition: Attitudes, self-esteem, and stereotypes. *Psychological Review, 102,* 4–27.

Greenwald, A. G., & Farnham, S. D. (2001). Using the Implicit Association Test to measure self-esteem and self-concept. *Journal of Personality and Social Psychology, 79,* 1022–1038.

Greenwald, A. G., McGhee, D. E., & Schwartz, J. L. K. (1998). Measuring individual differences in implicit cognition: The Implicit Association Test. *Journal of Personality and Social Psychology, 74,* 1464–1480.

Heine, S. J., Lehman, D. R., Markus, H. R., & Kitayama, S. (1999). Is there a universal need for positive self-regard? *Psychological Review, 106,* 766–794.

Hinton, G. E. (1990). Mapping part-whole hierarchies into connectionist networks. *Artificial Intelligence, 46,* 47–76.

Hogarth, R. M. (2001). *Educating intuition.* Chicago: University of Chicago Press.

Hoshino-Browne, E., Zanna, A. S., Spencer, S. J., & Zanna, M. P. (2004). Investigating attitudes cross-culturally: A case of cognitive dissonance among East Asians and North Americans. In G. Haddock & G. R. Maio (Eds.), *Contemporary perspectives on the psychology of attitudes* (pp. 375–397). New York: Psychology Press.

Jankowski, M. S. (1991). *Islands in the street: Gangs and American urban society.* Berkeley: University of California Press.

Jones, J. T., Pelham, B. W., Mirenberg, M. C., & Hetts, J. J. (2002). Name letter preferences are not merely mere exposure: Implicit egotism as self-regulation. *Journal of Experimental Social Psychology, 38,* 170–177.

Jordan, C. H., Logel, C., Spencer, S. J., & Zanna, M. P. (2006). Nonconscious self-esteem: Is there something you're not telling yourself? In M. H. Kernis (Ed.), *Self-esteem issues and answers: A source book of current perspectives* (pp. 60–68). Philadelphia: Psychology Press.

Jordan, C. H., Spencer, S. J., & Zanna, M. P. (2003). "I love me...I love me not": Implicit self-esteem, explicit self-esteem, and defensiveness. In S. J. Spencer, S. Fein, M. P. Zanna, & J. M. Olson (Eds.), *Motivated social cognition: The Ontario Symposium* (Vol. 9, pp. 117–145). Mahwah, NJ: Erlbaum.

Jordan, C. H., Spencer, S. J., & Zanna, M. P. (2005). Types of high self-esteem and prejudice: How implicit self-esteem relates to ethnic discrimination among high explicit self-esteem individuals. *Personality and Social Psychology Bulletin, 31,* 693–702.

Jordan, C. H., Spencer, S. J., Zanna, M. P., Hoshino-Browne, E., & Correll, J. (2003). Secure and defensive high self-esteem. *Journal of Personality and Social Psychology, 85,* 969–978.

Jordan, C. H., Whitfield, M., & Zeigler-Hill, V. (2007). Intuition and the correspondence between implicit and explicit self-esteem. *Journal of Personality and Social Psychology, 93,* 1067–1079.

Kernis, M. H. (2003). Toward a conceptualization of optimal self-esteem. *Psychological Inquiry, 14,* 1–26.

Kernis, M. H., Abend, T. A., Goldman, B. M., Shrira, I., Paradise, A. N., & Hampton, A. (2005). Self-serving responses arising from discrepancies between explicit and implicit self-esteem. *Self and Identity, 4,* 311–330.

Kernis, M. H., & Paradise, A. W. (2002). Distinguishing between fragile and secure forms of high self-esteem. In E. L. Deci & R. M. Ryan (Eds.), *Self-determination: Theoretical issues and practical applications.* Rochester, NY: University of Rochester Press.

Kernis, M. H., & Waschull, S. B. (1995). The interactive roles of stability and level of self-esteem: Research and theory. In M. P. Zanna (Ed.), *Advances in experimental social psychology* (Vol. 27, pp. 93–141). San Diego: Academic Press.

Kohut, H. (1971). *The analysis of the self.* New York: International University Press.

Koole, S. L., Dijksterhuis, A., & van Knippenberg, A. (2001). What's in a name: Implicit self-esteem and the automatic self. *Journal of Personality and Social Psychology, 77*, 111–125.

Koole, S. L., & Pelham, B. W. (2003). On the nature of implicit self-esteem: The case of the name-letter effect. In S. J. Spencer, S. Fein, M. P. Zanna, & J. M. Olson (Eds.), *Motivated social cognition: The Ontario Symposium* (Vol. 9, pp. 93–116). Mahwah, NJ: Erlbaum.

Lieberman, M. D. (2000). Intuition: A social cognitive neuroscience approach. *Psychological Bulletin, 126*, 109–137.

Lobel, T. E., & Teiber, A. (1994). Effects of self-esteem and need for approval on affective and cognitive reactions: Defensive and true self-esteem. *Personality and Individual Differences, 16*, 315–321.

Logel, C., Spencer, S. J., Holmes, J. G., & Wood, J. V. (2004, January). *Low self-esteem and the downside of success.* Poster presented at the 4th annual conference of the Society for Personality and Social Psychology, Austin, Texas.

Logel, C., Spencer, S. J., Zanna, M. P., Jordan, C. H., & Sadler, P. (2006). Low self-esteem and depression: How implicit self-esteem can buffer the evaluative implications of school performance. Unpublished data, University of Waterloo.

McGregor, I., & Marigold, D. C. (2003). Defensive zeal and the uncertain self: What makes you so sure? *Journal of Personality and Social Psychology, 85*, 838–852.

McGregor, I., Nail, P. R., Marigold, D. C., & Kang, S.-J. (2005). Defensive pride and consensus: Strength in imaginary numbers. *Journal of Personality and Social Psychology, 89*, 978–996.

Morf, C. C., & Rhodewalt, F. (2001). Unraveling the paradoxes of narcissism: A dynamic self-regulatory processing model. *Psychological Inquiry, 12*, 177–196.

Murray, S. L., Holmes, J. G., MacDonald, G., & Ellsworth, P. C. (1998). Through the looking glass darkly? When self-doubts turn into relationship insecurities. *Journal of Personality and Social Psychology, 75*, 1459–1480.

Olweus, D. (1994). Bullying at school: Long-term outcomes for the victims and an effective school-based intervention program. In R. Huesmann (Ed.), *Aggressive behavior: Current perspectives* (pp. 97–130). New York: Plennum Press.

Paulhus, D. L. (1998). Interpersonal and intrapsychic adaptiveness of trait self-enhancement: A mixed blessing? *Journal of Personality and Social Psychology, 74*, 1197–1208.

Pelham, B. W., & Hetts, J. J. (1999). Implicit and explicit personal and social identity: Toward a more complete understanding of the social self. In T. Tyler & R. Kramer (Eds.), *The psychology of the social self* (pp. 115–143). Mahwah, MJ: Erlbaum.

Perruchet, P., & Baveux, P. (1989). Correlational analyses of explicit and implicit memory performance. *Memory and Cognition, 17,* 77–86.

Petty, R. E., & Briñol, P. (2006). A meta-cognitive approach to "implicit" and "explicit" evaluations: Comment on Gawronski and Bodenhausen (2006). *Psychological Bulletin, 132,* 740–744.

Petty, R. E., & Briñol, P. (in press). Implicit ambivalence: A meta-cognitive approach. In R. E. Petty, R. H. Fazio, & P. Briñol (Eds.), *Attitudes: Insights from the new implicit measures.* Hillsdale, NJ: Erlbaum.

Raskin, R. N., & Hall, C. S. (1988). The narcissistic personality inventory. *Psychological Reports, 40,* 590.

Raskin, R., Novacek, J., & Hogan, R. (1991). Narcissism, self-esteem, and defensive self-enhancement. *Journal of Personality, 59,* 19–38.

Reasoner, R. (2005). *The true meaning of self-esteem* [On-line]. National Association for Self-Esteem website: www.self-esteem-nase.org/what.php.

Rosenberg, M. (1965). *Society and the adolescent self-image.* Princeton, NJ: Princeton University Press.

Rubin, M., & Hewstone, M. (1998). Social identity theory's self-esteem hypothesis: A review and some suggestions for clarification. *Personality and Social Psychology Review, 2,* 40–62.

Rudman, L. A. (2004). Sources of implicit attitudes. *Current Directions in Psychological Science, 13,* 79–82.

Salmivalli, C., Kaukiainen, A., Kaistaniemi, L., & Lagerspetz, K. M. J. (1999). Self-evaluated self-esteem, peer-evaluated self-esteem, and defensive egotism as predictors of adolescents' participation in bullying situations. *Personality and Social Psychology Bulletin, 25,* 1268–1278.

Schneider, D. J., & Turkat, D. (1975). Self-presentation following success or failure: Defensive self-esteem models. *Journal of Personality, 43,* 127–135.

Shrauger, J. S., & Rosenberg, S. E. (1970). Self-esteem and the effects of success and failure feedback on performance. *Journal of Personality, 38,* 404–417.

Sloman, S. A. (1996). The empirical case for two systems of reasoning. *Psychological Bulletin, 119,* 3–22.

Smith, E. R., & DeCoster, J. (2000). Dual-process models in social and cognitive psychology: Conceptual integration and links to underlying memory systems. *Personality and Social Psychology Review, 4,* 108–131.

Smolensky, P. (1988). On the proper treatment of connectionism. *Behavioral and Brain Sciences, 11,* 1–23.

Spalding, L. R., & Hardin, C. D. (1999). Unconscious unease and self-handicapping: Behavioral consequences of individual differences in implicit and explicit self-esteem. *Psychological Science, 10,* 535–539.

Spencer, S. J., Jordan, C. H., Logel, C., & Zanna, M. P. (2005). Nagging doubts and a glimmer of hope: The role of implicit self-esteem in self-image maintenance. In A. Tesser, J. V. Wood, & D. A. Stapel (Eds.), *On building, defending and regulating the self* (pp. 153–170). New York: Psychology Press.

Steele, C. M. (1988). The psychology of self-affirmation: Sustaining the integrity of the self. In L. Berkowitz (Ed.), *Advances in experimental social psychology* (Vol. 21, pp. 261–302). San Diego: Academic Press.

Steele, C. M., & Lui, T. J. (1983). Dissonance processes as self-affirmation. *Journal of Personality and Social Psychology, 45*, 5–19.

Steele, C. M., Spencer, S. J., & Lynch, M. (1993). Self-image resilience and dissonance: The role of affirmational resources. *Journal of Personality and Social Psychology, 64*, 885–896.

Strack, F., & Deutsch, R. (2004). Reflective and impulsive determinants of social behavior. *Personality and Social Psychology Review, 8*, 220–247.

Swann, W. B. (1992). Seeking "truth," finding despair: Some unhappy consequences of a negative self-concept. *Current Directions in Psychological Science, 1*, 15–18.

Tajfel, H. (1981). *Human groups and social categories.* Cambridge: Cambridge University Press.

Tajfel, H., & Turner, J. C. (1979). An integrative theory of intergroup conflict. In W. G. Austin & S. Worchel (Eds.), *The social psychology of intergroup relations* (pp. 33–47). Monterey, CA: Brooks/Cole.

Wilson, T. D., Lindsey, S., & Schooler, T. Y. (2000). A model of dual attitudes. *Psychological Review, 107*, 101–126.

Wood, J. V., Heimpel, S. A., Newby-Clark, I. R., & Ross, M. (2005). Snatching defeat from the jaws of victory: Self-esteem differences in the experience and anticipation of success. *Journal of Personality and Social Psychology, 89*, 764–780.

Zeigler-Hill, V. (2006). Discrepancies between implicit and explicit self-esteem: Implications for narcissism and self-esteem instability. *Journal of Personality, 74*, 119–143.

Section V

Attitude Change

10

Changing Attitudes on Implicit Versus Explicit Measures
What Is the Difference?

Pablo Briñol
Richard E. Petty
Michael J. McCaslin

Introduction

In the typical situation in which persuasion is possible, a person or a group of people (i.e., the recipient or audience) receives an intervention (e.g., a persuasive communication) from another individual or group (i.e., the source) in a particular setting (i.e., the context). Successful persuasion is said to occur when the recipients' attitudes are modified in the desired direction. After a long tradition of assessing the impact of persuasion treatments on attitudes with deliberative self-reports (Eagly & Chaiken, 1993; Petty & Wegener, 1998), more recent work has assessed change with measures that tap the more automatic evaluations associated with objects, issues, and people. Measures that assess automatic associations without a person's knowledge of what is being assessed are often referred to as *implicit measures,* and assessments that tap a person's more deliberative and acknowledged evaluations are referred to as *explicit measures.*

In describing changes in attitudes measured with explicit and implicit techniques, we also examine the nature (explicit or implicit) of the psychological processes that underlie those changes. We define an *implicit process* as one in which the persuasion elements tend to operate automatically and often outside of awareness. In contrast, we refer to an *explicit process* as involving persuasion elements that require some deliberation and of which people are more likely to be aware. This distinction is, of course, not perfect, and most persuasion techniques will use elements of both.

Our specific goals in this chapter are to (a) briefly note the dominant persuasion finding that explicit measures are affected by deliberative processes, (b) describe how explicit measures also can be affected
by automatic processes requiring little thought, (c) examine research
revealing that implicit measures can assess changes brought about
through both low and high deliberative processes, (d) explore strength-
related consequences associated with those changes, and (e) identify
cases in which deliberative and automatic processes are jointly activated and what their impact is on explicit and implicit measures.

Single-Process Changes

Explicit Measures: Changes by Deliberative Processes

By far, most work in attitude change has focused on relatively deliberative processes affecting explicit measures of attitudes. There are a number of persuasion theories suggesting that deliberative processes can
produce change in explicitly assessed attitudes (see reviews by Eagly &
Chaiken, 1993; Petty & Wegener, 1998). For example, one of the earliest
deliberative theories argued that message learning was an important
precursor to opinion change (Hovland, Janis, & Kelley, 1953). According to this framework, for example, distracting someone from the message was predicted to reduce persuasion because it would interfere with
comprehending and learning the message. Similarly, providing a person
with a credible source would increase the impact of a communication
on persuasion because it would motivate people to learn the message.

Another of the influential deliberative theories of persuasion, cognitive response theory (Greenwald, 1968; Petty, Ostrom, & Brock, 1981),
similarly postulated a relatively thoughtful mechanism. This theory
contended that persuasion depended on the extent to which individuals
articulated and rehearsed their own idiosyncratic thoughts to the information presented. Consistent with this framework, extensive research
has shown that aspects of the source (e.g., credibility), message (e.g.,
quality of arguments), recipient (e.g., mood), and context (e.g., presence
of distraction) can influence persuasion by affecting the explicit and
measurable thoughts people generate in response to persuasive appeals
(for a review, see Petty, Ostrom et al., 1981).

In addition to these two approaches, many other classic theories of
persuasion proposed deliberative mechanisms to account for changes
on explicitly measured attitudes. For example, according to dissonance

theory (Festinger, 1957), explicit attitudes can change due to effortful cognitive reorganization stemming from the psychological tension induced by engaging in a discrepant action. Although people are not necessarily aware of their dissonance reduction efforts, our assumption is that dissonance reduction is facilitated by cognitive effort and inferential reasoning (see also Gawronski & Strack, 2003; Petty & Cacioppo, 1986; Wilson, Lindsey, & Schooler, 2000). Early research on role-playing (e.g., Janis & King, 1954) also showed that active generation of a message, which involves an effortful process of biased scanning (Janis, 1968), can be a successful strategy for producing explicit change. The probabilogical (e.g., McGuire, 1981) and the expectancy/value (e.g., Fishbein & Ajzen, 1975) approaches to attitude change also provide examples of thoughtful change because they imply that people deliberatively assess the likelihood and desirability of attributes of the attitude object and then integrate this information into a coherent impression (for a review, see Petty & Wegener, 1998).

Explicit Measures: Change by Less Thoughtful and Automatic Processes

Although many early theories of persuasion focused on deliberative processes and provided considerable evidence for the fact that these processes could produce change on explicit measures, according to other early theories of persuasion, attitude change need not require much thinking. For example, one of the most primitive means of changing attitudes involves the direct association of affect with objects through *classical conditioning*. Thus, people's evaluations of words, other people, political slogans, products, and persuasive communications have been modified by pairing them with a variety of stimuli about which people already feel positively or negatively (e.g., Staats & Staats, 1958). Explicit measures of attitudes also can be changed through other processes that require relatively little thinking. Some inference-based approaches, such as self-perception theory (Bem, 1972), illustrate this possibility by demonstrating that people sometimes infer their attitudes directly, and perhaps even automatically, in a manner similar to that by which they infer the attitudes and traits of others (i.e., from observed behavior and the context in which it occurred; Uleman, 1987).

Also consistent with the idea that attitude change can occur when thinking is low, explicitly assessed attitudes have been affected as a result of mere exposure (Zajonc, 1968) and the use of simple heuristics (Chaiken, 1980). For example, when objects are presented—even subliminally—to an individual on repeated occasions, this mere exposure is capable of making the person's explicit attitude toward the objects more positive (Kunst-Wilson & Zajonc, 1980). In addition, people can base acceptance of a message on the expertise of the message or the mere number of arguments it contains by retrieving the heuristic "Experts are usually correct." (e.g., Chaiken; Petty, Cacioppo, & Goldman, 1981) or "The more arguments, the better." (Petty & Cacioppo, 1984).

Thus, the accumulated work on persuasion reveals that a variety of low deliberation processes can produce attitude change on explicit measures. Taken together with the high deliberation processes described earlier, it seems clear that explicit attitudes can be modified by both high and low thinking processes. For expository purposes, we have described persuasion processes as if they can be neatly categorized into high versus low thought mechanisms. However, it is important to note that the various persuasion processes fall along a thinking continuum and are not invariably at the extremes (Petty & Cacioppo, 1986). For example, at the low end of the thinking continuum are relatively pure automatic processes (e.g., subliminal mere exposure) as well as some other processes (e.g., use of simple heuristics) that could require at least some controlled reflection.

The Elaboration Likelihood Model (ELM; Petty & Cacioppo, 1981) and the Heuristic-Systematic Model (HSM; Chaiken, Liberman, & Eagly, 1989) of persuasion were proposed to establish the conditions under which relatively thoughtful versus nonthoughtful processes would affect explicit change.[1] Furthermore, these theories noted that although persuasion can occur when thinking is relatively high or low, the consequences of the attitude change induced are different in each situation. In particular, the ELM holds that the process by which an attitude is formed or changed is consequential for the strength of the attitude (see Petty & Cacioppo, 1986; Petty & Wegener, 1999). For example, when a variable such as source credibility produces persuasion through a relatively low thinking process (e.g., by serving as input to an expertise heuristic; e.g., Petty, Cacioppo et al., 1981), the attitude formed is less persistent, resistant to change, and predictive of behavior than when the same amount of change is produced by credibility because of a relatively high thinking process (e.g., biasing the thoughts generated; e.g., Chaiken & Maheswaran, 1994). Thus, understanding the processes by which variables have their impact on attitude change has been essential because it is informative about the immediate and long-term consequences of persuasion (Petty, Haugtvedt, & Smith, 1995).

Implicit Measures: Change by Automatic Processes

To summarize so far, throughout the history of persuasion work, theories of attitude change focused on processes that varied in the extent of deliberative thought they required to operate (low to high). Theories of persuasion such as the ELM and HSM attempted to integrate both high and low thought processes into one conceptual framework. Regardless of the amount of thinking, however, a common feature of most prior work is that attitude change was assessed with deliberative measures because that was all there was. In the last decade, however, there have been a growing number of new measures of automatic attitudes available (e.g., evaluative priming; Fazio, Jackson, Dunton, & Williams, 1995; Implicit Association Test, or IAT; Greenwald, McGhee, & Schwartz, 1998).

Fazio's MODE model (Fazio & Towles-Schwen, 1999) provided an influential early account of the relationship between deliberative and automatic measures. According to the MODE model, automatic measures of attitudes are more likely to reflect the true attitude than are explicit measures because deliberative measures also tap any downstream cognitive activity in addition to the stored evaluative association (see Chapter 2, this volume). One important downstream consideration is the perceived validity of the activated evaluation. This validity assessment is sometimes assumed to be conducted entirely on-line (e.g., Gawronski & Bodenhausen, 2006). In other approaches, however, such as the Meta-Cognitive Model (MCM) of attitudes (Petty & Briñol, 2006; Petty, Briñol, & DeMarree, 2007), people are assumed to store validity assessments—at least for some attitude objects—that can be retrieved with additional cognitive effort. These validity assessments are important in determining the attitudes reported on explicit measures (see Chapter 5, this volume).

Early assumptions about the nature of automatic evaluations suggested that such attitudes would be very difficult to change, in part because the underlying object-evaluation associations were assumed to be learned over a long period of time. For example, automatic evaluations reflecting prejudice have been viewed as resulting from passive, long-term exposure to negative portrayals in the media (Devine, 1989) and longstanding status differences between groups. In accord with this view, Wilson et al. (2000) argued that "explicit attitudes change relatively easily, whereas implicit attitudes, like old habits, change more slowly" (p. 14). As a result of this assumption, a common proposal was that automatic evaluations were more enduring and resistant to change than were deliberative attitudes (i.e., attitudes reported on explicit measures; e.g., Banaji, 2004; Bargh, 1999; Greenwald et al., 1998; Rydell, McConnell, Strain, Claypool, & Hugenberg, 2007).

Given these considerations, how should automatic attitudes be changed? If anything, based on their origin and nature, measures of automatic evaluation have been assumed to be sensitive to automatic, implicit processes that can require multiple exposures for success (e.g., Rydell & McConnel, 2006). Classical conditioning and mere exposure are two relatively low thought or automatic processes that rely on multiple exposures. Consistent with the idea that automatic attitudes can be changed with these mechanisms, Olson and Fazio (2001) showed that automatic evaluations were sensitive to classical conditioning procedures that used 20 pairings of the target attitude objects and CS. Using a similar paradigm, Dijksterhuis (2004) found that automatic evaluations of the self can be affected by subliminal evaluative conditioning trials (15 pairings) in which the word *I* is repeatedly associated with positive or negative trait terms (see also Petty, Tormala, Briñol, & Jarvis, 2006; Walter, 2002).

Also consistent with this approach, research on automatic prejudice has shown that implicit measures can change through other paradigms that involve exposing individuals repeatedly to either positive or negative information about outgroup members. For example, automatic evaluations of Blacks have been shown to be affected by exposure to admired Black individuals (Dasgupta & Greenwald, 2001), to a Black professor (Rudman, Ashmore, & Gary, 2001), to a Black experimenter (Lowery, Hardin, & Sinclair, 2001), or to a Black partner who occupied a superior task role (Richeson & Ambady, 2003; for reviews, see Blair, 2002; Fazio & Olson, 2003; Gawronski & Bodenhausen, 2006).

Thus, the accumulated research is generally consistent with the idea that automatic measures of attitudes can be affected by relatively low thought and automatic attitude change processes. In fact, implicit measures of attitudes have sometimes been assumed to change *only* as a result of low thought processes (cf. Smith & DeCoster, 1999). In other words, just as automatic attitudes have been postulated to predict more automatic behaviors than controlled attitudes (e.g., Dovidio, Kawakami, & Beach, 2001), so too has it been assumed by some theorists that automatic attitudes should be changed by more automatic processes than deliberative attitudes (e.g., Rydell & McConnell, 2006). For example, Dasgupta and Greenwald (2001) expressed that "it is conceivable that whereas explicit attitudes may be best tackled with techniques that involve deep cognitive processing, automatic prejudice may benefit from the frequent use of techniques that involve shallower processing" (see Rudman et al., 2001, for a similar view).

In another illustration of this view, Gawronski, Strack, and Bodenhausen (Chapter 4, this volume) have argued that automatic evaluations are sensitive to associative processes that are fast and require little cognitive capacity but not to propositional thinking that often requires a large amount of cognitive capacity. In contrast with low effort associative processes, propositional thinking is assumed to require more extensive thinking because it implies an evaluation of declarative knowledge as true or false (see Gawronski & Bodenhausen, 2006, for a review). According to Gawronski and Strack (2003), for example, dissonance-related phenomena are inherently propositional, with inconsistency between two or more propositions being resolved either by explicitly rejecting one proposition as being false or by finding an additional proposition that resolves the inconsistency (Kruglanski, 1989). Based on these considerations, Gawronski and Strack predicted and found that counterattitudinal behavior under conditions of low situational pressure affected deliberative but not automatic attitudes. Although the null effect on automatic measures across conditions is open to multiple interpretations, this finding was explained as a matching effect between the extent (and type) of thinking in the attitude change induction and the nature of the measure. According to Gawronski and Strack, controlled attitudes changed as a result of counterattitudinal behavior because the process of dissonance reduction requires a thoughtful consideration of the propositional representation of cognitive elements. In contrast, automatic attitudes would not change as a function of counterattitudinal behavior unless dissonance reduction processes were operating through a low effort mechanism such as self-perception (Bem, 1972) or the activation of simple counterattitudinal associations (e.g., Blair, Ma, & Lenton, 2001).

Implicit Measures: Change by Deliberative Processes

Although there is now considerable agreement that automatic and low thought attitude change processes—especially those involving multiple trials—can affect automatic attitudes, it is less clear if deliberative processes can affect those same measures. As noted above, some theorists have argued that this should be rather difficult.

The general notion of the need to match certain change strategies with attitude measures has received considerable theoretical attention and some empirical support. However, a variety of findings call into question the general idea that automatic and deliberative measures respond only to matched persuasion techniques. For example, as described previously, extensive research has shown that low effort (relatively nonthoughtful) processes such as classical conditioning and mere exposure can influence both deliberative (e.g., Zajonc, 1968; Staats & Staats, 1958) and automatic (Olson & Fazio, 2001) measures of attitudes. However, it is possible that although deliberative attitudes are affected by both high and low thought processes, perhaps automatic attitudes are influenced only (or primarily) by low thought processes. Or, if deliberative processes have an impact on automatic measures, then it must be that this effect is mediated by deliberative attitudes (Gawronski & Bodenhausen, 2006).

Some evidence against strict matching effects for automatic attitude measures comes from research on attitude accessibility. That is, it is well known that mere rehearsal and repetition of an attitude without thinking can increase its accessibility (Fabrigar, Priester, Petty, & Wegener, 1998; Fazio, 1995; Judd & Brauer, 1995). However, it is less well known that attitudes changed as a result of highly thoughtful processes can be more accessible than attitudes changed to the same extent by less thoughtful processes (see Petty et al., 1995). For example, Bizer and Krosnick (2001, Experiment 3) manipulated extent of thinking by varying the personal importance of a topic (i.e., participants were led to believe that the proposed new policy would affect them personally or not; Petty & Cacioppo, 1979) and found a significant effect on attitude accessibility, such that those in the high (vs. low) thinking condition had more accessible attitudes. Because attitude accessibility is a dimension that operates automatically and outside conscious awareness (Fazio, 1995), it suggests that perhaps measures of attitudes assessing automatic associations can similarly be affected by deliberative processes.

To examine this issue more directly, we conducted a series of studies to test whether automatic evaluations can be affected by thoughtful processing of persuasive messages (Briñol, Petty, & Horcajo, 2008). In all experiments participants received a persuasive message, and in some the extent to which they were motivated to think about these messages was also manipulated. We assessed if extensive message processing can change an implicit measure of attitudes related to the proposal. Different IATs (Greenwald et al., 1998) were used to approximate the strength of association between the attitude object and an evaluation.

Pilot test of implicit change from deliberation. In a pilot test, participants read a persuasive message composed of compelling arguments in favor of consuming vegetables. In a control condition, they read a neutral message. An example argument in favor of vegetable consumption was that vegetables have more vitamins than most supplements on the market, making them particularly beneficial during exam and workout periods. The neutral topic was an editorial related to interior design and decoration in which the word *vegetable* was also mentioned explicitly to control for the accessibility of the attitude object itself. All participants were asked to think carefully about the message. After thinking about the message, participants had to complete an apparently unrelated task (an IAT) that was designed to assess automatic evaluations relevant to the proposal of the message. In the IAT (Greenwald et al., 1998), participants classified target concepts (represented by *vegetable* or *animal*) and attributes (represented by *good* or *bad*).

Consistent with the idea that deliberative processes can influence implicit measures, we found automatic evaluations toward vegetables to change as a result of the persuasive message. These findings are consistent with some prior research showing that automatic evaluations as measured by the IAT can sometimes change in response to advertisements (Czyzewska & Ginsburg, 2007; Park, Felix, & Lee, 2007; Maio, Haddock, Watt, & Hewstone, this volume), and other treatments involving verbal information (e.g., Petty et al., 2006; Teachman & Woody, 2003; see Gawronski & Bodenhausen, 2006, for a review). Although this research demonstrates that automatic evaluations can be influenced by traditional persuasive messages, it is unclear what the psychological processes were underlying the obtained effects.

In our pilot study, because we asked participants to read the content of the arguments, we argue that the observed changes on automatic evaluations were likely due to the careful consideration of their merits. However, it is also possible that participants just counted and relied on the number of arguments presented in favor of the proposal (e.g., Petty & Cacioppo, 1984), or they might have followed some other low effort process, such as mere exposure or classical conditioning. For example, just by looking at the message superficially (e.g., simply attending to the advocated position of the message without reading the content of the arguments), a person might have reasoned that the culture favors vegetables (e.g., Olson & Fazio, 2004). Because the findings of our pilot study, like other research in this domain, do not allow us to examine whether (and how much) participants elaborated the information received, we designed a second study in which the extent of thinking and argument quality were manipulated.

Experiment 1: Manipulating extent of thinking and argument quality. This study was designed to provide evidence that thoughtful processing can impact automatic evaluations and do so in a way that is not subject to the most salient alternative explanations. Participants in this second study received a persuasive message in favor of a new policy to integrate more African-American professors into the university. This message was composed of either strong or weak arguments in favor of the proposal. The gist of one of the strong arguments was that because the number and quality of professors would increase with this program (without any tuition increase), the number of students per class could be reduced by 25%. Examples of the gist of weak arguments, on the other hand, included that implementing the program would allow the university to take part in a national trend, and that with the new professors, current professors might have more free time to themselves. By manipulating argument quality, we aimed to examine the role of elaboration on the malleably of automatic evaluations because the relative effect of strong versus weak arguments on attitudes is reflective of the amount of thinking devoted to the content of the message (Petty, Wells, & Brock, 1976). That is, if people are not thinking carefully about the message, the quality of the arguments will not influence their attitudes, but if they are thinking carefully about the message content, it will (Petty & Cacioppo, 1986). Importantly, any effects of argument quality on automatic evaluations should indicate the extent of thinking rather than the use of any other low thought associative mechanisms. This is because the strong and weak messages are equivalent in terms of the aspects of the message to which simple associative mechanisms are presumably sensitive (e.g., direction of the message, number of arguments, and mere repetition of the attitude object).

Furthermore, in this study the extent of thinking was manipulated directly by making the message personally relevant (or irrelevant; e.g., Petty & Cacioppo, 1979) and by enhancing (or undermining) personal responsibility to think about the proposal (e.g., Petty, Harkins, & Williams, 1980). Participants in the high elaboration condition were told that the integration policy was being considered for implementation at their own (vs. a remote) university and in the next academic year (vs. in 10 years), and they were in a small (vs. a large) group of participants who were being asked to complete this survey (see Tormala, Petty, & Briñol, 2002, for successful use of this combined manipulation). After reading the message, participants were asked to complete an automatic measure related to the program to hire more African-American professors.[2]

The implicit measure consisted of a race IAT, in which participants classified target concepts (represented by White or Black) and attributes (represented by pleasant or unpleasant categories of words). Just as prior research had shown that mere exposure to positive Black exemplars could modify automatic racial attitudes (e.g., Dasgupta & Greenwald, 2001), we aimed to show that processing a message about Black professors could modify these attitudes. Importantly, if the mere activation of the Black professor subtype is sufficient to modify attitudes, those exposed to both the strong and weak arguments should show similar levels of favorability toward Blacks. Similarly, if the IAT was simply responding to an expressed "cultural" opinion regarding integration, then the IAT would show more favorable attitudes even in the weak arguments condition (see Han, Olson, & Fazio, 2006). However, if careful elaboration and acceptance (or rejection) of the idea based on its merits is capable of affecting automatic attitudes, then argument quality should have an impact on automatic evaluation, with strong arguments producing more favorable evaluations than weak ones.

Consistent with previous literature on traditional message-based attitude change (see Petty & Wegener, 1998), we expected and found argument quality to influence automatic evaluations depending on the extent of message processing. That is, under high elaboration conditions, automatic evaluations were found to be more positive toward Blacks for the strong than the weak message. In contrast, for low elaboration conditions, we did not find as much attitudinal responsiveness to the manipulation of argument quality. This is presumably because when not processed carefully, the strong and weak message conditions are comparable in terms of the persuasive cues that are present (e.g., number of arguments, length, complexity, number of stereotype related words, and use of positive language) and also equivalent in terms of the opinion expressed and the mere activation of the Black professor subtype.

Although not directly tested in this study, we argue that the effect of argument quality obtained under high elaboration on automatic evaluations is due to the fact that the strong message led to many favorable thoughts associated with the integration program and Blacks, whereas the weak message led to many unfavorable thoughts associated with the integration program and Blacks. We speculate that, at least in this persuasion paradigm, the generation of each positive (negative) thought provides people with the opportunity to rehearse a favorable (unfavorable) evaluation of Blacks, and it is the rehearsal of the evaluation allowed by the thoughts (not the thoughts directly) that are responsible for the effects on the implicit measure. Thus, the automatic change might involve just getting the link between the attitude object and good (bad) rehearsed by each favorable (unfavorable) thought. Thus, automatic measures would reflect the valence of the thoughts generated.

Experiment 2: The effect of thoughts on implicit change. We conducted another study in order to examine the role of thoughts in response to the message on implicit measures. All participants in this experiment received a persuasive message composed of strong or weak arguments in favor of including more vegetables in their diet (adopted from Briñol, Petty, & Wheeler, 2006). The strong arguments were the same as those used in the pilot study described previously. The gist of one of the weak arguments in favor of vegetables was that vegetables are becoming more popular for wedding celebrations because they are colorful and look beautiful on plates. As described earlier, the greater the thinking about the information presented, the bigger the difference strong versus weak messages should have on people's attitudes.

As in the previous study, the extent of thinking was manipulated by making the message personally relevant or irrelevant. Thus, the message was introduced as part of an article about personal habits with potential consequences for academic performance (personally relevant frame) or as part of an article about plant properties (personally irrelevant frame). Importantly, after reading the message framed as relevant or irrelevant, participants were asked to list their thoughts about the proposal. After the thought-listing, and as part of an ostensibly unrelated study, participants were then asked to complete the IAT used in our pilot study to assess automatic evaluations of vegetables.

The results of this study were consistent with our previous experiments in showing that automatic evaluations (as assessed by the IAT) can change as a result of processing persuasive messages. We first found that elaboration increased the impact of argument quality on automatic evaluations just as past research has shown this pattern for deliberative evaluations (e.g., Petty & Cacioppo, 1979). That is, under high elaboration conditions, automatic evaluations of vegetables were more impacted by argument quality than they were under low elaboration conditions. More importantly, under high elaboration conditions, the obtained changes on automatic evaluations from argument quality were mediated by the valence of the thoughts (i.e., positive or negative) that participants generated in response to the message.

Thus, this study provides preliminary evidence for thoughtful mediation of changes on implicit measures. As noted earlier, it seems plausible that the generation of thoughts (positive or negative) in the high elaboration conditions allowed participants to rehearse their evaluative links repeatedly, leading to the obtained changes on the automatic measure. In contrast, participants in the low elaboration conditions presumably did not think about the merits of the arguments in the message and thus did not have many valenced thoughts that would allow for attitude rehearsal.

Processes underlying explicit and implicit change. Taken together, our experiments reveal that automatic evaluations as assessed with an IAT can be affected by deliberative forms of persuasion. That is, just as explicit attitudes have been more affected by the quality of message arguments when conditions foster elaboration, so too were automatic attitudes more affected by argument quality when the likelihood of thinking was high. Given that the available research clearly indicates that implicit and explicit measures are both sensitive to similar deliberative (and automatic) processes of persuasion, an important question is to what extent are automatic and deliberative measures related to each other? Although the present studies focused on automatic measures, there are several possibilities for this relationship that we outline next.

On the one hand, changes on implicit and explicit measures might be related to each other because they plausibly respond to some of the same mediators. That is, the valence of the thoughts generated in response to a persuasive message has been found to determine both automatic changes (in Experiment 2 above) and deliberative changes (as described earlier in this chapter and illustrated by two decades of research). If changes on implicit and explicit measures are related, then it is possible that changes in one determine the other. For example, according to the APE model (Chapter 4, this volume), any change on implicit measures obtained through deliberative (i.e., propositional) processes should be a function of changes in explicit measures (Gawronski & Bodenhausen, 2006; see Case 4). Applied to the present research, this would suggest that the obtained changes on the automatic measure due to argument quality under high elaboration conditions must be mediated by the changes that presumably first occurred in explicit attitudes.

Alternatively, according to the MODE model (Chapter 2, this volume), changes on automatic measures that result from deliberative processes should be due to the creation of an evaluative association with the attitude object. That is, automatic changes do not depend upon or require any changes in a deliberative attitude to occur. In fact, according to this view, change in the stored evaluative association is precisely what serves as the basis of the deliberative response (in addition to other downstream cognitive activities). Applied to the present research, this view suggests that changes in the automatic measure would mediate any change that was observed in the explicit measure. Although to our knowledge it has not been tested experimentally in a traditional persuasion paradigm, it seems quite plausible that automatic changes can potentially mediate deliberative changes in many situations. Thus, in contrast to some theorists who would not expect deliberative processes to impact automatic measures, the MODE and APE models agree with the idea that change on implicit measures through deliberative processes is possible, though these two models postulate different mediating sequences.

It is also possible to speculate about a third possibility. That is, the automatic and deliberative changes that result from deliberative treatments might be unrelated to each other. This implies that deliberation about message arguments can produce change in both implicit and explicit measures, but neither would mediate the other. If true, then thinking about message arguments is leading to the same outcome on implicit and explicit measures, but by different processes. Although early theories of persuasion held that any one variable (e.g., an expert source, a happy emotional state) was likely to have just one effect on persuasion (i.e., either enhancing or reducing it), through just one single process, within contemporary multiprocess models of persuasion such as the ELM and HSM, there is recognition that the same outcome for any one variable can be due to very different processes (see Petty, 1997; Petty & Briñol, 2008).

Consider, for example, persuasion research on source credibility that has uncovered a number of different mechanisms by which this variable can produce attitude change. Depending on the extent of thinking, source credibility has been found to produce changes in deliberative measures of attitudes by serving as a simple cue or heuristic (e.g., Petty, Cacioppo, et al., 1981), by affecting the direction (e.g., Chaiken & Maheswaran, 1994) and the amount (e.g., Priester & Petty, 1995) of thoughts generated, by influencing the confidence people have in those thoughts (Briñol, Petty, & Tormala, 2004), and by serving as a piece of evidence relevant to the merits of an issue (Kruglanski & Thompson, 1999; for a review, see, e.g., Tormala, Briñol, & Petty, 2007). Source credibility is only one of the factors that can produce changes through different processes in different situations. According to the elaboration likelihood model, many variables serve in these same roles. To take one more example, consider the emotional state of the communication recipient. Depending on elaboration and other conditions, a person's emotions have been found to serve in the same diverse roles as observed for source credibility (for reviews, see Briñol, Petty, & Rucker, 2006; Petty, Fabrigar, & Wegener, 2003).

Note that according to the ELM, both external (e.g., source credibility) and internal (e.g., one's emotions) information can be processed as cues or arguments or serve in other roles depending on the elaboration likelihood. Thus, we speculate that a person's own thoughts can also serve in these different roles as well. The most simplistic treatment of one's thoughts would only consider their number and valence: two qualities that are relatively easy to extract (e.g., see Betsch, Plessner, & Schallies, 2004). As described earlier, it is possible that when processing a persuasive message, a person generating mostly positive thoughts would rehearse mostly positive evaluative associations to the attitude object, and a person generating mostly negative thoughts would rehearse mostly negative evaluative associations. This would lead strong arguments to show more positive evaluations on an implicit measure than weak arguments. Thus, when the measurement conditions involve low thinking, as is the case with measures of automatic evaluation, thoughts might have an impact on attitudes because of the relatively low effort extraction of their evaluative information.

Importantly, when conditions foster more thinking, as is the case with deliberative measures, it is possible to extract additional information (besides valence) from one's thoughts. For example, in addition to the desirability (valence) involved in a thought about a persuasive proposal, a person can consider other aspects of that thought, such as the likelihood of the consequence it implies (e.g., Fishbein & Ajzen, 1975), and the overall confidence one has in the thought (see Petty, Briñol, & Tormala, 2002; Briñol et al., 2004). These additional features of thoughts should be less likely to emerge in an automatic measure of attitudes. Thus, when the measurement conditions involve high thinking, not only the valence of a thought, but other information associated with that thought, should be more likely to have an impact. In this analysis we note that there are similarities between how variables have an impact on attitudes when thinking is varied during response to the attitude measure and when thinking is varied during processing of the persuasive message.[3]

In brief, our speculation is that when deliberation at the time of attitude responding is low (as is the case with automatic measures), the valence of thoughts is most critical, but as responding allows more thinking, other aspects of one's thoughts come into play. This is analogous to saying that thoughts are treated as simple evaluative cues when the likelihood of thinking is low, but are analyzed more fully as arguments when thinking is high. These different processes can sometimes lead to different outcomes, but sometimes the outcome can be the same. For example, under low elaboration conditions a negative emotion is likely to reduce persuasion because it serves as a negative evaluative cue, but under high elaboration, the same negative emotion can produce a favorable outcome depending on how it is evaluated (e.g., sadness induced by a sad movie leads one to like the movie). The same is true with respect to thoughts. Thus, under low thinking conditions (automatic measure), a negative thought, like a negative emotion, will lead to more unfavorable attitudes, but under high thinking conditions (deliberative measure), a negative thought will not necessarily lead to negative attitudes. It will also depend on the perceived likelihood of the negative consequence and the overall confidence in the thought (see also Chapter 5, this volume). If the thoughts are clearly favorable (or unfavorable), the likelihood of the consequences is high, and people have high confidence in their thoughts, both implicit and explicit measures will show the same outcome, but the process underlying each will be different (i.e., the explicit measure taps more aspects of the thoughts than does the implicit measure). Because the processes underlying change on implicit and explicit measures might not be identical, it may not be the case that the implicit measure mediates the explicit, or vice versa.

Experiment 3: The effect of thought-confidence on implicit change. As described above, we propose that thoughts generated in response to a message can influence automatic measures of attitudes by providing the opportunity to rehearse the evaluative link (e.g., object-good) repeatedly. Consistent with this view, the automatic measure used in Experiment 2 was sensitive to the valence of the thoughts generated. We further speculated that automatic measures might not reflect the confidence that people have in the validity of newly generated thoughts, as this is a unique feature reflected in deliberative measures. We conducted another study in order to examine the assumption that automatic measures are affected by the valence of the thoughts (primary cognition) but not by the confidence people have in those thoughts (secondary, meta-cognition; see Petty, Briñol, Tormala, & Wegener, 2007, for a review of meta-cognition and persuasion).

All participants in this experiment were placed in a high elaboration condition and received a persuasive message composed of strong or weak arguments on the topic of including more vegetables in the diet. Importantly, after listing their thoughts in response to the proposal, and before measuring automatic responses toward it, we manipulated the confidence with which participants held their thoughts by asking them to remember past events in which they felt confidence or doubt in their thinking. Previous research has established that recalling past episodes of confidence or doubt can influence thought-confidence and, therefore, affect deliberative measures of attitudes by affecting use of one's thoughts (Petty et al., 2002).

As expected, participants generated more favorable thoughts toward the proposal of the message and showed more positive automatic evaluations for the strong than for the weak message. Also replicating Experiment 2, changes on automatic evaluations were mediated by the valence of the thoughts generated. Importantly, the manipulation of thought-confidence, which significantly affected an explicit manipulation check on the perceived validity of the thoughts, did not influence automatic evaluations. These findings thus suggest that the IAT, and perhaps other implicit measures, might reflect only the valence but not the confidence people have in their newly generated thoughts. Providing further support for this idea is recent research showing that implicit measures are sensitive to the valence of persuasive treatments but not to correction processes (Forehand & Perkins, 2005) or the subjective ease associated with one's thoughts (Gawronski & Bodenhausen, 2005).[4]

Summary. Taken together, these studies demonstrated that automatic evaluations as assessed with an IAT can be affected not only by relatively simple associative processes (as amply documented in prior research) but also by traditional elaborative forms of rhetorical persuasion. Across several different studies, manipulations, topics, and messages, we found automatic evaluations to be sensitive to the direction and the quality of the persuasive arguments contained in the message. Furthermore, the changes on automatic evaluations were more evident for situations of high rather than low elaboration. These findings qualify previous views, which suggested a need to match experimental treatments and measures such that automatic measures would only be malleable to the extent to which the induction was also relatively unconscious or nonpropositional (e.g., Gawronski & Strack, 2003; Dasgupta & Greenwald, 2001). Finally, changes in automatic evaluations were independent of properties of the thoughts other than valence. These findings open the possibility that changes in implicit measures produced by deliberative processes might differ from changes in explicit measures produced by the same persuasive treatments.

Finally, our approach might also provide a new avenue to reinterpret some of the earlier findings about the malleability of automatic evaluations. For example, in the context of the classic contact hypothesis in the domain of prejudice (Allport, 1954), Rudman et al. (2001) studied the automatic and controlled attitudes of people who participated in a seminar on diversity training. Interestingly, compared to controls, participants changed their self-reported attitudes (but not their automatic evaluations) after learning during the seminar that they might possess prejudicial attitudes and deciding that they would like to become more egalitarian. Automatic evaluations only changed for participants in the conflict seminar who also evaluated the professor and the course positively, who made friends with outgroup members, and who reported feeling less threatened by outgroup members. Rudman et al. (p. 866) interpreted these findings in terms of the matching hypothesis in stating that "the present findings, although speculative, suggest that explicit intergroup orientations may be linked more to cognitive or direct processes, whereas implicit intergroup orientations may be linked more to affective or indirect processes." The current research suggests another possibility, namely that liking the professor and making friends enhanced the motivation of participants to think carefully about the information received, leading to changes in both deliberative and automatic measures associated with the outgroup.

Implicit Measures: Consequences of Deliberative and Automatic Processes

The research we have reviewed suggests that deliberative and automatic measures of attitudes can change through low thought (e.g., subliminal classical conditioning; Dijksterhuis, 2004) and deliberative (e.g., biasing the thoughts generated) processes. As noted earlier, traditional research on explicit measures of change has shown that although both high and low thought attitude change processes are possible, the consequences of those processes are different. According to the ELM, attitudes formed or changed through low thinking processes are less persistent, resistant to change, and predictive of behavior than attitudes changed via high thinking processes. This is because elaboration typically involves accessing relevant information from both external and internal sources, making inferences, generating new arguments, and drawing new conclusions about the merits of the attitude object (Petty & Cacioppo, 1986). These mental activities involve people adding something of their own to the information available and are likely to lead to the integration of all relevant information into the underlying structure for the attitude object, therefore making the adopted evaluation not only stable, but also coherent and resistant. Thus, deliberative attitudes based on high amounts of thinking are stronger than attitudes based on little thought (see Petty et al., 1995, for a review).

It is important to distinguish between strength-like consequences that result from relatively high versus low thought processes. For example, because elaboration strengthens the object-evaluation associations, the more thinking a person does, the more likely the evaluation is not only to persist over time and have an impact on judgment and behavior, but also to be resistant when challenged. On the other hand, a large number of conditioning trials would also produce a stronger evaluative association than would a small number of trials in the absence of any issue-relevant thinking. Thus, pairing an attitude object with positive stimuli 20 times would result in more accessible and consequential attitudes than pairing those stimuli one or two times (e.g., Fazio, 1995). These evaluations would also be stable and resistant to extinction in the absence of compelling challenges. However, because these attitudes are based only on mere association rather than substantive information, they are not likely to be resistant when challenged with cogent evidence. Similarly, presenting 20 attractive sources endorsing a proposal would likely produce stronger attitudes (e.g., in terms of accessibility) than using just one attractive source. However, compared with attitudes based on issue-relevant thinking, those resulting attitudes would still be relatively weak when challenged. Thus, people who possess accessible attitudes bolstered by considerable attitude-congruent knowledge are better able to defend their attitudes compared to those who have equally accessible attitudes that resulted from low thinking processes.

Although considerable research has demonstrated that extensive thinking enhances the strength of explicit attitudes, it is less clear that the same consequences would hold for automatic attitudes. Thus, just as understanding the nature of the processes by which explicit measures of attitudes change has been essential because it is informative about the immediate and long-term consequences of these changes, so too might it also be relevant for understanding the consequences associated with changes in automatic measures of attitudes. A preliminary question to explore would be the extent to which the changes in implicit measures obtained as a result of deliberative processes show evidence of strength. As noted, attitude strength can be demonstrated in many different ways, ranging from enhanced accessibility to influence on related thought processes and behavior.

We conducted a number of studies to test whether automatic attitudes might show some properties associated with strength when changed through high elaboration processes (Horcajo, Briñol, Petty, & Wheeler, 2007). For example, we noted earlier that attitude change processes that require thinking deeply about the attitude object are likely to result in attitude representations that are well integrated and connected with other relevant material in memory (see, e.g., McGuire, 1981; Tesser, 1978). Because of the strong linkage among constructs associated with high thinking, activating one mental representation should activate related cognitive elements easily. Indeed, within the literature on explicitly assessed attitudes, there is some suggestive evidence that it is easier to activate related constructs for high than low need for cognition (NC) individuals (Petty, DeMarree, Briñol, Horcajo, & Strathman, 2008; Smith, Haugtvedt, & Petty, 1994). An important question to examine would be to what extent this argument holds for automatic attitudes. As a first step in examining this issue, we tested whether changes on automatic attitude measures induced by deliberative processes showed evidence of spreading activation to related constructs.

Experiment 1: Spreading automatic activation as a function of measured thinking (need for cognition). The main goal of this study was to test whether deliberative attitude change processes would be consequential in terms of spreading activation when assessed with measures of automatic evaluation. Participants were told that they were helping out with research designed to assess possible changes in the institutional color of their university. Half of the participants were randomly assigned to receive a persuasive message containing strong arguments in favor of using green as the institutional color for the university. The other half of the participants, who composed the control group, received an irrelevant message (also containing the word *green*, but not advocating it). Participants' need for cognition (Cacioppo & Petty, 1982) was measured in order to assess the participants' preferences and motivation to process the information provided. Then, instead of assessing the impact of this persuasive induction directly on automatic evaluations of the color green, we assessed the impact of the treatment on an automatic measure that was only indirectly related to that concept.

Specifically, to assess indirect (associated) change, we constructed an IAT on the brand *Heineken* (because the logo of that brand is green and uses the slogan "Think in green" in many of its marketing campaigns). In this implicit measure, participants classified target concepts, represented by Heineken (e.g., *Heineken, Dutch, European, Amsterdam,* and *regular*) or Corona (e.g., *Mexican, lemon, Coronita, Mexico,* and *mild*), and attributes, represented by *good* and *bad*. We predicted and found that implicitly measured attitudes toward Heineken were significantly affected by the message for participants high in NC (but not for those low in NC). Thus, high NC individuals not only presumably changed their automatic responses toward green, but also their automatic responses to other objects related to green. That is, for individuals with high motivation to think, we found more favorable automatic evaluations of Heineken for the group that received the arguments in favor of the color green than for the control group. These findings provide

preliminary evidence that suggests that for implicit measures, deliberative processes can lead to associated changes on automatic measures
though a process of spreading activation (from green to Heineken).

As discussed in the earlier section, it seems plausible that the generation of thoughts allowed high NC participants to rehearse their evaluative links to green repeatedly, leading to changes in evaluation of this
color that spread to related constructs such as Heineken. In contrast,
the automatic evaluations of participants low in NC did not reveal any
impact of the manipulation. This finding suggests that participants in
the low elaboration conditions did not think about the merits of the
arguments contained in the message (i.e., did not generate thoughts that
allowed them to rehearse their attitudes) and therefore did not show
any indirect automatic changes.[5] The present findings are interesting in
showing that automatic changes that result from deliberative thinking
are consequential in terms of spreading activation. The next study replicates and extends this finding to a different generalization target.

*Experiment 2: Spreading automatic activation to the self as a func-
tion of thinking.* As noted previously, within the literature on explicitly
assessed attitudes, there is some preliminary evidence for easier related
construct activation under high than low thinking conditions (Petty,
DeMarree et al., 2008; Smith et al., 1994). The above study suggests that
receiving a persuasive treatment can affect automatic attitudes toward
a construct that is only indirectly related to the focal construct in the
message for relatively high thinking individuals. The main purpose of
our next study was to provide further evidence for this strength-related
consequence but using a different attitude object. In this study, we
asked participants to generate arguments in favor of or against including more vegetables in their diet. Need for cognition was measured in
this study as in the prior one to assess the extent of thinking. Following
the argument generation task, instead of measuring automatic attitudes
toward vegetables, however, we measured the automatic link between
vegetables and the self. As would be expected if deliberative processes
lead to changes that are consequential, those with high NC showed
more automatic self-vegetable associations after thinking about the
benefits (rather than the negative consequences) of consuming vegetables. Because most people like themselves, if vegetables are good rather
than bad, they would be more likely to be linked to the self.[6]

In this study, individuals with high NC generated more issue-relevant
thoughts than individuals low in NC. The difference in the number of
thoughts might have led to more automatic change toward vegetables
for high than low NC individuals (i.e., because it allows for more oppor-

tunities to rehearse the evaluative link), which in turn might explain the differences observed in the indirect, automatic measure toward the self. Even in the case that participants high and low in NC were engaging in the same amount of thinking, however, the spreading activation effect might still be due to other differences between these individuals.[7] For example, it might be easier to activate links between mental constructs among high (vs. low) NC individuals because of their well-developed knowledge structures (e.g., Petty, 2001). Alternatively, individuals high in NC are more likely to translate their thoughts into judgments and their judgments into behaviors because judgments formed through careful thought tend to be better represented in memory and are more stable and impactful (Petty et al., 1995; for reviews, see Briñol & Petty, 2005; Cacioppo, Petty, Feinstein, & Jarvis, 1996). In order to rule out some of these structural differences between high and low NC individuals, we conducted another study in order to replicate the preliminary findings on spreading activation that results from elaboration by manipulating (rather than measuring) the extent of thinking.

Experiment 3: Spreading automatic activation as a function of group status. Consider the classic paradigm on minority influence in which participants receive persuasive information that is endorsed by either a minority or a majority source. The traditional result for this paradigm is that although minorities do not tend to produce change on explicit measures directly linked to the attitude object, they can sometimes produce change on explicit measures indirectly related to the proposal (e.g., changing on birth control when the message is on abortion; see Alvaro & Crano, 1997; Mugny & Perez, 1996). Among other possible alternatives, this finding has been interpreted in terms of elaboration differences with minority sources leading to more deliberative processing of the information compared to majority sources (Baker & Petty, 1994; Moscovici, Mucchi-Faina, & Maass, 1994; Tormala, DeSensi, & Petty, 2007). If participants exposed to minority sources engage in greater message processing, then change on indirect topics becomes more likely.

To examine the implications of these findings for automatic attitudes, we conducted a number of experiments in which strong and weak arguments were presented by sources of different majority/minority status and then assessed automatic attitudes with respect to an attitude object only indirectly related to the target object. For example, in one study (Horcajo, Tormala, Petty, & Briñol, 2007), participants received a strong or weak message in favor of the color green endorsed by either a majority or a minority status source. We measured the indirect automatic change (IAT toward Heineken) and found that only the minority source condition was associated with spreading automatic activation from green to Heineken.

Summary. In sum, in cases of high elaboration (i.e., high need for cognition individuals, minority source) indirect change on automatic measures was observed. These findings are conceptually similar to those obtained with explicit measures when attitude changes were induced with deliberative processes. Although our preliminary studies have focused exclusively on the examination of the spreading activation effect, future studies should also explore other potential consequences of the strength of automatic attitude changes as a function of extensive thinking. It seems plausible to argue that automatic changes, like explicitly assessed changes (Petty et al., 1995), induced through relatively deliberatively processes might also be particularly stable, resistant, and impactful on information processing and behavior.

Finally, the studies described in this section not only might have implications for automatic attitudes, but also might provide some potential insights for the study of explicit persuasion. For example, recent research has demonstrated that when people appear to have resisted persuasion on traditional measures, there might be some potentially important, yet previously hidden, persuasive effects on the confidence with which people hold those apparently unaffected attitudes (e.g., Tormala & Petty, 2002; Rucker & Petty, 2004; Rucker, Petty, & Briñol, 2008). It is plausible to imagine that under some circumstances, although participants were not influenced by persuasive messages on explicit self-report measures (e.g., as a result of demand characteristics, evaluation apprehension, impression management, social judgeability concerns, and self-awareness limitations), automatic evaluations might still be affected (Tormala, Briñol, & Petty, 2004). Thus, when people appear to have resisted persuasion on explicit measures, there might still be some potentially hidden, persuasive effects on the automatic evaluative associations that exist with respect to the attitude object (e.g., see Forehand & Perkins, 2005). If true, then researchers might sometimes be able to use automatic measures as researchers have used attitude confidence as a way of indicating that a message has had some hidden persuasive effect.

Dual-Process Changes

We have now reviewed evidence that both relatively high and low thought processes appear to be capable of affecting both automatic and deliberative measures of attitudes. Despite the volume of research demonstrating cross-domain effects that we have already mentioned, it is still the case that a number of models and supporting empirical evidence have emerged recently that suggest that such cross-domain effects should be difficult or impossible to obtain (e.g., Rydell, McConnell, Mackie, & Strain, 2006; DeCoster, Banner, Smith, & Semin, 2006) or should only be found if change in either explicit or implicit attitudes mediates change in the other (Gawronski & Bodenhausen, 2006). According to these theories, the evaluations captured by implicit and explicit measures reflect the operation of two different, independent systems of reasoning. After briefly outlining this dual-systems view, we review evidence in favor of it and then our own studies that challenge common derivations from this approach.

Dual-Systems Models

Drawing on evidence from studies on learning, memory, and judgment, a number of psychologists have proposed different dual-systems models of cognition. Each of these models posits the existence of two distinct information processing systems: a relatively automatic system and a more consciously deliberative one. The nomenclature used to differentiate one system from the other varies from model to model (e.g., System 1 vs. System 2, Kahneman & Frederick, 2005; associative vs. rule-based systems, Sloman, 1996; slow-learning vs. fast-learning, Smith & DeCoster, 2000; impulsive vs. reflective, Deutsch & Strack, 2006; experiential vs. rational, Epstein, 1991), but the description of the fundamental features of these systems is similar across theories (Carver, 2005). In a general dual-systems view, the automatic system is characterized by associative or heuristic processing that occurs rapidly, spontaneously, and with little (or no) conscious awareness or cognitive effort. In contrast, the deliberative system controls more complex processing involving symbolic or logic-based thinking. This system functions at the conscious level but requires both the motivation and ability to process to perform its mental operations. Although some associative processes may take time and repetition to produce evaluative change and some propositional processes can occur very quickly, in general the associative processes will require less mental effort than the deliberative ones. Notably, the new dual-systems approaches share features with the dual-process models of judgment proposed earlier (e.g., ELM; Petty & Cacioppo, 1986; HSM; Chaiken et al., 1989). One difference is that the latter theories focus on a continuum approach to information processing (i.e., variations in the extent of thinking), whereas the former postulate discrete systems of judgment. Second, the more recent systems theories highlight differences in mental architecture (i.e., brain systems), whereas the earlier theories focus on mental processes.

When the dual-systems approaches are applied to implicit versus explicit attitudes (e.g., Rydell et al., 2006), implicit (automatic) attitudes are presumed to be formed and changed through the *impulsive system*, in which simple associations based on similarity and contiguity develop gradually (and with little effort) as more information about the attitude object is acquired over time. Explicit (deliberative) attitudes, on the other hand, are thought to be the products of a *reflective system* that relies on rule-based thinking and symbolic representation to quickly (but effortfully) generate or modify self-reported evaluations (see also Chapter 4, this volume). Because implicit and explicit attitudes are believed to stem from orthogonal systems of information processing, some dual-systems theorists have claimed that it is possible for an individual to concurrently hold two very different independent attitudes about the same attitude object that are stored in separate brain regions (e.g., DeCoster et al., 2006; Rydell et al., 2006; see also Wilson et al., 2000). Indeed, in this view, a single persuasion treatment can in some cases elicit opposite responses on implicit and explicit measures.[8]

To test the idea that a single persuasion treatment can produce opposite effects on implicit and explicit measures, Rydell and colleagues (2006) conducted an experiment in which participants were simultaneously exposed to deliberative and associative information about a target person named *Bob*. Note that in all of the prior research on implicit and explicit change summarized earlier, participants were exposed to either only deliberative (e.g., traditional persuasive message; Hovland et al., 1953) or only nonthoughtful (e.g., classical conditioning; Staats & Staats, 1958) persuasion treatment, or if exposed to both the treatments, they were administered sequentially with separate measures after each (e.g., Petty et al., 2006; Gregg, Seibt, & Banaji, 2006). In contrast to this, Rydell et al. exposed participants to both types of treatments simultaneously prior to assessing deliberative and automatic attitudes.[9]

In the Rydell et al. (2006) research, the deliberative information was presented by having participants read 100 statements describing a positive or negative behavior performed by Bob. After reading each sentence, participants were given information about whether the behavior described was characteristic of Bob or not. For half the participants, positive behaviors were labeled as characteristic and negative behaviors were designated as uncharacteristic of Bob (positive deliberative information). For the remaining participants, Bob's positive behaviors were said to be uncharacteristic, and his negative behaviors were identified as characteristic (negative deliberative information). In addition, prior to the presentation of each sentence, participants received associative information in the form of a subliminal word prime that had a valence opposite that of the deliberative statements. That is, participants who received positive deliberative information about Bob were primed with negative words, and those who were presented with negative deliberative information were primed with positive words. In this way, the information about Bob requiring high versus low amounts of thinking to process was always opposite in valence.

In line with their view that implicit and explicit attitudes are the products of independent systems of reasoning, Rydell et al. (2006) hypothesized that the deliberative information would only influence responses on explicit self-report measures, whereas the associative information would only produce effects on an implicit measure (IAT). Just as predicted, Rydell et al. found that explicit self-reports reflected the valence of the behavioral sentences, and IAT responses were affected only by the valence of the associative information. The authors interpreted these results as clear evidence for the existence of two dissociated attitudinal representations of the same attitude object in accord with their strict dual-systems approach.[10]

Limitations of a Strict Dual-Systems Perspectives

Although the work of Rydell et al. (2006) and the data from other dual-systems theorists (e.g., DeCoster et al., 2006) appear to offer a strong case for the predictions derived from the two-systems framework, this approach does not appear to account well for the wealth of literature reviewed earlier documenting cross-domain effects. In a strict orthogonal dual-systems approach, it would not be possible for associative information to influence an explicit measure or for deliberative information to impact an implicit measure. Nevertheless, such effects have been shown in a number of studies, as illustrated above. So, how can this discrepancy be resolved?

A potential solution to this quandary begins to emerge when one considers the precise nature of the information available in each attitude change scenario. As described earlier, when only one kind of information or process (associative or deliberative) is present, cross-domain attitude change effects appear to be relatively easy to obtain. Specifically, nondeliberative persuasion treatments, such as classical conditioning or subliminal mere exposure in the absence of explicit information to deliberate upon, have effects on explicit as well as implicit measures. Furthermore, as was the case in our research reviewed earlier, deliberative persuasion treatments, such as processing verbal messages in the absence of strong associative cues, can have effects on implicit as well as explicit measures. On the other hand, when associative and deliberative information are of comparable strength, opposite in valence, and jointly at hand, the typical pattern of results appears to support the predictions derived from a dual-systems approach, such that associative information only has an impact on implicit measures and deliberative information seems to only affect explicit measures.

Why did cross-domain effects emerge when people were exposed to either associative or deliberative persuasion treatments alone, and why did cross-domain effects not occur when deliberative and associative treatments were combined? One possible explanation for the latter question resides in the particular methodological designs used in tests of the strict dual-systems approach. For example, Rydell et al. (2006) found that presenting participants with oppositely valenced associative and deliberative information produced opposing implicit and explicit attitudes. However, it is not entirely clear from this research whether the implicit measures were completely uninfluenced by the deliberative information and the explicit measures were uninfluenced by the associative information, because no experimental conditions were included where the associative and deliberative information were of the same valence.

In a strict dual-systems approach, the content of the deliberative information at hand is irrelevant when forming implicit evaluations, just as the content of the associative information present is irrelevant when making explicit evaluations. Adding congruent conditions where the associative and deliberative information are matched in valence to the design used by Rydell et al. (2006) would allow for a more definitive test of the dual-systems hypotheses. Specifically, if fully independent systems exist that do not influence each other, one would predict that in a 2 × 2 fully crossed design (associative information: positive vs. negative × deliberative information: positive vs. negative), an implicit measure would only show a main effect of the associative information, and an explicit measure would only show a main effect of the deliberative information. However, if implicit and explicit measures of attitudes are multiply determined, this full design should reveal a main effect of both the associative and deliberative information on both implicit and explicit responses.

Experimental Test of the Dual-Systems Hypothesis

To investigate these possibilities, McCaslin, Loersch, and Petty (2007) conducted a conceptual replication of Rydell et al. (2006) that included two additional conditions where the associative and deliberative information was of the same valence (positive-positive, negative-negative). In this experiment, participants were given deliberative information by reading a 108-word paragraph that described a target person named *Paul* in either a positive or negative way. The paragraph was presented on a computer screen one word at a time with each new word of the paragraph added to the preceding text. To manipulate the associative information related to Paul, participants were subliminally shown a positive or negative image after the presentation of each new word of the paragraph.[11] This resulted in the individual presentation of either 108 positive or 108 negative images. By presenting the subliminal images alongside the deliberative information about Paul in this manner, it was expected that the positivity (or negativity) primed by the images would condition participants to hold positive (or negative) associations toward Paul. Once this procedure was finished, participants completed both implicit (IAT; Greenwald et al., 1998) and explicit (semantic differential) measures of their attitudes.

It was predicted that using a more complete design would reveal an effect of both associative and deliberative processing on participants' implicit attitudes. In contrast to the dual-systems approach by Rydell et al. (2006), it was expected that both the deliberative statements about Paul and the subliminal images would shape participants' implicit evaluation of him. Results confirmed this hypothesis, such that participants' IAT scores reflected significant main effects of both the associative (implicit) and the deliberative (explicit) information (see Figure 10.1).[12]

A different pattern of results was expected to emerge on the explicit measure. Like implicit attitudes, we expected that explicit evaluations would also be multiply determined. That is, both deliberative and associative information would inform participants' self-reported attitudes. However, self-reported attitudes can also be affected by momentary considerations (e.g., see Chapter 2, this volume). In particular, with respect to forming evaluations of people, according to the social judgeability model (Yzerbyt, Schadron, Leyens, & Rocher, 1994) individuals only use information that they feel is of socially acceptable quality and quantity. To determine if the information they possess can be used, people will refer to known social rules about what is and is not appropriate for making judgments about others in a particular situation. If

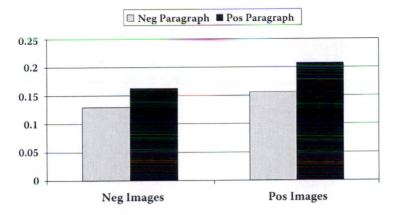

FIGURE 10.1 Effects of positive and negative explicit information and positive and negative subliminal images on attitudes as assessed with an IAT. More positive values reflect more positive standardized attitude scores (data from McCaslin, Loersch, & Petty, 2007).

the information available is deemed acceptable, it will be incorporated into the impression. If the information is determined to be inappropriate, it will be considered unusable (Croizet & Fiske, 2000) and will not influence explicit judgments about the target. In the McCaslin et al. (2007) study, it was thought that participants might be reluctant to use any evaluative reactions that stemmed from the subliminal images in their explicit assessments of Paul because they would be unaware of any valid source of these reactions (because they were elicited by consciously unavailable images). Furthermore, it seemed quite possible that participants would hold the lay belief that judging another person based on a vague sense of positivity or negativity would be inappropriate especially in light of the very explicit information provided (Yzerbyt et al.). As a result, participants were expected to focus their explicit judgments only on the evaluative implications of the consciously available statements about Paul and not any reaction to the subliminal images.

However, even though social judgeability concerns were predicted to inhibit participants' use of the associative information in their explicit judgments, we hypothesized that perhaps the subliminal images would still affect deliberative responses in an indirect way. Thus, similar to the minority influence literature, where minorities do not show any effects on attitude measures obviously related to the advocacy, but the impact of minorities is nonetheless observed on more indirect (but still deliberative) assessments (e.g., Crano & Chen, 1998; Perez & Mugny, 1996), we expected that the associative information would influence explicit measures that assessed Paul in a less direct manner. To test this possibility, McCaslin et al. (2007) had participants complete two items (averaged into one index) typically used to tap subjective ambivalence (i.e., "To what extent is your reaction toward Paul one-sided or mixed?" and "To what extent are your reactions towards Paul conflicted?"). Importantly, because the associative information was presented subliminally and previous research has shown that individuals tend to be unaware of any conflict between their implicit and explicit evaluations (Petty, Tormala et al., 2006; Briñol, Petty, & Wheeler, 2006), it was predicted that these items would not reflect any explicit ambivalence toward Paul for those who received mismatched (i.e., positive-negative, negative-positive) associative and deliberative information. On the other hand, it seemed plausible that any negativity participants experienced regarding their feelings toward Paul would be captured by these items. Indeed, prior research has shown a positive correlation between measures of negativity and ambivalence (Cacioppo, Gardner, & Berntson, 1997), suggesting that ambivalence measures may be sensitive to negativity as well as explicit conflict. Thus, we reasoned that even if participants did not use the associative information in their self-reported attitudes, the ambivalence items would tap negativity in an indirect way because the items did not ask about participants' feelings toward Paul directly, but assessed their evaluations of their attitude toward Paul (an assessment that would not be bound by the explicit Paul-relevant information provided).

As expected if our reasoning was correct, participants' explicit attitudes about Paul were influenced only by the deliberative information presented about Paul. This result was consistent with that obtained by Rydell and colleagues (2006). In contrast, both the associative and deliberative information impacted participants' responses on the ambivalence index. In particular, those who read the negative paragraph reported higher scores on this index than those who read the positive paragraph, and those who had been shown negative subliminal images reported higher scores than those who had seen the positive images.

The results of this experiment show that even when associative and deliberative information are simultaneously presented, cross-domain effects can occur. First, by adding two new conditions in a conceptual replication of Rydell et al. (2006), it was possible to see an effect of both the associative and deliberative information on participants' implicit evaluations. Second, by including measures of subjective ambivalence (which in the absence of explicit conflict were expected to only capture negativity), it was shown that associative (as well as deliberative) information can influence explicit judgments, albeit indirectly. Furthermore, it seems possible that the absence of a direct effect of associative information on explicit evaluation is due to social judgeability concerns. In addition, such concerns might also explain the results of a similar experiment by Rydell and McConnell (2006, Experiment 5), where participants were simultaneously exposed to positive or negative word primes along with many neutral behavioral statements about Bob. As the authors predicted, participants' implicit evaluations reflected the valence of the primes, but their explicit attitudes were neutral regardless of the kind of associative information they received.[13] The authors viewed these results as evidence in support of their dual-systems perspective, but it is also possible that the participants in this experiment relied solely on the neutral behavioral information about Bob to form their explicit judgments because they did not feel it was appropriate to make use of the positive or negative reactions elicited by the word primes because there was no explicit basis for a valenced judgment.[14]

Conclusion

In sum, it seems that perhaps implicit and explicit measures of attitudes are not independently impacted by different processes, as suggested by a number of recent papers. Instead, it appears that regardless of whether one or both types of information are available, implicit and explicit evaluations have the potential to be influenced by multiple sources. Based on classic and contemporary studies, the presence of only one (associative or deliberative) kind of information seems to facilitate the occurrence of cross-domain effects. When both types of information are present, however, the picture becomes more complicated, but both implicit and explicit evaluations still are capable of being multiply determined. In particular, we showed that implicit measures of attitudes can be impacted by both associative and deliberative information even when both are presented together. In addition, both kinds of information were also shown to influence explicit responses, though it appears that social judgeability concerns (and other downstream consequences) have the potential to eliminate any direct effect that associative information has on explicit measures of attitudes. Based on the existing evidence, it seems clear that the different kinds of evaluative processing are interrelated, and future research should further examine the nature of this relationship. In the meantime, researchers should exhibit caution before assuming that implicit and explicit measures only capture certain kinds of information or access certain processing systems.

References

Allport, G. W. (1954). *The nature of prejudice*. New York: Addison-Wesley.

Alvaro, E. M., & Crano, W. D. (1997). Indirect minority influence: Evidence for leniency in source evaluation and counterargumentation. *Journal of Personality and Social Psychology, 72,* p. 949–964.

Axsom, D., Yates, S. M., & Chaiken, S. (1987). Audience response as a heuristic cue in persuasion. *Journal of Personality and Social Psychology, 53,* 30–40.

Baker, S. M., & Petty, R. E. (1994). Majority and minority influence: Source-position imbalance as a determinant of message scrutiny. *Journal of Personality and Social Psychology, 67,* 5–19.

Banaji, M. R. (2004). The opposite of a great truth is also true. In J. T. Jost, M. R. Banaji, & D. A. Prentice (Eds.), *Perspectivism in social psychology: The yin and yang of scientific progress* (pp. 127–140). Washington, DC: American Psychological Association.

Bargh, J. A. (1999). The cognitive monster: The case against the controllability of automatic stereotype effects. In S. Chaiken & Y. Trope (Eds.), *Dual-process theories in social psychology*. New York: Guilford Press.

Bem, D. J. (1972). Self-perception theory. In L. Berkowitz (Ed.), *Advances in experimental social psychology* (Vol. 6, pp. 1–62). San Diego, CA: Academic Press.

Betsch, T., Plessner, H., & Schallies, E. (2004). The value-account model of attitude formation. In G. R. Maio & G. Haddock (Eds.), *Contemporary perspectives on the psychology of attitudes* (pp. 252–273). Hove, England: Psychology Press.

Bizer, G. Y., & Krosnick, J. A. (2001). Exploring the structure of strength-related attitude features: The relation between attitude importance and attitude accessibility. *Journal of Personality and Social Psychology, 81,* 566–586.

Blair, I. V. (2002). The malleability of automatic stereotypes and prejudice. *Personality and Social Psychology Review, 6,* 242–261.

Blair, I. V., Ma, J. E., & Lenton, A. P. (2001). Imagining stereotypes away: The moderation of implicit stereotypes through mental imagery. *Journal of Personality and Social Psychology, 81,* 828–841.

Briñol, P., & Petty, R. E. (2005). Individual differences in persuasion. In D. Albarracín, B. T. Johnson, & M. P. Zanna (Eds.), *Handbook of attitudes and attitude change* (pp. 575–616). Hillsdale, NJ: Erlbaum.

Briñol, P., Petty, R. E., & Horcajo, J. (2008). *Automatic change through deliberative processing of persuasive messages*. Working paper. Ohio State University, Columbus.

Briñol, P., Petty, R. E., & Rucker, D. D. (2006). The role of meta-cognitive processes in emotional intelligence. *Psicothema, 18,* 26–33.

Briñol, P., Petty, R. E., & Tormala, Z. L. (2004). The self-validation of cognitive responses to advertisements. *Journal of Consumer Research, 30,* 559–573.

Briñol, P., Petty, R. E., & Tormala, Z. L. (2006). The meaning of ease and its malleability. *Psychological Science, 17,* 200–206.

Briñol, P., Petty, R. E., & Wheeler, S. C. (2006). Discrepancies between explicit and implicit self-concepts: Consequences for information processing. *Journal of Personality and Social Psychology, 91,* 154–170.

Cacioppo, J. T., Gardner, W. L., & Berntson, G. G. (1997). Beyond bipolar conceptualizations and measures: The case of attitudes and evaluative space. *Personality and Social Psychology Review, 1,* 3–25.

Cacioppo, J. T., & Petty, R. E. (1982). The need for cognition. *Journal of Personality and Social Psychology, 42,* 116–131.

Cacioppo, J. T., Petty, R. E., Feinstein, J., & Jarvis, W. B. G. (1996). Dispositional differences in cognitive motivation: The life and times of individuals varying in need for cognition. *Psychological Bulletin, 119,* 197–253.

Carver, C. S. (2005). Impulse and constraint: Some perspectives from personality psychology, convergence with theory in other areas, and potential for integration. *Personality and Social Psychology Review, 9,* 312–333.

Chaiken, S. (1980). Heuristic versus systematic information processing and the use of source versus message queues in persuasion. *Journal of Personality and Social Psychology, 39,* 752–766.

Chaiken, S., Liberman, A., & Eagly, A. H. (1989). Heuristic and systematic information processing within and beyond the persuasion context. In J. S. Uleman & J. A. Bargh (Eds.), *Unintended thought* (pp. 212–252). New York: Guilford Press.

Chaiken, S., & Maheswaran, D. (1994). Heuristic processing can bias systematic processing: Effects of source credibility, argument ambiguity, and task importance on attitude judgment. *Journal of Personality and Social Psychology, 66,* 460–473.

Chaiken, S., & Trope, Y. (Eds.) (1999). *Dual-process theories in social psychology.* New York: Guilford Press.

Crano, W. D., & Chen, X. (1998) The leniency contract and persistence of majority and minority influence. *Journal of Personality and Social Psychology, 6,* 1437–1450.

Croizet, J. C., & Fiske, S. T. (2000). Moderation of priming by goals: Feeling entitled to judge increases judged usability of evaluative primes. *Journal of Experimental Social Psychology, 36,* 155–181.

Czyzewska, M., & Ginsburg, H. J. (2007). Explicit and implicit effects of antimarijuana and anti-tobacco TV advertisements. *Addictive Behaviors, 32,* 114–127.

Dasgupta, N., & Greenwald, A. G. (2001). On the malleability of automatic attitudes: Combating automatic prejudice with images of admired and disliked individuals. *Journal of Personality and Social Psychology, 81,* 800–814.

DeCoster, J., Banner, M. J., Smith, E. R., & Semin, G. R. (2006). On the inexplicability of the implicit: Differences in the information provided by implicit and explicit tests. *Social Cognition, 24*, 5–21.

De Houwer, J. Comparing measures of attitudes at the functional and structural level: Analysis and implications. In R. E. Petty, R. H. Fazio, & P. Briñol (Eds.), *Attitudes: Insights from the new implicit measures.* Hillsdale, NJ: Erlbaum.

Deutsch, R., & Strack, F. (2006). Duality models in social psychology: From dual processes to interacting systems. *Psychological Inquiry, 17*, 166–172.

Devine, P. G. (1989). Stereotypes and prejudice: Their automatic and controlled components. *Journal of Personality and Social Psychology, 56*, 5–18.

Dijksterhuis, A. (2004). I like myself but I don't know why: Enhancing implicit self-esteem by subliminal evaluative conditioning. *Journal of Personality and Social Psychology, 86*, 345–355

Dovidio, J. F., Kawakami, K., & Beach, K. (2001). Implicit and explicit attitudes: Examination of the relationship between measures of intergroup bias. In R. Brown & S. L. Gaertner (Eds.), *Blackwell handbook of social psychology, Vol. 4, Intergroup relations* (pp. 175–197). Oxford, England: Blackwell.

Dovidio, J. F., Kawakami, K., Johnson, C., Johnson, B., & Howard, A. (1997). On the nature of prejudice: Automatic and controlled processes. *Journal of Experimental Social Psychology, 33*, 510–540.

Eagly, A. H., & Chaiken, S. (1993). *The psychology of attitudes.* Fort Worth, TX: Harcourt, Brace, Jovanovich.

Epstein, S. (1991). Cognitive-experiential self-theory: An integrative theory of personality. In R. Curtis (Ed.), *The self with others: Convergences in psychoanalytical, social, and personality psychology* (pp. 111–137). New York: Guilford Press.

Fabrigar, L. R., Priester, J. R., Petty, R. E., & Wegener, D. T. (1998). The impact of attitude accessibility on cognitive elaboration of persuasive messages. *Personality and Social Psychology Bulletin, 24*, 339–352.

Fazio, R. H. (1995). Attitudes as object-evaluation associations: Determinants, consequences, and correlates of attitude accessibility. In R. E. Petty & J. A. Krosnick (Ed), *Attitude strength: Antecedents and consequences* (pp. 247–282). Hillsdale, NJ: Erlbaum.

Fazio, R. H., Jackson, J. R., Dunton, B. C., & Williams, C. J. (1995). Variability in automatic activation as an unobtrusive measure of racial attitudes: A bona fide pipeline? *Journal of Personality and Social Psychology, 69*, 1013–1027.

Fazio, R. H., & Olson, M. (2003). Implicit measures in social cognition research: Their meaning and uses. *Annual Review of Psychology, 54*, 297–327.

Fazio, R. H., & Towles-Schwen, T. (1999). The MODE model of attitude-behavior processes. In S. Chaiken & Y. Trope (Eds.), *Dual-process theories in social psychology* (pp. 97–116). New York: Guilford Press.

Festinger, L. (1957). *A theory of cognitive dissonance.* Stanford, CA: Stanford University Press.

Fishbein, M., & Ajzen, I. (1975). *Belief, attitude, intention, and behavior.* Reading, MA: Addison-Wesley.

Forehand, M. R., & Perkins, A. (2005). Implicit assimilation and explicit contrast: A set/reset model of response to celebrity voiceovers. *Journal of Consumer Research, 32,* 435–441.

Gawronski, B., & Bodenhausen, G. V. (2005). Accessibility effects on implicit cognition: The role of knowledge activation and retrieval experiences. *Journal of Personality and Social Psychology, 89,* 672–685.

Gawronski, B., & Bodenhausen, V. (2006). Associative and propositional processes in evaluation: An integrative review of implicit and explicit attitude change. *Psychological Bulletin, 132,* 692–731.

Gawronski, B., Bodenhausen, G. V., & Becker, A. P. (2007). I like it, because I like myself: Associative self-anchoring and post-decisional change of implicit evaluations. *Journal of Experimental Social Psychology, 43,* 221–232.

Gawronski, B., & Strack, F. (2003). On the prepositional nature of cognitive consistency: Dissonance changes explicit, but not implicit attitudes. *Journal of Experimental Social Psychology, 40,* 535–542.

Gawronski, B., Strack, F., & Bodenhausen, G. V. (in press). Attitudes and cognitive consistency: The role of associative and propositional processes. In R. E. Petty, R. H. Fazio, & P. Briñol (Eds.), *Attitudes: Insights from the new implicit measures.* Hillsdale, NJ: Erlbaum.

Greenwald, A. G. (1968). Cognitive learning, cognitive response to persuasion, and attitude change. In A. Greenwald, T. Brock, & T. Ostrom (Eds.), *Psychological foundations of attitudes.* New York: Academic Press.

Greenwald, A. G., & Banaji, M. (1995). Implicit social cognition: Attitudes, self-esteem, and stereotypes. *Psychological Review, 102,* 4–27.

Greenwald, A. G., Banaji, M. R., Rudman, L. A., Farnham, S. D., Nosek, B. A., & Mellott, D. S. (2002). A unified theory of implicit attitudes, stereotypes, self-esteem, and self-concept. *Psychological Review, 109,* 3–25.

Greenwald, A. G., McGhee, D. E., & Schwartz, J. L. K. (1998). Measuring individual differences in implicit cognition: The Implicit Association Task. *Journal of Personality and Social Psychology, 74,* 1464–1480.

Gregg, A. P., Seibt, B., & Banaji, M. R. (2006). Easier done than undone. Asymmetry in the malleability of implicit preferences. *Journal of Personality and Social Psychology, 90,* 1–20.

Han, H. A., Olson, M. A., & Fazio, R. H. (2006). The influence of experimentally created extrapersonal associations on the Implicit Association Test. *Journal of Experimental Social Psychology, 42,* 259–272.

Horcajo, J., Briñol, P., Petty, R. E., & Wheeler, S. C. (2007). *Deliberative automatic attitude change: Consequences for spreading activation.* Working paper. Ohio State University, Columbus.

Horcajo, J., Tormala, Z. L., Petty, R. E., & Briñol, P. (2007). *The effects of minority influence on indirect automatic evaluations.* Working paper. Ohio State University, Columbus.

Hovland, C. I., Janis, I. L., & Kelley, H. H. (1953). *Communication and persuasion: Psychological studies of opinion change.* New Haven, CT: Yale University Press.

Janis, I. L. (1968). Attitude change via role playing. In R. Abelson, E. Aronson, W.M. McGuire, T. Newcomb, M. Rosenberg, & P. Tannebaum (Eds.), *Theories of cognitive consistency: A sourcebook.* Chicago: Rand McNally.

Janis, I. L., & King, B. T. (1954). The influence of role-playing on opinion change. *Journal of Abnormal and Social Psychology, 49,* 211–218.

Jordan, C. H., Whitfield, M., & Zeigler-Hill, V. (2007). Intuition and the correspondence between implicit and explicit self-esteem. *Journal of Personality and Social Psychology, 93,* 1067–1079.

Judd, C. M., & Brauer, M. (1995). Repetition and evaluative extremity. In R. E. Petty & J. A. Krosnick (Eds.), *Attitude strength: Antecedents and consequences* (pp. 43–71). Hillsdale, NJ: Lawrence Erlbaum Associates.

Kahneman, D., & Frederick, S. (2005). A model of heuristic judgment. In K. J. Holyoak & R. G. Morrison (Eds.), *The Cambridge handbook of thinking and reasoning* (pp. 267–293). New York: Cambridge University Press.

Kruglanski, A. W. (1989). The psychology of being "right": The problem of accuracy in social perception and cognition. *Psychological Bulletin, 106,* 395–409.

Kruglanski, A. W., & Thompson, E. P. (1999). Persuasion by a single route: A view from the unimodel. *Psychological Inquiry, 10,* 83–110.

Kunst-Wilson, W. R., & Zajonc, R. B. (1980). Affective discrimination of stimuli that cannot be recognized. *Science, 207,* 557–558.

Lowery, B. S., Hardin, C. D., & Sinclair, S. (2001). Social influence effects on automatic racial prejudice. *Journal of Personality and Social Psychology, 81,* 842–855.

Maio, G. R., Haddock, G., Watt, S. E., & Hewstone, M. (in press). Implicit measures in applied contexts: An illustrative examination of antiracism advertising. In R. E. Petty, R. H. Fazio, & P. Briñol (Eds.), *Attitudes: Insights from the new implicit measures.* Hillsdale, NJ: Erlbaum.

McCaslin, M. J., Loersch, C., & Petty, R. E. (2007, January). *Attitude dissociation? The interplay of associative and deliberative attitude processes.* Presented at the annual meeting of the Society for Personality and Social Psychology, Memphis, TN.

McGuire, W. J. (1981). The probabilogical model of cognitive structure and attitude change. In R. E. Petty, T. M. Ostrom, & T. C. Brock (Eds.), *Cognitive responses in persuasion* (pp. 291–307). Hillsdale, NJ: Erlbaum.

Moscovici, S., Mucchi-Faina, A., & Maass, A. (1994). *Minority influence.* Chicago: Nelson-Hall.

Olson, M. A., & Fazio, R. H. (2001). Implicit attitude formation through classical conditioning. *Psychological Science, 12*, 413–417.

Olson, M. A., & Fazio, R. H. (2004). Reducing the influence of extrapersonal associations on the Implicit Association Test: Personalizing the IAT. *Journal of Personality and Social Psychology, 86*, 653–667.

Olson, M. A., & Fazio, R. H. (in press). Implicit and explicit measures of attitudes: The perspective of the MODE model. In R. E. Petty, R. H. Fazio, & P. Briñol (Eds.), *Attitudes: Insights from the new implicit measures*. New York: Psychology Press.

Park, J., Felix, K., & Lee, G. (2007). Implicit attitudes toward Arab-Muslims and the moderating effects of social information. *Basic and Applied Social Psychology, 29*, 35–35.

Perez, J. A., & Mugny, G. The conflict elaboration theory of social influence. In E. H. Witte & J. H. Davis (Eds) *Understanding group behavior, Vol. 2: Small group processes and interpersonal relations* (pp. 191–210). Hillsdale, NJ: Lawrence Erlbaum Associates.

Petty, R. E. (1997). The evolution of theory and research in social psychology: From single to multiple effect and process models. In C. McGarty & S. A. Haslam (Eds.), *The message of social psychology: Perspectives on mind in society* (pp. 268–290). Oxford, England: Blackwell.

Petty, R. E. (2001). Subtle influences on judgments and behaviors: Who is most susceptible? In J. Forgas & K. D. Williams (Eds.), *Social influence: Direct and indirect processes* (pp. 129–146). Philadelphia: Psychology Press.

Petty, R. E., & Briñol, P. (2006). A meta-cognitive approach to "implicit" and "explicit" evaluations: Comment on Gawronski and Bodenhausen (2006). *Psychological Bulletin, 132*, 740–744.

Petty, R. E., & Briñol, P. (in press). Implicit ambivalence: A meta-cognitive approach. In R. E. Petty, R. H. Fazio, & P. Briñol (Eds.), *Attitudes: Insights from the new implicit measures*. Hillsdale, NJ: Erlbaum.

Petty, R. E., & Briñol, P. (2008). Persuasion: From single to multiple to meta-cognitive processes. *Perspectives on Psychological Science, 3*, 137–147.

Petty, R. E., Briñol, P., & DeMarree, K. G. (2007). The Meta-Cognitive Model (MCM) of attitudes: Implications for attitude measurement, change, and strength. *Social Cognition, 25*, 609–642.

Petty, R. E., Briñol, P., & Tormala, Z. L. (2002). Thought confidence as a determinant of persuasion: The self-validation hypothesis. *Journal of Personality and Social Psychology, 82*, 722–741.

Petty, R. E., Briñol, P., Tormala, Z. L., & Wegener, D. T. (2007). The role of meta-cognition in social judgment. In E. T. Higgins & A. W. Kruglanski, (Eds.) *Social psychology: A handbook of basic principles* (2nd ed., pp. 254–284). New York: Guilford Press.

Petty, R. E., & Cacioppo, J. T. (1979). Issue involvement can increase or decrease persuasion by enhancing message-relevant cognitive responses. *Journal of Personality and Social Psychology, 37*, 1915–1926.

Petty, R. E., & Cacioppo, J. T. (1981). *Attitudes and persuasion: Classics and contemporary approaches.* Dubuque, IA: Win. C. Brown.

Petty, R. E., & Cacioppo, J. T. (1984). The effects of involvement on responses to argument quantity and quality: Central and peripheral routes to persuasion. *Journal of Personality and Social Psychology, 46,* 69–81.

Petty, R. E., & Cacioppo, J. T. (1986). *Communication and persuasion: Central and peripheral routes to attitude change.* New York: Springer-Verlag.

Petty, R. E., Cacioppo, J. T., & Goldman, R. (1981). Personal involvement as a determinant of argument-based persuasion. *Journal of Personality and Social Psychology, 41,* 847–855.

Petty, R. E., DeMarree, K. G., Briñol, P., Horcajo, J., & Strathman, A. J. (2008). Need for cognition can magnify or attenuate priming effects in social judgment. *Personality and Social Psychology Bulletin, 34,* 900–912.

Petty, R. E., Fabrigar, L. R., & Wegener, D. T., (2003). Emotional factors in attitudes and persuasion. In R. J. Davidson, K. R. Scherer, & H. H. Goldsmith (Eds.), *Handbook of affective sciences* (pp. 752–772). Oxford: Oxford University Press.

Petty, R. E., Harkins, S. G., & Williams, K. D. (1980). The effects of group diffusion of cognitive effort on attitudes: An information processing view. *Journal of Personality and Social Psychology, 38,* 81–92.

Petty, R. E., Haugtvedt, C., & Smith, S. M. (1995). Elaboration as a determinant of attitude strength: Creating attitudes that are persistent, resistant, and predictive of behavior. In R. E. Petty & J. A. Krosnick (Eds.), *Attitude strength: Antecedents and consequences* (pp. 93–130). Hillsdale, NJ: Erlbaum.

Petty, R. E., & Krosnick, J. A. (1995). *Attitude strength: Antecedents and consequences.* Hillsdale, NJ: Erlbaum.

Petty, R. E., Ostrom, T. M., & Brock, T. C. (Eds.). (1981). *Cognitive responses in persuasion.* Hillsdale, NJ: Erlbaum.

Petty, R. E., Tormala, Z. L., Briñol, P., & Jarvis, W. B. G. (2006). Implicit ambivalence from attitude change: An exploration of the PAST model. *Journal of Personality and Social Psychology, 90,* 21–41.

Petty, R. E., & Wegener, D. T. (1998). Attitude change: Multiple roles for persuasion variables. In D. Gilbert, S. Fiske, & G. Lindzey (Eds.), *The handbook of social psychology* (4th ed., Vol. 1, pp. 323–390). New York: McGraw-Hill.

Petty, R. E., & Wegener, D. T. (1999). The Elaboration Likelihood Model: Current status and controversies. In S. Chaiken & Y. Trope (Eds.), *Dual-process theories in social psychology* (pp. 41–72). New York: Guilford Press.

Petty, R. E., Wegener, D. T., & White, P. (1998). Flexible correction processes in social judgment: Implications for persuasion. *Social Cognition, 16,* 93–113.

Petty, R. E., Wells, G. L., & Brock, T. C. (1976). Distraction can enhance or reduce yielding to propaganda: Thought disruption versus effort justification. *Journal of Personality and Social Psychology, 34,* 874–884.

Priester, J. R., & Petty, R. E. (1995). Source attributions and persuasion: Perceived honesty as a determinant of message scrutiny. *Personality and Social Psychology Bulletin, 21*, 637–654.

Richeson, J. A., & Ambady, N. (2003). Effects of situational power on automatic racial prejudice. *Journal of Experimental Social Psychology, 39*, 177–183.

Rucker, D. D., & Petty, R. E. (2004). When resistance is futile: Consequences of failed counterarguing on attitude certainty. *Journal of Personality and Social Psychology, 86*, 219–235.

Rucker, D. D., Petty, R. E., & Briñol, P. (2008). What's in a frame anyway? A meta-cognitive analysis of one- versus two-sided message framing. *Journal of Consumer Psychology, 18*, 137–149.

Rudman, L. A., Ashmore, R. D., & Gary, M. L. (2001). "Unlearning" automatic biases: The malleability of implicit prejudice and stereotypes. *Journal of Personality and Social Psychology, 81*, 856–868.

Rydell, R. J., & McConnell, A. R. (2006). Understanding implicit and explicit attitude change: A system of reasoning analysis. *Journal of Personality and Social Psychology, 91*, 995–1008.

Rydell, R. J., McConnell, A. R., Mackie, D. M., & Strain, L. M. (2006). Of two minds: Forming and changing valence-inconsistent implicit and explicit attitudes. *Psychological Science, 17*, 954–958.

Rydell, R. J., McConnell, A. R., Strain, L. M., Claypool, H. M., & Hugenberg, K. (2007). Implicit and explicit attitudes respond differently to increasing amounts of counterattitudinal information. *European Journal of Social Psychology, 37*, 867–878.

Schwarz, N., Bless, H., Strack, F., Klumpp, G., Rittenauer-Schatka, H., & Simons, A. (1991). Ease of retrieval as information: Another look at the availability heuristic. *Journal of Personality and Social Psychology, 61*, 195–202.

Sloman, S. A. (1996). The empirical case for two systems of reasoning. *Psychological Bulletin, 119*, 3–22.

Smith, E. R., & DeCoster, J. (1999). Associative and rule-based processing: A connectionist interpretation of dual-process models. In S. Chaiken & Y. Trope (Eds.), *Dual-process theories in social psychology*. New York: Guilford Press.

Smith, E. R., & DeCoster, J. (2000). Dual-process models in social and cognitive psychology: Conceptual integration and links to underlying memory systems. *Personality and Social Psychology Review, 4*, 108–131.

Smith, S. M., Haugtvedt, C. P., & Petty, R. E. (1994). Need for cognition and the effects of repeated expression on attitude accessibility and extremity. *Advances in Consumer Research, 21*, 234–237.

Staats, A. W., & Staats, C. K. (1958). Attitudes established by classical conditioning. *Journal of Abnormal and Social Psychology, 11*, 187–192.

Teachman, B. A., & Woody, S. R. (2003). Automatic processing in spider phobia: Implicit fear associations over the course of treatment. *Journal of Abnormal Psychology, 112*, 100–109.

Tesser, A. (1978). Self-generated attitude change. In L. Berkowitz (Ed.), *Advances in experimental social psychology* (Vol. 11, pp. 289–338). New York: Academic Press.

Tormala, Z. L, Briñol, P., & Petty, R. E. (2004). Hidden effects of persuasion. *Advances in Consumer Research, 31*, 75–76.

Tormala, Z. L., Briñol, P., & Petty, R. E. (2007). Multiple roles for source credibility under high elaboration: It's all in the timing. *Social Cognition, 25*, 536–552.

Tormala, Z. L., DeSensi, V. L., & Petty, R. E. (2007). Resisting persuasion by illegitimate means: A meta-cognitive perspective on minority influence. *Personality and Social Psychology Bulletin, 33*, 354–367.

Tormala, Z. L., Falces, C., Briñol, P., & Petty, R. E. (2007). Ease of retrieval effects in social judgment: The role of unrequested cognitions. *Journal of Personality and Social Psychology, 93*, 143–157.

Tormala, Z. L., & Petty, R. E. (2002). What doesn't kill me makes me stronger: The effects of resisting persuasion on attitude certainty. *Journal of Personality and Social Psychology, 83*, 1298–1313.

Tormala, Z. L., Petty, R. E., & Briñol, P. (2002). Ease of retrieval effects in persuasion: The roles of elaboration and thought-confidence. *Personality and Social Psychology Bulletin, 28*, 1700–1712.

Uleman, J. S. (1987). Consciousness and control: The case of spontaneous trait inference. *Personality and Social Psychology Bulletin, 13*, 337–354.

Walther, E. (2002). Guilty by mere association: Evaluative conditioning and the spreading attitude effect. *Journal of Personality and Social Psychology, 82*, 919–934.

Walther, E., & Trasselli, C. (2002). I like her, because I like myself: Self-evaluation as a source of interpersonal attitudes. *Experimental Psychology, 50*, 239–246.

Wilson, T. D., Lindsey, S., & Schooler, T. Y. (2000). A model of dual attitudes. *Psychological Review, 107*, 101–126.

Yzerbyt, V. Y., Schadron, G., Leyens, J., & Rocher, S. (1994). Social judgeability: The impact of meta-informational cues on the use of stereotypes. *Journal of Personality and Social Psychology, 66*, 48–55.

Zajonc, R. B. (1968). Attitudinal effects of effort and improvisation on self-persuasion produced by role-playing. *Journal of Experimental Social Psychology, 1*, 103–120.

Endnotes

1 The ELM and the HSM are early examples of what became an explosion of dual-process and dual-systems theories that distinguished

thoughtful from non-thoughtful determinants of judgment (see Chaiken & Trope, 1999).

2 Extensive prior literature has already demonstrated that explicit measures of attitudes are sensitive to argument quality manipulations (see Eagly & Chaiken, 1993; Petty & Wegener, 1998), and thus these measures were not of interest in this line of research.

3 For example, just as source attractiveness is more likely to impact an explicit measure as a simple cue when thinking during the message is low than high, when thinking is high during the message, source attractiveness might impact an implicit but not an explicit measure because of the positive associations with the message topic.

4 Using a classic ease-of-retrieval paradigm (Schwarz et al., 1991) in which people have to generate either a few (easy) or many (difficult) thoughts, Gawronski and Bodenhausen (2005) found that implicit measures based on stimulus compatibility processes (e.g., semantic priming with a lexical/decision task) were affected exclusively by the valence of the thoughts generated but not by the ease associated with those thoughts (a metacognitive property of the thoughts that can affect attitudes by increasing thought-confidence; Tormala, Petty, & Briñol, 2002). In contrast, implicit measures based on response compatibility processes (e.g., IAT; see Chapter 12, this volume) were affected by the subjective sense of ease. Although the finding of a significant ease effect on an IAT might seem to contradict our reasoning, it is important to note that in the classic ease-of-retrieval paradigm, ease and valence are confounded; that is, the cognition that one's thoughts are easy to generate is a positive one, whereas difficulty is a negative one (Briñol, Petty, & Tormala, 2006). Furthermore, when people generate a small number of requested thoughts, they also generate even more thoughts in the opposite direction, which can, in part, account for the ease effect (see Tormala, Falces, Briñol, & Petty, 2007). Thus, automatic measures could be sensitive to these aspects of the ease of manipulation.

5 Because we did not measure automatic evaluation of the color green, it is not clear if low need for cognition individuals did not show change to this color or if, as hypothesized, they did show change to this color but it did not spread to related concepts such as Heineken.

6 Indeed, in another study in this line of research we found that these results were moderated by implicit self-esteem, such that only those with high (but not low) implicit self-esteem showed the automatic spreading activation effect as a function of thinking. This finding is consistent with the idea that automatic spreading activation responds to balance principles (for similar examples, see Gawronski, Bodenhausen, & Becker, 2007; Greenwald, Banaji, Rudman, Farnham, Nosek, & Mellott, 2002; Walter & Trasselli, 2002).

7 High and low NC individuals might have engaged in the same degree of thinking if situational constraints to think were operating or other factors encouraged thinking (e.g., see Axson, Yates, & Chaiken, 1987).

8 It is also possible to explain discordant explicit and implicit attitudes from a single, integrated systems approach (e.g., see Chapter 2 and Chapter 5, this volume).

9 In some research guided by the dual-process perspective, deliberative information has also been paired with associative information of opposite valence (e.g., strong arguments are paired with an unattractive source or weak arguments are paired with an attractive source; e.g., see Petty, Wegener, & White, 1998). In this research, the associative (simple cue) information affects deliberative attitudes when it is processed under low deliberation conditions (versus affecting low deliberation measures even when processed under high deliberation conditions).

10 After the implicit and explicit measures of attitudes toward Bob, the authors exposed participants to another 100 experimental trials where the valence of the associative and deliberative information was flipped (i.e., positive to negative and vice versa). Implicit and explicit evaluations of Bob were then collected a second time. As before, implicit measures reflected only (the most recent) associative information, and explicit measures reflected only (the most recent) deliberative information.

11 Each image appeared onscreen for 13 ms and was followed by a 52-ms presentation of a pattern mask. The images were randomly drawn from a bank of either 75 positive or 75 negative pictures (see Petty et al., 2006, Study 1).

12 The fact that the informational sentences affected responses on the IAT is consistent with the idea that both cognitively and affectively based attitudes can have an impact on automatic measures. Furthermore, the earlier studies reviewed on cognitive responses mediating the impact of persuasive messages on implicit measures of attitudes are also consistent with this idea.

13 Corresponding results were found following a change manipulation similar to that used in Rydell et al. (2006).

14 A similar experiment was conducted in our lab where participants were repeatedly exposed to subliminal positive or negative images while they read a neutral paragraph about Paul on the computer screen. Participants were asked to form an impression of Paul and to "go with their gut" when doing so (see also Jordan, Whitfield, & Zeigler-Hill, 2007). In this case, explicit attitudes toward Paul were affected by the associative information presented. It was presumed that this was because the special instructions alleviated social judgeability concerns about using the reactions elicited by the subliminal images to judge Paul.

11

Implicit Measures in Applied Contexts[*]
An Illustrative Examination of Antiracism Advertising

Gregory R. Maio
Geoffrey Haddock
Susan E. Watt
Miles Hewstone

Introduction

The earliest research on attitude formation and change was inspired by important social problems. What factors can cause people to like each other in social housing? How can people be made to remain favorable to the war against the Third Reich? How can we reduce prejudice? The list of applied research on attitude formation and change has grown over the years and now examines issues in the formation and change of attitudes toward a variety of objects, policies, and behaviors. These include employment (e.g., job satisfaction, organizational commitment), health promotion (e.g., food attitude, sunscreen use), politics (e.g., campaign design, policy preference), product consumption (e.g., brand preference, methods of marketing), the environment (e.g., recycling, reduction of consumption), and sexual behavior (e.g., condom use), among other topics. It is now safe to say that the volume of applied research on attitude formation and change is truly enormous and important.

As in most applied domains of research, the methods that are used often involve novel extensions of work that has taken place in laborato-

* The research reported in this chapter was supported by the Economic and Social Research Council. The authors also wish to thank the U.K. Commission for Racial Equality for its advice and donation of materials at various stages of the research.

ries. It is therefore important to revisit periodically the fit between the applied research and the concepts and tools that have been developed in the lab. With this in mind, there is a clear methodological discrepancy between the conduct of most past research on applied interventions to change attitudes and the focus of laboratory research in the past decade. In particular, most of the applied research has tended to utilize self-report scales to assess the attitudes of interest, whereas the laboratory research has been increasingly developing and using numerous implicit measures of attitude that do not rely on self-reports. Of course, part of the reason for the discrepancy is the inevitable lag between developments in the lab and their dissemination (including training) to practitioners. Another reason pertains to the practical difficulties posed by using most implicit measures in applied settings.

Nonetheless, there are several reasons to incorporate implicit measures in applied settings. In this chapter, we briefly consider evidence highlighting these reasons across a range of applied domains. After noting a relative lack of evidence about the use of implicit measures to evaluate the effects of applied interventions, we focus on a set of experiments that used these measures to help evaluate the effects of a specific set of applied interventions to reduce prejudice.

Importance of Implicit Measures in Applied Contexts

One reason to examine implicit measures in applied research is their unique role in the prediction of behavior. This role has been illustrated in several domains of study, including consumer behavior, health behavior, clinical disorders, and prejudice. In the domain of consumer behavior, Maison, Greenwald, and Bruin (2001) found that women who preferred the taste of low-calorie products over high-calorie products on an Implicit Association Test (IAT) habitually restricted their high-calorie-food intake. These researchers subsequently found that preferences for brands of yoghurt (Danone vs. Bakoma), fast-food restaurant (McDonald's vs. Milk Bar), and colas (Coca-Cola vs. Pepsi) significantly predicted brand preference, product usage, and even brand recognition in a blind taste test. Moreover, although explicit self-report measures of attitude were also powerful predictors of behavior in these experiments, the implicit measures predicted behavior even after controlling for the explicit ratings. Thus, implicit measures have a unique relationship with common, everyday brand-related behavior.

Of interest, there is also evidence that implicit measures predict different types of behavior compared with explicit measures. Research on the use of condoms provides interesting evidence in support of this idea. In this research, explicit self-report measures of condom use tended to better predict hypothetical decisions and behaviors regarding steady dating partners rather than casual dating partners. In contrast, IAT measures of favorability toward condoms tended to predict hypothetical decisions and behavior for condom use with casual partners, but not hypothetical decisions and behavior for condom use with steady partners (Czopp, Monteith, Zimmerman, & Lynam, 2004; Marsh & Julka, 2000). This evidence has been interpreted as support for the notion that explicit measures are better predictors of behavior that is relatively deliberative and controlled (e.g., sex with a steady partner), whereas implicit measures are better predictors of behavior that is relatively spontaneous and automatic (e.g., sex with a casual partner).

Other interesting evidence indicates that implicit measures are able to detect effects of mood: Formerly depressed individuals who are made to experience a negative mood subsequently exhibit negative evaluative bias on self-relevant items in the IAT (Gemar, Segal, Sagrati, & Kennedy, 2001). It is therefore not surprising that these measures can also predict behaviors regarding mood-altering substances, such as nicotine, cannabis, and alcohol. For instance, smokers exhibit preferences for smoking-related cues on an implicit measure (Bradley, Field, Mogg, & De Houwer, 2004; Mogg, Bradley, Field, & De Houwer, 2003). In addition, nicotine deprivation affects attitude scores on the evaluative priming measure (Sherman, Rose, Koch, Presson, & Chassin, 2003). Similarly, users of cannabis exhibit less negative reactions to cannabis-related words on the IAT than do nonusers (Field, Mogg, & Bradley, 2004), and a greater preponderance of positive implicit associations to alcoholic beverages predicts more alcohol consumption, over and above a frequently used explicit measure of alcohol expectancies (Jajodia & Earleywine, 2003).

This ability to account for unique variance is evident even in studies of extreme antisocial behaviors, such as murder and child sexual abuse (Gray, Brown, MacCulloch, Smith, & Snowden, 2005; Snowden, Gray, Smith, Morris, & MacCulloch, 2004). For example, in one study (Snowden et al.), implicit measures revealed reduced negative associations with violence among psychopathic murders compared with nonpsychopathic murderers and offenders (low or high in psychopathy) who are convicted of other crimes; explicit measures did not detect this difference. Such results indicate that implicit measures might eventually help to assess the effects of incarceration and treatment on recidivism.

Nevertheless, there are comparatively few studies of the effects of interventions on implicit evaluations. Exceptions have been provided by Teachman and her colleagues. For instance, people with spider phobia typically exhibit stronger implicit associations between spiders and words such as *afraid* and *disgusting* than do matched controls, but this difference is eliminated after exposure therapy (Teachman & Woody, 2003). Paralleling the other evidence in applied settings, the implicit associations also predict phobic behavior independently of self-reported fear (Teachman & Woody). Most relevant to the present chapter, Teachman, Gapinski, Brownell, Rawlins, and Jeyaram (2003) found that procedures designed to highlight genetic contributions to obesity and to instigate empathy for obese individuals did not reduce prejudice on an implicit measure. Yet, the implicit measure revealed more evidence of antifat bias than a comparable explicit measure, on which participants largely denied any bias. Of course, the tendency for people to deny bias on an explicit measure, but show it on an implicit measure, is one important reason why there has been abundant research on the use of implicit measures in the study of prejudice (see the third section of this volume). This pattern also highlights the general relevance of implicit measures to applied settings, which are often precisely the domains where the vulnerability of self-report measures to socially desirable responding is most apparent. Thus, the lack of an effect on the implicit measure of antifat bias is disconcerting.

Ultimately, most applied research is oriented toward yielding successful interventions. Most interventions directed at large-scale attitude change involve public information campaigns, including marketing and advertising approaches. Yet, there is a lack of evidence evaluating the effects of such interventions using implicit measures of attitude. For this reason, the remainder of this chapter focuses on a set of studies that have examined the effects of persuasive interventions on implicit and explicit measures of prejudice. By describing this program of research, we hope to highlight the kinds of insights that can be gained by using both implicit and explicit measures to evaluate applied interventions.

Antiracism Interventions

Most research on interventions to reduce prejudice has focused on Allport's (1954) contact hypothesis, which stipulates that direct contact with members of other ethnic groups reduces prejudice in special circumstances, such as equal status contact (Hewstone, Rubin, & Willis, 2002). Although this approach appears to reduce prejudice and stereotyping in some circumstances, a practical disadvantage of this method is the requirement of strong institutional and legislative support and the high cost of directing intergroup contact (e.g., through rezoning of schools, and housing and legislative changes). An easier and more common option is to utilize social marketing techniques, which involve the distribution of antiracism advertisements. In Britain, where the present research took place, the Commission for Racial Equality (CRE) has distributed numerous clever pictorial advertisements, which attract attention using simple, emotional arguments. For instance, one advertisement shows a picture of the world beside the caption, "Don't like your neighbors?" and the word "Move" shown at a location in outer space (see Figure 11.1). Another ad shows pictures of grotesque physical injuries to ethnic minority children, along with the caption, "Children from ethnic minorities often get the worst marks at school." A third advertisement shows a mop and pail, garbage bag, and open toilet, along with the caption, "Who says ethnic minorities can't get jobs? There are openings everywhere."

Despite their creative, provocative nature, one common element of these appeals is the ease with which they can be counterargued by someone who is motivated to scrutinize the messages. For example, in the third advertisement, many individuals might wonder what is wrong with the forms of labor depicted in the advertisement. This potential for easy counterargument is an almost-inescapable feature of most simple print messages, and not just messages used in the antiracism domain. In general, the use of cheaper print formats constrains the amount of argumentation that can be included in the advertisements, and marketers often have good reason to suspect that their message recipients will not attend to messages that present abundant text. Because people often lack the motivation and opportunity to read long print ads, these messages are often kept short and facile.

Marketers have stressed two disparate answers to this limitation. On the one hand, the simple appeals may help to fulfill an important function of advertising, which is to attract attention to a brand or issue (e.g., prejudice) in a memorable way (Ehrenberg, Barnard, Kennedy, & Bloom, 2002). This awareness might be regarded as a necessary first step in the process of eliciting attitude change and as a step that should be supplemented by other interventions (e.g., education campaigns). On the other hand, some experts argue that such brand awareness is an insufficient objective of advertising: Its most important function is to change attitudes as much as possible (Kover, 2002). Some advocates of this view argue that messages can successfully change attitudes in

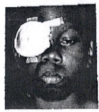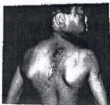

FIGURE 11.1 Sample antiracism advertisements used by Britain's Commission for Racial Equality.

people whose initial attitudes are mixed or ambivalent (e.g., individuals who favor one brand while being loyal to another; Rossiter & Percy, 1997). Ambivalence is clearly described in the social psychological literature on attitude change, which asserts that ambivalence is the simultaneous presence of strong positive and negative elements in attitudes (Conner & Sparks, 2002; Thompson, Zanna, & Griffin, 1995). This literature also describes research indicating that people with ambivalent attitudes toward the topic of a message should be more affected by the content of a message than people with nonambivalent attitudes (Armitage & Conner, 2000).

Nonetheless, there are reasons to doubt the ostensible amenability of ambivalent people to change. Many researchers have predicted that message recipients who are ambivalent toward the topic of a message should scrutinize it more carefully than message recipients who are not ambivalent toward the topic (Bell & Esses, 2002; Jonas, Diehl, & Bromer, 1997; Maio, Bell, & Esses, 1996; Maio, Greenland, Bernard, & Esses, 2001; Petty, Tormala, Briñol, & Jarvis, 2006). There are several bases for this prediction. One reason emerges from cognitive dissonance theory (Festinger, 1957), which stipulates that ambivalence creates an aversive state of tension. Indeed, there is evidence that ambivalence toward ethnic groups in particular is associated with increased aversive arousal (Britt, Boniecki, Vescio, Biernat, & Brown, 1996; Hass, Katz, Rizzo, Bailey, & Moore, 1992). In theory, resolving the attitude so that it becomes entirely positive or negative can reduce this tension. Therefore, ambivalent people may be motivated to scrutinize relevant messages more carefully in order to resolve their ambivalence, and this scrutiny should cause the ambivalent individuals to become more sensitive to the quality of the message arguments.

Another reason for this prediction is that ambivalence lowers subjective confidence in the individual's attitude. Contemporary models of persuasion indicate that people are often motivated to form an accurate attitude (Albarracín, 2002; Chen & Chaiken, 1999; Kruglanski, Fishbach, Erb, Pierro, & Mannetti, 2004; Petty & Wegener, 1999), and lower attitude certainty can motivate increased scrutiny of arguments in order to achieve a more confident attitude (Chen & Chaiken; Jonas et al., 1997).

A third reason is that ambivalent individuals are more able to process relevant messages because of their greater wealth of knowledge about both sides of an issue (Maio et al., 1996). This knowledge could confer a greater ability to understand and counterargue the message. As a result, ambivalent people should be more able to pick up strengths and weaknesses in the arguments, increasing attitude change from cogently argued messages and decreasing attitude change from weakly argued messages.

Consistent with the notion that ambivalence elicits argument scrutiny, people who are ambivalent toward a group exhibit more positive attitudes toward the group after reading a message containing six strong arguments in favor of the group than after reading a message containing six weak arguments in favor of the group, independently of relevant individual differences (e.g., need for cognition) and several attitude properties (e.g., attitude valence); nonambivalent message recipients do not exhibit this increased message scrutiny (Maio et al., 1996, 2001). Thus, the evidence indicates that it may be particularly difficult (and not easier) for most antiracism advertisements to change the attitudes of people who are ambivalent toward an ethnic group. This difficulty would arise because most antiracism advertisements use the simple, easy-to-process print format that we described above. This format is simply meant to pithily claim that racism is wrong. The ads are usually similar to the famous "Just say no" theme present in 1980s American anti-drug-abuse advertising: the antiracism ads imply that people should not be prejudiced but often do not add cogent argumentation. The lack of cogent argumentation in many antiracism advertisements may cause them to backfire for ambivalent individuals, who responded negatively to weakly argued messages in the past research. This backfire is especially important because many individuals possess ambivalent attitudes toward ethnic minority groups (Bell, Esses, & Maio, 1996; Katz & Hass, 1988).

Nevertheless, several issues need to be considered before becoming certain about the dangers of message backfire among ambivalent people. First, past research has not compared postmessage attitudes to those that would have emerged after participants receive no message in favor of ethnic minorities, so this research is unable to reveal whether weak antiracism messages actually can cause more negative attitudes than would have existed without the messages. Second, it is not clear whether the effects of intergroup ambivalence on reactions to antiracism messages are explained by other attitude properties not included in the past research, such as self-reported attitude strength or attitude certainty. As explained above, both constructs are potential mediating mechanisms for the effects of ambivalence. Alternatively, the effects of ambivalence might be independent of these variables, suggesting that the correct explanation has more to do with the unique ability of ambivalence to reflect evaluative conflict or dissonance than these other attitude properties. The answers to these questions would help explain how ambivalence exerts its effects, which is an important step to understanding its impact in the first place.

Finally, and most relevant to the present volume, the past research only employed explicit measures of attitude, which rely on self-reports and are susceptible to socially desirable responding, particularly in the context of prejudice (Fazio & Olson, 2003). Implicit measures of attitude can help to circumvent these biases, and therefore, it is important to understand the effects on both implicit and explicit attitude measures.

Evidence about the Impact of Antiracism Advertisements on Explicit and Implicit Measures of Prejudice

We have attempted to address these issues in a large program of research funded by the Economic and Social Research Council in Britain. These experiments tested the basic idea that weak messages backfire on ambivalent individuals, using text-based and pictorial antiracism advertisements, and using assessments of attitudes that were presented immediately after exposure to the advertisement or after a delay.

Effects of Tainted Text-Based Antiracism Messages

One experiment presented participants with a modified version of the strong pro-ethnic-minority editorial that was used by Maio et al. (1996). This new version contained four of the original six arguments that were used in the strong editorial, but replaced two of the original six arguments with weak claims designed to taint the overall strength of the appeal. If ambivalence elicits a heightened sensitivity to the flaws in this weakened antiracism message, then this tainted editorial should elicit more negative attitudes among ambivalent participants than among ambivalent participants who receive a control message on an irrelevant topic. In other words, small flaws may be sufficient to affect ambivalent participants' attitudes negatively. In contrast, nonambivalent people should be less negatively (or perhaps even positively) affected by the tainted message.

In this study, psychology undergraduates completed measures of numerous properties of their attitudes toward ethnic minority people. The valence of pretest attitudes toward ethnic minority people was assessed using an evaluation thermometer (Haddock & Zanna, 1998).

Attitude extremity was assessed by calculating the absolute value of the difference between participants' ratings on the attitude thermometer (from 0 to 100) and the neutral point on the thermometer (50).

Additional attitude properties were calculated using responses to an open-ended measure that examined three components of participants' attitudes toward ethnic minorities: emotions, stereotypes, and symbolic beliefs (Bell & Esses, 2002; Stangor, Sullivan, & Ford, 1991). To assess emotions, participants were asked to list emotions and feelings that they experienced when they saw, met, or thought about ethnic minority people. To assess stereotypes, participants listed adjectives or short phrases that described characteristics of ethnic minority people. To assess symbolic beliefs, participants listed the values, customs, and traditions that they believed were held by ethnic minority people. For each component, participants were asked to list as many responses as necessary to convey their impression of ethnic minority people (to a maximum of 10 for each component). After indicating responses for a particular component (e.g., emotions), participants were asked to assign a valence (favorability rating) to each of their responses for that component. Valences ranged from –3 (extremely negative) to +3 (extremely positive).

These valence scores were then used in previously validated formulas for calculating ambivalence (Bell & Esses, 2002; Bell et al., 1996; Maio, Esses, & Bell, 2000), evaluative inconsistency (Chaiken, Pomerantz, & Giner-Sorolla, 1995), and embeddedness (Wood, Rhodes, & Biek, 1995). The formula for calculating ambivalence summed the z-transformed average of the ambivalence within each component (Positivity + |Negativity| – 2 |Positivity + Negativity|) with the z-transformed average of the ambivalence between the pairs of components (|Valence of Component 1| + |Net Valence of Component| – 2 |Net Valence of Component 1 + Net Valence of Component 2|). Scores using this formula are perfectly correlated with scores formed using the formula used by Thompson et al. (1995), which correlates almost perfectly with scores derived using a formula developed by Priester and Petty (1996). The formula for calculating evaluative inconsistency reflected the average absolute value of the differences between each participant's attitude rating (z-transformed) and his or her net favorability within each component (z-transformed). The formula for calculating embeddedness simply sums the total number of feelings, stereotypes, and symbolic beliefs listed.

An additional attitude property, attitudinal openness, was assessed by examining participants' responses to a list of nine statements that ranged from expressing extreme unfavorability toward ethnic minority people ("I am extremely unfavorable toward ethnic minority people.")

to extreme favorability ("I am extremely favorable toward ethnic minority people."). Participants indicated whether they found each statement to be unacceptable, neither acceptable nor unacceptable, or acceptable. As in prior research (Bell & Esses, 2002), we subtracted the number of statements that were rated as being unacceptable from the number of statements that were rated as being neither acceptable nor unacceptable (see Sherif, Sherif, & Nebergall, 1965, for the origins of this approach). Finally, subjective attitude strength was assessed by asking participants to complete five items that assessed the certainty and importance of their attitudes (see Wegener, Downing, Krosnick, & Petty, 1995).

Before examining the effects of ambivalence and other attitude attributes on postmessage implicit and explicit attitudes, we examined the correlations among our strength-relevant attitude attributes (extremity, ambivalence, evaluative inconsistency, embeddedness, openness, and subjective attitude strength). As expected, the correlations between the attitude attributes were small to moderate in magnitude, with all correlations being lower than .40. Thus, the attributes were related, but distinct, constructs.

Five to seven months after completing these measures, participants read either a message in support of ethnic minority people or a control article. The experimenter indicated that he was conducting a study of newspaper evaluations and gave participants a fictitious editorial that was formatted to look like a copy of an actual leading page in a popular magazine. The editorial was entitled "Solutions to Immigration from India?" It began with a general paragraph describing a steep rise in immigration from India, to which the British government has responded by quietly developing new laws that could bring immigration down to unprecedented lows. Then, similar to real-life articles advocating greater immigration (e.g., Conner, Sparks, Povey, James, Shepherd, & Armitage, 2002), this editorial made use of statistical arguments in favor of permitting more immigration from India. We manipulated the arguments so that they indicated a high probability (four arguments) or a very low probability (two arguments) that ethnic minority people possess positive emotions, personality traits, and values. A portion of the editorial that contained a strong argument and a weak argument is presented below, with the weak argument presented in italics.

> [R]esearch has been carried out by Professor Michael Jones and Dr. Hannah Edwards in the Cross-Cultural Research Laboratory at York University. Their findings are quite positive: In general, ethnic immigrants tend to be friendly and polite (a recent government survey found that 78% of shoppers regarded Asian shopkeepers as the most helpful and polite); they make others feel com-

fortable and happy. Young people generally rate their friendships with ethnic immigrants as 4% more satisfying than other friendships.

The control article merely described the annual British Royal Commendations. That is, the article briefly summarized the achievements of a large list of people (e.g., actors, politicians, sports stars) who had received honors (e.g., knighthoods, OBEs) from the queen. This article was similar in length and readability to the editorial.

After exposure to the experimental or control message, participants completed an implicit measure and an explicit measure of prejudice. The implicit measure of prejudice was based on a priming technique used by Fazio, Jackson, Dunton, and Williams (1995) and by Wittenbrink, Judd, and Park (1997). Across trials, a prime was shown on the screen for 10 to 20 ms (randomly depending on the state of screen refresh), which was too fast for participants to report the content of the prime. This prime was followed by a mask (which was a string of seven X's) for 2000 ms and a subsequent target letter sequence for 250 ms. On 93 critical trials, the prime was either *British*, *Ethnic*, or the masking stimulus itself. After each prime, participants were exposed to a target letter sequence that was a nonword, one of eight positive evaluative words (e.g., *good*), or one of eight negative evaluative words (e.g., *bad*). Participants used one of two keys to indicate as quickly as possible whether the target letter sequence was a word or nonword. After excluding responses greater than 1500 ms (Wittenbrink et al.), we calculated the extent to which the British and Ethnic primes facilitated (quickened) responses to each adjective, compared to the nonword primes. The implicit index of prejudice was then calculated by subtracting (a) the sum of facilitation for positive adjectives after the Ethnic prime and for negative adjectives after the British prime from (b) the sum of facilitation for negative adjectives after the Ethnic prime and for positive adjectives after the British prime. Thus, high scores on this measure indicated more implicit prejudice.

For the explicit measure of attitude, participants first rated their attitudes toward the immigration of ethnic minority groups to the UK on bipolar semantic differential scales (e.g., *bad/good*, *negative/positive*). Attitudes toward the group's immigration were used as an indicator of participants' subsequent explicit attitudes toward the group because prior research has indicated that unfavorability toward a group's immigration is a useful, indirect indicator of prejudice (e.g., Katz & Hass, 1988; Maio et al., 1996; Wittenbrink et al., 1997). The experimenter then asked participants to imagine that they were evaluating two excellent candidates for a position as a senior executive manager and that one of the candidates was an ethnic immigrant and the other was British. Participants were asked to indicate who they would choose, their degree of preference for the person, and the difficulty of their choice. Participants' responses were used to calculate the extent to which they chose and preferred the ethnic candidate, while finding it easy to do so. In all of the experiments using this measure, the pattern of results was similar across the semantic differential items and the discrimination score. We therefore used factor analyses (which revealed a single latent factor among the items) to compute a score reflecting the latent evaluation underlying participants' responses to all of the items. This score was used as the indicator of explicit prejudice in the analyses, such that higher scores indicated more explicit prejudice.

Of interest, past research indicates that measures of implicit and explicit prejudice should be unrelated or moderately related at best (Greenwald, McGhee, & Schwartz, 1998; McConnell & Leibold, 2001), perhaps because of people's high motivation to control prejudice (Fazio & Olson, 2003). Consistent with this prediction, our indices of implicit prejudice were not significantly related to the index of explicit prejudice. (These null relations were replicated in each of our experiments.) Thus, it was justifiable to include these measures as separate dependent variables in our examination of the effects of the tainted antiracism article.

For each dependent variable (i.e., the explicit and implicit measures of attitude), we conducted a regression analysis with the experimental message (antiracism vs. control), the attitude attribute of interest (e.g., ambivalence, strength), pretest attitude valence, and the two- and three-way interactions between these variables entered as predictors of attitude. We singled out attitude valence for control because valence is often considered the defining attribute of attitudes, making it important to ensure that any effects of the other attitude properties were independent of attitude valence. In addition, most of the attitude attributes were moderately correlated with attitude valence, such that positive intergroup attitudes tended to be stronger and less ambivalent. Thus, it was important to eliminate this shared variance as an alternative explanation for any effects of the other attitude attributes. Main effects or interactions involving only the pretest attitude properties (e.g., extremity, valence) are irrelevant to our hypotheses and are not described below.

In all of the analyses, the results indicated no significant main effects of the manipulation and no interactions involving pretest attitude valence. However, in the analysis examining implicit prejudice and ambivalence, there was a significant interaction between the message

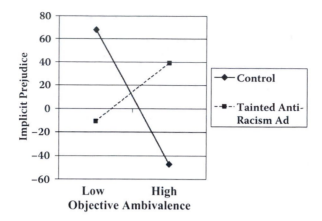

FIGURE 11.2 Effects of a tainted antiracism message and objective ambivalence on scores from the implicit measure of prejudice. The endpoints of the lines are based on the predicted attitudes one standard deviation below and above the mean level of objective ambivalence in each condition.

manipulation and ambivalence. As shown in Figure 11.2, the antiracism message increased implicit prejudice among ambivalent participants, whereas the message decreased implicit prejudice among nonambivalent participants. None of the other attitude attributes interacted with the message manipulation. Of interest, however, the analyses of responses to the explicit measure of prejudice revealed no significant main effects, two-way interactions, or three-way interactions involving any of the attitude properties, including ambivalence.

To summarize, the tainted antiracism message was sufficient to cause people who were ambivalent toward ethnic minority groups to exhibit more prejudice on our implicit measure. In contrast, nonambivalent people expressed less prejudice on the implicit measure after receiving the tainted antiracism message than after receiving the control message. We were uncertain what conclusions could be drawn from this direction of the effects for the nonambivalent participants. Prior to conducting this program of research, we were unsure whether nonambivalent participants should exhibit a weaker negative effect of the messages or a positive effect. In theory, a weaker negative effect could emerge because nonambivalent people fail to scrutinize the messages, or a positive effect could emerge because nonambivalent people quickly perceive the antiracism messages' egalitarian gist, with which most people strongly agree (e.g., Maio & Olson, 1998). The results revealed a positive effect of the messages on nonambivalent participants. Before interpreting both the backlash effect (on ambivalent individuals) and the positive effect (on nonambivalent individuals), however, it was important to see whether these effects were replicable using different messages. We therefore return to this issue later in the chapter.

In the meantime, it is worth noting that ambivalence moderated the impact of the tainted antiracism message on only the implicit measure of attitude. Thus, ambivalent participants grew more prejudiced after seeing the antiracism message, but they appeared either unwilling or unable to consciously acknowledge and report this increase in negativity. Nevertheless, null effects are inherently difficult to interpret, especially without results of additional studies that use different procedures. Therefore, the next experiment again included the explicit measures of attitude together with the implicit measures.

Effects of Simple Pictorial Antiracism Advertisements

An interesting issue was whether backlash effects would be obtained using a different measure of ambivalence. The prior experiment and prior research (e.g., Maio et al., 1996) have focused on objective ambivalence, which exists when people's attitudes subsume many positive and negative elements (e.g., "The group is witty and kind, but unintelligent and lazy.").

In our next experiment, we added a measure of subjective ambivalence, which exists when people report feeling ambivalent using semantic differential and Likert scales. Similar to the frequent lack of significant relations between explicit and implicit measures of attitude, there are often only moderate correlations between subjective and objective measures of ambivalence toward different attitude targets (Newby-Clark, McGregor, & Zanna, 2002; Priester & Petty, 1996). There has been some suggestion that subjective ambivalence may be akin to a "gold standard" measure of ambivalence (Priester & Petty) and some suggestion that objective measures are better because of their closer relation to nonconscious and spontaneous mental processes (Bassili, 1996). At the very least, the inclusion of both measures simultaneously helps to establish more power in the estimation of ambivalence and to examine their relative efficacy at predicting responses to the messages.

Most important, it was necessary to extend the investigation to simple antiracism advertisements, rather than employ the more detailed antiracism message that was used in the first experiment. Because antiracism advertisements often contain a simple picture and caption, we created ads that used this approach and closely followed an advertisement used previously by Britain's Commission for Racial Equality.

In an experiment designed to assess the effectiveness of simple pictorial antiracism advertisements, participants completed measures of objective and subjective ambivalence several months prior to manipulating their exposure to antiracism advertisements. Objective ambivalence was assessed as in the previous study, whereas subjective ambivalence was assessed using items adapted from Jamieson (1988), including "I find myself feeling torn between positive and negative feelings toward Ethnic Minorities." and "My head and my heart seem to be in disagreement in my attitude toward Ethnic Minorities." In addition to completing these measures, the valence of pretest attitudes toward ethnic minority people was assessed once again using the evaluation thermometer.

Several months after completing these measures, participants arrived at a different lab and were exposed to one of four antiracism advertisements or a control advertisement. The antiracism advertisements featured a picture of people from different ethnic groups. Below the picture was one of four captions that presented arguments similar to those used in past antiracism advertisements: "How do you feel about these people? They have much to offer" (Figure 11.3), "How do you feel about these people? Respect for others is important," "Multicultural = Prosperity + Progress," or "Multicultural = Equality + Respect." The control advertisement simply displayed the word *Orange* in the middle of the page (Orange is a British mobile phone company). Most important, all of the advertisements were presented unobtrusively. Participants were asked to open a magazine to the table of contents and count all of the words that appeared on this page and the adjacent inside cover, which featured one of the advertisements. To count the words, participants had to examine the advertisement briefly (6 to 17 words); the far majority of the words were in the adjacent page (461 words).

After exposure to a message, participants completed the explicit measure and the implicit measure of prejudice from the prior experiment, except that the length of the mask presentation in the implicit measure of prejudice was shortened from 2000 ms to 135 ms. Preliminary analyses revealed similar effects across the different types of antiracism messages that were presented. Consequently, our principal analyses examined their effects simultaneously using regression analyses with the experimental message (antiracism vs. control), the ambivalence score of interest (subjective or objective), pretest attitude valence, and the two- and three-way interactions between these variables entered as predictors of attitude (assessed with either the implicit or explicit measure). In all of the analyses, the results indicated no significant main effects of the manipulation and no interactions involving pretest atti-

FIGURE 11.3 An example of simple pictorial antiracism advertisements examined in our research.

tude valence. However, the manipulation significantly interacted with objective ambivalence in the analysis of responses to both measures of attitude. As shown in Figures 11.4 and 11.5, the antiracism advertisements increased prejudice among ambivalent participants, but decreased prejudice among nonambivalent participants.

The regression analyses that examined subjective ambivalence revealed a similar interaction when participants' responses to the explicit measure were examined. Specifically, the antiracism advertisements decreased prejudice among nonambivalent participants, but increased prejudice among ambivalent participants (see Figure 11.6). Subjective ambivalence did not moderate the impact of the antiracism messages on the implicit measure.

These results have important implications for the practice of antiracism advertising. Although the most popular format that we have seen involves using a picture and caption that are attention grabbing and simple, our advertisements using this format did not reduce prejudice.

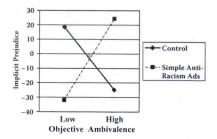

FIGURE 11.4 Effects of simple antiracism advertisements and objective ambivalence on scores from the implicit measure of prejudice. The endpoints of the lines are based on the predicted attitudes one standard deviation below and above the mean level of objective ambivalence in each condition.

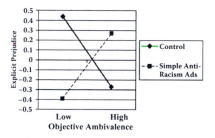

FIGURE 11.5 Effects of simple antiracism advertisements and objective ambivalence on scores from the explicit measure of prejudice. The endpoints of the lines are based on the predicted attitudes one standard deviation below and above the mean level of objective ambivalence in each condition.

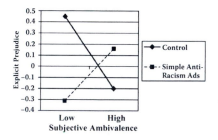

FIGURE 11.6 Effects of simple antiracism messages and subjective ambivalence on scores from the explicit measure of prejudice. The endpoints of the lines are based on the predicted attitudes one standard deviation below and above the mean level of subjective ambivalence in each condition.

Instead, these advertisements negatively influenced the message recipients who were ambivalent toward ethnic minority people before seeing the messages. These results support our suspicion that simple antiracism advertisements do not withstand scrutiny from ambivalent individuals. These people present a formidable barrier to the effectiveness of antiracism messages, instead of being a group that is more amenable to change from the messages. It is also interesting that these results were obtained using pictorial messages; these findings fit prior evidence that implicit measures of attitude can be influenced by visual imagery (Blair, Ma, & Lenton, 2001; Dasgupta & Asgari, 2004), while adding the caveat that the nature of these effects may depend on ambivalence before contemplation of the images.

Varying Message Content: Effects of Group-Focused versus Individual-Focused Ads

It was important to test whether ambivalent people present an obstacle to other types of antiracism messages. One dimension on which pictorial antiracism advertisements can differ is whether they focus on individuals (i.e., exemplars) or ethnic minority people as a group. We expected that individual-focused advertisements would be more likely to backfire for ambivalent participants than advertisements that targeted ethnic minority people as a group. In theory, individual-focused advertisements require that recipients generalize from the information about the single individual to their impression of the group. This would provide more opportunity for ambivalent participants to counterargue the message. As noted by abundant research on the use of information about group members on judgments of groups as a whole (Kunda & Oleson, 1995; Rothbart & Park, 1986), recipients of this information can mentally represent the presented target as an exception to the stereotypes, feelings, and symbolic beliefs that define the group.

With this in mind, one study manipulated whether the antiracism advertisements were individual versus group focused. At the same time, this study included several other changes. First, consistent with the nature of most advertising, we repeated the presentation of the antiracism advertisements by using different advertisement variants in two presentations. That is, there was a 30-min group discussion of an irrelevant topic in between two message exposures, which were presented in the same unobtrusive manner as before (i.e., on the inside cover of a magazine used for a different task). Second, we tested whether backfire effects would be evident several days after the presentation of the advertisements in a different laboratory. Third, because of practical restrictions imposed by our repeated presentations and separated lab sessions, we assessed only subjective ambivalence.

Each participant saw a group-focused antiracism advertisement before and after the 30-min discussion or an individual-focused advertisement before and after the 30-min discussion. The group-focused condition used two of the advertisements described earlier in the chapter and focused on ethnic minority people in general. The ads that were presented in the individual-focused condition are shown in Figure 11.7. One of the individual-focused advertisements showed an Asian headteacher (principal) and the slogan, "Improve Your English." The other individual-focused advertisement showed a young member of a religious minority and the slogan "No One Respects Me: I'm an Arsenal Fan." (Arsenal is a popular English soccer team.) Both of the individual-focused advertisements had been used by the CRE in some areas of Britain prior to our research. In the control condition, the Orange advertisement was presented twice. Two to five days later, participants completed the second session, which included the same implicit and explicit measures of attitude as in the previous studies.

Using regression analyses, we found no significant effects or interactions in our analysis of the implicit measure, but there was a significant main effect of the manipulation in the analysis of the explicit measure. Compared to the control condition, the group-focused advertisements exhibited a marginal negative impact on explicit attitudes, and the individual-focused advertisements exerted a significant negative impact. In addition, high subjective ambivalence predicted more negative explicit attitudes than low subjective ambivalence. These effects remained significant even after controlling for pretest differences in attitude valence.

Of interest, even though our previous research showed backfire effects for the group-focused advertisements immediately after message presentation, these advertisements did not backfire more strongly for ambivalent participants 2 days after message presentation (Figure 11.8). In contrast, the individual-focused advertisements elicited more negative attitudes toward ethnic minority people among ambivalent participants than among nonambivalent participants after the delay, consistent with our expectation that the individual-based advertisements are more likely to have negative effects on ambivalent individuals. This latter result extended the moderating effect of subjective ambivalence that was observed in the experiment using the tainted appeal, and it demonstrates that attitude change in experimental settings need not

FIGURE 11.7 The individual-focused, simple, pictorial antiracism advertisements examined in our research. (The ads were deployed by the Commission for Racial Equality and passed to us for the purpose of this research.)

lack persistence over time (cf. Gruder, Cook, Hennigan, Flay, Alessis, & Halamaj, 1978; see also Chapter 10, this volume). Nonetheless, an interesting issue is why there was evidence of these effects after a delay for the explicit measure of prejudice, but not for the implicit measure. We discuss this issue further at the end of the chapter, because we believe it may reflect an important difference in the types of mental operations required by the measures.

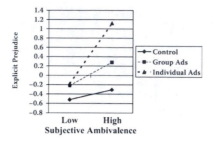

FIGURE 11.8 Effects of group-based and individual-based antiracism messages and subjective ambivalence on scores from the explicit measure of prejudice. The endpoints of the lines are based on the predicted attitudes one standard deviation below and above the mean level of subjective ambivalence in each condition.

Explaining the Effects on Implicit and Explicit Measures of Intergroup Attitude

The effects of the antiracism messages on the implicit and explicit measures provided a number of interesting effects. First, the tainted text-based antiracism message did not affect scores on the explicit measure of attitude, but it did elicit message backfire among ambivalent participants on the implicit measure of attitude. Second, the weak pictorial antiracism messages evoked message backfire among ambivalent participants on the implicit measure of attitude and on the explicit measure of attitude. Third, when we added a delay between the presentation of the advertisements and the assessment of attitudes, the weak antiracism messages elicited message backfire among ambivalent participants on the explicit measure of attitude. Thus, the implicit measure and the explicit measure were influenced in the predicted manner most of the time across experiments, and only one of the experiments failed to reveal an effect on the implicit measure.

Before considering the general implications of these findings, it may help to first focus on why the implicit measure was unaffected in the third experiment. Many factors may help to explain this result. In any applied program of research that examines multiple interventions and diverse contexts (e.g., temporal delays), it is not surprising to see results that vary. In our case, the use of different types of antiracism message and different experimental designs are relevant to explaining the variation in effects across the implicit and explicit measures, and it is worth considering each factor in turn.

With regard to the differences between messages, our experiments included messages that varied from detailed text to simple pictures with captions. Nonetheless, all of the messages were expected to be relatively weak. To verify this assumption, a separate group of participants were asked to list their thoughts in response to the messages. These participants indicated a large number of positive and negative responses to the messages, and our tainted editorial was regarded as being significantly less persuasive than the strong editorial included in the prior research. Overall, then, these results are consistent with our assumption that all of the messages were somewhat flawed. Nonetheless, it is unclear why there were no effects on implicit attitudes for the group-focused posters that were used in the last experiment, even though these posters did predict responses to the implicit measure in the prior experiment.

Perhaps two other design issues are more relevant to the lack of findings for the implicit measure in this experiment. First, the inclusion of a delay of several days between the antiracism posters and the implicit measures might have attenuated the effect on them. However, lab-induced changes in implicit measures of attitude have been found to persist in other research (Dasgupta & Greenwald, 2001), so implicit measures are vulnerable to effects of delay per se. Second, this experiment included the subjective measure of ambivalence and not the objective measure of ambivalence. Indeed, the objective measure consistently predicted responses to the implicit measure in the other experiments, whereas the subjective measure did not. For this reason, we suspect that the null effect on the implicit measure has more to do with the type of ambivalence measure that was used to predict the measure than the measure per se, and this possibility is elaborated below.

So what have we learned by including the implicit measures with the explicit measures? We believe that the answer is that a great deal was learned. First, by obtaining effects on these measures, we can have greater confidence that antiracism campaigns have the potential to influence the spontaneous, nondeliberative behaviors that tend to be more strongly associated with these measures than with explicit measures. Thus, at least in the time soon after people see such messages, their nonverbal and spontaneous behaviors toward the targets of prejudice may change. This potential consequence is important because intergroup contact often occurs in informal settings, where interaction is unlikely to be fully deliberate and controlled.

Second, in our experiment using the tainted antiracism message, we learned that the implicit measures were able to reveal effects that were hidden on the explicit measures. This result converges with the aforementioned evidence that implicit measures predict unique variance in consumer decisions (e.g., Maison et al., 2001). If we had just relied on

an explicit measure, we would have missed an important potential consequence of the message.

Third, it is interesting that the effects of ambivalence on implicit
attitudes were reliable when we measured objective ambivalence, but
not when we measured subjective ambivalence. In contrast, subjective
ambivalence moderated the impact of the antiracism messages on the
explicit measures of attitude in the experiments that assessed subjective
ambivalence. This pattern supports past contentions that the measurement of objective ambivalence is more reflective of other implicit, spontaneous responses than other explicit, deliberative responses (Bassili,
1996), and it supports the claim that both types of measures should
be included in experiments examining the effects of ambivalence (e.g.,
Bell & Esses, 2002).

Before finishing this discussion of the effects across the implicit and
explicit measures, it is worth considering the direction of the effects
for the nonambivalent participants. As noted earlier, we were initially
uncertain whether the nonambivalent participants would simply show a
less negative effect of the messages or a positive effect. Because a variety
of experimental paradigms using several measures of message scrutiny
have found that nonambivalent people are more likely to avoid message
scrutiny (Jonas et al., 1997; Maio et al., 1996, 2000, 2001), one possibility was that nonambivalent people would show little influence of the
messages because they failed to process them. Another possibility was
that the antiracism message would be quickly accepted among nonambivalent people, because most individuals unquestioningly agree with
the general importance of equality and egalitarian attitudes (Maio &
Olson, 1998), even if they harbor strong negative or strong positive feelings about ethnic minorities (Gaertner & Dovidio, 1986; Katz & Hass,
1988). Both prejudiced and nonprejudiced nonambivalent individuals
may spontaneously accept the ideal of being less prejudiced, and this
acceptance may help them avoid the burden of recognizing additional
complexities by further scrutinizing the antiracism message. In contrast,
ambivalent individuals' mixed feelings may motivate them to consider
the message more fully, thereby exposing its flaws and inadvertently
creating more prejudice. The results of our experiments examining the
effects of the tainted editorial and simple, pictorial advertisements supported this reasoning, because nonambivalent participants exhibited
more positive attitudes following the weak messages than following the
control messages. That said, nonambivalent people exhibited no significant effects of the group-based and individual-based pictorial ads after
a 2-day delay. Nonetheless, even this divergent result fits the hypothesis

that nonambivalent participants were responding to the simple gist of the message, which was not salient in the experimental context after the delay was imposed.

Implications for Antiracism Advertising

To assess the implications of our results for antiracism advertising, it is important to consider the range of advertisements that were examined, the power of the effects, and the sample of participants. Across experiments, individuals who were ambivalent toward ethnic minority people exhibited significantly more negative attitudes after exposure to three types of antiracism messages that lacked cogent argumentation: a tainted antiracism editorial; simple, group-focused antiracism posters; and individual-focused antiracism posters. Thus, across the studies, a variety of messages were employed, helping to yield a broader picture of the potential effects of antiracism messages.

The power of the effects can be assessed by considering the statistical strength of the results, the effects across measures, and the duration of the effects. The negative effects of the tainted editorial and the simple, pictorial antiracism advertisements on ambivalent participants were nontrivial in size (mean $r = .33$; see Cohen, 1988). In addition, as described above, the effects occurred on implicit and explicit measures of attitude, though not always on both. Also, ambivalence was measured several months prior to message exposure in two of the experiments, and effects of ambivalence were observable several days after message exposure in one of the experiments. It is also interesting that numerous additional attitude properties (attitude extremity, self-reported attitude strength, acceptance of alternative attitude positions, evaluative inconsistency, embeddedness) did not moderate the positive or negative effects of the antiracism messages (see also Maio et al., 1996). Thus, the impact of the antiracism messages depends crucially on message recipients' initial ambivalence toward ethnic minority people.

Notwithstanding the wide range of advertisements employed and the general power of the effects, we believe it is important for this research to study more diverse and heterogeneous participant samples. Because real-world advertisements reach diverse sectors of the population, it is imperative that research examines the effects of the messages across these sectors. The moderating role of ambivalence may be a basic moderating principle that operates across diverse populations, but this hypothesis remains to be tested.

In the meantime, it is worth considering the additional ways in which antiracism messages may be strengthened. One possible way to address the negative impact on ambivalent people is to utilize messages that acknowledge the negative aspects of their attitudes in a way that allows some validation of their concerns, while arguing that these concerns are weak in comparison to the basis for responding positively to the group. Ambivalent people may be particularly responsive to two-sided messages, which are more reflective of their capacity to think and reason than are one-sided messages. Indeed, scholars have long suspected that the effects of two-sided messages are more effective than one-sided messages when message recipients' attitudes at least partly refute the message position (e.g., Hovland, Lumsdaine, & Sheffield, 1949; cf. Allen, 1991).

Another possible way to address the negative impact on ambivalent people is to utilize messages that present more of an emotional, affective message. For example, people might be more convinced by a message that shows the suffering that results from subtle and blatant forms of prejudice. Ambivalent people may be particularly responsive to such emotional appeals, because they circumvent the more complex and conflicting evaluative beliefs that these individuals possess. In the present research, the antiracism messages were not designed to elicit strong emotion. It is important to examine the effects of these messages if antiracism campaigns and other social marketing efforts are to achieve their goals.

General Implications for Applied Interventions

At a more general level, our results demonstrate the importance of empirically examining the effects of messages on implicit and explicit measures of attitude, which is an approach that is hardly ever employed by social marketers. Of course, it is possible to retort that the implicit measures did not reveal unique effects in all of the experiments. Clearly, future research is needed to help interpret these differences. More important for the present volume, however, the bottom line from our studies is that attempts to evaluate interventions without both types of measures would have yielded only a partial picture of the total effects. This incomplete picture may be especially nonproductive in instances where the attitude of interest is expected to predict fairly automatic, nondeliberative behaviors. For example, in many wealthy nations, governments are developing campaigns to help battle rising levels of obesity by changing dietary and exercise attitudes. Diet and exercise may be precisely the kinds of behaviors that are often controlled by automatic impulses and habit, making it important to ensure that interventions affect both explicit and implicit measures of attitude that are relevant to these behaviors. Thus, as implicit measures grow in simplicity and ease of use, we hope to see more research incorporate them in evaluations of such campaigns.

References

Albarracín, D. (2002). Cognition in persuasion: An analysis of information processing in response to persuasive communications. *Advances in Experimental Social Psychology, 34,* 61–130.

Allen, M. (1991). Meta-analysis comparing the persuasiveness of one-sided and two-sided messages. *Western Journal of Speech Communication, 55,* 390–404.

Allport, G. W. (1954). *The nature of prejudice.* New York: Addison-Wesley.

Armitage, C. J., & Conner, M. (2000). Attitudinal ambivalence: A test of three key hypotheses. *Personality & Social Psychology Bulletin, 26,* 1421–1432.

Bassili, J. N. (1996). Meta-judgmental versus operative indexes of psychological attributes: The case of measures of attitude strength. *Journal of Personality and Social Psychology, 71,* 637–653.

Bell, D. W., & Esses, V. M. (2002). Ambivalence and response amplification: A motivational perspective. *Personality and Social Psychology Bulletin, 28,* 1143–1152.

Bell, D. W., Esses, V. M., & Maio, G. R. (1996). The utility of open-ended measures to assess intergroup ambivalence. *Canadian Journal of Behavioural Science, 28,* 12–18.

Blair, I. V., Ma, J. E., & Lenton, A. P. (2001). Imagining stereotypes away: The moderation of implicit stereotypes through mental imagery. *Journal of Personality and Social Psychology, 81,* 828–841.

Bradley, B. P., Field, M., Mogg, K., & De Houwer, J. (2004). Attentional and evaluative biases for smoking cues in nicotine dependence: Component processes of biases in visual orienting. *Behavioral Pharmacology, 15,* 29–26.

Briñol, P., Petty, R. E., & McCaslin, M. Changing attitudes on implicit versus explicit measures: What is the difference? In R. E. Petty, R. H. Fazio, & P. Briñol (Eds.), *Attitudes: Insights from the new implicit measures.* Hillsdale, NJ: Erlbaum.

Britt, T. W., Boniecki, K. A., Vescio, T. K., Biernat, M., & Brown, L. M. (1996). Intergroup anxiety: A person X situation approach. *Personality and Social Psychology Bulletin, 22,* 1177–1188.

Cohen, J. (1988). *Statistical power analysis for the behavioral sciences.* Mahwah, NJ: Erlbaum.

Chaiken, S., Pomerantz, E. M., & Giner-Sorolla, R. (1995). Structural consistency and attitude strength. In R. E. Petty & J. A. Krosnick (Eds.), *Attitude strength: Antecedents and consequences* (pp. 387–412). Hillsdale, NJ: Erlbaum.

Chen, S., & Chaiken, S. (1999). The heuristic-systematic model in its broader context. In S. Chaiken & Y. Trope (Eds.), *Dual-process theories in social psychology* (pp. 73–96). New York: Guilford Press.

Conner, M., & Sparks, P. (2002). Ambivalence and attitudes. *European Review of Social Psychology, 12*, 37–70.

Conner, M., Sparks, P., Povey, R., James, R., Shepherd, R., & Armitage, C. J. (2002). Moderator effects of attitudinal ambivalence on attitude-behaviour relationships. *European Journal of Social Psychology, 32*(5), 705–718.

Czopp, A. M., Monteith, M. J., Zimmerman, R. S., & Lynam, D. R. (2004). Implicit attitudes as potential protection from risky sex: Predicting condom use with the IAT. *Basic and Applied Social Psychology, 26*, 227–236.

Dasgupta, N., & Asgari, S. (2004). Seeing is believing: Exposure to counter-stereotypic women leaders and its effect on the malleability of automatic gender stereotyping. *Journal of Experimental Social Psychology, 40*, 642–658.

Dasgupta, N., & Greenwald, A. G. (2001). On the malleability of automatic attitudes: Combating automatic prejudice with images of admired and disliked individuals. *Journal of Personality and Social Psychology, 81*, 800–814.

Ehrenberg, A. J., Barnard, N., Kennedy, R., & Bloom, H. (2002). Brand advertising as creative publicity. *Journal of Advertising Research, 42*, 7–18.

Fazio, R. H., Jackson, J. R., Dunton, B. C., & Williams, C. J. (1995). Variability in automatic activation as an unobtrusive measure of racial attitudes: A bona fide pipeline? *Journal of Personality and Social Psychology, 69*, 1013–1027.

Fazio, R. H., & Olson, M. A. (2003). Implicit measures in social cognition research: Their meaning and use. *Annual Review of Psychology, 54*, 297–327.

Festinger, L. (1957). *A theory of cognitive dissonance.* Evanston, IL: Row, Peterson.

Field, M., Mogg, K., & Bradley, B. P. (2004). Cognitive bias and drug craving in recreational cannabis users. *Drug and Alcohol Dependence, 74*, 105–111.

Gaertner, S. L., & Dovidio, J. F. (1986). The aversive form of racism. In J. F. Dovidio & S. L. Gaertner (Eds.), *Prejudice, discrimination, and racism* (pp. 61–89). San Diego: Academic Press.

Gemar, M. C., Segal, Z. V., Sagrati, S., & Kennedy, S. J. (2001). Mood-induced changes on the Implicit Association Test in recovered depressed patients. *Journal of Abnormal Psychology, 110*, 282–289.

Gray, N. S., Brown, A. S., MacCulloch, M. J., Smith, J., & Snowden, R. J. (2005). An implicit test of the associations between children and sex in pedophiles. *Journal of Abnormal Psychology, 114*, 304–308.

Greenwald, A. G., McGhee, D. E., & Schwartz, J. K. L. (1998). Measuring individual differences in implicit cognition: The Implicit Association Test. *Journal of Personality and Social Psychology, 74*, 1464–1480.

Gruder, C. L., Cook, T. D., Hennigan, K. M., Flay, B. R., Alessis, C., & Halamaj, J. (1978). Empirical tests of the absolute sleeper effect predicted from the discounting cue hypothesis. *Journal of Personality and Social Psychology, 36*, 1061–1074.

Haddock, G. G., & Zanna, M. P. (1998). On the use of open-ended measures to assess attitudinal components. *British Journal of Social Psychology, 37*, 129–149.

Hass, R. G., Katz, I., Rizzo, N., Bailey, J., & Moore, L. (1992). When racial ambivalence evokes negative affect, using a disguised measure of mood. *Personality and Social Psychology Bulletin, 18*, 786–797.

Hewstone, M., Rubin, M., & Willis, H. (2002). Intergroup bias. *Annual Review of Psychology, 53*, 575–604.

Hovland, C. I., Lumsdaine, A. A., & Sheffield, F. D. (1949). *Experiments on mass communication.* Princeton, NJ: Princeton University Press.

Jajodia, A., & Earleywine, M. (2003). Measuring alcohol expectancies with the Implicit Association Test. *Psychology of Addictive Behaviors, 17*, 126–133.

Jamieson, D. W. (1988, June). *The influence of value conflicts on attitudinal ambivalence.* Paper presented at the annual conference of the Canadian Psychological Association, Montreal.

Jonas, K., Diehl, M., & Bromer, P. (1997). Effects of attitudinal ambivalence on information processing and attitude-intention consistency. *Journal of Experimental Social Psychology, 33*, 190–210.

Katz, I., & Hass, R. G. (1988). Racial ambivalence and American value conflict: Correlational and priming studies of dual cognitive structures. *Journal of Personality and Social Psychology, 55*, 893–905.

Kover, A. J. (2002). What does advertising do? *Journal of Advertising Research, 42*, 5.

Kruglanski, A. W., Fishbach, A., Erb, H.-P., Pierro, A., & Mannetti, L. (2004). The parametric unimodel as a theory of persuasion. In G. Haddock & G. R. Maio (Eds.), *Contemporary perspectives on the psychology of attitudes* (pp. 399–422). New York: Psychology Press.

Kunda, Z., & Oleson, K. (1995). Maintaining stereotypes in the face of disconfirmation: Constructing grounds for subtyping deviants. *Journal of Personality and Social Psychology, 68*, 565–579.

Maio, G. R., Bell, D. W., & Esses, V. M. (1996). Ambivalence and persuasion: The processing of messages about immigrant groups. *Journal of Experimental Social Psychology, 32*, 513–536.

Maio, G. R., Esses, V. M., & Bell, D. W. (2000). Examining conflict between components of attitudes: Ambivalence and inconsistency are distinct constructs. *Canadian Journal of Behavioural Science, 32*(1), 58–70.

Maio, G. R., Greenland, K., Bernard, M. M., & Esses, V. M. (2001). Effects of intergroup ambivalence on information processing: The role of physiological arousal. *Group Processes and Intergroup Relations, 4*, 355–372.

Maio, G. R., & Olson, J. M. (1998). Values as truisms: Evidence and implications. *Journal of Personality and Social Psychology, 74*, 294–311.

Maison, D., Greenwald, A. G., & Bruin, R. H. (2001). The Implicit Association Test as a measure of implicit consumer attitudes. *Polish Psychological Bulletin, 32*, 61–69.

Marsh, K. L., & Julka, D. L. (2000). A motivational approach to experimental tests of attitude functions theory. In G. R. Maio & J. M. Olson (Eds.), *Why we evaluate: Functions of attitude* (pp. 271–294). Mahwah, NJ: Erlbaum.

McConnell, A. R., & Leibold, J. M. (2001). Relations among the Implicit Association Test, discriminatory behavior, and explicit measures of racial attitudes. *Journal of Experimental Social Psychology, 37*, 435–442.

Mogg, K., Bradley, B. P., Field, M., & De Houwer, J. (2003). Eye movements to smoking-related pictures in smokers: Relationship between attentional biases and implicit and explicit measures of stimulus valence. *Addiction, 98*, 825–836.

Newby-Clark, I. R., McGregor, I., & Zanna, M. P. (2002). Thinking and caring about cognitive inconsistency: When and for whom does attitudinal ambivalence feel uncomfortable? *Journal of Personality and Social Psychology, 82*, 157–166.

Petty, R. E., Tormala, Z. L., Briñol, P., & Jarvis, W. B. G. (2006). Implicit ambivalence from attitude change: An exploration of the PAST model. *Journal of Personality and Social Psychology, 90*, 21–41.

Petty, R. E., & Wegener, D. T. (1999). The elaboration likelihood model: Current status and controversies. In S. Chaiken & Y. Trope (Eds.), *Dual-process theories in social psychology* (pp. 41–72). New York: Guilford Press.

Priester, J. R., & Petty, R. E. (1996). The gradual threshold model of ambivalence: Relating the positive and negative bases of attitudes to subjective ambivalence. *Journal of Personality and Social Psychology, 71*, 431–449.

Rossiter, J. R., & Percy, L. (1997). *Advertising communications and promotion management* (2nd ed.). London: McGraw-Hill.

Rothbart, M., & Park, B. (1986). On the confirmability and disconfirmability of trait concepts. *Journal of Personality and Social Psychology, 50*, 131–142.

Schuette, R. A., & Fazio, R. H. (1995). Attitude accessibility and motivation as determinants of biased processing: A test of the MODE model. *Personality and Social Psychology Bulletin, 21,* 704–710.

Sherif, C. W., Sherif, M., & Nebergall, R. E. (1965). *Attitudes and attitude change.* Philadelphia: Saunders.

Sherman, S. J., Rose, J. S., Koch, K., Presson, C. C., & Chassin, L. (2003). Implicit and explicit attitudes toward cigarette smoking: The effects of context and motivation. *Journal of Social and Clinical Psychology, 22,* 13–39.

Snowden, R. J., Gray, N. S., Smith, J., Morris, M., & MacCulloch, M. J. (2004). Implicit affective associations to violence in psychopathic murderers. *Journal of Forensic Psychiatry and Psychology, 15,* 620–641.

Stangor, C., Sullivan, L. A., & Ford, T. E. (1991). Affective and cognitive determinants of prejudice. *Social Cognition, 9,* 359–380.

Teachman, B. A., Gapinski, K. D., Brownell, K. D., Rawlins, M., & Jeyaram, S. (2003). Demonstrations of implicit anti-fat bias: The impact of providing causal information and evoking empathy. *Health Psychology, 22,* 68–78.

Teachman, B. A., & Woody, S. R. (2003). Automatic processing in spider phobia: Implicit fear associations over the course of treatment. *Journal of Abnormal Psychology, 112,* 100–109.

Thompson, M. M., Zanna, M. P., & Griffin, D. W. (1995). Let's not be indifferent about (attitudinal) ambivalence. In R. E. Petty & J. A. Krosnick (Eds.), *Attitude strength: Antecedents and consequences* (pp. 361–386). Hillsdale, NJ: Erlbaum.

Wegener, D. T., Downing, J., Krosnick, J. A., & Petty, R. E. (1995). Measures and manipulations of strength-related properties of attitudes: Current practice and future directions. In R. E. Petty & J. A. Krosnick (Eds.), *Attitude strength: Antecedents and consequences* (pp. 455–487). Hillsdale, NJ: Erlbaum.

Wittenbrink, B., Judd, C. M., & Park, B. (1997). Evidence for racial prejudice at the implicit level and its relationship with questionnaire measures. *Journal of Personality and Social Psychology, 72,* 262–274.

Wood, W., Rhodes, N., & Biek, M. (1995). Working knowledge and attitude strength: An information-processing analysis. In R. E. Petty & J. A. Krosnick (Eds.), *Attitude strength: Antecedents and consequences* (pp. 283–313). Hillsdale, NJ: Erlbaum.

Section VI

Implicit Measurement: Conceptual Issues

12

Comparing Measures of Attitudes at the Functional and Procedural Level[*]
Analysis and Implications

Jan De Houwer

Introduction

During the past decade, many new measures of attitudes have been proposed, several of which received the label *implicit measure*. The most commonly known implicit measures are probably the affective priming task (e.g., Fazio, Jackson, Dunton, & Williams, 1995), the Implicit Association Test (IAT; e.g., Greenwald, McGhee, & Schwartz, 1998), the Extrinsic Affective Simon Task (EAST; e.g., De Houwer, 2003b; De Houwer & Eelen, 1998), and the Go/No-Go Association Task (GNAT; Nosek & Banaji, 2001; see Fazio & Olson, 2003, for a review). Given this increase in the number of available measures, there is a risk of not being able to see the proverbial forest for the trees. Although each of the measures is assumed to reveal attitudes, it is often difficult to understand how the different measures are related to each other, whether they can be expected to converge, and if so, under which conditions. There is thus a need for criteria that can be used to compare and describe the different measures.

In this chapter, I will discuss two levels at which measures can be compared. As I recently pointed out in another book (De Houwer, 2006), it is crucial to realize that the term *measure* can be used in different ways. It can be used to refer to either the outcome of a measurement

---

[*] Preparation of this chapter was supported by Grant G.0356.03 of the Fund for Scientific Research (Flanders, Belgium). The final version was completed on March 8, 2006.

procedure (e.g., a particular score on a questionnaire or a particular pattern of reaction-time performance such as an IAT effect) or the objective measurement procedure itself (e.g., the questionnaire itself as consisting of certain instructions and certain questions or the exact instructions and stimuli that are presented during an IAT task). The outcome of a measurement procedure has certain functional properties; that is, it functions as an index of an attitude under certain conditions. In the first part of this chapter, I will argue that the distinction between *implicit* and *explicit* measures is situated at this functional level. I will also argue that one needs to specify and examine the functional properties of (implicit) measures in order to (a) reduce conceptual confusion regarding the concept *implicit measure*, (b) arrive at a better understanding of the processes that underlie the measure, and (c) have a better understanding of which measures might predict which types of behaviors.

The second and longer part of this chapter focuses on the measurement procedure rather than the functional properties of the measurement outcome. A first aspect of the procedure that can be used to differentiate measures is related to whether participants are asked to self-assess their attitudes. This aspect determines the distinction between direct and indirect measures. The second procedural aspect involves the structural properties of the measurement procedures. As I argued in an earlier book (De Houwer, 2003a), reaction-time measures of attitudes can be characterized on the basis of the type of compatibility that is manipulated. In this chapter, I focus on two implications of the structural analysis, namely (a) the issue of whether measures (in particular the IAT) reflect the attitudes toward categories (e.g., *flowers*) or toward the exemplars of those categories (e.g., *tulip*) and (b) the issue of the validity and reliability of measures that are based on different types of compatibility.

The Functional Level

Many of the attitude measures that have been proposed during the past decade have been called implicit measures. Despite the immense popularity of these measures, it is rarely spelled out what sets these implicit measures apart from more traditional (explicit) measures of attitudes such as questionnaires. When we look at the definitions of implicit measures that can be found in recent psychological literature, researchers often argue that implicit measures provide an index of a certain attitude or cognition even though participants (a) are not aware of the fact that the attitude or cognition is being measured (e.g., Brunel, Tietje, & Greenwald, 2004), (b) do not have conscious access to the attitude or cognition (e.g., Asendorpf, Banse, & Mücke, 2002), or (c) have no control over the measurement outcome (e.g., Fazio & Olson, 2003). What is clear from these definitions is that they do not refer to objective properties of the measurement procedure itself. A procedure is merely a set of guidelines about what one should do as a researcher (e.g., present certain instructions and stimuli and record certain responses). Rather, the definitions of implicit measure that can be found in the literature refer to the conditions under which the outcome of the procedure functions as an index of the to-be-measured attitude or cognition. In line with the available definitions, one can therefore say that the term implicit measure refers to certain functional properties of measurement outcomes: The outcome functions as an index of an attitude or cognition under certain conditions, for instance, despite the fact that participants are unaware of the impact of the attitude or cognition on the outcome, are not aware of the attitude or outcome, or have no control over the outcome.

It is not entirely clear which functional properties can be considered as typical for implicit measures. Most often, the term implicit is used to refer to properties related to (un)awareness. However, much can be said for using it in the broader sense of *automatic* (see De Houwer, 2006). The concept automatic can be linked to a variety of functional properties of which properties related to (un)awareness are only a subset. Each property refers to certain conditions such as the presence or absence of (a) goals (i.e., [un]controlled, [un]intentional, goal-[in]dependent, autonomous, purely stimulus driven), (b) awareness of an input, output, goal, or process, (c) processing resources, or (d) time (i.e., speed). For instance, a process can be said to be automatic in the sense of unintentional if the process operates even when the person does not have the goal to start the process (see Moors & De Houwer, 2006, for an in-depth discussion of the exact meaning of these properties). In a similar manner, implicit measures can be defined as measurement outcomes that reflect to-be-measured attitude in an automatic manner, that is, even in the absence of certain goals, awareness of certain elements, processing resources, or time. For instance, a measurement outcome can be described as implicit in the sense of uncontrolled if it reflects the attitude even when participants have the goal to avoid expressing their attitude (see De Houwer & Moors, 2007, for a detailed discussion of how properties related to automaticity can be applied to the concept of implicit measures).

One can thus examine the functional properties of a measure by testing whether the measurement outcome provides a valid index of the to-be-measured outcome when certain conditions are or are not met. Many of these conditions refer to mental states of the person (e.g., goals, awareness) but others refer to objective properties of the situation (e.g., the time during which a stimulus is presented) or can be phrased both in terms of mental states (e.g., resources) or objective properties of the situation (e.g., the presence of demanding secondary tasks). The crucial issue is not whether functional properties refer to mental states or objective properties of the situation. I also do not want to make strong claims about which functional properties are central to the concept automatic or implicit. This is in large part a matter of convention. But what is crucial is the idea to define implicit measures as measurement outcomes with certain functional properties, that is, by specifying which conditions do or do not need to be fulfilled in order for the measurement outcome to function as a valid index of the to-be-measured construct.

There is also no one-to-one mapping between the functional properties of attitude measures and the functional properties of attitude activation. Just like one can examine the conditions under which a measurement outcome functions as a valid index of an attitude, one can also examine the conditions under which the to-be-measured attitude can be activated (e.g., when participants do not have the goal to activate the attitude, are not aware of the attitude, or are engaged in other demanding tasks).* The conditions under which a measurement outcome reflects the to-be-measured attitude are not necessarily the same

---

* Just as implicit measures can be seen as measures that capture the attitude in an automatic manner, one can define *implicit attitudes* as attitudes that influence behavior in an automatic manner. One could object that automaticity and awareness are to a certain extent orthogonal. For instance, an attitude can in principle be activated automatically (e.g., in the sense of unintentionally or efficiently) regardless of whether the participant is aware of the attitude. But the same is true for any other functional feature of automaticity. For instance, an attitude might be activated automatically in the sense of unintentionally regardless of whether resources are available. Hence, awareness of the attitude is just one of several functional properties related to automaticity. I see no reason to assign a special status to the property *awareness* or to reserve the term implicit attitudes for attitudes that are unaware. First, awareness of the attitude is not central in existing definitions of implicit attitudes (e.g., Greenwald & Banaji, 1995; Wilson et al., 2000; also see De Houwer, 2006). Second, there are important problems in assessing whether people are unaware of an attitude. Third, defining implicit attitudes as unaware implies that these attitudes are somehow fundamentally different from others, a claim for which there are neither sound arguments nor empirical data. I thus prefer to define implicit attitude as *automatically activated attitude*. But regardless of this personal preference, it would be good if researchers would clarify their use of the term *implicit measure*.

as the conditions under which the to-be-measured attitude is activated. On the one hand, a measurement outcome can function as a valid index of an attitude only when the attitude has been activated. Hence, the functional properties of an attitude measure (i.e., the conditions under which a measure is valid) can provide important information about the functional properties of attitude activation (i.e., conditions under which the underlying attitude can be activated). On the other hand, situations in which a measure is not valid do not necessarily provide information about the conditions under which the underlying attitude is activated. This is because each measure depends not only on the activation of the crucial attitude but also on additional processes by which this attitude is translated into behavior. Hence, conclusions about the functional properties of measurement outcomes cannot be based solely on knowledge about the functional properties of attitude activation.

It is important to realize that it only makes sense to say that a measure is implicit if one is explicit about the functional properties of the measure and if one has evidence to back up that claim. One cannot simply say that a measure is implicit, because the different functional properties do not always co-occur (Bargh, 1992; Moors & De Houwer, 2006). For instance, existing evidence suggests that participants have little intentional control over the outcome of the IAT (e.g., Steffens, 2004) but are often aware of what a certain IAT is meant to measure (e.g., Monteith, Voils, & Ashburn-Nardo, 2001). Therefore, an IAT effect can be called an implicit measure in the sense that the size and direction of the IAT effect is difficult to control, but not in the sense that participants are typically unaware of the fact that the IAT effect measures the target attitude. In order to claim that a measure is implicit, it is thus not only necessary to demonstrate that the measure is valid and reliable (otherwise it is not a measure in the real sense of the word), one also needs to specify its functional properties and collect evidence to support these claims about functional properties (otherwise it cannot be called implicit).

There are several reasons why it is important to examine the functional properties of (implicit) measures. First, as is clear from the previous paragraph, without empirical evidence regarding the functional properties of a measure, it is not possible to specify the sense in which the measure can be regarded as implicit. In fact, without such evidence, one cannot even claim that the measure is implicit. Hence, research about the functional properties of measures is necessary before one can reach an acceptable level of conceptual clarity.

Second, examining functional properties will also increase our understanding of the processes that underlie the measures. As I pointed out above, a measurement outcome can reflect a construct or entity (such as an attitude) only if it is (partially) produced or determined by the construct or entity. In other words, there are some underlying processes through which the construct or entity is activated and influences the outcome of the measurement procedure. When one says that an (implicit) measure has certain functional properties, that is, functions as an index of an attitude or cognition under certain conditions, it means that the processes that underlie the measure (e.g., the automatic activation of the attitude) operate under those conditions. Hence, research about the functional properties can help us to understand the processes that underlie the measure and provide the much-needed measurement theory that is needed in order to consider a measure as valid (see Borsboom, Mellenbergh, & van Heerden, 2004, for an excellent discussion of this issue).

Finally, understanding the functional properties of a measure could also help us get an insight into the conditions under which the measure can be used to predict behavior. Let us consider the MODE model of Fazio (1990) that provides a useful framework for understanding the possible benefits of implicit measures in predicting behavior (see Chapter 2, this volume). As Fazio and Olson (2003, p. 301) pointed out, the MODE model:

> ... proposes that attitudes can exert influence through relatively spontaneous or more deliberative processes. The former involve judgments of, or behavior toward, an object being influenced by one's construal of the object in the immediate situation—perceptions that themselves can be affected by individuals' attitudes having been automatically activated upon encountering the attitude object. In contrast, deliberative processing involves a more effortful, cost-benefit analysis of the utility of a particular behavior.

Importantly, deliberative processing will take place only when participants have the opportunity and are motivated to engage in such processing.

Most often, people do not analyze their attitudes toward stimuli in a conscious and deliberate manner. Rather, their behavior is guided by a spontaneous, automatic affective appraisal of the environment (e.g., Zajonc, 1980). Whereas traditional questionnaires typically tap into the consciously constructed and expressed attitudes, implicit measures could index the spontaneous, automatic evaluation of stimuli. Hence, implicit measures could be particularly suited to predict spontaneous, uncontrolled behavior. Fazio and Olson (2003) reviewed evidence that suggests that implicit measures are indeed particularly helpful in predicting behavior that is intrinsically difficult to control or behavior in situations where people are not motivated or do not have the opportunity to control the impact of automatically activated attitudes on behavior.

From the perspective of the MODE model, implicit measures can be regarded as laboratory equivalents of the automatic influence of attitudes on real-life behavior. Hence, implicit measures can provide a unique perspective on real-life behavior. This argument is closely related to the idea of transfer-appropriate processing (e.g., Roediger, 1990). That is, the closer the overlap between the processes that determine the measurement outcome and those that determine the actual behavior that one wants to predict, the more that the measurement outcome will be able to predict the behavior (also see Vargas, 2004). In fact, one could say that both the measurement outcome and the real-life behavior have certain functional properties (i.e., the conditions under which the attitude influences the outcome or behavior). One could thus argue that the predictive value of the measurement outcome depends on the extent to which its functional properties overlap with the functional properties of the real-life behavior that one wants to explain. For instance, real-life attitude-driven behavior that occurs when people do not have the conscious goal to evaluate stimuli in the environment might be related most to measurement outcomes that occur in the absence of a conscious evaluation goal.

Despite the importance of knowing the functional properties of (implicit) measures, relatively little research has been conducted to examine these properties (see De Houwer, 2006, and De Houwer & Moors, 2007, for a more detailed overview). There is some, albeit limited, evidence that affective priming effects can capture attitudes even when participants do not have the conscious goal to evaluate the stimulus (uncontrolled, unintentional), when they do not have the general conscious goal to evaluate stimuli in the environment (partial goal-independence), when they are unaware of the presented stimuli (awareness), when resources are limited (efficient), and when there is little time to process the stimuli (fast; see Klauer & Musch, 2003, for a review). Surprisingly, even less research has been conducted to examine the functional properties of IAT effects even though the IAT is currently the most popular implicit measure. There are some studies showing that it is difficult to fake IAT effects (e.g., Steffens, 2004, but see Fiedler & Bluemke, 2005). This suggests that IAT effects are relatively uncontrollable in that they provide a valid measure of attitudes even when participants have the goal to alter the impact of their attitude on behavior. There is one study showing that many participants are aware of what an IAT measures (Monteith et al., 2001), but little is known about whether this kind of awareness influences the validity of the IAT. Because of the reasons given above, it is imperative that more research is conducted to test the functional properties of the various implicit measures.

The Procedural Level

Direct versus Indirect Measures

Whereas the terms *implicit measure* and *explicit measure* refer to functional properties of a measurement outcome, the terms *indirect measure* and *direct measure* refer to an objective property of a measurement procedure (see De Houwer, 2006). Direct measures are procedures (tasks) in which the participant is asked to self-assess the to-be-measured construct (e.g., an attitude) by selecting a certain response (e.g., a rating) and in which the attitude is inferred on the basis of that response. Indirect measures, on the other hand, are procedures in which the participant is not asked to self-assess the to-be-measured construct, or if the participant is asked to self-assess the construct by selecting a certain response, the construct is not inferred on the basis of selected response. Whether a measure is direct or indirect is thus an objective property of the task or procedure. There is no need to do research about whether a measure is direct or indirect. It can be determined simply by looking at the procedure.

Consider the following example (see De Houwer, 2006). In a typical study on the name-letter effect (Nuttin, 1985), participants are asked to express their liking of each letter of the alphabet using a Likert-type rating scale. This measurement procedure is a direct measure of attitudes toward letters because participants are asked to self-assess their attitude toward each letter by selecting a certain rating and the attitudes are inferred on the basis of the ratings that the participants select. However, on the basis of the letter ratings, researchers can indirectly infer self-esteem by comparing how much a person likes the letters of his or her name better than other letters. This procedure (i.e., asking participants to rate letters and then comparing ratings for name letters with ratings for other letters) is an indirect measure of self-esteem because participants are not asked to self-assess their self-esteem. There is indeed evidence that this indirect procedure of assessing self-esteem results in valid estimates of self-esteem (e.g., Koole, Dijksterhuis, & van

Knippenberg, 2001).* When the participant is asked to self-assess self-esteem, for instance, by giving a rating on a Likert scale but self-esteem is inferred from another behavior such as the activity of certain facial muscles or the degree of eye contact with the experimenter during the rating task, the procedure can still be classified as an indirect measure. This is because the to-be-measured construct is assessed on the basis of a behavior or index that is different from the one that was said to be relevant for the self-assessment.

It should be clear that indirect measures are not a separate class of measures next to the class of implicit measures. The qualification direct/indirect refers to the measurement procedure, whereas the qualification implicit/explicit refers to the functional properties of the outcome of the measurement procedure. Each direct and indirect measure produces an outcome with certain functional characteristics. Not all indirect measures produce outcomes that have (all the) functional properties typical of implicit measures. For instance, asking person A to self-report how much time she or he spends with person B can provide an indirect way of assessing how much person A likes person B, but chances are that it does not provide an implicit measure of that attitude (in the sense of, e.g., uncontrollable, unintentional, or unaware). Likewise, the IAT task is an indirect measure because participants are not asked to self-assess the construct of interest. But evidence suggests that IAT effects are implicit only with regard to some functional features. For instance, IAT effects appear to be implicit measures in the sense that they are relatively difficult to control, but not in the sense that participants are unaware of what is being measured. Whether and in what sense indirect measures are implicit is thus a matter of research. Direct measures also do not by definition provide explicit measures. For instance, one can ask participants to express their liking of a certain attitude object as quickly as possible or while performing a demanding secondary task. In such cases, participants might have little control over the expressed attitude (e.g., Wilson, Lindsey, & Schooler, 2000). But regardless of whether a measure is direct or indirect, one should always verify what the functional properties of the measurement outcome are before claiming that it is an implicit measure.

---

* Note that the procedure of indirectly measuring self-esteem on the basis of the ratings of letters is not identical to the procedure of directly measuring attitudes toward letters. In the former but not latter case, the procedure entails that one compares the ratings for name letters with rating of letters that are not in the name. This also illustrates that the calculation of the dependent variable is part of the procedure.

The fact that context variables can influence the functional features of a measurement outcome while leaving intact the indirect nature of the measurement procedure also shows that the concepts indirect and implicit do not overlap. Take the example of asking person A to report how much time he or she spends with person B. The extent to which person A is aware of the fact that the answer to this question is meant to reflect his or her attitude toward person B can depend on the context in which the question is given (e.g., when it follows after questions about the positive or negative traits of person B versus questions related to physical attributes of person B). But the context in which the question is given has no impact on the fact that person A is not asked to self-assess the attitude toward person B. Hence, context can change the sense in which a measurement outcome is implicit while leaving intact the indirect nature of the measurement procedure.

Structural Properties

A taxonomy. Many of the so-called implicit measures that have been proposed during the past decade are reaction-time-based measures. That is, attitudes are inferred on the basis of the speed or accuracy with which participants respond to presentation of certain stimuli. I previously proposed a heuristic framework or taxonomy for describing and comparing reaction-time-based tasks at the structural level (De Houwer, 2003a). The structure of a task refers to procedural elements that remain constant in different implementations of the task. Hence, like the distinction between direct and indirect measures, a structural description of reaction-time-based measures is situated at the procedural level.

The framework that I proposed originated from an analysis of standard stimulus-response (S-R) compatibility tasks. These tasks can be characterized on the basis of which types of compatibility vary over trials: relevant S-R compatibility, irrelevant S-R compatibility, and stimulus-stimulus (S-S) compatibility. In traditional S-R compatibility tasks (e.g., Fitts & Seeger, 1953; Kornblum & Lee, 1995), on some trials, the relevant stimulus feature that determines the response is somehow related or similar to the correct response, whereas on other trials, both elements differ or are less related (see Table 12.1). Consider a task in which participants are required to say "left" or "right" in response to the location of stimuli. In one part of the task, participants are instructed to give the corresponding responses (i.e., say "left" when a stimulus appears on the left side of a screen and say "right" when a stimulus appears on the right

TABLE 12.1 A Taxonomy of the Stimulus-Response Compatibility Tasks and Indirect Measures

| Task | Is there a manipulation of | | |
	S-S Compatibility?	Irrelevant S-R Compatibility?	Relevant S-R Compatibility?
Traditional S-R Compatibility	No	No	Yes
Stroop	Yes	Yes	No
IAT	No	Yes	Yes
Affective Priming	Yes	Yes	No
Affective Simon	No	Yes	No

side; compatible task), whereas in the other part, they give the opposite responses (i.e., say "left" to right stimuli and "right" to left stimuli; incompatible task). The two parts of the task differ with regard to the compatibility between the relevant stimulus feature (left or right position) and the responses (say "left" or "right"). Hence, in this task, relevant S-R compatibility is manipulated: On some trials (i.e., all trials in the compatible task) the relevant stimulus feature and the to-be-emitted response are compatible (both refer to left or both refer to right), whereas on the other trials (i.e., all trials in the incompatible task) the relevant stimulus feature and the response are incompatible (one refers to left and the other to right). The typical outcome of these studies is that performance is better when the relevant stimulus feature and the response correspond than when they differ (i.e., faster performance in the compatible task than in the incompatible task).

Irrelevant S-R compatibility and S-S compatibility can be illustrated on the basis of the well-known Stroop color-word task. In this task, participants name the ink color of color words while ignoring their meaning. On congruent trials, the word refers to the ink color (e.g., say "blue" to the word *blue* in blue ink). On incongruent trials, the word refers to a different color than the ink color (e.g., say "green" to the word *blue* in green ink). Unlike to what is the case in traditional S-R compatibility tasks, the compatibility between the relevant feature and the correct response does not vary over trials because response always corresponds to the ink color. Hence, relevant S-R compatibility is not manipulated. The compatibility between an irrelevant stimulus feature and the correct response, however, does vary over trials: On congruent trials, the correct response corresponds to the (task-irrelevant) meaning of the word, whereas on incongruent trials, both elements differ. Hence, the Stroop task can be characterized as a task in which irrelevant S-R compatibility is manipulated. In addition, the compatibility between an irrelevant stimulus feature (i.e., the meaning of the word) and the relevant stimulus feature (i.e., the color of the word) also varies over trials. On congruent but not incongruent trials, the irrelevant meaning of the word corresponds to the ink color. Hence, in Stroop tasks, S-S compatibility also varies over trials. Moreover, the manipulation of irrelevant S-R compatibility and S-S compatibility is confounded. That is, when the irrelevant meaning of the word corresponds to the correct response, it also corresponds to the ink color (congruent trials), and when word meaning differs from the correct response, it also differs from the ink color (incongruent trials). The Stroop task can therefore be described as a task in which irrelevant S-R compatibility and S-S correspondence are manipulated in a confounded manner (see Table 12.1).

Reaction-time-based measures of attitudes can also be characterized according to this taxonomy (see De Houwer, 2001, 2003a, for a more detailed discussion). The IAT, for example, is a task in which both irrelevant S-R compatibility and relevant S-R compatibility are manipulated, most often in a confounded manner (see De Houwer, 2001, 2003a). Consider the flower-insect IAT as introduced by Greenwald et al. (1998) in their seminal paper. Participants were asked to categorize names of flowers, names of insects, positive words, and negative words by pressing one of two keys. Results showed that performance was better when flowers and positive words were assigned to one key and insects and negative words to the other key (flower+positive task) than when the first key was assigned to insects and positive words and the second key to flowers and negative words (insect+positive task). Importantly, all exemplars of the category flowers had a positive valence (e.g., *tulip*), whereas all exemplars of the category insects had a negative valence (e.g., *cockroach*).

Because of the task instructions, one response became extrinsically associated with positive valence (i.e., the response assigned to positive words), whereas the other response was extrinsically associated with negative valence (i.e., the response assigned to negative words; see Proctor & Vu, 2002; De Houwer, 2003b, 2004). Therefore, in the flower+positive task, the valence of the correct response always corresponded to the valence of the relevant category (flower or insect), whereas in the insect+positive task, the valence of the correct response always differed from the valence of the relevant category. Hence, the degree of compatibility between the correct response and the relevant stimulus feature (i.e., the category of the word) varied over trials. Put more formally, relevant S-R compatibility is manipulated. Because all flower exemplars were positive and all insect exemplars were negative, the task-irrelevant valence of the presented flower names and insect names also corresponded to the valence of the correct response in the flower+positive task but not in the insect+positive task. Hence, irrelevant S-R compatibility is also manipulated. Because there is a perfect confound between the valence of the category and the valence of the items in each category (i.e., all flower names are positive and all insect names are negative), the flower-insect IAT as implemented by Greenwald et al. (1998) is a task in which relevant S-R compatibility and irrelevant S-R compatibility are manipulated in a confounded manner (see Table 12.1).

Other reaction-time-based implicit measures have a different structure. Consider the affective priming task. In a typical affective priming study, a prime stimulus is presented briefly and followed immediately by a target that needs to be classified on the basis of its valence (see Klauer & Musch, 2003, for a review). In this task, the valence of the prime is a task-irrelevant feature, the valence of the target is the task-relevant feature, and the responses are related to positive or negative valence. On congruent trials, the prime and the target have the same valence, whereas on incongruent trials, they have a different valence. Hence, S-S compatibility is manipulated. The valence of the prime is also compatible with the valence of the response on congruent trials but not on incongruent trials. Hence, irrelevant S-R compatibility is also manipulated. Because the valence of the target is always identical to the valence of the response, just as in the Stroop task, S-S compatibility and irrelevant S-R compatibility are manipulated in a confounded manner (see Table 12.1).

Finally, the affective Simon task has yet another underlying structure. In this task, participants give a valenced response on the basis of a nonaffective feature of valenced stimuli (De Houwer & Eelen, 1998). For instance, participants can be asked to say "good" when they see an adjective and "bad" when they see a noun, irrespective of the valence of the word. The irrelevant valence of the word and the response match on congruent trials (e.g., say "good" to the word *happy* because it is an adjective) but differ on incongruent trials (e.g., say "good" to the word *sad* because it is adjective). Hence, the (affective) Simon task is a task in which irrelevant S-R compatibility is manipulated. Relevant S-R compatibility is not manipulated because the responses are always unrelated to the relevant feature. S-S compatibility is also kept constant because the irrelevant valence of the words is unrelated to their relevant grammatical category (see Table 12.1).

Characterizing implicit measures at the structural level offers a way
to see important commonalities and differences between different measures and thus has a clear heuristic value. In the remainder of this chapter, I will argue that it can also have implications for understanding
how these measures work. First, I will discuss evidence regarding the
role of exemplars and categories in the IAT and the affective priming
task. Next, I will look at the implications of the structural analysis for
the validity and reliability of different measures.

On the role of exemplars and categories in the IAT. The effect in a
reaction-time task is always based on a comparison of performance on
certain types of trials. The effect (i.e., the difference in performance on
certain types of trials) can arise because of the structural differences
between the trial types that are compared. Therefore, when there is a
confound between the valence of the categories and the valence of the
exemplars in the IAT, the IAT effect can arise either because the trials
in the two IAT tasks differ with regard to relevant S-R compatibility or
because those trials differ with regard to irrelevant S-R compatibility.
In the former case, IAT effects would depend on the properties (e.g.,
valence) of the categories; in the latter case, IAT effects will reflect the
properties of the exemplars.* Consider the flower-insect IAT as introduced by Greenwald et al. (1998). If the IAT effect is driven by relevant
S-R compatibility, then the typical flower-insect IAT effect is due to
the fact that participants have a more positive attitude toward the concept flowers than toward the concept insects. If the IAT depends on
variations in irrelevant S-R compatibility, the flower-insect IAT effect
reflects more positive attitudes toward flower exemplars such as tulip
than toward insect exemplars such as cockroach.

I examined the relative contribution of variations in relevant and
irrelevant S-R compatibility by designing an IAT in which the confound between the valence of the categories and the valence of the
exemplars was removed (De Houwer, 2001). British participants were
asked to classify names of British persons, names of foreign persons,
positive words, and negative words by pressing one of two keys on the
basis of the nationality of the persons (British or foreign) or the valence
of the words (positive or negative). Importantly, half of the British and
foreign persons were liked by the participants (e.g., Princess Diana;

---

* It is possible that the IAT (sometimes) does not reflect the valence of the categories
  or exemplars, but other features such as salience (see Rothermund & Wentura, 2004;
  De Houwer, Geldof, & De Bruycker, 2005). To simplify the discussion, I will assume
  that IAT effects do reflect valence.

Mahatma Gandhi), whereas the other British and foreign persons were disliked (e.g., Harold Shipman, a well-known British mass murderer; Adolf Hitler). Results showed that the British participants were faster in the task where British names and positive words were assigned to one key and foreign names and negative words to the other key than when the foreign and positive words were assigned to the first key and British and negative words to the second key. This effect was not influenced by the valence of the exemplars. On the basis of these results, I concluded that IAT effects are driven primarily by the properties of the categories (i.e., British participants have a more positive attitude toward the concept *British* than toward the concept *foreign*), whereas properties of the exemplars seem to have little or no effect. Similar results were found in subsequent studies (e.g., Mitchell, Nosek, & Banaji, 2003, Experiment 1; Rothermund & Wentura, 2004, Experiment 4).

The conclusion that properties of the exemplars have little influence on IAT effects was, however, based on a null finding. Moreover, in a footnote of the paper, I described an experiment in which the categories had a more or less neutral valence (i.e., *person* and *animal*) but the exemplars were positive or negative (e.g., *friend, enemy, swan, snake*). In this experiment (which actually was the first Extrinsic Affective Simon experiment ever conducted; see De Houwer, 2003b), I did observe a significant effect of exemplar valence (see De Houwer, 2001, footnote 4). The discrepancy between the results of the two studies can be explained as follows: When the categories are clearly positive or negative, category valence might be much more salient than the valence of the exemplars. Hence, exemplar valence might not have much effect on performance. But when the categories are fairly neutral, exemplar valence might be salient and have an effect on performance (see below for a discussion of data showing that salience of stimulus features can matter).

Research suggests that there are also other ways in which exemplar properties might influence IAT performance. For instance, Steffens and Plewe (2001) presented names of women, names of men, positive words, and negative words. When the positive words referred to stereotypic positive attributes of women (e.g., *empathic*) and the negative words to stereotypic negative attributes of men (e.g., *brutal*), the IAT revealed more positive attitudes toward women than toward men in female participants. This IAT effect was, however, significantly reduced when the positive attribute words were associated with men (e.g., *independent*) and the negative attribute words associated with women (e.g., *bitchy*). Likewise, Mitchell et al. (2003, Experiment 2; also see Govan & Williams, 2004, Experiment 1b) presented names of well-known White persons, well-known Black persons, positive words, and negative words. When all White persons were liked and all Black persons disliked, the IAT revealed a strong preference for White people. When all White persons were disliked and all Black persons liked, the IAT effect disappeared. Finally, Govan and Williams (Experiment 1a) found a normal flower-insect IAT effect (faster in the flower+positive task than in the insect+positive task) when all flower exemplars had a positive valence and all insect exemplars a negative valence (e.g., *daffodil, cockroach*). But this effect reversed when the flower exemplars were negative and the insect exemplars positive (e.g., *poison ivy, butterfly*).

It is important to note, however, that the impact of exemplars on IAT performance does not necessarily provide evidence for the hypothesis that IAT effects are partially determined by irrelevant S-R compatibility. An alternative explanation for these effects is that the nature of the exemplars has an impact on how the categories are conceptualized or on the attitude toward the categories. For instance, when participants are repeatedly exposed to (unusual) names of negative flowers (e.g., *poison ivy*) and positive insects (e.g., *butterfly*), it is possible that participants recode the categories in terms of *nasty plants* and *nice animals* or that their attitude toward the concept flower temporarily becomes more negative and the attitude toward insects more positive. If this is true, then the impact of exemplars on IAT performance is mediated by relevant S-R compatibility effects (i.e., effects of manipulations of relevant S-R compatibility). That is, performance on an IAT trial would be determined by the match between the relevant stimulus feature (i.e., the valence of the categories) and the responses on that trial rather than by the match between an irrelevant stimulus feature (i.e., the valence of the presented category exemplar).

Govan and Williams (2004) obtained some evidence to support this alternative explanation. Their participants first completed an IAT in which names of plants, names of animals, positive words, and negative words were presented. In one condition, all animals had a positive valence (e.g., *swan*) and all plants a negative valence (e.g., poison ivy), whereas the reverse was true in the other condition (e.g., *crocodile, daffodil*). Afterwards, they completed a second IAT that was identical to the first except that only the words animal and plant were used as exemplars for the category animals and the category plants, respectively. This category IAT removed any possible impact of exemplars (simply because only the category labels were presented) and could therefore provide an estimate of the attitude toward the concepts animals and plants. Results showed that performance in both IATs was influenced in the same way by the nature of the exemplars in the first IAT. That is, both IATs revealed a preference for plants over animals when plant exemplars were positive and animal exemplars negative but a preference for animals over plants when plant exemplars were negative and animal exemplars positive. Because the second IAT could be based only on the properties of the categories, these results suggest that the nature of the exemplars in the first IAT changed the way in which the categories were conceptualized or resulted in a change in the attitude toward these categories.

One way to prevent these changes at the category level, and thus to test whether irrelevant S-R compatibility can have a direct effect on IAT performance, is to manipulate the valence of the exemplars on a within-subjects basis rather than a between-subjects basis. This is exactly the approach that was followed in the British-foreign experiment described above (De Houwer, 2001). Because half of the British and foreign names were positive and half were negative, it is unlikely that participants recoded the categories or that the attitudes toward the categories would have changed. The fact that no impact of exemplar valence was found therefore raises doubts about whether irrelevant S-R compatibility can have a direct effect.*

Regardless of whether irrelevant S-R compatibility does contribute to IAT effects, it is clear that relevant S-R compatibility is an important source of IAT effects. This conclusion has important implications. First, it provides at least a partial explanation for why an IAT measure of attitudes often does not correlate with other measures of the same attitudes. For instance, Bosson, Swann, and Pennebaker (2000) found little or no correlation between an IAT measure of self-esteem and self-esteem as measured in an affective priming task. This lack of correspondence could be partially due to the fact that IAT effects are

---

* In a recent study, Bluemke and Friese (2006, Experiment 2) did find an effect of the nature of the exemplars when this was manipulated on a within-subjects basis. The presented words related to East Germany, West Germany, positive words, and negative words. Unlike the case in the British-foreign experiment, they manipulated not only the valence of the East German (e.g., *Weimar, surveillance*) and West German (e.g., *freedom, greed*) items, but also the extent to which the positive words (e.g., *modest, optimistic*) and negative words (e.g., *unproductive, greedy*) were related to the concept *East German* and *West German*. Note, however, that because of these manipulations, participants probably found it difficult to decide whether an item should be classified according to region (East or West German) or valence (positive or negative). This was evidenced by a high percentage of errors. It would therefore be interesting to see whether this pattern of results can be replicated with other categories and stimuli (see De Houwer, Geldof, & De Bruycker, 2005, for related evidence).

predominantly driven by relevant S-R compatibility, whereas affective priming effects are due mainly to effects of irrelevant S-R compatibility (see Klauer & Musch, 2003, for a review). This means that the IAT will generally reflect the attitudes toward the categories, whereas affective priming will reflect the attitude toward the exemplars that are used to instantiate the categories (De Houwer, 2003a; Fazio & Olson, 2003).

Olson and Fazio (2003) obtained strong support for this hypothesis. Their participants completed an affective priming task and an IAT that were both directed at measuring attitudes toward White and Black people. When participants were asked to merely pay attention to the primes (faces of persons from different racial groups), there was no correspondence between the affective priming measure and the IAT measure. This is probably due to the fact that the IAT measured attitudes toward the concepts *Whites* and *Blacks*, whereas the priming measure reflected the attitude toward the individual exemplars (e.g., how attractive each individual face was). When participants were asked to process the race of the primes (in order to keep a mental tally of the number of faces from each group), the IAT and priming measures did converge. By making race salient, it is likely that the priming effect reflected the racial category of the exemplars rather than other properties of the primes such as attractiveness.

Olson and Fazio (2004) pointed to a second implication of the fact that IAT effects are driven by relevant S-R compatibility. In most IATs, the words *positive* and *negative* (or related words such as *pleasant/unpleasant* or *good/bad*) are used to label the category of positive words and the category of negative words, respectively. Moreover, when participants categorize a positive or negative word in a manner that is inconsistent with the categorization intended by the experimenter, they receive error feedback. Because of these task characteristics, it is possible that participants conceptualize the categories *positive* and *negative* in the sense of *normatively positive* and *normatively negative*. Because of this, the IAT might reflect not the personal attitudes of the participants (e.g., how much someone likes to smoke) but rather knowledge that they have about the normative societal views regarding the attitude object (e.g., the fact that most people in Western societies nowadays strongly disapprove of smoking). Olson and Fazio therefore developed a personalized version of the IAT in which the labels *I like* and *I dislike* are used for the category of positive words and the category of negative words, respectively, and in which error feedback is no longer given. They reported the results of four experiments that support the hypothesis that such a personalized IAT is influenced less by societal views than a standard IAT.

It is interesting to note that both the studies on the effects of exemplars in the IAT (e.g., Govan & Williams, 2004) and the studies of Olson and Fazio (2004) suggest that IAT effects are susceptible to the manner in which participants conceptualize the categories in the IAT. On the one hand, this is a drawback because it introduces a potential source of error variance that the experimenter cannot control completely. But on the other hand, it also offers possibilities. For instance, in some cases it might be difficult to find a label that unequivocally represents the category or concept of interest. In that case, one can select a label that approaches the intended concept as closely as possible and explain to the participant what the exact meaning of the label is. For instance, in a recent study conducted at our lab (Dewitte, De Houwer, & Buysse, 2007), we used an IAT to measure the attachment dimension of anxiety (Brennan, Clark, & Shaver, 1998). Because it is difficult to represent this complex concept in just one or two words, we used the labels *relationally worthful* and *relationally worthless* and explained to our participants that the labels and items did not refer to general self-esteem but only to feelings of worth in the context of close relationships. Under these conditions, we found that our IAT measure of relational anxiety did correlate with several questionnaire measures of this attachment dimension (but not other attachment dimensions).

Implications for the validity and reliability of implicit measures. It has been reported repeatedly that affective priming and affective Simon measures of interindividual differences have a lower split-half and test-retest reliability than IAT measures of the same constructs (e.g., Bosson et al., 2000; Banse, Seise, & Zerbes, 2001; Teige, Schnabel, Banse, & Asendorpf, 2004). In this section, I will argue that this could be due to the fact that both affective priming and affective Simon measures are based on irrelevant S-R compatibility effects (i.e., effects of the manipulation of irrelevant S-R compatibility; see De Houwer, 2003a; Klauer & Musch, 2003), whereas IAT measures primarily rely on effects of relevant S-R compatibility (see above). When a measure is based on irrelevant S-R compatibility effects, the target concept is implemented at the level of the irrelevant stimulus feature. For instance, in affective priming studies, one can measure the attitude toward the concept *smoking* by presenting the word *smoking* as the task-irrelevant prime stimulus and examining whether this facilitates positive or negative responses. Likewise, an affective Simon measure of attitudes toward smoking could entail that one asks participants to say "good" or "bad" on the basis of the grammatical category of the words whose task-irrelevant meaning is related to smoking (e.g., *cigarette, smoking*; De Houwer, 2003b; De Houwer & Eelen, 1998). Importantly, because the concept that one wants to measure (i.e., the target concept) is implemented at the level of an irrelevant stimulus or stimulus feature, participants do not need to process it or take it into account when selecting their response. But the measure can work only if the target concept is processed and if its associated properties have an impact on the selection of the responses. If these conditions are not met, then logically the target concept cannot have an effect on performance and thus cannot be revealed by the measure. It is likely that a variety of factors will influence whether, when, and to which extent these conditions are fulfilled and thus whether, when, and to which extent the measure is valid and reliable.

First, certain aspects of the procedure can determine the likelihood that the target concepts are processed or have an impact on performance. For instance, Musch and Klauer (2001) demonstrated that affective priming effects are smaller when the prime is consistently presented at a different location than the target. They argued that this effect is due to the fact that automatic processing of valence depends on the allocation of spatial attention. Likewise, De Houwer, Crombez, Baeyens, and Hermans (2001) showed that the magnitude of the affective Simon effect depends on the nature of the relevant feature. This is probably due to the fact that the relevant feature determines the extent to which participants process the irrelevant target feature (and thus the target concepts). Both findings suggest that procedural parameters can influence the likelihood that the target concept is processed. Hence, one should make sure to use a procedure that is known to allow for a sufficient processing of the target concepts. Otherwise, irrelevant S-R tasks such as the affective priming and affective Simon task cannot provide a valid measure of the properties of the target concepts.

Second, whether the target concept is processed and has an impact on response selection will also depend on the salience of the concept. Consider the study of Olson and Fazio (2003) discussed above. They found a higher correspondence between an affective priming measure of racial attitudes and an IAT measure of those same attitudes when participants were asked to determine the race of the prime stimuli in the priming task than when participants were instructed to merely pay attention to the primes. Olson and Fazio attributed this difference to differences in the salience of the racial features of the primes compared to other features such as attractiveness or gender. Note, however, that until now there have been hardly any studies in which the valence of multiple features of the same stimulus have been manipulated independently. It is thus unclear how the valence associated with different features and concepts interacts and how this interaction is influenced by salience or instructions. Nevertheless, the results of Olson and Fazio are at least in line with the possibility that the impact of the target concept on priming effects depends on the salience of that concept.

Olson and Fazio (2003) argued that the degree of salience of the target concept could also influence the reliability of the measure. For instance, in their priming measure of racial attitudes, the measure corresponds to the differences in responses on trials with a Black face as prime compared to trials with a White face as prime. But those participants who pay more attention to the physical attractiveness of the faces will add noise to the measure, which will reduce reliability. Noise can also be added by variations in the type of feature that participants pay attention to over the course of the task or during different administrations of the task.

Based on these considerations, it seems important to ensure that the target concept is salient. This can be achieved through instructions (e.g., Olson & Fazio, 2003), but one should also not neglect the selection of the stimuli. For instance, rather then presenting exemplars of the target category (e.g., pictures of different Black men or different names typical of Black people), it could be better to present the label of the category itself (e.g., the word *Blacks*) or at least to present the label as one of the stimuli. Whereas exemplars are rarely exemplars of a single category, labels often do represent a single category or concept. This reduces the probability that participants start paying attention to features other than the target feature (also see Livingston & Brewer, 2002). Note, however, that repeated presentation of category labels might generate awareness about the purpose of the task.

The third factor that influences whether the target concept is processed and influences performance concerns interindividual differences in the capacity to ignore irrelevant information. It is likely that participants will often try to ignore the target concept either because it distracts them from their task or because they are explicitly instructed to ignore it. There is clear evidence from Stroop studies that participants who differ in working memory capacity also differ in their ability to ignore irrelevant information (see Long & Prat, 2002). It is therefore likely that these interindividual differences will reduce the validity and reliability of measures that are based on irrelevant S-R compatibility such as the affective priming task and the affective Simon task. But as far as I know, this hypothesis has not yet been tested empirically.

The fourth factor relates to effects of the order in which trials are presented. Studies on the spatial Simon effect have demonstrated strong effects of trial order on the magnitude of irrelevant S-R compatibility effects. For instance, it has now been demonstrated repeatedly that the spatial Simon effect is much stronger after a congruent trial (e.g., press left because of the color of a stimulus on the left) than after an incongruent trial (e.g., press left because of the color of a stimulus on the right; e.g., Hommel, Proctor, & Vu, 2004). In many studies, the Simon effect even disappeared completely after an incongruent trial. Provided that these findings generalize to other tasks in which irrelevant S-R compatibility is manipulated, such order effects could have a profound effect on the reliability of affective priming and affective Simon measures of attitudes and other constructs. One way to reduce the adverse impact of these order effects on reliability is to control rather than randomize the order of the trials, for instance, by keeping the order of the trials fixed. Another option would be to ensure that each type of trial is presented a large number of times so that the noise due to order effects is leveled out by averaging across trials. But the effects of trial order could interact in complex ways with interindividual differences in the ability to ignore irrelevant information and other factors such as the duration of the test. Therefore, there is no guarantee that such solutions will be successful.

All the factors that I have discussed jeopardize the validity and reliability of reaction-time-based measures such as the affective priming and affective Simon task that are based on a manipulation of irrelevant S-R compatibility. In contrast, the validity and reliability of measures that are based on a manipulation of relevant S-R compatibility such as the IAT (Greenwald et al., 1998; also see the approach-avoid task as implemented by Mogg, Bradley, Field, & De Houwer, 2003, and the Implicit Association Procedure by Schnabel, Banse, & Asendorpf, 2006) is not endangered by factors that determine whether the target concept is processed. The reason is simple: By definition, in relevant S-R measures, participants must process the target concept in order to select the correct response. For instance, in a flower-insect IAT, participants are instructed to respond on the basis of whether a presented name refers to a flower or an insect.*

The hypothesis that the task-relevance of the target concepts is a crucial determinant of the validity and reliability of implicit measures is also supported by a recent series of studies on the Extrinsic Affective Simon Task (De Houwer, 2003b) that was conducted at our lab (De Houwer & De Bruycker, 2007a, 2007b). In a typical EAST study, participants see words that are presented in white, blue, or green. They are asked to categorize white words on the basis of the valence and colored words on the basis of color. By assigning one key to positive words and the other key to negative words, the keys become associated with positive and negative valence, respectively. As such, the trials with colored words are equivalent to affective Simon trials: Participants give valenced responses on the basis of a nonaffective stimulus feature (color) while ignoring the valence of the words. Results typically show that participants respond more quickly and accurately when the irrelevant valence of the word corresponds to the (extrinsic) valence of the response than when the stimulus and response have a different valence (e.g., De Houwer, 2003b).

---

* Note that measures based on relevant S-R compatibility could to some extent be influenced by interindividual differences in working memory capacity and by trial order effects. First, although participants need to process the target concept in order to select the correct response (e.g., tulip is a flower, therefore push the left button), they do not need to process the property of the target concept that one wants to measure (e.g., that the concept flower has a positive valence). On incompatible trials, participants probably try to ignore the target property in active manner because it is associated with the incorrect response. For instance, in the flower+negative task of a flower-insect IAT, the word tulip has a positive valence and thus activates the incorrect positive response. Hence, performance on incompatible trials (and thus the measurement outcome) will depend on the ability to ignore the task-irrelevant property of the target concept. This ability is probably determined by working memory capacity. But the role of working memory capacity will most likely be larger in irrelevant S-R measures than in relevant S-R measures because the former depend not only on the capacity to ignore the target property but also on the capacity to ignore the irrelevant feature that contains the target concept. Second, the extent to which the target property can be ignored probably also depends on task order, for instance, whether, on the previous trial, the target property was compatible or incompatible with the correct response. Note, however, that in most relevant S-R tasks, all compatible trials are grouped in one block and all incompatible trials in another block, whereas in most irrelevant S-R tasks, compatible and incompatible trials are presented in a random order. Hence, the noise introduced by order effects is probably larger in irrelevant S-R tasks than in relevant S-R tasks.

In principle, the EAST can be used to measure individual differences in attitudes. For instance, if a person needs less time to respond to a certain colored stimulus (e.g., the word *smoking*) by pressing the positive key than by pressing the negative key, one can infer that that person has a positive attitude toward the stimulus. Although some studies have found evidence for the validity of the EAST as a measure of individual differences in attitudes (e.g., Huijding & de Jong, 2006; Ellwart, Becker, & Rinck, 2005), in a recent series of experiments, we consistently failed to find any evidence for the reliability and validity of the Extrinsic Affective Simon Task as a measure of attitudes toward food items, political parties, and homosexuality. These failures were even more striking because in the same studies we did obtain evidence for the validity and reliability of IAT measures of these attitudes (De Houwer & De Bruycker, 2007a).

In light of these disappointing findings and the arguments presented above, we decided to create a variant of the EAST in which participants were forced to identify the target concept before they could select the correct response (De Houwer & De Bruycker, 2007b). For instance, in order to measure the attitude toward the concepts *beer* and *sprouts* (a cabbage-like vegetable), we presented the words beer and sprouts intermixed with positive and negative adjectives. All words were sometimes presented in uppercase letters and sometimes in lowercase letters. Participants were instructed to evaluate all adjectives by pressing one key for positive adjectives and the other key for negative adjectives, irrespective of the letter case in which the adjective was presented. The function of these trials was to link the responses with positive or negative valence. Participants were also told that there were two special words, namely the word beer and the word sprouts (both nouns), for which the task would be different. When the word beer or the word sprouts was presented, participants were asked to respond not on the basis of valence but on the basis of the letter case in which the word was presented (e.g., press the positive key when the word beer was presented in uppercase letters but press the negative key when it was presented in lowercase letters). Hence, in order to decide whether they should respond on the basis of stimulus valence while ignoring letter case (as was the case for all adjectives) or on the basis of letter case while ignoring valence (as was the case for the target words beer and sprouts), participants first needed to identify the word. If the word beer or sprouts was presented, then letter case was relevant. If it was another word, valence was relevant. Whereas the standard EAST failed to provide a reliable (split-half reliability) or valid (correlations with explicit ratings) measure of these attitudes, the EAST that required identification (we therefore call it the Identification EAST, or ID-EAST) did provide scores that were fairly reliable (split-half correlations of about $r = .55$) and valid (correlations with explicit ratings and expected differences between heavy and light drinkers for beer but not sprouts). In fact, the ID-EAST performed at a level close to that of the IAT while overcoming some of the limitations of the IAT (e.g., the ID-EAST provides a measure of single attitudes; see De Houwer, 2003b). The fact that making the target concept relevant in an EAST seems to improve the psychometric qualities of the EAST supports the idea that irrelevant S-R measures (such as the EAST) are often inferior to relevant S-R measures (such as the IAT) because the target concepts are typically not relevant in irrelevant S-R measures but are relevant in relevant S-R measures. Nevertheless, more recent studies at our lab have shown that the ID-EAST is still too unreliable to provide a useful measure of interindividual differences.

One should note, however, that relevant S-R measures are not by definition better than measures based on irrelevant S-R compatibility effects. Relevant S-R measures have their own limitations and potential weaknesses. For instance, most often, relevant S-R compatibility is varied between tasks. That is, in one task (e.g., the flower+positive task in a flower-insect IAT), the mapping between the responses and the relevant target feature is compatible, whereas in a separate second task (e.g., the flower+negative task), the mapping is incompatible. The measure is therefore derived from a comparison of performance in different tasks. This allows for the possibility that performance in the two tasks does not rely on the same processes and that the difference between the tasks therefore does not (only) reflect the construct that one wants to measure. For instance, participants might succeed in finding a shortcut to simplify one of the tasks (e.g., by finding a feature such as valence or salience that is common to all stimuli assigned to the same response regardless of category) but could fail to find such a shortcut in the other task (e.g., De Houwer, 2003b; Mierke & Klauer, 2003). Another potential weakness is that the target concepts need to be made explicit in relevant S-R measures. This could increase the probability that participants are aware of what is being assessed (e.g., Monteith et al., 2001). Hence, while relevant S-R measures might often be more valid and reliable than irrelevant S-R measures, they might be less implicit in the sense that fewer of the functional characteristics of implicit processes apply to relevant S-R measures than to irrelevant S-R measures. Given the current lack of research on the functional properties of implicit measures, this hypothesis is, however, still speculative.

Conclusion

In this chapter, I describe two levels at which measures of attitudes can be described and compared. The first level is that of the functional properties of the outcome of a measurement procedure. These properties relate to the conditions under which the outcome of a measurement procedure provides an index of the to-be-measured construct. So far, little research has been conducted about these functional properties. Nevertheless, it could help (a) reduce confusion about the concept implicit measures, (b) clarify the processes underlying the measures, and (c) make clear the conditions under which a measure can be used to predict behavior. The second level is that of the procedure. There are at least two ways in which measurement procedures can be classified. The first is related to whether participants are asked to self-assess the construct that is measured. If the answer to that question is affirmative, the measurement procedure can be labeled as direct. If the answer is negative, the measure is indirect. The second aspect refers to the structural properties of the task. Here I make a distinction between measures that are based on a manipulation of relevant S-R compatibility and measures based on a manipulation of irrelevant S-R compatibility. I then argue that this distinction has important implications with regard to what is measured and with regard to the reliability and validity of the measures.

It should be clear that there are undoubtedly other ways of characterizing and comparing measures. Likewise, our characterization of measures at the functional and procedural level might have implications that were not yet recognized. Nevertheless, I hope that the analysis and discussion presented in this chapter goes at least some way in clarifying the nature of and relation between different measures of attitudes. The analysis also led to the identification of some important gaps in our knowledge about (implicit) measures of attitudes. Hopefully, this chapter will provide an impetus for addressing these unresolved questions.

References

Asendorpf, J. B., Banse, R., & Mücke, D. (2002). Double dissociation between implicit and explicit personality self-concept: The case of shy behavior. *Journal of Personality and Social Psychology, 83*, 380–393.

Banse, R., Seise, J., & Zerbes, N. (2001). Implicit attitudes towards homosexuality: Reliability, validity, and controllability of the IAT. *Zeitschrift für Experimentelle Psychologie, 48*, 145–160.

Bargh, J.A. (1992). The ecology of automaticity. Toward establishing the conditions needed to produce automatic processing effects. *American Journal of Psychology, 105*, 181–199.

Bluemke, M., & Friese, M. (2006). Do features of stimuli influence IAT effects? *Journal of Experimental Social Psychology, 42*, 163–176.

Borsboom, D., Mellenbergh, G. J., & van Heerden, J. (2004). The concept of validity. *Psychological Review, 111*, 1061–1071.

Bosson, J.K., Swann, W.B., & Pennebaker, J.W. (2000). Stalking the perfect measure of implicit self-esteem: The blind men and the elephant revisited? *Journal of Personality and Social Psychology, 79*, 631–643.

Brennan, K. A., Clark, C. L., & Shaver, P. R. (1998). Self-report measurement of adult romantic attachment: An integrative overview. In J. A. Simpson & W. S. Rholes (Eds.), *Attachment theory and close relationships* (pp. 46–76). New York: Guilford Press.

Brunel, F. F., Tietje, B. C., & Greenwald, A. G. (2004). Is the Implicit Association Test a valid and valuable measure of implicit consumer social cognition? *Journal of Consumer Psychology, 14*, 385–404.

De Houwer, J. (2001). A structural and process analysis of the Implicit Association Test. *Journal of Experimental Social Psychology, 37*, 443–451.

De Houwer, J. (2003a). A structural analysis of indirect measures of attitudes. In J. Musch & K. C. Klauer (Eds.), *The psychology of evaluation: Affective processes in cognition and emotion* (pp. 219–244). Mahwah, NJ: Lawrence Erlbaum.

De Houwer, J. (2003b). The Extrinsic Affective Simon Task. *Experimental Psychology, 50*, 77–85.

De Houwer, J. (2004). Spatial Simon effects with non-spatial responses. *Psychonomic Bulletin & Review, 11*, 49–53.

De Houwer, J. (2006). What are implicit measures and why are we using them? In R. W. Wiers & A. W. Stacy (Eds.), *The handbook of implicit cognition and addiction* (pp. 11–28). Thousand Oaks, CA: Sage Publishers.

De Houwer, J., Crombez, G., Baeyens, F., & Hermans, D. (2001). On the generality of the affective Simon effect. *Cognition and Emotion, 15*, 189–206.

De Houwer, J., & De Bruycker, E. (2007a). The IAT outperforms the EAST as a measure of interindividual differences in attitudes. *British Journal of Social Psychology, 46*, 401–421.

De Houwer, J., & De Bruycker, E. (2007b). The Identification-EAST as a valid measure of implicit attitudes toward alcohol-related stimuli. *Journal of Behavior Therapy and Experimental Psychiatry, 38*, 133–143.

De Houwer, J., & Eelen, P. (1998). An affective variant of the Simon paradigm. *Cognition and Emotion, 12*, 45–61.

De Houwer, J., Geldof, T., & De Bruycker, E. (2005). The Implicit Association Test as a general measure of similarity. *Canadian Journal of Experimental Psychology, 59*, 228–239.

De Houwer, J., & Moors, A. (2007). How to define and examine the implicit-ness of implicit measures. In B. Wittenbrink & N. Schwarz (Eds.), *Implicit measures of attitudes: Procedures and controversies* (pp. 179–194). New York: Guilford Press.

Dewitte, M., De Houwer, J., & Buysse, A. (2007). *On the role of the implicit self-concept in adult attachment*. Manuscript submitted for publication.

Ellwart, T., Becker, E. S., & Rinck, M. (2005). Activation and measurement of threat associations in fear of spiders: An application of the Extrinsic Affective Simon Task. *Journal of Behavior Therapy and Experimental Psychiatry, 36*, 281–299.

Fazio, R. H. (1990). Multiple processes by which attitudes guide behavior: The MODE model as an integrative framework. In M. P. Zanna (Ed.), *Advances in experimental social psychology* (Vol. 23, pp. 75–109). San Francisco: Academic Press.

Fazio, R. H., Jackson, J. R., Dunton, B. C., & Williams, C. J. (1995). Variability in automatic activation as an unobtrusive measure of racial attitudes: A bona fide pipeline? *Journal of Personality and Social Psychology, 69*, 1013–1027.

Fazio, R. H., & Olson, M. A. (2003). Implicit measures in social cognition research: Their meaning and use. *Annual Review of Psychology, 54*, 297–327.

Fiedler, K., & Bluemke, M. (2005). Faking the IAT: Aided and unaided response control on the Implicit Association Test. *Basic and Applied Social Psychology, 27*, 307–316.

Fitts, P. M., & Seeger, C. M. (1953). SR compatibility: Spatial characteristics of stimulus and response codes. *Journal of Experimental Psychology, 46*, 199–210.

Govan, C. L., & Williams, K. D. (2004). Changing the affective valence of the stimulus items influences the IAT by redefining the category labels. *Journal of Experimental Social Psychology, 40*, 357–365.

Greenwald, A. G., McGhee, D. E., & Schwartz, J. L. K. (1998). Measuring individual differences in implicit cognition: The Implicit Association Test. *Journal of Personality and Social Psychology, 74*, 1464–1480.

Hommel, B., Proctor, R. W., & Vu, K.-P. (2004). A feature-integration account of sequential effects in the Simon task. *Psychological Research, 68*, 1–17.

Huijding, J., & de Jong, P. J. (2006). Specific predictive power of implicit associations for automatic fear behavior. *Behavior Research and Therapy, 44*, 161–176.

Klauer, K. C., & Musch, J. (2003). Affective priming: Findings and theories. In J. Musch & K. C. Klauer (Eds.), *The psychology of evaluation: Affective processes in cognition and emotion*. Mahwah, NJ: Lawrence Erlbaum.

Koole, S. L., Dijksterhuis, A., & van Knippenberg, A. (2001). What's in a name? Implicit self-esteem and the automatic self. *Journal of Personality and Social Psychology, 80*, 669–685.

Kornblum, S., & Lee, J.-W. (1995). Stimulus-response compatibility with relevant and irrelevant stimulus dimensions that do and do not overlap with the response. *Journal of Experimental Psychology: Human Perception and Performance, 21,* 855–875.

Livingston, R. W., & Brewer, M. B. (2002). What are we really priming? Cue-based versus category-based processing of facial stimuli. *Journal of Personality and Social Psychology, 82,* 5–18.

Long, D. L., & Prat, C. S. (2002). Working memory and Stroop interference: An individual differences investigation. *Memory & Cognition, 30,* 294–301.

Mierke, J., & Klauer, K. C. (2003). Method specific variance in the Implicit Association Test. *Journal of Personality and Social Psychology, 85,* 1180–1192.

Mitchell, J. P., Nosek, B. A., & Banaji, M. R. (2003). Contextual variations in implicit evaluation. *Journal of Experimental Psychology: General, 132,* 455–469.

Mogg, K., Bradley, B. P., Field, M., & De Houwer, J. (2003). Eye movements to smoking-related pictures in smokers: Relationship between attentional biases and implicit and explicit measures of stimulus valence. *Addiction, 98,* 825–836.

Monteith, M. J., Voils, C. I., & Ashburn-Nardo, L. (2001). Taking a look underground: Detecting, interpreting, and reacting to implicit racial bias. *Social Cognition, 19,* 395–417.

Moors, A., & De Houwer, J. (2006). Automaticity: A conceptual and theoretical analysis. *Psychological Bulletin, 132,* 297–326.

Musch, J., & Klauer, K. C. (2001). Local uncertainty moderates affective congruency effects in the evaluative decision task. *Cognition and Emotion, 15,* 167–188.

Nosek, B. A., & Banaji, M. R. (2001). The Go/No-Go Association Task. *Social Cognition, 19,* 625–666.

Nuttin, J. M. (1985). Narcissism beyond Gestalt awareness: The name-letter effect. *European Journal of Social Psychology, 15,* 353–361.

Olson, M. A., & Fazio, R. H. (2003). Relations between implicit measures of prejudice: What are we measuring? *Psychological Science, 14,* 636–639.

Olson, M. A., & Fazio, R. H. (2004). Reducing the influence of extra-personal associations on the Implicit Association Test: Personalizing the IAT. *Journal of Personality and Social Psychology, 86,* 653–667.

Olson, M. A., & Fazio, R. H. (in press). Implicit and explicit measures of attitudes: The perspective of the MODE model. In R. E. Petty, R. H. Fazio, & P. Briñol (Eds.), *Attitudes: Insights from the new implicit measures.* Hillsdale, NJ: Erlbaum.

Proctor, R. W., & Vu, K.-P. L. (2002). Eliminating, magnifying, and reversing spatial compatibility effects with mixed location-relevant and irrelevant trials. In W. Prinz & B. Hommel (Eds.), *Common mechanisms in perception and action: Attention and performance XIX* (pp. 443–473). Oxford, England: Oxford University Press.

Roediger, H. L. (1990). Implicit memory: Retention without remembering. *American Psychologist, 45*, 9, 1043–1056.

Rothermund, K., & Wentura, D. (2004). Underlying processes in the Implicit Association Test (IAT): Dissociating salience from associations. *Journal of Experimental Psychology: General, 133*, 139–165.

Schnabel, K., Banse, R., & Asendorpf, J. B. (2006). Employing automatic approach and avoidance tendencies for the assessment of implicit personality self-concept: The Implicit Association Procedure (IAP). *Experimental Psychology, 53*, 69–76.

Steffens, M. C. (2004). Is the Implicit Association Test immune to faking? *Experimental Psychology, 51*, 165–179.

Steffens, M. C., & Plewe, I. (2001). Items' cross-category associations as a confounding factor in the Implicit Association Test. *Zeitschrift für Experimentelle Psychologie, 48*, 123–134.

Teige, S., Schnabel, K., Banse, R., & Asendorpf, J. B. (2004). Assessment of multiple implicit self-concept dimensions using the Extrinsic Affective Simon Task (EAST). *European Journal of Personality, 18*, 495–520.

Vargas, P. T. (2004). On the relationship between implicit attitudes and behavior: Some lessons from the past, and directions for the future. In G. Haddock & G. R. Maio (Eds.), *Contemporary perspectives on the psychology of attitudes*. New York: Psychology Press.

Wilson, T. D., Lindsey, S., & Schooler, T. Y. (2000). A model of dual attitudes. *Psychological Review, 107*, 101–126.

Zajonc, R. B. (1980). Feeling and thinking. Preferences need no inferences. *American Psychologist, 35*, 151–175.

13

Controlled Influences on Implicit Measures[*]
Confronting the Myth of Process-Purity and Taming the Cognitive Monster

Jeffrey W. Sherman

Introduction

Though implicit measures often are portrayed as *process-pure* measures of automatic attitudes, instead, they reflect the joint contributions of automatic and controlled processes. As such, automatic and controlled components of attitudes are better measured, not with two separate measures, but with process dissociation (PD) techniques that extract independent estimates of automatic and controlled influences from performance on a single task. I will describe such approaches for analyzing responses on implicit tasks, concentrating on our own Quadruple Process (Quad) model (Sherman, Gawronski, Hugenburg, & Groom, 2005; Sherman, Gawronski, Conrey, Hugenburg, & Groom, 2008). The application of the Quad model provides important insights into central questions surrounding the conceptualization, measurement, and interpretation of implicit attitudes. Among these, Quad model analyses shed new light on Bargh's (1999) provocative claim that the "cognitive monsters" of implicit attitudes and stereotypes cannot be controlled. I will reexamine the status of this claim, concluding that, in general, the controllability of such biases has been underestimated. However, some forms of control may be more attainable than others. In particular, I

* This research was supported by NIMH grant R01 MH59774.

will argue that a failure to consider the multifaceted nature of implicit task performance has led to both an overestimation of the ease with which people can control the initial automatic activation of relevant associations and an underestimation of the extent to which the expression of those associations subsequently can be controlled.*

The Myth of Process-Purity and the Trouble with Tasks

People may be unaware of their attitudes or unwilling to report them truthfully. The "willing and able" issues are two of the most difficult problems for research on attitudes. The advent of implicit measures of attitudes has offered promising new ways to avoid these obstacles by measuring attitudes without directly requesting that respondents report those attitudes. In many cases, people are unaware that their attitudes are being measured with such tasks.† Many proponents of these measures further argue that, even if made aware of the nature of the task, people are unable to control their responses. Thus, these measures are seen as reflecting the unintended, automatic activation of stored attitudes, whose expression largely cannot be altered or inhibited (e.g., Bargh, 1999; Devine, 1989; Fazio, Jackson, Dunton, & Williams, 1995; Greenwald, McGhee, & Schwartz, 1998; Kim, 2003). Taken

---

* In this chapter, I will use the term *implicit measure* to refer to measures that assess attitudes and knowledge indirectly (i.e., without explicitly asking people to report their attitudes and knowledge). The term *indirect measure* may be technically more accurate for my intended meaning, but I will nevertheless use the common terminology of *implicit*.

I will use the term *implicit attitude* to refer simply to an attitude that is measured with an implicit measure. Here, the term implicit attitude implies nothing about the status of that attitude in terms of subjective awareness, intention, controllability, and so on. In my view, those are empirical questions that may be asked about any measured attitude, rather than definitional criteria. Critically, though implicit attitudes are defined as the behavioral outcomes of implicit measures (e.g., reaction time effects), they are not assumed to be isomorphic with the underlying evaluative associations (or *evaluative generators*) that instigate responses on the measures. Rather, behavioral biases on implicit measures (i.e., implicit attitudes) may or may not correspond closely with underlying associations, depending on the intervention of other processes that translate the associations into behavioral responses on the implicit measures. Thus, I call the behavioral bias an implicit attitude in the common vernacular, but distinguish this attitude from evaluative associations.

† The IAT may be a notable exception to this state of affairs (e.g., Fazio & Olson, 2003; Monteith, Voils, & Ashburn-Nardo, 2001).

in conjunction with explicit measures (e.g., questionnaires), implicit measures are used to compare and contrast automatic and controlled aspects of attitudes.

The Specter of Task Confounds

Though this *task dissociation* approach has certainly proven to be productive (see the contents of this book), it has significant drawbacks. First, assessing automatic and controlled components of attitudes with separate measures introduces a confound between process type (automatic vs. controlled) and measurement task (e.g., IAT vs. questionnaire). Undoubtedly, implicit measures are less subject to the whims of awareness and intention than are explicit measures. However, there may be other important differences between any pair of implicit and explicit tasks beyond the extent to which they tap automatic versus controlled processing.

As an example, consider the case of research on implicit and explicit memory. As in the attitudes domain, for years, different measures were used to assess what were thought to be independent implicit and explicit types or systems of memory. However, Roediger and his colleagues determined that, whereas implicit measures of memory had tapped perceptual encoding processes, explicit measures had tapped conceptual encoding processes (e.g., Roediger, 1990). Instantaneously, a whole generation of research depicting differences between implicit and explicit types of memory was open to reinterpretation as reflecting, instead, differences in measures that tapped perceptual and conceptual encoding processes. As of yet, no one has provided a similar reinterpretation of dissociations between implicit and explicit measures of attitudes. However, Roediger's example should serve as a cautionary tale for social psychologists' approach to studying implicit attitudes. Even if there is no overarching confound across all implicit and explicit measures of attitudes, within any pair of measures, there are bound to be significant differences beyond the extent to which they tap automatic and controlled processes. Thus, assessing automatic and controlled aspects of attitudes via task dissociations is problematic.

On Process-Purity

The more general point is that no task is process-pure. Any task that requires an observable response (e.g., a button press) cannot be entirely automatic, and no task is immune from the influence of automatic processes (e.g., Jacoby, Toth, & Yonelinas, 1993). Rather, all tasks involve an ongoing interplay among simultaneously occurring automatic and controlled processes. As such, a behavioral response, in and of itself, is incapable of specifying the nature of the underlying processes that produced the response.

Consider the Stroop Task (Stroop, 1935). A fully literate adult and a young child who knows colors but does not know how to read may make an equally small number of errors on the task. However, very different processes are at work for the adult and the child. On incompatible trials (e.g., the word *blue* written in red ink), the adult must overcome a habit to read the word in order to name the color of the ink correctly. In contrast, the child has no habit to overcome; she or he simply responds to the color of the ink.

The same principle applies to implicit measures of attitudes, many of which have a Stroop-like structure of compatible (e.g., pairing Black faces with negative words and White faces with positive words) and incompatible (e.g., pairing Black faces with positive words and White faces with negative words) trials. The performance of two people who appear to have equally strong implicit attitudes on such measures may reflect very different underlying processes. Whereas one person may have strong automatic evaluative associations that are successfully overcome in responding, the other may have weaker associations that are not overcome so well. The measure itself cannot distinguish between the two cases. The distinction is well worth making because the causes, consequences, and cures of having strong automatic associations versus weak self-regulatory abilities are very different.

An important methodological implication of this analysis is that, when taken as pure reflections of automatic associations, implicit measures underestimate the extent of cognitive control. The equally important corollary is that a strong ability to overcome automatic associations on implicit measures may mask the true extent of automatic bias (e.g., Conrey et al., 2005; Sherman et al., 2008).

The Poverty of Task Dissociation

A related drawback to the task dissociation approach is that it cannot reveal the simultaneous contributions of automatic and controlled processes to attitudinal responses. If we assume that responses on any attitude measure reflect the joint contributions of automatic and controlled processes, then it would be advantageous to have a means to track those contributions independently. However, because implicit and explicit measures are taken as self-contained, process-pure estimates of automatic and controlled processes, there is no way to assess the ongoing interplay of these processes in producing a discrete attitudinal response on a particular task. This necessarily produces an overly simplified depiction of the processes that underlie the production of attitudinal responses.

Implicit Attitudes are Constructed, Not Revealed

The preceding discussions all converge on the important point that responses on implicit measures of attitudes are just that: responses on measures. As such, there are all sorts of factors and processes that may intervene in the translation of evaluative associations into responses on implicit measures. Though the constructive nature of responses on explicit measures of attitudes has been well appreciated (e.g., Wilson & Hodges, 1992), the same has not been true for implicit measures. Because responses on implicit measures are typically viewed as inevitable and uncontrollable (e.g., Bargh, 1999; Devine, 1989), they have been portrayed as reflecting a real, true, and singular underlying representation to a much greater extent than have responses on explicit tasks (e.g., Dovidio & Fazio, 1992; Fazio et al., 1995). It is as if implicit measures crawl inside our heads and locate a treasure chest that contains the One Real Attitude, revealing the buried truth that people may be unable or unwilling to report.

However, though implicit measures are certainly less susceptible to intention and less reliant on awareness than are explicit measures, recent evidence makes clear that implicit attitudes are not the singular, stable entities they once were thought to be. For example, there is now considerable evidence that responses on implicit measures may be influenced by a variety of personal and contextual factors (e.g., Blair, 2002). Moreover, implicit measures of attitudes show poorer test-retest reliability than do explicit measures and show smaller correlations across measures of the same attitude object than do explicit measures (e.g., Cunningham, Preacher, & Banaji, 2001; Kawakami & Dovidio, 2001). These findings are hard to reconcile with the view that implicit measures directly tap singular, true attitudes. Instead, these results indicate that implicit measures are no different than all other psychological measures; there is a translational gap between the construct and the way it is measured.

There are many possible explanations for the apparently large size of this gap in implicit measures of attitudes. To be sure, random measurement error is one important contributor to the lack of reliability and convergent validity among implicit measures (e.g., Cunningham et al., 2001). The lack of convergent validity also likely reflects structural differences in the extent to which different measures tap attitudes toward particular category exemplars versus categories as a whole (e.g., Fazio & Olson, 2003; Olson & Fazio, 2003). In this case, the lack of validity does not represent the failure of two measures of the same attitude to correlate, but rather the fact that the two measures simply tap different attitudes.

However, implicit measures differ not only in the content that they tap, but also in the processes that they recruit for task completion. That is, different tasks (e.g., IAT, evaluative priming, Weapons Identification Task, or WIT; Shooter Task), and even different stimuli within a single task, recruit different processes to differing degrees. For example, implicit tasks may differ widely in the extent to which they require accurate perception of a stimulus or are susceptible to regulatory efforts at overcoming automatically activated associations (e.g., Conrey et al., 2005; Sherman et al., 2008). As such, low levels of reliability and construct validity in implicit measures reflect more than random noise in the measurement of a true, singular attitude. They also reflect more than the fact that different implicit measures may tap different singular, true attitudes. Even if random noise and activated content can be controlled, the fact remains that different measures of the exact same content will vary in the procedural demands they make on the respondent. Once again, implicit attitudes are constructed in response to the demands of the task; they are not revealed truths.

This is not meant to suggest that there is no such thing as a stable evaluation that is represented in memory. In any given case, the extent to which responses on an implicit measure are influenced by strong and stable evaluative or descriptive associations will vary (e.g., Conrey et al., 2005; Sherman et al., 2008). The point is that these underlying associations must be translated into what we call implicit attitudes via performance on some task. There are significant drawbacks to treating these task outcomes as direct reflections of automatically activated and uncontrollable associations, rather than as constructed responses that reflect the influence of multiple component processes. These drawbacks are particularly consequential when implicit and explicit measures are compared for the purpose of drawing conclusions about the automatic versus controlled nature of attitudes. As summarized above, this approach increases the risk of misinterpreting task confounds, increases the risk of misrepresenting the extent of automatic and controlled influences on an attitude, and thwarts the identification of joint, ongoing automatic and controlled processes.

Process Dissociation

These same concerns about task dissociation paradigms in the implicit memory literature led Jacoby (1991; Lindsay & Jacoby, 1994; see Jacoby, Kelley, & McElree, 1999, for a review) to develop process dissociation (PD) techniques for separating the automatic and controlled components of behavior from performance on a single task. The PD approach assumes that no measure is process-pure, and that automatic and controlled processes exert independent and simultaneous influences on any task. Because estimates of the two components are derived from behavior on a single task, PD techniques avoid confounding task and process.

Initially, Jacoby and his colleagues developed two different models of process dissociation (Jacoby, 1991; Lindsay & Jacoby, 1994). Both models rely on the method of opposition, which contrasts performance on compatible trials, on which a controlled process and an automatic process should lead to the same response, with performance on incompatible trials, on which the two processes should lead to different responses. Estimates of automatic and controlled processing are derived by subtracting performance on the incompatible trials from performance on the compatible trials. The primary difference between the two models is whether automatic or controlled processes are assumed to be primary.

The Control Default Model

One model is designed to account for tasks in which automatic processes are thought to influence behavior only when control fails (Jacoby, 1991). For example, in recognition memory, Jacoby proposed that controlled, effortful recollective processes will determine judgments whenever possible. Only when controlled recollection fails to provide a response will automatically generated perceptions of an item's familiarity drive recognition judgments. Estimates of the contributions of recollection (control) and familiarity (automaticity) are derived by comparing trials in which the two processes produce the same recognition judgment with trials in which the two processes lead to different recognition judgments (e.g., an item that is familiar but was not presented as part of the to-be-remembered list). This model of process dissociation is frequently applied to separating the automatic and controlled components of interracial attitudes and behavior on Weapons Identification Tasks (e.g., Amodio, Harmon-Jones, Devine, Curtin, Hartley, & Covert, 2004; Lambert, Payne, Jacoby, Shaffer, Chasteen, & Khan, 2003; Payne, 2001; Payne, Lambert, & Jacoby, 2002; Plant, Peruche, & Butz, 2005).

The primary limitation of this model is that it permits no role for automatic processes that influence behavior even though the correct response can be determined. Thus, this model is not well suited to implicit measures of attitude, such as evaluative priming or the IAT, or for the Stroop Task, in which most people can determine the correct response easily, but an automatic association or habit nevertheless interferes with that response (for a more thorough discussion, see Conrey et al., 2005; Sherman, 2006; Sherman et al., 2008).

As such, when applying this model, researchers should understand clearly exactly what type of automaticity and what type of control the model estimates, and should interpret their results accordingly. The automatic component estimated in this model represents an automatic process that influences responses only when control has already failed (i.e., on a Weapons Identification Task, the automatic component of stereotypes will influence responses only when participants are unable to discern whether a presented object is a gun or a tool). In contrast, most research on automatic attitudes and beliefs seeks to understand the extent to which these constructs are automatically activated in the first place and influence perception and behavior, regardless of the status of control. The controlled component in this model represents control as reflected in the effort expended to accurately identify the nature of a stimulus or situation (e.g., "Is it a gun?"). Thus, control in this model does not represent the type of self-regulatory control that seeks to overcome the influence of unwanted automatic processes.

The Automatic Default model The other original PD model (Lindsay & Jacoby, 1994) is designed to account for tasks in which automatic processes are thought to influence behavior, regardless of whether or not control succeeds. In these tasks, controlled processes drive responses only in the absence of automatic bias. Thus, the model proposes that, in the Stroop Task, if present, an automatic habit to read the word will determine responses. Only in the absence of such a habit will the controlled process of determining the color drive responses. Estimates of the contributions of color perception (control) and reading habit (automaticity) are derived by comparing trials in which the two processes produce the same response (e.g., the word *blue* written in blue ink) with trials in which the two processes would lead to different responses (e.g., the word *blue* written in red ink). This model of process dissociation would appear to be well suited for Stroop-like implicit measures of attitude, such as evaluative priming and the IAT, in which automatic associations influence behavior, regardless of whether or not control succeeds.

The primary limitation of this model is that it does not distinguish between cases in which an automatic association is not activated at all from cases in which the association is activated but is overcome. On the Stroop Task, people provide correct responses on most trials despite the fact that they have an automatic habit to read the word. In these cases, the habit is overcome. In contrast, as described above, a child who cannot read will make few errors simply because he or she has no reading habit to overcome in the first place. This PD model cannot distinguish between these two cases. Likewise, on implicit measures of attitude, the model cannot distinguish between a person who is able to overcome a strong automatic bias and a person who has no bias in the first place (for a more thorough discussion, see Conrey et al., 2005; Sherman et al., 2008).

Again, researchers should be careful to interpret the meaning of the automatic and controlled estimates derived from this model appropriately. In this case, the automatic estimate reflects the extent to which a construct or habit is automatically activated. The controlled estimate reflects the same type of control as in the Control Default model—control exerted to accurately identify a stimulus or situation. Thus, this model also does not estimate control that works to overcome the influence of the automatic process. As described above, this model does not permit automatic biases to be overcome; if the bias is activated, it will drive responses.

The Quad Model

We developed the Quad model (Conrey et al., 2005; Sherman et al., 2008) to address some of the limitations of other PD models, and to provide a more comprehensive analysis of the automatic and controlled components of behavior. The Quad model relies on the method of opposition articulated by the PD approach, and owes a substantial intellectual debt to Jacoby and his colleagues. Like other PD models, the Quad model seeks to separate multiple processing components from performance on a single task. However, the Quad model also differs in important ways from those models.*

Most obviously, whereas original PD analyses produce single estimates of automatic and controlled processing, we believe it is critical to distinguish between two distinct automatic processes and two distinct controlled processes.† In our view, each of these processes represents a ubiquitous and fundamental component of behavior. Indeed, the four processes identified by the Quad model appear repeatedly across a wide spectrum of dual-process models of social psychology (e.g., Chaiken & Trope, 1999; Sherman, in 2008). Of course, by definition, all four processes never appear within any particular dual-process model. Thus, although the shared aim of dual-process models is to assess the extent to which a given judgment reflects relatively automatic or controlled processing, the particular types of automaticity and control of interest vary across models.

Two Types of Control

Dual-process models have generally been concerned with one of two different types of control. In some models, control is characterized by stimulus detection processes that attempt to provide an accurate depiction of the environment. For example, in dual-process models of persuasion, the controlled process discriminates between strong and weak arguments (e.g., Chaiken, 1980; Petty & Cacioppo, 1981; Fazio, 1990). In models of impression formation, the controlled process attends to and integrates target behaviors, providing an individuated (and, presumably, relatively accurate) impression of the person (e.g., Brewer, 1988; Fiske & Neuberg, 1990). This is the type of control represented in Jacoby's PD models.

However, in other dual-process models, control is characterized by self-regulatory processes that attempt to inhibit unwanted or inappropriate information. For example, in Devine's (1989) model of stereotyping, control must be exerted to overcome the automatic influence of stereotypes. In Wegner's (1994) model of thought suppression, control

---

* See Sherman (2008) for a discussion of the conditions under which two-component PD models and the Quad model may be applied most appropriately.

† Recently, Jacoby and his colleagues (e.g., Jacoby, Bishara, Hessels, & Toth, 2005) have proposed a new PD model that incorporates the two types of automatic processes represented in the Quad model. However, the model does not provide roles for both of the controlled processes estimated by the Quad model and, as a result, cannot separate strength of activation from ability to overcome activation.

must be exerted to inhibit unwanted thoughts. In many models of social judgment, self-regulatory control is exerted when people try to correct their judgments for subjectively expected biases (e.g., Martin, 1986; Wegener & Petty, 1997).

Both detection and regulation processes are controlled processes in that they require intention and cognitive resources, and can be terminated at will (e.g., Bargh, 1994). However, they are very different types of control, and it is clear that, on many occasions, they operate independently and simultaneously. For example, a police officer's decision whether or not to shoot a Black man who may or may not have a gun may depend both on his ability to discriminate whether or not the man has a gun and, when there is no gun, on his ability to overcome an automatic bias to associate Black men with guns and to shoot. Thus, we believe there is much to be gained by distinguishing between these types of control and measuring their contributions to behavior independently.

Two Types of Automaticity

Dual-process models also have generally been concerned with one of two different types of automaticity. Most commonly, automaticity is represented as simple associations that are triggered by the environment without the perceiver's awareness or intent. Stereotypes play this role in dual-process models of impression formation (e.g., Brewer, 1988; Fiske & Neuberg, 1990). In models of persuasion (e.g., Chaiken, 1980; Petty & Cacioppo, 1981) and judgment (e.g., Epstein, 1991; Sloman, 1996), heuristics function in much the same way. This is the kind of automaticity that implicit measures of attitudes and stereotypes are meant to assess (e.g., Devine, 1989; Fazio et al., 1995; Greenwald et al., 1998).

In other dual-process models, however, automatic processes influence behavior only when control fails. Jacoby's (1991) depiction of the role of familiarity in recognition memory is a prominent example of this type of process. Others have portrayed automatic processes in Weapons Identification and Shooter Tasks in this manner (e.g., Amodio et al., 2004; Lambert et al., 2003; Payne, 2001; Payne et al., 2002; Plant et al., 2005). Another example is the implicit preference shown for items on the right side of a display when conscious introspection provides no rational basis for preference (Nisbett & Wilson, 1977).

Though both types of automatic processes may operate without intention, awareness, or the use of cognitive resources, clearly they are different kinds of processes. It also is clear that they frequently operate simultaneously. For example, a police officer's decision to shoot might be influenced by automatically activated associations between Black men and aggression. In the absence of such associations, however, the officer's decision still might be influenced by a secondary automatic bias to presume danger in the absence of clear evidence to the contrary, and guess that the person is holding a gun. We believe it is important to distinguish between these types of automatic processes and to measure their contributions to behavior independently.

How the Quad Model Works

The Quad model (Conrey et al., 2005; Sherman et al., 2008) is a multinomial model (see Batchelder & Riefer, 1999) designed to estimate the independent contributions of each of the four components described above to a given behavior. More formally, the four components of the model are the automatic activation of an association (*Association ACtivation*, AC), the ability to determine correct and incorrect responses (*Detection*, D), the success at overcoming automatically activated associations, when necessary (*Overcoming Bias*, OB), and the influence of a general response bias that might guide responses in the absence of other available guides to response (*Guessing*, G). Whereas AC and G are automatic processes (though G need not be), D and OB are controlled processes.

The structure of the Quad model is depicted as a processing tree in Figure 13.1. In the tree, each path represents a likelihood. Processing parameters with lines leading to them are conditional upon all preceding parameters. For instance, overcoming bias is conditional upon both association activation and detection. Similarly, guessing is conditional upon the lack of association activation (1-AC) and the lack of detection (1-D). Note that these conditional relationships do not imply a serial order in the onset and conclusion of the different processes. Rather, these relationships are mathematical descriptions of the manner in which the parameters interact to produce behavior. Thus, attempts to detect a correct response and attempts to overcome automatic biases may occur simultaneously. However, in determining a response on a trial of a given task, the influence of attempts to overcome bias will be seen only in cases in which detection is successful.

The conditional relationships described by the model form a system of equations that predict the number of correct and incorrect responses in different conditions. The model's predictions are then compared with actual data to determine the model's ability to account for participants' behavior. A χ^2-estimate is computed for the difference between the predicted and observed errors. In order to best approximate the model to

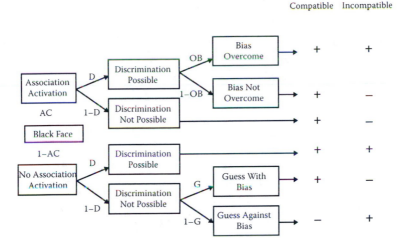

FIGURE 13.1 The Quadruple Process Model (Quad Model). Each path represents a likelihood. Parameters with lines leading to them are conditional upon all preceding parameters. The table on the right side of the figure depicts correct (+) and incorrect (−) responses as a function of process pattern and trial type.

the data, the four parameter values are adjusted through maximum likelihood estimation until they produce a minimum possible value of χ^2. The final parameter values that result from this process are interpreted as relative levels of the four processes. For a complete description of data analysis within the Quad model, see Conrey et al. (2005).

An Example and Range of Application

As an example of how the model works, consider performance on a standard Black-White/positive-negative IAT (Greenwald et al., 1998). The presentation of a Black face may automatically activate negative associations, predisposing the participant to press the *negative* button. Depending on whether the trial is part of a compatible (Black/bad and White/good) or incompatible (Black/good and White/bad) block, this automatic bias will be either congruent or incongruent with the correct answer *Black* achieved through detection. On compatible trials, there is no conflict between what is automatically activated and what is detected. As such, there is no need to overcome the bias in order to produce the correct response. However, on incompatible trials, AC and D generate conflicting responses. Which of these two processes ultimately directs the outcome is determined by whether or not the participant succeeds in overcoming his or her bias. Finally, if no association is activated and the correct response cannot be ascertained, then participants must guess. Guessing need not be random and may, for example, reflect a bias to respond with the positive key when all else fails (Conrey et al., 2005).

The Quad model may be used to analyze data from any measure that compares compatible and incompatible trials, in which automatic and controlled processes are placed in concert with, and in opposition to, one another. Though I have used the IAT as an example, the logic is the same with any implicit measure that compares compatible and incompatible trials, including Stroop Tasks (Kawakami, Dovidio, Moll, Hermsen, & Russin, 2000), evaluative priming tasks (e.g., Fazio et al., 1995), the Weapons Identification Task (e.g., Payne, 2001), the Shooter Task (e.g., Correll, Park, Judd, & Wittenbrink, 2002), and the Go/No-Go Association Task (Nosek & Banaji, 2001). Though the model also may be applied in the same way to explicit measures, we have focused, thus far, on applications to implicit measures. Because of their oft-reputed property of being pure measures of automatic activation, implicit measures are particularly interesting contexts in which to examine the independent contributions of multiple automatic and controlled processes. In contrast, most everyone would probably agree that explicit measures reflect the influence of both automatic and controlled processes.

Results. The viability of a mutinomial model depends on four critical elements: model fit (Can the model adequately approximate the behavioral data?), parameter independence (Can the model's parameters be influenced independently?), construct validity of the parameters (Do the parameters signify the processes claimed by the model?), and predictive validity of the parameters (Do the parameters predict meaningful behaviors?). Without going into great detail, the Quad model has succeeded on all elements (for a full description, see Sherman et al., 2008).

The model has shown its ability to accurately predict performance on a variety of priming tasks, IATs, and the GNAT, demonstrating good model fit for these tasks (Conrey et al., 2005; Sherman et al., 2008). The parameters also have been shown to vary independently of one another. For example, implementing a response deadline in an IAT reduced D and OB, but left AC and G unaffected. Manipulating the base rate of left-hand versus right-hand responses in the same task affected G, but none of the other three parameters (AC, D, OB). The expectation that one's performance on the weapon identification task (Lambert et al., 2003) would be observed by others decreased participants' ability to accurately detect the stimuli (D), but increased success at overcoming bias (OB). These results indicate that the four parameters of the Quad model can vary independently (for a review, see Sherman et al., 2008).

The construct validity of the model parameters has also been established by a number of findings (Conrey et al., 2005; Sherman et al., 2008). The fact that D and OB were reduced by a response deadline supports the claim that the two parameters reflect controlled processes that require cognitive capacity. In contrast, the finding that AC and G were unaffected by the response deadline is consistent with their depiction as relatively automatic processes that do not require significant cognitive capacity. The validity of OB as a measure of self-regulation was further established by demonstrations that it is impaired by alcohol consumption and decreases with age, two factors associated with impairments in self-regulation. The fact that altering the base rate of left-hand and right-hand responses influenced G corroborates the portrayal of that parameter as a general response bias. Finally, a neuroimaging study of performance on an IAT (Beer et al., 2008) showed that AC was correlated with activity in the amygdala and insula, which are involved in emotional processing and arousal. This finding is consistent with the depiction of AC as measuring evaluative associations in such a task. At the same time, D was associated with activation in both the dorsal anterior cingulate cortex and the dorsolateral prefrontal cortex, areas of the brain associated with detecting the need for control and implementing control, respectively. This is consistent with the Quad model's depiction of D as a controlled process that selects appropriate behavior and feeds into efforts to overcome inappropriate automatic influences. Altogether, there are now considerable behavioral and neuroscientific data indicating that the Quad model's parameters reflect the processes that they are intended to assess (see Sherman et al., 2008 for a full review).

Finally, two studies provide evidence for the predictive validity of the parameters. First, estimates of individual subjects' AC parameters derived from an IAT were positively correlated with reaction time impairment in the same task (Conrey et al., 2005). Thus, the higher the AC, the greater the association-based impairment in performance. At the same time, estimates of OB were negatively correlated with reaction time impairment. Thus, the higher the OB, the better able were participants to avoid association-based impairments in performance.

In another study (Gonsalkorale, von Hippel, & Sherman, 2008), a Muslim confederate's ratings of how much he liked interaction partners were predicted by an interaction between AC and OB, derived from participants' GNAT performance. Specifically, when participants had low AC estimates of negative associations with Muslims, their level of OB was unrelated to how much they were liked by the confederate. In contrast, participants with high AC estimates of negative associations with Muslims were liked to the extent that they had high OB parameter estimates. Thus, the ability to overcome automatic negative associations on the GNAT predicted the quality of the social interaction when those associations were strong.

Summary

In this section, I have argued that implicit measures should not be taken as direct reflections of the automatic activation of associations in memory. Furthermore, contrasting performance on implicit and explicit measures as a means to estimate automatic and controlled aspects of attitudes is problematic in many ways. Instead, I recommend the use of process dissociation techniques that permit the independent estimation of automatic and controlled components of processing within a single measure of attitude. The Quad model is particularly useful in this regard, as it permits the assessment of multiple automatic and controlled processes that have been shown to be important in many domains of social psychology.

Controlled Influences on Implicit Measures

Perhaps the most controversial claim of the process dissociation approach for implicit attitude researchers is that responses on implicit measures are influenced by controlled processes. Certainly, this view is inconsistent with the common portrayal of implicit measure performance as wholly unintentional, resource-independent, and uncontrollable (e.g., Bargh, 1999; Devine, 1989; Fazio et al., 1995; Greenwald et al., 1998; Kim, 2003). Bargh offered a particularly spirited challenge to the view that implicit attitudes and stereotypes could be controlled. In his entertaining and thought-provoking chapter, he compared these implicit concepts to "cognitive monsters" that social psychologists were desperate to prove could be controlled. In turn, he depicted claims on this controllability as well-meaning but, ultimately, fictional tales. The two central claims of his argument were that (a) the initial activation of implicit attitudes and stereotypes could not be altered through conscious intent, and that (b), once activated, the use of these concepts could not be inhibited deliberately.

Though the limited data available at the time were vulnerable to skepticism, the intervening years have yielded growing evidence that the fable of the cognitive monster can have a happier ending than Bargh (1999) deemed likely. Still, under careful scrutiny, some aspects of the case for controllability remain fragile, and the cognitive monster is not yet completely subdued. An examination of this literature through the lens of the Quad model helps to clarify which aspects of controllability do and do not have strong empirical support. First, I will discuss conceptual reasons to believe that the extent of controllability has been underestimated. I also will discuss problems in distinguishing between controlling the initial activation versus application of automatic associations. Then, I will review the empirical evidence for controllability. In so doing, I will consider both indirect evidence gleaned from studies on the malleability of implicit attitudes as well as more direct evidence of controllability.

Reasons for the Underestimation of Controllability

For a number of reasons, the extent of control over implicit attitudes has probably been underestimated. Most basically, there is the almost universal view that, by definition, responses on implicit measures cannot be controlled. Given this stance, it is not surprising that researchers have been reluctant to attribute fluctuations in implicit attitudes to the influence of controlled processes. Again, this view may be contrasted with that of the process dissociation approach, which assumes that all measures, including implicit ones, are influenced by both automatic and controlled processes.

Another factor in the underestimation of controllability is the standard treatment of stimulus onset asynchronies (SOAs) and reaction-time data. In priming studies, the SOA is the amount of time that elapses between the onset of a prime and the appearance of the target. Neely (1977) first reported that at SOAs shorter than 500 ms, priming effects occurred, regardless of participants' intentions to respond otherwise. This formed the basis for what has since become the standard view that control is not possible with short SOAs. However, there are two significant problems with this assumption. First, it is not only the SOA, but also the time taken to respond to the target that influences the extent of controllability. This is easily demonstrated with a simple thought experiment. Imagine that a face is presented as a prime for 200 ms and, after a brief pause of 200 ms, a positive word is presented, to which participants must respond by pressing a positive key on their computers. That would be a 400-ms SOA and, in the eyes of many, would, therefore, be uncontrollable. But imagine that a participant sits there looking at the positive word, thinking about her response for 1, 2, 3, 10 seconds. After 10 seconds, she finally presses the key. Is this an automatic response? Certainly not. Thus, a brief SOA does not guarantee that a participant will not sit there consciously pondering the nature of her response long past the time at which it could reasonably be considered to be "automatic."

There are many findings in the implicit attitudes and stereotyping literature that are interpreted as reflecting automatic bias on the basis of brief SOAs, even though the subsequent target reaction times may be as long as 1000 ms or more. A 500-ms SOA plus a 1000-ms reaction time represents a response that has taken place a full second and a half after the initial presentation of the prime. Even an SOA of 200 ms plus a 500-ms reaction time likely leaves more room for control than has been acknowledged. The point is that a brief SOA is no guarantee of uncontrollability, and we do not have careful metrics of what SOA/reaction-time combinations do and do not permit control on different tasks. This lack of neat boundaries between automatic and controlled SOAs/reaction times is yet another incentive to apply process dissociation techniques to identify the automatic and controlled components of implicit task performance.

The second problem with this treatment of SOAs and reaction times is that there are now a number of documented cases where control appears to be present at very brief SOAs (e.g., Blair & Banaji, 1996; Devine, Plant, Amodio, Harmon-Jones, & Vance, 2002; Glaser & Banaji, 1999; Kawakami et al., 2000; Maddux, Barden, Brewer, & Petty, 2005; Moskowitz, Gollwitzer, Wasel, & Schall, 1999). There are two possible interpretations of such findings. One is that participants engage in *automatic control* or *automatic inhibition*. Though inhibition can surely be routinized to the point of automaticity, this explanation raises the specter of circularity. That is, if control is, by definition, not possible at brief SOAs, then these effects must be attributed to automated control. The second interpretation—that participants are actually able to apply control in these situations—has rarely been invoked.

Another reason for the underestimation of control concerns the role of awareness in implementing controlled processes. It is generally assumed that biases may be controlled only if a person is consciously aware both that control is necessary and of how to correct for the bias (e.g., Bargh, 1999; Strack, 1992; Tesser & Martin, 1996; Wegener &

Petty, 1997). The lack of either or both kinds of awareness is one of the central bases for the designation of implicit measures as implicit (e.g., Fazio et al., 1995; Greenwald et al., 1998; see this volume) and one of the key sources for the conclusion that responses on these measures cannot be controlled.* However, the process dissociation perspective views the role of awareness differently. For example, both of Jacoby's models and the Quad model propose that one type of controlled process, stimulus detection, plays a role in all responses on implicit measures, regardless of whether participants are intentionally trying to correct a perceived bias. Factors that influence these detection processes, such as a speeded judgment task or an enhanced motive to perform a task accurately, affect implicit task performance even if participants are not aware of implicit bias or how to control it. There are now many process dissociation results demonstrating such effects on controlled components of implicit responses (see below; Conrey et al., 2005; Lambert et al., 2003; Payne, 2001; Payne et al., 2002; Plant et al., 2005).

The Quad model proposes that overcoming the influence of automatic associations is an additional controlled process that regularly occurs during implicit task performance. This process does not depend on conscious awareness that overcoming bias is necessary or on applying a conscious strategy to overcome such bias. Rather, overcoming bias may occur whenever there is a conflict between responses suggested by automatic associations and stimulus detection, even if there is no awareness of the bias or of a strategy for countering it. Thus, on a priming task, a Black face may activate negative content and push responses in that direction. When a positive target word appears, participants must overcome the influence of the prime to respond correctly to the target. However, they need not be consciously aware that the prime is affecting their responses or that the prime is related in any way to the target. Indeed, overcoming the influence of an entirely subliminal prime should proceed in much the same way. All participants need to know is that they would like to provide a particular response on the task. The fact that that response happens to be incompatible with a prime engages overcoming bias processes. These processes are controlled in that they require time and resources, and may be influenced by intention (Conrey et al., 2005). Thus, from the process dissociation perspective, the

---

* Some researchers have argued that people generally are aware of their implicit biases (e.g., Fazio & Olson, 2003; Monteith et al., 2001). However, even when this is true, people are not typically aware of how that bias influences responses on implicit measures and cannot formulate conscious strategies to counteract it (e.g., Kim, 2003).

stipulation that control requires awareness has led to an underestimation of the extent of control.

Controlled Activation Versus Application

A key distinction in considering the controllability question is the extent to which control is exerted over the initial automatic activation of underlying associations versus the application of already-activated associations (e.g., Bargh; 1999; Brauer, Wasel, & Niedenthal, 2000). The common view that implicit measures provide a direct, uncontaminated picture of the information that is automatically activated in memory complicates assessments of this distinction. Namely, this view dictates that any evidence of controlled influences on implicit task performance must be taken as a reflection that the initial activation of associations can be controlled (e.g., Blair, Ma, & Lenton, 2001; Govan & Williams, 2004; Kawakami et al., 2000; Lepore & Brown, 1997; Maddux et al., 2005; Moskowitz et al., 1999; Lowery, Hardin, & Sinclair, 2001). The possibility that variations in implicit task performance might be due to controlled processes that alter the expression of the same activated content is, generally, not considered. As a result, research on implicit attitudes has likely overestimated the ease with which people can intentionally alter their underlying associations and underestimated the extent to which these automatically activated associations can be controlled, once activated.

Viewed from the perspective of the Quad model, demonstrations of controlled influences on implicit measures may reflect control of activation, application, both, or neither. Specifically, according to the Quad model, attempts at control may change the underlying associations that are automatically activated, the ability to accurately detect and represent the environment, the ability to overcome activated associations, or the nature of response biases. In the case of D and G, implicit task performance may be altered even if there are no associations automatically activated in the first place (see Figure 13.1). Of course, one of the most significant advantages of the Quad model is that these different effects of control need not be exclusive. All four components may be influenced by attempted control, and the Quad model is able to identify each of these independent effects from performance on a single implicit measure.

Evidence for Controllability: Implicit Attitude Malleability

The preceding discussions suggest that control influences implicit attitudes to a greater extent than has been recognized. What evidence is there to support this claim? One potential source is the now extensive body of research showing that various experimental, contextual, motivational, and personal factors can alter the nature of responses on implicit measures. Indeed, these findings have been regarded as a challenge to the view that implicit attitudes cannot be controlled (e.g., Blair, 2002). However, there are two key questions to consider in evaluating these findings. First, when such effects are observed, does control play any role at all? There is an important distinction between showing that implicit task performance is malleable and showing that it is controllable. The fact that the identical implicit attitude is not inevitably produced on a measure, regardless of variations in stimuli, context, motives, or individual differences, does not necessarily invoke the presence of control. For example, these variations may passively alter the accessibility of different contents in memory, regardless of any exertion of intent or control. Second, if control is involved, at what stage is it exerted? Is it exerted over the initial automatic activation of associations or is it exerted over the application of those associations in responding to the implicit task demands?

The extent to which the malleability findings answer these questions is obscured by the common position that, by definition, implicit measures reflect only the automatic activation of content from memory, and they cannot be controlled. As detailed above, this view has likely led to a general underestimation of the role of control and an overemphasis on the control of activation versus application of automatic associations. Deciphering the role of control in these findings also is difficult because the same behavioral outcome may be explained by a variety of different underlying processes, some of which are controlled, and some of which are automatic. For example, fluctuations in implicit attitudes may reflect fluctuations in any of the four underlying processes in the Quad model. A major advantage of the process dissociation approach is that it can separate these components and specify their independent contributions. However, with only the behavioral data to consider, what follows necessarily will be largely speculative.

Stimulus feature effects. In some cases, controlled processes would seem to play a modest role, at best. For example, contextual variations in stimulus features (e.g., Barden, Maddux, Petty, & Brewer, 2004; Wittenbrink, Judd, & Park, 1997) may influence performance on implicit tasks by altering the associations that are automatically activated without affecting controlled processes at all. In this case, variations in implicit task performance would reflect the simple fact that different stimuli activate different associations in memory. As such, these data may not imply that a given attitude is either malleable (i.e., the data do not show that a given attitude is changed but that different attitudes are activated) or controllable. Such demonstrations of contextual variation in implicit activations are certainly important for understanding the nature of category representation and the specificity of automatic processes. However, it is not clear that they have much to do with the debate on controllability.

Accessibility and context effects. Controlled processes may play a larger role in other demonstrations of fluctuations in implicit measures. For example, variations in accessible category exemplars (Dasgupta & Greenwald, 2001; Govan & Williams, 2004), accessible category features (e.g., Blair et al., 2001; Livingston & Brewer, 2002), situational contexts (Lowery et al., 2001; Richeson & Ambady, 2003; Richeson & Nussbaum, 2004; Rudman, Ashmore, & Gary, 2001; Sechrist & Stangor, 2001), or situationally induced motives (e.g., Sinclair & Kunda, 1999) may influence implicit measures by enhancing efforts at controlling what associations are activated in memory, efforts to perform the task more accurately, efforts to overcome associations, or guessing biases. However, it also is possible that these effects are driven entirely by passive changes in the associations that are activated by the different conditions, without the intervention of control at all. If so, then these effects would, again, represent the contextual specificity of association activation rather than the malleability or controllability of a given attitude. Indeed, these findings have most commonly been interpreted as reflecting unintended changes in activation (e.g., Dasgupta & Greenwald; Govan & Williams; Livingston & Brewer; Lowery et al.; Rudman et al.). As described below, we have preliminary evidence that this is, in fact, the case (Sherman et al., 2008).

Individual differences. Another potential source of evidence for controllability are the numerous studies demonstrating individual differences in implicit attitudes (e.g., Devine et al., 2002; Maddux et al., 2005; Moskowitz et al, 1999). The favored explanation for such differences is that people who are properly motivated and, therefore, practiced at overcoming unwanted biases may automate the process to the extent that they can control their responses even on implicit measures. However, though the development of such expertise is clearly one way to gain control over implicit biases, interpreting such individual differences can be difficult. In particular, it often is difficult to rule out the possibility that people who show less bias on implicit measures do so, not because they are efficient at regulation, but because they simply have weaker or different associations to regulate in the first place (e.g., Conrey et al.,

2005; Lepore & Brown, 1997; Sherman et al., 2008). Even person X situation interactions may be interpreted as showing that in different contexts, different associations are accessible for different people. Simply put, it is difficult to distinguish differential activation from differential inhibition (for other examples, see Sinclair & Kunda, 1999; Kawakami et al., 2000). This suggests that the role of controlled processes in these individual differences may be smaller than has been proposed.

At the same time, other considerations and findings suggest that the role of control may have been underestimated in explaining these individual differences. First, as described above, what is typically described as automatic control may, in fact, be standard control (e.g., is subject to intention, resources, etc.). The designation of this control as automatic is based almost entirely on the a priori assumption that control is simply not possible on implicit measures. From the perspective of the Quad model, an increased ability among some individuals to overcome bias need not represent an automatic process (e.g., automatic inhibition), per se. That is, skill at overcoming bias may be enhanced even though the process retains features of a controlled process (e.g., influenced by intent, resource availability, etc.).

Research by Amodio and his colleagues indicates that individual differences in implicit biases may have more to do with controlled conflict detection processes than with either automatic activation or inhibition processes (see below; Amodio, Devine, & Harmon-Jones, 2008; Amodio et al., 2004; Sherman et al., 2008). In particular, these studies have provided evidence that what sets apart people who show weaker or no implicit bias is neither the strength of their automatic associations (but see Sherman et al., 2008) nor their ability to overcome those associations. Rather, their particular skill appears to lie in their increased sensitivity to detecting conflict among behavioral impulses (e.g., conflicts between automatically activated associations and controlled determinations of accurate responses). Detecting such conflict is itself a controlled process, and superior detection skills may facilitate the application of other self-regulatory controlled processes that help to overcome intrusive biases that thwart desired (or task-accurate) responses (see below; Monteith, Ashburn-Nardo, Voils, & Czopp, 2002).

Summary. In summary, these demonstrations of implicit attitude malleability certainly refute any claim that the exact same implicit attitude will be educed inevitably by all stimuli, for all people, and in all contexts. Much less clear is the extent to which these findings represent a significant challenge to the claim of Bargh (1999) and others that implicit attitudes cannot be controlled. Due, in part, to the standard conceptions of implicit measures, few researchers have interpreted their results as demonstrating controlled processes. Instead, the results primarily have been interpreted as reflecting either changes in the content that is automatically activated or the application of automatized control. Initial attempts to address these questions with the Quad model suggest that both automatic and controlled processes are involved in these effects.

One way to better understand the bases of these different malleability effects is through the application of process dissociation techniques. In our own research, we have attempted to do so by examining changes in the Quad model parameters that correspond to changes in implicit task performance (i.e., implicit attitudes). Thus, we are directly measuring the extent to which a change in the behavioral measure is related to changes in the activation of different associations, changes in participants' ability to detect correct and incorrect responses, changes in overcoming associations, or changes in response biases.

As one example, we have applied the Quad model to examine the effects of altering the accessibility of category exemplars on implicit bias (Sherman et al., 2008). Replicating past research, participants exposed to positive Black and negative White exemplars showed weaker implicit pro-White bias than participants who were shown positive White and negative Black exemplars. Our modeling results suggest that this effect is because different associations are activated in the pro-Black condition than in the pro-White condition. Thus, exposure to different exemplars alters the nature of the associations that are automatically brought to mind in performing the IAT, but not participants' ability to detect correct responses or overcome bias. Other applications of the Quad model to questions of malleability are ongoing, including research aimed at understanding the bases of individual differences in implicit attitudes (Sherman et al., 2008).

Direct Evidence of Control

Process Dissociation Findings

More direct evidence of controlled influences on implicit attitudes comes from a variety of sources. First, there is the accumulating body of evidence from process dissociation analyses. Researchers applying Jacoby's models have reported a number of contributions of the controlled component to responses on implicit measures. The tasks that have produced such effects include Payne's Weapons Identification Task (e.g., Amodio et al., 2004; Lambert et al., 2003; Payne, 2001; Payne et al., 2002) and the Shooter Task (Plant et al., 2005). These findings have shown not only that PD can be applied to such tasks but also that the controlled component of PD within these tasks responds in predictable ways. For example, factors that diminish the opportunity for controlled processing, such as rapid responding (e.g., Payne, 2001; Payne et al., 2002) or social distraction (e.g., Lambert et al., 2003), have been shown to diminish the PD estimates of control, whereas factors that should enhance control, such as extensive practice (e.g., Plant et al., 2005), have been shown to increase the PD estimate of control.

Application of the Quad model (Conrey et al., 2005) has further shown that multiple controlled processes contribute to implicit task performance. Both stimulus detection and overcoming bias have been shown to play a role in the IAT, the GNAT, the WIT, and other priming tasks (Conrey et al., 2005; Sherman et al., 2008). These studies also have shown that the controlled components of the Quad model respond to manipulations in predicted ways. Thus, both D and OB are reduced by a short response window. In contrast, the expectation of an audience diminishes D but enhances OB. Finally, OB is reduced both by aging and alcohol consumption.

Detection and Overcoming Bias also have demonstrated meaningful predictive validity. In the IAT, the extent of OB was negatively correlated with the strength of the reaction time bias, suggesting the role of overcoming automatic associations in the extent of that bias. In our Muslim interaction study (Gonsalkorale et al., 2008), OB (from a GNAT) interacted with automatic associations to influence a confederate's impressions of participants. When participants had weak associations, OB was unrelated to the confederate's impressions. In contrast, participants with strongly biased associations were liked to the extent that they had high OB parameter estimates. Thus, the ability to overcome automatic negative associations predicted impressions when those associations were strong.

The role of D in reducing implicit prejudice has been demonstrated recently by examining a group of people that Devine and her colleagues have identified as better able to respond without bias on implicit measures of prejudice (Devine et al., 2002). These "good regulators" have been distinguished from "poor regulators" (who wish to be non-prejudiced, but fail to achieve that goal on implicit measures) and "non-regulators" (who are not concerned about responding in prejudiced ways). Good regulators have been defined as those who are high on Internal Motivation to Respond Without Prejudice (IMS) but low on External

Motivation to Respond Without Prejudice (EMS; see Devine et al., 2002 for further details). Poor regulators are high on both IMS and EMS. Non-regulators are those who are low on IMS and, thus, have no internal motivation to be non-prejudiced. What accounts for the differences among these groups? One possibility is that they differ in the nature of their automatic associations (AC), with good regulators possessing less biased associations than the other groups. Another possibility is that good regulators are better at determining correct and incorrect responses (D) than the other groups. Finally, a third possibility is that good regulators, as their name would suggest, are better at overcoming their biases (OB) than the other groups. The Quad model provides a means for distinguishing among these accounts, and we (Sherman et al., 2008) applied the model to data collected from a WIT (Amodio et al., 2008). There were two major findings. First, we found that both good and poor regulators had less biased automatic associations than non-regulators. Second, we found that the key factor separating the good and poor regulators was the detection parameter (D), and not the underlying associations (AC) or the ability to overcome them (OB).

Further Evidence for an Implicit Task Cognitive Skill

Other evidence also indicates that general cognitive abilities may underlie performance on implicit measures. In particular, McFarland and Crouch (2002) reported high within-participant correlations on a wide range of IATs. Thus, participants who showed strong or weak bias on one kind of IAT (e.g., having to do with race) tended to show a similar strength of bias on other IATs (e.g., having to do with taste).* These data cannot be explained in terms of the strength of the underlying associations, but rather must be due to differing levels of skill at meeting the task demands of the IAT (e.g., resolving incompatible influences on response). It also seems unlikely that these skilled individuals have automatized control in each of the different content domains tested in the research. Instead, it would appear that some individuals are simply better able to implement control in performing the task.

---

* Though the extent of these correlations was reduced by the application of a different scoring procedure, they were not eliminated (Cai, Sriram, Greenwald, & McFarland, 2004).

Intentional Regulation

Other research has demonstrated that conscious intentions to avoid bias can be effective. Kawakami et al. (2000) showed that, after hundreds of trials of intentionally negating stereotypes, participants showed weaker automatic stereotyping effects. We (Sherman et al., 2008) performed a similar training study and examined the effects on IAT performance. Replicating Kawakami et al. (2000), we found that negation training reduced implicit bias. Application of the Quad model to the data showed that the training not only weakened participants' automatically activated associations (AC), but also improved their ability to determine the correct response (D).

Neuroscientific evidence of control. Finally, there also is growing neuroscientific evidence for the role of control in implicit attitudes. Using fMRI, Chee and his colleagues (Chee, Sriram, Soon, & Lee, 2000; see also Luo et al., 2006) showed that performing an insect-flower IAT involves the left dorsolateral prefrontal cortex (DLPFC) and the anterior cingulate cortex (ACC). Whereas the DLPFC is associated with inhibitory processes, the ACC is associated with conflict detection and resolution processes. Both types of processes are considered to be executive, controlled operations.

Using fMRI, Richeson and her colleagues (Richeson, Baird, Gordon, Heatherton, Wyland, Trawalter, & Shelton, 2003) showed the involvement of the DLPFC when White participants were simply exposed to Black faces. This suggests that mere exposure to targets of potential bias is sufficient to instigate controlled processes. Moreover, the extent of DLPFC activation was related to the strength of implicit prejudice. Thus, participants with the strongest implicit prejudice apparently worked the hardest to control their behavior. These efforts were shown to deplete regulatory resources on a subsequent Stroop Task.

Also using fMRI, Cunningham and his colleagues (Cunningham, Johnson, Raye, Gatenby, Gore, & Banaji, 2004) reported the involvement of the PFC and the ACC when White participants were exposed to Black and White faces. Moreover, activation in these regions modulated the extent of amygdala activation when the faces were presented for 525 ms (vs. 30 ms). The amygdala is associated with automatic emotional reactions and has been shown to correlate with implicit racial bias (see also Phelps et al., 2000). This suggests that the PFC and ACC were actively regulating affective responses produced by exposure to Black and White faces, at least when there was sufficient time for control to engage.

Finally, using both a different behavioral measure and a different neurocognitive measure, Amodio and his colleagues (Amodio et al., 2004) also found evidence that the ACC is active during implicit task performance. In particular, Amodio et al. used electroencephalographic (EEG) recording to measure brain activity as participants performed a Weapons Identification Task (Payne, 2001). Their analysis focused specifically on the extent of error-related negativity (or ERN) during the task. The ERN is sensitive to response conflicts that result in task errors, and has been shown to originate from neural activity in the ACC (Dehaene, Posner, & Tucker, 1994) and to predict subsequent behavioral control (e.g., Gehring, Goss, Coles, Meyer, & Donchin, 1993). The results showed enhanced ERN activity during the commission of race-based errors on incompatible trials (i.e., Black faces priming pictures of tools). Amodio et al. also performed a process dissociation analysis and found that the extent of race-bias ERNs was associated with higher estimates of the controlled component of PD. These results strongly suggest the involvement of controlled processes in the execution of the priming task (see also Sherman et al., 2008).

Summary. In summary, there is growing direct evidence that controlled processes do influence responses on implicit measures. The process dissociation findings show that controlled processes are a fundamental component of implicit task performance. Moreover, the extent of this control is influenced by motivated intentions. Specifically, the likelihood of overcoming automatic associations is enhanced by efforts to appear nonprejudiced in a social context (Conrey et al., 2005). Also, the ability to detect appropriate behavior is related to internal motivations to act in nonprejudiced ways (Amodio et al., 2008; Sherman et al., 2008) and reduces implicit prejudice. Obversely, those who lack such detection skills demonstrate implicit prejudice even though they would prefer not to. The work of McFarland and Crouch (2002) similarly implicates the role of controlled skills in performing implicit tasks. There is also evidence that conscious training may facilitate this process (e.g., Kawakami et al., 2000; Sherman et al., 2008). Finally, there is now considerable neuroscientific evidence that brain regions associated with control are actively engaged upon exposure to bias-prone targets and during implicit task performance (Amodio et al., 2004; Chee et al., 2000; Luo et al., in press; Richeson et al., 2003), and that the activity of these regions modulates automatic affective responses (Cunningham et al., 2004).

These data provide evidence of control over both the initial activation of automatic associations and their subsequent application. The Quad model analyses reported by Sherman et al. (2008) showed that both good and poor regulators had less biased associations than non-regulators. These different associations could have resulted from motives to be non-prejudiced or through long-term practice aimed at altering those associations. However, as with the other individual difference data (e.g., Devine et al., 2002; Maddux et al., 2005; Moskowitz et al, 1999), it is impossible to rule out the possibility that the good and poor regulators simply never had strongly biased associations. Relatedly, and perhaps more compelling, the Quad model analysis of our negation study (Sherman et al., 2008) showed that negation training reduced the activation of biased associations in a subsequent IAT. Whether the training led to "automatic inhibition" of the associations, altered those associations, or instead activated alternate associations is unclear. However, in any case, the intentional training did alter the associations that were automatically activated.

Most of the other findings suggest control over the application of activated associations. For example, the skills of good regulators (i.e., high IMS/low EMS ability to detect appropriate behavior) identified by Sherman et al. (2008) and the general skills identified by McFarland (McFarland & Crouch, 2002) appear to correspond to controlled processes that exert influence during implicit task performance. Other research showed that impairments in the ability to control the application of activated associations were associated with increased implicit bias. For example, increased implicit bias in public (vs. private) settings seems to be related, at least in part, to diminished ability to determine correct behavior in such contexts (Conrey et al., 2005; Lambert et al., 2003). In contrast, the effects of aging and alcohol consumption on implicit bias were shown to be related to failures in the ability to overcome activated associations (Sherman et al., 2008). Diminished ability to overcome activated associations was also shown to be related to increased reaction time bias on the IAT and to making poor impressions during an interaction with a Muslim confederate (Sherman et al., 2008). Finally, the brain regions shown to be active during the performance of implicit tasks and during exposure to race-prone targets are those that influence behavior post-activation. Specifically, they have to do with detecting conflict produced by opposing activations and resolving that conflict with self-regulatory control (e.g., Amodio et al., 2004; Chee et al., 2002; Cunningham et al., 2004; Richeson et al., 2003). Other research has also shown that people can control the application of stereotypes that have been activated via thought suppression without awareness or intent (e.g., Wyer, Sherman, & Stroessner,

2000, Experiment 2). In sum, this research indicates that the ability to control the influence of automatic associations once they have been activated has been significantly underestimated and that, perhaps, the ability to control the nature of the associations that are activated has been overestimated.

Conclusion

The advent of implicit measures has revolutionized research on attitudes by offering a solution to the perpetual problems of willing and able. Though the advances produced by this approach are undeniable, there are significant drawbacks with the manner in which these tasks are commonly used and interpreted. In particular, the use of task dissociation paradigms to estimate the automatic and controlled components of attitudes introduces a number of significant methodological and conceptual problems. In this chapter, I argue that there are many advantages to a process dissociation approach that provides independent estimates of the simultaneous contributions of automatic and controlled processes to a single task. The Quad model (Conrey et al., 2005; Sherman et al., 2008) provides a nuanced depiction of the operation of multiple, distinct automatic and controlled contributions to behavior.

I also argue that, for a variety of reasons, the extent to which implicit attitudes are subject to control has been underestimated substantially. The process dissociation approach provides a very different perspective than the standard view on the role of control in implicit attitudes and measures, and provides means of estimating the extent of this control. The Quad model, in particular, also permits a much clearer distinction between controlling the automatic activation of content from memory and controlling the subsequent application of that content in performing a given task. From this view, it appears that the extent to which people are able to control the initial activation of automatic associations has been overestimated and that the ability to control the expression of those associations (including on the implicit tasks themselves) has been underestimated. This unacknowledged role for control also has likely concealed the true extent of automatic bias. Thus, the cognitive monster of automatic associations (Bargh, 1999) may be controlled once it has been summoned, but altering the nature of the beast that arrives may be very difficult.

References

Amodio, D. M., Devine, P. G., & Harmon-Jones, E. (2008). Individual differences in the regulation of intergroup bias: The role of conflict monitoring and neural signals for control. *Journal of Personality and Social Psychology, 94,* 60–74.

Amodio, D. M., Harmon-Jones, E., Devine, P. G., Curtin, J. J., Hartley, S. L., & Covert, A. E. (2004). Neural signals for the detection of unintentional race bias. *Psychological Science, 15,* 88–93.

Barden, J., Maddux, W. W., Petty, R. E., & Brewer, M. B. (2004). Contextual moderation of racial bias: The impact of social roles on controlled and automatically activated attitudes. *Journal of Personality and Social Psychology, 87,* 5–22.

Bargh, J. A. (1994). The four horsemen of automaticity: Awareness, intention, efficiency, and control in social cognition. In R. S. Wyer & T. K. Srull (Eds.), *Handbook of social cognition: Vol. 1. Basic processes* (2nd ed., pp. 1–40). Hillsdale, NJ: Erlbaum.

Bargh, J. A. (1999). The cognitive monster: The case against the controllability of automatic stereotype effects. In S. Chaiken & Y. Trope (Eds.), *Dual-process theories in social psychology* (pp. 361–382). New York: Guilford Press.

Batchelder, W. H., & Riefer, D. M. (1999). Theoretical and empirical review of multinomial process tree modeling. *Psychonomic Bulletin and Review, 6,* 57–86.

Blair, I. V. (2002). The malleability of automatic stereotypes and prejudice. *Personality and Social Psychology Review, 6,* 242–261.

Blair, I. V., & Banaji, M. R. (1996). Automatic and controlled processes in stereotype priming. *Journal of Personality and Social Psychology, 70,* 1142–1163.

Blair, I. V., Ma, J. E., & Lenton, A. P. (2001). Imagining stereotypes away: The moderation of implicit stereotypes through mental imagery. *Journal of Personality and Social Psychology, 81,* 828–841.

Brauer, M., Wasel, W., & Niedenthal, P. (2000). Implicit and explicit components of prejudice. *Review of General Psychology, 4,* 79–101.

Brewer, M. B. (1988). A dual process model of impression formation. In T. K. Srull & R. S. Wyer (Eds.), *Advances in social cognition* (Vol. 1, pp. 1–36). Hillsdale, NJ: Erlbaum.

Cai, H., Sriram, N., Greenwald, A. G., & McFarland, S. G. (2004). The Implicit Association Test's D measure can minimize a cognitive skill confound: Comment on McFarland and Crouch (2002). *Social Cognition, 22,* 673–684.

Chaiken, S. (1980). Heuristic versus systematic information processing and the use of source versus message cues in persuasion. *Journal of Personality and Social Psychology, 39,* 752–766.

Chaiken, S., & Trope, Y. (Eds.). (1999). *Dual-process theories in social psychology*. New York: Guilford Press.

Chee, M. W. L., Sriram, N., Soon, C. S., & Lee, K. M. (2000). Dorsolateral prefrontal cortex and the implicit association of concepts and attributes. *NeuroReport, 11*, 135–140.

Conrey, F. R., Sherman, J. W., Gawronski, B., Hugenberg, K., & Groom, C. (2005). Separating multiple processes in implicit social cognition: The Quad Model of implicit task performance. *Journal of Personality and Social Psychology, 89*, 469–487.

Correll, J., Park, B., Judd, C. M., & Wittenbrink, B. (2002). The police officer's dilemma: Using ethnicity to disambiguate potentially threatening individuals. *Journal of Personality and Social Psychology, 83*, 1314–1329.

Cunningham, W. A., Johnson, M. K., Raye, C. L., Gatenby, J. C., Gore, J. C., & Banaji, M. R. (2004). Separable neural components in the processing of Black and White faces. *Psychological Science, 15*, 806–813.

Cunningham, W. A., Preacher, K. J., & Banaji, M. R. (2001). Implicit attitude measures: Consistency, stability, and convergent validity. *Psychological Science, 121*, 163–170.

Dasgupta, N., & Greenwald, A. G. (2001). On the malleability of automatic attitudes: Combating automatic prejudice with images of admired and disliked individuals. *Journal of Personality and Social Psychology, 81*, 800–814.

Dehaene, S., Posner, M. I., & Tucker, D. M. (1994). Localization of a neural system for error detection and compensation. *Psychological Science, 5*, 303–305.

Devine, P. G. (1989). Stereotypes and prejudice: Their automatic and controlled components. *Journal of Personality and Social Psychology, 56*, 5–18.

Devine, P. G., Plant, E. A., Amodio, D. M., Harmon-Jones, E., & Vance, S. L. (2002). The regulation of explicit and implicit race bias: The role of motivations to respond without prejudice. *Journal of Personality and Social Psychology, 82*, 835–848.

Dovidio, J. F., & Fazio, R. H. (1992). New technologies for the direct and indirect assessment of attitudes. In J. M. Tanur (Ed.), *Questions about questions: Inquiries into the cognitive bases of surveys* (pp. 204–237). New York: Russell Sage Foundation.

Epstein, S. (1991). Cognitive-experiential self theory: An integrative theory of personality. In R. Curtis (Ed.), *The self with others: Convergences in psychoanalytical, social, and personality psychology* (pp. 111–137). New York: Guilford Press.

Fazio, R. H. (1990). Multiple processes by which attitudes guide behavior: The MODE model as an integrative framework. *Advances in Experimental Social Psychology, 23*, 75–109.

Fazio, R. H., Jackson, J. R., & Dunton, B. C., & Williams, C. J. (1995). Variability in automatic activation as an unobstrusive measure of racial attitudes: A bona fide pipeline? *Journal of Personality and Social Psychology, 69*, 1013–1027.

Fazio, R. H., & Olson, M. A. (2003). Implicit measures in social cognition research: Their meaning and use. *Annual Review of Psychology, 54*, 297–327.

Fiske, S. T., & Neuberg, S. L. (1990). A continuum of impression formation, from category-based to individuating processes: Influences of information and motivation on attention and interpretation. *Advances in Experimental Social Psychology, 23*, 1–74.

Gehring, W. J., Goss, B., Coles, M. G. H., Meyer, D. E., & Donchin, E. (1993). A neural system for error detection and compensation. *Psychological Science, 4*, 385–390.

Glaser, J., & Banaji, M. R. (1999). When fair is foul and foul is fair: Reverse priming in automatic evaluation. *Journal of Personality and Social Psychology, 77*, 669–687.

Gonsalkorale, K., von Hippel, W., Sherman, J. W., & Klauer, K. C. (2008). Bias and regulation of bias in intergroup interactions: Implicit attitudes toward Muslims and interaction quality. Unpublished manuscript.

Govan, C. L., & Williams, K. D. (2004). Changing the affective valence of the stimulus items influences the IAT by redefining the category labels. *Journal of Experimental Social Psychology, 40*, 357–365.

Greenwald, A. G., McGhee, D. E., & Schwartz, J. L. K. (1998). Measuring individual differences in implicit cognition: The Implicit Association Test. *Journal of Personality and Social Psychology, 74*, 1464–1480.

Jacoby, L. L. (1991). A process-dissociation framework: Separating automatic from intentional uses of memory. *Journal of Memory and Language, 30*, 513–541.

Jacoby, L. L., Bishara, A. J., Hessels, S., & Toth, J. P. (2005). Aging, subjective experience, and cognitive control: Dramatic false remembering by older adults. *Journal of Experimental Psychology: General, 134*, 131–148.

Jacoby, L. L., Kelley, C. M., & McElree, B. D. (1999). The role of cognitive control: Early selection versus late correction. In S. Chaiken & Y. Trope (Eds.), *Dual-process theories in social psychology* (pp. 383–402). New York: Guilford Press.

Jacoby, L. L., Toth, J. P., & Yonelinas, A. P. (1993). Separating conscious and unconscious influences of memory: Measuring recollection. *Journal of Experimental Psychology: General, 122*, 139–154.

Kawakami, K., & Dovidio, J. F. (2001). The reliability of implicit stereotyping. *Personality and Social Psychology Bulletin, 27*, 212–225.

Kawakami, K., Dovidio, J. F., Moll, J., Hermsen, S., & Russin, A. (2000). Just say no (to stereotyping): Effects of training in the negation of stereotypic associations on stereotype activation. *Journal of Personality and Social Psychology, 78*, 871–888.

Kim, D. Y. (2003). Voluntary controllability of the Implicit Association Test (IAT). *Social Psychology Quarterly, 66*, 83–96.

Lambert, A. J., Payne, B. K., Jacoby, L. L., Shaffer, L. M., Chasteen, A. L., & Khan, S. R. (2003). Stereotypes as dominant responses: On the "social facilitation" of prejudice in anticipated public contexts. *Journal of Personality and Social Psychology, 84,* 277–295.

Lepore, L., & Brown, R. (1997). Category and stereotype activation: Is prejudice inevitable? *Journal of Personality and Social Psychology, 72,* 275–287.

Lindsay, D. S., & Jacoby, L. L. (1994). Stroop process-dissociations: The relationship between facilitation and interference. *Journal of Experimental Psychology: Human Perception and Performance, 20,* 219–234.

Livingston, R. W., & Brewer, M. B. (2002). What are we really priming? Cue-based versus category-based processing of facial stimuli. *Journal of Personality and Social Psychology, 82,* 5–18.

Lowery, B. S., Hardin, C. D., & Sinclair, S. (2001). Social influence effects on automatic racial prejudice. *Journal of Personality and Social Psychology, 81,* 842–855.

Luo, Q., Nakic, M., Wheatley, T., Richell, R., Martin, A., & Blair, R. J. R. (2006). The neural basis of implicit moral attitude—An IAT study using event-related fMRI. *NeuroImage, 30,* 1449–57.

Maddux, W. W., Barden, J., Brewer, M. B., & Petty, R. E. (2005). Saying no to negativity: The effects of context and motivation to control prejudice on automatic evaluative responses. *Journal of Experimental Social Psychology, 41,* 19–35.

Martin, L. L. (1986). Set/reset: Use and disuse of concepts in impression information. *Journal of Personality and Social Psychology, 51,* 493–504.

McFarland, S. G., & Crouch, Z. (2002). A cognitive skill confound on the Implicit Association Test. *Social Cognition, 20,* 483–510.

Monteith, M. J., Ashburn-Nardo, L., Voils, C. I., & Czopp, A. M. (2002). Putting the brakes on prejudice: On the development and operation of cues for control. *Journal of Personality and Social Psychology, 83,* 1029–1050.

Monteith, M. J., Voils, C. I., & Ashburn-Nardo, L. (2001). Taking a look underground: Detecting, interpreting, and reacting to implicit racial biases. *Social Cognition, 19,* 395–417.

Moskowitz, G. B., Gollwitzer, P. M., Wasel, W., & Schaal, B. (1999). Preconscious control of stereotype activation through chronic egalitarian goals. *Journal of Personality and Social Psychology, 77,* 167–184.

Neely, J. H. (1977). Semantic priming and retrieval from lexical memory: Roles of inhibitionless spreading activation and limited-capacity attention. *Journal of Experimental Psychology: General, 106,* 226–254.

Nisbett, R. E., & Wilson, T. D. (1977). Telling more than we can know: Verbal reports on mental processes. *Psychological Review, 84,* 231–259.

Nosek, B. A., & Banaji, M. R. (2001). The Go/No-Go Association Task. *Social Cognition, 19,* 625–666.

Olson, M. A., & Fazio, R. H. (2003). Relations between implicit measures of prejudice: What are we measuring? *Psychological Science, 14,* 636–639.

Payne, B. K. (2001). Prejudice and perception: The role of automatic and controlled processes in misperceiving a weapon. *Journal of Personality and Social Psychology, 81,* 181–192.

Payne, B. K., Lambert, A. J., & Jacoby, L. L. (2002). Best laid plans: Effects of goals on accessibility bias and cognitive control in race-based misperceptions of weapons. *Journal of Experimental Social Psychology, 38,* 384–396.

Petty, R. E., & Cacioppo, J. T. (1981). *Attitudes and persuasion: Classic and contemporary approaches.* Dubuque, IA: Win. C. Brown.

Phelps, E. A., O'Connor, K. J., Cunningham, W. A., Funayama, E. S., Gatenby, J. C., Gore, J. C., & Banaji, M. R. (2000). Performance on indirect measures of race evaluation predicts amygdala activation. *Journal of Cognitive Neuroscience, 12,* 729–738.

Plant, E. A., Peruche, B. M., & Butz, D. A. (2005). Eliminating automatic racial bias: Making race non-diagnostic for responses to criminal suspects. *Journal of Experimental Social Psychology, 41,* 141–156.

Richeson, J. A., & Ambady, N. (2003). Effects of situational power on automatic racial prejudice. *Journal of Experimental Social Psychology, 39,* 177–183.

Richeson, J. A., Baird, A. A., Gordon, H. L., Heatherton, T. F, Wyland, C. L., Trawalter, S., & Shelton, J. N. (2003). An fMRI examination of the impact of interracial contact on executive function. *Nature Neuroscience, 6,* 1323–1328.

Richeson, J. A., & Nussbaum, R. J. (2004). The impact of multiculturalism versus color-blindness on racial bias. *Journal of Experimental Social Psychology, 40,* 417–423.

Roediger, H. L. (1990). Implicit memory: Retention without remembering. *American Psychologist, 45,* 9, 1043–1056.

Rudman, L. A., Ashmore, R. D., & Gary, M. L. (2001). "Unlearning" automatic biases: The malleability of implicit prejudice and stereotypes. *Journal of Personality and Social Psychology, 81,* 856–868.

Sechrist, G. B., & Stangor, C. (2001). Perceived consensus influences intergroup behavior and stereotype accessibility. *Journal of Personality and Social Psychology, 80,* 645–654.

Sherman, J. W., Gawronski, B., Gonsalkorale, K., Hugenberg, K., Allen, T. J., & Groom, C. J. (2008). The self-regulation of automatic associations and behavioral impulses. *Psychological   Review, 115,* 314–335.

Sherman, J. W. (2006a). Clearing up some misconceptions about the Quad Model. *Psychological Inquiry, 17,* 269–276.

Sherman, J. W. (2006b.0). On building a better process model: It's not only how many, but which ones and by which means. *Psychological Inquiry, 17,* 173–184.

Sherman, J. W., Gawronski, B., Conrey, F. R., Hugenberg, K., & Groom, C. (2006). *The Quad Model of impulse and self-regulation.* Unpublished manuscript.

Sinclair, L., & Kunda, Z. (1999). Reactions to a Black professional: Motivated inhibition and activation of conflicting stereotypes. *Journal of Personality and Social Psychology, 77*, 885–904.

Sloman, S. A. (1996). The empirical case for two systems of reasoning. *Psychological Bulletin, 119*, 3–22.

Steffens, M. C. (2004). Is the Implicit Association Test immune to faking? *Experimental Psychology, 5*, 165–179.

Strack, F. (1992). The different routes to social judgments: Experiential versus informational strategies. In L. L. Martin & A. Tesser (Eds.), *The construction of social judgments*. Hillsdale, NJ: Erlbaum.

Stroop, J. R. (1935). Studies on the interference in serial verbal reactions. *Journal of Experimental Psychology, 59*, 239–245.

Tesser, A., & Martin, L. (1996). The psychology of evaluation. In E. T. Higgins & A. W. Kruglanski (Eds.), *Social psychology: Handbook of basic principles* (pp. 400–432). New York: Guilford Press.

Wegener, D. T., & Petty, R. E. (1997). The flexible correction model: The role of naive theories of bias in bias correction. *Advances in Experimental Social Psychology, 29*, 141–208.

Wegner, D. M. (1994). Ironic processes of mental control. *Psychological Review, 101*, 34–52.

Wilson, T. D., & Hodges, S. D. (1992). Attitudes as temporary constructions. In L. Martin and A. Tesser (Eds.), *The construction of social judgment* (pp. 37–65). Hillsdale, NJ: Erlbaum.

Wittenbrink, B., Judd, C. M., & Park, B. (1997). Evidence for racial prejudice at the implicit level and its relationship with questionnaire measures. *Journal of Personality and Social Psychology, 72*, 262–274.

Wyer, N. A., Sherman, J. W., & Stroessner, S. J. (2000). The roles of motivation and ability in controlling the consequences of stereotype suppression. *Personality and Social Psychology Bulletin, 26*, 13–25.

Section VII

Additional Measures

14

Linguistic Markers of Implicit Attitudes

William von Hippel
Denise Sekaquaptewa
Patrick T. Vargas

Introduction

Much of the richness of language arises from the fact that there are so many ways to say the same thing, and many statements have multiple meanings, depending on grammar, punctuation, intonation, and context. Shakespeare made a living off this principle, as did the oracle at Delphi. Speakers and listeners are generally aware of this principle (Holtgraves, 1997), although differences in experience or expectancies can make it difficult if not impossible to perceive another person's intended meaning (Bartlett, 1932) or even that multiple meanings are possible (Dunning & Sherman, 1997). Additionally, because people often unconsciously rely on context, schemas, and stereotypes when producing and interpreting language, it sometimes appears that a particular meaning was directly communicated when it was only one of many possible implications (Dunning & Sherman, 1997). The content of a message obviously has a major impact on these interpretative issues, but the style of a communication can also influence the type of automatic inferences made from it.

Although people occasionally use grammar or word choice in an unusual manner to make a joke or emphasize a specific point, in general the gist of the communication is the focus and the specifics of grammar or word choice are just the backdrop in conversation, receiving little direct attention (Schmalhofer & Glavanov, 1986; Zwaan & Radvansky, 1998). Nevertheless, even though the details of a communication often go largely unnoticed, changes in these details can have dramatic effects on the meaning inferred. For this reason, researchers have proposed that linguistic markers can be used to measure attitudes implicitly, as people will occasionally show evidence of their attitudes in the manner of their communication but not in the content (e.g., Franco & Maass, 1996; von Hippel, Sekaquaptewa, & Vargas, 1997). In the current chapter we explore the use of linguistic markers as implicit measures of attitudes. In service of this goal, we also review linguistic research on topics other than attitudes when the findings of that research suggest methods that could be of use to attitude researchers.

Our review of linguistic research in the current chapter is organized by the type of linguistic marker under study. First we consider parts of speech, specifically pronouns, verbs, adjectives, and nouns, and then we review research on different qualities of the description itself, specifically stereotype-biased explanatory processing; ease of communication effects; passive versus active voice; word pattern and word count; and speech hesitations, tag questions, errors, and hedges. In all of this research, the focus is on what can be interpreted from how people communicate, and not just from what they communicate. This research demonstrates clearly not only that people are expert at communicating via content, but that they are also quite facile at manipulating linguistic style to communicate their attitudes about the object of their speech. Because variability in linguistic style appears to be a largely nonconscious aspect of language use (Semin, 2006), linguistic markers can serve as implicit measures of attitudes in a manner that is high in external validity, easily assessed in a variety of settings, and even suitable for historical analysis.

Pronouns, Verbs, Adjectives, and Nouns

Collective versus Personal Pronouns

You and I are not us. When people feel part of a meaningful group or committed to a dyadic relationship, they tend to use the collective pronoun *us*, but when they do not feel part of a group or committed to a dyadic relationship, they tend to separate us into *you* and *me*. A large number of researchers have assessed this differential pronoun use to measure commitment to a collective or a relationship, typically by computing the ratio of collective to personal pronouns (for use of this technique in various contexts, see Agnew, Van Lange, Rusbult, & Langston, 1998; Boals & Klein, 2005; Cialdini, Borden, Thorne, Walker, Freeman, & Sloane, 1976; Conrad & Conrad, 1956; Hoover, Wood, & Knowles, 1983; Moreland, 1999; Sillars, Shellen, McIntosh, & Pomegranate, 1997; Veroff, Sutherland, Chadiha, & Ortega, 1993). For example, in Agnew et al. participants were asked to write thoughts about their relationships. Examples containing an equivalent number of plural and singular pronouns were provided. The thoughts provided by participants were then coded for whether they contained plural or singular pronouns, both, or neither. The number of plural pronouns provided by participants was a strong predictor of relationship commitment and centrality among romantic partners, but less so among close friends. In contrast, Aron, Aron, and Smollan's (1992) Inclusion of the Other in the Self Scale was similarly predictive of relationship commitment and centrality for both romantic partners and close friends. If this sort of result replicates across samples (an open question, as it was not the focus of Agnew et al.'s research), it would provide evidence that collective versus personal pronoun usage taps aspects of relationship closeness that are not assessed by explicit measures such as the Inclusion of the Other in the Self Scale.

As is often the case with subtle linguistic characteristics, collective pronouns not only reflect attitudes toward the group or relationship, but they can also be used to manipulate them. For example, priming people with collective versus personal pronouns leads to reliable differences in feelings of interdependence versus independence (Brewer & Gardner, 1996; Gardner, Gabriel, & Lee, 1999). These feelings of interdependence appear to impact ongoing social relationships such that, for example, social comparison with a high-performing friend leads to gratification rather than threat after collective priming (Gardner, Gabriel, & Hochschild, 2002). In addition to influencing the use of collective versus personal pronouns, interdependence is also reflected in the use of single versus multiple addressees when speaking (e.g., addressing your sister vs. all of your siblings simultaneously; Ng, Loong, He, Liu, & Weatherall, 2000). It seems likely that this effect can also be reversed, such that number of addressees can be used as an implicit measure of collectivism, and perhaps as a manipulation of interdependence as well.

Verbs and Adjectives

The Linguistic Intergroup Bias (LIB; Maass, Salvi, Arcuri, & Semin, 1989) is the tendency to describe positive ingroup and negative outgroup behaviors at a more abstract level than negative ingroup and positive outgroup behaviors. LIB was developed based on the Linguistic Category Model (LCM; Semin & Fiedler, 1991), which identifies levels of abstraction at which people may describe individuals and their behaviors. At the least abstract (i.e., most concrete) level, behavioral events may be described in terms of descriptive action verbs ("She grasped the child's hand."), followed by interpretive action verbs ("She guided the child."), state verbs ("She loved the child."), and finally adjectives ("She is nurturing.").

The level of abstraction at which we describe the behaviors of others exposes how we think and feel about them because it implies what we believe to be the enduring versus fleeting qualities of the person. For example, in the least abstract description above, "She grasped the child's hand.", the behavior does not have clear positive or negative connotations, nor does it generalize to other settings or times. In contrast, as the descriptions become more abstract, the positive versus negative connotations become clearer, and the descriptions also generalize more readily to other times and places. LIB is present when levels of abstraction systematically vary depending on the valence of the behavior and the group membership of the target relative to the perceiver. For example, a woman may show LIB by describing positive female behaviors and negative male behaviors in more abstract terms ("She is kind.", "He is stingy.") but positive male behaviors and negative female behaviors in more concrete terms ("He donated some money.", "She grabbed the last piece."). In this way, consistent with the "ultimate attribution error" (Pettigrew, 1979), LIB expresses ingroup favorability by conveying positive ingroup and negative outgroup qualities as stable and enduring, but negative ingroup and positive outgroup qualities as fleeting and situationally specific.

LIB is evidenced not only in response to the valence of outgroup and ingroup behaviors, but also in response to their stereotypicality. Stereotype-consistent behaviors of group members tend to be described in abstract trait terms ("Latoya is athletic."), and stereotype-inconsistent behaviors in concrete terms ("Lee-Mei placed first in the 100-meter dash."; Schanke & Ruscher, 1998; von Hippel et al., 1997).* In this manner, abstract inferences are made and communicated from instances of stereotype confirmation but not stereotype disconfirmation, contributing to maintenance of the original stereotype or expectancy (Karpinski & von Hippel, 1996; Wigboldus, Semin, & Spears, 2000). Thus, a seemingly incidental feature of the way individuals describe and relate the behaviors of others may communicate ingroup favorability and maintain stereotypes as well.

---

* This version of LIB has been referred to as the Linguistic Expectancy Bias, or LEB (Wigboldus, Semin, & Spears, 2000), but for the sake of simplicity we collapse these two biases under the original label of LIB.

LIB is typically assessed by examining responses to behaviors attributed to ingroup and outgroup members. These behaviors are often depicted in cartoons displaying positive or negative behaviors enacted by individuals described as ingroup and outgroup members (or as one's best friend and one's worst enemy; Werkman, Wigboldus, & Semin, 1999; see also Karpinski & von Hippel, 1996). Other researchers have used behavioral descriptions (Schanke & Ruscher, 1998), stories (ostensibly newspaper articles indicating the actors' social group membership via photographs or names; von Hippel et al., 1997), or videotaped footage of social interactions (Watson & Gallois, 2002) to relate the target's behaviors. The descriptions that participants generate of the behaviors depicted are coded according to LCM guidelines (i.e., as descriptive action verbs, interpretive action verbs, state verbs, or adjectives). Another more streamlined method requires respondents to rate the appropriateness of a description of the behavior shown; typically four descriptions are provided that vary in their level of abstraction (from descriptive action verb to adjective). Researchers then simply compare the ratings of the concrete versus abstract descriptions of behaviors attributed to ingroup and outgroup members (von Hippel, 2006; von Hippel et al., 1997).

Two theoretical explanations have been offered for why perceivers show biased communication in the form of LIB (Maass, Milesi, Zabbini, & Stahlberg, 1995). First, a motivational explanation suggests that individuals engage in this bias because it supports a more positive view of one's ingroup relative to the outgroup. Indeed, some research indicates that the need to communicate this perspective to others is critical in determining whether LIB emerges; descriptions provided with no intended recipient in mind show little evidence of LIB (Semin, de Montes, & Valencia, 2003). A motivation for ingroup protection is also evidenced in increased LIB in reaction to perceived threat to one's social identity (Maass, Ceccarelli, & Rudin, 1996).

Second, a cognitive account of LIB proposes that because stereotypes are more positive for ingroups than for outgroups, LIB emerges because positive ingroup and negative outgroup behaviors are more expected, and thus described abstractly, whereas negative ingroup and positive outgroup behaviors are more unexpected, and thus described concretely (Maass et al., 1995; see also Fiedler, Bluemke, Friese, & Hofmann, 2003). LIB evinced in regard to stereotypic behaviors, regardless of valence, supports the differential expectancy account (Karpinski & von Hippel, 1996; Maass et al., 1995; Rubini & Semin, 1994). The differential expectancy explanation may also be related to the finding that individuals high in need for cognitive closure tend to show greater LIB (Webster, Kruglanski, & Pattison, 1997). In sum, LIB appears to be a linguistic strategy that serves to communicate our preferred or expected group representations to others.

LIB has been documented among many social groups including Italian *contrada* (Maass et al., 1989), Japanese baseball fans (Tanabe & Oka, 2001), nations (Maass, Montalcini, & Biciotti, 1998), and doctor-patient interactions (Watson & Gallois, 2002). LIB has even been shown to emerge when previously unacquainted people cooperate versus compete with each other (de Montes, Semin, & Valencia, 2003). To the extent that LIB supports favorable ingroup perception and maintains outgroup stereotypes, LIB may be considered an implicit marker of intergroup attitudes and stereotyping.

In one example of LIB as an implicit indicator of stereotyping, von Hippel et al. (1997) asked White participants to report their level of endorsement of abstract and concrete descriptions of behaviors congruent and incongruent with Black stereotypes. Greater endorsement of abstract descriptions of Black stereotype-congruent than stereotype-incongruent events indicated greater LIB. Participants then viewed a video clip showing a White man on a street corner being asked for money by either a White or Black panhandler. Because direct applications of racial stereotypes in judgment are often influenced by the motivation to appear nonprejudiced (Kunda, Davies, Adams, & Spencer, 2003), an indirect measure of stereotypic judgment was used. Specifically, participants were asked to rate not the aggressiveness of the panhandler, but the level of meekness they perceived in the White person who was asked for money, under the assumption that lower meekness ratings would reflect perceptions of the panhandler as particularly threatening (see also Kunda et al.). In line with this reasoning, White individuals who engaged in LIB rated the Black panhandler as indirectly more threatening than the White panhandler (as evidenced in lower meekness ratings of the White man asked for money by the Black than the White panhandler), even though the man displayed identical behavior in the two film clips. An explicit measure of racial bias (the Modern Racism Scale) did not predict these ratings.

Although some research has shown LIB to be correlated with self-reported prejudice (Schanke & Ruscher, 1998), other research has failed to find a relationship between the two (von Hippel et al., 1997). The relationship between explicit prejudice and LIB may be moderated by social desirability concerns, as explicit prejudice and LIB have been found to be more highly correlated for groups that are not protected by social norms of nondiscrimination (e.g., ratings of Islamic fundamentalists by Catholic respondents) than for groups that are normatively protected (e.g., Jews; Franco & Maass, 1999). One interpretation of this result is that social desirability norms influence self-reported but not implicit measures of attitudes, and individuals are largely unaware they are engaging in LIB (Franco & Maass, 1996).

Language abstraction has been used most extensively to study intergroup and interpersonal relations, but it has also been used to study other attitudinally relevant phenomena. For example, abstract language is associated with a promotion focus, whereas concrete language is more typical of a prevention focus (Semin, Higgins, de Montes, Estourget, & Valencia, 2005). This pattern is thought to occur because promotion-focused individuals are inclusive and broad in their emphasis on a successful outcome, whereas prevention-focused individuals are more concerned with concrete details that may go awry. Additionally, abstract language also leads to recall of earlier information than concrete language, because older memories are stored in more abstract form than more recent memories (Semin & Smith, 1999).

These sorts of studies suggest that attitude researchers may be able to manipulate or measure factors such as regulatory focus and temporal distance of recalled information via language abstraction in a manner that is largely outside conscious awareness. To the degree that regulatory focus is relevant to the attitude measure in question (e.g., see research on *value from fit*; Higgins, 2000), or to the degree that attitudes may have differed over time (e.g., see Petty, Tormala, Briñol, & Jarvis, 2006), language abstraction might enable researchers to access information unavailable by other methods. Nevertheless, because language abstraction is sensitive to both of these factors, as well as congruity with expectations, for language abstraction to be useful in inferring any of these factors it will be necessary for alternative influences on abstraction to be ruled out or controlled.

Adjective breadth. This term refers to the number of behaviors that could be subsumed by a particular adjective; for example, *friendly* is a broader descriptor than *punctual* (Hampson, John, & Goldberg, 1987). As with LIB, people describe attitude-consistent behaviors with broader adjectives than they use for attitude-inconsistent behavior. This effect has been shown with ingroups and outgroups (Hamilton, Gibbons, Stroessner, & Sherman, 1992), with liked and disliked politicians (McGraw, Fischle, Stenner, & Lodge, 1996), and with the self (Karpinski, Steinberg, Versek, & Alloy, 2007). For example, in Hamilton et al. participants rated liked and disliked nationalities on a series of broad and narrow desirable and undesirable traits. Hamilton et al. found that participants believed that liked nationalities exhibited more of the broad desirable traits than the narrow desirable traits, whereas disliked nationalities exhibited more of the narrow than broad desirable traits. Although there is not yet any research demonstrating that this measure is particularly well suited for the implicit assessment of attitudes, it has the advantage that differential evaluations can be measured even though people are only providing positive evaluations of groups. Thus, it seems possible that the measure may be nonreactive and suitable for implicit measurement when social desirability is an important concern.

Nouns. Nouns play a role that is similar to adjectives, in that using nouns rather than descriptive action verbs to describe others gives the impression that the attitudes underlying the person's behavior are stronger, more stable, and more resilient (Walton & Banaji, 2004). For example, describing someone as a *movie buff* makes the quality seem more essentialist than simply saying that the person *watches movies a lot*. Furthermore, this effect extends to evaluations of the self, as people rated their own preferences as stronger, more stable, and more resilient when they were led to describe their preferences with nouns rather than descriptive action verbs (Walton & Banaji). These findings suggest that nouns carry an essentialist quality to them, and that this rather subtle essentialism results in self-perception effects that change the way people understand their own attitudes. It would be an interesting question to assess whether describing oneself with nouns rather than verbs also has behavioral consequences, such that people show more attitude-consistent behavior in the former condition than in the latter.

Qualities of the Description

Stereotypic Explanatory Bias

Research on Stereotypic Explanatory Bias (SEB) emerged from findings showing that expectancy violations are often interpreted in a manner that resolves or dismisses the inconsistency, thereby maintaining the original expectancy (Hastie, 1984; Stangor & McMillan, 1992). For example, people are more likely to provide explanations for behaviors that disconfirm their expectancies than for behaviors that confirm their expectancies. Thus, if one expects a Black male "Marquis" to be dishonest, learning that "Marquis refused to take part in the looting ..."

may instigate attributional processing, in an attempt to make sense of the incongruity ("... because he spied police nearby."). Learning that "Marquis broke the window and stole the items," on the other hand, is unlikely to be met with an explanation. In this way, explanatory bias allows the perceiver to reconcile discrepant information with stereotypic expectations of the individual.

As this example illustrates, expectancies about people are often based on stereotypes; therefore, SEB is defined as the tendency to engage in greater attributional processing when confronted by stereotype inconsistency rather than stereotype consistency (Sekaquaptewa, Espinoza, Thompson, Vargas, & von Hippel, 2003). To assess whether SEB may serve as a linguistic marker of intergroup bias, von Hippel et al. (1997) adapted a sentence completion task from Hastie (1984), in which participants are given a series of sentence stems and are asked to add more words to form a grammatically correct sentence. The sentence stems describe group members performing behaviors that are either consistent or inconsistent with group stereotypes. To create an SEB score, independent raters code the sentence completions as a function of whether they explain the behavior in the sentence stem. SEB is evidenced when more explanations are provided for stereotype inconsistency over stereotype consistency.

One advantage of the SEB measure is that it can be easily modified for implicit assessment of stereotyping of different social groups, simply by developing sentence stems that reflect behaviors consistent or inconsistent with stereotypes relevant to the target group of interest (gender, race, etc.). Indeed, this measure could easily serve as an indirect indicator of attitudes toward many social groups (e.g., political conservatives, drug abusers) and even social issues (e.g., abortion rights) to the extent that stereotypic expectations exist about the behaviors of group members or issue supporters. Thus, SEB could potentially serve as a linguistic marker of social attitudes as well as social stereotyping.

To date, research has primarily focused on SEB as an implicit linguistic marker of gender and racial stereotyping. In one study (Sekaquaptewa et al., 2003), the relationships between SEB and measures of implicit racial prejudice and stereotyping were examined. Implicit prejudice has been conceived as an implicit association between racial categories and negative concepts regardless of stereotypicality, whereas implicit stereotyping has been conceived as an implicit association between racial categories and stereotypic attributes, regardless of valence (Greenwald, McGhee, & Schwartz, 1998; Wittenbrink, Judd, & Park, 1997). SEB was found to correlate with a measure of implicit stereotyping (Wittenbrink et al.'s priming measure) but not a measure of implicit prejudice (the race Implicit Association Test; Greenwald et al.), suggesting that SEB may have convergent validity as a measure of implicit stereotyping.*

SEB is also increased by factors known to augment stereotyping, such as mortality salience (Schimel et al., 1999; Espinoza & Sekaquaptewa, 1999), threats to collective self-esteem (Gonsalkorale et al., 2007), positive mood (Chartrand, van Baaren, & Bargh, 2006), and subtle suggestions that stereotyping is normative (Gonsalkorale, 2005). SEB is also greater in response to low than high social status targets (Sekaquaptewa & Espinoza, 2004). Evidence also suggests that SEB is useful as a predictor of cognitive responses to outgroup members, in that SEB predicts stereotype-congruent recall (Espinoza & Sekaquaptewa, 2001; Sekaquaptewa, Vargas, & von Hippel, 1996).

Perhaps most important in establishing SEB as an indicator of bias are findings supporting its utility to predict the nature of intergroup interactions. Consistent with studies showing that implicit measures are particularly good predictors of subtle nonverbal behaviors displayed toward outgroup members (Dovidio, Kawakami, Johnson, Johnson, & Howard, 1997), SEB has been shown to predict such subtle intergroup behaviors. In one study regarding African-American SEB (Sekaquaptewa et al., 2003, Experiment 1), White participants engaged in a mock job interview with a White or African-American job applicant. Following a procedure described by Rudman and Borgida (1995), White interviewers chose their interview questions from pairs of questions designed such that one question was worded in a subtly racist fashion, whereas the other was neutrally worded. SEB predicted White participants' choice of racist question over neutral questions, such that Whites who showed greater SEB were more likely to ask racist questions of the African-American, but not the White, job applicant. This result was conceptually replicated in a second study using a measure of gender SEB and male or female job applicants (Vargas, Sekaquaptewa, & von Hippel, 2004). In both studies, explicit measures of bias (the Modern Racism Scale and Attitudes toward Women Scale) did not emerge as significant predictors of these outcomes.

SEB toward African-American targets was also used to predict the quality of an interracial interaction (Sekaquaptewa et al., 2003, Experi-

---

* It should be noted that priming measures may assess associations that differ from those assessed by the IAT (i.e., personal beliefs vs. extrapersonal or unendorsed associations; Olson & Fazio, 2004), which could also account for their differential relationships to SEB.

ment 2). In this study, White participants engaged in a social interaction that involved playing a game with either a White or African-American male partner, who was actually a confederate. During the course of the game, the experimenter left the two alone for a period of 2 min, to give the participant unstructured interaction time with the confederate. Then the experimenter returned and the participant and confederate were separated. While the participant completed questionnaires about the game, the confederate rated the participant's social interaction on various dimensions including the confederate's liking for the participant and nonverbal behaviors (e.g., amount of eye contact, open vs. closed posture).

We found that participants' SEB predicted the Black but not the White confederate's rating of the social interaction, and that this effect differed depending on the type of explanation provided for stereotype inconsistency on the SEB measure. Explanations for stereotype-relevant behaviors can be categorized as internal (attributed to the person) or external (attributed to the situation). By categorizing SEB into its internal and external forms, we found that engaging in external SEB (attributing stereotype inconsistency to external or situational forces) predicted having a more negative social interaction with an African-American interaction partner. Conversely, engaging in internal SEB (attributing stereotype inconsistency to internal dispositions) predicted having a more positive social interaction with an African-American confederate. This pattern may have emerged because external SEB is associated with stereotype maintenance, as stereotype inconsistency is attributed to less controllable and perhaps fleeting situational forces. Internal SEB, on the other hand, is associated with stereotype change, as stereotype inconsistency is attributed to stable and enduring characteristics of the actor. Therefore, an important feature of the SEB measure is that it appears to predict positive as well as negative social interaction outcomes, depending on the locus of explanation.

Ease of communication. If communication plays an important role in evaluations of groups, and much of the evidence reviewed so far suggests that it does, then it may also be the case that communicability plays a role in group stereotypes as well. That is, if some stereotypes are more readily communicated than others, then more communicable stereotypes may be more widely disseminated and longer lasting. Schaller, Conway, and Tanchuk (2002) examined this possibility by operationalizing trait communicability as an index of the perceived likelihood that people would discuss someone having a particular trait with others and how commonly they find themselves doing so. In their terms, communicability refers to "gossip worthiness" (Schaller et al., p. 863), and consistent with this notion, communicability of traits was highly correlated with their interest value.

More importantly, Schaller et al. (2002) demonstrated not only that more communicable traits (e.g., *athletic, intelligent*) are more widely spread than less communicable traits (e.g., *rhythmic, sly*) in stereotypes of different groups, but they are also more likely to persist as part of the group stereotype over time. Furthermore, this effect was moderated by the conversational prominence of the target group, such that stereotypes of groups that are more frequently the subject of social discourse (e.g., African Americans and Jews) were more likely to show effects of communicability than groups that are only infrequently discussed (e.g., Italians and Japanese). These results provide evidence for the important role that communication plays in stereotyping, particularly for groups that are frequently the topic of conversation.

Passive versus active voice. People use passive voice to communicate that the person being described is not so much the actor as the acted upon. Because most communications can be provided in either active or passive voice, using the passive voice allows people to insinuate that the target person is not responsible for the behavior or situation in which she or he was engaged. Research on perceptions of causality for rape provides evidence demonstrating just how adroit people are in using passive voice to communicate their perceptions of causality and blame. In one study, people who subscribe to rape myths that the victim really wants to be forced into sexual relations tended to describe the rape itself in the passive rather than the active voice (Bohner, 2001). In so doing, they communicated that the rape is something that just happened, rather than something that a perpetrator did to a victim. Furthermore, this communicative style was associated with judgments of responsibility, in that use of the passive voice was positively associated with victim blame and negatively associated with assailant blame.

This relationship between assessment of responsibility and use of the passive voice can also be seen in the related tendency to vary whether a person is the subject versus object of a sentence. In an impressive demonstration of the impact of subject versus object sentence construction, Semin and De Poot (1997a) put participants in the role of an investigating police officer and had them question the victim about events that had happened prior to the alleged rape. Participants read a scenario in which a woman accused a man of date rape. The accused acknowledged that they had engaged in sexual intercourse, but he argued that it was consensual. One fact that participants were to gather was whether the assailant and victim had danced together earlier that evening. When participants were led to believe that the sexual contact was in fact consensual, they tended to ask her, "Did you dance with him?" When participants were led to believe that the sexual contact was forced, they tended to ask her, "Did he dance with you?" The active versus passive role of the female in these competing versions of the sentence implied that the causality for dancing rested with her in the first version, and with him in the second version. As a consequence, when she answers "yes" to both versions of the question, her dancing seems indicative of greater sexual interest on her part in response to the first question than the second (see Semin & De Poot, 1997b). Thus, despite the fact that the behavior was always the same (the two people danced together prior to the alleged rape), the inferences that were made from this behavior varied as a function of whether the sentence construction put the female in the role of subject versus object.

Similar to active versus passive voice, a related effect has been documented whereby people are led via language to focus on internal versus external factors as the cause of their behavior. For example, Salancik (1974) had participants complete sentences beginning with either "I generally do X because I ..." (intrinsic mindset) or "I generally do X in order to ..." (extrinsic mindset). He then measured attitudes toward college courses and assessed two critical types of behaviors: contingent (behaviors that could impact performance in the course), and noncontingent (behaviors that reflected personal interest in the course, but would not have a direct impact on performance in the course). Extrinsic set participants' attitudes were more closely related to contingent behaviors than noncontingent behaviors, and the opposite was true for intrinsic set participants. Similarly, Seligman, Fazio, and Zanna (1980) asked dating couples to complete sentences beginning "I seek out my girlfriend/boyfriend because I ..." or "I seek out my girlfriend/boyfriend in order to ..." and then assessed liking and loving among partners. Extrinsic set participants reported feeling less love, but not less liking, and they also reported reduced likelihood of marriage. We are aware of no research in which assessment of active versus passive voice, or internal versus external focus, was demonstrably used as an implicit rather than explicit assessment or manipulation of attitudes, but studies such as the ones described above suggest that this should be possible.

Coding for Content: Projective Measures and the Thematic Apperception Test

Based on Freud's arguments that people project their own feelings onto their perceptions of others, attitude theorists moved quickly from the explicit measurement of attitudes (Thurstone, 1928) to an implicit approach. For example, in a classic study of projective measures of attitude, Proshansky (1943) presented students known to have pro- and antilabor union attitudes with a series of images previously judged to be neither pro- nor antilabor and asked the students to write about each picture. Judges coded the responses as either favorable or unfavorable toward labor. Proshansky's projective technique was found to be highly correlated with a traditional measure of attitudes toward labor unions.

Early personality theorists were perhaps even more steeped in Freudian theory, and although trait theorists have long relied on self-report, many aspects of personality have been assumed to be consciously inaccessible. Indeed, the influence of consciously inaccessible constructs has more consistently remained a concern in the study of personality than in the domain of attitudes. For example, motives, or "dispositions to strive for a particular kind of goal-state or aim, e.g., achievement, affiliation, power" (Atkinson, 1965, p. 435), have been construed as consciously accessible or inaccessible (McClelland, Koestner, & Weinberger, 1989). The psychodynamic tradition posited the existence of unacknowledged motives resulting from biological drives; a more cognitive approach posits that motives may be situationally aroused and consciously inaccessible. Consciously inaccessible motives must be measured implicitly, and the most commonly used tool is the Thematic Apperception Test (TAT).

The TAT was developed by Morgan and Murray (1935), and administration of the test remains strikingly simple. Participants are presented with a series of vague or ambiguous images and asked to write stories about them. Murray himself described the procedure in an address to the annual meeting of the American Psychiatric Association (1950/1965):

> The technique is very simple, if you happen to be the kind of person who is disposed to hearten people in their creative efforts. All you have to do is to recite a short paragraph of plain instructions and with an encouraging expression—I won't say with a grin—hand the patient Picture No. 1 (p. 427).

The stories are then content coded according to a predetermined scheme (for a brief review of different coding methods see Lilienfeld, Wood, & Garb, 2000). Unfortunately, the coding schemes are not nearly as simple as TAT administration.

The TAT's association with Freudian psychodynamic theory and challenging coding instructions have led some psychologists to express concern over the measure's psychometric properties (e.g., Entwisle, 1972; Lilienfeld et al., 2000). Indeed, early research examining test-retest correlations for the TAT obtained unacceptably low scores, and although various remedies have been suggested for low reliability (e.g., Lundy, 1985; Winter & Stewart, 1977), these issues remain largely unresolved.

Despite problems with reliability, the predictive ability of TAT measures can be quite remarkable. McClelland (1985) reported a study by Constantian (1981) demonstrating the interactive effects of self-reported preferences for affiliation versus solitude (an explicit measure) and TAT assessment of the need for affiliation (see also Jacobs & McClelland, 1994). Respondents were factorially split into groups who showed an explicit preference for either affiliation or solitude, and either a high or low implicit need for affiliation. Thus, implicit and explicit measures of affiliation were arranged orthogonally, forming groups who had either consistent (low explicit, low implicit; high explicit, high implicit) or inconsistent (high explicit, low implicit; low explicit, high implicit) affiliative dimensions. There were two critical dependent measures: self-reported liking for "taking a country walk with friends" (p. 818) and the proportion of people who were actually writing letters to friends when beeped (more or less randomly from 9 a.m. to 11 p.m.). Among participants with a high implicit need for affiliation, those who also explicitly preferred affiliation (i.e., those who showed implicit-explicit consistency) were most likely to report liking the country walk with friends; those who explicitly preferred solitude (i.e., showed implicit-explicit inconsistency) were most likely to be writing to friends. The consistent individuals reported enjoying an obviously affiliative act. The inconsistent individuals were engaged in an affiliative act that could be performed in solitude. More difficult to interpret, among participants low in implicit need for affiliation there were no differences between high and low explicit need for affiliation participants on either dependent measure.

A remarkable longitudinal study on the TAT involved women who studied at Mills and Radcliffe colleges (Winter, John, Stewart, Klohnen, & Duncan, 1998). The women in this study were administered TATs assessing both affiliation and power motives at ages 18 (Radcliffe) and 21 (Mills), and were followed up with other measures, including an explicit measure of extraversion and critical life-outcome dependent measures, at ages 43 (both samples) and 48 (Radcliffe). As in the study reported above, the TAT and explicit personality measures were examined in a factorial design (Winter et al. reported correlations among the TAT and explicit personality measures for both samples that range from –.09 to +.10, and averaged +.025).

Findings involving the affiliation motive were most clear and consistent. Winter et al. (1998) obtained a series of trait by motive interactions, whereby women displaying implicit-explicit consistency (e.g., high affiliation/high extraversion) generally fared better than those who displayed implicit-explicit inconsistency (e.g., high affiliation/ low extraversion). The consistent women (regardless of whether they were low affiliation/introverted or high affiliation/extraverted) in both samples were more likely to be involved in volunteer work and more successful at combining multiple roles (e.g., work and home). The consistent Radcliffe women had fewer marriages and divorces than their inconsistent counterparts, while the consistent Mills women were less likely to report a disrupted marriage than their inconsistent counterparts. Additionally, the consistent Radcliffe women reported fewer intimacy low points than their inconsistent counterparts, while the consistent Mills women reported less relationship dissatisfaction than their inconsistent counterparts.

These findings speak to the ability of the TAT to predict very long-term outcomes in combination with explicit measures, but at the same time they reveal that implicit measurement with the TAT is still poorly understood. Perhaps for this reason, current research using TAT measures remains somewhat scarce despite the impressive findings reviewed above (but see Saragovi, Aubé, Koestner, & Zuroff, 2002; Tuerlinckx, De Boeck, & Lens, 2002). Presumably many researchers are reluctant to use the measures because of the complexity and difficulty in correctly coding responses, with no guarantee of meaningful findings. Sokolowski, Schmalt, Langens, and Puca (2000) recognized this limitation of the TAT and have developed a new measure designed to assess achievement, affiliation, and power motives simultaneously. Their measure, the Multi-Motive Grid (MMG), retains two critical aspects of the TAT, viz., a series of ambiguous images and the instruction to think creatively; but it eliminates the essay coding by presenting standardized response options that reflect different aspects of achievement, power, and affiliation motives. Respondents are simply asked to indicate whether each option describes the way people in the image might think or feel, e.g., "hoping to get in touch with other people," "being afraid of being overpowered by other people." As yet there is insufficient work on the predictive validity of this approach, but initial results suggest that it might provide a useful alternative to the TAT (e.g., Puca & Schmalt, 1999).

In both the traditional and MMG versions of the TAT, the focus is on the content of the respondents' stories. For the MMG, respondents are provided with fixed-alternative response options. For the traditional TAT, the consistent use of a particular set of ambiguous images presumably constrains story content somewhat. Without a specific set of images, respondents' stories would likely vary so widely that content coding would be all but meaningless. In response to this difficulty with a priori content coding of natural language use, other researchers have tried to assess the underlying structure without the aid of pre-existing theories of what that structure should look like. We now consider this alternative approach to mining language content for implicit evidence of attitudes.

Word Pattern and Word Count

Rather than approach linguistic analysis from a top-down, or thematic content-based, approach, some scholars have turned to a bottom-up technique. There are at least two broad frameworks for bottom-up approaches: word pattern and word count. Word pattern analysis is not unlike a factor analysis of natural language use, in which the covariation of words is of critical interest. Word count analysis examines word frequencies and may involve either content (what is said) or style (how something is said). Pennebaker, Mehl, and Neiderhoffer (2003) offered a concise review of both approaches and software that has been employed in the different approaches.

Pennebaker and colleagues have used a program called Linguistic Inquiry and Word Count (LIWC) to examine word use as both independent (i.e., individual differences; Pennebaker & King, 1999) and dependent (e.g., changes following traumatic events; Pennebaker & Lay, 2002) variables. The program was developed to examine which aspects of emotional writing (often following traumatic life events) were most likely to predict subsequent health outcomes; its use has been expanded to examine literature, media coverage of various events, press conferences, and natural conversation. The LIWC program can be used to search any computer text file for more than 2,300 words or word stems. The words are sorted into more than 70 different categories (e.g., parts of speech; first, second, and third person; words indicating positive and negative emotion), and categories may be hierarchically organized (e.g., sad words are categorized as such, and also as negative emotion, overall affect, and past-tense [part of speech]; Pennebaker et al., 2003, p. 553).

Age and sex differences have emerged in studies of language use. Pennebaker and Stone (2003) found that as people age across the life span they tend to use "more positive and fewer negative affect words, use fewer self-references, use more future-tense and fewer past-tense verbs, and demonstrate a general pattern of increasing cognitive complexity" (p. 291). In a study supporting reliability of different linguistic markers over a 4-week span, Mehl and Pennebaker (2003b) found that males and females used different patterns of language in their daily conversations. Among other differences, males tended to use more swear words, more big words (i.e., greater than six letters), and more negative emotion and anger words, whereas females used more references to positive emotions and more filler words. In a pair of longitudinal case studies examining writing styles of individuals undergoing testosterone therapy, Pennebaker, Groom, Loew, and Dabbs (2004) found a reduction in the use of words describing social connections, but no increase in words relating to anger, sexuality, or achievement.

Several interesting extensions of these demographic differences may be considered. For example, the findings regarding age paint a picture of a kindly, other-centered, forward-thinking, and wise elderly person. One may imagine a younger individual who shows a similar pattern of language use—would this individual be described as "wise beyond her years" or perceived as a leader, nurturing guide, or teacher by others? To what extent do these linguistic markers indicate wisdom, intelligence, or thoughtfulness among younger individuals? The linguistic patterns differentiating males and females could be assessed as an implicit measure of masculinity, femininity, or possibly even sexual orientation (see Bailey, Kim, Hills, & Linsenmeier, 1997; Gangestad, Bailey, & Martin, 2000).

Very few studies have examined language use as a measure of individual differences. Pennebaker and King (1999) factor-analyzed 15 of 72 linguistic categories and found support for four reliable dimensions: immediacy (including first-person singular, present tense), making distinctions (including discrepancies, words to indicate exclusiveness), the social past (including social words, past tense), and rationalization (including insight and causation-related words). They correlated LIWC factors with a variety of other personality measures, including TAT measures of the needs for achievement, affiliation, and power. Correlations were modest, and not entirely intuitive, ranging from –.33 (immediacy and need for achievement) to +.23 (the social past and need for achievement). The social past was negatively related to need for affiliation (–.25), and no LIWC items were correlated with need for power. LIWC factors were also largely uncorrelated with explicit measures of achievement, affiliation, and dominance and with dimensions from the Five-Factor Model of Personality, suggesting that the LIWC items may tap novel dimensions of personality. Pennebaker et al. (2003) reviewed relations between language use and other dimensions of personality (moods and emotions, self-esteem, etc.) and summarized the findings by noting that correlations between word use and traditional measures of personality were generally quite small.

The influence of extraneous variables on word use has also been extensively studied. Linguistic politeness and immediacy are influenced by setting; people tend to be more polite and less immediate in formal compared to informal settings (e.g., Morand, 2000; Pennebaker & King, 1999). In formal settings people tend to use more honorific titles, hedges, apologies, and so forth. Surprisingly, immediacy was unrelated to TAT-assessed need for power and negatively related to explicit dominance (Pennebaker & King). These linguistic tendencies could be analyzed to assess an individual's comfort in a particular setting, or perhaps his or her acceptance of a vertical power hierarchy. One might imagine assessing racial prejudice or sexism by randomly assigning participants to work under a supervisor who is male, female, of ethnic minority status, or otherwise stigmatized, and then analyzing speech patterns using LIWC. Presumably individuals who reject the status of non-White, nonmale supervisors would show less politeness, more immediacy, fewer apologies, and so on.

Similarly, linguistic markers of emotional distress include increased use of first-person pronouns, negative emotion words, and decreased use of big words (Gortner & Pennebaker, 2003; Mehl & Pennebaker, 2003a). Although students may be reluctant to report homesickness or difficulty adjusting to the new environment, linguistic markers may provide an implicit measure for identifying at-risk students (see Pennebaker, Mayne, & Francis, 1997; Rude, Gortner, & Pennebaker, 2004; Stirman & Pennebaker, 2001). LIWC analyses could be run on incoming college freshmen, and change could be indicated by comparing college entrance statements and essays assigned in class. Individuals showing linguistic evidence of emotional distress could be identified and given additional assistance, counseling, or other attention.

Language use can also be influenced by the speaker's intention to deceive. Newman, Pennebaker, Berry, and Richards (2003) analyzed data from five studies involving deceptive and nondeceptive participants. Participants were instructed to provide truthful and untruthful information about themselves. For example, in one study students discussed their own views on abortion, and then discussed the opposite view as if it were their own. Newman et al. found that deceptive participants were less likely to speak in the first person and more likely to use the third person and to use exclusive words; they were more likely to use negative emotion and motion verbs. Bond and Lee (2005) likewise asked prisoners to tell deceptive and truthful statements and found that liars were less likely to use sensory, perceptual, and temporal words, but more likely to use spatial and affective words. The extent to which prisoners differ from members of the general population notwithstanding, both sets of findings should be treated with caution, as demonstrating a measure's construct validity (i.e., differentiating between known groups) is quite different from demonstrating predictive validity. Whether these criteria could be used to predict individual levels of dishonesty remains an open question. Clearly there are numerous reasons—apart from deceptive intent—why individuals would be more likely to speak in the third person, use negative emotion, and so forth. Nevertheless, these results certainly point to interesting directions for future research.

Speech hesitations, tag questions, errors, and hedges. The manner in which a statement or request is made communicates information about the power relationship between the speaker and the audience. Speakers relatively low in power are more likely to include tag questions (e.g., "It's warm out, isn't it?") and hedges (e.g., "It sort of seems …"), more likely to show hesitations in speech (e.g., "um" or "uh"), and more likely to make minor speech errors (see Newcombe & Arnkoff, 1979). These various forms of powerless speech make speakers appear less competent and credible, and make their arguments appear less persuasive (Blankenship & Holtgraves, 2005; Holtgraves & Lasky, 1999). These forms of speech are not only associated with power, but also with politeness, as less powerful forms of requests are typically perceived as more polite (Brown & Levinson, 1987). Presumably through their association with power and politeness, these forms of speech are also associated with gender, as women tend to use tag questions, hedges, and so on, particularly when talking to men (Carli, 1990; Lakoff, 1973).

At least two different types of data suggest that people are sensitive to the role of these forms of speech in generating messages that appear powerful or polite. First, people in sad moods use more hesitations, tag questions, and so on than people in happy moods when making a request, thereby causing the request to be more polite (Forgas, 1999). This effect is more pronounced when the request is socially difficult rather than simple to formulate, suggesting that although people may not consciously manipulate the use of these forms of speech, when they put more effort into a request they show greater sensitivity to these communication styles. Second, when women are put under stereotype threat that they are poor leaders, they shift their style of speech to a more powerful or masculine style, with their directions containing fewer hedges, hesitations, and so on (von Hippel, 2005). This reactance against stereotype threat has been shown in other situations when the threat is explicit and people have the necessary resources to meet the situational demands (e.g., Kray, Reb, Galinsky, & Thompson, 2004). These data suggest that hesitations, tag questions, and so on can be used as implicit measures of factors that influence feelings of power or politeness. Thus, depending on context, the use of hedges, tag questions, hesitations, and so on may be indicators of feelings of power, positive mood, or even stereotype threat (so long as the alternative possibilities can be effectively ruled out).

Conclusion

More than 20 years ago, Zajonc and Adelmann (1987) argued that cognition and communication are interwoven in such a manner as to make the study of one construct incomplete without the study of the other. For Zajonc and Adelmann, the study of cognition required the study of communication because "communication is an essential aspect of cognition and a full understanding of either process requires the understanding of the other" (p. 4). They further proposed that the study of both constructs had been conducted largely in isolation of the other and referred to this as "a story of missed opportunities." As is evident from the research reviewed in this chapter, that opportunity is no longer missed. Substantial research now indicates that a variety of different types of linguistic markers exist that reveal who and what people believe, how they feel about themselves and others, how they perceive their relationships, and even the motivations that underlie some of their most important behaviors and decisions.

This linguistic research provides techniques that can be useful for the implicit measurement of attitudes when situations or budgets preclude a high-tech approach (see also Vargas, Sekaquaptewa, & von Hippel, 2007). This linguistic research also provides entrée to implicit measurement of attitudes that may not be accessible with the measures and techniques reviewed elsewhere in this volume (for example, in the communications of historical figures). For these reasons, linguistic measures are likely to become increasingly important tools in the arsenal of implicit attitude researchers.

References

Agnew, C. R., Van Lange, P. A. M., Rusbult, C. E., & Langston, C. A. (1998). Cognitive interdependence: Commitment and the mental representation of close relationships. *Journal of Personality and Social Psychology*, 74, 939–954.

Aron, A., Aron, E. N., & Smollan, D. (1992). Inclusion of Other in the Self Scale and the structure of interpersonal closeness. *Journal of Personality and Social Psychology*, 63, 596–612.

Atkinson, J. W. (1965). Thematic apperceptive measurement of motives within the context of a theory of motivation. In B. I. Murstein (Ed.), *Handbook of projective techniques* (pp. 433–456). New York: Basic Books.

Bailey, J. M., Kim, P. Y., Hills, A., & Linsenmeier, J. A. W. (1997). Butch, femme, or straight acting? Partner preferences of gay men and lesbians. *Journal of Personality and Social Psychology*, 73, 960–973.

Bartlett, F. C. (1932). *Remembering: A study in experimental and social psychology*. Cambridge: Cambridge University Press.

Blankenship, K. L., & Holtgraves, T. (2005). The role of different markers of linguistic powerlessness in persuasion. *Journal of Language and Social Psychology*, 24, 3–24.

Boals, A., & Klein, K. (2005). Word use in emotional narratives about failed romantic relationships and subsequent mental health. *Journal of Language and Social Psychology*, 24, 252–268.

Bohner, G. (2001). Writing about rape: Use of the passive voice and other distancing text features as an expression of perceived responsibility of the victim. *British Journal of Social Psychology*, 40, 515–529.

Bond, G. D., & Lee, A. Y. (2005). Language of lies in prison: Linguistic classification of prisoners' truthful and deceptive natural language. *Applied Cognitive Psychology*, 19, 313–329.

Brewer, M. B., & Gardner, W. L. (1996). Who is this "we"? Levels of collective identity and self representations. *Journal of Personality and Social Psychology*, 71, 83–93.

Brown, P., & Levinson, S. C. (1987). *Politeness: Some universals in language usage*. New York: Cambridge University Press.

Carli, L. L. (1990). Gender, language, and influence. *Journal of Personality and Social Psychology*, 59, 941–951.

Chartrand, T. L., van Baaren, R. B., & Bargh, J. A. (in press). Linking automatic evaluation to mood and information processing style: Consequences for experienced affect, impression formation, and stereotyping. *Journal of Experimental Psychology: General*.

Cialdini, R. B., Borden, R. J., Thorne, A., Walker, M. R., Freeman, S., & Sloane, L. R. (1976). Basking in reflected glory: Three (football) field studies. *Journal of Personality and Social Psychology*, 34, 366–375.

Conrad, D. C., & Conrad, R. (1956). The use of personal pronouns as categories for studying small group interaction. *Journal of Abnormal and Social Psychology, 52,* 277–279.

Constantian, C. A. (1981). Attitudes, beliefs, and behavior in regard to spending time alone. Unpublished doctoral dissertation, Harvard University, Cambridge, MA.

de Montes, L. G., Semin, G. R., & Valencia, J. F. (2003). Communication patterns in interdependent relationships. *Journal of Language & Social Psychology, 22,* 259–281.

Dovidio, J., Kawakami, K., Johnson, C., Johnson, B., & Howard, A. (1997). On the nature of prejudice: Automatic and controlled processes. *Journal of Experimental Social Psychology, 33,* 510–540.

Dunning, D., & Sherman, D. A. (1997). Stereotypes and tacit inference. *Journal of Personality and Social Psychology, 73,* 459–471.

Entwisle, D. R. (1972). To dispel fantasies about fantasy-based measures of achievement motivation. *Psychological Bulletin, 77,* 377–391.

Espinoza, P. E, & Sekaquaptewa, D. (1999, June). *The role of biased processing in assessing prejudice.* Paper presented at the 11th annual convention of the American Psychological Society, Denver.

Espinoza, P., & Sekaquaptewa, D. (2001, May). *Perceiving racial outgroup members as "All the Same": Outgroup homogeneity as an individual-difference racial bias.* Paper presented at the 73nd annual meeting of the Midwestern Psychological Association, Chicago.

Fiedler, K., Bluemke, M., Friese, M., & Hofmann, W. (2003). On the different uses of linguistic abstractedness: From LIB to LEB and beyond. *European Journal of Social Psychology, 33,* 441–453.

Fiske, S. T. (1998). Stereotypes, prejudice, and discrimination. In D. T. Gilbert, S. T. Fiske, & G. Lindzey (Eds.), *The handbook of social psychology* (4th ed.). New York: McGraw-Hill.

Forgas, J. P. (1999). On feeling good and being rude: Affective influences on language use and request formulation. *Journal of Personality and Social Psychology, 76,* 928–939.

Franco, F. M., & Maass, A. (1996). Implicit versus explicit strategies of outgroup discrimination: The role of intentional control in biased language use and reward allocation. *Journal of Language & Social Psychology, 15,* 335–359.

Franco, F. M., & Maass, A. (1999). Intentional control over prejudice: When the choice of the measure matters. *European Journal of Social Psychology, 29,* 469–477.

Gangestad, S. W., Bailey, J. M., & Martin, N. G. (2000). Taxometric analyses of sexual orientation and gender identity. *Journal of Personality and Social Psychology, 78,* 1109–1121.

Gardner, W. L., Gabriel, S., & Hochschild, L. (2002). When you and I are "we," you are not threatening: The role of self-expansion in social comparison. *Journal of Personality & Social Psychology, 82,* 239–251.

Gardner, W. L., Gabriel, S., & Lee, A. Y. (1999). "I" value freedom, but "we" value relationships: Self-construal priming mirrors cultural differences in judgment. *Psychological Science, 10,* 321–326.

Gonsalkorale, K. (2005). *The relationship between ingroup positivity and outgroup negativity under threat.* Unpublished doctoral dissertation, University of New South Wales, Sydney.

Gonsalkorale, K., Carlisle, C., & von Hippel, W. (2007). Intergroup threat increases implicit stereotyping. *International Journal of Psychology and Psychological Therapy, 7,* 189–200.

Gortner, E., & Pennebaker, J. W. (2003). The archival anatomy of a disaster: Media coverage and community-wide health effects of the Texas A&M bonfire tragedy. *Journal of Social and Clinical Psychology, 22,* 580–603.

Greenwald, A. G., McGhee, D. E., & Schwartz, J. K. L. (1998). Measuring individual differences in implicit cognition: The Implicit Association Test. *Journal of Personality and Social Psychology, 74,* 1464–1480.

Hamilton, D. L., Gibbons, P. A., Stroessner, S. J., & Sherman, J. W. (1992). Stereotypes and language use. In G. R. Semin & K. Fiedler (Eds.), *Language, interaction and social cognition* (pp. 102–128). Thousand Oaks, CA: Sage Publications.

Hampson, S. E., John, O. P., & Goldberg, L. R. (1987). Category-breadth and social desirability values for 573 personality terms. *European Journal of Personality, 1,* 37–54.

Hastie, R. (1984). Causes and effects of causal attribution. *Journal of Personality and Social Psychology, 46,* 44–56.

Higgins, E. T. (2000). Making a good decision: Value from fit. *American Psychologist, 55,* 1214–1230.

Holtgraves, T. (1997). Styles of language use: Individual and cultural variability in conversational indirectness. *Journal of Personality & Social Psychology, 73,* 624–637.

Holtgraves, T., & Lasky, B. (1999). Linguistic power and persuasion. *Journal of Language and Social Psychology, 18,* 196–205.

Hoover, C. W., Wood, E. E., & Knowles, E. S. (1983). Forms of social awareness and helping. *Journal of Experimental Social Psychology, 19,* 577–590.

Jacobs, R. L., & McClelland, D. C. (1994). Moving up the corporate ladder: A longitudinal study of the leadership motive pattern and managerial success in women and men. *Consulting Psychology Journal: Practice and Research, 46,* 32–41.

Karpinski, A., Steinberg, J. A., Versek, B., & Alloy, L. B. (2007). The breadth-based adjective rating task (BART) as an indirect measure of self-esteem. *Social Cognition, 25,* 778–818.

Karpinski, A., & von Hippel, W. (1996). The role of the linguistic intergroup bias in expectancy maintenance. *Social Cognition, 14,* 141–163.

Kray, L. J., Reb, J., Galinsky, A. D., & Thompson, L. (2004). Stereotype reactance at the bargaining table: The effect of stereotype activation and power on claiming and creating value. *Personality & Social Psychology Bulletin, 30,* 399–411.

Kunda, Z., Davies, P. G., Adams, B. D., & Spencer, S. J. (2003). The dynamic time course of stereotype activation: Activation, dissipation, and resurrection. *Journal of Personality and Social Psychology, 82,* 283–299.

Lakoff, R. (1973). Language and woman's place. *Language in Society, 1,* 45–80.

Lilienfeld, S. O., Wood, J. M., & Garb, H. N. (2000). The scientific status of projective techniques. *Psychological Science in the Public Interest, 1,* 27–66.

Lundy, A. (1985). The reliability of the Thematic Apperception Test. *Journal of Personality Assessment, 49,* 141–145.

Maass, A., Ceccarelli, R., & Rudin, S. (1996). Linguistic Intergroup Bias: Evidence for ingroup-protective motivation. *Journal of Personality and Social Psychology, 71,* 512–526.

Maass, A., Milesi, A., Zabbini, S., & Stahlberg, D. (1995). Linguistic Intergroup Bias: Differential expectancies or ingroup protection? *Journal of Personality and Social Psychology, 68,* 116–126.

Maass, A., Montalcini, F., & Biciotti, E. (1998). On the (dis-)confirmability of stereotypic attributes. *European Journal of Social Psychology, 28,* 383–402.

Maass, A., Salvi, D., Arcuri, L., & Semin, G. (1989). Language use in intergroup contexts: The Linguistic Intergroup Bias. *Journal of Personality and Social Psychology, 57,* 981–993.

McClelland, D. C. (1985). How motives, skills, and values determine what people do. *American Psychologist, 40,* 812–825.

McClelland, D. C., Koestner, R., & Weinberger, J. (1989). How do self-attributed and implicit motives differ? *Psychological Review, 96,* 690–702.

McGraw, K. M., Fischle, M., Stenner, K., & Lodge, M. (1996). What's in a word? Bias in trait descriptions of political leaders. *Political Behavior, 18,* 263–287.

Mehl, M. R., & Pennebaker, J. W. (2003a). The social dynamics of a cultural upheaval: Social interactions surrounding September 11, 2001. *Psychological Science, 14,* 579–585.

Mehl, M. R., & Pennebaker, J. W. (2003b). The sounds of social life: A psychometric analysis of students' daily social environments and natural conversations. *Journal of Personality and Social Psychology, 84,* 857–870.

Morand, D. A. (2000). Language and power: An empirical analysis of linguistic strategies used in superior-subordinate communication. *Journal of Organizational Behavior, 21,* 235–248.

Moreland, R. L. (1999). Transactive memory: Learning who knows what in work groups and organizations. In L. Thompson, D. Messick, & J. Levine (Eds.), *Shared cognition in organizations: The management of knowledge* (pp. 3–31). Mahwah, NJ: Erlbaum.

Morgan, C. D., & Murray, H. A. (1935). A method for investigating fantasies: The Thematic Apperception Test. *Archives of Neurology and Psychiatry, 34*, 289–304.

Murray, H. A. (1950/1965). Uses of the thematic apperception test. In B. I. Murstein (Ed.), *Handbook of projective techniques* (pp. 425–432). New York: Basic Books.

Newcombe, N., & Arnkoff, D. B. (1979). Effects of speech style and sex of speaker on person perception. *Journal of Personality and Social Psychology, 37*, 1293–1303.

Newman, M. L., Pennebaker, J. W., Berry, D. S., & Richards, J. M. (2003). Lying words: Predicting deception from linguistic styles. *Personality and Social Psychology Bulletin, 29*, 665–675.

Ng, S. H., Loong, C. S. F., He, A. P., Liu, J. H., & Weatherall, A. (2000). Communication correlates of individualism and collectivism talk directed at one or more addressees in family conversations. *Journal of Language and Social Psychology, 19*, 26–45.

Olson, M. A., & Fazio, R. H. (2004). Reducing the Influence of Extrapersonal Associations on the Implicit Association Test: Personalizing the IAT. *Journal of Personality and Social Psychology, 86*, 653–667.

Pennebaker, J. W., Groom, C. J., Loew, D., & Dabbs, J. M. (2004). Testosterone as a social inhibitor: Two case studies of the effect of testosterone treatment on language. *Journal of Abnormal Psychology, 113*, 172–175.

Pennebaker, J. W., & King, L. A. (1999). Linguistic styles: Language use as an individual difference. *Journal of Personality and Social Psychology, 77*, 1296–1312.

Pennebaker, J. W., & Lay, T. C. (2002). Language use and personality during crises: Analyses of Mayor Rudolph Giuliani's press conferences. *Journal of Research in Personality, 36*, 271–282.

Pennebaker, J. W., Mayne, T. J., & Francis, M. E. (1997). Linguistic predictors of adaptive bereavement. *Journal of Personality and Social Psychology, 72*, 863–871.

Pennebaker, J. W., Mehl, M. R., & Neiderhoffer, K. G. (2003). Psychological aspects of natural language use: Our words, our selves. *Annual Review of Psychology, 54*, 547–577.

Pennebaker, J. W., & Stone, L. D. (2003). Words of wisdom: Language use over the life span. *Journal of Personality and Social Psychology, 85*, 291–301.

Pettigrew, T. F. (1979). The ultimate attribution error: Extending Allport's cognitive analysis of prejudice. *Personality and Social Psychology Bulletin, 5*, 461–476.

Petty, R. E., Tormala, Z. L., Briñol, P., & Jarvis, W. B. G. (2006). Implicit ambivalence from attitude change: An exploration of the PAST model. *Journal of Personality and Social Psychology, 90*, 21–41.

Proshansky, H. M. (1943). A projective method for the study of attitudes. *Journal of Abnormal and Social Psychology, 38*, 393–395.

Puca, R. M., & Schmalt, H. D. (1999). Task enjoyment: A mediator between achievement motives and performance. *Motivation and Emotion, 23*, 15–29.

Rubini, M., & Semin, G. R. (1994). Language use in the context of congruent and incongruent ingroup behaviours. *British Journal of Social Psychology, 33*, 355–362.

Rude, S. S., Gortner, E., & Pennebaker, J. W. (2004). Language use of depressed and depression-vulnerable college students. *Cognition and Emotion, 18*, 1121–1133.

Rudman, L. A., & Borgida, E. N. (1995). The afterglow of construct accessibility: The behavioral consequence of priming men to view women as sexual objects. *Journal of Experimental Social Psychology, 6*, 493–517.

Salancik, J. R. (1974). Inference of one's attitude from behavior recalled under linguistically manipulated cognitive sets. *Journal of Experimental Social Psychology, 10*, 415–427.

Saragovi, C., Aubé, J., Koestner, R., & Zuroff, D. (2002). Traits, motives, and depressive styles as reflections of agency and communion. *Personality and Social Psychology Bulletin, 28*, 563–577.

Schaller, M., Conway, L. G., & Tanchuk, T. L. (2002). Selective pressures on the once and future contents of ethnic stereotypes: Effects of communicability of traits. *Journal of Personality and Social Psychology, 82*, 861–877.

Schanke, S. B., & Ruscher, J. B. (1998). Modern racism as a predictor of the linguistic intergroup bias. *Journal of Language and Social Psychology, 17*, 484–491.

Schimel, J., Simon, L., Greenberg, J., Pyszczynski, T., Solomon, S., Waxmonsky, J., & Arndt, J. (1999). Stereotypes and terror management: Evidence that mortality salience enhances stereotypic thinking and preferences. *Journal of Personality and Social Psychology, 77*, 905–926.

Schmalhofer, F., & Glavanov, D. (1986). Three components of understanding a programmer's manual: Verbatim, propositional, and situational representations. *Journal of Memory and Language, 25*, 279–294.

Schultheiss, O. C. (2001). *Manual for the assessment of hope of success and fear of failure (English translation of Heckhausen's need achievement measure)*. Unpublished manuscript, Department of Psychology, University of Michigan, Ann Arbor.

Sekaquaptewa, D., & Espinoza, P. (2004). Biased processing of stereotype-incongruency is greater for low than high status groups. *Journal of Experimental Social Psychology, 40*, 128–135.

Sekaquaptewa, D., Espinoza, P., Thompson, M., Vargas, P., & von Hippel, W. (2003). Stereotypic explanatory bias: Implicit stereotyping as a predictor of discrimination. *Journal of Experimental Social Psychology, 39*, 75–82.

Sekaquaptewa, D., Vargas, P., and von Hippel, W. (1996, May). *Process prejudice predicts biased processing of information about women*. Paper presented at the 68th annual meeting of the Midwestern Psychological Association, Chicago.

Seligman, C., Fazio, R. H., & Zanna, M. P. (1980). Effects of salience of extrinsic rewards on liking and loving. *Journal of Personality and Social Psychology, 38*, 453–460.

Semin, G. R. (2006). Modelling the architecture of linguistic behavior: Linguistic compositionality, automaticity, and control. *Psychological Inquiry, 17*, 246–255.

Semin, G. R., de Montes, L. G., & Valencia, J. F. (2003). Communication constraints on the Linguistic Intergroup Bias. *Journal of Experimental Social Psychology, 39*, 142–148.

Semin, G. R., & De Poot, C. J. (1997a). Bringing partiality to light: Question wording and choice as indicators of bias. *Social Cognition, 15*, 91–106.

Semin, G. R., & De Poot, C. J. (1997b). The question-answer paradigm: You might regret not noticing how a question is worded. *Journal of Personality and Social Psychology, 73*, 472–480.

Semin, G. R., & Fiedler, K. (1991). The linguistic category model, its bases, applications, and range. In W. Stroebe & M. Hewstone (Eds.), *European review of social psychology* (Vol. 2, pp. 1–50). Chichester, England: Wiley.

Semin, G. R., & Smith, E. R. (1999). Revisiting the past and back to the future: Memory systems and the linguistic representation of social events. *Journal of Personality and Social Psychology, 76*, 877–892.

Semin, G. R., Higgins, E. T., de Montes, L. G., Estourget, Y., & Valencia, J. F. (2005). Linguistic signatures of regulatory focus: How abstraction fits promotion more than prevention. *Journal of Personality and Social Psychology, 89*, 36–45.

Sillars, A., Shellen, W., McIntosh, A., & Pomegranate, M. (1997). Relational characteristics of language: Elaboration and differentiation in marital conversations. *Western Journal of Communication, 61*, 403–422.

Sokolowski, K., Schmalt, H., Langens, T. A., & Puca, R. M. (2000). Assessing achievement, affiliation, and power motives all at once: The Multi-Motive Grid (MMG). *Journal of Personality Assessment, 74*, 126–145.

Stangor, C., & McMillan, D. (1992). Memory for expectancy-congruent and expectancy-incongruent information: A review of the social and social developmental literatures. *Psychological Bulletin, 1*, 42–61.

Stirman, S. W., & Pennebaker, J. W. (2001). Word use in the poetry of suicidal and nonsuicidal poets. *Psychosomatic Medicine, 63*, 517–522.

Tanabe, Y., & Oka, T. (2001). Linguistic Intergroup Bias in Japan. *Japanese Psychological Research, 43*, 104–111.

Thurstone, L. L. (1928). Attitudes can be measured. *American Journal of Sociology, 33*, 529–554.

Tuerlinckx, F., De Boeck, P., & Lens, W. (2002). Measuring needs with the Thematic Apperception Test: A psychometric study. *Journal of Personality and Social Psychology, 82*, 448–461.

Vargas, P. T., Sekaquaptewa, D., & von Hippel, W. (2004). It's not just what you think, it's also how you think: Prejudice as biased information processing. In W. N. Lee & J. Williams (Eds.), *Diversity in advertising* (pp. 93–119). Mahwah, NJ: Lawrence Erlbaum.

Vargas, P. T., Sekaquaptewa, D., & von Hippel, W. (2007). Armed only with paper and pencil: "Low-tech" implicit measures of attitudes, prejudice, and self-esteem. In B. Wittenbrink & N. Schwarz (Eds.), *Implicit attitude measures*. New York: Guilford Press.

Veroff, J., Sutherland, L., Chadiha, L., & Ortega, R. M. (1993). Newlyweds tell their stories: A narrative method for assessing marital experiences. *Journal of Social and Personal Relationships, 10*, 437–457.

von Hippel, C. (2005, August). *The three C's of stereotype threat: Communication, coping, and consequences*. Presentation at the 13th annual Brisbane Symposium on Social Identity, Brisbane, Australia.

von Hippel, C. (2006). When people would rather switch than fight: Out-group favoritism among temporary employees. *Group Processes and Intergroup Relations, 9*, 533–546.

von Hippel, W., Sekaquaptewa, D., & Vargas, P. (1997). The Linguistic Intergroup Bias as an implicit indicator of prejudice. *Journal of Experimental Social Psychology, 33*, 490–509.

Walton, G. M., & Banaji, M. R. (2004). Being what you say: The effect of essentialist linguistic labels on preferences. *Social Cognition, 22*, 193–213.

Watson, B., & Gallois, C. (2002). Patients' interactions with health providers: A Linguistic Category Model approach. *Journal of Language & Social Psychology, 21*, 32–52.

Webster, D. M., Kruglanski, A. W., & Pattison, D. A. (1997). Motivated language use in intergroup contexts: Need-for-closure effects on the Linguistic Intergroup Bias. *Journal of Personality and Social Psychology, 72*, 1122–1131.

Werkman, W. M., Wigboldus, D. H. J., & Semin, G. R. (1999). Children's communication of the Linguistic Intergroup Bias and its impact upon cognitive inferences. *European Journal of Social Psychology, 29*, 95–104.

Wigboldus, D., Semin, G. R., & Spears, R. (2000). How do we communicate stereotypes? Linguistic bases and inferential consequences. *Journal of Personality and Social Psychology, 78*, 5–18.

Winter, D. G., John, O. P., Stewart, A. J., Klohnen, E. C., & Duncan, L. E. (1998). Traits and motives: Toward an integration of two traditions in personality research. *Psychological Review, 105*, 230–250.

Winter, D. G., & Stewart, A. J. (1977). Power motive reliability as a function of retest instructions. *Journal of Consulting and Clinical Psychology, 45*, 436–440.

Wittenbrink, B., Judd, C. M., & Park, B. (1997). Evidence for racial prejudice at the implicit level and its relationship with questionnaire measures. *Journal of Personality and Social Psychology, 72*, 262–274.

Zajonc, R. B., & Adelmann, P. K. (1987). Cognition and communication: A story of missed opportunities. *Social Science Information/sur les sciences socials, 26,* 3–30.

Zwaan, R. A., & Radvansky, G. A. (1998). Situation models in language comprehension and memory. *Psychological Bulletin, 123,* 162–185.

15

Attitude Misattribution

Implications for Attitude Measurement and the Implicit–Explicit Relationship

B. Keith Payne

Introduction

Nuremberg, Germany, 1945. A young American intelligence officer and psychologist named Gustave Gilbert passes through a prison corridor with an American soldier standing guard outside every cell. Entering a cell, he greets the prisoner in fluent German. The prisoner is amiable as Gilbert starts the interview, joking, "Oh, those crazy cards again.... you know, one of the old gents said you showed him a lot of vulgar pictures" (Miale & Selzer, 1975, p. 84). Gilbert has opened a set of Rorschach inkblots.

Sitting across from Gilbert is Hermann Goering, head of the *Luftwaffe*, architect of the first concentration camps, and at one time Hitler's hand-picked successor. Gilbert has the unprecedented opportunity of conducting psychological studies of not only Goering, but all of the Nazi officials on trial for war crimes at Nuremberg. One of his main tools for probing the minds of these war criminals is the Rorschach inkblot test.

On the first two cards Goering gives unremarkable interpretations, the answers that most people give. "A bat," he says on the first one, which almost everyone sees as a bat or a butterfly. "Two people dancing," he says on the second. Looking at the third card in the series of 10, Goering holds the card, turns it on its side and then back again. The inkblot makes a symmetrical pattern in black with three red splotches, most commonly described as two human figures facing each other. Goering's response: "An opened figure of one man ... opened up, with two identical halves and the insides in the middle" (p. 87). What does this response reveal about the mind of Hermann Goering? It seems tempting to infer that there must be a lurid personality lurking behind such a response.

The Rorschach test works on the assumption that how people interpret an ambiguous figure says more about the interpreter than about the figure. Based in psychodynamic theory, the notion is that people project their own traits, attitudes, and motivations onto the inkblot in order to give form to a formless shape. In the process, they reveal something about themselves. What they reveal is presumed to be hidden deep in the Freudian unconscious, inaccessible to self-report. In Gilbert's interpretation, "there is much sadism and brutality as well in his response; Goering's ability to inflict great pain on others has its roots in his own pain" (Miale & Selzer, 1975, p. 88).

But is Goering's personality really revealed in his interpretation of an inkblot? After all, the psychologist already knew that the prisoner across from him was charged as a mass murderer. Perhaps the sequence was reversed, and Gilbert's interpretation of the response was shaped by his beliefs about the Nazi leader. Would he be inclined to give the same interpretation if he did not know who made the response? Would other psychologists consistently interpret the response in the same way? And would the interpretations made from such responses accurately predict Goering's behavior? These questions surrounding the interpretation of Goering's test illustrate the criticisms that have been frequently raised against projective tests more generally.

My intention here is not to defend the validity of the Rorschach test. Careful empirical studies have shown that although more than 80% of practicing therapists report using the Rorschach test (Watkins, Campbell, Nieberding, & Hallmark, 1995), the evidence for its validity is weak at best (Dawes, 1994; Lilienfeld, Wood, & Garb, 2000). There is also little evidence that the tendencies revealed by the Rorschach and other projective tests reflect deep, unconscious traits or motivations. However, I will argue that a fundamental premise behind the measure—that interpretations of ambiguous objects can reveal important insights about the interpreter—remains valuable (see also Chapter 14, this volume). When combined with the precision and experimental control of recent methods in social cognition, the approach can be very powerful.

This chapter describes research developing a novel approach to implicit attitude measurement based on interpretations of ambiguous objects. The first section describes evidence that the method provides a valid assessment of attitudes and shows why it has advantages over other techniques. The second section explores some startling new implications of this approach for the differences and similarities between attitudes measured using implicit and explicit tests.

Affect Misattribution

From the halls of Nuremberg, we move 45 years and 4,000 miles to the University of Michigan, early 1990s. Sheila Murphy and Robert Zajonc have conducted a remarkable experiment. Using a tachistiscope to precisely control the timing of stimuli, they projected prime pictures of happy and angry faces on a screen for 4 ms and followed each face with a Chinese pictograph, presented more slowly. The faces were flashed so quickly as to be undetectable by participants in the experiment. They could discriminate only the pictographs. Participants were asked to make an interpretation of the ambiguous pictographs, rating each for pleasantness. Even though participants subjectively experienced only the pictographs, the faces exerted a significant effect. Pictographs were rated as more pleasant following a happy face than an angry face.

Murphy and Zajonc (1993) argued that the subliminally presented faces sparked an emotional reaction, leaving subjects in a curious position. On the one hand, they experienced a pleasant or unpleasant emotional reaction, depending on the flashed face. On the other hand, they experienced only one stimulus that could have engendered that reaction: the pictograph. As a result, subjects attributed their emotional reactions to the pleasantness of the pictographs.

The purpose of the study was to explore the minimal psychological requirements for engendering an emotional reaction. There were several nuances to the paper that are not covered here, because the point I want to make is different from the point the authors were making. Although Murphy and Zajonc's (1993) paper was striking in showing how little input is required to engender emotional responses, there was another interesting fact uncovered but largely unnoticed in that paper. Evaluations of the pictographs can provide an indirect reflection of subjects' attitudes toward the primes.

Given an ambiguous object to interpret as pleasant or unpleasant, subjects drew on their spontaneous reactions toward the prime pictures. Though far removed from the psychodynamic theories and clinical diagnoses of the Rorschach test, this experiment represented an interesting instance of projective measurement. We have found that a procedure based on these same principles—which we call the *Affect*

Misattribution Procedure (AMP)—can provide an excellent method of implicit attitude measurement. Of course, attitudes can include non-emotional elements as well as emotional elements. We focus first on affective responses—pleasantness judgments and feelings ratings—and later in the chapter we examine the possibility of using the same approach to measure nonemotional aspects of attitudes.

Consider what would happen if we changed the happy and angry faces of the Murphy and Zajonc study to the faces of individuals who are either liked or disliked. Presumably, liked individuals would spark a pleasant reaction, whereas disliked individuals would spark an unpleasant reaction. If those reactions could be captured by ratings of ambiguous pictographs, that should provide a way to make inferences about attitudes toward the individuals. My collaborators and I took this approach in a study of political attitudes (Payne, Cheng, Govorun, & Stewart, 2005).

An indirect poll. The faces in this study belonged to U.S. President George W. Bush and the Democratic challenger John Kerry. The study was conducted just weeks before the 2004 presidential election, at a time when attitudes toward the presidential candidates were heavily on the minds of most people. The nation was highly polarized in their opinions of the two candidates, and the election would turn out to be one of the closest in American history. The sample of university volunteers reflected this sharply divided populace. Almost exactly half of the subjects said they would vote for Bush, and half said that they would vote for Kerry. Our question was whether we could use the affect misattribution procedure to distinguish between the two groups.

We selected photos of Bush and Kerry from various Internet news sources. After matching the photos on several extraneous factors (e.g., wearing a suit, smiling, presence of American flags) we selected 12 photos of each candidate. We constructed a priming task similar to that of Murphy and Zajonc, but with several alterations (see Figure 15.1). On each trial a candidate photo was flashed, followed by a randomly selected Chinese pictograph, which was followed by a black-and-white pattern mask. Subjects were asked to evaluate each pictograph as either "more pleasant than average" or "less pleasant than average." One difference from the Murphy and Zajonc (1993) procedure was that we flashed the prime photos visibly rather than subliminally. In such a situation, subjects might discount or correct for the influence of the primes when judging the pictographs. Judgmental correction refers to attempts to prevent or to remove the influence of bias from one's judgment. Correction is a well-established finding, commonly found

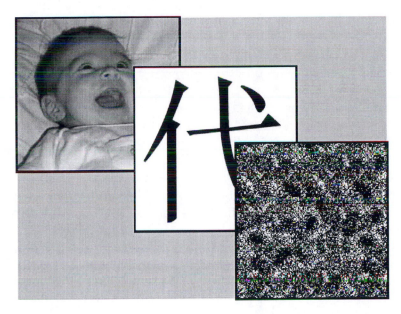

FIGURE 15.1 Representative prime, target, and mask stimuli from the Affect Misattribution Procedure.

when individuals perceive that their judgments might be biased by an unwanted influence (see Wegener & Petty, 1997, for a review). In contrast to other research using either projective measurement or implicit attitude measurement, we employed such correction attempts as part of the design rather than trying to avoid them. We did so by warning subjects that the primes might influence their responses and urging subjects to avoid any such influence.

This approach pits intentionally controlled correction processes directly against automatically activated attitudes. To the extent that people have control over the expression of attitudes on the task, they should be able to eliminate any influence of the prime when warned. Critically, whatever systematic effect of the prime persisted despite correction attempts could then be taken as an indication of automatic influence of attitudes evoked by the primes.

Results of the study were clear: Bush-voters found the pictographs more pleasant following a Bush prime, whereas Kerry-voters found the pictographs more pleasant following a Kerry prime. Individual differences in automatic attitudes were measured by taking the difference between pleasant responses on Bush versus Kerry trials. The correlation between individual AMP scores and voting intention was strong: $r = .58$. Using a discriminant analysis, it was possible to test how well the AMP score could discriminate between Bush-voters and Kerry-voters. Based on only this score, the model correctly classified 80% of subjects.

These results provided initial evidence that evaluations of the pictographs reflected subjects' attitudes toward the primes. The relation between AMP responses and voting intentions suggests that the method provides a valid estimate of attitudes, because it successfully predicted behavior. Moreover, further analyses showed that the measure provided a highly reliable estimate of attitudes (.90 using Cronbach's *alpha* coefficient). Given the high correspondence between the implicit measure of attitudes and people's self-reported voting intentions, one might wonder about the relationship between people's motivations and the attitudes captured by the AMP. On an issue as polarizing as the 2004 presidential election, it is possible that people disregarded the warning to avoid being influenced by the primes because they wanted to express their attitudes. If so, then the findings might not reflect high-quality implicit measurement, but instead, explicit attitudes deliberately expressed using an implicit task. To disentangle these explanations we needed a kind of attitude that people were less enthusiastic about expressing. We chose to study racial attitudes, one of the most socially sensitive attitude topics in American culture, and a sine qua non of implicit/explicit discrepancies.

Race and the Implicit/Explicit Divide

To establish that the AMP was capable of detecting attitudes that people may be unwilling or unable to directly report, we selected a sample of both White and Black college students and replaced the faces of Bush and Kerry with the faces of 12 White and 12 Black young men (Payne, Cheng et al., 2005). All subjects were told that the study concerned how people make simple judgments while avoiding distraction. This provided a cover story to explain why two images were presented on each trial. Half of the subjects were told simply that the faces presented were unimportant "warning signals" that would precede the Chinese pictographs and that they should rate the pictographs as more or less pleasant than average. They were not alerted to potential biasing influence of the faces. The other half were told that the race of the faces might influence their evaluations of the pictographs, and they were urged to avoid any such influence. The warning was blatant, reading, "Because we are interested in studying how people can avoid being biased, *please try your absolute best not to let the real-life images bias your judgment of the drawings!* Give us an honest assessment of the drawings, regardless of the images that precede them." Warnings of this sort have proven very effective at eliciting corrections in previous research (Wegener & Petty, 1997). Correcting judgments in this paradigm would intuitively seem to be easy—there was no time pressure or cognitive load. On any given trial, if a participant believed that the face was influencing the judgment, he or she could simply press the other key. With conditions so favorable for correction, any influences that persist nonetheless can provide strong evidence that the influence is unintentional.

Following an approach pioneered by Fazio and colleagues (1995), we compared responses on the implicit measure with responses on an explicit measure of racial attitudes and examined how that relationship changed as a function of subjects' motivations to control prejudice. Following the AMP, participants completed a set of questionnaires in what was described as a separate and unrelated study. These included a "feeling thermometer" rating of their attitudes toward Whites and Blacks, and the Motivation to Control Prejudiced Responses Scale (Dunton & Fazio, 1997). We expected to find a pattern similar to that of Fazio and colleagues (1995), in which the implicit and explicit measures corresponded for individuals who were not motivated to control prejudiced responses. However, for those who were more motivated, we expected the correlation to be obscured because they would complete the explicit measure in a way that would hide any negative racial attitudes.

The results were telling: On both the self-report measure and on the AMP, participants showed a slight ingroup preference. On the feelings ratings, Blacks rated their feelings as more favorable toward Blacks than Whites, whereas Whites rated their feelings as more favorable toward Whites than Blacks. On the AMP, Blacks rated the pictographs as more pleasant following Black faces compared to White faces, whereas Whites showed the opposite pattern. Importantly, the warning manipulation made no significant difference on AMP performance. The same ingroup preference was observed in both the warned and unwarned groups, suggesting that AMP responses may reflect something different than deliberately expressed attitudes.

Given that an ingroup bias was found on both implicit and explicit tasks, it is important to know whether the same individuals produced the parallel patterns on both tasks. In fact, the correlation between implicit and explicit measures was strong, $r = .58$, much stronger than is typically found on the topic of racial attitudes (e.g., Hofmann, Gawronski, Gschwendner, Le, & Schmitt, 2005). However, that correlation depended on individuals' motivations to control prejudice. Figure 15.2 shows the regression lines relating AMP performance and self-reported

Racial Attitudes

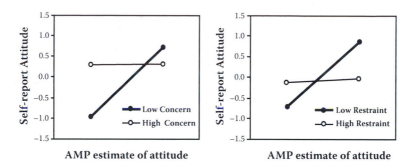

FIGURE 15.2 Relationships between AMP estimates of racial attitudes and self-reported feelings, as a function of motivation to control prejudice. Lines are regression lines plotted at one standard deviation above and below the mean of AMP and motivation variables. Concern = Concern with acting prejudiced. Restraint = Restraint to avoid dispute.

attitudes for individuals high and low (one standard deviation above and below the mean) on motivation to control prejudice. The same relationship was found for both subscales of the measures Concern with Acting Prejudiced and Restraint to Avoid Dispute. Among individuals who were highly motivated to control prejudice, the implicit-explicit correlation was near zero. However, among those who were unmotivated to control prejudice, the correlation was very high.

At first glance, this pattern might suggest that highly motivated individuals may have altered their AMP responses, which would argue against the use of the AMP to circumvent socially desirable responding. However, AMP scores and motivation scores were uncorrelated. Instead, the motivations correlated only with the self-report measure. Why were the highly motivated unable to rein in the revealing of their attitudes on the AMP? In part, it was because they did not know they were expressing any attitudes. When participants were asked whether the prime photos influenced their response, and how hard they tried to correct for any influence of the primes, their responses to these questions were uncorrelated with actual performance on the AMP. Regardless of whether subjects showed a consistent pro-White bias or a consistent pro-Black bias, their perceptions of their own performance were not at all tuned in to their behavior. Together, the presidential election study and the racial attitude study provided evidence (a) that AMP responses indirectly reflect attitudes toward the primes, (b) that these attitudes were strongly related to self-reported attitudes and behavior when motivation to conceal those attitudes was low, and (c) that these attitudes were very weakly related to self-reports when motivation to conceal the attitude was high. That is, among those who were motivated to conceal their attitudes, the AMP provided very different information than did self-report.

These studies provided initial evidence that the misattribution approach offers a viable means of attitude measurement. But the field of implicit attitude measures is crowded, with many measurement techniques for researchers to choose from. Can the AMP reveal anything about people's spontaneous evaluations that other measures do not? To answer this question we turned to a topic where implicit attitudes seem clearly relevant, but where their role is poorly understood: addictive behaviors. Potentially addictive behaviors such as smoking and alcohol abuse often reflect counterproductive automatic impulses that are difficult to control. Implicit measures seem well suited to provide valuable insight into the processes underlying these impulses.

Liking and drinking. Previous research on drinking and smoking has shown complex patterns of results that depend on many factors, including what implicit measure is used. As an example, one study found that an Implicit Association Test (IAT; Greenwald, McGhee, & Schwartz, 1998) differentiated smokers from nonsmokers but a priming task (Fazio, Sanbonmatsu, Powell, & Kardes, 1986) did not. In contrast, the priming measure was sensitive to nicotine deprivation but the IAT was not (Sherman, Rose, Koch, Presson, & Chassin, 2003). Another study using the IAT found that heavy drinkers showed a greater association between alcohol and arousal expectancies than light drinkers (Wiers, van Woerden, Smulders, & de Jong, 2002). However, the same study found no association between drinking and evaluative associations. Both heavy and light drinkers showed similarly negative associations to alcohol.

The varied results arising from different techniques suggest that idiosyncratic aspects of different measures may have influenced results. An important strength of the reaction-time-based priming procedure is its simplicity. The relationship between evaluations of the primes and responses to the targets is relatively straightforward and intuitive. However, a weakness is that reaction-time priming is often low in reliability (Fazio & Olson, 2003), which can lead to underestimation of the true relationship with other variables. A strength of the IAT is large effect sizes, which make it relatively easy to detect effects. However, a potential weakness is that the IAT is complex, requiring two different categorizations mapped onto a single set of response keys. Research subjects faced with this difficult task may develop strategies to simplify the task.

The assumption behind the IAT is that the relative speed of responses reflects how strongly the person associates the target concepts with *good* and *bad*. However, researchers have also identified other strategies that subjects might use to solve this mapping problem independent of associative strength (Karpinski & Hilton, 2001; Olson & Fazio, 2004; Rothermond & Wentura, 2004). These proposals raise questions about how to interpret IAT effects. For example, when both heavy drinkers and light drinkers show equally negative associations to alcohol, does that reflect dislike of alcohol among both groups, or something else?

It has often been argued that addictive behaviors are driven by automatic appetitive responses to the drug, which one might expect to be revealed in positive implicit attitudes. But a model in which appetitive automatic responses mediate drug-taking behavior is inconsistent with the data that show negative implicit attitudes toward drugs even among those who use the drug. Such a pattern is important for theories of addictive behavior, because it suggests that people use drugs despite an automatic aversion to them, rather than because of an automatic attraction.

The lack of clarity about the relationship between implicit attitudes and addictive behavior led us to examine the subject using the AMP (Payne, Govorun, & Arbuckle, 2006). Like the IAT, the AMP has large effect sizes, but it also has the advantage of simplicity. Like reaction-time priming, the transfer of evaluations from prime to target items in the AMP is straightforward, but it also has high reliability. Given these advantages, we expected to find a relatively simple and systematic pattern of findings. First, we expected that people with more positive automatic responses toward addictive substances would be more likely to use them. Second, we expected the relationship to be clearest under conditions of low motivation to conceal such preferences, where we could expect people to express their substance use openly. This is the same pattern found in the study reported earlier of racial attitudes. Finding that addictive behaviors follow that same pattern would suggest that they too can be understood in terms of automatic impulses, coupled with controlled efforts to manage those impulses.

In the first study testing whether AMP responses could predict drinking behavior, we recruited volunteers who were over 21 years of age for a study on drinking preferences. Subjects first completed an AMP in which the primes showed photos of beer, photos of drinking water, and a blank gray square as a baseline. Next subjects were asked to participate in a taste test. They could choose either to taste beer or to taste bottled water. The question of interest was whether AMP responses could predict the choice to drink beer versus water.

Overall, about half of the sample chose to taste beer. However, that choice was significantly related to individual differences in AMP responses. At one standard deviation above the mean of liking for beer, 70% of subjects chose beer. In contrast, at one standard deviation below the mean, only 36% chose beer. Spontaneous affective reactions measured by the AMP proved to be a good predictor of who would choose beer.

In the second study, we included several items to measure subjects' motivation to conceal drinking behavior (e.g., "I attempt to appear as though I do not drink much in order to avoid negative reactions from others."). By the same logic as applied in the racial attitudes study, we expected the relationship between AMP responses and self-reported drinking behavior to depend on people's motivation to conceal drinking. In this study we measured drinking behavior using a self-report measure of frequency (how often one drinks alcohol) and quantity (how much one drinks when drinking). An overall estimate of drinking behavior was derived by multiplying these two sets of items.

As expected, individual differences in AMP performance significantly correlated with drinking behavior. However, the correlation was significantly stronger among those who were not motivated to conceal drinking, as shown in Figure 15.3. Motivation to conceal drinking correlated with self-reported drinking, but not with AMP responses.

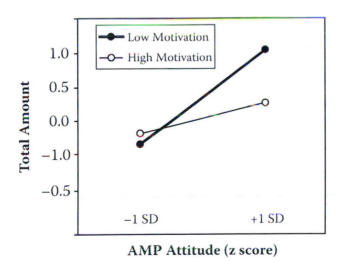

FIGURE 15.3 Drinking behavior. Relationship between AMP estimate of attitude toward alcohol and total drinking amount, as a function of motivation to conceal drinking. Lines are regression lines plotted at one standard deviation above and below the mean of AMP and motivation variables.

Among those who were not motivated to conceal drinking, individuals who reported drinking a lot showed very favorable implicit responses to alcohol cues. These results nicely match those regarding racial attitudes, showing a simple systematic pattern in contrast to some previous investigations of drinking attitudes.

This study also included explicit attitudes toward alcohol to test whether evaluations measured by the AMP and self-reported attitudes each uniquely predicted variance in drinking behavior. The explicit attitude items asked subjects to rate the extent to which they liked beer, liquor, and wine. Both explicit and implicit measures of attitudes related to the amount subjects reported drinking. Moreover, when partial correlations were examined, both were uniquely associated with reported drinking.

Given the differences between these results and previous studies using other measures, it seemed important to directly compare the behavior of different measures in the same context. To do so, we conducted another study in which we included not only the AMP, but also the IAT and a reaction-time-based sequential priming task. These measures all used the same stimuli (alcohol and water pictures) and were completed in a counterbalanced order to control for practice and fatigue effects. In addition to these three implicit tasks, we measured six variables related to drinking behavior and life problems associated with drinking.

Reaction-time priming showed a significant relationship with one of the six variables, with an average correlation of $r = .15$. The IAT also showed a significant relationship with one of the six variables, with an average correlation of $r = .20$. Finally, the AMP showed a reliable correlation with all six drinking measures, averaging $r = .35$. The correlation between AMP scores and drinking behavior was significant even after controlling for attitudes measured using the other two tasks.

The AMP, but not the other measures, related also to a measure of serious drinking-related life consequences, such as missing exams because of drinking and being arrested for drinking and driving. Though negative consequences might generally be expected to lead to negative attitudes, the relationship may be different when it comes to potentially addictive drugs. Not surprisingly, life problems were highly correlated with the amount participants reported drinking: Those who drank more suffered more problems. The relationship between AMP responses and life problems was fully mediated by the amount subjects drank. This pattern suggests that subjects with positive automatic responses to alcohol drink more, and as a result they have more alcohol-related problems. As in the study described earlier, this relationship was independent of explicitly reported attitudes toward alcohol, with both explicit and implicit measures uniquely predicting alcohol-related problems.

The results from the alcohol studies are important because they demonstrate that attitudes revealed by the AMP provide novel information beyond what may be gained by other commonly used implicit measures. Previous research using other measures has produced a puzzling pattern of results, leaving questions about whether automatic evaluative responses have anything to do with drinking behavior. In the case of reaction-time priming, the complex results may be related to high error variance. In the case of the IAT, the complex results may stem from IAT scores reflecting multiple factors, such as cultural associations that may differ from personal associations, cognitive skills, figure-ground asymmetries, or other factors. Based on the AMP studies, it appears that people who have spontaneous pleasant reactions to alcohol are the ones who tend to drink more and to have more negative life consequences from drinking.

The line of thought laid out so far began with the fascinating potential of projective tests and some of their disappointing failures to live up to it. Yet, I have tried to salvage one critical aspect of projective logic—that interpretations reveal qualities of interpreters. I made the case that interpretations of ambiguous objects primed by attitude objects can reveal attitudes toward the primes. By moving out of the Freudian unconscious and into more modern concepts and techniques of social cognition, this approach offers a new potential for indirectly assessing attitudes, even in socially sensitive situations where individuals may be less than candid on direct measures. The evidence presented suggests that the AMP performs as one would theoretically expect an implicit measure to perform and compares favorably with other indirect measures. But the most exciting prospect for this new approach is not simply that it does a good job doing the same things that other implicit measures do. The most exciting prospect is that this approach opens up new possibilities for studying the similarities and differences between directly expressed and indirectly measured attitudes. The next section describes how those possibilities unfold from the research summarized above.

The Importance of Intent

What is it that all implicit measures have in common with each other, and that all explicit measures have in common? The distinction between implicit and explicit attitudes has been variously described as the difference between unconscious and conscious, spontaneous and deliberate, unobtrusive and obtrusive, and automatic and controlled, among others. Although the preferred distinction depends on one's theoretical perspective, it is worth noting that all implicit measures share a common feature. They all measure attitudes without asking subjects to report them. All explicit measures share the feature that they directly ask subjects to express their attitude. The critical difference between these two classes of measures boils down to a question of intent. On direct or explicit attitude measures, subjects intend to express an attitude. On indirect or implicit measures, they do not.

Ideally, a comparison of indirect and direct attitude measures would hold all other factors constant and vary only intent (Schacter, Bowers, & Booker, 1989). This is, of course, standard experimental methodology—only the variable of interest should vary. Differences in behavior when subjects intend to express an attitude toward John Kerry or Jack Daniels, versus when they do not intend to express an attitude, can then be taken as evidence for a distinction between intentionally expressed attitudes versus unintentionally expressed attitudes.

Now consider the implicit and explicit tasks that are the state of the art, and how many ways they differ beyond intent. Explicit attitude measures are nearly always self-report questions in which subjects read a set of sentences and express their agreement or favorability on a numerical scale. For example, an item from the commonly used Modern Racism Scale (MRS) reads, "Blacks have more influence upon school desegregation plans than they ought to have." Participants are asked to consider this statement and indicate their agreement or disagreement. Compare that with what participants are asked to do on the race IAT. They are presented with a word (e.g., *awful*) and asked to classify it using keys that are either designated for Black-or-bad versus White-or-good, or Black-or-good versus White-or-bad pairings. On priming tasks, participants simply evaluate the word as good or bad, after being primed with a relevant image or word. The dependent variable for both is reaction time.

In addition to intentional versus unintentional expressions of attitudes, these tasks differ in at least (a) the stimuli presented (complex propositions versus simple words), (b) the abstractness of judgments subjects make (endorsement of complex ideas versus word classifications), and (c) the dependent variables measured (Likert scales versus reaction times). These measures differ in many ways besides the implicit/explicit distinction (Payne, 2001; Payne, Jacoby, & Lambert, 2005).

What if the low correlations often reported between implicit and explicit measures (e.g., Poehlman, Uhlmann, Greenwald, & Banaji, 2005; Hofmann et al., 2005; Fazio & Olson, 2003) were due as much to these differences as to the implicitness or explicitness of the measurement? There is precedent for such a suggestion. For example, on the question of attitude-behavior consistency, Ajzen and Fishbein (1977) argued persuasively that attitudes and behaviors must be "conceptually correspondent"; that is, defined and measured at comparable levels of specificity. Otherwise, the correlation observed between an attitude measure and a behavioral measure would spuriously underestimate the relationship. Closer to the issue at hand, a meta-analysis by Hofmann and colleagues found that the degree of conceptual correspondence between implicit and explicit measures was a significant moderator of the implicit/explicit correlation. In fact, it was a stronger moderator than social desirability.

If implicit/explicit correlations have been generally underestimated because of a lack of correspondence between measures, then equating measures on extraneous features should increase the relationship. With most measures it is impossible to equate these features because the structure of implicit tasks is essential to their operation. However, the structure of the AMP allows new possibilities.

Consider the sequence of events on a typical AMP trial. First a prime picture (say, the face of an African American) is flashed. Then a fraction of a second later a pictograph is flashed, followed by a pattern mask. At that point, subjects evaluate whether the pictograph is pleasant or unpleasant, trying to avoid any influence from the prime. This is the sequence that produces an indirect measure of attitudes toward the face flashed as a prime. Now consider the same sequence of events, alike in all ways except this time after the prime is flashed, the pictograph is flashed, and the mask is flashed, subjects evaluate whether the face is pleasant or unpleasant. By comparing these two types of trials, we can gain both an indirect measure of attitudes toward the face and a direct measure of attitudes toward it. The stimuli, the abstractness of the judgment, and the response scale are all identical. The only difference is that in the direct rating, subjects intend to express an evaluation of the face. In the indirect rating, they intend not to do so.

A study comparing direct and indirect ratings serves to illustrate the similarities and differences between them. Payne et al. (2008) presented participants with Black and White faces as primes, followed by Chinese pictographs, followed finally by a black-and-white pattern mask. In one block of trials, subjects were instructed to evaluate the pictographs on a 4-point scale ranging from –2 (very unpleasant) to +2 (very pleasant). (Pilot testing showed that a continuous scale versus a binary choice made virtually no difference. Therefore, we chose a continuous scale.) They were warned that the prime pictures could influence their

TABLE 15.1 Correlations among Self-Report Scales of Racial Attitudes, and Direct and Indirect AMP Ratings

	ATB	MRS	Direct AMP	Indirect AMP
ATB	—	.68**	.25*	.25*
MRS		—	.26*	.24*
Direct AMP			—	.64**

Note: *= p < .05; **= p < .001; ATB = Attitudes toward Blacks scale; MRS = Modern Racism Scale.

responses and were urged to avoid any influence. In a second block of trials (counterbalanced for order) participants saw the same kinds of trials, with new pictographs. This time they were instructed to evaluate how the person whose face was flashed made them feel, on the same 4-point scale. They were warned that the pictographs could influence their ratings of the faces and that they should avoid any such influence. Finally, after completing both rounds of ratings (which took about 10 min), subjects completed two self-report scales measuring racial attitudes: the Modern Racism Scale (McConahay, 1983) and the Attitudes toward Blacks (ATB) scale (Brigham, 1993).

These measures allow several interesting comparisons. The two self-report scales are both explicit measures and they are also similar conceptually, both asking propositional questions about African Americans as a social group. The comparison between these scales and the indirect ratings provides an implicit/explicit comparison of the sort that is typically made. The measures differ both on intent (i.e., implicitness versus explicitness) and on other features (stimuli, abstractness, etc.), although they are comparable on the use of rating scales as the dependent measure. Finally, the comparison between indirect and direct AMP ratings provides an implicit/explicit comparison that differs only in intent. Table 15.1 displays the pattern of correlations.

Not surprisingly, the two self-report scales were highly correlated. However, replicating much previous work, these scales were only weakly related to the indirect ratings (average implicit-explicit r = .25). So far, these results are just as most researchers would expect. The traditional interpretation is that these correlations represent a dissociation between implicit and explicit attitudes, because they reflect either different constructs or different degrees of self-regulation.

That interpretation suggests that the direct ratings should be related to the self-report scales much more strongly, because direct ratings, like the scales, are explicit reports of racial attitudes. But counter to this pre-diction, the direct ratings were no more related to the self-report scales than were the indirect ratings (average $r = .26$). These small correlations cannot be explained based on differences between implicit and explicit attitudes. Like the indirect ratings, the direct ratings differed from the self-report scales on other extraneous factors. Could those extraneous factors be responsible for the low implicit/explicit correlation between the scales and the indirect ratings? If so, the direct ratings and indirect ratings should be significantly correlated, despite the fact that they are on opposite sides of the implicit/explicit divide. In fact, the correlation between indirect and direct ratings was $r = .64$. The strong correlation between indirect and direct ratings suggests that when measures are equated on extraneous factors, implicit and explicit evaluations might be more closely related than previously thought.

The strong implicit/explicit correlation was observed with two tasks using pictures of individual group members. In contrast, the scales were verbal measures that assessed attitudes toward racial groups as a whole. A person's attitude toward an entire social group may be quite different from their affective responses to a sample of individuals from the group (Olson & Fazio, 2003). Of course, this is one of the ways that many implicit and explicit measures lack structural correspondence, because most explicit tests refer to entire groups, whereas many implicit tests measure responses to individual exemplars. Our analysis suggests that implicit-explicit correspondence for attitudes toward racial groups may also be high, so long as both implicit and explicit tests measure attitudes toward the same group labels. To test this idea, we conducted a sec-ond study. In addition to the face primes, verbal group labels were also used as primes (African Americans, Black Americans, Blacks; Euro-pean Americans, White Americans, Whites). This study fully crossed whether the primes were faces versus group labels, and whether ratings were direct (rating the primes) or indirect (rating pictographs).

The rating scale for ratings of all items (both primes and pictographs) was a four-point feeling thermometer ranging from "Very cold/unfa-vorable feelings" to "Very warm/favorable feelings." When verbal labels were used with direct ratings, this amounted to a traditional feeling thermometer rating because participants were shown a group label (e.g., African Americans) and asked to rate their feelings toward the group. Thus, this technique provides both direct and indirect versions of a classic method of attitude assessment. As a standard of comparison, a traditional feeling thermometer measure for the same group labels was also administered in a separate phase of the experiment. As expected,

TABLE 15.2 Correlations Between Direct and Indirect AMP
Ratings Using Pictures and Verbal Labels as Primes

	Indirect—verbal	Direct—picture	Indirect—picture
Direct—verbal	.65**c	.39*b	.39*a
Indirect—verbal		.17a	.50**b
Direct—picture			.48**c

Note: * = p < .01; ** = p < .001; Cells with subscript *a* differ in both prime type (picture vs. verbal) and intent (direct vs. indirect). Cells with a subscript *b* differ only in prime type. Cells with a subscript *c* differ only in intent.

the feeling thermometer correlated strongly with the verbal label/direct rating, $r = .72$. This strong correlation confirms that the verbal/direct rating was assessing something very similar to what traditional feeling thermometers assess.

The main questions of interest were whether verbal labels led to strong implicit/explicit correlations similar to the picture primes, and whether comparing verbal measures to picture measures reduced the correlations. The results are shown in Table 15.2. The measures that differed in both intent and conceptual correspondence (denoted with subscript *a*) showed relatively weak relationships, with an average correlation of only .28. The measures that differed in prime type but were matched on intent (denoted by subscript *b*) showed stronger relationships, averaging .45. Finally, the measures that differed in intent but were matched on prime type as well as all other features (denoted by subscript *c*) showed the strongest correlations, averaging .57.

Together, these findings suggest that noncorresponding irrelevant features such as the kinds of primes used can greatly underestimate relationships between implicit and explicit measures. Low correlations based on these measurement features may sometimes be mistaken for weak relationships between the constructs of implicit and explicit evaluations themselves.

That implies that when measures are equated on irrelevant features, the implicit/explicit correlation can be much greater than previously thought. The strong implicit/explicit correlations described here were on the topic of racial attitudes, a topic known to produce low implicit/explicit correlations (Hofmann et al., 2005). The relationships in other domains are likely to be even stronger.

Such strong correlations between direct and indirect ratings raise the question of whether the indirect ratings are really all that indirect. Perhaps the AMP correlates with explicit measures because it is not very implicit. Or alternatively, perhaps the direct ratings were not very explicit. To test these ideas, Payne et al. (2008) conducted a final study. If indirect AMP ratings are simply a thinly veiled explicit measure, then indirect and direct ratings should both respond in similar ways to social pressure, which is known to influence explicit attitude measures. If, on the other hand, indirect and direct ratings are really both implicit measures, then neither should be influenced much by social pressure. But if, as we predicted, indirect ratings acted as an implicit test whereas direct ratings acted as an explicit test, then social pressure should affect direct but not indirect ratings.

This study manipulated social pressure to avoid expressing prejudice. Subjects in the low-pressure group had their attitudes validated by instructions emphasizing that everyone's opinion is valid. They were asked to be open and honest even if their attitudes were not "politically correct," and they were reminded that their responses would be kept strictly confidential. The high-pressure group received instructions emphasizing that racial prejudice and discrimination continue to exist, and that the study was motivated by the goal of "eliminating the scourge of racial prejudice." High-pressure subjects were asked to complete the experiment while keeping in mind that everyone is vulnerable to racial biases.

Black and White faces were used as primes. In one block of the experiment subjects made indirect ratings, evaluating the pictographs after being warned to avoid the influence of the prime photos. In the other block (counterbalanced for order) subjects directly evaluated the faces. We expected the social pressure manipulation to influence direct ratings. More interesting was the question of whether indirect ratings would be similarly affected.

Supporting the hypothesis that indirect ratings provided a valid implicit measure of race attitudes, social pressure affected the direct ratings but not indirect ratings. As a result, the two were highly correlated in the low-pressure condition, $r = .61$, but only weakly correlated in the high-pressure condition, $r = .26$ (see Figure 15.4). Even when implicit and explicit measures are equated so that they differ only in intent, the strong implicit/explicit correlation can be greatly reduced by introducing social pressure.

Affective and cognitive bases of attitudes and the AMP. The studies described thus far all focused on affective responses, in part because the AMP grew out of a research tradition focused on the misattribution of emotion. There is no reason, however, that the techniques described here should be limited to emotional responses alone. Some theories consider attitudes to include cognitive and behavioral components in addition

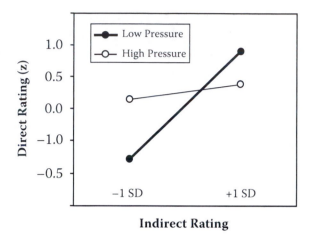

FIGURE 15.4 Racial attitudes. Relationship between indirect and direct AMP ratings as a function of social pressure. Lines are regression lines plotted at one standard deviation above and below the mean of AMP and social pressure variables.

to affect (Zanna & Rempel, 1988). Though most of our research has focused on affective judgments such as pleasantness or feelings ratings, the method can easily be used with any kind of judgment.

Some preliminary research suggests that cognitive responses can be measured effectively. To extend this analysis to cognitive aspects of intergroup attitudes, one study in our lab examined the usefulness of trait judgments for implicitly measuring stereotypes. The procedure for indirect ratings was similar to the racial attitude studies described earlier, in that faces of Black and White individuals were used as primes, followed by Chinese pictographs. In this study, however, subjects were asked to guess whether each pictograph meant *aggressive* or *friendly* in the Chinese language. For direct ratings, subjects saw the same prime faces and were asked to judge how friendly or aggressive each person looked.

As a way to validate these indirect and direct measures of stereotypes, the study also examined how subjects formed impressions of a target person described as performing several behaviors pretested to be ambiguous in aggressiveness. One group of participants was told that the person described was Black, whereas the other group was told he was White. Participants rated the person on aggressiveness and friendliness, and also on global evaluative terms such as *likeable*. The main question in this study was whether indirect or direct measures of stereotyping were associated with the kinds of impressions participants formed of the person described.

In fact, both indirect and direct stereotype ratings were correlated with judgments of the target character, but only when he was described as Black. As expected, they related more strongly to the specific traits of aggressive and friendly than to global evaluations. Interestingly, indirect ratings were uniquely associated with aggression judgments of the target person when controlling for direct ratings.

Although there is much more work to be done here, these initial results suggest that semantic concepts such as traits can be measured using misattributions in the same ways that affective responses can be. Explicit measures of attitudes often include both cognitive and affective components, as in semantic differential scales. These scales might ask subjects to rate an object on affective items such as *pleasantness* and on more cognitive items such as *useful* or *wise*. This same measurement procedure could easily be used with the AMP, producing both direct and indirect semantic differentials. Doing so may help better integrate research on implicit evaluation with traditional attitude research.

Implications for the nature of implicit and explicit evaluation. Based on many empirical findings of low correlations between implicit and explicit attitude tests, theories have often emphasized the differences between implicitly measured attitudes and explicitly measured attitudes. The present findings suggest, though, that when methodological differences between implicit and explicit tests are removed, the correlations can become much greater. Does this imply the processes underlying implicit and explicit tests are really the same? Probably not.

First, it is important to recognize that even when two tests are correlated in the .60 range, nearly two thirds of the variance in scores on each test remains unexplained. Findings of such high correlations are important because they suggest that implicit and explicit tests might measure underlying processes that are much more closely related than previously thought. But that does not necessarily mean that the two are identical. There remains room for the kinds of distinctions between automatic and controlled aspects of evaluation described by dual-process theories of attitudes.

Beyond these psychometric considerations, there are other reasons to suspect that implicit and explicit tests reflect distinct processes. The most obvious one is the effects of social desirability described in the studies above. Directly expressed evaluations were shaped by social desirability much more than indirectly assessed evaluations. This fact implies that direct attitude expressions incorporated motivated adjustments more so than indirect ratings did, consistent with much prior research (e.g., Fazio, 1990). In this sense, the processes underlying direct and indirect assessments differed in an important and systematic way.

There are reasons beyond the studies reported here to expect that equating measurement structures will not render implicit and explicit measures redundant. Some research has demonstrated differences between implicitly and explicitly measured attitudes that cannot easily be explained by method differences. For example, discrepancies between implicit and explicit tests may lead people to process more information, presumably in an effort to resolve the discrepancy (Briñol, Petty, & Wheeler, 2006; see Chapter 5, this volume). Because it is not obvious how structural differences would explain such patterns, these findings provide evidence that the processes underlying implicit and explicit tests differ in some ways.

If implicit and explicit evaluations are neither completely independent nor completely redundant, then the important question is how strongly they overlap (and under what conditions). Answering that question requires accurate measurements, uncontaminated by structural differences. It is important to sort out when low correlations between implicit and explicit measures reflect real differences between accurately measured constructs, and when they reflect stronger relationships obscured by methodological differences. The more closely implicit and explicit tests are matched in their structures, the more confidence researchers will have that whatever differences they observe reflect differences in the underlying processes rather than test structures.

Conclusion

By equating implicit and explicit tests on everything but intent, the AMP showed uncommonly strong correspondence with explicit measures. Strong correspondence with explicit measures is not necessarily the best quality for an implicit measure. After all, if implicit attitudes are qualitatively different from explicit attitudes—a fundamental theoretical question—then we might expect little or no relationship. However, the AMP does not always show strong relationships with explicit measures. Under conditions such as high social pressure or low conceptual correspondence, correlations were quite low. What is critically important is the ability to detect strong relationships when they are present, so that one can be confident in concluding when they are not. It is the pattern of correspondence and noncorrespondence under specific conditions that will shed light on the nature of implicit evaluation.

Sparse relationships between implicit and explicit measures have formed the backdrop for a great deal of theorizing about the nature of attitudes, conscious choice, and the self. The questions that arise are important ones: What if a test of race bias suggests that I am less fair minded than I would describe myself to be? Should my minority students worry? What does it mean if a test shows that your child's implicit response to beer is more favorable than he might report to you? Should you worry when he heads away to college? The answers will depend on how we understand implicit and explicit measures and how we interpret the meaning of their divergences. As structural differences between tests can be ruled out with more confidence, remaining discrepancies between implicit and explicit tests become more meaningful in answering these important questions.

References

Ajzen, I., & Fishbein, M. (1977). Attitude-behavior relations: A theoretical analysis and review of empirical research. *Psychological Bulletin, 84*, 888–918.

Brigham, J. C. (1993). College students' racial attitudes. *Journal of Applied Social Psychology, 23*, 1933–1967.

Briñol, P., Petty, R. E., & Wheeler, S. C. (2006). Discrepancies between explicit and implicit self-concepts: Consequences for information processing. *Journal of Personality and Social Psychology, 91*, 154–170.

Dawes, R. M. (1994). *House of cards: Psychology and psychotherapy built on myth*. New York: The Free Press.

Dunton, B. C., & Fazio, R. H. (1997). An individual difference measure of motivation to control prejudiced reactions. *Personality and Social Psychology Bulletin, 23*, 316–326.

Dunton, B. C., & Fazio, R. H. (1990). Multiple processes by which attitudes guide behavior: The MODE model as an integrative framework. In M. P. Zanna (Ed.), *Advances in experimental social psychology* (Vol. 23, pp. 75–109). New York: Academic Press.

Fazio, R. H., Jackson, J. R., Dunton, B. C, & Williams, C. J. (1995). Variability in automatic activation as an unobtrusive measure of racial attitudes: A bona fide pipeline? *Journal of Personality and Social Psychology, 69*, 1013–1027.

Fazio, R. H., & Olson, M. A. (2003). Implicit measures in social cognition research: Their meaning and uses. *Annual Review of Psychology, 54*, 297–327.

Fazio, R. H., Sanbonmatsu, D. M., Powell, M. C., & Kardes, F. R. (1986). On the automatic activation of attitudes. *Journal of Personality and Social Psychology, 50*, 229–238.

Greenwald, A. G., McGhee, D. E., & Schwartz, J. L. K. (1998). Measuring individual differences in implicit cognition: The Implicit Association Test. *Journal of Personality and Social Psychology, 74*, 1464–1480.

Hofmann, W., Gawronski, B., Gschwendner, T., Le, H., & Schmitt, M. (2005). A meta-analysis on the correlation between the implicit association test and explicit self-report measures. *Personality and Social Psychology Bulletin, 31,* 1369–1385.

Karpinski, A., & Hilton, J. L. (2001). Attitudes and the Implicit Association Test. *Journal of Personality and Social Psychology, 81*, 774–788.

Lilienfield, S. O., Wood, J. M., & Garb, H. N. (2000). The scientific status of projective techniques. *Psychological Science in the Public Interest, 1*, 27–66.

Miale, F., & Selzer, M. (1975). *The Nuremberg mind: The psychology of the Nazi leaders.* New York: Quadrangle.

McConahay, J. B. (1983). Modern racism and modern discrimination: The effects of race, racial attitudes, and context on simulated hiring decisions. *Personality and Social Psychology Bulletin, 9*, 551–558.

Murphy, S. T., & Zajonc, R. B. (1993). Affect, cognition, and awareness: Affective priming with optimal and suboptimal stimulus exposures. *Journal of Personality and Social Psychology, 64*, 723–739.

Olson, M. A., & Fazio, R. H. (2003). Relations between implicit measures of prejudice: What are we measuring? *Psychological Science, 14*, 36–39.

Olson, M. A., & Fazio, R. H. (2004). Reducing the influence of extrapersonal associations on the Implicit Association Test: Personalizing the IAT. *Journal of Personality and Social Psychology, 86*, 653–667.

Payne, B. K. (2001). Prejudice and perception: The role of automatic and controlled processes in misperceiving a weapon. *Journal of Personality and Social Psychology, 81*, 181–192.

Payne, B. K., Burkley, M., & Stokes, M. B. (2008). Why do implicit and explicit attitude tests diverge? The role of structural fit. *Journal of Personality and Social Psychology, 94*, 16–31.

Payne, B. K., Cheng, C. M., Govorun, O., & Stewart, B. (2005). An inkblot for attitudes: Affect misattribution as implicit measurement. *Journal of Personality and Social Psychology, 89,* 277–293.

Payne, B. K., Govorun, O., & Arbuckle, N. L. (2008). Automatic attitudes and alcohol: Does implicit liking predict drinking? *Cognition and Emotion, 22*, 238–271.

Payne, B. K., Jacoby, L. L., & Lambert, A. J. (2005). Attitudes as accessibility bias: Dissociating automatic and controlled components. In R. Hassin, J. Uleman, & J. Bargh (Eds.), *The new unconscious* (pp. 393–420). New York: Oxford University Press.

Petty, R. E., & Briñol, P. (in press). Implicit ambivalence: A meta-cognitive approach. In R. E. Petty, R. H. Fazio, & P. Briñol (Eds.), *Attitudes: Insights from the new implicit measures*. Hillsdale, NJ: Erlbaum.

Poehlman, T. A., Uhlmann, E., Greenwald, A. G., & Banaji, M. R. (2005). *Understanding and using the Implicit Association Test: III. Meta-analysis of predictive validity.* Unpublished manuscript, Yale University, New Haven, CT.

Rorschach, H. (1921). *Psychodiagnostics: A diagnostic test based on perception.* New York: Grune & Stratton.

Rothermond, K., & Wentura, D. (2001). Figure-ground asymmetries in the Implicit Association Test (IAT). *Zeitschrift fur experimentelle Psychologie, 48,* 94–106.

Schacter, D.L., Bowers, J., & Booker, J. (1989). Intention, awareness, and implicit memory: The retrieval intentionality criterion. In S. Lewandowsky, J. C. Dunn, & K. Kirsner (Eds.), *Implicit memory: Theoretical issues* (pp. 47–65). Hillsdale, N.J: Erlbaum.

Sherman, S. J., Rose, J. S., Koch, K., Presson, C. C., & Chassin, L. (2003). Implicit and explicit attitudes toward cigarette smoking: The effects of context and motivation. *Journal of Social and Clinical Psychology, 22,* 13–39.

von Hippel, W., Sekaquaptewa, D., & Vargas, P. T. (in press). Linguistic markers of implicit attitudes. In R. E. Petty, R. H. Fazio, & P. Briñol (Eds.), *Attitudes: Insights from the new implicit measures.* Hillsdale, NJ: Erlbaum.

Watkins, C. E., Campbell, V. L., Nieberding, R., & Hallmark, R. (1995). Contemporary practice of psychological assessment by clinical psychologists. *Professional Psychology: Research and Practice, 26,* 54–60.

Wegener, D. T., & Petty, R. E. (1997). The flexible correction model: The role of naive theories of bias in bias correction. In M. P. Zanna (Ed.), *Advances in experimental social psychology* (Vol. 29, pp. 141–208). Mahwah, NJ: Erlbaum.

Wiers, R. W., Van Woerden, N., Smulders, F. T. Y., & De Jong, P. J. (2002). Implicit and explicit alcohol-related cognitions in heavy and light drinkers. *Journal of Abnormal Psychology, 111,* 648–658.

Zanna, M. P., & Rempel, J. K. (1988). Attitudes: A new look at an old concept. In D. Bar-Tal & A. Kruglanski (Eds.), *The social psychology of knowledge* (pp. 315–334). New York: Cambridge University Press.

16

Implicit Measurement of Attitudes
A Physiological Approach

William A. Cunningham
Dominic J. Packer
Amanda Kesek
Jay J. Van Bavel

Introduction

Psychology has a long history of developing methods to study mental states that avoid reliance on introspective self-report. Psychoanalysts, for instance, used word choice errors (Freud, 1933) or narratives generated after viewing ambiguous images (e.g., the TAT; Morgan & Murray, 1935) to infer unconscious motivations and preferences. Similarly, recognizing that verbal reports of attitudes only provide information regarding a subset of evaluative processes, social cognition researchers have developed a large arsenal of implicit attitude measures, such as the Implicit Association Test (Greenwald, McGhee, & Schwartz, 1998), bona fide pipeline (see Chapter 2, this volume), and Affect Misattribution Procedure (see Chapter 15, this volume). These measures have the potential to uncover aspects of evaluative processing that occur automatically (Fazio, Sanbonmatsu, Powell, & Kardes, 1986) and outside of conscious awareness (Draine & Greenwald, 1998). Thus, in addition to having the advantage that they circumvent obvious social desirability concerns (especially in sensitive domains such as prejudice), these types of indirect measures may also provide information regarding aspects of evaluative processing that people do not have accurate or complete introspective access to (e.g., processes that occur within hundreds of milliseconds). For this chapter, we define an implicit measure of attitude as one that does not require a self-report or conscious introspection.

From their earliest definitions, attitudes were thought to invoke a readiness for behavioral action and, as such, were expected to have physiological consequences supported by specific emotional states (Allport, 1935). Most simply stated, Thurstone (1931) defined an attitude as "the affect for or against a psychological object." Because the activation of an attitude often leads to an emotional reaction, it was assumed that one could understand the evaluative state of a person by monitoring various bodily responses, an assumption predicated on the following sequence of events:

$$\text{Stimulus} \rightarrow \text{Attitude} \rightarrow \text{Emotional Response} \rightarrow \text{Measurement}$$

Thus, if a person with a negative attitude toward spiders should come across one, a negative emotional response is assumed to follow the activation and processing of the spider attitude. Following this logic, psychologists have measured physiological states to make inferences about attitudes for nearly a century. For example, electrodermal activity (i.e., the skin's ability to conduct electricity) has been shown to vary as a function of the emotionality (Smith, 1922) and attitude extremity (Dysinger, 1931) of presented stimuli, and agreement with attitude statements (Dickson & McGinnies, 1966).

The Evaluative System and Physiology

At root, attitude research is concerned with the prediction of behavior, a task that has proven to be much more complicated than initially imagined by psychologists. Accordingly, the history of attitude research has shifted from a focus on the general relationship between attitudes and behavior to a more precise investigation and delineation of different attitudinal components, and their relation to the prediction of different aspects of behavior. Research in this vein has found, for instance, that more specific attitudes predict more specific behaviors (Ajzen & Fishbein, 1977) and that more automatic attitudes tend to influence more spontaneous behaviors (Dovidio, Kawakami, & Gaertner, 2002). These findings reveal the utility of studying the complexity of the evaluative system and suggest that multiple components of the evaluative system play relatively unique roles in driving behavior.

Understanding the evaluative system may allow us to dissect the complex relationship between specific stimuli and particular behavioral outcomes. As noted by Cacioppo and Berntson (1992), the relationships among psychological events and their causes can take many forms, and the physiological measurement of attitudes necessitates a careful understanding of the relationships between any particular measurement and inferences about process and representation (i.e., inferences about how the evaluative system works). Thus, in order to make appropriate and productive use of physiological measures, it is necessary to ground their use and interpretation in an understanding of the evaluative system. Naturally, our understanding of the evaluative system will be continually revisited and revised based on the findings generated from physiological and other measures.

Evaluation is not the result of a single process that occurs within a fixed interval of time. Some judgments may be quick and remain stable after just a moment or two, whereas others can take a lifetime to develop. For example, an attitude toward a dishonest car salesman may consist of a fleeting impression that is constructed with minimal processing, whereas attitudes toward complex issues like immigration policy or environmental conservation may be slowly and continuously updated. Upon encountering a stimulus (whether a person, object, abstract concept, or situation), a sequence of evaluative processes is involved in the decoding and interpretation of a particular stimulus and the retrieval of appropriate and contextually meaningful memories that can be used to construct an evaluative state (see Figure 16.1).

We take an imperialist view of the concept of attitude—including all forms of associative or propositional representations that may guide or aid evaluative processing. That is, we use the term attitude to refer to all pre-existing evaluative information a person has about a stimulus, due to prior learning (directly experienced or socially communicated; conditioned stimuli) and maybe even innate preferences (unconditioned stimuli). These attitude representations may take the form of semantic information (cognitive aspects), emotional associations (affective

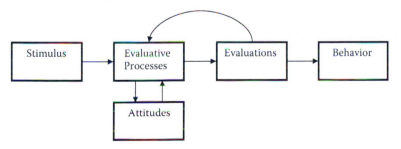

FIGURE 16.1 Process depiction demonstrating the conceptual differences and relationships among attitudes, evaluations, and evaluative processes.

aspects), or scripts for action (behavioral aspects; Eagly & Chaiken, 1993). The fact that evaluations are constructed from multiple representations, contexts, and states does not imply that attitude representations are themselves constructed; relatively stable representations are needed to have consistency from situation to situation (and especially for novel contexts).

This conceptualization allows us to disentangle concepts that tend to be interchangeable in attitude research. Whereas the terms attitude and evaluation are often used synonymously, we have recently proposed a framework in which these constructs are assumed to be conceptually distinct aspects of the evaluative system (Cunningham, Zelazo, Packer, & Van Bavel, 2007). Whereas an attitude refers to a relatively stable set of representations (only some of which may be active at any time), an evaluation reflects the current processing state of the evaluative system (which is determined by the aspects of the attitude that are currently active).

Evaluative processes help determine the motivational significance of a stimulus as well as its expected reward or punishment value. These processes draw upon pre-existing attitudes, as well as novel information about the stimulus, contextual information, and current goal states. Evaluative states arise out of highly dynamic interactions between these elements. In our framework, we propose that this sequence is iterative and this information is weighted and reweighted multiple times with the goal of arriving at an optimal match between a stimulus and its evaluation. In other words, current evaluative states can serve as information to guide the next iteration of evaluative processing. In contrast to traditional dual-process models, we propose a continuum of implicit and explicit attitudes, in which implicit evaluations involve few iterations and a reduced set of cognitive operations and explicit evaluations involve many iterations and relatively more cognitive operations (see Cunningham & Johnson, 2007; Cunningham & Zelazo, 2007; Cunningham et al., in press). Thus, implicit, like explicit, evaluations may be rapidly constructed from a relatively stable set of attitudes in line with context and in accordance with motivational states (see Wilson & Hodges, 1992).

An advantage of physiological measures is that they are able to examine evaluative processes at multiple stages of information processing. Using different measures, with various spatial and temporal resolutions, the multiple components of this complex system can be disentangled. By turning to physiology, we can examine the antecedents (e.g., stimulus decoding, attention, and memory retrieval) and consequences (e.g., emotional and behavioral) of evaluative processing.

An important challenge for attitude researchers has been to identity the various functional properties of these processes and to understand how they integrate to form coherent evaluations.

Valence versus Arousal

In this review, we focus primarily on the concepts of valence and arousal/intensity. We acknowledge that this is a simplification of a highly complex system and do not wish to imply that these are the only important aspects of attitudes—multiple characteristics of attitudes, such as accessibility, certainty, elaboration, knowledge, personal relevance, and structural consistency, are all likely to be important (Petty & Krosnick, 1995). Yet, the concepts of valence (good vs. bad) and arousal (the amount of energy associated with the state of readiness induced by a stimulus) are currently among the best understood biological aspects of evaluation. A reliable distinction between emotional valence and arousal has been found in self-reports (Russell, 1979), behavior (Schacter & Singer, 1962), and more recently, neural signatures (Anderson et al., 2003; Cunningham, Raye, & Johnson, 2004; Small, Gregory, Mak, Gitelman, Mesulam, & Parrish, 2003).

In their classic work on meaning, Osgood, Suci, and Tannenbaum (1957) found that the concepts of valence and potency were almost always the two most dominant sources of variance in any set of stimuli. The constant presence of a valence factor is easily understood: Knowing what is good or bad has implications for immediate survival, as well as goal development and attainment. On the other hand, increased states of arousal (which are associated though not necessarily synonymous with potency) direct attention toward motivationally relevant stimuli in complex environments and prepare an organism for behavior. Because different stimuli may be deemed important at different times, a general arousal or vigilance system that is independent of valence might function efficiently; in this type of dual system, a stimulus can maintain a consistent valence across situations although its relevance changes.

The Peripheral Nervous System and Attitudes

At one level, the output of evaluative processing is highly complex. The potential behavioral outcomes of evaluative processing approach the infinite; evaluative processing impacts the products people buy, the politicians they vote for, the proximity with which they sit to others, their body language, the newspapers they read, the places they travel to, the numbers they select on attitude scales, and so on. That said, at a more general level of analysis, behavioral responses can be divided into either approach or avoidance responses (see, for example, Gray, 1982). Loosely speaking, approach responses serve to increase the presence of a particular stimulus in an individual's environment, whereas avoidance responses serve to decrease its presence.

Although there is great variety in the specifics of different behaviors, these behaviors reflect more general orientations or directions of action. As behavioral responses are made (as products are put into shopping carts, ballots are cast, etc.), the peripheral nervous system coordinates the complex movement of muscles throughout the body. However, before behavior is even initiated, the peripheral nervous system is already preparing for action; indeed, this preparation for action occurs even if the action itself never takes place. Importantly for our purposes, the pattern of peripheral nervous system preparation appears to differ depending on the intended direction of action. For example, because the physiological requirements of approaching versus avoiding presumably differ, preparatory responses in the peripheral nervous system are likewise assumed to be different.

Attitude researchers are able to capitalize on this behavioral readiness by measuring indices of peripheral nervous system activity; different patterns of activity can be taken to indicate the organism's current orientation toward a stimulus. Because the peripheral nervous system prepares the body for action before behavior takes place, these measures can provide an assessment of a person's current evaluative state even in relatively impoverished laboratory environments. In general, we suggest that peripheral nervous system measures are most likely to tap current evaluative states, the outcome of evaluative processing, as opposed to the more cognitive aspects of processing itself.

Sympathetic and Parasympathetic Activity

The state of readiness for action that results from evaluative processing of a stimulus depends largely on the activity of the sympathetic (SNS) and parasympathetic (PNS) nervous systems. Historically, these systems were thought to be associated with opposite patterns of behavioral readiness, such that an increase in one system is associated with a decrease in the other. Whereas the SNS generally serves to mobilize bodily resources, the PNS generally serves to conserve resources or restore the body to equilibrium/homeostasis. More recently, although the SNS and PNS can be reciprocally activated, they may operate more independently than previously thought (see Berntson, Cacioppo, & Quigley, 1993; Berntson, Cacioppo, Quigley, & Fabro, 1994).

One index of sympathetic activation is sweat gland activity, which can be measured using a small electrical current passed through electrodes attached to the hand; as the sweat glands fill with sweat, the skin is better able to conduct electricity (Cacioppo, Petty, Losch, & Crites, 1994). More sweat flowing to the glands (and the corresponding increase in electrical conductivity) is thought to indicate greater SNS activation. Stimuli in the environment that induce evaluative processing, and a subsequent state of behavioral readiness, differ in the extent to which they arouse the SNS. A great deal of research has demonstrated the association between arousal and the skin conductance response (SCR). For example, Codispoti, Bradley, and Lang (2001) found that skin conductance responses were positively associated with the arousal ratings of briefly presented pleasant and unpleasant pictures.

Although the state of preparedness induced by the peripheral nervous system is influenced by both the valence and arousal associated with the stimulus, skin conductance is typically used only as a measure of arousal. The skin conductance response does not vary as a function of whether an arousing stimulus is positive or negative, and is therefore a poor indicator of valence. That is, although skin conductance responses can serve as a measure of the intensity of the state of behavioral readiness, it is difficult to determine from skin conductance responses alone whether an individual is primed to approach or avoid the stimulus (see Cacioppo, Bernston, Klein, & Poehlmann, 1997). Despite these limitations, skin conductance has often been used as an indirect measure of attitudes. In an early example, Cooper and Singer (1956) observed greater skin conductance in response to hearing complimentary statements about their least liked group and derogatory statements about their most liked group, relative to complimentary and derogatory statements about an intermediately rated group.

Skin conductance responses have the potential to provide information about relatively implicit evaluations. For example, in the Iowa Gambling Task (see Bechara, 2004, for a review), participants select cards from a number of decks, each of which is associated with different reward contingencies and levels of risk. Typical participants show anticipatory skin conductance responses when making risky decisions and begin to switch toward advantageous strategies, even before they are able to articulate a specific strategy. The implicit nature of the skin conductance response is evidenced by the fact that these physiological changes occur before participants are able to give an introspective, verbal report of their strategy.

Whereas SCR only indexes SNS activity, measures of cardiac activity have been shown to be sensitive to both SNS and PNS activity. As such, these measures may be able to better differentiate the valence of different responses (Blascovich & Kelsey, 1990; Boiten, 1996). Although attitudes that evoke approach and avoidance response tendencies may both be associated with increased arousal (and correspondent SNS activity), they may be distinguished from one another by unique patterns of peripheral blood flow. For example, preparations to fight versus flee a foe may both increase heart rate (HR), and yet be distinguishable by the patterns of blood flow to different muscle groups.

Similarly, researchers have used aspects of cardiovascular activity to distinguish between challenge and threat responses. Depending on one's current evaluations or existing attitudes, an object or situation may be perceived as a threat or challenge. This perception may be activated relatively automatically or occur following reflective processing. In either event, both threat and challenge are likely to enhance arousal (indexed by constriction and dilation at the arterioles), but can be distinguished by the easy (challenge) or restricted (threat) passage of blood through the vessels (e.g., Blascovich, Mendes, Hunter, Lickel, & Kowai-Bell, 2001). In this context, different forms of arousal have different physiological consequences: Whereas a threatening stimulus may evoke an intense affective response, a challenging stimulus may evoke greater potential energy to act.

Within the emotion literature, there is a great deal of research examining the potential for indices of cardiovascular activity, such as heart rate, to discriminate between types of emotions and aspects of evaluation (for reviews of cardiovascular variability measurement and analysis, see Berntson et al., 1997; Blascovich & Kelsey, 1990). Arguing that discrete emotions may possess relatively unique physiological signatures, Levenson (1992) found greater HR acceleration to fear, anger, and sadness than disgust; to anger and fear than happiness; and to negative than positive emotions. In contrast, Lang, Greenwald, Bradley, and Hamm (1993) found that HR acceleration was related to positive valence. Providing some resolution to these contradictory findings, a meta-analysis found that although current measures of cardiovascular activity do not appear to reliably distinguish between discrete emotions, certain indices do discriminate between positive and negative valence

(Cacioppo, Berntson, Larsen, Poehlmann, & Ito, 2000). For example, HR and other cardiovascular indices were more strongly associated with negative than positive emotional states.

Interestingly, the activation of an attitude may result in less automatic activity when making preference judgments. Blascovich, Ernst, Tomaka, Kelsey, Salomon, and Fazio (1993) had participants make quick preference judgments about two abstract paintings. In one condition, participants first "rehearsed" their attitudes prior to the judgment task. In the other condition, participants rehearsed their attitudes toward one set of paintings, but were presented with novel paintings during the test phase. In the rehearsal condition, autonomic activity when making the preference decisions was similar to baseline. In contrast, when participants were responding to novel paintings, they exhibited autonomic reactivity that was consistent with threat motivation: increased contractility and vasoconstriction. Presumably, the accessible attitudes facilitated decision making and, thus, reduced threat by making responses less ambiguous.

Facial Electromyography

Facial expressions of emotion (e.g., smiles and frowns) have long been used to communicate personal evaluations and infer the emotional states of others. Indeed, several emotional states (e.g., fear, anger, disgust) are believed to remain relatively consistent in visual representation across cultures (Ekman, 1989). Given the strong relationship between emotional displays and evaluations, facial expressions have long been assumed to reflect (e.g., Darwin, 1872) or communicate (Kraut & Johnston, 1979) personal attitudes. Facial electromyography (EMG) measures the electrical impulses that result from the activation of selected facial muscles. Muscle activity is generally measured by placing electrodes (in pairs) over the muscles in the brow (*corrugator supercilii*), cheek (*zygomaticus major*), and forehead (*medial frontalis*); near the lips (*orbicular oris*); and near the eye (*orbicularis oculi*); for a review of surface electromyography, see Tassinary and Cacioppo (2000).

Facial EMG has been used to measure emotional expressions, including those too subtle or fleeting to observe. For example, participants exposed to mild and moderate positive and negative images revealed EMG activity near the brow, eye, and cheek that could not be detected by independent judges (Cacioppo, Petty, Losch, & Kim, 1986). Subtle EMG activity near the brow (frowning) was higher for moderately than mildly negative images and lower for moderately than mildly positive images. In contrast, EMG activity near the eye (smiling) was higher for moderately than mildly positive images. Together, these interactions between valence and intensity provide evidence that facial EMG can differentiate the valence and intensity of emotional reactions and may allow relatively independent assessments of the intensity of positivity and negativity (Cacioppo et al., 1986).

Facial EMG has also been shown to index automatically and unconsciously evoked emotional responses. In one study, people were presented with happy, neutral, and angry faces for 30 ms, followed by a 500-ms neutral face mask (Dimberg, Thunberg, & Elmehed, 2000). Despite the fact that participants could not consciously recognize the rapidly presented emotional faces, they showed greater cheek (smiling) activity to happy than neutral faces, and greater activity to neutral than angry faces approximately 500 ms after stimulus presentation. Conversely, there was greater brow (frowning) activity to angry than neutral faces, and greater activity to neutral than happy faces. In a related study, brow activity increased for negative stimuli and cheek activity increased to positive stimuli even when participants were instructed not to respond to these stimuli (Dimberg, Thunberg & Grunedal, 2002). This research provides additional evidence that EMG may provide an index of relatively automatic and unconscious responses to valenced stimuli (distinguishing between positive, neutral, and negative stimuli).

There is also some evidence that facial EMG may provide a valid indirect measure of individual attitudes. For example, when White participants rated the friendliness of White and Black faces, they reported a preference for Blacks in spite of facial EMG activity suggesting a preference for Whites (Vanmen, Paul, Ito, & Miller, 1997). Similarly, participants were most likely to choose a partner from a politically sensitive outgroup (African-American or homosexual) despite greater facial EMG negativity (cheek less brow activity) compared to less sensitive outgroup targets (business major or graduate student). However, after being insulted, self-reported partner preference converged with facial EMG negativity, such that participants were least positive toward politically sensitive outgroup members (Ensari et al., 2004). More recently, cheek EMG activity was found to be a stronger predictor of selecting a White over a Black applicant for a teaching fellowship ($r = .40$) than the IAT ($r = .09$; Vanman, Saltz, Nathan, & Warren, 2004). Taken together, these studies provide evidence of the utility and predictive validity of facial EMG as an indirect attitude measure.

A related measure is the startle response. The startle response represents a quick launch into a state of behavioral readiness in response to a negative stimulus. Although the startle response involves a full body response, the eyeblink is a quick, reliable, and easily measured aspect of the startle response (Lang, Bradley, & Cuthbert, 1990). The startle response is typically evoked by a loud, aversive noise; the subsequent eyeblink is recorded by an electrode placed on the forehead. Although a startle response is always evoked, this response is potentiated or enhanced when it occurs in conjunction with negative or threatening stimuli. Conversely, the startle response is likely to be attenuated when presented in a positive context (Lang et al., 1990).

In the section that follows we turn to discussion of the central nervous system, including the role that the amygdala appears to play in evaluative processing. The startle response is highly associated with amygdala activity. Patients with lesions to the amygdala often show attenuated or absent startle responses (Angrilli et al., 1996; Funayama, Grillon, Davis, & Phelps, 2001). To the extent that the amygdala is involved in the processing of fear or threat, the startle response can be used to assess evaluations of this type. Phelps and colleagues (2000) found that a greater startle response when viewing Black faces was correlated with amygdala activation to Black faces (measured using functional magnetic resonance imaging, or fMRI) and IAT-assessed racial bias scores.

The Central Nervous System and Attitudes

In recent years, technological advances such as electroencephalography (EEG) and functional magnetic resonance imaging have allowed us to examine more directly the ways that specific brain regions are involved in evaluative processes. These methods have the potential to allow us to dissect the evaluative system into its various processing subcomponents, which will increase understanding of the various ways that people make evaluative judgments. If, as mentioned earlier, evaluations are the outcome of multiple affective and cognitive processes, we now have the opportunity to examine directly the evaluative processes that are recruited to meet situational and motivational constraints. In combination with other methods, brain imaging should help illuminate how prior attitudes are dynamically transformed into evaluative states.

In this part of our review, we will examine methods and findings regarding how the central nervous system is involved in evaluative processing. Specifically, we will review research (a) from functional brain imaging that allows us to make inferences about the brain correlates of evaluative processing, (b) using event-related potentials (ERPs) derived from EEG to make inferences regarding the time course of evaluative processing, and (c) examining frontal EEG asymmetries to map evaluative responding to approach and avoidance motivational tendencies.

Brain Correlates of Evaluative Processing

In the last 10 years, there has been a rapid expansion in cognitive neuroscience research using fMRI to study the brain correlates of complex thought and feeling. Researchers use fMRI under the assumption that following neural activity in a brain region, the ratio of oxygenated to deoxygenated hemoglobin changes, resulting in a measurable change in magnetic signal. Although fMRI has very poor temporal resolution (the magnetic signal resulting from mere milliseconds of neural activity can lag for up to 12 to 16 s), it provides a relatively fine-grained (within 10 mm or so) index of where neural activity occurs. By carefully designing tasks for participants to perform while being scanned, we can observe evidence that may support dissociations between processes (i.e., two processes have distinct neural generators), associations among processes (i.e., two processes have the same neural generator), and interactions among processes (i.e., interdependencies between processes). In addition, research such as this may reveal that different psychological phenomenon share common underlying processes and causes.

Of most relevance to our understanding of evaluation is research on emotional processing, in particular, the processing of emotional facial expressions, as well as the neural circuits involved in reward and punishment. Although little work has been conducted on attitudes per se, research on emotion can guide the development of hypotheses regarding evaluative processes. More directly, to the extent that implicit attitudes are learned through principles of evaluative conditioning (Olson & Fazio, 2001), animal models that have mapped the neural circuits of fear and reward conditioning should be relevant for our understanding of implicit evaluation. Below, we focus our discussion on several brain regions that are thought to be important for evaluation. As in the previous section, we highlight the distinction between the processing of valence and arousal as it is reflected in central nervous system activity.

Although the neural networks involved in evaluation are likely to be widely distributed, a logical starting point for our discussion is the amygdala: a small almond-shaped structure in the medial temporal lobe at the tip of the hippocampus. The amygdala is one of the key components of the limbic system, which is involved in various aspects of emotional learning and memory (LeDoux, 1996). Damage to the amygdala has been shown to have dramatic effects on one's ability to automatically learn affective associations and on the ability to generate automatic physiological responses to stimuli (Davis, 1997). In addition, the amygdala appears to be critical for the decoding of emotional facial expressions. Damage to the amygdala is associated with impairments in the ability to correctly identify emotional facial expressions, especially the negatively valenced expressions of fear, anger, and disgust (Adolphs et al., 1999). Extending this, research using fMRI has consistently found greater amygdala activity to negative than positive stimuli. Interestingly, these effects have been shown in multiple stimulus and sensory modalities, including faces (Morris et al., 1996), scenes (Paradiso et al., 1999), words (Isenberg et al., 1999), odors (Small et al., 2003), and tastes (Anderson et al., 2003). Research using subliminal stimuli has shown that these processes are (at least somewhat) automatic. In a conceptual replication of previous research on supraliminal emotional face processing (Morris et al., 1996), Whalen, Rauch, Etcoff, McInerney, Lee, and Jenike (1998) demonstrated that subliminal presentations of emotionally fearful faces led to significant amygdala activation. In addition, Morris, Öhman, and Dolan (1998) found, using both subliminal and supraliminal presentations, that after participants were classically conditioned to associate particular angry faces with an aversive stimulus, the amygdala showed greater activity to these conditioned faces than control faces. In the domain of race, subliminal presentations of Black faces (compared to White faces) are associated with amygdala activation (Cunningham, Raye et al., 2004). Moreover, the degree of this amygdala activation to Black faces was significantly correlated with responses to the IAT.

Although it is tempting to think of the amygdala as the *valence region*—simply activating as a direct function of stimulus negativity— recent imaging research suggests otherwise. In addition to activating to negative stimuli, the amygdala also appears to activate to positive stimuli when compared with neutral stimuli (Liberzon, Phan, Decker, & Taylor, 2003; Hamann, Ely, Hoffman, & Kilts, 2002; Hamann & Mao, 2002; Garavan, Pendergrass, Ross, Stein, & Risinger, 2001; see Zald, 2003, for a review). In three fMRI studies that manipulated or parametrically analyzed both valence and arousal such that the two could be examined orthogonally, different brain areas were associated with valence and arousal (Anderson et al., 2003; Cunningham, Raye et al., 2004; Small et al., 2003). In each of these studies, arousal was associated with amygdala activation and negative valence was associated with right prefrontal activation.

Although these findings suggest that amygdala activity may be more a function of arousal or emotional intensity than valence, caution needs to be taken regarding fMRI studies of amygdala activation in general. The amygdala is a highly complex structure and has 12 separate nuclei, each with different inputs and outputs. Unfortunately, the spatial resolution of fMRI is not yet fine enough to separate out these individual nuclei. It is quite possible that each nucleus has a different information processing function and pattern (see Whalen, 1998). As such, attributing a global role to the whole amygdala may not be accurate. It is possible that some amygdalic regions are involved in arousal, whereas others are specific to fear, reward, or punishment. Future research using higher field strength MRIs may be able to sort out these potentially unique functional areas.

Several other brain regions have been more directly associated with the processing of valence. For example, the ventral striatum—part of the basal ganglia located just above the amygdala—has been proposed to be part of a fear conditioning circuit (Davis & Whalen, 2001). In addition, several cortical areas appear to be involved in the processing of negatively valenced information. Sutton, Davidson, Donzella, Irwin, and Dottl (1997) found, using positron emission tomography (PET), that viewing negatively valenced pictures was associated with activation in the right orbital frontal cortex (OFC) and the right inferior frontal cortex, whereas viewing positively valenced pictures was associated with activation in the left pre- and postcentral gyri. More recently, evidence for right lateralized processing of negative information has been found using fMRI (Anderson et al., 2003; Cunningham, Johnson, Gatenby, Gore, & Banaji, 2003; Cunningham, Raye et al., 2004). Specifically, areas of the right inferior frontal cortex and anterior insula consistently appear to be involved more in processing negative than positive valenced stimuli.

The brain regions associated with reward may be distinct from those involved in the processing of threat or negativity. Animal models suggest a limbic reward circuit made up of the amygdala, hippocampus, nucleus accumbens, ventral pallidum, and ventral tegmental area. Neuroimaging research in humans has replicated this work, finding greater activation in these regions when receiving or learning about rewards (Delgado, Nystrom, Fissell, Noll, & Fiez, 2000). In addition, regions of posterior orbital frontal cortex appear to be involved in the processing of reward or positive valence more generally (Anderson et al., 2003; Nitschke, Nelson, Rusch, Fox, Oakes, & Davidson, 2003; Kringelbach, O'Doherty, Rolls, & Andrews, 2003). Although such findings do not necessarily imply that the processing of positive and negative information is fully dissociated, this suggests that they may involve at least partially separable circuits.

The Time Course of Evaluative Processing

Whereas fMRI provides detailed information regarding the location of neural processing, it provides little to no information regarding the time course of such processing. In contrast, EEG methods provide the opposite type of information—millisecond-by-millisecond timing information with poor spatial resolution.* Given that claims that a particular process is implicit often depend on the speed of processing (i.e., the process appears to occur before conscious awareness), EEG methods can help determine the automaticity of a neural process.

In one of the first studies to examine evaluation using EEG, Cacioppo and colleagues (Cacioppo, Crites, & Gardner, 1996) identified an event-related potential wave associated with the processing of valenced stimuli presented in an emotionally incongruous context. A series of valenced stimuli were presented before a critical stimulus that was of the same or different valence. Of interest were EEG signals that differentiated the stimuli presented in congruous versus incongruous contexts. Cacioppo and colleagues identified a particular type of wave form termed a late positive potential (LPP) when participants saw a stimulus that was incongruous with a context; in these studies, a negative stimulus in the context of positive stimuli, or a positive stimulus in the context of negative stimuli. The amplitude of the LPP wave in these studies was shown to vary as a function of the degree of difference between the valence of the stimulus and the valence of the context in which it occurs. For example, when presented in the context of positive stimuli, a strongly negative stimulus will result in a larger LPP than a mildly negative stimulus (Cacioppo et al., 1996; Cacioppo, Crites, Gardner, & Berntson, 1994). The LPP associated with evaluative

---

* New source localization techniques are now allowing us to estimate likely neural generators of EEG signals, but these estimates are still controversial and at their best still cannot provide the resolution of fMRI.

incongruity is widely distributed across scalp electrodes but is more pronounced over posterior (parietal) scalp regions than over frontal sites. There is also evidence that the amplitude of this posterior LPP is greater over the right hemisphere than over the left—for both positive and negative stimuli presented in an incongruous evaluative context (Cacioppo et al., 1996).

Although the timing of the posterior LPP varies as a function of context, it typically begins around 500 to 600 ms after stimulus presentation. Researchers using this paradigm have shown that the posterior LPP is evident when participants are making both evaluative and non-evaluative judgments, suggesting that evaluative incongruity may be detected automatically (Cacioppo et al., 1996; Ito & Cacioppo, 2000; see also Crites & Cacioppo, 1996). Providing further evidence for the LPP to be involved in evaluative extremity, Schupp, Cuthbert, Bradley, Cacioppo, Ito, and Lang (2000) found that the amplitude of the LPP was largest for stimuli that were the most arousing—presumably the stimuli with the greatest motivational relevance.

ERP data also has provided evidence for hypotheses suggesting that negative stimuli have more motivational force than positive stimuli. Showing evidence for this negativity bias, LPPs are typically larger for negative stimuli in a positive context than positive stimuli in a negative context (Ito, Larsen, Smith, & Cacioppo, 1998), and the degree of hemispheric asymmetry (right greater than left) is greater for these stimuli as well (Cacioppo et al., 1996). In addition, several studies have found that the processing of negative information may occur more rapidly than the processing of positive information. Some have suggested that negative information is privileged such that it is processed more quickly than positive information—a temporal negativity bias (Cacioppo & Gartner, 1999). For example, Kawasaki et al. (2001) found that the processing of negative, but not neutral or positive, stimuli occurred 120 to 160 ms after stimulus presentation in single cell recordings of the human orbital frontal cortex. Negative stimuli appear to be differentiated from positive stimuli in posterior perception areas as indexed by an early ERP component in visual areas occurring in the first 100 ms after stimulus presentation (Smith, Cacioppo, Larsen, & Chartrand, 2003). In one study using magnetoencephalography (MEG), researchers found that negative stimuli were processed 200 ms more quickly than positive stimuli in the OFC (Carretie, Martin-Loeches, Hinojosa, & Mercado, 2001). Similarly, some ERP components such as the P200 appear to occur more rapidly to negative than positive stimuli (Carretie, Mercado, Tapia, & Hinojosa, 2001).

Given the importance of arousal in directing attention, it is not surprising that these effects occur at a very early stage of information processing. In a study of face perception, Asley, Vuilleumier, and Swick (2004) found that ERP signals differed between emotional and nonemotional faces as early as 120 to 160 ms after stimulus presentation (see also Pizzagalli, Lehmann, Hendrick, Regard, Pascual-Marqui, & Davidson, 2002; Eimer & Holmes, 2002). In fact, ERP differences to emotional stimuli compared to neutral stimuli have been observed as early as 94 ms after stimulus presentation in occipital regions (Batty & Taylor, 2003). What is particularly interesting about this rapid emotional processing is that identification of facial structure and features is thought to not occur until 170 ms after stimulus presentation (Sagiv & Bentin, 2001), suggesting that the processing of emotional expression, a signal that can denote safety or danger, may occur in parallel with the encoding of facial structure. In other words, emotional significance may be processed before a stimulus has been fully identified (see Niedenthal & Kitayama, 1994). In addition to occurring rapidly, these early emotional processes may also occur in the absence of conscious awareness. Several studies have now demonstrated emotional processing of stimuli that participants do not report even having seen. For example, skin conductance and ERP signals index the subliminal presentation of emotional faces as rapidly as 100 ms after stimulus presentation (Öhman & Soares, 1994; Williams et al., 2004).

EEG Asymmetry and Evaluative Processing

Following this research, Cunningham, Espinet, DeYoung, and Zelazo (2005) found an LPP occurring approximately 450 ms after stimulus presentation that was greater in frontal electrodes on the right for concepts later rated on an explicit attitude scale as bad, and greater on the left for concepts later rated as good. The amplitude of the LPP effects did not differ between tasks for the first few hundreds of milliseconds of the LPP whether participants were making evaluative (good-bad) or control (abstract-concrete) judgments. Only later (approximately 750 ms after stimulus presentation) did the effects become amplified for the good-bad task. This suggests that early differences in right versus left frontal sites may differentiate implicit positive versus negative evaluations, whereas later differences differentiate explicit positive versus negative evaluations (see Davidson & Irwin, 1999).

Although initial theories linked frontal EEG alpha (8 to 12 Hz) asymmetries to valence, more recent research strongly suggests that frontal asymmetries index motivational tendency, rather than valence. Early research confounded valence with motivational tendency, finding that greater right hemisphere activation is associated with a tendency toward withdrawal behavior (and negative stimuli) and that greater left hemisphere activation is associated with a tendency for approach behavior (and positive stimuli; Sobotka, Davidson, & Senulis, 1992; Sutton & Davidson, 1997, 2000; see Davidson, 2004, for a review). Moreover, frontal EEG alpha asymmetries have been shown to predict depression (Davidson, 1988), emotion regulation ability (Jackson et al., 2003), and general well-being (Urry et al., 2004). Recent research has unconfounded valence with motivational tendency, showing that anger, an approach motivation with a negative valence, is associated with greater left frontal EEG activity (Harmon-Jones & Allen, 1998). The relationship between anger and left frontal asymmetries has been replicated extensively, suggesting that left hemispheric activity is primarily involved in approach motivation, regardless of valence (e.g., Harmon-Jones, Lueck, Fearn, & Harmon-Jones, 2006). Although these alpha power estimates have not yet been examined in the context of attitudes, it seems plausible that attitude valence should predict the direction of asymmetry and attitude strength variables should predict the intensity of the asymmetry. It may also prove fruitful to explore whether motivational tendencies mediate attitudes and behavior.

Conclusion

In this chapter, we review a number of physiological measures that can be used to investigate attitudes and evaluations and the processes that underlie them. Specifically, these measures allow us to examine the neural architecture and processes (central nervous system) that support attitude activation and evaluative processing, and how the outcomes of evaluative processing are reflected in the body's readiness to act (peripheral nervous system). One of the central themes of this chapter has to do with the complexity of the evaluative system and the necessity of matching physiological measures with the specific aspect(s) of evaluation under investigation. The recent distinction between relatively implicit and explicit evaluations (Fazio, 1990; Greenwald & Banaji, 1995) captures some of this complexity, but a more complete understanding of the evaluative system is an ongoing goal. We believe that physiological measures and methods, appropriately used, have enormous promise to help us achieve this objective by allowing researchers to more precisely explore specific processes of evaluation. These measures will represent useful tools as social psychologists investigate evaluation with increasing specificity.

In the introduction, we discuss the utility of distinguishing between attitudes as representations, evaluations as states, and evaluative processes as the computations that connect attitudes and evaluations (see Figure 16.1). In this framework, peripheral nervous system measures are more likely to be associated with evaluations and central nervous system measures with attitudes and evaluative processes. Within the peripheral nervous system, SNS and PNS activity are associated with patterns of readiness for action (e.g., approach or avoidance responses). EMG activity reflects the current emotional state of the perceiver, which includes aspects of valence (i.e., positive vs. negative affect) and arousal. fMRI and EEG, on the other hand, directly examine the neural processes that give rise to these bodily responses and, as such, likely reflect the evaluative processing component of our model. It is important to note that, at present, no physiological method directly measures the attitude representation itself. Evaluations arise out of evaluative processes that draw not only upon pre-existing attitudes, but also upon novel information about the stimulus, contextual information, current goals, and so on (see Schwarz & Bohner, 2001). The presence and strength of a pre-existing representation has to be inferred by its impact on evaluative processing and ultimately the current evaluation.

Admittedly, a one-to-one mapping of evaluation onto the peripheral nervous system and evaluative processing onto the central nervous system is somewhat overstated, especially considering the iterative nature of the evaluative system. According to our model, the evaluation of a particular stimulus is continually updated, with the current evaluation providing a source of information that feeds forward into future evaluative processing. This means that the links between the peripheral and central nervous systems are not unidirectional; rather, the individual's current state of behavioral readiness can feed into subsequent evaluative processing. For example, in the SCR section we describe research using the Iowa Gambling Task, which finds that participants show anticipatory skin conductance responses immediately before choosing from a risky deck of cards. Importantly, these anticipatory physiological responses occur before participants have begun to construct a conscious strategy for selecting appropriate cards and appear to feed into the on-line evaluative processes that occur as individuals attempt to develop a strategy. The importance of this peripheral nervous system feedback is revealed by research on orbital frontal patients, who show normal skin conductance responses when receiving rewards and punishments, but do not show the normal anticipatory physiological responses prior to their decisions. Patients with these types of lesions, unlike normal adults, typically continue to make disadvantageous decisions by choosing from risky decks of cards (see Bechara, 2004), perhaps because their ongoing evaluations do not include peripheral nervous system feedback from previous trials.

For social psychologists to make the best possible use of physiological measures, it will be necessary to validate them in the same manner as traditional attitude measures. Specifically, although there are direct associations between biology and each measurement technique, each measure also has its own sources of error. For example, although the amygdala and orbital frontal cortex are likely to play an important role in evaluative processing, fMRI signals from these regions are distorted due to signal interference from the surrounding sinus cavities. In addition, these regions are too distant from the scalp to provide reliable EEG signals (note that both of these problems are more severe for OFC than amygdala). Just as an answer on a questionnaire or a reaction time on a response latency measure can be influenced by various factors, only part of a physiological response is "caused" by the evaluation or process it is presumed to measure. Therefore, as for any other attitude measure, a careful analysis of the reliability of each method is necessary to ensure that our conclusions are justified, particularly if we want to make claims about individual, as opposed to group-level, differences.

The potential for measurement error highlights the need to use these measures in conjunction with traditional explicit and recently developed implicit attitude measures. In addition, because each physiological measure taps different aspects of the evaluative system, these measures should also be used in complement with one another to explore the entire evaluative system. Physiological measures should not replace or supersede other methods; rather, their greatest promise lies in helping to elucidate the processes that support and underlie behavior. In doing so, biologically informed research will enhance current models of attitudes. Although a relatively new approach, social neuroscience has already made insights into the complexity of the biological systems underlying evaluation (see Cunningham & Zelazo, 2007; Ito & Cacioppo, 2001). As social neuroscience further integrates the theories and methods of social psychology and cognitive neuroscience, it promises to advance our understanding of attitudes and evaluation.

References

Adolphs, R., Tranel, D., Hamann, S., Young, A. W., Calder, A. J., Phelps, E. A., Anderson, A., Lee, G. P., & Damasio, A. R. (1999). Recognition of facial emotion in nine individuals with bilateral amygdala damage. *Neuropsychologia, 37,* 1111–1117.

Ajzen, I., & Fishbein, M. (1977). Attitude-behavior relations: A theoretical analysis and review of empirical research. *Psychological Bulletin, 84,* 888–918.

Allport, G. W. (1935). Attitudes. In C. Murchison (Ed.), *Handbook of social psychology* (pp. 798–844). Worcester, MA: Clark University Press.

Anderson, A. K., Christoff, K., Stappen, I., Panitz, D., Ghahremani, D. G., Glover, G., & Sobel, N. (2003). Dissociated neural representations of intensity and valence in human olfaction. *Nature Neuroscience, 6,* 196–202.

Angrilli, A., Mauri, A., Palomba, D., Flor, H., Birbaumer, N., Sartori, G., & di Paola, F. (1996). Startle reflex and emotional modulation impairment after a right amygdala lesion. *Brain: A Journal of Neurology, 119,* 1991–2000.

Asley, V., Vuilleumier, P., & Swick, D. (2004). Time course and specificity of event-related potentials to emotional expressions. *NeuroReport, 15,* 211–216.

Batty, M., & Taylor, M. J. (2003). Early processing of the six basic facial emotional expressions. *Cognitive Brain Research, 17,* 613–620.

Bechara, A. (2004). The role of emotion in decision-making: Evidence from neurological patients with orbitofrontal damage. *Brain and Cognition, 55,* 30–40.

Berntson, G. G., Bigger, J. T., Eckberg, D. L., Grossman, P., Kaufmann, P. G., Malik, M., Nagaraja, H. N., Porges, S. W., Saul, J. P., Stone, P. H., & van der Molen, M. W. (1997). Heart rate variability: Origins, methods, and interpretive caveats. *Psychophysiology, 34,* 623–648.

Berntson, G. G., Cacioppo, J. T., & Quigley, K. S. (1993). Cardiac psychophysiology and autonomic space in humans: Empirical perspectives and conceptual implications. *Psychological Bulletin, 114,* 296–322.

Berntson, G. G., Cacioppo, J. T., Quigley, K. S., & Fabro, V. T. (1994). Autonomic space and psychophysiological response. *Psychophysiology, 31,* 44–61.

Blascovich, J., Ernst, J. M., Tomaka, J., Kelsey, R. M., Salomon, K. L., & Fazio, R. H. (1993). Attitude accessibility as a moderator of autonomic reactivity during decision making. *Journal of Personality and Social Psychology, 64,* 165–176.

Blascovich, J., & Kelsey, R. M. (1990). Using electrodermal and cardiovascular measures of arousal in social psychological research. In C. Hendrick & M. S. Clark (Eds.), *Review of personality and social psychology* (Vol. 11, pp. 45–73). Newbury Park, CA: Sage.

Blascovich, J., Mendes, W. B., Hunter, S. B., Lickel, B., & Kowai-Bell, N. (2001). Perceiver threat in social interactions with stigmatized others. *Journal of Personality and Social Psychology, 80,* 253–267.

Boiten, F. (1996). Autonomic response patterns during voluntary facial action. *Psychophysiology, 33,* 123–131.

Cacioppo, J. T., & Berntson, G. G. (1992). Social psychological contributions to the decade of the brain: Doctrine of multilevel analysis. *American Psychologist, 47,* 1019–1028.

Cacioppo, J. T., Berntson, G. G., Klein, D. J., & Poehlmann, K. M. (1997). The psychophysiology of emotion across the lifespan. *Annual Review of Gerontology and Geriatrics, 17,* 27–74.

Cacioppo, J. T., Berntson, G. G., Larsen, J. T., Poehlmann, K. M., & Ito, T. A. (2000). The psychophysiology of emotion. In R. Lewis & J. M. Haviland-Jones (Eds.), *The handbook of emotion (2nd ed.,* pp. 173–191). New York: Guilford Press.

Cacioppo, J. T., Crites, S. L., Jr., & Gardner, W. L. (1996). Attitudes to the right: Evaluative processing is associated with lateralized late positive event-related brain potentials. *Personality and Social Psychology Bulletin, 22,* 1205–1219.

Cacioppo, J. T., Crites, S. L., Jr., Gardner, W. L., & Berntson, G. G. (1994). Bioelectrical echoes from evaluative categorizations: I. A late positive brain potential that varies as a function of trait negativity and extremity. *Journal of Personality and Social Psychology, 67,* 115–125.

Cacioppo, J. T., & Gardner, W. L. (1999). Emotion. *Annual Review of Psychology, 50,* 191–214.

Cacioppo, J. T., Petty, R. E., Losch, M. E., & Crites, S. L. (1994). Psychophysiological approaches to attitudes: Detecting affective dispositions when people won't say, can't say, or don't even know. In S. Shavitt & T. C. Brock (Eds.), *Persuasion: Psychological insights and perspectives* (pp. 43–69). New York: Allyn & Bacon.

Cacioppo, J. T., Petty, R. E., Losch, M. E., & Kim, H. S. (1986). Electromyographic activity over facial muscle regions can differentiate the valence and intensity of affective reactions. *Journal of Personality and Social Psychology, 50,* 260–268.

Carretie, L., Martin-Loeches, M., Hinojosa, J. A., & Mercado, F. (2001). Emotion and attention interaction studied through event-related potentials. Journal of Cognitive Neuroscience, 13, 1109–1128.

Carretie, L., Mercado, F., Tapia, M., & Hinojosa, J. A. (2001). Emotion, attention, and the "negativity bias," studied through event-related potentials. *International Journal of Psychophysiology, 41,* 7–85.

Codispoti, M., Bradley, M. M., & Lang, P. J. (2001). Affective reactions to briefly presented pictures. *Psychophysiology, 38*, 474–478.

Cooper, J. B., & Singer, D. N. (1956). The role of emotion in prejudice. *Journal of Social Psychology, 44*, 241–247.

Crites, S. L., Jr., & Cacioppo, J. T. (1996). Electrocortical differentiation of evaluative and nonevaluative categorizations. *Psychological Science, 7*, 318–321.

Cunningham, W. A., Espinet, S. D., DeYoung, C., & Zelazo, P. D. (2005). Attitudes to the right—and left: Frontal ERP asymmetries associated with stimulus valence and processing goals. *NeuroImage, 28*, 827–834.

Cunningham, W. A., & Johnson, M. K. (2007). *Attitudes and evaluation: Toward a component process framework.* In E. Harmon-Jones & P. Winkielman (Eds.), *Fundamentals of social neuroscience.* New York: Guilford Press.

Cunningham, W. A., Johnson, M. K., Gatenby, J. C., Gore, J. C., & Banaji, M. R. (2003). Neural components of social evaluation. *Journal of Personality and Social Psychology, 85*, 639–649.

Cunningham, W. A., Johnson, M. K., Raye, C. L., Gatenby, J. C., Gore, J. C., & Banaji, M. R. (2004). Separable neural components in the processing of Black and White faces. *Psychological Science, 15*, 806–813.

Cunningham, W. A., Raye, C. L., & Johnson, M. K. (2004). Implicit and explicit evaluation: fMRI correlates of valence, emotional intensity, and control in the processing of attitudes. *Journal of Cognitive Neuroscience, 16*, 1717–1729.

Cunningham, W. A., Raye, C. L., & Johnson, M. K. (2005). Neural correlates of evaluation associated with promotion and prevention regulatory focus. *Cognitive, Affective, & Behavioral Neuroscience, 5*, 202–211.

Cunningham, W. A., & Zelazo, P. D. (2007). Attitudes and evaluations: A social cognitive neuroscience perspective. *TRENDS in Cognitive Sciences. 11*, 97–104.

Cunningham, W. A., Zelazo, P. D., Packer, D. J., & van Bavel, J. J. (2007). The Iterative Reprocessing model: A multilevel framework for attitudes and evaluation. *Social Cognition, 25*, 736–760.

Darwin, C. (1872). *The expression of the emotions in man and animals.* London: John Murray.

Davidson, R. J. (1988). EEG measures of cerebral asymmetry: Conceptual and methodological issues. *International Journal of Neuroscience, 39*, 71–89.

Davidson, R. J. (2004). What does the prefrontal cortex "do" in affect? Perspectives in frontal EEG asymmetry research. *Biological Psychology, 67*, 219–234.

Davidson, R. J., & Irwin, W. (1999). The functional neuroanatomy of emotion and affective style. *Trends in Cognitive Science, 3*, 11–21.

Davis, M. (1997). Neurobiology of fear responses: The role of the amygdala. *Journal of Neuropsychiatry and Clinical Neurology, 9*, 382–402.

Davis, M., & Whalen, P. J. (2001). The amygdala: Vigilance and emotion. *Molecular Psychiatry, 6*(1), 13–34.

Delgado, M. R., Nystrom, L. E., Fissel, C., Noll, D. C., & Fiez, J. A. (2000). Tracking the hemodynamic responses to reward and punishment in the striatum. *The American Physiological Society*, 3072–3077.

Dickson, H. W., & McGinnies, E. (1966). Affectivity in the arousal of attitudes as measured by galvanic skin response. *American Journal of Psychology*, *79*, 584–587.

Dimberg, U., Thunberg, M., & Elmehed, K. (2000). Unconscious facial reactions to emotional facial expressions. *Psychological Science*, *11*, 86–89.

Dimberg, U., Thunberg, M., & Grunedal, S. (2002). Facial reactions to emotional stimuli: Automatically controlled emotional responses. *Cognition and Emotion*, *16*, 449–471.

Dovidio, J. F., Kawakami, K., & Gaertner, S. L. (2002). Implicit and explicit prejudice and interracial interaction. *Journal of Personality and Social Psychology*, *82*, 62–68.

Draine, S. C., & Greenwald, A. G. (1998). Replicable unconscious semantic priming. *Journal of Experimental Psychology: General*, *127*, 286–303.

Dysinger, D. W. (1931). A comparative study of affective responses by means of the impressive and expressive methods. *Psychological Monographs*, *41*, 14–31.

Eagly, A. H., & Chaiken, S. (1993). *The psychology of attitudes*. Forth Worth, TX: Harcourt Brace Jovanovich.

Eimer, M., & Holmes, A. (2002). An ERP study on the time course of emotional face processing. *NeuroReport*, *13*, 427–431.

Ekman, P. (1989). The argument and evidence about universals in facial expressions of emotion. In H. Wagner & A. Manstead (Eds.), *Handbook of social psychophysiology* (pp. 143–164). Chichester, England: John Wiley.

Ensari, N., Kenworthy, J. B., Urban, L., Canales, C. J., Vasquez, E., Kim, D., & Miller, N. (2004). Negative affect and political sensitivity in crossed categorization: Self-reports versus EMG. *Group Processes and Intergroup Relations*, *7*, 55–75.

Fazio, R. H. (1990). Multiple processes by which attitudes guide behavior: The MODE model as an integrative framework. In M. P. Zanna (Ed.), *Advances in experimental social psychology* (Vol. 23, pp. 75–109). New York: Academic Press.

Fazio, R. H., Sanbonmatsu, D. M., Powell, M. C., & Kardes, F. R. (1986). On the automatic activation of attitudes. *Journal of Personality and Social Psychology*, *50*, 229–238.

Freud, S. (1933). *New introductory lectures on psycho-analysis*. New York: Norton.

Funayama, E. S., Grillon, C., Davis M., & Phelps, E. A. (2001). A double dissociation in the affective modulation of startle in humans: Effects of unilateral temporal lobectomy. *Journal of Cognitive Neuroscience*, *13*, 721–729.

Garavan, H., Pendergrass, C., Ross, T. J., Stein, E. A., & Risinger, R. (2001). Amygdala response to both positively and negatively valenced stimuli. *NeuroReport*, *12*(12), 1–5.

Gray, J. A. (1982). *Neuropsychological Theory of Anxiety: An investigation of the septal-hippocampal system*. Cambridge, England: Cambridge University Press.

Greenwald, A. G., & Banaji, M. R. (1995). Implicit social cognition: Attitudes, self-esteem, and stereotypes. *Psychological Review, 102*, 4–27.

Greenwald, A. G., McGhee, D. E., & Schwartz, J. L. K. (1998). Measuring individual differences in implicit cognition: The Implicit Association Test. *Journal of Personality and Social Psychology, 74*, 1464–1480.

Hamann, S. B., Ely, T. D., Hoffman, J. M., & Kilts, C. D. (2002). Ecstasy and agony: Activation of human amygdala in positive and negative emotion. *Psychological Science, 13*, 135–141.

Hamann, S., & Mao, H. (2002). Positive and negative emotional verbal stimuli elicit activity in the left amygdala. *NeuroReport, 13*(1), 15–19.

Harmon-Jones, E., & Allen, J. J. B. (1998). Anger and prefrontal brain activity: EEG asymmetry consistent with approach motivation despite negative affective valence. *Journal of Personality and Social Psychology, 74*, 1310–1316.

Harmon-Jones, E., Lueck, L., Fearn, M., & Harmon-Jones, C. (2006). The effect of personal relevance and approach-related action expectation on relative left frontal cortical activity. *Psychological Science, 17*, 434–440.

Isenberg, N., Silbersweig, D., Engelien, A., Emmerich, S., Malavade, K., Beattie, B., Leon, A. C., & Stern, E. (1999). Linguistic threat activates the human amygdala. *Proceedings of the National Academy of Sciences, U.S.A., 96*, 10456–10459.

Ito, T. A., & Cacioppo, J. T. (2000). Electrophysiological evidence of implicit and explicit categorization processes. *Journal of Experimental Social Psychology, 36*, 660–676.

Ito, T. A., & Cacioppo, J. T. (2001). Affect and attitudes: A social neuroscience approach. In J. P. Forgas (Ed.), *The handbook of affect and social cognition* (pp. 50–74). Mahwah, NJ: Lawrence Erlbaum & Associates.

Ito, T. A., Larsen, J. T., Smith, N. K., & Cacioppo, J. T. (1998). Negative information weighs more heavily on the brain: The negativity bias in evaluative categorizations. *Journal of Personality and Social Psychology, 75*, 887–900.

Jackson, D. C., Mueller, C. J., Dolski, I., Dalton, K. M., Nitschke, J. B., Urry, H. L. et al. (2003). Now you feel it, now you don't: Frontal EEG asymmetry and individual differences in emotion regulation. *Psychological Science, 14*, 612–617.

Kawasaki, H., Kaufman, O., Damasio, H., Damasio, A. R., Granner, M., Bakken, H. et al. (2001). Single-neuron responses to emotional visual stimuli recorded in human ventral prefrontal cortex. *Nature Neuroscience, 4*, 15–16.

Kraut, R. E., & Johnston, R. E. (1979). Social and emotional messages of smiling: An ethological approach. *Journal of Personality and Social Psychology, 37*, 1539–1553.

Kringelbach, M. L., O'Doherty, J., Rolls, E. T., & Andrews, C. (2003). Activation of the human orbitofrontal cortex to a liquid food stimulus is correlated with its subjective pleasantness. *Cerebral Cortex, 13*, 1064–1071.

Lang, P. J., Bradley, M. M., & Cuthbert, B. N. (1990). Emotion, attention and the startle reflex. *Psychological Review, 97*, 377–395.

Lang, P. J., Greenwald, M. K., Bradley, M. M., & Hamm, A. O. (1993). Looking at pictures: Affective, facial, visceral, and behavioral reactions. *Psychophysiology, 30*, 261–273.

LeDoux, J. E. (1996). *The emotional brain: The mysterious underpinnings of emotional life.* New York: Simon & Schuster.

Levenson, R. W. (1992). Autonomic nervous system difference among emotions. *Psychological Science, 3*, 23–27.

Levenson, R. W., Ekman, P., & Friesen, W. V. (1990). Voluntary facial action generates emotion-specific autonomic nervous system activity. *Psychophysiology, 27*, 363–384.

Liberzon, I., Phan, K. L., Decker, L. R., & Taylor, S. F. (2003). Extended amygdala and emotional salience: A PET investigation of positive and negative affect. *Neuropsychopharmacology, 28*, 726–733.

Morgan, C. D., & Murray, H. A. (1935). A method for investigating fantasies: The Thematic Apperception Test. *Archives of Neurology and Psychiatry, 34*, 298–306.

Morris, J. S., Frith, C. D., Perrett, D. I., Rowland, D., Young, A. W., Calder, A. J., & Dolan, A. J. (1996). A differential neural response in the human amygdala to fearful and happy facial expressions. *Nature, 383*, 812–815.

Morris, J. S., Öhman, A., & Dolan, R. J. (1998). Conscious and unconscious emotional learning in the human amygdala. *Nature, 393*, 417–418.

Niedenthal, P., & Kitayama, S. (Eds.). (1994). *The heart's eye: Emotional influences in perception and attention.* New York: Academic Press.

Nitschke, J. B., Nelson, E. E., Rusch, B. D., Fox, A. S., Oakes, T. R., & Davidson, R. J. (2003). Orbitofrontal cortex tracks positive mood in mothers viewing pictures of their newborn infants. *NeuroImage, 21*, 583–592.

Öhman, A., & Soares, J. J. F. (1994). Unconscious anxiety: Phobic responses to masked stimuli. *Journal of Abnormal Psychology, 103*, 231–240.

Olson, M. A., & Fazio, R. H. (2001). Implicit attitude formation through classical conditioning. *Psychological Science, 12*, 413–417.

Olson, M. A., & Fazio, R. H. (in press). Implicit and explicit measures of attitudes: The perspective of the MODE model. In R. E. Petty, R. H. Fazio, & P. Briñol (Eds.), *Attitudes: Insights from the new implicit measures.* Hillsdale, NJ: Erlbaum.

Osgood, C. E., Suci, G. J., & Tannenbaum, P. H. (1957). *The measurement of meaning.* Urbana: University of Illinois Press.

Paradiso, S., Johnson, D. L., Andreasen, N. C., O'Leary, D. S., Watkins, G. L., Ponto, L. L., & Hichwa, R. D. (1999). Cerebral blood flow changes associated with attribution of emotional valence to pleasant, unpleasant, and neutral visual stimuli in a PET study of normal subjects. *American Journal of Psychiatry, 156,* 1618–1629.

Payne, B. K. (in press). Attitude misattribution: Implications for attitude measurement and the implicit-explicit relationship. In R. E. Petty, R. H. Fazio, & P. Briñol (Eds.), *Attitudes: Insights from the new implicit measures.* Hillsdale, NJ: Erlbaum.

Petty, R. E., & Krosnick, J. A. (Eds.). (1995). *Attitude strength: Antecedents and consequences.* Hillsdale, NJ: Erlbaum.

Phelps, E. A., O'Connor, K. J., Cunningham, W. A., Funayama, E. S., Gatenby, J. C., Gore, J. C., & Banaji, M. R. (2000). Performance on indirect measures of race evaluation predicts amygdala activation. *Journal of Cognitive Neuroscience, 12,* 729–738.

Pizzagalli, D. A., Lehmann, D., Hendrick, A. M., Regard, M., Pascual-Marqui, R. D., & Davidson, R. J. (2002). Affective judgments of faces modulate early activity (~160 ms) within the fusiform gyri. *NeuroImage, 16,* 663–677.

Russell, J. A. (1979). Affective space is bipolar. *Journal of Personality and Social Psychology, 37,* 345–356.

Sagiv, N., & Bentin, S. (2001). Structural encoding of human and schematic faces: Holistic and part-based processes. *Journal of Cognitive Neuroscience 13,* 937–951.

Schachter, S., & Singer, J. E. (1962). Cognitive, social, and physiological determinants of emotional state. *Psychological Review, 69,* 379–399.

Schupp, H. T., Cuthbert, B. N., Bradley, M. M., Caciopo, J. T., Ito, T., & Lang, P. J. (2000). Affective picture processing: The late positive potential is modulated by motivational relevance. *Psychophysiology, 37,* 257–261.

Schwarz, N., & Bohner, G. (2001). The construction of attitudes. In A. Tesser & N. Schwarz (Eds.), *Blackwell handbook of social psychology, Vol. 1, Intraindividual processes* (pp. 436–457). Oxford, England: Blackwell.

Small, D. M., Gregory, M. D., Mak, Y. E., Gitelman, D., Mesulam, M. M., & Parrish, T. (2003). Dissociation of neural representation of intensity and affective valuation in human gestation. *Neuron, 39,* 701–711.

Smith, N. K., Caciopo, J. T., Larsen, J. T., & Chartrand, T. L. (2003). May I have your attention please? Electrocortical responses to positive and negative stimuli. *Neuropsychologia, 41,* 171–183.

Smith, W. (1922). *The measurement of emotion.* London: Kegan Paul.

Sobotka, S. S., Davidson, R. J., & Senulis, J. A. (1992). Anterior brain electrical asymmetries in response to reward and punishment. *Electroencephalography and Clinical Neurophysiology, 83,* 236–247.

Sutton, S. K., & Davidson, R. J. (1997). Prefrontal brain asymmetry: A biological substrate of the behavioral approach and inhibition systems. *Psychological Science, 8*, 204–210.

Sutton, S. K., & Davidson, R. J. (2000). Prefrontal brain electrical asymmetry predicts the evaluation of affective stimuli. *Neuropsychologia, 38*, 1723–1733.

Sutton, S. K., Davidson, R. J., Donzella, B., Irwin, W., & Dottl, D. A. (1997). Manipulating affective state using extended picture presentations. *Psychophysiology, 34*, 217–226.

Tassinary, L. G., & Cacioppo, J. T. (2000). The skeletomotor system: Surface electromyography. In J. T. Cacioppo, L. G. Tassinary, & G. G. Berntson (Eds.), *Handbook of psychophysiology* (2nd ed., pp. 163–199). New York: Cambridge University Press.

Thurstone, L. L. (1931). Measurement of social attitudes. *Journal of Abnormal and Social Psychology, 26*, 249–269.

Urry, H. L., Nitschke, J. B., Dolski, I., Jackson, D. C., Dalton, K. M., Mueller, C. J., Rosenkranz, M. A., Ryff, C. D., Singer, B. H., & Davidson, R. J. (2004). Making a life worth living: Neural correlates of well-being. *Psychological Science, 15*, 367–372.

Vanman, E. J., Paul, B. Y., Ito, T. A., & Miller, N. (1997). The modern face of prejudice and structural features that moderate the effect of cooperation on affect. *Journal of Personality and Social Psychology, 73*, 941–959.

Vanman, E. J., Saltz, J. L., Nathan, L. R., & Warren, J. A. (2004). Racial discrimination by low-prejudice Whites: Facial movements as implicit measures of attitudes related to behavior. *Psychological Science, 15*, 711–714.

Whalen, P. J. (1998). Fear, vigilance, and ambiguity: Initial neuroimaging studies of the human amygdala. *Current Directions in Psychological Science, 7*, 177–188.

Whalen, P. J., Rauch, S. L., Etcoff, N. L., McInerney, S. C., Lee, M. B., & Jenike, M. A. (1998). Masked presentations of emotional facial expressions modulate amygdala activity without explicit knowledge. *The Journal of Neuroscience, 18*, 411–418.

Williams, L. M., Liddell, B. J., Rathjen, J., Brown, K. J., Shevrin, H., Gray, J. A., Phillips, M., Young, A., & Gordon, E. (2004). Mapping the time course of nonconscious and conscious perception of fear: An integration of central and peripheral measures. *Human Brain Mapping, 21*, 64–74.

Wilson, T. D., & Hodges, S. D. (1992). Attitudes as temporary constructions. In L. Martin & A. Tesser (Eds.), *The construction of social judgment* (pp. 37–65). Hillsdale, NJ: Erlbaum.

Zald, D. H. (2003). The human amygdala and the emotional evaluation of sensory stimuli. *Brain Research Reviews, 41*, 88–123.

Author Index

A

Abelson, R. P., 85
Abend, T. A., 52, 274
Abler, B., 214
Adams, B. D., 434
Adelmann, P. K., 449
Adolphs, R., 201, 205, 206, 211, 497
Adorno, T. W., 166
Agnew, C. R., 430
Agocha, V. B., 182
Ajzen, I., 23, 48, 287, 299, 473, 486
Albarracín, D., 106, 143, 333
Albers, L. W., 234, 246
Alessis, C., 347
Alfieri, T., 105
Allen, J. J. B., 502
Allen, M., 352
Allen, T. J., 394, 396, 398, 399, 404, 405, 412,
      413, 414, 415, 416, 417, 418, 419,
      420
Alloy, L. B., 435
Allport, G. W., 165, 166, 194, 301, 330, 486
Alvaro, E. M., 306
Ambady, N., 290, 412
Amodio, D. M., 183, 198, 200, 201, 202, 204,
      206, 208, 211, 398, 401, 408, 412,
      413, 415, 416, 418, 419
Anagnostaras, S. G., 205
Anastasio, P. A., 167
Anderson, A., 497
Anderson, A. K., 489, 497, 498, 499
Anderson, N. H., 143
Andreasen, N. C., 497
Andrews, C., 499
Angrilli, A., 495
Arbuckle, N. L., 468
Arcuri, L., 431, 434
Armitage, C. J., 333, 337

Arndt, J., 438
Arnkoff, D. B., 448
Aron, A., 431
Aron, E. N., 431
Aronson, E., 85, 103, 259
Asendorpf, J. B., 78, 141, 254, 363, 379, 382
Asgari, S., 345
Ashburn-Nardo, L., 210, 365, 368, 385, 392,
      409, 413
Ashmore, R. D., 178, 207, 290, 291, 301, 412
Asley, V., 501
Atkinson, J. W., 442
Aubé, J., 444

B

Baccus, J. R., 233, 234, 235, 236, 273
Baer, L., 201
Baeyens, F., 235, 380
Bailey, J., 125, 333
Bailey, J. M., 446
Baird, A. A., 183, 417, 418, 419
Baker, J. R., 201
Baker, S. M., 306
Bakken, H., 500
Baldwin, M. W., 233, 234, 235, 236, 270, 273
Banaji, M., 8, 10, 170
Banaji, M. R., 67, 68, 70, 77, 79, 86, 94, 95, 98,
      99, 110, 131, 138, 144, 170, 171,
      173, 182, 183, 198, 199, 200, 201,
      202, 204, 206, 207, 208, 253, 273,
      290, 309, 361, 375, 395, 396, 404,
      408, 417, 418, 419, 436, 472, 495,
      498, 502
Banner, M. J., 10, 133, 143, 308, 309, 310
Banse, R., 47, 78, 141, 254, 363, 379, 382
Barden, J., 129, 130, 408, 410, 411, 412, 419

513

Author Index

T

U

Subject Index

A

ACC, *see* Anterior cingulate cortex
Addictive behavior, implicit attitudes and,
        467, 468
Advertising, *see* Antiracism advertising
Affect Misattribution Procedure (AMP), *see*
        also Misattribution, attitude
    advantage of, 468
    affective and cognitive bases of attitudes
        and, 477
    alcohol studies, 469–471
    correspondence with explicit measures,
        480
    description of technique, 14
    direct and indirect ratings, 474, 476
    implicit attitude measurement using, 462
    ingroup bias and, 465
    misattribution of emotion and, 477
    motivation scores and, 466
    racial attitudes and, 478
    representative stimuli, 463
    responses, life problems and, 470
    semantic differentials, 479
    sequence of events, 473
    spontaneous evaluations and, 467
African Americans
    approach/avoidance responses toward,
        210
    attitude discrepancies, 135
    Attitudes toward Blacks scale, 474
    college freshmen dyads with White
        Americans, 42
    commercial ads depicting, 33
    commonly reported stereotypes about,
        207, 208
    conferedate, social interaction with, 439
    faces, priming measure, 31

faces as primes, 473, 477
IAT effect, 208, 376
Implicit Association Test and, 137
ingroup preference, 465
negative associations regarding, 87
policies that disadvantage, 210
positive reactions to in sports context,
        129
professors, 294
propositional evaluations, 91
SEB toward, 438
verbal labels, 475
Ambivalence, implicit, 119–161
    attitude validation as on-line process, 130
    bipolar scales, 123
    change of attitudes, 127
    classical conditioning procedure, 143
    conflict of new and old attitudes, 127
    creation of implicit ambivalence by
        changing attitudes, 140–150
    criticism of studies, 142
    discomfort, 135
    discrepancy in attitude valence, 133
    dominant evaluative reaction, attitude
        objects and, 122
    explicit ambivalence, 120–126
        antecedents, 120–122
        consequences, 122–124
        experience of ambivalence, 125–126
    false rumor, 131
    hypothesis, 136
    implications of changed attitude, 149
    implicit ambivalence, 126–140
        antecedents, 126–128
        diagnosis with discrepancies between
            implicit and explicit measures,
            132–135
        discrepancies in domain of racial
            attitudes, 135–138

T

U

V